Chris,
may you enjoy
this journey into
my past.
sincerely,
Carolyn Bennett-

MW01274252

The Oceanview Matter

by

Carolyn Bennett-Hunter

INDEX

Other Books by Carolyn Bennett-Hunter:

City Beyond the Deep

The Widow's Four

ACKNOWLEDGMENTS

My heartfelt thanks to the family and friends who carefully reviewed this story, including but not limited to my husband David R. Hunter, my mother Charlene Bennett, court reporter friend Melissa Berman, attorney friend Rachel Bertoni, paralegal friend Julie Cohen, and film producer and long-time dear friend Sherry Collins, for their extraordinary efforts in proofing the pages of this book. I am grateful for their unique insights and many helpful suggestions.

Of special mention is the moral support and encouragement from Sherry Collins as this project progressed on an almost daily basis. And, I can't tell you how excited I am that Sherry has agreed to be featured as one of the main characters in this book's sequel!

Many thanks to Lynn Larsen for permission to use the beautiful photo of Devil's Elbow State Park that he took himself and generously allowed me to use on the cover. Though not the actual location of the place depicted as "Oceanview Academy" in the pages of this book, the "Devil's Churn" parcel of beach by Florence, Oregon was indeed a perfect choice to help illustrate it. Thanks also to my dear friend Susan for permission to include her photo from forty-three years ago, as well. And, despite Susan's permission to use her real last name in this book, an alias last name has been used instead to protect her privacy.

Deepest thanks and appreciation to my husband's distant cousin and dear friend Laurey Lee for her help with "cleaning up" the photos used on the cover of this book, and for finalizing the lettering and other cover artwork. I could not have managed this without her!

Unlike the old days when it was necessary for writers to make repeated trips to the local library while researching various topics, a vast realm of knowledge is literally at one's fingertips in today's modern electronic age. I am especially grateful for the marvelous "Wikipedia" feature on my computer.

My thanks to Charon Johnson and her friend Nohely Sanchez, and to friend Heather Shepherd, for their help translating several small speaking parts from English into Spanish for The Daisy Patch, and to Armando Ruiz for his expertise in proofing the final result.

Imagine my surprise when learning that my friend and proofer Rachel Bertoni also speaks Italian! I am grateful for her skills in reviewing several brief speaking parts that were originally "machine translated" from English into Italian but now have the human touch.

Special thanks to my dear friend Mary Bliss, founder of a local wildlife center, for her extremely helpful suggestions about the wild bird rescue sequence in chapter seven.

Many thanks to former classmate and email friend Bert Higa for his aeronautic expertise, and for looking over the flight sequence in chapter ten. Bert was a chief inspector at an aircraft repair station for commercial airliners, and inspected propulsion systems for orbiting spacecraft. Bert is now semi-retired but actively participates in piloting small planes on humanitarian aid missions of mercy to third world countries.

Special thanks to church friend Kent Garrett for confirming the factual accuracy of the flight sequence in chapter ten, and for his helpful suggestions. Kent just happens to be a retired Air Traffic Controller and commercial pilot with experience flying many different airplanes.

Thanks also to Mike, Joshua and Richard from BestBuy for showing me the latest voice-activated smartwatches with independent internet access that are available now, in 2016. Will smartwatches have perfect internet browsing capabilities by the year 2023?

FOREWORD

More than forty years have come and gone since many of the events in this story, yet it will not rest from my thoughts and insists upon being told. It is my hope that doing so can finally bring peace to those nagging memories once and for all.

It should be mentioned before we go on that any semblance to events, places or persons either living or dead within the pages of this book are purely coincidental, and that those whose real names are used have graciously given their explicit consent and permission to do so.

That said, I also wish to acknowledge my dear friend Susan for her part in this story, and for her encouragement in the telling of it. Not only was Susan my high school roommate, confidant and cohort in one unplanned adventure after another back then, but also an inspiration to succeed in life and rise against whatever circumstances arose thereafter.

Finally, I was deeply saddened to learn from my friend "Pete" (whose real name I am not at liberty to disclose) of the untimely death of my friend "Lenny" on the very day I finished writing this book – though I did not learn of it until two weeks later. How in the world could something like that even be possible? It is my sincere, heartfelt prayer and hope that "Lenny" did accomplish his dreams and was happy in this life. He will be greatly missed by all who knew him.

It is therefore to the memory of my late father Wesley Bennett and to my friend "Lenny Owens" (whose real name cannot be revealed) that I dedicate this book. May they both rest in peace.

PROLOGUE

Understandably, finding the time to meet with her long-time friend Susan after so long had been nearly as challenging for Carolyn as coordinating their schedules. Though retired from her full time teaching career at a local elementary school, Susan was currently in the midst of a nasty divorce and busy dealing with all the various details when she and Carolyn first reconnected in March of 2016. Even time with her two preschool age granddaughters was mostly on hold for the moment.

Surprised and pleased to learn that Susan would be able to meet with her in spite of her circumstances, Carolyn wasted no time setting her affairs in order to take the trip to see her friend Susan. Still working full-time as a legal secretary for a busy law firm, Carolyn had only three weeks of vacation time available. She intended to make the most of it. Making sure her busy husband would be able to feed and care for her "high needs" rescue animals during her absence was also necessary before Carolyn could leave.

Two sixty-year-old women might be conspicuous showing up at the doors of an isolated parochial school in the middle of nowhere, so naturally they needed to come up with an excuse for being there.

Susan just plain needed to get away and was as anxious as Carolyn was to look into the Oceanview matter. They would soon learn whether there was any hope of discovering the truth about what had happened to two of their closest friends, schoolmates that had vanished without a trace forty-three years ago.

1. Beach Party

Winding past windswept ocean cliffs overgrown with aging cypress trees, the Bennett family car slowly made its way toward Oceanview Academy. Their daughter Carolyn would now attend the remote coed boarding school, designed primarily to keep its students as far as possible from the wayward influences of the outside world.

The year was 1972. Seagulls announced their presence overhead as one of them managed to drop and leave a small present on the otherwise clean windshield that Mr. Bennett was so proud of. In fact, every insect in the area seemed to decide at that very moment to arrive on the scene and add to the situation at an alarming rate. Cursing under his breath as he rolled up his window to prevent stragglers from entering the interior of his vehicle, Mr. Bennett continued without stopping.

"Are we there yet?" asked Carolyn, anxious to stop and use the restroom facilities. It seemed as if her father would never stop for his passengers to relieve themselves, and it had become unbearable.

"We're almost there," assured her mother. If only Carolyn could get along with her father, she thought to herself. Their increasing clash of wills was part of the reason for this decision in the first place. Perhaps the disciplinary style at Oceanview Academy might be more effective for Carolyn than home had been. Only time would tell.

Mr. Bennett slowed as he drove the white Dodge Dart with the bug-splattered windshield beneath the main entrance arch to Oceanview Academy, debating on whether to stop and clean his windshield before proceeding onto campus. Appearances could be important.

"I really need to use the restroom," reminded Carolyn.

Without reply, Mr. Bennett proceeded on without stopping, but driving ever so slowly through the arch and down the long winding entryway until finally reaching a sprawling compound of unmarked white buildings.

"Which one's the restroom?" asked Carolyn's mother. "I need to use one, too."

"Take your pick," Mr. Bennett slowly began to smile, clearly amused by their dilemma. "Let's stop here," he decided aloud as he noticed another family unloading a small trunk from their car.

"That must be the girls' dormitory," recognized Mrs. Bennett.

Unable to wait any longer, Carolyn opened the back door, jumped from her parents' car, and raced for the building's entrance.

"Excuse me," called a young woman at the front counter. "Only students and faculty are allowed beyond this point."

"I need to use the restroom!" explained Carolyn, not caring what the young woman thought of her at that moment. "I am going to be a student here," she explained further, realizing it was necessary.

"Okay then. Down the hall, half-way down," directed the girl at the desk. "Then please come right back."

Without further comment, Carolyn raced to the location indicated, barely making it there in time to relieve herself. Only moments passed before Carolyn could hear the distinct sound of her mother's white patent leather high heeled shoes on the black and white tiled floor of the large restroom.

"Carolyn?" called her mother. "Are you still here?" Mrs. Bennett quickly surveyed the long row of toilet stalls before deciding which one to use.

"In here," replied Carolyn as she flushed the peculiar toilet before standing back to study it. Pull chains hanging from the ceiling above the toilets were something Carolyn had seen in a museum once, and she was surprised to see them still in use.

"I think we'd better get back as quickly as we can," advised Mrs. Bennett while she and her daughter washed their hands. "The Dean of Girls is waiting for us."

"We just got here," answered Carolyn as she stopped to search for a paper towel dispenser. "Really? Look at this!"

"I haven't seen one of those for years," smiled Carolyn's mother as she reached for the reusable cloth towel dispenser.

"Oh, that's horrible!" frowned Carolyn as she watched her mother grab the dirty blue cloth and yank on it several times before managing to pull down an allegedly clean portion to use. "You have no idea whether what comes out is really clean."

"Well, it looks like that's all there is," replied her mother.

"I'll make do," responded Carolyn while she wiped her clean wet hands on the sides of her new blue jeans. "It's only water."

2

"Oh, look at that," noticed Mrs. Bennett as they turned to leave. "They must be renovating the showers."

"Seems like they'd be done by now, with all the new students arriving this weekend," mused Carolyn as she approached to get a closer look. "I don't see any actual construction going on."

The huge shower stall was twenty feet square with only a single water dispensing pole in the middle containing multiple heads that pointed in various directions.

"Surely they must intend to put up shower curtains between them," commented Mrs. Bennett, surprised to see six individual shower heads attached to the single water pole. "They don't even have places to hang any curtains!"

"Look! There's another big shower stall just like this one over at the other end," observed Carolyn. "And it hasn't got any shower curtains, either. But it's got six heads on it, too."

Modesty was something Carolyn's parents had always insisted upon, so clearly she and her daughter were both shocked by what they saw now. Why, even in PE class back home, there had always been individual shower stalls separated by dividers for the students to use, as well as individual dressing rooms by each locker where the students could dress again before returning to class.

"Perhaps we need to ask the Dean about this when we talk to her," suggested Carolyn.

"Indeed we shall," agreed Mrs. Bennett.

"Ah, there you are," greeted Miss Dixon as Carolyn and her mother entered the Dean's office. "There are some things we need to go over before you head down to the Registrar's Office."

"Are they planning to hang up curtains in the girls' shower room?" asked Mrs. Bennett, deciding to find out now.

"Shower curtains?" laughed the Dean. "No, why?"

"It doesn't seem very modest," explained Mrs. Bennett. "Surely you don't expect the girls to shower like that?"

"They all seem to be doing just fine," chuckled the Dean, clearly amused by Mrs. Bennett's question. "One less thing they have to worry about cleaning up afterwards."

"Cleaning?" Mrs. Bennett was clearly puzzled.

"In the shower stalls," clarified Miss Dixon. "As it is now, all the girls have to do is grab a bucket and a mop and clean the floor when they are finished. No shower curtains to worry about."

"I see," nodded Carolyn's mother, obviously displeased.

"We can go over the housekeeping issues later," proceeded Miss Dixon as she turned to Carolyn. "Have you read the student handbook yet?"

"Well, yeah, on the four-hour drive over here," replied Carolyn. "A lot of rules."

"Yes, there are," assured the Dean. "For example, we do not normally allow any of our students to wear blue jeans on campus."

"Excuse me?" Mrs. Bennett interjected. "We just finished purchasing new clothes for Carolyn to wear, including several new pairs of blue jeans like the pair she has on now."

"Exactly," grinned Miss Dixon. "There are, of course, situations where blue jeans are considered acceptable, with permission from the Dean. That would be me."

"I see," sighed Mrs. Bennett, sensing already that Miss Dixon was not someone to be argued with.

"As you know," continued the Dean, "we have a work-study program here where the Freshmen and Juniors work in the mornings and attend class in the afternoons. The Sophomores and Seniors are just the reverse, attending class in the mornings and working in the afternoons."

"Carolyn will be working in the mornings then?" clarified Mr. Bennett, quiet until now.

"Exactly!" beamed Miss Dixon. "You seem like a typical upper middle class family, driving a better than average vehicle."

Mr. Bennett cringed slightly, certain the Dean must be implying that she disapproved of the bug splattered windshield on his car. He knew he should have stopped to clean it off.

"Finances," continued the Dean, "are something you will work out with the Registrar's Office. But, what I can tell you is that you will need to make sure your daughter has a wardrobe acceptable to our standards. The only time she would be wearing blue jeans would be if she were assigned to work in one of the manual labor jobs where that type of attire is appropriate."

"What type of manual labor jobs?" frowned Carolyn.

"Your father tells me you have worked as a tray girl in a rest home after school each day for the past two years," mentioned Miss Dixon. "That would qualify you to work as a server in the food line at the cafeteria."

"That sounds like an acceptable job," approved Mr. Bennett.

"Regular school dress is what she would wear for that particular job," revealed the Dean. "No blue jeans in the cafeteria."

"So, what type of jobs do require blue jeans?" persisted Carolyn, curious whether she might be able to wear them at all, and anxious to earn some extra spending money.

"There are some jobs at a local lumber mill," began Miss Dixon.

"My daughter is not working in any lumber mill!" interrupted Carolyn's mother indignantly. "Does she really have to work? Won't going to classes and doing her homework be enough?"

Carolyn's mother was tall, slender and well-endowed in all the right places. Her short dark hair was arranged in a stylish wedge haircut, with steep-angled layers cut all around the sides and back. The fashionable pink and white paisley cotton shift she wore was sleeveless but modest, complimented well by her white patent leather high heeled shoes and matching white handbag. Fashion was clearly important to Mrs. Bennett. Her smooth alabaster skin was accentuated by the latest style in eyewear, white framed glasses with large round lenses. It was hard to believe the Dean was still wearing horn-rimmed glasses from two decades ago! But at the moment, Mrs. Bennett's greatest concern was the possibility that her beautiful sixteen-year-old daughter might be thrust into some type of common labor job when she really should be focusing on her school work instead.

"All students are encouraged to work as part of their educational experience," informed the Dean. "That's part of what makes our institution such a success. It helps teach responsibility and good work ethics that each student can carry with them throughout their lives."

"Sounds good to me," Mr. Bennett remarked.

"There are also jobs in the farming industry, such as picking or caring for crops. And of course, there is the dairy," smirked the Dean.

"The dairy?" Carolyn obviously was not enthused.

"The candle factory, bakery and laundry jobs are all taken," added Miss Dixon. "For you see, everyone is anxious for an opportunity to wear their blue jeans when they can."

"What about in our room?" questioned Carolyn.

"No blue jeans are allowed on campus, inside or outside of the dormitory, without explicit permission from the Dean," responded the Dean with finality.

"I see," mumbled Carolyn, clearly not happy about it.

"Nor do we allow jewelry of any kind," continued the Dean.

"Jewelry?" frowned Carolyn.

"You will need to take off the earrings that you have on now, and you may as well send them home with your parents," suggested Miss Dixon. "A wristwatch is about the only type of jewelry you'll be wearing around here."

"What about makeup?" quizzed Carolyn, suddenly recalling having read something about it in the never-ending handbook she had perused during the drive over.

"We certainly discourage it," replied Miss Dixon with an even tone, "but tasteful and natural looking like you have on now is allowable, just not encouraged."

"Anything else?" Mr. Bennett sighed deeply, clearly annoyed by the direction of the conversation and anxious to get to the Registrar's Office so he could get the financial arrangements taken care of before lunch.

"Tell you what," offered the Dean as she turned to Carolyn, ignoring Mr. Bennett completely. "You may wear the blue jeans you have on now while you unload your things and get settled."

"Thank you," Carolyn tried to force a smile.

"After that, you will be expected to change into something that complies with the rules in our student handbook, which you have read," reminded the Dean.

"Yes, ma'am," agreed Carolyn.

"Excellent!" beamed Miss Dixon. "Come, let me show you which room will be yours. Then when you are finished at the Registrar's Office, you may want to have lunch before you begin bringing in your things."

"Can't we just see the room when we come back?" scowled Mr. Bennett. "And after lunch?"

"I have an idea," proposed the Dean to Mr. Bennett. "You go ahead and go to the Registrar's Office while I show the ladies where Carolyn's room will be and then take them over to the cafeteria. They can meet you there."

"So, which building is the Registrar's Office?" questioned Mr. Bennett. "They all look alike."

"Indeed they do," smiled Miss Dixon, amused by the comment. "This campus used to be a military base in its previous life. Many of the buildings we use now were a part of it."

"Including the showers?" questioned Carolyn's mother.

"Including the showers," confirmed the Dean as she arose and opened an entrance door leading directly from her apartment to the outside world. "The Registrar's Office is the large building in the middle, just down that flight of stairs by the lamp post."

Mr. Bennett looked to see where Miss Dixon was pointing. "The buildings are quite a distance from one another."

"Yes, they are," responded the Dean. "We have approximately 400 acres of land here, much of it farmland now. Our school is largely self-sustaining, and many of the products are used right here."

"Nice view of the ocean," approved Mr. Bennett, pleased with the well-kept landscaping.

"Do the students ever get to go to the beach?" Mrs. Bennett suddenly asked.

"Absolutely," smiled Miss Dixon. "But only on certain days. We can go over all of that later. Right now we'd better get on our way or none of us will make it in time for lunch. They only serve at specific times."

"No exceptions?" asked Mr. Bennett.

"No exceptions," responded the Dean. "We'll see you at the cafeteria, right next door to the dormitory. It's 11:30 now, so you should have plenty of time. They serve from 11:45 until 12:45 and what you need to do at the Registrar's Office should only take about 15 minutes."

Nodding his consent, Mr. Bennett headed toward the building indicated.

Miss Dixon then turned to the other entrance door to her apartment – the one leading back into the dormitory – and motioned for Carolyn and her mother to follow.

Dean Dixon was a short stout woman with unusually heavy legs, thankfully hidden above the knees by her straight pink cotton dress. The rest of the world may have been wearing mini-skirts back in 1972, but thank goodness Miss Dixon had chosen not to be in style with the times. The short harsh haircut and horn rimmed glasses did not do much for her appearance, either, though she walked with a confidence that did not go unnoticed by Carolyn or her mother.

There was just something about Dean Dixon that neither of them liked, though they could not exactly explain why. It may have been an arrogance of sorts, coupled with the threatening manner in which she wielded her position of authority over those within her domain.

"This is Carolyn Bennett," introduced Dean Dixon as they approached the young woman at the front desk whom Carolyn had spoken with earlier upon her arrival.

"Yes, we've met," greeted the girl with an insincere smile. She clearly did not like Carolyn or her mother and it was obvious to them. If the Dean noticed it, she gave no indication.

"Carolyn will be in room 124," added Miss Dixon, patiently waiting while the receptionist wrote down the information in a small black notebook she had in front of her. "I'm taking them to see the room now, after which they will be having lunch at the cafeteria."

"Nice to meet you both," added the young woman. "My name is Diana." Diana was a frail looking girl with pale skin, closely cropped hair and horn-rimmed glasses, much like the ones worn by Dean Dixon. She could easily have passed as a Freshman.

"Diana's job is to work at the front desk on weekday afternoons and on every other Sunday," elaborated the Dean. "Diana is a Senior this year, and her father is the chemistry and math teacher."

"I see," nodded Carolyn, silently disapproving of the favoritism shown to Diana because of her father's position.

"Oh yes," Miss Dixon mentioned to Diana, "Carolyn has my permission to wear her blue jeans to lunch, and while she unloads her things and gets settled, but she will be expected to be in proper dress for the get-acquainted party down on the beach tonight."

Diana then made another notation in her little book, glancing at Carolyn with obvious disapproval.

"This way," Miss Dixon nodded as she headed down the same hallway Carolyn and her mother had walked down earlier. Room 124 was only two doors down from the restroom. Miss Dixon gingerly opened the door and stood aside for Carolyn and her mother to enter.

Stunned with silence as they surveyed the tiny room, Carolyn and Mrs. Bennett saw that there was only one small sink, two small beds, two small dressers, and two very small closets. Nothing else. Clearly, she would be using the restroom down the hall again.

Like her mother, Carolyn was indeed tall, but also just downright skinny, greatly embarrassed by her long skinny legs and knobby knees. Though grateful for the opportunity to cover her unsightly legs with the stylish new bell-bottomed blue jeans for just a few hours more, Carolyn could not help but worry what she would do after that. Carolyn had brought only two pairs of pantyhose with her, intending to use them for special occasions. She would now need to wear them on a daily basis, even while working in the cafeteria! Hopefully her first paycheck would somehow arrive in time to enable her to purchase more. Carolyn's long, golden blonde hair was parted in the middle and hung loosely over her bony shoulders, disguised well by the puffy caps on her long-sleeved peasant style blouse.

Mrs. Bennett finally asked, "Where will Carolyn be able to put all her things? There's no room!"

"You'll probably need to take my cedar chest back with you," suggested Carolyn. "It's mostly full of blue jeans, anyway."

"Perhaps you should have read the handbook more carefully before deciding what to bring," countered Miss Dixon. "And as you know, students are not allowed to have televisions, stove burners, space heaters, candles, incense, or anything else that might be a fire hazard."

"And where would I get a key to the room?" Carolyn suddenly asked, though not enthused at all about it.

"We do not use keys here," informed the Dean. "Each hall has a monitor, just like the one at the front desk, and all the outside doors and windows remain locked at all times for security purposes."

"What if she wants to open her window for fresh air at night?" Mrs. Bennett was concerned.

"Well, actually the window will open, but only about a half an inch," chuckled the Dean. "There is a lock to prevent it from opening any farther, and it should only be opened if both occupants of the room are in agreement. However, your new roommate may not want the window open at night. The weather here can be quite foggy and damp, being so close to the water like we are."

"Do we know who her roommate will be?" Mrs. Bennett suddenly wanted to know.

"Her name is Sheree Wilkins," revealed Miss Dixon, "and she is also a Junior. Very nice young lady. You'll meet her tonight. The Wilkins have not arrived just yet but should be here soon."

"We should get to the cafeteria now," suggested the Dean.

Without further discussion, Miss Dixon proceeded down the long hallway, walked outside, and headed toward the cafeteria building pointed out earlier. Students had already begun to line up at the doors. Carolyn could not help but notice that only girls were lined up on the side of the building closest to the girls' dormitory. The line on the other side of the building was of only boys.

"Is that the boys' dorm on the other side of the cafeteria?" asked Carolyn, though already suspecting the answer.

"Your daughter is very perceptive," grinned the Dean. "Yes, it is. And there is a girls' food line and a boys' food line. But, they do allow the boys and girls to eat together now."

"Now?" repeated Carolyn. "You mean they didn't always allow them to?"

"Not until this past year," responded Miss Dixon. "We found that allowing them this liberty helps discourage sneaking off to the woods or the beach to socialize in a less acceptable manner."

"Wouldn't you know it if they did?" quizzed Mrs. Bennett, feeling less and less fond of the idea of leaving her only daughter behind at such a place.

"Oh yes," promised the Dean. "Absolutely, we would."

"Yeah, it mentions all the consequences of that in your little handbook, too," added Carolyn evenly.

"Good," Dean Dixon smiled with a less than sincere smile. "Then we understand each other."

Mr. Bennett was deep in thought as he climbed the meandering stairway leading uphill from the Registrar's Office to the cafeteria. Should he mention to Carolyn that the earnings from her school job would be applied directly to the cost of her tuition, and that she would never see an actual paycheck or hold a penny of it in her hands?

10

The day had been difficult enough already. He would bring that up later. Carolyn did not need to know that part of it, not just yet. This might not give her the experience of handling her own money as he had hoped, but perhaps it might help teach her that life is not always fair.

Born and raised as a "meat and potatoes" man, Mr. Bennett felt certain that the strict vegetarian cuisine at Oceanview Academy was one of those unfair things in life, and that he would not have wanted to be a student there himself.

Mr. Bennett's distinct carrot red colored hair was well trimmed, parted on the left side, and neatly combed into place with an oil based hair tonic. Slow and deliberate in his pace, and usually quiet unless he had something specific to say, Mr. Bennett was a man of few words. A firm believer in corporal punishment when necessary to maintain order and discipline within his home, it saddened him to think of his inability to control his own daughter's strong will. Carolyn must get it from me, he thought. Mr. Bennett then smiled imperceptibly, which was how he usually smiled when he did. Perhaps a semester or two at a place like this was just what Carolyn needed to help her appreciate life at home.

At least it is beautiful here, noticed Mr. Bennett as he paused to admire the freshly mowed lawn on either side of the steep, winding walkway he was ascending. Noisy seagulls were still circling overhead as they made their way toward the beach below. Cypress and eucalyptus trees grew in abundance along the windswept cliffs nearby, their pungent odors distinct upon the balmy ocean breeze as it continued to blow away the usual morning fog. Brilliant rays of sun could now be seen. Mr. Bennett tended to sunburn easily due to his fair complexion, so he proceeded to head indoors without further delay.

A hearty mat of creeping succulent ice plants with hot pink blooms lined the walkway, accented along the outer edge by golden yellow coreopsis, lavender and sedum plants where they met the edges of the expansive but well-kept lawn. Many of the plants which did well here in the cooler coastal environment would never have survived back in the valley he called home four hours away. Especially lovely were the colorful flowers planted around the cafeteria and dormitories. Red Salvia flowers grew intermingled with bright yellow Shasta Daisies, Lamb's Ears and Lavender Cotton. Juniper, hydrangea and creeping cypress shrubs stood out in relief against many of the freshly white washed military style buildings now being used by the school.

Behind the school and farthest from the cliff lined beach was a towering stand of old growth trees, mostly spruce, cedar and various varieties of fir. Off to either side of the main campus area sprawled endless fields of crops and various other white washed military style buildings. Some were used for farming or dairy equipment, while other buildings served as facilities for physical education, woodshop, auto mechanics, photography, equestrian stables, an aviation hangar, and of course the laundry, bakery and candle making factory. No doubt there were more. Mr. Bennett nodded with satisfaction as he tried to imagine the many opportunities that might be available to his daughter Carolyn, if only she would take advantage of them. He decided at that moment that he would let Carolyn find out for herself that the earnings from her school job would be applied directly to the cost of her tuition, and that she would never see an actual paycheck. The last thing he needed was to part with his only daughter on a negative note. They had quarreled enough already. Besides, it would be good for her, a valuable lesson.

After lunch, Carolyn and her parents quickly unloaded what was left of her possessions. The cedar chest, along with all but two pairs of new blue jeans and the new space heater, were left in their car while the Bennett family went for a walk together on the beach. The Dean had informed them that it was actually "boys' beach" that particular weekend, but that they could have special permission to go there together as a family and say their farewells.

"It really is a beautiful campus," pointed out Carolyn's mother, trying to lighten the mood. "And you should be able to come to the beach on Tuesdays and Thursdays when it's girls' beach and you're not working or attending classes."

"And every other weekend," added Mr. Bennett.

"Yep," nodded Carolyn. "Provided there's time after doing all my homework."

"Oh Carolyn," sobbed her mother, suddenly grabbing and holding her daughter close. "Are you sure this is what you want?"

After a long pause, Carolyn replied, "Yes, I'm sure. I love you both, but Dad and I need some time apart."

"I agree," Mr. Bennett spoke up. While usually quiet and rarely able to show his affection for anyone, Mr. Bennett loved his daughter deeply and did want the best for her. "Let us know if you need anything at all," he added as he unexpectedly hugged his daughter and wife close to him for a long embrace.

The three of them silently watched while the warm afternoon sun painted its bright reflection across the vast ocean beside them.

Relieved to have first pick of beds, closets and dressers in her small dormitory room, Carolyn decided to also make sure her toiletries and other items were neatly arranged on the side closest to her chosen half of the room, just in case there was any question about it.

Without warning, a voice could be heard on the inside wall intercom speaker beside her dormitory door. "Carolyn?" It was Miss Dixon. Until now, Carolyn had assumed the speaker was a universal speaker that sent announcements to all of the rooms simultaneously.

"Miss Dixon?" responded Carolyn, puzzled at how the Dean had been able to have direct access to the speaker in just her room.

"Good, you're there!" responded the voice of Dean Dixon. "Your new roommate is here, are you dressed?"

"I am," replied Carolyn, suddenly wondering if the Dean was also able to listen in on the conversations in individual rooms without the occupants being any the wiser. She would definitely have to find out about that!

Within moments, the door to her room swung open and in walked Sheree Wilkins. Again, the horn-rimmed glasses. Did everyone wear them here? And not only that, the coke-bottle eyeglasses were so thick they made Sheree's eyes appear like large insect eyes. Sheree's acne problem was quite noticeable, and her buck teeth were firmly attached to an unsightly orthodontic headgear device that wrapped around her head. Sheree's clothes were hideous, too, and hung on her like nothing more than a plain brown sack. Sheree was extremely flat chested, knock-kneed, wore flat shoes with thick braces on them, and also wore a special brace on her back.

"Pleased to meet you," greeted Sheree with a lisp, unable to speak clearly with the cumbersome orthodontic device in her mouth.

"I'm Carolyn," responded her new roommate, not certain what to make of the situation.

"Sheree has a few physical disabilities," explained Dean Dixon, "but it should not interfere with her ability to be a good roommate. In fact, I think you two will get along famously."

"Where are your parents?" asked Carolyn, trying not to stare too much at the hardware on her new roommate.

"They couldn't stay," apologized Sheree.

"Where are your things?" wondered Carolyn aloud. All Sheree had was a single suitcase, and nothing else.

"I haven't had a chance to pick up my books yet," explained Sheree, assuming that must be what Carolyn was asking about.

"Oh," nodded Carolyn. "Me, neither."

"Well, I'll just leave you two to get acquainted then," smiled Miss Dixon as she turned to leave. "Oh yes, we are having a special get-acquainted dinner and beach party down by the water at 6:30 for all the students. A chance for everyone to meet and get to know one another."

"That should be fun," smiled Carolyn, hoping for an opportunity to ditch her new roommate so she would not be seen with her at the party. It could definitely affect her ability to make a good impression on any new friends she might meet.

Seeming to read Carolyn's thoughts, Dean Dixon then added, "So, I'll expect to see the two of you up in the chapel at 6:00. That's where we normally hold the mandatory morning vesper services. But tonight, we'll just meet there so everyone can walk down to the beach together. Carolyn, please look out for Sheree, as she cannot see too well at night, especially on the long walk back uphill after the party."

"Yes, ma'am," muttered Carolyn, clearly displeased.

After Miss Dixon had gone, Sheree did her very best to convince Carolyn that she did not want to go to the party, seeming to sense that she might be in the way.

Nevertheless, Carolyn managed to persuade Sheree to come anyway, knowing deep down that her failure to make it happen might somehow anger the new Dean, and it appeared to be the lesser of two evils as Carolyn saw it.

The walk across campus took nearly more than half an hour. Sheree had to be especially careful on the uneven terrain as they left the carefully manicured campus walkways. The rock covered roadway ahead of them had been cut between the cliffs with an excavator at some previous time and now was a convenient access point leading

14

down to the sandy beach. The steep grade became sandier with every step, but Carolyn patiently waited as her new roommate negotiated it.

Finally reaching the beach, Carolyn and Sheree could see the other students several hundred yards away on a flat section of beach set back far enough from the water to avoid any incoming tide until well after the party would be over. Most of them had made the trek in fifteen to twenty minutes.

Gathered around a huge bonfire and seated on logs arranged in a large semicircle around it, the students of Oceanview Academy waited while their new principal climbed on top of a weather beaten tree stump that had a portable microphone placed in front of it.

"Greetings, everyone!" came the booming voice of Principal Roth over a loudspeaker attached to the microphone from which he was speaking. "We will be taking a photo of each of you individually as you wait in line for your vegetarian hot dogs."

"The Seashell is a small publication with everyone's picture in it that each of you will receive by the end of the week. That way you will know who everyone is and be able to look up those you missed," explained the Principal.

"I can't have my picture taken," muttered Sheree with genuine terror, clearly ready to make a bolt for it. "I'm going back."

"Oh no, you're not," argued Carolyn. "We both need to eat, and there will be nothing else to eat until the cafeteria opens again in the morning. Besides, I promised Miss Dixon I would help you get back. Would you deprive me of eating my dinner?"

After realizing the futility of arguing further, Sheree finally nodded and agreed to stay.

Carolyn really did need to keep an eye on her, she realized, or Sheree might just try and go back by herself. Then Dean Dixon would really be upset, and that's the last thing Carolyn needed right now. As it was, she and the new Dean did not seem to have gotten off on the best foot.

Once pictures had been taken and dinner consumed by the large group of hungry new students, Principal Roth could be heard again.

"Next week will be the first of our three official date nights this semester, a coed Saturday night activity where you and your date will be able to sit together and watch a Disney movie at the gymnasium," announced the Principal. "To make it interesting, we are passing out compatibility questionnaires to each of you now who would like to participate. You will want to answer the questions honestly."

"I can't do that," mumbled Sheree.

"He said it's optional," reminded Carolyn, tired already of Sheree's deadbeat attitude.

"Once you have completed your questionnaire, just drop it in the box beside the stage here," indicated Principal Roth. "Then you can return to your rooms for the night."

"A compatibility questionnaire?" grinned Carolyn, hoping sincerely that whoever she would be paired with would not have seen her here with her new roommate.

"Are you going to do it?" asked Sheree with surprise.

"Absolutely," responded Carolyn. "It sounds like fun."

"Okay," sighed Sheree, realizing they would not be leaving until Carolyn had completed and turned in her questionnaire.

Once Sheree was safely back inside the confinement of their dormitory room, Carolyn decided she would head back to the beach by herself and started to make her way back down the long hallway.

"You're not going anywhere," informed Diana, who was just in the process of being relieved by the next hall monitor.

"Excuse me?" replied Carolyn.

"Curfew is usually at 6:00, anyway, and it is already past 8:00," pointed out the hall monitor.

"So?" argued Carolyn. "Aren't we supposed to be able to be down there for the party until we decide to come back?"

"Which you did," reminded Diana. "Dean's orders are that once a student returns from the beach, they are to remain in their rooms for the night."

"We usually have to be in our rooms by 6:00?" Carolyn was stunned by this information, certainly not something from the handbook she had read.

"No, just inside the dormitory," clarified Diana. "Room curfew is not until 8:00. Students are usually free to use the showers and laundry rooms between 6:00 and 8:00, provided their homework has been completed."

"Tell me you're kidding?" asked Carolyn.

"People must be in their rooms by 8:00 to get ready for bed, as the lights go off at 9:00," elaborated the hall monitor. "You're new, but you'll get used to it."

"Lights go off at 9:00?" repeated Carolyn as she shook her head and returned to her room. "I don't believe it!"

Carolyn slowly returned to her dormitory room and mentioned what she had learned to her new roommate.

Sheree, who was already aware of it from the previous year, merely smiled.

"Fine!" muttered Carolyn as she set her alarm clock and went to bed, unable to sleep right away while considering her busy day and whether coming here was a wise choice.

Finally drifting off to sleep, Carolyn was suddenly awakened by an unearthly banging noise.

"It's just the heaters," mumbled Sheree from the darkness.

"Why are the heaters making a noise like that?" demanded Carolyn, unhappy with the interruption in her sleep.

"They're steam heaters," replied Sheree. "They always do that."

"Why would they have steam heaters in this day and age?" persisted Carolyn. "That's absurd!"

"That's all that works with the electricity turned off," revealed Sheree. "And it was probably too expensive to convert them all to gas."

"Steam heaters?" Carolyn could not believe it. This whole situation was going from bad to worse. "Wait a minute! Is that why my night light isn't working? And why I can't see the face of my alarm clock? How are we supposed to know what time it is to get up in the morning?"

"Looks like you're going to need a wind-up model," chuckled Sheree, clearly amused by Carolyn's predicament.

"I can't afford to buy another clock right now!" Carolyn was angry. Why hadn't the Dean bothered to reveal that tidbit of information while she was busy yammering on about everything else?

"My clock is a wind-up," assured Sheree, "and I have it set for 4:45 in the morning."

"Excuse me? Why so early?" Carolyn was perplexed.

"To make it to the required dormitory vesper service at 5:15 in the morning," replied Sheree.

"I didn't realize it would be that early," scowled Carolyn.

"They have them every morning at that time," responded Sheree. "And they take roll. If you miss more than two of them in a semester, they will withhold your grades."

"Unbelievable." Carolyn shook her head in the darkness. "And the breakfast line starts serving at 6:15?"

"Yeah, but I think you have to be there at 6:00 for your new job serving food," mentioned Sheree. "Sorry, I forgot to pass that message along. You'll be working in the boys' line, though. You ought to like that. Maybe you'll get to meet whoever it is you're compatible with from your questionnaire – before you find out who it is, of course."

"Huh," mumbled Carolyn. "Well, maybe it won't be so bad after all. At least I won't have to work in the dairy shoveling animal poop, or in the lumber mill doing who knows what."

"Good night," said Sheree.

"Say, if you don't mind my asking," queried Carolyn, "but, why do you wear a back brace, anyway?"

Silent for several moments before answering, Sheree revealed, "My parents were in an auto accident and my back was broken. I was in the hospital for several months before I could even walk again."

"Oh, I'm sorry!" responded Carolyn, unable to help but feel sorry for her new roommate after learning what she had just been told.

"Many times I even hoped I would not make it," added Sheree.

"Why?" pressed Carolyn.

"You've seen what I look like," reminded Sheree. "The buck teeth, the thick glasses. I know I'm not much to look at, and I don't blame you for being embarrassed to have me with you at the beach party tonight. But, it's the way things are."

"I'm the one who owes you an apology," countered Carolyn. "You're not so bad."

"In the darkness," chuckled Sheree.

"No, really, you're not so bad. I'm honored to have you as my roommate," replied Carolyn.

"Thanks!" replied Sheree, beaming from the darkness. "Have a good sleep."

2. The Substitute

Deeply inhaling the crisp ocean breeze before opening her eyes again, Carolyn was amazed at how delightful the warm soft sand actually felt between her toes. Carrying her new white tennis shoes to prevent them from getting dirty, she made her way toward a large semi-circle of weather beaten logs that were neatly arranged around an old tree stump in the middle.

"I can't believe it's all still here," commented Susan from beside her. "What's it been, forty years now?"

"Forty-three," replied Carolyn as they approached and sat down on one of the logs.

"A lifetime," marveled Susan. "And who ever thought we'd be back?"

"At least we get to wear our blue jeans this time around," chuckled Carolyn, grateful to learn that blue jeans were no longer considered a societal ailment in this isolated community.

"Except when I'm teaching classes, of course," grinned Susan, amazed that she had managed to land the substitute teacher job so easily. "Who better than a retired school teacher with current credentials for them to hire while their regular teacher is out for six weeks following an unexpected surgery?" And how timely that the opening should come up just now when she and Carolyn were trying to find an acceptable excuse for being there. They would now be free to poke around and learn what they came here to find out, without drawing any suspicious attention to themselves.

"And they're fine with me being your roommate while you're here? And with both of us staying in that teacher's house?" questioned Carolyn. "Won't it look strange when I need to leave after only three weeks?"

"They're absolutely fine with it," assured Susan. "Family members are more than welcome to stay with faculty and staff, for as long as they like, and most of them still live in the staff housing right here on campus."

"Convenient, but what if they find out we're not even related?" worried Carolyn, not liking the idea of misleading anyone.

"I only told them we are like sisters," added Susan. "Is it my fault if they took it literally? We have nothing to worry about. Trust me."

"Oh, Susan," Carolyn shook her head, recalling the many times Susan had told her that in the past. "Trust you? I just hope you know what you're doing."

"It'll be fine," added Susan. "Hey, we've got to find out what happened to Joyce and Veronica. That's why we're here. Remember?"

"You're right," agreed Carolyn, "it's the best shot we have."

"More like the only one," nodded Susan.

Carolyn stared idly at the incoming ocean waves beside them as she reflected upon the fact that it was 2016 already, and that many things at Oceanview Academy had indeed changed since 1972. For one thing, students were actually allowed to wear blue jeans, any time they chose. Even to class! Stereos, cell phones and even computers were allowed, as well, even in the dormitory rooms. More surprisingly, male and female students were allowed to hold hands in public, provided of course that it was in the presence of a properly authorized adult.

"They still have separate dormitories, though," chuckled Susan, as if reading her thoughts.

"I wouldn't hold your breath on that one," laughed Carolyn. "They'll never have coed dormitories at this place! But, at least they have one serving line now."

"Oh yeah, for the food," smirked Susan. "I'd almost forgotten about that part. Remember Lenny Owens? You two ate almost every single meal together, when the school year first started."

"I do remember Lenny," sighed Carolyn as she shook her head. "Just like it was yesterday."

"Look here," pointed out Susan as she brushed a dead piece of seaweed off the end of the log on which they sat. "LO and CB."

"Let me see that," demanded Carolyn as she got up and came closer to where Susan was. "Oh, my goodness! Look at that. It's even got a heart carved around it now. That wasn't there before. Lenny must have come back later."

"Lenny Owens and Carolyn Bennett," smiled Susan. "That was the night you and I were down here with Lenny and his cousin Pete. Pete built a big bonfire while Lenny carved your initials onto that log. Then the four of us roasted marshmallows and watched the sunset."

"And listened to the transistor radio we managed to smuggle onto campus so we could appreciate all that worldly music," laughed Carolyn. "And now the kids are allowed to have stereos in their rooms!"

"Ironic, isn't it?" nodded Susan.

"I wonder if Lenny ever made it to medical school like he had planned," mused Carolyn.

"You should look him up and find out," grinned Susan. "He really did have it bad for you, you know."

"Indeed," added Carolyn with a deep sigh.

"I wonder if Lenny ever really knew how crazy you were about him?" wondered Susan.

"I think he knew," replied Carolyn. "The sad part is that I never even had the courage to tell Lenny how I really felt about him before it was too late. But, I've been happily married for 33 years now, and I wouldn't trade my husband for anyone else in the world!"

"Still, don't you ever wonder sometimes how things might have turned out, had you and Lenny worked up the courage to tell each other how you really felt back then, before it was too late?" reminisced Susan.

"Actually, we kind of did, during that last week," revealed Carolyn, "but in all the time we hung out together, Lenny never once said anything about being more than just friends."

"That's just sad," remarked Susan as she ran her hand over the carved initials on the log.

"Even then," added Carolyn, "Lenny said he just couldn't make any promises about the future. Still, I always wondered why Lenny carved our initials on this log, or if he knew at the time how his dad was going to react to our relationship."

"Both your dads!" reminded Susan with a sardonic grin.

"Life isn't always fair," answered Carolyn.

"Touché!" laughed Susan. "Hey, let's just eat at the house, shall we? Faculty and their families are not required to eat in the cafeteria, unless they just want to. And we want to be the ones asking the questions, not the other way around."

"Good point," agreed Carolyn as they headed back toward the rocky access road leading down from tree lined cliffs above.

Like Susan, Carolyn had been fortunate enough to find a good hair dresser. Maintaining her natural hair color was important to Carolyn, especially in today's competitive world. Exercising and maintaining her ideal weight had not hurt anything, either. Still wearing her golden blonde hair parted in the middle and hanging loosely over her shoulders, Carolyn appeared much younger than she actually was.

Several inches shorter than Carolyn, Susan was also still quite shapely for her age. Her ample cleavage, small butt, and long muscular legs were nicely proportioned for a person of her size. Susan's exotic facial features and hazel colored eyes hinted of Latin heritage. Her medium brown hair was neatly pulled back into a French braid with long bangs hanging down to one side in the front. Pleased that the school now allowed jewelry in moderation, Susan wore an elegant pair of sterling silver posts with dolphins on them. Though most of her outfits at home were designed to show off her cleavage to its best advantage, Susan now wore a loose fitting baby blue blouse with elbow length sleeves sporting button looped cuffs.

"Look," pointed Carolyn as she paused on the clifftop, adjacent to a large field of corn that overlooked the beach below. "They still use the tunnels for all that farming equipment!"

Susan turned just in time to notice a well-built teenage boy with well-tanned arms and a wide brimmed cowboy hat driving a rather modern looking tractor into one of the many bunker tunnels on campus.

"Do you think it's really true all those tunnels are connected?" wondered Carolyn aloud.

"The bunkers are supposed to be an underground tunnel system, left over from when this was a military base," recalled Susan.

"From what I remember, they all have iron-barred gates with locks on 'em," mentioned Carolyn. "At least all the ones we were able to find back then."

"That was a long time ago, though," reminded Susan. "Perhaps they don't keep them all locked anymore."

"Well, it would make sense to lock up such expensive farming equipment," recognized Carolyn. "What we need is a way to get inside and look around. I read somewhere that many bunkers from that time period served a dual purpose."

"Didn't they have barred cells where prisoners of war could be kept?" asked Susan. "Seems like they would."

"Remember Ray Dixon?" queried Carolyn as they continued past the campus farm buildings and toward the small airstrip used by students who were wealthy and fortunate enough to enroll in the school's elite aviation course. Naturally, it was offered only to those whose tuition had been prepaid in full and who maintained a grade point average of 3.8 or above.

"Wasn't Ray Dixon the Dean's nephew?" asked Susan. "Or her younger brother, or something like that?"

"Something like that," agreed Carolyn, though not sure which. "He was an ex-convict, though. I do remember that. I heard he was in prison for twenty years, for something terrible. No one seemed to know what it was."

"I'm still surprised the school even let him hang around a girls' dormitory like he did," commented Susan. "He sure gave me the creeps, anyway. Something just wasn't right about him."

"You could tell he worked out, though," recalled Carolyn.

"And had tattoos over every inch of those muscular arms," added Susan. "But those glasses!"

"He did wear those thick horn-rimmed glasses that everyone seemed to wear back then," laughed Carolyn.

"But only here!" reminded Susan. "Remember, that was 1972, and nobody else in the world was wearing horn-rimmed glasses by then."

"Except here," nodded Carolyn knowingly. "But he did wear blue jeans and white t-shirts."

"Oh yeah, white t-shirts were like blue jeans, weren't they? Another forbidden clothing item, at least as outerwear," snorted Susan. "And that horrible crewcut he had, when all the other guys were trying to grow their hair as long as they could without getting into trouble."

"Didn't it have to be at least two inches above their ears and shirt collar?" smiled Carolyn.

"No, I think it was only an inch above the ears, but it was two inches above the shirt collar," verified Susan. "And the girls' dresses had to be no shorter than two inches from the floor when we knelt down for them to measure it."

"Oh, I remember that!" exclaimed Carolyn.

"Me too," recalled Susan. "Three times. They'd pull you out of class, send you to the Principal's office, make you wear one of those long burlap gunnysacks tied around your waist for the rest of the day."

"I broke out into hives the time it happened to me," reflected Carolyn, not fond of the memory. "Those certainly were the days."

"But, back to that Ray guy," resumed Susan. "Didn't he usually just show up in the middle of the night, at the outside entrance to Miss Dixon's apartment?"

"Yeah, he did." responded Carolyn. "We sure had a good view of it from our window, didn't we? I always wondered what was in all those boxes they loaded up into his ratty old pickup truck in the middle of the night."

"Contraband, what else?" guessed Susan. "You know, transistor radios, flashlights, record players, and anything else Miss Dixon managed to confiscate from those girls because it wasn't allowed."

"Yeah, I know," replied Carolyn. "I lost a transistor radio to her once, a really nice one."

"Some of those boxes really were pretty big, though," continued Susan. "She couldn't possibly have confiscated that much stuff, not even from the entire dormitory."

"Didn't Ray have a job at the dairy once?" Carolyn suddenly asked. "The dairy kept some of their equipment in the bunkers, too."

"Yes, Ray did work at the dairy," realized Susan as they reached the main administration building. "We absolutely must get into those tunnels. If we're going to find anything, that's where it will be."

"And just how are we going to manage it?" asked Carolyn.

"Trust me," grinned Susan.

"May I have your attention," shouted Miss Snow above the loudly chattering students. "Class!"

Silence descended upon the classroom as Miss Snow motioned toward their new substitute teacher.

"This is Susan Rives," she introduced.

"You may call me Miss Rives," corrected Susan with a crooked smile. "As you know, I will only be here for six weeks, but we will manage to make the most of it, won't we?"

24

The young man she and Carolyn had noticed earlier driving the tractor by the corn field seemed quite interested in his new teacher, something that did not escape Susan's attention. She then rewarded him with one of her promising smiles. In fact, several of the young men in the class seemed quite interested in their new substitute teacher. If only they knew she could be old enough to be their grandmother!

An opportunity was presenting itself, and Susan intended to somehow make the most of it.

"Let's introduce ourselves, starting with you," suggested Susan as she reached for and picked up a clipboard on the desk in front of her and glanced at the young tractor driver.

"Ted Jensen," responded the young man, aware that she was studying him.

"Ted, nice to meet you," Susan smiled, just a touch too warmly.

"I'm Ann Roth," informed the young lady behind him, not happy about the unusual interest the new substitute teacher was taking in her long-time boyfriend. She and Ted had been dating for two years now and it was her hope the relationship might lead to something more.

"Roth?" repeated Susan. "Didn't your father used to be the principal here?"

"That was my grandfather," replied the young woman proudly. "My father is the theology instructor now. Grandpa passed away last year, but he will be missed by all of us."

"Oh, I'm sorry," Susan made sure her response seemed sincere, though she had really never liked Principal Roth. He was an arrogant man, mean spirited, and had enjoyed making her life as miserable as possible forty-three years ago.

"Were you a student here?" asked Ann, curious to know how the substitute teacher knew about Principal Roth. She certainly had never seen Ms. Rives before, and would remember someone like her.

"I must have heard about him from a friend of mine who was," mentioned Susan evasively. After all, Carolyn was a friend of hers, and had been a student here, too, so she technically was being truthful. Besides, there was no way of knowing just yet who could be trusted.

Wasting no time turning her attention to the next student, Susan prompted, "And you are?"

"Jon Dunwoody," revealed a tall, lanky young man with blonde curly hair and small round glasses.

"Thank you," smiled Susan. "This is what we're going to do. Let's back up, starting with Ted, and work our way around the room. I'd like each of you to stand, tell me your first and last name, where you're from, and what you plan to be someday when you grow up."

Interrupted by the laughter of several students, mostly guys, Susan patiently waited until they were finished before continuing. "Then, please tell me what job you are currently working now, and in a sentence or two, how you feel it will be of value to you in that occupation."

"Well, you already know my name is Ted Jensen," reminded Ted. "I'm from down south, born and raised in the same place as my dad and his two sisters."

"That would be Los Angeles," added Ann with a slight bit of sarcasm, not caring for Ms. Rives one bit.

"Let Ted finish, please," chided Susan, positive that Ann would become a serious problem unless dealt with swiftly and appropriately.

"What else?" questioned Ted. "Oh yeah, what I'm doing now. Well, when I'm not plowing crops, I can usually be found boogie boarding down on the beach, and hope someday to be a world-class surfer. Once I get a real surfboard, that is."

The classroom erupted into laughter once again, this time nearly everyone, including Susan, continued to laugh for several moments.

"Thank you, Ted," Susan replied with another of her promising smiles. "I shall certainly have to come watch that boogie boarding sometime. But, for the rest of you, let's please keep it a little briefer, or we'll never make it through the introductions before class is over. Just name, place of origin, current occupation, and future career goal."

"Ann Roth, Oceanview Academy, Administrative Secretary, Dean of Girls," revealed Ann rather curtly after standing. Then with an arrogant toss of her chin, Ann sat back down just as abruptly. Like her late grandfather, Ann had straight dark hair, pale skin and a rather long hooked nose. Her long bony arms and legs reminded Susan of a skin covered skeleton, which made Susan's eyes twinkle with amusement.

"Is something funny?" demanded Ann with a note of hostility.

26

"I just find it amusing that on my very first day, it could actually become necessary to send someone to the principal's office for having a rude and inappropriate attitude," responded Susan evenly.

The classroom became very quiet. Purposely pausing for a few moments for effect before continuing, Susan grinned a crooked smile. "Ann, I will expect you to remain after class so we can chat privately and get to know one another a little better."

"Yes, ma'am," agreed Ann, hopeful that she and Ms. Rives might be able to resolve this without involving the principal.

Introductions then continued around the classroom without further incident until all thirty-three names had been marked off on the clipboard. A loud buzzer suddenly rang that could be heard up and down the long hallway outside and in each of the adjoining classrooms.

"Well, that sure went by fast," noted Susan. "Tomorrow we'll just pass the clipboard around while we get started on the lesson. Class dismissed."

Waiting while everyone except Ann grabbed their laptops and notebooks, Susan could not help but think of a time when such computer equipment would no doubt have been seized as contraband by old Dean Dixon. Whatever had happened to her, anyway? Hopefully Carolyn would be able to find out.

Turning her attention to Ann Roth, Susan sighed deeply before saying anything. "You obviously have a problem with me?"

"No, ma'am," replied Ann, clearly scared to her senses.

"Ms. Rives," corrected Susan. "But, if you promise to give me a fair chance, you may call me Susan when we're not in class."

Ann looked up at Susan, surprised to see her smiling with amusement at the entire situation. "You weren't going to send me to the principal's office?"

"If you had persisted, yes," answered Susan. "I'm glad it wasn't necessary."

"Thank you, Ms. Rives." Ann was genuinely sorry for how she had acted earlier. "Susan."

"No problem." Susan studied Ann for a moment. "If you're worried about your boyfriend, rest assured I'm old enough to be his grandmother."

"How old are you?" Ann suddenly asked.

"That, my dear, is none of your business," Susan smiled with a mischievous look. "I'll look forward to seeing you tomorrow."

"Yes, Susan. Ms. Rives," bid Ann as she got up with relief and made a hasty but awkward exit.

That wasn't too bad, mused Susan to herself. But whoever thought taking roll could use up an entire class period? Hopefully she would get a chance to read the next lesson herself and be prepared by tomorrow. History was definitely not one of her favorite subjects. But, it was about to be! Susan frowned as she thought of the real purpose for being there.

The original faculty housing block had first been established in 1948, though some of the homes had been built as late as 1965. Prior to that, all faculty members had resided in some of the various buildings left behind by the military from when the property had been used as a defensive seaside outpost during World War II.

Located at least two crop fields to the north, over at the far edge of the school's property, most of the existing faculty homes had been constructed in a charming cottage cove style around 1950. Even though well kept, all were beginning to show definite signs of wear from constant exposure to the harsh ocean climate.

The constant battle with mildew, humidity and acrid salt air had taken its toll on many of the metal roofs and satellite dishes. Car engines often rusted out in far too short a period of time. Soggy foundations and garden spaces around them had caused serious structural problems with some of the faculty homes. Yet, succulents and other moisture loving plants thrived in the naturally cool damp soil, making constant yard maintenance more of an option than a necessity.

Views of the ocean itself were now mostly blocked by the ever thickening grove of cypress and eucalyptus trees along the windswept cliffs beside them. Carolyn was deep in thought as she slowly climbed the steps to what had once been the Eggersol home. Ms. Eggersol, the English Literature instructor, had been one of the few teachers Carolyn really liked forty-three years ago. Now the place belonged to a Miss Neilson, the Religious Spiritual Care Coordinator, who had flown back home to stay with her parents while recovering from hip surgery.

Grateful that someone would be staying at and caring for her home, Miss Neilson had graciously given her permission for the substitute teacher to treat the home as if it were her own.

At least there were no animals here to care for, noticed Carolyn, though suddenly missing the ones at home that her husband was caring for now in her absence. An unbidden tear trickled down her cheek. She already missed them terribly.

I sure hope Miss Neilson has internet access, thought Carolyn as she opened the door to the charming cove style cottage in which she and Susan were staying.

The furniture, like the house, was definitely showing signs of age. It was no doubt the same furniture that had been there forty-three years ago. At least it sure looked like it, thought Carolyn as she walked over to the sink to get herself a glass of water and hopefully enjoy a glimpse of the sunset. Disappointingly, the ocean view of years ago was now obscured by the dense coastal forest surrounding Miss Neilson's small home. Something else suddenly captured Carolyn's attention. It was movement from among the nearby trees! The usual evening fog was already rolling in for the night, so it was impossible to get a clear view of what or who it was.

There were no curtains in the kitchen, worried Carolyn as she considered that someone could be out there looking in. At least there were curtains in the other rooms, but that did not help ease her concern as Carolyn glanced at the front door and thought about the fact that there was no locking mechanism other than the interior deadbolt. And, would their things be safe each day while they were out and about? She would either need to take her laptop with her or lock it in the car.

Rather than wait for Susan to return, Carolyn quickly turned the handle on the deadbolt and flipped on the front porchlight. She certainly hoped Susan would be safe walking past the two isolated crop fields during her return.

3. The Big Splash

Date night had finally arrived at Oceanview Academy. New and returning students alike were gathered anxiously at the entrance to the school's large gymnasium. Countless rows of hard folding chairs could be seen inside, neatly set up on the well shellacked wooden floor.

"May I have your attention," called Principal Roth, his loud bass voice easily carried above the noise. After waiting patiently until he had everyone's attention, he continued. "We have here the results of the questionnaires you filled out earlier. My lovely wife Edith will read the names of each couple from the clipboard she is holding. Once your names are called, please come forward to meet your date for tonight. You will then remove your shoes and accompany your date into the gymnasium where you will be able to sit together during the movie."

"Here goes," smiled Mrs. Roth as she opened the metal covered clipboard. "Susan Rives. Is Susan here?"

Carolyn watched with a tinge of envy as Susan made her way to the front while everyone clapped enthusiastically, especially the boys. Stunningly beautiful, confident and obviously popular, Susan rewarded her audience with a mischievous smile. Susan was definitely someone Carolyn needed to meet. Perhaps Susan could help introduce her to some of the more popular guys that seemed to be so interested in Susan at the moment.

"Karl Branson," called Mrs. Roth after checking off Susan's name. "Karl?" Renewed clapping erupted as a short but handsome and well-built young man came forward.

"He's only a Freshman!" hooted someone from the audience.

Relieved to see that Karl was not any shorter than she was, Susan nodded and smiled as she grasped Karl's hand.

"Oh, one other thing," interrupted the Principal as he reached over to pull their hands apart. "I'm sure all of you have read your student handbook by now, and holding hands is something we do not allow here at Oceanview. It has been our experience that such contact can encourage and lead to behavior that will not be tolerated. In fact, if you do get caught holding hands with a member of the opposite sex while here at this institution, there will be serious consequences."

By the expressions on their faces, it was clear that few of the new students had even read their entire handbook, especially the part at the very end addressing this particular issue.

"So," resumed Mr. Roth, "please remember to limit your contact with your chosen date for tonight to the pleasant conversations I know you will have when not actually watching the movie."

"What're we gonna watch, anyway?" snickered a young man's voice from the audience. "Bambi?"

Laughter erupted at once among the students but quickly died when they noticed Principal Roth's austere gaze.

"Just kidding," added the youth, to smooth things over.

"Apology accepted," replied the Principal, making a mental note of the youth's face for possible future reference. Then turning to Karl and Susan, he directed, "You may remove your shoes and go on in. No street shoes are allowed on the gym floor."

Mrs. Roth continued reading names until finally Carolyn heard hers. "Carolyn Bennett?"

"Here," responded Carolyn as she made her way to the gymnasium steps and proceeded to remove her shoes.

"Lenny Owens," read Mrs. Roth. Most of the names had been read already and nearly everyone else was inside, patiently waiting for the movie to begin.

"Lenny?" repeated Carolyn with surprise as she carefully placed her light beige suede sandals on the steps and slowly stood up.

Lenny was indeed tall, dark and handsome! In fact, Carolyn had met Lenny on her second day while serving breakfast in the boys' food line, drawn to his sensitive warm face from the start. Lenny never did have much to say. He was the strong silent type. But, Lenny was an excellent listener and always seemed to hang on Carolyn's every word when they had breakfast together each morning. Lenny would usually manage to stay around until after Carolyn's serving duties were over so he could keep her company while she ate. By then, most of the other students had usually finished their meals and were already on their way to work, class or their respective dormitories.

Carolyn had wondered what Lenny would think of her date that night, secretly wishing that it could be him.

"Lenny!" smiled Carolyn, resisting the urge to reach out and take his hand, especially under the watchful eyes of faculty members standing nearby.

"Carolyn," acknowledged Lenny, obviously pleased. Six feet five inches in height, Lenny had been a basketball champion at his previous school. Sadly, the Oceanview basketball class had already been filled to capacity by the time Lenny registered for classes, forcing him to sign up for track and field instead.

Suffering from a similar predicament, Carolyn had wanted to take the badminton course and was disappointed to find it full. Carolyn had fond memories of playing badminton with her father after school each day in junior high school, before the clash of wills had arisen between them. Physical Education was mandatory, though, so Carolyn finally ended up registering for the Senior Life Saving Course.

Lenny and Carolyn were both tall and slender, noticed by everyone as they entered the gymnasium together and sat down in two hard metal chairs at the end of row four. The knees on Lenny's long powerful legs butted up against the back of the chair in front of him.

"At least we didn't end up in the first row," commented Carolyn, noticing at once how large the makeshift movie screen was that had been placed only a few feet away from the seats up front.

"Good thing," agreed Lenny, shifting his legs to a sideways position as the lights were dimmed and the movie began to play.

The Absent-Minded Professor was a 1961 Walt Disney movie appropriate for family entertainment, but definitely on the cutting edge for Oceanview Academy viewing back in 1972.

After a short time, Lenny tenderly reached for Carolyn's hand. Nothing was said as they grasped and continued to hold hands while watching the movie. Lenny and Carolyn felt comfortable with each other, and grateful for the cover of darkness to avoid getting into trouble for holding hands.

Without warning, the lights came on and the movie suddenly stopped. Several faculty members could be seen patrolling around the perimeter of the gymnasium, carefully searching the audience for any students who might be holding hands, or worse. One young girl had been resting her head on the shoulder of the boy beside her, and both were immediately called out.

Lenny and Carolyn had instantly let go of one another's hand the moment the lights had come on, so had not been noticed. The unfortunate pair who had been called out was each sent to his or her respective dormitory room without being allowed to watch the remainder of the movie. They were then put on "all boy" and "all girl" social status for the rest of that week. She would not be allowed to speak to any members of the male sex for an entire week, with the exception of teachers during open class period. The young man in turn was not allowed to speak to any member of the female sex for the rest of that week, particularly the one with whom he had been caught. Further incursions could lead to possible suspension and finally to expulsion from school. Principal Roth was obviously a man of his word.

Waiting for the cover of darkness again, Lenny finally resumed holding Carolyn's hand as the movie continued, though remaining alert for any sign of spying faculty members lurking nearby.

Fearful of suffering a fate similar to that of the other couple, Lenny and Carolyn stopped holding hands the moment the credits began to appear on the large, wavy, out-of-focus movie screen.

"May I walk you up?" asked Lenny. "It is dark out."

"Sure," replied Carolyn. "But we'd better not push our luck, there's way too much light from the lamp post up there."

Lenny smiled and nodded as he quickly put on his shoes. Then, after waiting for Carolyn to retrieve and put on her sandals, Lenny quietly walked beside her as they climbed the meandering stairway leading uphill from the central campus area to the cafeteria above. Lenny's neat dark hair glistened beneath the lamp post as he bid Carolyn good night and headed for the boys' dormitory.

"Well?" pressed Sheree as Carolyn entered her dormitory room. "How was the movie?"

"It was okay," answered Carolyn absentmindedly.

"So, are you going to keep me in suspense?" demanded Sheree. "Who was it? Who was your date?"

"Oh," grinned Carolyn, "sorry. It was Lenny Owens."

"Lenny Owens?" repeated Sheree excitedly. "Isn't he the guy you've been having breakfast with each morning, almost every day since you got here?"

"Well, yeah, he is," confirmed Carolyn. "All except for the first day, before we met."

"You are so lucky!" pointed out Sheree. "What I wouldn't give to have something like that."

"You could have filled out a questionnaire, too," reminded Carolyn. "Just like anyone else."

"No, it's not the same," differed Sheree. "Besides, just look at me! Who'd want to get stuck with someone who looks like this?"

Sighing deeply as she carefully washed and hung up her last remaining pair of pantyhose on the small towel rod by the sink, Carolyn nearly stumbled and fell as the lights went out. "Oh, no!"

"What is it?" called Sheree from the darkness.

"I can't believe they'd actually turn off the lights right at 9:00, especially while people are still in the middle of coming back from the movie!" exclaimed Carolyn. "I think I just snagged my only pair of pantyhose. They caught on my watchband."

"You don't have any more?" Sheree sounded surprised.

"Well, I sure can't wear my blue jeans," mentioned Carolyn. "And I don't have any cords."

Corduroy pants and cotton slacks were the only types of pants Oceanview Academy did allow, though not in class and certainly not for worship service. Unfortunately, Carolyn did not own any.

"What are you going to do?" quizzed Sheree. "I have an extra pair of nylons, but they are the kind you need a girdle with."

"Well, I don't happen to have one of those, either," sighed Carolyn. "I'm just going to have to wear the pantyhose like they are."

"Maybe your parents can send you some?" suggested Sheree.

"That could take a week or more," realized Carolyn. She would have to phone her parents first thing in the morning.

Still tired from lying awake and worrying about her nylons last night, Carolyn was startled by the sound of Miss Dixon's voice on the intercom speaker box in her room.

"Carolyn?" came the Dean's deep raspy voice.

"Miss Dixon?" Carolyn was startled to see that Sheree's bed was already made and that it was nearly noon. How had she failed to hear her alarm clock that morning?

"Are you all right?" questioned Miss Dixon. "You were missed at vespers this morning. And at your cafeteria job."

34

Carolyn suddenly worried what Lenny might think of her not showing up for breakfast that morning, especially after their date night. Lenny might think I don't like him anymore, worried Carolyn.

"Carolyn?" pressed the Dean.

"I'm sorry, Miss Dixon," apologized Carolyn. "I'm not feeling well. I had no idea it was this late."

"Why don't you get dressed and stop by my office after that?" requested Miss Dixon.

"Yes ma'am," responded Carolyn, certain she must be in terrible trouble now.

Hurriedly getting ready, Carolyn headed toward Miss Dixon's apartment at the far end of the long hallway. The run in her pantyhose was far worse than expected, running up the entire length of her long skinny right leg and across the top of her knobby knee. After taking a deep breath, Carolyn timidly knocked on the Dean's door.

"Come in," called Miss Dixon, motioning for Carolyn to sit on the couch in her sitting room.

Carolyn silently waited for the stern lecture she expected.

"Sheree informs me you ruined your last pair of pantyhose last night when the lights went off," smiled the Dean.

"Yes, Miss Dixon," confirmed Carolyn, puzzled that her roommate would have come to the Dean with this information.

"Sheree was worried about you," revealed Miss Dixon. "She said you did not appear to be feeling well this morning, so she turned off your alarm clock before it rang in order that you might get your rest. You're not in trouble."

"I see," Carolyn was surprised, yet also upset that Sheree would presume to touch her things without asking.

"I also know that you were one of the only girls at movie night that was not appropriately dressed for the damp foggy weather we have here," added the Dean. "Sheree tells me you do not even own a pair of corduroy or cotton slacks."

"Well, I had been expecting to wear my blue jeans," reminded Carolyn. "My dresses and pajamas are the only other things I have to wear. I don't even have a swimsuit of my own for PE class yet. The one I'm using now is a lender, and it's two sizes too big."

"And I told your father that he needed to make sure you had an adequate wardrobe acceptable to our standards!" the Dean was clearly irritated about it. "But, that's not your fault. And it is unfortunate, but the only time you could wear your blue jeans would be if you were assigned to work in one of the manual labor jobs where that type of attire is appropriate."

"Am I being transferred to another job?" asked Carolyn with concern, worried about not being able to see Lenny as much.

"Of course not," replied Miss Dixon. "But I will be calling your parents today to request that they send you some adequate clothing. I certainly can't have you getting sick because you aren't properly dressed for the weather around here."

"May I call them?" questioned Carolyn, hoping to ask for some other items, as well.

"Absolutely," agreed the Dean. "You can use the pay phone in the hallway by the front desk."

"I don't have any more money," mentioned Carolyn. "And I'm not sure how long it is until payday."

"Oh, Carolyn," sighed the Dean. "Your father didn't tell you?"

"Tell me what?" frowned Carolyn.

"That any money you earn at your school job is applied directly toward your tuition," revealed the Dean. "There are no paychecks here. Besides, how would the students even cash them? They certainly don't cash checks or take credit at the campus store. It's cash only."

Carolyn sat in stunned silence, angry and wondering why she had not been told this important bit of information until now. And just how was she going to get more soap or shampoo?

Yes, even the tiny, utilitarian store on campus required money in exchange for the few goods it carried! Included among its inventory were one brand of shampoo, one brand of soap, one brand of deodorant, one brand of toothpaste, and one – and only one - of each and every other item the school administration office felt was absolutely necessary for the students to have available to them. Naturally, school books, notepads, pencils, PE uniforms and other required items were included among the merchandise offered.

Trips to town in an old refurbished prison bus were also made twice each semester, when students in good standing were allowed an afternoon shopping trip at Ocean Bluff. The half hour drive there did offer scenic views of the ocean below as the rickety old bus wound its way along the windswept ocean cliffs. Unfortunately, the next shopping expedition was still a month away.

36

Reaching for the switch on her intercom device, Miss Dixon pressed the lever marked "front desk" and leaned in close to the speaker. "Diana? Are you there?"

"Yes, Miss Dixon," responded the young lady at the front desk. "How may I help you?"

"Carolyn Bennett needs to make an important phone call to her parents," explained the Dean. "Please let her use the phone key for that call. There will be no charge."

The phone key was earmarked for emergencies only, or when authorized by the Dean, to override the coin operated payment slot on the old black rotary-dial wall phone. Interestingly, there was no phone booth surrounding the out-of-date wall phone, and no stool on which to sit while using it.

Irritated that Diana would be able to eavesdrop on her private conversation, Carolyn considered what she would say.

"This is the operator. How may I direct your call?"

After giving the operator her home phone number, Carolyn waited as it began to ring.

"Hello?" it was her mother.

"Yes, this is the operator. I have a collect call from Carolyn Bennett. Will you accept the charges?"

"Yes! Put her through," replied Mrs. Bennett. "Carolyn? Are you there?"

"Hi, it's just me," whispered Carolyn, undesirous of Diana knowing what the conversation was about.

"Are you all right?" questioned her mother. "Can you talk any louder? I can barely hear you."

"Is Dad there?" inquired Carolyn, not anxious to talk to him.

"No, he's out on a job right now," revealed Mrs. Bennett. "He should be back in a couple hours."

"The Dean called me into her office today," notified Carolyn.

"Oh, Carolyn! Are you in trouble?" worried her mother.

"No, I'm not in trouble," responded Carolyn. "The reason she called me in is because I'm coming down with a cold and don't have the right clothing to wear in a place like this. She's concerned about me. It's cold, damp and foggy all the time here, and all I have left that I can wear are these cotton and polyester dresses."

"Can't you get any other clothes at that little store?" questioned her mother.

"Not at that store," replied Carolyn. "All it carries is school books, pencils, notebooks and toiletries, that kind of thing. The only way I can get more clothes would be next month when they make a bus trip into town for the kids to shop for an afternoon. And they sure don't give stuff away for free. It takes money."

"When do you get your first paycheck?" quizzed Mrs. Bennett.

"I don't," answered Carolyn. "Apparently, everything the students earn at their jobs is applied directly to their tuition. I'll never see a penny of it."

"You're kidding!" exclaimed her mother, displeased that she had not been advised of this before now.

"According to the Dean," continued Carolyn, "my father was well aware of it."

"He certainly never mentioned it to me!" Mrs. Bennett was clearly upset.

"Nor to me," added Carolyn. "Meanwhile, my last pair of pantyhose has a huge run up the front, and I have only enough soap and shampoo to last until the end of the week."

"I'll send you some by special delivery today!" promised her mother, clearly incensed that her husband had not bothered to share this very important piece of information with her. She would make sure that Carolyn had a decent selection of warm practical clothing, as well.

Afraid that Carolyn might become spoiled, since she was an only child, Mr. Bennett had always insisted that she not be over indulged. During the eighth grade, Carolyn had grown through three dress sizes in one semester, reaching her full adult height of five feet ten inches by the time she was thirteen years old. That was when Carolyn's father enlisted the help of his mother to teach Carolyn how to sew. Store bought items were just becoming way too expensive. Naturally, most of the clothing Carolyn wore now was homemade, and thick fabrics such as blue jeans or corduroy pants would have been too much for the family's aging sewing machine to handle, causing her current wardrobe to be made of mostly cotton or polyester.

It was only three days before the large box of supplies from home arrived, much to Carolyn's relief. Still recovering from the cold she had come down with after being inadequately dressed during date night, Carolyn was only just now feeling better. But, she had not seen

Lenny since date night. Was he sick, too? Why had that awful Sheree turned off her alarm clock that next morning? What if Lenny thought Carolyn was no longer interested in him? Come to think of it, Carolyn had not seen Lenny at breakfast for two days now and knew of no way to contact him to find out if he was all right. Phone calls between the dormitories were prohibited and Carolyn knew of no one she could ask. Unknown to Carolyn, Lenny's job at the lumber mill had been switched to the extra early shift and Lenny's busy class schedule often forced him to eat in his room for the other meals. So, breakfast was usually the only meal Lenny could still take the time to eat during regular serving hours at the cafeteria, and only if he hurried.

Inside the box from Carolyn's mother were two pairs of light green corduroy pants, one pair of maroon colored cotton slacks, several pairs of tall size pantyhose, three pullover sweaters, a soft white cardigan sweater, a warm hooded navy blue jacket, a pair of dark brown waffle stompers, and several pair of thick wool socks. Also inside the box was soap, shampoo, a flashlight with extra batteries, homemade oatmeal cookies, and various other nutritious snacks including nuts, dried fruit and crackers.

Sheree watched with curiosity as Carolyn searched through the box. "You're not allowed to have a flashlight," mentioned Sheree.

"Excuse me?" Carolyn was becoming increasingly irritated by Sheree's constant reminders of all the rules and regulations, and started to wonder if some of them were made up as she went along. "I'm sure that's not in the handbook!"

"It was announced," countered Sheree.

"Really? Well, I could need it some night to keep from stubbing my toe, if there were ever an emergency and we had to get up in the middle of the night. Besides, there was never any announcement about flashlights. I would remember something like that," snapped Carolyn.

"Yes there was!" persisted Sheree. "And they would turn the electricity back on if there ever were an actual emergency."

"What if the power going off was part of the emergency?" pointed out Carolyn. "Then what?"

"Well, it's still against the rules," argued Sheree.

"You know, perhaps you should just mind your own business," recommended Carolyn. "I know you meant well, but turning off someone's alarm clock without their permission is another thing I've been meaning to talk to you about. I'd really like you to keep your hands off of my things!"

"I'm sorry you feel that way," mumbled Sheree, tears slowly began to run down her cheeks.

"I'm going to need a swimsuit that fits, too," mumbled Carolyn, deciding for now to ignore Sheree's crocodile tears. Clearly she would need to find somewhere to hide her new flashlight so it would not be confiscated during one of the routine room raids she had heard other girls talking about during gym class. "My PE teacher lent me an old swimsuit that was left behind by a previous student, but it's two sizes too big and tries to come off when I'm in the water. I'm never going to pass Senior Lifesaving Class without a swimsuit that fits."

"Sounds like you've got a problem, then," recognized Sheree, not happy with Carolyn's changed attitude toward her.

Hurrying to make it in time for PE class, Carolyn stumbled and nearly twisted her ankle when the strap on one of her light beige suede sandals unexpectedly broke. Removing her other sandal, and tossing both into her gym bag, Carolyn continued barefooted down the rocky path as quickly as she could. She definitely needed to obtain a pair of zorries to keep in her bag. The swimming facility was located several hundred yards past the gymnasium, in another of the many military style buildings still left on campus.

"There you are!" greeted Mrs. Bovinae.

"One of my sandals broke," apologized Carolyn as she raced for the locker room. Too bad there were no locks on any of the lockers, but leaving a wet swimsuit behind in her PE locker each day would have been out of the question anyway. There would be no way for it to dry. Everyone else had already changed into their swimsuits and were standing in line by the pool, waiting for class to begin. The one-piece blue striped swimming outfits reminded Carolyn of photos she had once seen that had been taken at the turn of the last century, where people wore striped swimsuits resembling these. The only thing these swimsuits lacked were the long sleeves and leg coverings!

"Veronica and Susan," directed Mrs. Bovinae, "you will be backups for Carolyn when it comes time to pull her assigned swimming partner from the pool."

"Why would I need a backup?" questioned Carolyn as she emerged from the locker room in her loose fitting borrowed swimsuit.

"Carolyn, this is Karol Weeble," introduced the PE teacher. "Badminton was not working out for her, so Karol will be in Senior Life Saving Class from now on."

Carolyn stared with amazement at her new swimming partner. Karol was the fattest person Carolyn had ever seen in her life.

"Hi," nodded Karol. "Sorry you didn't make it in time to get a better partner. But, 374 pounds shouldn't be too much of a problem once we're in the water, right?"

Karol did seem pleasant enough and had a good sense of humor about her condition, but 374 pounds was 374 pounds! Yikes.

Susan and Veronica smirked at Carolyn's predicament, aware that they would more than likely be needed when the time came. There was absolutely no way anyone could be expected to pull someone like Karol from the water without help.

Despite her size, Karol did swim rather well. Carolyn tried to envision how she would be able to pull someone that size from the water, uncertain it would even be possible. She would definitely have to use the underwater approach, but how would she ever get her arm around Karol for the cross chest carry?

"Girls," Mrs. Bovinae began. "Today we are going to review the procedure for lifting a rescued victim from the water. Has everyone reviewed their Life Saving and Water Safety handbooks?"

"Yes, Mrs. Bovinae," replied the class in unison.

"Excellent," smiled Mrs. Bovinae. She was a well-tanned, short but muscular woman with blonde curly locks worn in a stylish wedge haircut. Her intense blue eyes had kindness about them and she was well liked by her students. "As you know, the rescuer brings the victim to the edge and gets a hand hold, always holding the victim's head above water. Veronica, would you and Susan care to demonstrate?"

"Sure," grinned Veronica, always anxious to show off her skills. Veronica had worked as a lifeguard during the summer and knew what she was doing. Boogie boarding was also one of her favorite hobbies.

The class watched with interest as Susan was rescued by Veronica and brought to the edge of the pool.

"Note how Veronica braces her legs as she prepares to lift Susan from the water," pointed out the instructor. "She also avoids leaning backward as she lifts to avoid the danger of slipping. The rescuer should also be sure the victim's legs are not jackknifed under a platform or float device and avoid scraping the victim on the edge as they are raised out of the water to safety. The learning of this method requires nothing more than mastering the technique and lots of practice. It's just a matter of getting the victim safely from the water. Let's all try it."

Several of the girls in class tried to keep straight faces as Karol jumped into the large swimming pool. A huge wall of water splashed across everyone else that was still standing on the edge.

"Girls!" warned Mrs. Bovinae with a huge grin. She sincerely hoped they would all be able to stop laughing before Karol poked her head back up from the water.

"Whew hoo!" shouted Karol as she came to the surface. "And it's even heated!"

Laughter erupted among the group as everyone else jumped in, including Carolyn.

"Wanna be the victim first?" asked Karol with a grin.

"Yeah, sure," smiled Carolyn with relief. She knew Karol would have no trouble pulling her from the water.

When everyone was safely out of the water, Mrs. Bovinae called out, "Now let's switch."

To make it more interesting and fun, Karol loudly called, "Help! Help! I'm drowning! Help!"

Deciding to stay with the underwater approach, Carolyn circled around and grabbed Karol's huge swimsuit from behind. Despite her long arms, Carolyn was unable to reach far enough around her drowning victim for a cross chest carry. She would have to improvise. Pushing up on Karol's back from beneath with her hip, Carolyn used the arm on that side to maintain her grip on Karol's swimsuit while she kicked with all her might and used her free arm to swim to the edge of the pool.

Afraid she might drown herself, Carolyn suddenly let go of Karol to surface long enough for a breath of air.

"Never let go of the victim," reminded Mrs. Bovinae with an amused look on her face, not unsympathetic to Carolyn's predicament.

Able to touch the bottom of the pool from where they now were, Carolyn pushed up with all her might from beneath and managed to obtain another breath of air. Perhaps Karol could be rolled sideways up and onto the edge. After several failed attempts, Susan and Veronica then jumped into the water to try and assist. Even with the three of them pushing with all their might, they just were not able to get Karol out of the water.

"Let's try it from the edge," suggested Veronica.

Carolyn continued to support Karol's buoyant weight in the water while Susan and Veronica climbed back out of the water again, each taking one of Karol's hands in a wrist lock with both of theirs. "Okay, push!" yelled Veronica, bracing her legs and endeavoring to keep her back straight so she would not slip during the process.

"Try again," shouted Susan as she felt her feet giving way.

"Pull!" coached the instructor. "You can do it! You two help."

Two other students approached to assist. One grabbed Susan around the waist from behind for support while the other grabbed and hung onto Veronica. The four girls heaved with all their might as Carolyn tried one last time to shove Karol from the water.

All at once, the entire group of girls were overcome by Karol's gargantuan weightiness and pulled into the swimming pool, creating the biggest splash imaginable. The force of gravity had just been too much.

"Tsunami!" shouted Karol as she surfaced and swam over to the nearest steps before climbing from the pool. "Guess I'm dead, then?"

Back in the shower area of the locker room, the girls from Mrs. Bovinae's PE class could not stop laughing about the big splash. Similar to the showers up in the girls' dormitory, the huge shower stall was twenty feet square with only a single water dispensing pole in the middle containing multiple heads that pointed in various directions.

Karol was not the least bit shy about disrobing and joining the other naked girls in the military style shower to rinse off the strong odor of chlorine from their bodies before drying off and dressing again.

In spite of everything, Karol was well liked by everyone and quickly made friends with the other girls. Karol was anything but shy, and her goal in life was to become a standup comedian. Things were never dull when Karol was around, that was for sure!

"I'm Susan Rives," Susan introduced herself to Carolyn as they climbed into their dry clothes.

"Nice to meet you," smiled Carolyn. "I'm Carolyn Bennett."

"And I'm Karol Weeble, beached whale extraordinaire," howled Karol. "Hey, thanks for trying to save me."

"No problem," chuckled Carolyn.

"I'm Veronica Jensen," greeted the other girl standing beside Susan. "Lifeguard at the Los Angeles Aquatic Center this past summer, and boogie boarder extraordinaire."

The girls then laughed again, seeming to sense that they would become close friends.

"Have any more classes today?" asked Susan as they rung out and put their wet swimsuits into plastic bags before stuffing them into their gym bags.

"No," answered Carolyn. "This was it for me today."

"Indeed," grinned Veronica.

"Hey, it's girls' beach today," reminded Susan. "Wanna go down there for a while? We can watch Veronica do some boogie boarding. She usually practices each day after swim class."

"Any other time, but I won't be boogie boarding today," declined Veronica. "I need to get back to the dormitory. I have a paper due in history class tomorrow."

"I'm so glad not to be in that class!" replied Susan.

"I got the history paper to write, too," sighed Karol. "But, at least they say victims float better in the salt water. For next time."

"Oh my," Carolyn just shook her head. "Well, I don't have history class, and would love to go down to the beach, but broke the strap on my sandal coming down here. Now, I'm shoeless."

"Come with me," suggested Susan. "I think I have an extra pair of sandals that would fit you up in my room."

As Carolyn and Susan headed uphill toward the girls' dormitory, Susan suddenly asked, "Aren't you the girl that Lenny Owens had his date with last weekend?"

Surprised that Susan would remember, Carolyn asked, "Why?"

"Lenny and I went to high school together," revealed Susan. "Not my type, though. I'd have to climb up onto a step ladder just to kiss a guy that tall."

44

"And you had that short Freshman guy for your date?" recalled Carolyn. "Karl somebody."

"Karl Branson," said Susan. "Actually, a very nice guy. Too bad he is just a Freshman."

Carolyn suddenly seemed sad.

"Hey, what's wrong?" pumped Susan. "You didn't have your eye on him, did you?"

"Karl?" Carolyn was surprised. "Of course not. I'm just worried that Lenny will think I don't like him anymore."

"Why would he think that?" questioned Susan.

"Well, that stupid roommate of mine decided to turn off my alarm clock the very next morning after my date with Lenny," recalled Carolyn. "Without telling me, of course. She claimed I looked like I wasn't feeling well and needed my rest. I'm sure Lenny wondered why I didn't show up for breakfast that next morning, and now I haven't seen him since."

"Haven't you and Lenny been eating together almost every day since you got here?" quizzed Susan. "I just assumed the two of you were a couple."

"A couple?" Carolyn was surprised. "Well, as far as I know, we're just friends. Lenny's never mentioned anything about going steady or anything like that."

"Well, he is a man of few words," grinned Susan. "But trust me, I've known Lenny for years, and I've never seen him so taken with anyone before."

"Really? So, how come he's never told me about it?" demanded Carolyn. "And what's happened to him? Is he sick, too?"

"You didn't know?" smirked Susan.

"Tell me!" pressed Carolyn.

"They unexpectedly switched Lenny's hours to the extra-early shift. At least that's what his cousin Pete told me. We used to work at the mill together but all had a big stain fight in the assembly line." Susan chuckled at the memory. "It was a blast! Redwood stain, too."

"And?" Carolyn was anxious to learn what else Susan knew.

"Now they both start at 7:00 a.m. with little time for breakfast," revealed Susan. "No more hanging around until after the serving line closes. At least I don't have to be at the mill until 8:00."

"So Lenny has been at breakfast?" Carolyn seemed puzzled.

"Yes, but not for the past two days," explained Susan. "Lenny's been sick with that cold thing that's been going around, just like you. Pete's been taking trays back for Lenny. He's also his roommate."

"I know who you mean!" Carolyn recalled. "Pete is that short guy who's been filling up a second tray the past two days. Of course! So, how's Lenny now?"

"Like you, finally back on his feet again," chuckled Susan. "Today was Lenny's first day back on the extra-early shift at the mill."

"What does he do there?" grilled Carolyn, only now realizing how little she actually knew about the tall, dark, handsome young man she was interested in.

"I think he works in the nut house," answered Susan. "Either that or slats."

"The nut house?" repeated Carolyn.

"Counting metal washers as they come off of a conveyer belt and are put into little assembly packages," explained Susan. "The kind you find in do-it-yourself furniture kits."

"Lenny never mentioned what he does," pondered Carolyn.

"He's just very shy," informed Susan. "You didn't know? Say, who's that awful roommate of yours, anyway?"

"Sheree Wilkins," Carolyn mentioned with a roll of her eyes. "Dean's pet, always running to her with every little thing, and reminding me constantly of every rule in the handbook, including ones she makes up as she goes along."

"Isn't she that dweeb with the headgear and back brace?" Susan wrinkled her nose.

"Yeah, that's her," sighed Carolyn.

"Hey, you and I should be roommates," suggested Susan.

"Do you think they would let us?" Carolyn was hopeful.

"We could always ask," responded Susan.

"And if our roommates won't agree?" countered Carolyn.

"Then we make them want to agree," Susan grinned a crooked smile, seeming to know just how that might happen.

"What do you have in mind?" pressed Carolyn.

"Trust me," assured Susan. "I have a plan."

4. Demons in the Dorm

Sheree was clearly upset at learning that Carolyn did not want to be her roommate anymore.

"I'm sorry!" apologized Sheree after Carolyn told her that Lenny no longer was showing up for breakfast. "I should never have shut off your alarm clock and I'll never do it again."

"I just can't trust you anymore," responded Carolyn, deciding not to tell Sheree the rest of what she had learned from Susan about Lenny. After all, if Sheree wanted to feel bad about what she had done, then perhaps she should be allowed to do so.

"There aren't any extra rooms, except that single one down by the Dean's office," mentioned Sheree. "Are you suggesting one of us move down there?"

"If you had your own room," pointed out Carolyn, "then you could have more quiet time to do your studies."

"There aren't any windows in that room," frowned Sheree.

"But, you'd have it all to yourself," persisted Carolyn.

"Maybe you should be the one to move there," replied Sheree, determined to remain where she was. "I'm sure the Dean would let you if you asked."

"I guess nobody really wants that particular room, do they?" scowled Carolyn.

"No, they don't," confirmed Sheree with finality.

Susan, Carolyn and Veronica had come to the shower room in the east wing of the girls' dormitory restroom where they could freely talk without fear of being overheard by prying ears. One never knew when Dean Dixon might be listening over one of the dormitory room speaker boxes.

"Turn on the water so the hall monitor thinks we're taking a shower," instructed Susan.

Veronica quickly turned on the water and checked to be sure no one else was in the large restroom who might eavesdrop on them, including in each of the toilet stalls nearby.

After Carolyn related her encounter with Sheree to Susan and Veronica, a plan was hatched.

"This is not a problem," assured Susan.

"What do you have in mind?" worried Carolyn, not wanting to do anything that might land them in trouble with Dean Dixon.

"The punishment should fit the crime; don't you think?" Susan smiled an evil smile.

"The crime?" Veronica was unfamiliar with the alarm clock incident but was quickly brought up-to-date by Susan and Carolyn.

"Sheree wants someone else's alarm clock to turn off," began Susan. "Let's give her a few."

Veronica slowly began to smile with understanding. "Of course, the punishment should fit the crime, how perfect!"

"How many alarm clocks can we get?" questioned Susan.

"I've got one," offered Veronica.

"Karol might lend us one," suggested Susan.

"Are you planning what I think you are?" Carolyn could not believe what she was hearing.

"You should keep yours, Carolyn," added Susan. "Otherwise it might look suspicious."

"I should keep my alarm clock? And just what are we doing with the other alarm clocks?" quizzed Carolyn, very concerned about what her new friends were considering.

"Depending on how many we get," began Susan, "we can set them at different times, throughout the night. I have some favors to call in, not a problem. I'm sure I can get at least half a dozen clocks."

"And hide them in different places over on Sheree's side of the room?" howled Veronica. "I like it!"

"Then Sheree can have all the alarm clocks she wants to turn off," laughed Susan. "You just need to act surprised about it."

"She will go to the Dean," predicted Carolyn with trepidation. "And there's no way she'll believe I had nothing to do with it, especially after telling Sheree I don't want to be her roommate anymore."

"It's the only way," Susan replied seriously.

"And you really think Miss Dixon will let me pick who my new roommate will be after something like this?" Carolyn shook her head.

"Of course not," grinned Susan. "But, I suspect things may work out better than you think. It just so happens that my current roommate is a bit of a boring, studious, socially inept creature, too, and will probably be wanting to move somewhere else herself. Either that, or ask the Dean to move me out. And where else would she put me but with you? It's not like there's any other rooms available right now."

"Susan's gonna short sheet Jan's bed again, but this time a long slithery Garter snake will be part of the deal," revealed Veronica.

"Jan does hate snakes," smirked Susan. "You should have seen her in biology class the other day."

"They could end up putting one of us in that single room," feared Carolyn, not at all fond of the idea.

"I seriously doubt Dean Dixon would put one of us in that single room," assured Susan. "It's right next to her apartment, and that's the last place she would want one of us hanging out. Especially with everything going on over there late at night like it does."

"What do you mean?" asked Carolyn.

"You haven't seen that weird guy who comes to her apartment and carries boxes of stuff from her place out to his ratty old pickup truck?" marveled Susan.

"No, I haven't," admitted Carolyn.

"You really should peek out your window once in a while," recommended Veronica.

"Well, Carolyn probably wouldn't be able to see all that from where her room is anyway, but someone like Sheree or Jan would be too naive to even know what's going on if they saw it," explained Susan. "Whereas someone like one of us would figure it out and probably report her."

"Or have something to hold over her head," mused Veronica.

"Interesting," nodded Carolyn, curious to learn more about the illicit activities of Dean Dixon and her mysterious late-night friend that Susan and Veronica claimed were going on.

"I heard the guy's an ex-con," shuddered Veronica. "They say he was in prison for over twenty years for something really bad, but no one seems to know what it is."

"How would Miss Dixon know someone like that?" puzzled Carolyn. "Do you think he might be her son or a relative of some sort?"

"Anything's possible," agreed Susan, "but either she helps him because she wants to, or because he has something on her."

The girls shared a moment of silence while pondering that possibility.

"They probably take all those flashlights, radios, record players, and whatever else they steal from the girls' rooms and sell it at a pawn shop in town," speculated Veronica.

"He's real creepy, too," scowled Susan. "He's got a crewcut, horn-rimmed glasses so thick they make him look like super-fly, tattoos all over his huge muscular arms, and never wears anything but dirt-covered blue jeans and filthy white t-shirts."

"At least he's in compliance with the haircut code," Veronica was sarcastic. "Seriously, I don't see how Miss Dixon gets away with letting someone like that hang out by a girls' dormitory!"

"The school probably has no idea," guessed Susan.

"And I suppose you plan to tip 'em off?" questioned Carolyn. "Sounds dangerous."

"So about the alarm clock thing, are we a go?" grilled Susan.

After a long pause, Carolyn finally nodded her head, realizing it really was the only way. She just hoped the consequences would not be too dire.

Plausible deniability with an alibi. That's what Susan called it. Carolyn had followed Susan's suggestion and gone for a long walk along the bluffs after class with her friend Joyce the following day. Carolyn half hoped that Susan and Veronica might change their mind about the plan to sneak into her dormitory room so they could hide their collection of borrowed alarm clocks.

Sunlight streamed through the large, windblown cypress and eucalyptus trees as Carolyn and Joyce Troglite made their way single file along the narrow clifftop trail toward the Oceanview dairy. Seagulls circled high overhead while sandpipers, guillemots, murrelets and puffins could be heard in and around the craggy cliffs below. Countless numbers of migrating seabirds would spend years at sea, coming ashore only on particular beaches or cliffs to breed. Uniquely adapted to marine life with dense waterproof feathers and buoyant layers of fat, these birds possessed a desalinization system capable of removing minerals from saline water. It was fascinating to observe them.

Interspersed with the fresh ocean air was the increasing odor of pungent animal waste, a clear sign they were nearing their destination.

"Are you sure they won't mind if we watch?" asked Carolyn as she carefully stepped over a small boulder that had fallen onto the trail.

50

"Why would they?" Joyce shrugged her shoulders. "I come here all the time to watch them milk the cows and feed the chickens."

"Look!" noticed Carolyn. "A Siamese cat."

"They have a few barn cats, too," grinned Joyce.

"I have a Siamese cat at home," revealed Carolyn. "Her name is Socky, and I miss her so much I can hardly stand it!"

"That's tough," nodded Joyce. "I have a black one and a white one back home, but they both belong to the whole family."

Joyce was about five feet six inches tall, and well-tanned from spending time outdoors. Joyce had shoulder length wavy brown hair and hazel eyes, and was beautiful in a rugged sort of way. When not in class or boogie boarding with her friend Veronica, Joyce loved hiking along the bluffs and through the old growth forest at the other end of the campus, and was quite familiar with the best hiking trails Oceanview Academy had to offer.

"Here kitty, kitty, kitty," called Carolyn as she bent down to coax the elusive feline to come and be petted.

"That one's pretty shy," chuckled Joyce. "But, there are more at the barn. Most of them live up in the loft where the hay is kept."

"I never knew all this was here," marveled Carolyn as she approached and studied the dairy. "Wow!"

"The horses are over in the barn on the other side of that field," pointed out Joyce. "Some of the kids who come here have their own."

"Their own horses?" Carolyn was surprised.

"Yeah," sighed Joyce wistfully. "The lucky ones."

"Kind of like the ones who take aviation class or photography?" Carolyn inquired.

"Exactly like that," confirmed Joyce. "The rich and fortunate ones. At least those with a GPA of 3.8 or above."

"Whose tuition is paid in full," added Carolyn.

"And probably in advance," guessed Joyce.

"Maybe we better head back so we get there while dinner is still being served," suggested Carolyn.

"Good idea," agreed Joyce.

Carolyn and Joyce ate dinner with several of the other girls at the cafeteria, and enjoyed their time together. Susan and Veronica were not among them. Also missing was Karol Weeble. Carolyn wondered where they all might be but said nothing. Hopefully no one else would notice their absence at the evening meal.

One of the girls at Joyce and Carolyn's table told of her job at the candle factory, while another described what it was like working in the laundry facility. Two of the girls spoke of the many challenges they faced working in the bakery, just grateful not to be working in the produce area caring for and harvesting crops. Carolyn slowly began to realize that her job serving in the boys' food line for breakfast was actually one of the more desirable jobs here at Oceanview Academy and was thankful for it.

Occasionally Carolyn glanced around to see if Lenny Owens might be somewhere in the cafeteria, but he was nowhere to be seen. Will I ever see him again? Carolyn wondered to herself with a tinge of sadness. She truly missed Lenny and having breakfast with him each morning. Perhaps if she and Susan did become roommates, there might be an opportunity to see Lenny again and to find out whether there was a possible future to their relationship. After all, Susan did know Lenny from her previous school, so that made it imperative as far as Carolyn was concerned to remain in Susan's good graces.

Carolyn made sure she was seen by Diana coming into the dormitory with Joyce before heading directly to her room where Sheree was busy putting away her books and preparing for bed. In no time, the lights went off and it was time to climb into bed for the night.

Sleep would not come for Carolyn as she lay awake wondering when the first alarm clock would ring. Perhaps they hadn't done it after all, Carolyn silently hoped as midnight arrived and all was still silent save for the sound of Sheree's incessant snoring. Then, right at the stroke of midnight, the first alarm clock did ring.

"What in the world?" mumbled Sheree, confused that her clock would be ringing so early.

"Think you got the time wrong," mentioned Carolyn for effect.

"I'm sorry," apologized Sheree as she turned off the clock and tried to reset it in the dark. Just as she succeeded, yet another clock began to ring. "What's going on?"

"You tell me," snapped Carolyn. "Some people would like to get some rest around here! Is this your way of getting back at me for being upset with you about turning off my alarm clock?"

"No," assured Sheree, "but I'm pretty sure I know who did."

"Who?" questioned Carolyn.

"Diana told me she saw Susan Rives and her friend Veronica in here earlier," revealed Sheree. "They told her they thought they were in Karol Weeble's room and were waiting for her, but then left when they realized it was the wrong room."

"Really?" commented Carolyn as another alarm clock began to ring, this time hidden beneath Sheree's bed.

"All right, that's it!" Sheree was furious. "I know you're in on it, no matter what you might say! You know something!"

"I had nothing to do with any of this," Carolyn was honestly able to tell her. "I was out walking with Joyce on the cliffs all afternoon, over by the dairy. Diana saw us come in. You can ask her."

"It was boys' beach today," reminded Sheree.

"So," shrugged Carolyn in the darkness.

"Girls can only visit the dairy on girls' beach day," clarified Sheree, "because the dairy is on the beach half of the campus."

"What about any girls who might be working there?" questioned Carolyn as yet another alarm clock began to ring. This one was in Sheree's closet.

Carolyn felt helpless as she listened to Sheree fumble her way toward the closet to try and find the alarm clock.

"It really is too bad I don't have that flashlight anymore," reminded Carolyn. "You remember, the one you took out of my dresser without asking before you turned it over to the Dean!"

"Well, it was contraband!" shouted Sheree as she grabbed her bathrobe and decided to leave without bothering to turn off the clock after all. "You know what? You can turn off the rest of the alarm clocks by yourself! I have no doubt there are more, and I sincerely hope they keep you up the rest of the night! I'm going to see Miss Dixon, right now!" Sheree then left, slamming the dormitory room door as she went.

As Sheree predicted, several more clocks did ring as the night progressed. In fact, Carolyn was up the rest of the night finding and turning them off. By morning, Carolyn was so tired she could hardly keep her eyes open.

Suddenly, the voice of Miss Dixon could be heard over her room's intercom box. "Carolyn?"

"Yes, Miss Dixon," mumbled Carolyn.

"Please come to my office. I'll be waiting." It was not a request.

Carolyn hurriedly put on her robe and slippers without bothering to brush her hair or anything else and headed for Miss Dixon's apartment immediately. *Why did I ever agree to allow Susan and Veronica to do such a thing?* Carolyn chided herself. *Even Sheree did not deserve what they had tried to put her through last night. But, neither did she!* Carolyn was exhausted.

Carolyn lightly knocked on the Dean's familiar door, hoping sincerely that no one else was up. It was still half an hour until the mandatory morning vesper service at 5:15, though, so movement could be heard in some of the rooms.

"I'll get straight to the point," sighed Miss Dixon as she shook her head and motioned for Carolyn to sit on the small, worn, overstuffed couch in her office. "Sheree will be moving her things to the single occupant room next door to me while you are at your job this morning. Please wait until this afternoon before returning to your room."

"May I at least go there long enough to get dressed first?" questioned Carolyn.

"Of course," conceded the Dean. "And, it will continue to be your room after Sheree is out of it."

An awkward moment of silence pervaded the room. "I do realize you had nothing to do with hiding those alarm clocks," continued Miss Dixon. "But, I also know that you allowed it to happen."

Carolyn stared with shame at a bare spot on the carpet without comment.

"As your punishment," revealed the Dean, "you are going to have a new roommate. Her name is Susan Rives. I believe you already know one another."

"Oh, thank you," replied Carolyn with relief.

"Don't thank me yet," cautioned the Dean. "You may not be as well acquainted with Susan as you think you are. I've had nothing but problems with her since she's been here, and frankly I have nowhere else to put her just now. I just hope you fare better than some of her previous roommates. Perhaps you should have a chat with the last one."

"Yes, ma'am," nodded Carolyn somberly.

"Susan will be moving her things into your room after lunch," informed the Dean, "and she has a lot of them."

Carolyn was indeed familiar with the glamorous selection of clothing and shoes Susan would be bringing with her.

"Oh yes, another thing," continued Miss Dixon. "Susan and Veronica are both grounded for an entire week. That means they will only be allowed to leave their rooms for vespers, meals, classes and work. No walks on the beach, no boogie boarding, no hikes through the forest for them. But you, since you had nothing to do with hiding the clocks, will not be grounded. Perhaps while you're out and about, you will worry what your new roommate might be doing to the things in your room. And whatever it is, I do not want to hear about it."

"Yes, Miss Dixon," agreed Carolyn.

"Finally," the Dean studied Carolyn evenly, "you will start your new job assignment effective today."

"My new job?" Carolyn was flabbergasted.

"You wanted an opportunity to wear your new jeans," reminded Miss Dixon. "Well, now you'll have it. You will be working the extra-early shift at the lumber mill on the long side of the cut-off."

"The cut-off?" repeated Carolyn, unfamiliar with the term.

"The cut-off is where eight, ten and twelve foot boards are cut-off by lumbermen with commercial sized chop saws. The boards then ride on a conveyer belt to where the stackers are. You will be a stacker," Miss Dixon smiled at the thought. "You will have one fifteen-minute break mid-shift, so perhaps you'll have an opportunity to see Lenny when you aren't busy stacking eight, ten and twelve-foot boards onto a wooden pallet. Anyway, I understand Lenny's working the extra-early shift there, too."

"Thank you!" beamed Carolyn, grateful for the opportunity.

"Yeah, yeah," chuckled the Dean. "You can thank me later. And, I won't be the one mentioning this to your parents. That will be your responsibility. Come on, we'd both better hurry or we'll be late for vesper service."

Three weeks had come and gone since the alarm clock incident, but things were going better than expected for Carolyn with Susan as her new roommate. Sheree was rarely seen anymore, except at vesper services, but appeared to hold no ill will toward them. Susan had more new clothes and shoes than she could possibly ever wear and freely allowed Carolyn to borrow and wear them to classes. Susan also spent hours teaching Carolyn how to wear her clothes, hair and makeup more attractively, and how to walk with poise and distinction. Then, just as Susan predicted, many members of the male persuasion began to take notice of Carolyn that had not done so previously.

Despite everything, Carolyn was basically quite shy when it came to guys and thought of little else but Lenny. Had Carolyn done something to upset him? Had Lenny found someone else? Even during the 15-minute break they had at the lumber mill each morning, it was often necessary for Carolyn to continue working straight through the break in order to get "caught up" stacking boards that had accumulated into an unwieldy pile on the floor at her feet. Otherwise, she would have been unable to keep up with the renewed onslaught of approaching lumber once the machinery started back up again. That in itself made it nearly impossible to spend time with Lenny during breaks as she had hoped.

Located in the industrial section of the Oceanview campus near its bakery, laundry facility and candle making factory, the lumber mill had been built onto the back end of an abandoned airplane hangar with huge, manually operated bay doors. These were used for convenient access by truckers when making deliveries of fresh uncut lumber to the mill for processing. Kept closed except during deliveries or pleasant weather conditions, the open hangar bay doors offered clear views of the area outside where workers gathered for break and was easily seen by anyone inside near the cut-off or pallet stacking area.

When working through her break that morning, Carolyn was troubled by the sight of gorgeous Linda Shaver standing close to and visiting with Lenny outside. Linda was six feet tall with curved shapely legs, alabaster skin, blue eyes and dark brown shoulder length hair. Linda had a beautiful smile and eyes that twinkled with delight as she conversed with Lenny. Her interest in him was obvious.

Workers were not allowed to wear protective gloves while working near the conveyer belts or other machinery, lest their gloves should get caught in the mechanisms or pose a safety threat of some kind. Needless to say, most stackers had rough looking, sliver covered hands by the end of each shift. It was obvious that Linda did not work in a section of the mill that required handling wood. Her hands were absolutely lovely! From the apron she had on and the thread cutting ring she wore on her right hand, Carolyn recognized that Linda must be one of the sewers. Chaise lounge cushions were sewn on high powered sewing machines before being filled, tufted and packaged by hand in another section of the building. The place where boards were treated with redwood stain that Susan worked in was beyond that. Lenny's job was in the packaging portion of the mill where hardware packets were assembled that included various nuts, bolts, screws, washers and even instruction sheets. These were then sealed into plastic bags and included with each of the build-your-own patio furniture kits. That, of course, was located right beside the sewing area. Much too close to Linda's workstation, thought Carolyn.

Carolyn frowned as she hurried to get the rest of her fallen boards onto the wooden pallet before break was over, lest she get into trouble when the supervisor strolled by as he often did at just such times. While she did, Carolyn thought about the letter she had written to her parents the previous day. No doubt her father would be pleased about her new job with higher pay and longer hours, and how it would reduce the amount he needed to pay toward her tuition. The new roommate situation, however, was something else again. Carolyn would wait and tell her parents about that in person, next time they came out for a visit.

When her shift was over, Carolyn raced toward the timeclock where she waited in line for her turn to run her time card through the device so she could leave. Lenny and Linda were several places in line ahead of her, seemingly oblivious to her presence. Unbidden tears began to escape from Carolyn's eyes. Perhaps she would have an opportunity to see Lenny at lunch and could talk to him then. But, the opportunity did not present itself.

Why hadn't Lenny gone to lunch at the cafeteria? Come to think of it, she hadn't seen Linda Shaver at lunch, either, and was troubled by it. Afternoon classes seemed to drag by as Carolyn pondered the events of that morning.

The following morning, Susan and Carolyn raced straight from vesper service to the cafeteria to be there at 6:15 when the serving line opened. After wolfing down their breakfast in record time, they headed toward the lumber mill where the extra-early shift would begin promptly at 7:00.

"Hurry," urged Carolyn. "We can't be late again."

"What are they gonna do?" guffawed Susan as she raced to keep up. "Dock our pay? We don't see a penny of it anyway! So, what difference does it make?"

"There are worse jobs they could put us in," reminded Carolyn. "If we lose this one, who knows where we'll end up. Maybe cleaning out animal pens at the dairy, or handling dirty laundry from the mental institution."

"Oh yeah," laughed Susan. "The Ocean Bluff loony bin. I forgot about that."

"I'm serious!" Carolyn was upset at Susan's attitude. "As bad as working at the mill may be, doing that would definitely be worse!"

"At least you get to see Lenny," reminded Susan.

Stopping in her tracks, Carolyn turned to look at Susan with a cold hard stare. "Really?"

"Well, you do have the opportunity," added Susan as she took advantage of the chance to catch her breath.

"In a pig's eye!" snapped Carolyn as she turned and resumed her trek toward the mill where there would be a long line of fellow workers waiting to slide their time cards through the timeclock before hustling to their various workstations.

"Wait, hold on!" called Susan as she grabbed Carolyn's arm to get her to stop again. "What is it?"

"I'll tell you 'what is it,'" snapped Carolyn as she slowed down but continued walking. "It is Linda Shaver!"

"Ah ha," Susan nodded with understanding. "You really oughta take your breaks, you know. It's the law."

"Ya think?" Carolyn was frustrated. "I'm sorry, it's just that she has me so mad I can hardly think straight."

"Just because she talks to Lenny whenever she gets the chance?" questioned Susan. "Is that why you're so upset?"

"You weren't even there yesterday," reminded Carolyn. "You were up in your room pretending to be sick so you could finish that history paper!"

"True enough," admitted Susan. "But, it's not like you haven't seen this coming. And you never do anything about it."

"Like what?" pressed Carolyn.

"First of all, she's really no threat," pointed out Susan. "Just be sure you do take your breaks, and get over there before she does."

"What if Lenny won't even talk to me?" fretted Carolyn.

"Then you talk to him," suggested Susan. "You know how shy he is. Lenny never says much."

"Well, I wish he'd at least tell me where I stand with him," replied Carolyn. "First he holds my hand at date night...."

"Really?" interrupted Susan with a mischievous grin as they approached the mill. "You never mentioned that part."

"And then he just disappears from my life," finished Carolyn.

"Not entirely," assured Susan. "According to his cousin Pete, Lenny has it quite bad for you."

"Well, you'd never know it! You should have seen the way he and Linda were standing in line together at the timeclock yesterday," mentioned Carolyn.

"Was Lenny doing the talking, or was she?" questioned Susan.

"She was," recalled Carolyn.

"Then all you have to do is get there first and be the one to do the talking, instead of her," summed up Susan.

Carolyn and Susan then quietly waited in line for their turn to clock in before scurrying to their workstations.

Noticeably, Lenny was absent from work that day. Nonetheless, Carolyn did manage to take her break and made it a point to introduce herself to Linda Shaver to discover her true intentions toward Lenny.

"Hi, I don't think we've met," smiled Carolyn as she cautiously approached Linda Shaver. "I'm Carolyn."

"Oh hi, I'm Linda," greeted the stunning would-be rival. "You're Lenny's girlfriend." It was more of a comment than a question.

"Yes, she is," came Susan's voice from behind them. "And she certainly needs to be more diligent about remembering to take her breaks when that whistle blows."

"I'm sure Lenny would like that." Linda returned Susan's even but pleasant smile with one of her own.

"Where is Lenny, anyway?" questioned Susan, deciding it was not time to beat around the bush.

"He didn't tell you?" Linda seemed surprised. "Lenny and I are in Chemistry class together and I've been tutoring him on the side."

"Really?" Carolyn raised an eyebrow.

"Oh, it's not like that at all," assured Linda with an unexpected smile. "You didn't think...?" Linda broke off and began to laugh.

Susan then poked Carolyn in the side with her elbow and joined in the laughter. Linda's laugh was contagious and before long Carolyn was laughing, too.

"Lenny is probably studying for that Chemistry exam we have tomorrow," continued Linda when she was able to stop laughing. "But don't say anything or he might get into trouble. He's supposed to be out sick right now. They don't exactly let you miss work just to do your homework around here."

"No indeed, they don't," nodded Susan with understanding.

Later that night in their room, Susan decided it was time to let Carolyn in on a plan that she and Lenny's cousin Pete had come up with during dinner that evening. Lenny of course had remained in his room during the dinner hour to study for the following day's Chemistry exam. Likewise, Carolyn had missed the evening meal to finish writing a poem for her English Literature class.

Susan had asked her parents to send her a miniature chalkboard to use for "messages" to her roommate. In reality, it was a way for Susan and Carolyn to safely communicate without the risk of being overheard by Miss Dixon, should she ever happen to be listening in on their conversation without their knowledge. Unlike a pen and paper tablet, the chalkboard could easily be erased so there would be no evidence of their conversations left behind. After all, one never knew what might fall into the wrong hands later during an impromptu room search. It was actually an ingenious system.

"Would you mind helping me fold my laundry?" Susan suddenly asked aloud.

"What laundry?" Carolyn silently mouthed the words.

"That load you started for me when you first got back to the room?" whispered Susan.

"Oh yes, of course," nodded Carolyn, knowing full well there was no load of laundry to fold.

Once Susan and Carolyn were in the laundry room, Susan grabbed Carolyn by the arm and led her to the clothes dryer at the far end of the row of machines. There were six coin operated dryers in all. "Look!" nodded Susan.

Carolyn did not see anything at first. Susan then pointed to a large vent cover on the wall. "It's a wall vent. So?"

Susan carefully glanced behind them to be sure no one was approaching before pulling a nail file from her pocket. She then hoisted herself up onto the dryer and used her nail file to pry out the edge of the vent cover before pulling it the rest of the way out. "Look again."

Carolyn was puzzled.

"Come on," urged Susan as she pulled a small flashlight from her other pocket and handed it to Carolyn. "Come up here and have a look. Hurry, before somebody comes."

Carolyn carefully climbed onto the dryer and leaned close to peer inside the opening in the wall above it. Although the opening was only about two feet square in diameter, the space beyond was immense and extended in all directions as far as the eye could see. Cast-iron steam pipes connected by four inch conduits could be seen hanging from the floor above the four-foot high crawl area below. From the light of the small flashlight, Carolyn also noticed an upside down wooden crate on the ground inside, now being used as a stepstool.

"What am I looking for?" questioned Carolyn.

"I'm glad you asked," grinned Susan, still keeping a watchful eye behind them. "Follow me." Susan then wriggled through the opening and stepped down onto the box inside. "I'll hold the flashlight while you climb in."

"Oh Susan, you've got to be kidding!" objected Carolyn.

"Trust me," Susan smiled mischievously.

The sound of someone entering the large restroom complex was then heard. Whoever it was could be planning to take a shower or use one of the toilets. Or, they could come around the adjoining corner at any moment and be planning to do a load of wash.

"Hurry!" persisted Susan as she jumped off of the wooden crate and onto the ground below, to make room for Carolyn to follow.

Realizing the gravity of their situation, Carolyn quickly climbed through the opening and onto the wooden crate.

"Be sure to pull the vent cover in behind you, in case someone comes," added Susan. "We don't want anyone to see it open like that!"

The vent cover was just out of reach, so Carolyn had to climb part way back out to retrieve it before coming back into the secret area where Susan waited. Then, just as Carolyn managed to pull the vent into place behind her, she was able to see through the louvers in the vent cover and noticed Sheree Wilkins enter the laundry room with a basket of laundry. "Oh no! It's Sheree."

"Shhh!" hushed Susan as she clamped her hand over Carolyn's mouth. Then whispering closely into Carolyn's ear, Susan added, "Don't say a word! We'll just have to wait until she's gone."

It seemed to take forever for poor Sheree to retrieve her clean wash load from one of the washing machines on the opposite wall before bringing it over to put inside the dryer closest to where Susan and Carolyn were silently waiting behind the vent cover on the wall above it for her to leave. Sheree slowly reached inside her bathrobe pocket to find the quarter she had brought with her. Before managing to insert it into the dryer's coin slot, Sheree fumbled, dropped it, and helplessly watched as the coin rolled onto the floor beneath the machine.

Susan gripped Carolyn's arm tightly as they watched. "Oww!" whispered Carolyn as she wriggled free from Susan's grasp.

Sheree suddenly glanced around. It was clear she had heard something. Both Susan and Carolyn held their breath for an eternal moment, and hoped they would not be discovered.

Sighing deeply, Sheree then reached back into her pocket, this time more slowly than before, to retrieve another coin. This time she managed to insert it into the dryer's coin slot successfully and get the machine started.

Susan and Carolyn both let out the breath of air they had been holding and watched with relief as Sheree walked away.

"That was too close!" whispered Carolyn.

"Wait," advised Susan. "It sounds like she's getting ready to take a shower next."

"Then as soon as the water comes on, we need to get out of here," recommended Carolyn, not anxious at all to find herself back in Miss Dixon's apartment again.

"Before we leave," whispered Susan, "let me show you what we came here for."

Carolyn remained on the crate as she saw Susan on the ground below in the shadows, and noticed several boxes of items where Susan shined her small flashlight. Stepping down from the crate, Carolyn approached and sat on the ground beside Susan to watch while Susan silently showed her the collection of candles, matches, transistor radios, and even a small record player set up for 45 rpm singles.

"It's not like you have any electricity down here," chuckled Carolyn.

"Look at this," grinned Susan as she handed one of the 45 records to Carolyn. On the label it read, "Sherry Baby."

"Seriously?" Carolyn shook her head.

Susan began to sing the popular tune in animated whispers, "Sher-er-er-er-er-er-er-ee Bay-ay-bee. Sheree Baby, Sheree, won't you come out tonight?"

Carolyn and Susan then laughed as quietly as they could, unable to help themselves.

"Someone oughta hide that in her new room some night," suggested Susan with an evil laugh. "Too bad there's no way to set it on a timer."

"You're horrible!" chided Carolyn, beginning to wonder if Miss Dixon had been right about Susan.

"I'm just kidding," assured Susan. "And look over here. A whole box of flashlights with extra batteries, if we ever need any."

"So, why is all this stuff down here?" Carolyn became serious.

"It's just a safe place to keep stuff people don't want taken away when they come by and search the rooms," shrugged Susan. "It can get expensive to replace it all after a while."

"Who else knows this is here?" questioned Carolyn.

"Just Joyce and Veronica," revealed Susan. "Anyone else who wants their stuff kept in a safe place just gives it to us, for a small price."

"Why show me?" Carolyn was curious.

"Because, my dear," advised Susan, "this is how we'll get back into the dorm if we should ever be caught outside past curfew."

"You've gotten back in this way?" Carolyn was worried at what Susan might come up with next.

Without directly answering Carolyn's question, Susan merely nodded toward the far wall where a faint light could be seen streaming in through another louvered vent cover from outside. It was from one of the lamp posts.

"Wouldn't someone see you coming in that way?" Carolyn was astonished that Susan could even think of something like this, much less get away with it.

"Tomorrow afternoon you and I will be meeting Lenny and Pete down at the beach after classes," revealed Susan.

"What?" Carolyn could not believe what she was hearing. "Tomorrow is boys' beach! We can't go down there. Besides, what if we get caught down there? They'd throw the book at us for being there with two guys, no matter whose beach day it was!"

"Trust me," smirked Susan. "We have nothing to worry about."

The following afternoon after class, Susan and Carolyn met in their dormitory room where they quickly changed into more appropriate clothing for their rendezvous with Lenny and Pete.

"Wear the dark green cords," instructed Susan. "They'll be less noticeable. Wear a dark colored top, too."

Carolyn had hoped to wear the attractive baby blue pullover sweater her mother had sent her, as it fit nicely in all the right places and she wanted to look her best for Lenny.

"What about the dark blue one?" suggested Susan. "It looks fine, and goes with your navy blue jacket."

"All right," agreed Carolyn as she carefully folded and put her baby blue sweater back inside the dresser drawer.

"Wait!" Susan commanded. "Try this one."

Susan had grabbed and thrown various items of clothing onto her bed before finding the black and gold striped top she had been looking for. "Lenny will love this."

"I can't wear something like that!" objected Carolyn as she sat down to tie the laces on her dark brown waffle stompers.

"Sure you can," differed Susan as she tossed the top to Carolyn. "This is what you should wear."

Carolyn studied the gaudy piece of clothing and shook her head. "They'll see me coming from a mile away with the shiny gold threads in this thing."

"You'll have your navy blue coat over it," reminded Susan. "The only time anyone will see it is when we're down there, and only if you decide to unbutton or take off your coat."

"All right," agreed Carolyn, still unsure about the choice.

"Come on," urged Susan as she turned to leave. "Put it on! We need to hurry."

"Oh, no!" fretted Carolyn as she reached for the mini chalkboard they usually used when having conversations that were inappropriate for eavesdroppers.

"Don't worry, nobody heard us" laughed Susan. "I saw Miss Dixon drive away as I was coming back up here from class. She was with that crummy Ray character, and they were in his ratty old pickup. Probably headed for town."

"Really?" Carolyn was surprised.

"There's no way she'd be back yet," calculated Susan. "Come on! It's time for a walk in the woods. Besides, it is girls' woods today."

"Oh, okay," agreed Carolyn as she finally put on the top. It did fit in all the right places, too, but just a bit more so than Carolyn was accustomed to.

"Trust me," Susan raised a roguish eyebrow as she reached for Carolyn's arm and began to pull her toward the door. "Lenny's gonna like that on you!"

Susan and Carolyn stealthily made their way past the faculty housing area at the far edge of the campus before continuing through the towering stand of old growth trees, mostly spruce, cedar and various other varieties of fir. The dense coastal forest was already well on its way toward obscuring any possible view of the ocean from many of the faculty homes.

The last building was Ms. Eggersol's house. Carolyn had come here for special tutoring on poem writing after class last week. Unlike many of the faculty members, Ms. Eggersol seemed like someone who could be trusted. Carolyn had even considered telling Ms. Eggersol what she knew about the alarm clock incident, but decided against it.

"See that post?" Susan was pointing toward a boundary marker on the cliffs just ahead.

"Yeah, what about it?" asked Carolyn.

"It's the very edge of the school's property," indicated Susan. "Just beyond it, there's a negotiable trail down to the beach."

"But that's not on school property!" objected Carolyn.

"A little late for worrying about that now," remarked Susan as she began her descent on the rocky, switchback path.

The afternoon sun was making its way toward the horizon much too quickly for Carolyn's liking, and in their haste to leave earlier, she had left her wristwatch behind. "What time is it?"

"Who cares?" Susan shrugged her shoulders as she stopped to pick one of the hot pink ice plant blossoms that covered the steep hillside, and gingerly pulled back her hair as she placed it over her ear. Creeping cypress shrubs and wind sculptured juniper bushes also grew sporadically between the various sized boulders and loose rocks on the craggy hillside.

The crisp scent of salt water filled the air. A large ivory gull squealed overhead as it swooped toward the shoreline and suddenly dropped a large mussel shell onto a grouping of sharp boulders below. One scavenging method unique to gulls would involve dropping heavy shells of clams and mussels onto hard surfaces below. Gulls were known to fly considerable distances to locate suitable surfaces on which to accomplish this, as gulls had only a limited ability to dive below the water to feed on deeper prey.

"Hey!" called Pete from below. He and Lenny had been sitting on a weather beaten log waiting for them. "It's about time!"

"Can we still make it to the store and back?" asked Susan.

"What store?" asked Lenny, clearly unaware of the plan.

"Yeah, what store?" added Carolyn, certain they were taking enough of a risk as it was just being where they were. After all, someone living in one of the bluff-top houses nearby might see them. And what if those were some of the faculty houses? Anyone could be up there!

"It's only a few hundred yards in that direction, right past where the two large boulders are," grinned Susan as she and Pete began their trek toward the mysterious off-campus store.

"They're all down at the cafeteria right now, anyway," assured Pete, nodding toward the two houses above them. "We're fine."

"But there's nothing over there," doubted Carolyn as she noticed how rocky this section of beach had become, especially when compared to the soft sandy stretch of beach alongside the school's property. Of particular concern was the treacherous portion of trail that extended between the steep hillside and the two giant off-shore boulders.

"Yeah there is," maintained Susan. "See that second house up on the bluff? There's a trail down below it, right beside the water."

"What if the tide comes back in while we're over there?" worried Carolyn as she studied the rocky trail hugging the steep embankment. "How could we possibly get back?"

"We sure can't climb up there!" agreed Lenny, also concerned.

"Don't worry! It gets flat and sandy again, just on the other side. The store's practically right on the beach," informed Pete. "We've got money, too. Come on!"

"Why not?" shrugged Lenny as he reached over and grabbed Carolyn's hand.

Nothing was said as Lenny and Carolyn followed after Pete and Susan, though tender smiles and hand squeezes were exchanged. Any doubts Carolyn may have had about Lenny's feelings seemed to melt away and she suddenly wished this moment would last forever.

The brief hike around the rocky outcropping took longer than expected, but had been easier to negotiate than expected.

"The store's just closing," noticed Pete as he suddenly sprinted across the sand toward the weather beaten establishment.

"Hey!" shouted Susan as she raced along beside him. The proprietor had just pulled out his key ring to lock the door. "Is it too late to get some ice cream?"

"And some marshmallows, too?" pleaded Pete as he came to an abrupt stop, leaned over, and rested his hands on his knees to gasp for air. "We didn't realize it was so late."

"Oh sure, come on in," invited the store owner. "You got here just in time. I was actually closing early. Business has been slow."

After purchasing two bags of marshmallows, a small lighter, a bag of corn chips, and a six-pack of root beer, Pete suddenly realized, "Oh yeah, we came here for ice cream cones, too."

Lenny and Carolyn both ordered the walnut pistachio, while Pete decided on strawberry and Susan went for the chocolate.

"And some napkins, too!" laughed Susan as she grabbed a handful of them from a dispenser on the counter and distributed them to the others.

"We'd better get back," mentioned Carolyn, worried about what might happen if they were caught.

"We'll eat 'em on the way," agreed Susan as she grabbed one of the bags of groceries with her free hand.

"And I know just the place we can roast the marshmallows," added Pete as he grabbed the other bag from the proprietor after paying for the merchandise.

"Thanks," nodded Susan.

"Now you owe me one," grinned Pete.

Pete was barely five feet five inches tall, the same height as Susan. They laughed as they headed back, recounting the redwood stain fight experience that had gotten them into trouble at the mill earlier.

"I don't think I'd ever want to work in the stain section," chuckled Carolyn. "Way too messy for me."

Lenny truly was a good listener, but seldom had anything to say. He had resumed holding Carolyn's hand and smiled affectionately as he studied her with his warm, sensitive eyes.

"I wish he'd just take her in his arms and kiss her already," Susan whispered to Pete as they made their way along the rocky beach.

"Yeah, me, too," grinned Pete.

"You'd think he was a virgin or something," joked Susan, half seriously.

"Oh, he is," assured Pete.

"Really? Well, I have no doubt she is, too," guessed Susan. "Still, that's no reason he can't tell her how he feels about her."

"He's pretty shy," reminded Pete.

"So's she," sighed Susan with frustration.

"Hey you two, let's stop and do up the marshmallows before we go back," called Pete. Lenny and Carolyn had managed to fall behind.

Pete pulled the new lighter out of its package and built a big bonfire in the empty fire pit, managing to have it burning brightly before Lenny and Carolyn arrived.

"Won't someone see it?" worried Carolyn as she glanced nervously at the two houses on the bluffs above them.

"Relax. Both houses are dark," pointed out Susan. "Besides, they're probably just rentals or vacation homes. I think we're safe."

"Have you thought about how we're going to get back inside the dormitory?" Carolyn was vexed at the thought of getting called into the Dean's office for something like this.

"Remember my secret way back in?" reminded Susan.

68

"Seriously?" Carolyn realized at once that Susan was referring to the crawl area beneath the girls' dormitory.

"They don't check the rooms until eight," interjected Pete. "And there's no way we can just walk through the front doors now. It's after 6:00 already."

"We need to wait for the cover of darkness," explained Susan as she popped a handful of corn chips into her mouth and began to chew.

Lenny glanced at his wristwatch, noting that it was already 6:30. "I suppose you have a secret way back in, too?"

Everyone was surprised by Lenny's question, but after a moment of consideration Pete replied. "We are both on the track team, cousin. Remember those extra laps we were asked to do? No matter how long it took us?"

Lenny frowned, obviously displeased by their predicament.

"We're okay," assured Pete. "I got it covered. It'll be my fault I made you late."

Pete then grabbed and ate a handful of corn chips while Susan started putting marshmallows onto sticks she had found nearby.

"Here." Susan handed one of the marshmallow sticks to Carolyn as she pulled a bottle opener from her pocket and proceeded to remove the caps off four of the root beer soda bottles.

"We even got music," revealed Pete as he brought out the forbidden transistor radio and tuned it to a local radio station.

"*Nights in White Satin!*" exclaimed Carolyn. "I love that song!"

Lenny pulled Carolyn close to him and put his arm around her as they sat on one of the logs watching the sunset. Mesmerized by the music as it blended with the sound of waves on the shoreline, Carolyn put her head on Lenny's shoulder. Both of them seemed content to remain where they were.

Susan quickly retrieved the marshmallow stick from Carolyn's free hand and brought it back over to the fire where she and Pete proceeded to roast and eat the entire collection of marshmallows until they were gone. "I'd forgotten how good these could be."

Lenny unexpectedly pulled a pocketknife from his pocket and carved LO & CB onto the end of the log on which they were seated.

Carolyn fervently hoped this meant Lenny might finally tell her how he felt about their relationship. Perhaps Lenny would ask her to go steady with him as she had hoped for so long. After all, everyone else seemed to assume they already were.

Much to Carolyn's disappointment, Lenny said nothing of the sort, nor did he even try to kiss her. But, Lenny did continue to hold Carolyn's hand as they got up and returned to the warmth of the fire. "We need to get back," he advised his cousin.

"Maybe I'll see you at breakfast?" asked Lenny as he squeezed her hand one more time before letting go.

"I'd like that," Carolyn smiled warmly.

Carolyn sadly watched as Lenny and Pete dashed toward the rocky access road that led down from tree lined cliffs above. It did seem odd that Lenny was six feet five inches tall while his cousin Pete was an entire foot shorter.

Susan gulped down the last of the corn chips while she and Carolyn waited for the empty food packaging from the marshmallows and the corn chips to burn. Susan then rapidly poured the rest of her root beer onto the bonfire to extinguish it while Carolyn carefully hid the remaining two bottles of root beer in the bushes nearby. "We can get 'em later," called Susan as she headed for the trail on which they had come.

"How are we going to see where we're going?" worried Carolyn, noting that it was suddenly quite dark.

"Trust me," Susan had a crooked grin as she began climbing the rugged trail. "It's not as dark here as it will be in the forest."

Unexpectedly, a vehicle could be heard on the campus border road nearby, used only by security and just at night.

"Duck!" commanded Susan as she flattened herself on the trail.

"Who is that?" demanded Carolyn as she observed a bright spotlight scanning the area. "They must be looking for us!"

"Nonsense," replied Susan. "It's just campus security."

"Campus security?" Carolyn had never heard of it.

"Mr. Bovinae is the Chief of Security," explained Susan. "His wife may be a pushover in PE class, but not him. Just keep down."

Each night at dusk and continuing until dawn, Mr. Bovinae would patrol the campus in an old green Jeep. A huge rotating spotlight was securely mounted on top of the vehicle that systematically scanned the surrounding landscape for any sign of trouble. That included everything from coyotes who might be trying to infiltrate the henhouse over by the dairy, to prowlers or students that might be outside the dormitories after curfew. Mr. Bovinae also had a megaphone handy to use if needed.

Susan then explained to Carolyn that it took 35 minutes for Mr. Bovinae to complete a circuit of the campus. Once his vehicle was out of view, that would give them at least 30 minutes to make it to the next secure location where they could hide until he passed by again.

"I don't like this at all!" Carolyn was furious at Susan.

"You have no choice but to trust me now," rebutted Susan as she got up and began to jog past the faculty housing units. Faculty members could be seen inside the well-lit homes, going about their usual evening routines. "Let's just hope none of them sees us."

Clear of the housing area at last, Susan and Carolyn slowed their pace as they walked past the two isolated crop fields that separated them from the central campus complex where the administration building, cafeteria and dormitories were located.

"Look!" pointed Carolyn as she froze in her tracks. "Didn't you say we had 30 minutes before he came back? He must have seen us!"

"He couldn't have," assured Susan. "That's someone else. We still better hide. Over there, quick."

Susan and Carolyn secreted themselves inside the tall cornfield beside them and watched with curiosity as the ratty old pickup truck belonging to Ray Dixon crept by.

"Why doesn't he have his lights on?" wondered Carolyn aloud. "What is he looking for?"

"Shhh!" instructed Susan. "Not us! Must be something else."

Continuing past them without stopping, the pickup truck slowly pulled to a stop in front of an abandoned bunker tunnel entrance at the far end of the cornfield. Ray quickly jumped from the vehicle, pulled a jingling ring of keys from his detachable belt key holder, and unlocked the sturdy padlock at the tunnel's entrance.

"What's in there?" asked Carolyn.

"I have no idea," responded Susan. "Maybe that's where he takes those boxes."

"The ones he gets from the Dean?" quizzed Carolyn.

"Probably," guessed Susan. "Come on, let's get as far as we can before he comes back out."

Without waiting for Carolyn, Susan began to run as fast as she could past Ray's parked vehicle. Closing her eyes and taking a deep breath first, Carolyn followed.

Whatever Ray was doing inside the tunnel, it thankfully kept him in there long enough for them to make it by unnoticed.

"Here comes Mr. Bovinae!" Susan hurriedly leaped back into the cornstalks beside them for cover.

Ray Dixon came out of the tunnel just as Mr. Bovinae pulled up and came to a stop. "Greetings," nodded Ray.

The two men swiftly unloaded and carried several boxes from the back of Ray's pickup truck into the tunnel, making at least two trips between them. When they were finished, Mr. Bovinae grabbed a small duffle bag from his jeep and handed it to Ray Dixon, who then tossed it into the passenger side of his truck without bothering to look inside.

"Is everything satisfactory?" asked Mr. Bovinae.

"I'm sure it is," responded Ray as he shut the door to the tunnel, secured the padlock, and climbed back into his ratty old pickup truck. Ray then started the motor, and slowly drove away with his headlights still turned off.

Mr. Bovinae glanced around to make sure no one was watching before getting back into his jeep to resume his patrol duties.

The moment he was out of view, Susan and Carolyn ran as fast as they could, hoping to make it safely to their dormitory room before the 8:00 room check.

"Over here," directed Susan as she raced to the side of the girls' dormitory and knelt beside the outside louvered vent cover, hoping to easily pop it off so they could quickly get inside. "We're gonna need a screwdriver for this."

"There he comes!" panicked Carolyn as she saw the bright spotlight down by the administration building. "He's gonna be here in less than a minute!"

Carolyn and Susan leaped into a thick rhododendron bush nearby and silently waited while Mr. Bovinae continued his security sweep of the dormitory buildings. They held their breath as the spotlight swept past the bush in which they were hiding before moving on.

"How are we going to get back inside?" questioned Carolyn.

Susan pulled her nail file from her pocket and raced back over to the louvered vent cover, hoping her flimsy manicuring tool would not break as she proceeded to use it as a screwdriver. "It's working! Just three more to go."

"Hurry!" urged Carolyn as she dashed over to hold the vent cover in place while Susan loosened the remaining screws. "I can't believe it! There he comes again! How could he be back already?"

"Maybe he saw us? Quick inside," commanded Susan as she shoved Carolyn inside and then hopped inside behind her. "There's no way to put those screws back into it from this side."

"We can do it in the morning," suggested Carolyn. "Just pull it up against the building as close as you can get it and hope it doesn't fall down into the flowerbed."

"Or that Mr. Bovinae doesn't notice it with his spotlight!" added Susan with a deep sigh.

"We still have to get to our room before 8:00 and we have no idea what time it is," pressed Carolyn. "Which way?"

"I don't know," admitted Susan. "This is the first time I've ever actually come this way."

"Now you tell me!" chided Carolyn.

"I think we just follow the biggest pipe," hoped Susan. "Oh, this is horrible!"

Spider webs and signs of rodent droppings made the crawlway disgusting as Susan and Carolyn squatted to walk without hitting their heads on the hanging pipes and floor joists above them. Managing to maneuver the four feet high crawl area surrounded by steam pipes extending in every direction, they both were relieved to finally see a faint light ahead. "That's got to be the laundry room," hoped Carolyn.

"Remember that song about knocking three times on the ceiling?" Susan suddenly asked. "I think it came out just last year."

Susan was referring of course to "*Knock Three Times*," a catchy 1970 song release by Tony Orlando and Dawn that hit number one on the charts in 1971, eventually selling over six million copies.

"Yeah, why?" Carolyn was irritated.

"That's one of the 45 record singles we have down here," revealed Susan. "Hey, maybe we should try it."

"Try what?" asked Carolyn.

"Knocking on the ceiling three times," laughed Susan to break the tension. "I think this might be right about where Sheree's room is, right above us."

"And what if it's the Dean's apartment?" countered Carolyn. "Definitely not a good idea!"

Susan and Carolyn continued to squat-walk toward the light in silence until finally Susan said, "I dare you."

"You dare me to do what?" replied Carolyn.

"To knock three times on the ceiling," grinned Susan in the darkness. "Who's gonna hear it anyway? It's not like they're gonna come down here and find us."

They were within just a few yards of the light ahead when Carolyn finally agreed. "Okay, why not? Here goes."

Carolyn then knocked three times on the ceiling and paused, waiting to see if anyone would knock back. Only silence.

"Look!" Susan pointed out with relief. "There's the wooden crate, and the boxes of stuff!"

Carefully, Carolyn stood on the wooden crate and glanced inside the laundry room. "No one's there."

"Then hurry!" urged Susan. "Before someone comes."

"We smell like campfire smoke," Carolyn suddenly realized. "We can't go in there smelling like this."

"This is what we'll do," began Susan. "We'll throw our clothes into one of the washing machines and then hop in the shower."

"We don't have any towels or clean clothes," replied Carolyn.

"Then we'll just have to borrow some," decided Susan. "This is an emergency. As soon as we get to the room we can change and bring 'em back."

"If there are any there to borrow," cautioned Carolyn.

"Just go!" Susan gave Carolyn a shove.

Without further delay, Carolyn pushed the louvered vent cover out of the opening and both girls climbed into the laundry room. After carefully sliding the cover back into place, they quickly removed their clothes and tossed them into the nearest washing machine.

"Here's a load of towels," mentioned Susan as she grabbed two of them. "We can just wrap them around ourselves on our way back to the room. If anyone asks, we forgot our bathrobes."

"What about shampoo?" questioned Carolyn.

"They have liquid hand soap now, over at the sink," directed Susan as she raced over and put a couple handfuls of it onto her hair before scrambling toward the huge shower stall.

"So far so good," acknowledged Carolyn as they turned on two of the shower heads and proceeded to wash themselves.

"Girls?" came the voice of the hall monitor from behind them.

"What is it?" Susan tried to seem nonchalant as she finished rinsing her hair.

"I didn't realize anyone was still in here." It was Diana.

"Just us," responded Carolyn, also trying to appear unconcerned.

"It's five minutes until 8:00," reminded Diana.

"All right, we'll be there," complied Susan with a sigh of relief.

"I'd better wait," insisted Diana.

"What?" Susan was indignant. "We can't rinse and dry off by ourselves now?"

"Oh, it's not that." Diana was serious. "I probably shouldn't say anything yet. The Dean is going to make an announcement at a special vesper service we're having at 8:30."

"Tell us, please," urged Carolyn. "What's wrong?"

"Well," began Diana, leaning close to whisper. "I don't want to alarm you, but the dorm is on demon alert right now."

Susan had to swallow her smile and fight with every ounce of her being to appear serious, and especially to keep from breaking into hysterical laughter. The same was true for Carolyn. Both of them did an amazing job of trying to appear somber while they silently followed Diana to their room. Once inside, Susan and Carolyn laughed until they cried, rolling on their beds, holding their sides, and slapping their hands on their bed tops with hysterical glee.

"Demons in the dorm?" repeated Carolyn when she was finally able to catch her breath and sit up again.

"You demon, you!" howled Susan as they both erupted into a renewed round of mirth.

"Shhh!" cautioned Carolyn, suddenly fearful that they might be heard by the hall monitor outside or even worse, by Miss Dixon over their room's intercom box. "They might hear us."

"Girls," came the voice of Miss Dixon over the intercom.

Susan and Carolyn immediately stopped laughing. Certain at first that the Dean was addressing only them, they experienced a moment of panic.

"There will be a special vesper service in the second floor chapel at 8:30 tonight. I expect all of you to be there. Just come as you are. There is no need to get dressed again. Just come in your bathrobes and slippers." Miss Dixon was addressing the entire dormitory.

Susan and Carolyn let out a deep sigh of relief as they hurried to get their night clothes and bathrobes on. They would need to wait until the middle of the night to sneak back to the laundry room and return the borrowed towels. Hopefully they would be able to wait until morning to start up the washing machine, as it would undoubtedly be heard so late at night.

"Girls," began Miss Dixon from the podium. "This is a serious matter." Everyone waited for her to continue.

"Diana, can you please give us an opening prayer," requested the Dean.

"Absolutely," agreed Diana as she got up and came to the front of the small second floor chapel.

After Diana had said the prayer and was seated again, Miss Dixon stood in silence for several moments before speaking again. "Three of you were in one of your rooms having a séance tonight. A séance of all things! And now the entire dorm is on demon alert status."

The three girls to whom she was referring were seated together in the front row of the chapel. They were huddled together with tears streaming down their cheeks. The other girls all looked frightened.

"Oh, my!" whispered Susan with a grin.

Carolyn gently poked Susan in the side with her elbow, giving her a stern look.

"What were you girls thinking?" Miss Dixon shook her head. "Though I'm not sure whether to believe their entire story, these girls came screaming to my office a short while ago, pounding on my door, and told me that they had heard three knocks on their floor, right during their so-called séance."

Carolyn barely managed to stifle a giggle, this time being the recipient of Susan's elbow.

"Yes girls," continued Miss Dixon. "I'm afraid there may just be demons in the dorm."

Susan and Carolyn were unable to keep from smiling after the Dean's last remark. Naturally, Miss Dixon just happened to pick that particular moment to glance directly at Susan and Carolyn, and immediately noticed their huge grins.

5. The Ally

Susan knocked briskly on the front door to Ms. Neilson's small home, the one that had previously belonged to Ms. Eggersol back in 1972. "Hey, open up!"

"Sorry!" called Carolyn from inside, quickly getting up from the dining room table where she had been working on her laptop. After unlocking the deadbolt, Carolyn opened and held the door while Susan came inside.

"What's this? A bedsheet on the window?" chuckled Susan, nodding toward the kitchen window as she tossed a clipboard and thick history book she had been carrying onto the worn, overstuffed burgundy couch. "Nobody's out there."

"Well, actually," frowned Carolyn, "I did see something in the trees, over by where the old trail is. It was already too dark to make out who or what it was. It somehow felt as if they were looking in here."

"Really? It's getting foggy out there, too," admitted Susan as she walked over to the sink and pulled aside the bedsheet with one hand to glance outside. "I don't see anything out there now."

"Well, I hope Ms. Neilson won't mind, but I found this old bedsheet in the linen closet. There were some thumbtacks and a small hammer in one of the kitchen drawers, so I decided to put up a temporary covering for the window," explained Carolyn. "We may not be as safe here as we thought."

"You always did worry too much," laughed Susan as she kicked off her high heeled shoes, took off her dress clothes, and changed into a pair of blue jeans before pulling on a large, comfortable sweatshirt.

"Maybe next time you plan to come back after dark, you might want to take the car?" suggested Carolyn. "Remember that night we were walking past those particular crop fields when we were coming back from the beach?"

"Oh, yeah," recalled Susan. "That was the night Pete and I went to all that trouble to get you and Lenny hooked up, and then he didn't even bother to kiss you or anything!"

"That was also the night we had to hide in that cornfield to keep from being seen by Ray Dixon and Mr. Bovinae while we were on our way back! And they were definitely up to something questionable in that bunker," Carolyn added.

"Looks like there's squash over there now," guessed Susan.

"Well, they do rotate the crops," reminded Carolyn. "But I'll never forget what we saw that night."

"Mr. Bovinae and Ray Dixon carrying boxes into the bunker tunnel," recounted Susan.

"And Mr. Bovinae giving Ray Dixon a duffle bag of money, no doubt!" guessed Carolyn. "What if something like that's still going on, and we're stuck over here right by it with no one to help us?"

"You have your cellphone, right?" asked Susan.

"The laptop and the cellphone both work in here," revealed Carolyn. "But, it's a dead zone over there by that field. I tried it earlier while I was walking back."

"That's strange." Susan was deep in thought for a moment. "And what if Ray or that other guy did have something to do with Veronica and Joyce disappearing?"

"That's what we're here to find out," reminded Carolyn. "I also think when neither of us is here at the house, we should lock up anything we have of value in the car. I just wouldn't feel comfortable leaving my laptop in here where there's no outside lock on the door, or the research papers we have, either."

"Oh absolutely," agreed Susan as she noticed a pizza box on the coffee table and shoved the history book and clipboard aside to sit down on the couch. "I think you should keep the laptop with you. Say, can you toss me a water?"

"Oh sure," sighed Carolyn as she retrieved a bottle of water from the refrigerator and brought it to Susan. "Anything else, madam?"

"No, that'll be it for now," grinned Susan as she opened the box and grabbed a slice of pizza. "Hey, thanks."

"You're welcome." Carolyn just shook her head as she returned to the kitchen table to sit back down at her laptop.

"Find anything?" asked Susan with her mouth full of pizza.

"Actually, yes," replied Carolyn as she grabbed the computer mouse and began clicking while she studied the small computer screen.

"Well?" pressed Susan as she got up and came over to the table, pulled up a chair, and sat down beside Carolyn.

"Look at this!" commanded Carolyn as she brought up a screen she had recently viewed so Susan could see it for herself.

"OMG, it's Miss Dixon's obituary!" realized Susan. "Just when did she die, anyway?"

"It says here that she was almost 90 years old," read Carolyn. "She died right before Thanksgiving in 2009."

"So, she's been gone for seven years already," mused Susan. "What else does it say? Anything about Ray?"

"Let's see," responded Carolyn. "It says Miss Dixon died after a short illness. It doesn't say what it was. She had two brothers and one sister that preceded her in death, and was survived by two daughters, one granddaughter, and two great grandchildren."

"Names?" pressed Susan as she leaned closer to look at the screen, too. "It doesn't mention any Ray Dixon at all!"

"She was dean here for 25 years," chuckled Carolyn. "Wow!"

"Oh, this is good," noted Susan. "She was loved by all, and had an incredible warmth and love for all her students, just like a mom away from home."

"It also says that one student had a healthy fear of her because she always seemed to know what was going on," continued Carolyn. "And that you could never pull a fast one on her."

"That must have been us!" smirked Susan. "Remember that time back in 1972 when everyone thought there were demons in the girls' dormitory?"

"Yeah, everyone but her," reminded Carolyn.

"She probably knew it was us," agreed Susan.

Susan and Carolyn then began to laugh heartily at the memory, laughing almost as hard as they had forty-four years ago, back in 1972.

"Hey," Susan suddenly suggested, "let's look up her brothers, her daughters, and anyone else it mentions. Maybe one of them had kids who can tell us what happened to Ray, if he really was her nephew."

"That's right! We weren't even sure whether he was actually her nephew, or her son, or what he was to her," realized Carolyn.

"It says here she had two daughters, but doesn't mention a son," reasoned Susan, "so he must have been something else."

Carolyn and Susan spent the next two hours looking up each and every name associated with Miss Dixon, without success.

"So, where are these people?" demanded Susan. "It's like they all just dropped off the face of the earth or something."

"Well, that's exactly what happened to Joyce Troglite and Veronica Jensen," puzzled Carolyn, "and I can't find anything on either of them or their families on this thing, either."

"This is a total waste of time," scowled Susan as she got up and walked over to the refrigerator to retrieve herself another bottle of water. "Want one?"

"Sure," nodded Carolyn. "Thanks! Hey, look here. Oceanview Academy has a link on their website that lists all the current faculty members. I didn't notice that before."

"Really?" Susan was suddenly interested again. "Pull it up."

"Not a single one of the previous staff is still here," observed Carolyn. "Most of them are probably either dead or retired."

"And not necessarily in that order," chuckled Susan, trying to lighten the mood. "Hey, see if it lists any of the previous faculty on there, too, or says what might have happened to 'em."

"Nothing. But, this is interesting," paused Carolyn. "Jon Roth is the theology instructor here. I wonder if he's related to the Principal Roth that used to be here?"

"Oh yeah, that's what I forgot to mention," confessed Susan.

Carolyn looked at Susan with surprise, raised an eyebrow and waited for her to continue. "Well?"

"Today in class when I was taking roll," began Susan, "there was an Ann Roth. So, I asked her if she was Principal Roth's daughter."

"In open class?" pressed Carolyn.

"Yes, of course in open class," confirmed Susan. "That's when she advised me that her late great grandfather, Principal Roth, will be missed by all."

"What about Mrs. Roth?" wondered Carolyn.

"She didn't say," shrugged Susan. "Anyway, that's when Ann seemed to get suspicious and asked me if I'd ever been a student here."

"What'd you say?" urged Carolyn.

"That a friend of mine was," smirked Susan. "After all, you are my friend, and you were a student here once, so technically I was being truthful."

"You told her who I was?" Carolyn became concerned.

"No, of course not!" chuckled Susan. "She just kept pressing me for information so I had to give her something feasible. At first she was all snippy with me, jealous and thinking I was interested in her little boyfriend, too."

"Back up," interjected Carolyn. "Her boyfriend?"

"Remember that good-looking kid we saw earlier driving the tractor into one of the bunkers?" asked Susan. "His name is Ted Jensen."

"No way," mumbled Carolyn. "Do you think he might be related to Veronica Jensen somehow?"

"That's something else we need to find out, but it's a pretty common name," realized Susan.

"You are talking about the same well-built teenager with the big cowboy hat we saw driving the tractor over by the cornfield?" confirmed Carolyn. "You're old enough to be his grandmother!"

"That's what I told Ann Roth," continued Susan, "right before I threatened to send her to the principal's office if she didn't show me some more respect in class."

"Seriously?" Carolyn seemed worried.

"Relax," assured Susan. "I made her stay after class for a little chat, and the last thing she wants is to be sent to the principal's office. She was actually very compliant and respectful after that."

Carolyn took a deep breath. "So, how does that help us?"

"Ann has a job working in the Administration Office," informed Susan. "That could be useful."

"What'd she look like?" Carolyn was curious.

"Just like her father and her grandfather," responded Susan. "Ann has straight dark hair, pale skin, long bony arms and legs, a long hooked nose, and glasses."

"You've met her father?" quizzed Carolyn.

"Not recently," smiled Susan. "But you should remember him. Ever wonder what happened to Birdboy? That geek everyone used to make fun of at the mill? He worked over in tufting, right behind you, Joyce and Veronica."

"Oh, my God!" exclaimed Carolyn. "That was him?"

"Remember the day Birdboy went nuts and decided to take a flying leap off one of the tufting tables?" chuckled Susan.

"Birdboy?" Carolyn was flabbergasted. "You mean to tell me that Jon Roth and Birdboy were the same person? And that Principal Roth was his father? No way!"

"Way!" Susan had a crooked grin.

"I never knew they were his parents," informed Carolyn.

"I don't think the Roths were in any particular hurry to let people know who he was, either," chuckled Susan. "That was one weird dude!"

"Birdboy is Ann Roth's father? Making Principal Roth her grandfather?" Carolyn finally comprehended the significance of it. "What did you say his first name was again?"

"Jon Roth," repeated Susan. "It's right here on the website. Jon Roth also happens to be the theology instructor here right now."

Carolyn quickly pulled the faculty page back up and enlarged the photo of Jon Roth. "My, he has put on the pounds! Do you think he's seen you yet? He very well could recognize you, you know."

"Why thank you," smiled Susan. "But, no, he hasn't seen me yet. At least not that I know of. Perhaps you and I should visit the cafeteria for breakfast in the morning. He could be there. From this photo, he doesn't look like someone who'd dream of missing a meal."

Susan and Carolyn both laughed again.

"Seriously, do you think that's wise?" Carolyn became worried.

"Trust me," advised Susan with a devious wink.

Deciding to take the car with them the next morning, Susan and Carolyn slowly drove past the squash fields, studying the mysterious bunker where they had seen Ray Dixon and Mr. Bovinae forty-four years ago.

"It's still locked," noticed Susan as she brought the vehicle to a brief pause beside the bunker before continuing on.

"Maybe your friend Ann can get us a key?" suggested Carolyn.

"Or, her boyfriend can," smirked Susan. "Ted Jensen."

"Tractor boy?" joked Carolyn.

"Yes, tractor boy." Susan was serious. "He's the perfect one to get us a key! And, plowing crops just happens to be Ted's job. Not only that, Ted also mentioned that he likes to go boogie boarding down at the beach. I definitely think we should go watch him sometime."

"With Ann, of course?" chuckled Carolyn.

"Of course," smiled Susan, amused that Ann would even think of her as a possible threat.

"They probably will charge us for the food," reminded Carolyn as Susan pulled to a stop in front of the cafeteria in the new rental car they were using.

"Didn't your dad used to have one of these?" recalled Susan as she opened the door to get out.

"Yeah, I guess he did," replied Carolyn. "But his white Dodge Dart was definitely not a fuel efficient, compact model."

"Touché!" grinned Susan as she shut the door and used her remote car locking device to secure it. "Or one of these, either!" Two male students just happened to walk past right then, eyeing the smart looking 2016 vehicle with envy.

"Ms. Rives," acknowledged one of them.

"Jon Dunwoody," greeted Susan when she recognized the tall, lanky young man with blonde curly hair and small round glasses.

Jon and his friend stopped to get a better look at the vehicle. "Nice car," approved the other young man.

"This is Randy," introduced Jon.

"Randy Chekerman," grinned the lad, clearly as intrigued by the attractive substitute teacher as he was with the car.

"This is my friend Carolyn," Susan introduced. Then flirting with Jon and Randy just enough to maintain their interest, Susan turned to accompany Carolyn toward the cafeteria.

"May we join you?" offered Jon, anxious to learn more about the mysterious older woman who still held an irresistible appeal.

"Sure," shrugged Susan, trying to appear nonchalant.

"Do you think that's such a good idea?" Carolyn whispered closely into Susan's ear as they walked up to and through the entrance by the food line.

"Oh wait," apologized Susan as they got inside. "I promised Mr. Roth we'd join him for breakfast if he was here."

"That looks like him, right over there," recognized Carolyn.

"Okay, sure," acquiesced Randy. "Perhaps another time?"

"Absolutely," Susan gave them one of her encouraging smiles as they continued to the food line.

"Here, allow me," Jon grabbed one of the trays and handed it to Susan. "Hey, they're having fake bacon today!"

"You mean 'Doggie Strips' don't you?" Randy was sarcastic.

Susan and Carolyn exchanged an amused smile.

"It does seem strange to have just one food line now, doesn't it?" remarked Carolyn.

"You used to go to school here?" questioned Jon, curious now about Carolyn, too.

"What she means," clarified Susan, "is that back when I used to come here, they had two separate food lines. One for the girls and one for the boys."

"And Susan, ah, Ms. Rives always used to tell me about it," added Carolyn.

"More surprising is to see boys and girls walking around holding hands," noted Susan as she grabbed a warm plate from the stack of clean dishes, along with a set of silverware and a napkin.

"They used to be pretty strict here, didn't they?" realized Randy as he grabbed and placed a clean glass on Susan's tray for her.

"Very strict," confirmed Susan. "We never would have been allowed to have stereos, computers or anything like that in our rooms."

"They didn't even have computers back then anyway, did they?" questioned Jon. Right at that moment, the server suddenly slopped a huge pile of overly moist, reconstituted eggs onto Susan's plate and gained her attention at once.

"Is that too much?" asked the girl serving the food.

"No, that's fine." Susan tried to smile politely but became quiet as she studied the remaining food selections behind the clear acrylic safety glass on the stainless steel serving galley with trepidation.

"One or two?" pressed the server as she grabbed two slices of the fake bacon with a pair of tongs and hovered them over Susan's plate.

"Ah, just one," swallowed Susan, quickly cognizant of how unappetizing the food at Oceanview Academy actually still was.

"And tater tots," chuckled Carolyn. "Remember those?"

"Shhh!" cautioned Susan, not wanting to come up with any more explanations about Carolyn just then.

"Oh no," frowned Carolyn.

"What is it?" whispered Susan.

"Fruit cocktail," Carolyn made a face.

"But they do have pancakes," realized Susan as she tried in vain to scrape the horrible looking egg mess to one side of her plate to make room for one.

"Whole wheat," noticed Carolyn as she arrived at the pancake station where another server was busy plopping batter onto a huge griddle. "Those don't look too bad."

"And fresh whole milk from the dairy," commented Susan as she picked up her glass and held it to the solitary dispensing nozzle on the stainless steel drink dispenser.

"Didn't they used to have water, too?" questioned Carolyn, seeming to remember that they had.

"Water's over there by the condiments," indicated the server.

"Thanks," nodded Carolyn, quite certain her food intake would not include whole milk at this point in her life.

"That'll be $3.00 each," informed the cashier at the stainless steel cash register at the far end of the food serving galley.

"That's not too bad," realized Carolyn as she began to unzip her large purse.

"No, allow me," insisted Susan as she handed the cashier her credit card.

"Cash only," advised the cashier.

Carolyn then pulled out her wallet, removed a five-dollar bill and a one-dollar bill, and handed them to the red headed, freckle faced young lady working the cash register.

"Thanks," nodded the girl as she carefully placed the bills in her cash drawer.

"Thank you," responded Carolyn as she turned to follow Susan over to the condiment table, quickly filling her glass with some water.

"Oh boy, real butter, too." Susan was glib as she surveyed the various selections and decided against using any of the catsup, whipped butter, extra thick syrup, strawberry jam or whipped cream available. "A regular weight watching delight!"

"These are growing young teenagers," reminded Carolyn with amusement, also uninterested in the condiments. "They still have salt and pepper shakers on all the tables, though. I can't believe we actually used to eat this stuff!"

"Come on, there he is," nodded Susan as she spotted Jon Roth. "It's show time. And please, let me do the talking, at least at first."

"You're on," indicated Carolyn as they walked toward the table where Mr. Roth was busy shoveling a mountainous pile of scrambled eggs into his mouth directly from the edge of his plate.

"May we join you?" queried Susan, trying to appear demure yet friendly at the same time.

Immediately setting the plate back down on his food tray and grabbing a napkin to wipe any excess egg mess from his overstuffed face, Jon Roth nodded affirmatively. He then waved his hand toward the empty seats across from him while he finished chewing what was left in his mouth.

"Jon Roth?" inquired Susan as she set her tray down across from the large man.

"Yes," he nodded, studying Susan with interest. "I know you from somewhere."

"It's been a long time, hasn't it?" responded Susan with a twinkle in her eyes as she sat down.

Carolyn nodded and smiled pleasantly at Mr. Roth as she silently set her tray on the table beside Susan and sat down.

"I know you, too!" recognized Jon Roth. "Wait a minute, it's coming to me. No, it can't be!"

"I'm the new substitute teacher," grinned Susan mischievously. "For Ms. Neilson's history class."

"No, that's not where I know you from." Jon Roth furled his brow as he tried to remember. "And you!" he suddenly turned to Carolyn. "You used to work at the lumber mill. That's it! You used to be in tufting, with Joyce and Veronica! Carolyn, oh what was it? Carolyn Bennett! Of course. And you, you're Susan Rives? Oh, my God! I can't believe it! Just why are you here, anyway?"

"I just happen to be a retired school teacher," mentioned Susan.

"And they just happened to need one until Ms. Neilson gets back from her medical leave," added Carolyn, deciding it was time to speak. After all, the game was over. Jon Roth obviously knew who she was.

"And you?" Jon turned his full attention to Carolyn. "Why are you here?"

"She's my assistant," replied Susan, not wanting to reveal too much just yet.

"Your assistant?" Jon seemed suspicious.

"I'm actually assisting her with grading papers, research, and that kind of thing," elaborated Carolyn.

"Oh, I see," responded Mr. Roth, temporarily satisfied with her explanation. "Well, then, how nice to see you two. It has been a long time. What's it been, forty years?"

"Forty-three," clarified Susan without hesitation. "It was in March of 1973 that we saw each other last."

"Oh yes, so it has," nodded Jon Roth uncomfortably, and then wondered what Susan and Carolyn really wanted.

"I just learned today from Susan that Principal Roth was your father," mentioned Carolyn. "I never knew your last name."

"Or my first one, either, I'll bet," fumed Jon Roth as he suddenly stabbed a tater tot on his plate and stuffed it into his mouth.

"Birdboy, wasn't it?" snickered Carolyn, unable to help but smile with glee at the memory.

"Listen!" Jon Roth instantly became enraged and slammed his right fist onto the table as he started to get up and leaned toward Carolyn. "Don't you EVER call me that again! Do you hear me? Not EVER!"

The sudden change in Jon Roth's demeanor and the evil glare with which he stared at both of them made Susan and Carolyn very uncomfortable, and actually afraid. Both became serious and remained silent as they waited to see what he would say or do next.

"Hey, I'm sorry!" Jon Roth suddenly apologized and sat back down, feeling foolish when he noticed several of the students nearby had become quiet and were looking at him with curiosity. "It's just been so long since anyone has called me that...." Jon broke off in mid-sentence, unable to continue.

"No, I'm the one that's sorry." Carolyn was sincere. "It was a cruel and mean thing everyone did to call you that, and I shouldn't have reminded you of it. I hope you can forgive me."

Jon Roth cautiously studied Carolyn and Susan for several awkward moments more before responding. "Joyce and Veronica used to call me that. Especially Veronica."

"I remember them," replied Carolyn nervously, hoping Susan would not say something they both would regret.

"Oh, yes," acknowledged Susan. "The girls who disappeared. Some shark got 'em when they were boogie boarding one afternoon."

"Wasn't that the day Steve Fredrickson died on the beach after he was attacked by the shark?" Carolyn tried to control her breathing so she would not appear uneasy. The memory was extremely painful for her, even after forty-three years.

"Terrible thing, what happened to those kids," agreed Jon Roth, now appearing normal in his demeanor. His glaring rage seemed to have vanished as suddenly as it had appeared a few moments earlier.

"Everything okay over here?" questioned Ann from behind him as she approached the table. Ann had just finished eating and was getting ready to take her used food tray over to the return area to leave it with her dirty dishes, where other students whose job it was to wash them would then grab the dirty trays and dishes through an opening in the wall and whisk them to the back for processing.

"Mr. Roth," acknowledged Ted Jensen with a respectful nod. Ted was also holding a tray full of dirty dishes, waiting for Ann.

"Oh yes, everything's fine," assured Ann's father. "These are some old friends of mine, back from the good old days. This is Susan Rives and Carolyn Bennett. We all used to work in the lumber mill together, forty-three years ago."

"Forty-three years ago?" repeated Ted with amazement, not having realized that Ms. Rives was that old.

"So, you really did go to school here?" Ann did not seem too surprised. "Well, then, daddy must know you're our substitute teacher in history class?"

"Would you care to join us?" invited Susan hopefully.

"Ah, no, we really need to be on our way to English Literature class," declined Ann, "but perhaps daddy will invite you ladies over for the barbecue he plans to have on Sunday at noon? Daddy?"

"Ah, yes, please?" invited Mr. Roth, appearing most gracious about it. "We'd love to have you. We're just three houses down from Ms. Neilson's residence. I assume that's where you're staying now?"

"Ah, yes, it is," confirmed Susan uncomfortably.

"Excellent," replied Jon Roth with an almost triumphant grin. "Won't you join us Sunday at noon?"

"Well, sure, we'd love to," agreed Susan, hoping she didn't look as nervous as she felt. And, what made Birdboy assume they were staying at Ms. Neilson's house? They had never actually mentioned it.

Carolyn suddenly thought of the dark hooded figure she had seen in the forest by Ms. Neilson's home the previous night.

"Excellent," beamed Jon Roth. "We'll look forward to it. And Ted, will you be joining us?"

"Wouldn't miss it," promised Ted.

"Then it's a date," agreed Mr. Roth. "I hope you all can eat meat. We'll be having lamb burgers."

"Lamb burgers?" repeated Susan with interest. "That sounds delicious. Can we bring anything?"

"Just yourselves," insisted Jon Roth with a smile that truly appeared sincere.

"We'll see you then," accepted Susan as she got up to leave. "Sorry to eat and run, but I have to get ready for class today. I didn't realize how late it is."

"And I need to help," added Carolyn.

Neither of them had eaten a bite of their breakfast, a fact that did not go unnoticed by Birdboy as he watched their hasty departure.

Susan and Carolyn wasted no time dumping off their food trays at the tray return area before dashing outside to climb back inside the white Dodge Dart.

"We've got oatmeal back at the house," offered Carolyn as Susan started the engine, put the new rental car into gear, and slowly drove away from the cafeteria.

"Sixty minus sixteen comes to forty-four," muttered Susan as she calculated the figures in her head. "Do you realize Birdboy would have been forty-four years old when he fathered Ann? Assuming she's sixteen years old, and I'm pretty sure she is."

"I can hardly fathom that anyone would have married or even stayed with someone like that," replied Carolyn.

"And why so late in life?" wondered Susan aloud.

"I don't know," responded Carolyn, shaking her head. "I just think going to his house on Sunday could be a mistake. He seems like he could be very dangerous."

"I wonder if Ann has any brothers or sisters?" scowled Susan. "Can you imagine what their lives must be like? There's something seriously wrong with that man, and right now I'm concerned for Ann's safety. Especially if she agrees to help us. What would he do to her if he ever found out? And what about Ann's mother, if the woman was actually stupid enough to stay with him?"

"Ann doesn't seem foolish enough to tell him her plans if she did decide to help us," voiced Carolyn. "I just can't believe Birdboy's the theology instructor! Why in the world would they hire someone like him to work with a bunch of teenagers?"

"That is pretty odd," mused Susan, deep in thought as she pulled up in front of Ms. Neilson's home and came to a stop.

"Hey, what if he's the one that had something to do with Joyce and Veronica disappearing?" speculated Carolyn as she opened the car door to get out and go inside.

"I was just wondering that myself," admitted Susan as she got out of the car, too. "His reaction to the memory of what happened to them wasn't what it should have been. I don't care how long it's been, something like that doesn't just go away, and it haunts you for the rest of your life. Sure he put on a good act, but behind it all there was an unsettling coldness in his eyes."

"I felt it, too," agreed Carolyn as she opened the unlocked house door. "Now, I feel as if we need to search the entire house each time we come back, just to make sure no one's hiding inside."

"Perhaps we should just get a new door knob with a lock on it while we're in town," decided Susan. "I can always leave the key for Ms. Neilson when I go. At least the back door has a dead bolt on it."

"I agree. We do need to have a locking door knob, absolutely." The lack of security had been weighing heavily on Carolyn's mind, especially after spotting the shadowy figure in the forest last night.

"Birdboy never did like the way everyone always made fun of him," remembered Susan. "But, what about Ray Dixon and his boxes? How does he fit into all of this? And Mr. Bovinae? Seems like we have more questions now than we did when we got here."

"Well, it's only Tuesday," pointed out Carolyn as she completed her circuit of the home to be sure no one else was there. "That gives us five more days to track down some leads before Sunday."

"What do you have in mind?" questioned Susan.

"Let's grab that oatmeal and then head into town for some groceries," suggested Carolyn. "We've got at least three hours until you need to be back for your class. Maybe someone at the old store might know something."

"Sounds good," nodded Susan as she pulled two large bowls from the cupboard.

"You did study your lesson, didn't you?" smiled Carolyn.

"Trust me," chuckled Susan.

Carolyn drove while Susan took the opportunity to glance over her upcoming history class lesson.

"Did you know that Abraham Lincoln invented a device to keep steamboats from running aground?" asked Susan.

"No, I hadn't heard that," responded Carolyn as she admired the picturesque countryside surrounding them.

"It says he also wouldn't hunt or fish because he loved animals," continued Susan. "If he were alive today, he'd be running an animal shelter! Sounds like your kind of guy."

"My husband loves to hunt and fish," assured Carolyn as she slowed to read a small sign they were passing. "It just doesn't keep him from loving certain ones. In fact, he's caring for all seven of my outdoor cats and both of my indoor ones right now while I'm gone."

"He must love you," chuckled Susan. "My husband would have never done anything like that. He was a stupid, selfish pig! Can you believe it? He took up with some fat cow he met at an AA meeting!"

"That's really sad," commented Carolyn. "You deserve better."

"Hey, what'd that sign say back there?" Susan was suddenly interested and wanted to know.

"Silver Creek Trailer Park," replied Carolyn. "I think that's where the little ice cream shop used to be."

"Oh yes!" grinned Susan. "The one with the chocolate ice cream where we went with Pete and Lenny. We should stop there on the way back and see if they're still open. That was good ice cream."

"Yeah, let's," nodded Carolyn as she rounded the next hairpin turn and slowed to a stop by the huge wrought iron gate leading into Ocean Bluff Mental Institution.

"What are you doing?" Susan became excited when Carolyn turned into the long sweeping driveway.

"Small detour," informed Carolyn. "I'd like to see if there's anyone who can tell us more about Jon Roth. For some reason, I seem to remember something about Birdboy being in a mental institution. I never made the connection until now, since I never really knew who he was. How could I not have known the Roths were his parents!"

92

"It was a pretty well-kept secret. But, I remember that too, about Birdboy being put away!" Susan suddenly recalled. "In fact, it was right after Joyce and Veronica ...," she suddenly broke off in mid-sentence as an unbidden tear escaped the corner of one eye.

Carolyn and Susan remained silent as the new Dodge Dart made its way around the circular entrance drive before coming to a halt.

The Ocean Bluff Mental Institution was a large two-story brick building first established in 1887. Its white spiraled steeples and clock tower gave it a medieval appearance. Housed on the first floor of the building was its administration department where new patients and visitors alike were received. Situated on a high elevation of land overlooking the city below on one side and a vast expanse of ocean on the other, Ocean Bluff Mental Institution was a magnificent sight. The ample grounds with their fine trees, beautiful flowers and paved driveways were a veritable park. White wrought iron benches were strategically placed along its various walkways for visitors and less serious patients who were free to stroll through the gardens and enjoy the sound of crashing waves on the rocky hillside below.

"Come on," urged Carolyn as she opened the car door and started for the front entrance.

The huge white double doors were ornately curved on top with a large metal plaque centered over them that read: "When the waves reach to our heads we begin to listen to anything; no advice is too contemptible for us; no person too insignificant for us to be willing to listen." by Johann Peter Lange - 1872.

"Wow, that's nice," admired Susan as Carolyn lifted the huge brass lion-head door knocker and let it fall against the huge brass plate beneath it. After a few moments, footsteps could be heard inside.

An elderly woman with white hair, thick horn-rimmed glasses, and a white knee-length nurse's uniform answered the door. "Yes, may I help you?"

"We were wondering if you know of anyone who was here in 1972 that might be able to help us?" explained Carolyn.

"I was here in 1972," whispered the woman suspiciously. Her hearing was excellent for her age, and she had a keen alertness about her intense blue eyes that was disconcerting. "Please come in."

The nurse's clean rubber shoe soles made little sound as she walked on the hard linoleum floor. "Wait in there."

Carolyn and Susan had been led to a small sitting room with an antique Queen Anne style couch and matching chairs. All of them appeared to have been there since 1887 when the institution first opened. Nevertheless, the furniture was well kept and in excellent condition. A small coffee table displayed leaflets advertising the Ocean Bluff Mental Institution and its few amenities. Carolyn picked one up, studied it, and put it into her purse for possible future reference.

"What can I do for you?" asked a much younger nurse from the doorway to the sitting room. She appeared to be about thirty years of age with straight dark hair pulled back into a harsh bun. She also wore no makeup, and dressed identically to the older nurse who had first let them in. "I'm Nurse Redden." She did not sit down but remained where she was, obviously not wishing to engage in useless chitchat.

"We were hoping you could tell us something about a Ray Dixon?" began Carolyn, deciding to mention him first before bringing up Jon Roth.

"Never heard of him." Nurse Redden studied them with an even, hard gaze and tilted her head slightly back to see them more clearly through her bifocals as she placed her hands on her hips.

"Maybe in your records?" suggested Susan cautiously.

"No, he's not in our records," maintained Nurse Redden with finality. "Is that it?"

"Ah, we also were wanting to know if you know a man named Jon Roth," added Carolyn, surprised at the way Nurse Redden then lifted her eyebrows and narrowed her eyes. "Who wants to know?"

"I'm sorry," apologized Carolyn. "My name is Carolyn and this is Susan. We both used to go to school with Jon back in 1972, over at Oceanview Academy."

"We were just hoping to find out what might have happened to him?" Susan smiled with a sweet but pleading look.

"From what I understand," answered Nurse Redden, "Jon Roth is the theology instructor there right now."

"Ah, yes, we know," admitted Carolyn.

"We were just hoping to find out a little more about his past," clarified Susan hopefully.

Nurse Redden studied them both for several moments longer before responding. "You family?"

"Not exactly," replied Carolyn.

"Can't help you," answered Nurse Redden. "We have a strict policy here. Only blood relatives are entitled to see our files. Perhaps you should ask Jon Roth anything you want to know about him."

"Okay, we'll do that," smiled Carolyn as she got up to leave. "Thank you for your time."

Susan and Carolyn quickly left, not talking again until they were in the white Dodge Dart rental car, heading for the institution's main exit. "We're gonna have to get Ann's help now, whether we want to or not," pointed out Carolyn as she turned onto the narrow winding clifftop road that led to town.

"Maybe I can talk to Ann after class today," mentioned Susan. "Hey, we'd better hurry. My history class starts in just two hours."

"I'll get you there," promised Carolyn. "Trust me!"

Susan grinned and nodded her head as Carolyn continued toward the tiny town of Ocean Bluff.

"Hey, there's an old cemetery over there, too," noticed Carolyn.

"We'll have to do that later," regretted Susan. "There just isn't enough time today."

"Town still looks just the same," marveled Carolyn as she pulled into the tiny town of Ocean Bluff.

"Population 317," read Susan. "How did they come up with that? There can't be more than a dozen homes in the whole town."

"Probably scattered throughout the forest or along the bluffs," guessed Carolyn as she pulled to a stop and parked in front of the town's only store. There were very few cars parked along the main street, most of them older and showing signs of exposure to the harsh ocean climate. Traffic was almost non-existent. Parking was free.

"The ice cream shop looks like it's been shut down for years," marveled Susan. "I sure hope the one at Silver Creek is still open."

Indeed, the small town had but one store, one gas station, one post office, a recreation hall that doubled as a church on Sundays and as a senior center during the week, and a station house that doubled as both a fire station and a police department. But, it did have two restaurants. Kay's Diner and Patty's Pancake House.

"Wow!" Carolyn shook her head as she got out of the car. "It's like going back in a time machine. Nothing's changed!"

"Except for the ice cream shop," reminded Susan.

"Come on," urged Carolyn as they walked into the all-in-one grocery, bakery, hardware, basic clothing and knickknack store.

"They even have movies now," observed Susan as she studied the selection of outdated DVDs and videotaped movies available, most of them still in the original packaging. "That's new."

After filling their small shopping cart with an assortment of food items, Carolyn headed for the hardware section. Relieved to see new door knob sets among the selections, she quickly added one to the basket before heading up front to check out at the cash register.

"You ladies from around here?" asked the clerk. She was a middle-aged woman with rough leathery skin, frizzy unkempt graying hair, and badly worn clothing, yet friendly enough in an absent-minded sort of way.

"I'm Susan Rives," revealed Susan. "The substitute teacher over at Oceanview Academy while one of their teachers is out on leave."

"That would be Ms. Neilson, I suspect." The clerk already knew. "Nice lady. Too bad about that hip of hers. Long recovery for something like that."

After ringing up the food items without further comment, the clerk picked up and studied the new door knob kit. "You got the tools you'll need to install this?"

"I think so," replied Carolyn.

"Didn't get your name?" mentioned the clerk as she lowered her small square glasses to get a better look.

"I'm Carolyn, her assistant." Carolyn nodded toward Susan.

"I see," the clerk seemed surprised. "How long you ladies plan to be there? At Oceanview?"

"I'll only be there for a couple weeks or so," revealed Carolyn.

"I'm afraid they're stuck with me until Ms. Neilson returns," smiled Susan politely. "What tools do we need? For the door knob?"

"One moment," instructed the clerk as she headed for the back of the store, leaving her nearly empty cash drawer wide open.

"All rightie, then." Susan was as surprised as Carolyn that anyone would be so trusting of strangers.

The clerk returned and handed a small tool kit to Susan. "Here you go. Everything you'll need should be in there."

"We'll take it," agreed Carolyn.

"Good," nodded the clerk as she rung it up. "Anything else?"

"Ah, how long has the ice cream shop across the street been shut down?" inquired Carolyn as she brought out her wallet.

"Sad business there." The clerk shook her head. "Poor old Mr. Killingham died about … let me see … it was about six years ago, or was it seven? Anyway, he was just old. His step-son came to work one morning and found him dead on the floor in the back."

"How horrible!" exclaimed Susan.

"How old was he?" Carolyn was curious.

"Oh, let me see." The clerk put one hand on her chin and the other on her hip as she thought about it. "Well, his step-son was about seventy years old at the time. Maybe younger, I don't know."

"How old was the dad?" clarified Susan.

"Oh, he had to be at least ninety," recalled the clerk. "So, will there be anything else?"

"No, that'll do," replied Carolyn.

The clerk slowly finished totaling up the items on her aging cash register, after which Carolyn quickly paid the amount due in cash.

"Say, what about that other ice cream shop over at Silver Creek Trailer Park?" Susan suddenly asked. "Are they still open?"

"Hard to say," mumbled the clerk as she unhurriedly put their items into a recycled paper bag. "It belonged to the old man, too. Franchise of some sort."

"How many ice cream shops did he have?" prompted Carolyn.

"Just the two," answered the clerk as she carefully handed the bag of groceries to Carolyn.

"Okay, thanks," nodded Carolyn as she took the bag from the clerk and started toward the front door but then stopped, turning back to the clerk again. "Didn't there used to be a pawn shop here, too?"

"Oh, that was part of the ice cream shop," responded the clerk. "The step-son came and took all that stuff away when he closed the shop here in town, not too terribly long after Mr. Killingham passed."

"Any idea what he might have done with it?" Susan wanted to know. "The stuff from the pawn shop?"

"Nope. But, the old guy's step-son still lives out there at the trailer park, last I heard anyway. Can't remember his name off hand, but he might've decided to keep the other ice cream shop open. Could still have all that junk, too. Maybe you should stop and see."

"Thanks again," responded Susan as she and Carolyn turned to leave. "We very well might."

"We're here," informed Carolyn as she slowed down and turned onto the overgrown gravel road filled with deep ruts that led down to Silver Creek Trailer Park. Carolyn had been driving again, so Susan could continue studying the lesson for her history class.

The steep narrow road switched back and forth through the dense coastal forest and continued until reaching the sandy beachfront below where the rundown store still stood.

"What time is it?" Susan suddenly asked, though curious enough about the unkempt condition of the property to want to stop.

"We still have another hour," promised Carolyn.

"Just look at this place!" exclaimed Susan with dismay.

"I don't think it's a trailer park anymore," observed Carolyn. "The trailers are all gone, except for that abandoned one on the end."

"How sad," frowned Susan, recalling how beautiful the pristine trailer park had once been.

"But, the store's still here," pointed out Carolyn as she pulled to a stop in front of it. "There's even a light on inside!"

Indeed, there was still a sign hanging over the entrance door indicating that it was the Silver Creek Trailer Park Store. Unfastened on one end, the rickety wooden sign hung down precariously at an unsightly angle. The hinge from which it dangled squeaked whenever the sign banged against the post next to it, usually with each blast of wind on days when the weather was blustery.

"Wow! Now, that's sad." Carolyn merely shook her head, ready to drive away without further investigation.

"Wait, let's check it out first," grinned Susan as she inhaled a deep breath of fresh ocean air and stretched her hands above her head.

Carolyn turned off the car engine and slowly climbed out. She then patiently waited while Susan closed and tossed her history book into the back seat and put her shoes back on before getting out, too. It was hard to believe it had actually been forty-four years since their last visit to the small establishment in 1972. Perhaps it was no longer used as a store.

"Can I help you ladies?" came a voice from behind them. A man in his mid-seventies dressed in raggedy blue jeans, worn out steel tipped cowboy boots, and a dirty white t-shirt approached. After wiping his grease covered hands on a standard blue utility rag from his back pocket, he adjusted his thick, horn-rimmed glasses and ran one of his still-dirty hands through the overgrown crewcut on his well-tanned head. The years had not been kind to him. Faded tattoos of naked women adorned his muscular but leathery looking arms. A good shower wouldn't have hurt him much, either. It was obvious he had been doing engine work on the antique looking pickup truck parked nearby.

Susan was speechless and seemed frozen to the spot. "What is it?" asked Carolyn, not realizing the reason for her behavior at first.

"Ray Dixon?" mumbled Susan with disbelief.

"As I live and breathe," grinned the man as he approached and held out his dirty hand, waiting to shake Susan's in acknowledgment.

Susan remained motionless, choosing not to touch Ray Dixon's filthy hand.

"I'm sorry!" Ray chuckled. "What's wrong with me? Come inside. I guess I need to wash my hands, don't I?"

Carolyn remained silent and said nothing as she watched to see what would happen next.

"Hey?" Ray stopped to snap his dirty fingers in front of Susan's face. "You all right, ma'am? I still have some ice cream inside. Maybe that might help? Let me wash up and I'll get you some."

Carolyn and Susan exchanged a worried glance. "This is why we came here, after all," reminded Carolyn.

Susan nodded, swallowed hard, took a deep breath to regain her composure, and cautiously followed Ray Dixon up the wobbly steps and into the dilapidated structure.

"Haven't had many customers these days," mentioned Ray as he walked over to and washed his hands and arms over a huge sink in the corner of the room. Ray Dixon then grabbed and gingerly yanked several times on a dirty blue cloth hanging down from an aging reusable cloth towel dispenser on the wall beside him.

Carolyn's thoughts wandered immediately to a time forty-four years earlier when she had watched her own mother grab a similar dirty blue cloth from one of those wretched dispensers on which to dry her hands in the girls' dormitory during her first day there at Oceanview Academy in 1972.

"So, what can I get you ladies?" questioned Ray as he picked up an ice cream scooper and walked over to the small freezer galley in which only two gallons of ice cream remained. There was clearly room for at least a dozen more but the space was empty.

"Is it still good?" questioned Susan apprehensively.

"Of course it is," replied Ray. "Just made 'em last week."

"You made them by yourself?" Susan was surprised.

"Young lady, I've been making ice cream for that school next door for over fifty years," revealed Ray. "And my daddy, God rest his soul, was making it for as long as I can recall before that. It was he who taught me how to make it."

"You're Mr. Killingham's step-son?" realized Carolyn.

"Well, you ladies both seem to know who I am," reminded Ray as he proceeded to take the lid off one of the ice cream containers before scooping up some chocolate ice cream into a cone. "Who are you?"

"Oh, I'm sorry," apologized Susan. "I'm Susan Rives, the new substitute teacher at the school while Ms. Neilson is out on medical leave. And this is Carolyn."

"Here, have some ice cream," offered Ray as he handed the chocolate ice cream cone to Susan. "On the house."

"None for me, though," mentioned Carolyn. "I'm on a diet."

"Of course you are," laughed Ray as he scooped up another cone of chocolate ice cream for himself and slowly licked it, clearly pleased with the delicious flavor. "Well, I'm not."

Seeing that Ray was eating the ice cream himself, Susan relaxed and decided to go ahead. "Oh, this is delicious! Just as I remembered it. Carolyn, you should have some! This is really good."

"It's not that," persisted Carolyn. "I just can't have any."

"You're missing out," grinned Ray. "So, what can I really do for you ladies? No one ever comes out here anymore."

Susan nodded at Carolyn to go ahead.

"Well," began Carolyn. "We don't have time to beat around the bush. Ms. Rives has to get back to Oceanview Academy in less than an hour to teach her history class."

"Forty-five minutes now," interjected Susan with her mouth full.

"Just how are you related to Ms. Dixon, the lady who used to be Dean over there?" questioned Carolyn.

"Cat?" Ray seemed surprised.

"Cat?" repeated Carolyn, not understanding at first.

"Cathy Dixon," clarified Ray. "She was my aunt. Always called her Cat. Her sister Linda was my mother. The late Linda Killingham. Died in childbirth, delivering me."

Susan and Carolyn seemed puzzled for a moment.

"My real daddy abandoned her when he learned that she was pregnant," explained Ray. "They never married. Mark Killingham met and fell in love with my mother when she was six months pregnant."

"How sad that you never even knew her," remarked Susan as she grabbed the last napkin from the dispenser on the counter to wipe the excess ice cream from the corners of her mouth.

"Might've had a nice life together, too," added Ray sadly.

"How is it that you came to work at the school, then?" asked Carolyn, aware of their need to leave as soon as possible.

"Let me see," reflected Ray. "When I first got out of the military and came back to help out my daddy, that was when I found out Cat was Dean over there at the school. And, they needed a handyman."

"You were never in prison?" blurted Carolyn, embarrassed at once when she saw the look of astonishment on Ray's face.

After an awkward moment of silence, Ray broke into laughter before replying. "Where'd you ever get a notion like that? I've never been to prison in my life, not even to visit!"

"We just thought," Susan tried to smooth things over, "with the tattoos and blue jeans and such ...."

Ray continued to smile as he shook his head. "What year did you two say you went to school over there?"

"The 1972 to 1973 year," answered Carolyn, realizing at once that they had never actually mentioned going to school there.

"The demon girls, of course!" Ray laughed hysterically, so hard he began coughing, and slapped his free hand on his dirty pant leg as he stomped one of his worn out steel tipped cowboy boots on the rickety wooden floor.

"Demon girls?" Susan began to grin and raised an eyebrow.

"You were never in prison, then?" added Carolyn.

"I remember you now," realized Ray. "You were the two that crawled under the girls' dormitory and knocked on the floor that night."

"Your aunt told you about that?" queried Susan.

"I was there!" chucked Ray. "Cat wasn't the only one that used to listen in on them rooms. My favorite one was room 124, what a hoot! Cat and I laughed so hard that night I thought we'd bust a gut."

"So, she knew," Susan smiled and nodded with understanding. "No wonder she moved us up to the second floor after that."

"What I don't get," interjected Carolyn, "is why she never told our parents about it?"

"She liked you girls, both of you," assured Ray. "As I recall, Cat did everything she could to protect you, too."

"Protect us from what?" Susan became serious.

"There was some funny business going on over there, with the principal's son," Ray became serious, too. "We never could prove anything, but Cat and I both suspected he had something to do with them girls disappearing like they did. Two bodies don't just disappear into thin air, ocean or not. They would've found something."

"That's what we think, too," admitted Susan. "That's why we're here. We're hoping to find out what happened."

"After all this time?" Ray shook his head. "You'd have to know someone on the inside. I've been trying to manage that for years."

"Jon Roth's daughter Ann just happens to be one of my students. She's in my history class," divulged Susan. She suddenly had a good feeling about Ray Dixon and sensed that he could be trusted.

Carolyn, on the other hand, was not so sure and hoped that Susan had not made a mistake.

"Before we do become allies," stipulated Carolyn, "there's something else I need to know."

"Besides the fact that I've never been to prison, and that I've worked as a handyman and ice cream maker for Oceanview Academy for over fifty years?" chuckled Ray.

"And ran two ice cream shops on the side?" added Susan for effect. "You still do own them both, don't you?"

"Oh, the land, yes," confirmed Ray Dixon. "The shops went out of business after daddy died seven years ago. In fact, he died the same year Cat did, just a few months earlier. That was in 2009. So, there was no way I could keep up two ice cream shops, and a trailer park, and still work at the school. The school just seemed to need me the most."

"What else do you do at the school?" pressed Carolyn.

"Well, besides being an all-purpose handy man and fix-it person, I also do deliveries. When I'm not delivering or picking up produce, dairy, bakery or other supplies," informed Ray, "I also run the small ice cream facility they just built over by the dairy last year. It got to be too much for me to manufacture it here and then haul it all the way over there. Do you have any idea how much ice cream those kids can put away at one meal? There's over 320 kids over there! Plus faculty."

"I see," pondered Carolyn.

"Anything else?" asked Ray.

"Well," began Carolyn. "It was the same night the girls' dorm was put on demon alert."

Ray and Susan both began to smile.

"Susan and I were coming back from the beach when we just happened to see you unloading boxes from your pickup truck. You were putting them into one of those bunkers," recounted Carolyn.

Susan became serious. "That's right! And Mr. Bovinae pulled up to help you."

"So, that's how you got back," realized Ray. "My daddy called Cat after you left here, to let her know so she wouldn't worry. He knew you were from the school. I was there when Cat got the phone call."

"Really?" Susan was flabbergasted.

"You'd have to get up pretty early in the morning to put one over on old Dean Dixon," assured Ray.

"So, what kind of produce would you be putting into a bunker at night?" Carolyn directed the conversation back on track. "And why would Mr. Bovinae be paying you for it?"

"What?" puzzled Ray.

"The duffle bag full of money," clarified Susan. "Mr. Bovinae handed it to you after he finished helping you unload the boxes."

"A duffle bag full of money?" Ray shook his head and began to laugh again. "That's a good one!"

Susan and Carolyn became serious and waited for Ray Dixon to elaborate.

"You do know that Oceanview Academy was built on the site of a former military base?" questioned Ray.

Susan and Carolyn merely nodded.

"Those bunker tunnels that honeycomb the entire campus are all connected," continued Ray. "Most of them have been sealed off for years, and no one even knows what's inside some of them."

"And?" pressed Carolyn.

"Well, the military used to keep enough food and supplies in some of those tunnels to feed an entire Army during a siege," described Ray. "Literally."

"Go on," directed Susan with interest.

"There's a huge walk-in freezer just inside in the bunker over by the faculty housing," revealed Ray. "The school keeps a lot of its frozen goods in there. It takes a lot of food to feed all those kids, you know."

"So, what was in the boxes, then?" Carolyn wanted to know.

"Probably ice cream," chuckled Ray.

"And the duffle bag?" questioned Susan.

"Maybe rock salt," grinned Ray. "Who knows, that was over forty years ago!"

"Forty-four," corrected Susan. "It was in 1972."

"Why were the lights off on your pickup truck that night?" quizzed Carolyn. "When you drove up and when you left?"

"Oh yeah, I do remember that," recalled Ray. "The headlamps were burned out. There was some kind of an electrical short in 'em. Couldn't get 'em fixed until the next day. Had a heck of a time seeing to drive that night, too. I'd forgotten about that."

"So that's why you were going so slowly?" understood Susan.

"We got twenty minutes," advised Carolyn, suddenly noticing what time it was when she glanced at her wristwatch.

"Oh, my goodness! I've got to get to class right now," panicked Susan. "Let's go! Ray, I hope you can come over for dinner tonight. We're staying in Ms. Neilson's house. I trust you know where that is?"

"Ah, sure, I'd like that," agreed Ray.

"How 'bout six o'clock?" called Carolyn as she and Susan quickly got into the rental car to leave.

"I'll be there," promised their new ally.

6. The Daisy Patch

"Girls?" came the voice of Dean Dixon over the intercom speaker box in their room. "Are you there?"

Susan sighed deeply before responding. "Yes, Miss Dixon?"

"Is Carolyn there, too?" questioned the Dean.

"She hasn't come back yet from class," replied Susan nervously.

"When she does, I'd like to see the both of you in my office," replied Dean Dixon. "The sooner the better, please."

Just then the door to room 124 opened and in came Carolyn with Veronica and Joyce. Susan held her index finger to her lips to shhh them and nodded with her head toward the intercom.

Understanding immediately, they motioned for Susan to follow them and went at once to the large restroom and laundry facility down the hall. "Our stuff, it's all gone!" whispered Veronica.

"What do you mean?" questioned Susan with concern. "It was all down there yesterday!"

"Well, it's gone now," confirmed Joyce. "We just went down there to get a radio, but everything's gone now. We were gonna take it down to the beach with us."

Carolyn then whispered to Susan, "That reminds me. When I came back to the room after breakfast, I noticed the outside vent cover had already been put back into place. I thought we agreed I would fix it while everyone was at work or down in class." Carolyn hoped no one else besides Veronica or Joyce could overhear them. One of the toilets suddenly flushed, causing all of them to glance in that direction.

"I saw the outside vent cover back on, too, when I went out there after breakfast, and thought you'd put it back on," whispered Susan.

Carolyn shook her head in the negative.

"Let's go outside," insisted Veronica. "Nowhere's safe inside this dormitory anymore!"

"Hey, it's just me, ladies," grinned Karol Weeble when she saw them and approached, aware they were discussing something juicy.

"Whew!" sighed Carolyn with relief.

"So, you think the dorm is still on demon alert?" grinned Karol, already aware of what had really happened.

"Let's all go down to the beach," suggested Veronica. "I need to get in a little boogie boarding anyway."

"Sounds good to me," agreed Joyce. "Let's go."

"Hey, I saw that creepy weird Ray Dixon guy messing with that vent cover this morning," whispered Karol. "Right before breakfast."

"He's probably got all our stuff now, too!" Veronica was angry.

"And there's not a blessed thing we can do about it, either," recognized Susan with frustration.

The girls became quiet as they approached the front desk and headed for the front door.

"Wait!" called Diana. "Susan and Carolyn, the Dean would like to see you in her office. Now!"

"We'll see you later, then," nodded Susan as she and Carolyn split away from them to head down the long hallway. Then whispering so only Carolyn could hear, Susan muttered, "We're sunk!"

"Miss Dixon did look straight at us when we were grinning at the meeting last night," recalled Carolyn.

"She has to know it was us," guessed Susan.

"Well, she must know it was somebody," responded Carolyn. "We'll probably see all those boxes of stuff when we get to her office!"

"Oh, girls," greeted Miss Dixon from the open doorway of her office apartment. "Please, come in."

Never had Susan or Carolyn known Miss Dixon to open the door prior to it being knocked on, and frankly, they were both quite worried.

"Do sit down," motioned the Dean.

After they were all seated, Miss Dixon inhaled deeply and then exhaled again before she began. "Oh, girls." The Dean shook her head and looked first at Susan and then at Carolyn. It might have been their imagination, but Miss Dixon actually looked for a moment as if she were trying not to smile.

"Here's what's going to happen," continued the Dean. "A contractor has been hired to permanently seal off that false vent cover in the laundry room."

"False vent?" Susan tried to appear perplexed.

"One that leads to an open space beneath the girls' dormitory," clarified the Dean. "As opposed to an actual ventilation system, as one might expect."

"Why tell us?" Susan shrugged her shoulders while Carolyn remained silent and stared at the all-too-familiar bare spot on the carpet.

"Indeed," responded Miss Dixon with a tight lipped grin while she continued to shake her head.

Another awkward moment of silence pervaded the room as the Dean studied Susan and Carolyn more carefully.

"There also happened to be an exterior vent cover out of place on the west end of the dormitory that came unscrewed by itself last night. Perhaps by demons," the Dean was actually smiling with amusement.

"You certainly don't think ....," Susan broke off in mid-sentence, trying to seem shocked.

"Really?" Miss Dixon shook her head again and laughed for several moments before becoming serious again and continued. "Be assured, girls, that my handyman has already put that vent cover back into place, and that all of the items he found beneath the laundry room are on their way to the local pawn shop in town as we speak."

"Crawl space?" Carolyn tried to look as if she were puzzled.

"What kind of items?" Susan was curious.

"If they're not your items, then it doesn't matter," countered Miss Dixon squarely.

Susan and the Dean then maintained eye contact while Miss Dixon continued. "First the alarm clocks, and now this! I'm just not sure what to do with you girls!"

"Is there anything either of you would like to tell me?" pressed the Dean. "Before I decide what to do with you?"

Carolyn was clearly afraid but said nothing. Susan suppressed a smug grin, knowing that if the Dean could prove what she suspected, that Miss Dixon would already have issued her verdict.

"Very well, then," sighed the Dean with defeat. "Effective immediately, the two of you are being moved to the west wing on the second floor. You will be in room 230. That just happens to be on this side, right on the end where I can keep a better eye on you from here. Any time your room light is on, I will see it from my office window, and whenever it's off, I'll see that, too. Except when the electricity is off for the night, of course. And, there is no crawl space opening - or any other way - to sneak in or out of this dormitory in the middle of the night from that particular floor! Do we understand each other?"

"Apparently so," answered Susan as she glanced through Miss Dixon's office window at the second floor of the west wing.

"Yes, ma'am," mumbled Carolyn with relief, though amazed that the punishment had not been more severe. Not only that, she and Susan would still be roommates. Clearly, Miss Dixon had no concrete evidence of their guilt. Otherwise, their parents would have been called.

"Susan, you may go," instructed Miss Dixon. "I need to speak with Carolyn alone for a moment."

Without further comment, Susan quickly left.

Turning to Carolyn, the Dean advised, "I'm depending on you to make sure nothing like this happens again."

Carolyn merely nodded her acquiescence.

"And," revealed the Dean, "effective tomorrow, you will no longer be working in the lumber mill."

"Why not?" Carolyn was suddenly upset, worried that she would not be there to intervene should Linda Shaver try to monopolize Lenny's attention during breaks.

"Mr. Rosario, the Spanish instructor, informs me that you are not doing as well as hoped in his class," mentioned the Dean. "That was certainly a surprise to me, especially since you are doing so well in all your other subjects."

Carolyn did not comprehend what that had to do with working at the lumber mill but mutely waited for the Dean to continue.

"Your new job will be working in the daisy patch," smiled Miss Dixon enthusiastically. "You'll be picking, or should I say harvesting, flowers for a nearby florist."

"Picking daisies?" frowned Carolyn. "Whatever for?"

"Daisies are used for all sorts of things. I've seen them displayed at weddings, funerals, and all types of occasions," described Miss Dixon excitedly. "And most importantly, it is an entirely

Spanish-speaking jobsite. Mr. Rosario personally recommended you for the job so you might have the opportunity to improve your spoken Spanish."

"No one there speaks any English at all?" Carolyn was stunned.

"Absolutely no one!" confirmed the Dean with a mischievous grin. "Oh yes, you will still be able to wear your blue jeans. I thought you might like that."

"Yes, ma'am," replied Carolyn, though not sharing the Dean's zeal for her new job assignment.

"There you are!" called Susan as she watched Carolyn approach. "What's wrong? You look upset. What'd she say after I left?"

Carolyn quietly sat down on the weather beaten log before responding. "Veronica and Joyce are both quite good."

"Yeah, they are," agreed Susan. "So, are you gonna tell me?"

Carolyn watched her friends Joyce and Veronica boogie board for several moments longer before answering.

Boogie boarding, sometimes referred to as bodyboarding, was a casual form of wave riding that could also be participated in as a serious sport by those willing to devote sufficient time and patience to practice the skill. Similar to surfboarding, a boogie board would also need to be of proper size for the person using it. Most safely accomplished in an area of beach free from large rocks, boats or other obstructions, the sandy stretch of beach directly beside Oceanview Academy was an ideal location for recreational boogie boarding.

The average boogie board consisted of a short, rectangular piece of hydrodynamic foam, and often contained a short graphite rod within the core called a stringer. Boogie boarders typically would use swim fins for additional propulsion and control while riding a wave, usually on one's belly or knees, and in rare instances on their feet.

After strapping one's wrist to the board to avoid losing it in the current, the rider would then kick and paddle to where the waves were breaking. Just like in regular surfing, the boogie boarder would need to paddle to the highest point or crest of a breaking wave, and point the nose of the board toward the beach while lying flat on their belly and keeping their hands a couple inches down on the side from the top. With their shoulders parallel to their hands, and their elbows bent and

109

resting close to the outer edge of the board, the boogie boarder would then get ahead of the wave to "catch" it.

Being an experienced boogie board rider herself, Veronica knew just how to maintain the proper speed and wave direction, reveling in the sheer pleasure of feeling her body moving effortlessly toward the beach on her boogie board with no further need to kick or paddle. Almost as skilled as Veronica, Joyce was also well acquainted with the process of using wave momentum to propel herself forward.

Not only were both girls proficient at basic boogie boarding maneuvers, including "bottom turns" and "cut backs" but were currently trying out some newly acquired techniques that involved completing 360° turns while riding the wave.

"I'd be afraid of sharks," mentioned Carolyn. "They have had some sightings around here."

"So, tell me!" demanded Susan, anxious to learn what Dean Dixon had wanted to speak to Carolyn about in private.

"I finished moving all our stuff up to room 230, by the way," began Carolyn, irritated at having to complete the task by herself.

"I was just coming up to help you after this," explained Susan.

"Nevertheless," replied Carolyn, "Miss Dixon wanted it done right then. Don't worry, everything still needs to be put away. I tried to stack it all in neat piles."

"Hey man, I'm sorry," apologized Susan. "I'll help you put it all away after dinner, I promise."

"That's fine," nodded Carolyn, though clearly still upset about something else entirely.

"What else did she say?" pressed Susan.

"That I'm being transferred to the daisy patch!" fumed Carolyn.

"So, that's all it is?" teased Susan, to lighten the mood.

"What it means is that I'll no longer be there at the lumber mill!" snapped Carolyn.

"Maybe the daisy patch won't be so bad," suggested Susan.

"It also means that I won't be there to see Lenny during breaks anymore," fretted Carolyn. "Linda Shaver clearly has her eye on him, and now there'll be nothing I can do about it!"

"Oh, Carolyn," chuckled Susan. "You needn't worry! Pete and I will be there to keep an eye on things at the mill, no problem."

110

Carolyn rolled her eyes, shook her head, and sighed deeply as she continued to watch Joyce and Veronica in silence.

"Why the daisy patch?" Susan suddenly wanted to know.

"To help improve my Spanish-speaking skills," replied Carolyn. "Apparently, Mr. Rosario is concerned and mentioned it to Miss Dixon. And, he personally recommended me for the job."

"Lucky you!" grinned Susan.

"It's an entirely Spanish-speaking job site!" revealed Carolyn. "Absolutely none of them speaks English at all!"

Susan laughed heartily for several moments.

"It's not funny," pouted Carolyn before finally seeing the humor in it and began laughing herself.

"My dear Carolina la Gata," smiled Susan. "Mr. Rosario speaks nothing but Castilian Spanish from the old country. I doubt those people at the daisy patch would be able to understand him, either."

"What am I going to do, then?" worried Carolyn.

"I speak Spanish," assured Susan. "I'll help you! My parents are from Nicaragua, and the Spanish we speak is a lot closer to what these daisy pickers speak than what Mr. Rosario ever could."

"For extra credit, he had me read a book in Spanish called 'El Contrabandista de Dios' that was about a man who smuggled Bibles into Russia," revealed Carolyn. "At least that's what I think it was about. It seemed quite good. Someday I'll have to find one in English."

"Sí, usted puede leer y escribir el Español," reasoned Susan aloud, "then speaking it shouldn't be too hard at all."

"What?" frowned Carolyn, not understanding at all.

"If you can read and write Spanish," translated Susan, "then speaking it shouldn't be too hard at all. Being understood, of course, is another matter entirely."

"Hey you guys!" greeted Veronica as she and Joyce ran toward them. Both girls plopped their boogie boards down onto the sand, and grabbed their towels to dry off.

"Not bad at all," complimented Carolyn.

"You should try it sometime," suggested Joyce as she put on her zorries. Joyce then dried herself off the best she could before pulling on her blue corduroy pants and thick sweat jacket, leaving her wet one-piece swimsuit on underneath.

"Not me," declined Carolyn. "I'd be too afraid of sharks!"

"You don't know what you're missing," stated Joyce as she wrapped the damp towel around her wet hair and picked up her swim fins and boogie board to carry them back up to the dormitory.

"Besides, it's been over fifteen years since the last shark attack around here, and that was in 1957. I think we're pretty safe," reasoned Veronica while she, too, struggled to put her clothing back on over her wet swim attire.

"You just gotta keep an eye out for 'em," chuckled Joyce. "They're pretty easy to spot, especially in these shallow waters."

"You wouldn't catch me out there for anything," advised Susan, in total agreement with Carolyn's assessment of the possible danger.

"I just wish there were a place down here to stash our swim gear," mentioned Veronica. "That way we wouldn't have to haul it back and forth each time."

"Or go back in wet clothes," added Joyce. "Think how nice it would be to just come down in the mornings before breakfast, boogie board for an hour, and then change right here before heading up to class. We could just leave everything here!"

"There is a cave over there," noticed Carolyn with interest.

"We definitely should check that out when we have more time," realized Veronica, and wondered why she hadn't seen the cave before.

"Maybe it's a back way into one of the bunkers?" mused Susan. "Or an escape route for the military?"

"Perhaps it's an entrance for a secret invasion by the enemy, like at Normandy," imagined Joyce, who was a history buff.

"They very well could have kept a tank hidden in there," realized Susan, intrigued by the idea. "It looks big enough."

"Maybe they did! They could've been prepared for massive air strikes or even amphibious landings on the beach when they got here," grinned Joyce.

"I think you study your history book too much!" laughed Veronica as she started for the rocky access road leading down from the tree lined cliffs above.

Voices echoed throughout the cafeteria. The hungry crowd of students and faculty was seated here and there, at various tables, busy visiting while devouring their evening meal.

"There's Lenny," indicated Carolyn as she made her way toward his table with Susan, Joyce and Veronica close behind.

"Hey!" greeted Pete as they approached. "Sit down!"

Lenny merely smiled and nodded in acknowledgment at the other girls before focusing his attention exclusively on Carolyn alone. When their eyes met, Lenny's warm, sensitive face beamed with delight, causing Carolyn to blush ever so slightly as she sat down across from him.

"Carolyn's been reassigned to the daisy patch," announced Susan with a mischievous grin.

"The daisy patch?" repeated Lenny with disappointment, but maintaining eye contact with Carolyn. "When will I get to see you, then?" Lenny seemed for a moment to forget the others were there.

Carolyn secretly wondered if Lenny might finally ask her to go steady, perhaps when the others finished their dinner and were gone.

"Did you see the flyer about the Harvest Festival Prom coming up?" asked Joyce, of no one in particular.

"Don't they usually wait to have that closer to Thanksgiving?" questioned Veronica. "It's still two more weeks until Halloween."

"Is it a costume party, then?" questioned Susan with interest.

"Probably not. But, it did say on the flyer that they're having it on November 4th," recalled Joyce. "That's a Saturday night."

"Now that's different," commented Pete, wondering if it were some holiday he just was not familiar with.

Carolyn hoped with all her heart that Lenny would invite her to be his date for the upcoming Harvest Festival Prom, and gave him a pleading look. Lenny merely returned her gaze with a flirtatious smile, certain Carolyn understood his intentions without the need to spell it out. Carolyn began to wonder if Lenny would ever do more than string her expectations along.

"Carolyn?" It was Mrs. Bennett. "There you are!" Carolyn was roused immediately from her silent conversation with Lenny. In fact, she was absolutely stunned.

"Mom?" Carolyn stood to hug her mother before introducing her friends. "Mom, this is Susan, Joyce, Veronica, Pete and Lenny." Each of them smiled and acknowledged their introductions.

Carolyn looked around for a moment and then asked, "Where's dad?" It seemed strange that he was not with her.

"Your daddy is waiting out in the car," explained Mrs. Bennett uncomfortably. "He was hoping you could come out there so you two could chat. He just didn't feel like coming inside."

The moment was awkward as Carolyn's friends watched her pick up her tray to leave. Right at that moment, Lenny got up and came over to pull Carolyn's chair out for her. Then turning to Carolyn's mother, Lenny took one of her hands in both of his and said, "Very nice to meet you, Mrs. Bennett."

Carolyn's mother was somewhat surprised to see how tall Lenny actually was and smiled warmly in return. "My pleasure, Lenny. I hope we see each other again."

"Until then," bid Lenny as he watched Carolyn and her mother start to walk away.

Carolyn then paused and turned back to ask, "Will I see you at breakfast?"

"I'll look forward to it," grinned Lenny with irresistible charm, which surprised everyone at the table. Lenny was ordinarily quite shy.

"Your father is pretty upset," warned Carolyn's mother as she waited for Carolyn to leave her half eaten meal in the dish return area.

"So upset he couldn't even bother to come inside?" scowled Carolyn. Whatever it was, she was about to find out.

As soon as Carolyn and her mother were safely inside the white Dodge Dart, Mr. Bennett started the car's engine and slowly drove away, not bothering to stop until reaching the forested area by the bluffs. In fact, he had chosen a spot only feet from the entrance to the access trail by the school's property boundary. This was actually where Susan and Carolyn had made their way to and from the beach after their rendezvous with Lenny and Pete. It was hard to believe that had been only yesterday! It already seemed like a lifetime ago to Carolyn.

"Oh Carolyn," muttered her father as he shook his head.

"What is it?" asked Carolyn, seriously worried.

"This morning I received a phone call from the Administration Office letting me know that you've been reassigned to a new job – a job that will not pay anything near what you were making at the mill," began Mr. Bennett.

"Yes, Sir," replied Carolyn. "That's correct."

"Did something happen at your mill job that you're not telling us about?" pressed Carolyn's father.

"Not that I know of," answered Carolyn. "My supervisor at the lumber mill was quite happy with my work."

"Then why?" Mr. Bennett was perplexed. "Why would they transfer you to a minimum wage job when you were making three times that where you were?"

"It's not like I saw a penny of it anyway!" snapped Carolyn, sorry at once for doing so.

"Perhaps allowing you to come here was a mistake," mentioned Mr. Bennett sadly. "There's no way your mother and I can afford to make up the difference in your tuition now. If that Dean can't get you your job back at the mill, or some other job that pays a comparable rate, you very well might not be able to stay here."

"What your daddy is trying to say," elaborated Mrs. Bennett, "is that we both were troubled that it was the Administration Office who called us and not you."

"Or Miss Dixon," added Mr. Bennett, maintaining eye contact with Carolyn by looking at her in his rearview mirror, but not bothering to turn around.

"It was only this morning that the Dean called me in and told me about it," defended Carolyn. "I had planned on calling you tonight!"

"You knew nothing about this until today?" Carolyn's father sounded doubtful.

"No, Sir," maintained Carolyn. "It was apparently my Spanish teacher's idea. He recommended me for a Spanish-speaking job to help improve my spoken Spanish skills."

"What?" Carolyn's father was dumbfounded. "Whatever for?"

"The job involves picking daisies for a local florist shop," described Carolyn. "My first day is not until tomorrow."

"Picking daisies?" Mr. Bennett began to laugh, shaking his head with frustration. "We're going to have a chat with Miss Dixon about that, right now!"

Carolyn's father put the key back into the ignition but paused before starting the engine and added, "Another thing."

"What?" prompted Carolyn.

"I think you should choose your friends a little more carefully, young lady," he cautioned. "I didn't come into the cafeteria because I saw you sitting with some colored kids."

"Your father thinks you should be hanging out with your own kind," explained Mrs. Bennett.

"Excuse me?" Carolyn was flabbergasted. It was inconceivable that she had heard her parents say what they just had. What had come over them? This did not seem like her parents at all, especially her mother! Carolyn had never known her mother to support ideas of racial intolerance or prejudice, not ever!

Mr. Bennett then turned half-way around to look directly at his daughter. "No daughter of mine will be dating any colored boy! Do we understand each other?"

Carolyn was infuriated but remained silent, knowing better than to jeopardize her ability to remain at Oceanview Academy by upsetting her parents any worse than they already were.

"Well?" pressed Mr. Bennett.

"We understand each other," responded Carolyn, though certain she would not be giving up her friendship with Lenny!

"Let me make myself perfectly clear, Mr. Bennett," informed Miss Dixon. "We absolutely do not promote bigotry or racism here at Oceanview Academy! Any student in good standing is free to socialize in an acceptable manner with any other student in good standing, regardless of race, economic status, or other social difference."

"I do not want my daughter dating that colored boy!" persisted Mr. Bennett.

"That will be entirely up to Carolyn, at least while she's here!" informed the Dean with finality.

"And just why was she moved to a new room and given a new roommate without her parents being informed?" pressed Mr. Bennett. "Our daughter and anything that concerns her is our business!"

"Then I'm glad you understand that the decisions made about her room assignment, her roommate, or her school job, are up to us," Dean Dixon forced a smile. "I believe you also agreed to be responsible financially – in writing – for whatever part of her tuition that might not be covered by Carolyn's meager salary."

"Yes, that's correct," nodded Mr. Bennett.

"Then this is what I'll do," replied Miss Dixon. "I will contact the lumber mill today and have Carolyn's name put back on the roster for the first available opening. Will that be acceptable?"

Carolyn's father finally nodded in the affirmative.

"Good," smiled the Dean in a friendlier way. "Still, I should warn you, it could take a couple of weeks for another opening to come up. Carolyn's previous job has already been given to someone else."

"Why so long?" questioned Carolyn's mother, concerned that her husband might get upset again.

"Doesn't everyone want to work at the higher paying jobs?" asked the Dean with a smile. "Meanwhile, Carolyn will get the Spanish-speaking experience her teacher feels she needs to be more successful in that class."

"Also," Carolyn finally spoke up, "My new roommate speaks Spanish and said she'd be willing to help me practice it. Her name is Susan Rives."

"That's right," approved Miss Dixon. "Not only that, Carolyn was moved up to room 230 with her new roommate just today."

Carolyn was immensely relieved that Dean Dixon had been the one to inform her parents of the room change, as Carolyn had been quite worried about how to approach the subject with her father. Also strange was that the Dean chose not to mention to Carolyn's parents that Susan and Carolyn had been roommates already, before the room change.

The Bennett family car slowly pulled away from the small town of Ocean Bluff and proceeded north up the treacherously narrow road at a mere crawl. Oceanview Academy was already a good half hour behind them. Mr. Bennett usually drove much slower than the average driver anyway, and rarely made stops for restroom breaks. That, of course, created ample time for his passengers to enjoy the scenic ocean view below them while the vehicle unhurriedly continued north along the windswept cliffs overgrown with eucalyptus and aging cypress trees.

Located just two hours north of Oceanview Academy, the huge metropolis of Ocean Bay had a population approaching 300,000 people in 1972. The Bennett family and Susan, however, were headed for a destination that would arrive before reaching it.

"I'm glad you could join us," mentioned Carolyn's mother as she turned to smile sweetly at Susan, who was seated in the back seat beside Carolyn.

"It should be fun," nodded Susan politely.

"That was very nice of your Dean to make arrangements for the two of you to be excused from your classes and jobs today," added Mrs. Bennett pleasantly. She was looking forward to getting to know Carolyn's new roommate better, and also to be doing what she could to help smooth things over between Carolyn and her father.

"It was nice of Susan's parents to agree to it, too," pointed out Carolyn. "Too bad we weren't able to have breakfast at the cafeteria before taking off for the day, though. The food's really not bad."

"Patty's Pancake House wasn't too bad," replied Mrs. Bennett.

Susan and Carolyn both rolled their eyes as they looked at one another and shook their heads in the negative, clearly not in agreement with Mrs. Bennett's opinion of the food at Patty's Pancake House.

"We'll find a better place to have lunch when we get to the boardwalk," promised Carolyn's mother, secretly in agreement with them but not wanting to hurt her husband's feelings since he had chosen the establishment.

"Are you sure there's a boardwalk there?" Susan suddenly asked as they turned onto the main highway. "I've lived in Ocean Bay all my life but I've never seen a boardwalk along here."

"It's there," informed Mr. Bennett with a sly smile. Whenever he did smile, it was barely noticeable and usually only to those who knew him well enough to watch for the twinkle in his eyes.

Mr. Bennett loved his daughter with all his heart, and did regret the words that had been exchanged between them the previous day. But, he was normally not one to apologize or admit it when he was wrong. Carolyn's father truly hoped that taking his daughter and her new roommate for a fun-filled day at the boardwalk would help all of them move past what had happened.

Carolyn was worried what Lenny Owens would think of her for breaking their breakfast date, again.

"Are you all right?" questioned Carolyn's mother, aware that her daughter was preoccupied about something.

"I did promise some of our friends that I'd meet them for breakfast this morning," explained Carolyn, being careful not to mention Lenny in particular.

Mr. Bennett glanced studiously at his daughter in the rearview mirror as she conversed with her mother, purposely maintaining his best poker face.

Susan then endeavored to have a friendly conversation with Mr. Bennett, who was a man of few words.

"He's as bad as Lenny," Susan finally whispered to Carolyn.

"He never says much," responded Carolyn. "It's not you."

Mr. Bennett brought his car to a sudden stop so he could read an aging road sign that was barely noticeable amid the dense foliage surrounding it. The sign merely said, "Boardwalk."

The boardwalk of which Mr. Bennett spoke was indeed located half-way between Ocean Bluff and Ocean Bay.

"Wow!" exclaimed Susan. "Would you look at that! How'd you ever know this was here? I never even noticed it before."

"AAA book," explained Mr. Bennett as he turned onto the gravel road. Not fond of driving on unpaved roads, Carolyn's father proceeded at about five miles per hour and hoped to avoid getting any unnecessary dust on his white Dodge Dart.

"He'll stop to check for rocks in the tires when we get there," predicted Carolyn.

"You can count on it," promised Mr. Bennett with another of his sly grins, evidently unashamed of his fastidious habit of stopping completely after driving on any gravel road to check for unwanted rocks picked up by his tires and subsequently hidden within their grooves.

"He usually takes his car keys out and does a complete walk-around inspection of the car, using them to pry out each and every piece of gravel by hand," described Carolyn.

"You don't say," sighed Susan. She desperately needed to use the restroom as badly as Carolyn and her mother did already.

"And then he gets back in and pulls the car forward a few inches more before getting back out and checking all the tires again," added Carolyn.

"Gotta check both sides of the tires." Mr. Bennett was serious.

"The sides that were up under the wheel-well during his first inspection need to be checked, too," explained Carolyn's mother, just in case Susan did not understand.

Susan then gave Carolyn a look of sympathy and shook her head.

Mrs. Bennett did not notice Susan's reaction, but Mr. Bennett did. In fact, he almost seemed to take a sadistic delight in making his passengers wait while he performed his routine tire check each time he happened to drive through gravel of any kind.

Carolyn's mother was just grateful that her husband took such precautions against unwanted flat tires, which were never fun.

It took almost twenty minutes to finally reach the boardwalk, though it should have taken only five. Mr. Bennett eventually pulled to a stop by the parking lot entrance and got out to inspect his tires, just as predicted by Carolyn.

"I'm sorry," apologized Susan, "but I just can't wait any longer to use the ladies' room."

"Me, neither," agreed Carolyn as both of them hurriedly got out of the car, closed the back seat doors, and raced across the car lot toward a clearly marked restroom on the end of the boardwalk closest to the parking area. Times being what they were back in 1972, parking was unlimited and free.

"I can't wait, either," advised Carolyn's mother as she suddenly got out of the Bennett car, grabbed her handbag, and rushed after them. Mr. Bennett was left alone to finish checking his tires for rogue pieces of gravel before finding a parking spot.

Surprised by the number of cars parked in the huge parking lot, Mr. Bennett was forced to drive up and down several rows before finally finding an acceptable place to leave his white Dodge Dart for the day.

The sounds of merry-go-round music, laughing voices and other thrilling carnival rides were in sharp competition with the giant roller coaster and its many screaming passengers. Tantalizing aromas wafted through the air, constantly reminding any hungry boardwalk patrons of the many delicious food items for sale. Popcorn, chili dogs, shaved ice and cotton candy were available at a portable vendor near the parking lot entrance, along with several other delectable items.

After using the restroom first, Susan, Carolyn and Mrs. Bennett stopped to watch the taffy tumbler while they waited for Carolyn's father to join them.

Next to the taffy machine was a bright red, coin-operated soda pop dispenser where Coca Cola was offered at 25 cents per bottle. And, since a 10 ounce glass bottle of soda usually sold for 10 cents each back in 1972, that was expensive!

"Would you ladies like some fresh salt water taffy?" asked a handsome young man who was working the machine while it stretched the delicious taffy before their eyes.

Right then the young man was busy creating a batch of walnut pistachio taffy, which just happened to be Carolyn's favorite flavor. She thought for a moment of the walnut pistachio ice cream cones she and Lenny had enjoyed at the beach two nights ago.

Neither Susan nor Carolyn had any money, though the taffy was compelling. They glanced hopefully at Mrs. Bennett, but she was busy searching the crowd for any sign of her husband. It was usually fairly easy to spot Mr. Bennett in a crowd due to his bright red hair color and slow, meandering gait.

Carolyn's father had paused to watch the giant roller coaster as its train pulled slowly up the steep track to the uppermost pinnacle for its first drop. Some of the braver passengers held both hands high above their heads while the train plummeted down the first and farthest drop. Most of them shrieked with fear at first but then squealed with the delight of adrenaline and excitement as they sped forward over other inclines, descents and turns before finally coming to a screeching halt at its boarding station!

"There you are!" called Carolyn's mother as she went over to where her husband was and put her arm through his. "We were just getting ready to buy some taffy."

"I think I'd like to try a soft hot pretzel," preferred Mr. Bennett.

"The corn dogs look pretty good, too," mentioned Susan.

"You don't eat meat, do you?" questioned Carolyn's mother with abhorrence. She was an avid vegetarian and had been for years.

"When I get the chance," confessed Susan with a sheepish grin and a shrug of her shoulders.

"They do look good," agreed Carolyn's father, though he only ate meat once in a great while. He certainly seemed willing to make this one of those occasions.

"They even have chocolate covered bananas and soft serve ice cream!" noticed Carolyn. Even though it was still an hour yet before lunch time, all of them were hungry. The breakfast at Patty's Pancake House had left Susan and Carolyn, in particular, desirous of something else to eat. Unknown to Carolyn's parents, they had each managed to hurriedly dump a fair portion of their disgusting breakfast onto a waiter's cleanup tray at Patty's Pancake House when Mr. and Mrs. Bennett stepped away from the table to use the restroom.

"Why don't we just get some taffy now and wait until noon for lunch?" suggested Mrs. Bennett. "We should all be good and hungry by then." She had no idea!

Mr. Bennett merely nodded his agreement and allowed himself to be lead toward the taffy machine while he continued to study his surroundings in silence. The delicious taffy was quickly purchased and devoured by Susan and the Bennett family in short order.

Carolyn's parents then sat on a nearby bench to watch while Carolyn and Susan tried their hand at some of the games in a nearby video arcade. Despite her husband's objections, Mrs. Bennett pulled a small tube of suntan lotion from her purse, squirted some onto her hand, and gently applied it to his fair complexioned face and ears. Mr. Bennett then grabbed the tube of suntan lotion from her to put some of it on his own arms. Red headed people did tend to sunburn more easily than others, so he seemed quite pleased when Susan won and gave him a men's baseball cap. He had actually been thinking about purchasing one, anyway.

After playing several games of skee ball, which was Carolyn's favorite arcade game, she managed to win enough tickets to obtain a small yellow teddy bear that she secretly named "Lenny."

And, since they were having so much fun at the boardwalk, Susan and the Bennett family hastily decided on soft hot pretzels for lunch. They all held out hope that the evening meal would find them at a restaurant with adequate substantial food selections.

Carolyn and Susan then proceeded to go on as many rides as the twenty dollars her father had given them made possible. The remainder of their "fun money" was soon depleted after visiting the penny arcade, a giant building filled with vintage arcade game machines that each cost only one penny to operate.

"I think we should have an early dinner before we head back," suggested Mr. Bennett. "What sounds good?"

By then, they had walked the entire length of the boardwalk and were at the opposite end, farthest away from the parking lot and directly beside a long pier filled with small shops, fishermen and sightseers.

"Why don't we walk out onto the pier and take a look at that seafood place?" suggested Susan.

"They wouldn't have any vegetarian food at a place like that," objected Mrs. Bennett. She did not eat meat of any kind and was not about to start now!

"Even Jesus ate fish," grinned Susan.

"Not me," persisted Carolyn's mother.

"We should go walk on the beach before sundown," differed Carolyn. "It's only 5:00 now, and the sun doesn't go down until 6:30. We haven't had a chance to walk down on the sand yet."

"Ooh, yeah, we could go look for seashells!" Susan was pleased with the suggestion.

"Look at all those people down there!" pointed out Mr. Bennett, not desirous of getting sand into his shoes that might later fall out onto the floor mat of his car.

"That really does look like fun," agreed Carolyn's mother. "We haven't been down by the water yet, at all."

"Remember that time you stepped on a jellyfish when Carolyn was little, and we rushed you to the hospital?" reminded Mr. Bennett, not wanting to be confronted with an unexpected medical bill just now, especially after all the money that had been spent that day already.

Suddenly, there was a loud shriek from the beach, followed by screaming people grabbing their things and racing away from the water.

"What's going on?" questioned Carolyn's mother.

"Please step out of the water!" came a loud booming voice. It was the lifeguard, using his bullhorn to warn swimmers out of the water at once. "Everyone please come out of the water! Now!"

"Shark!" screamed someone.

"Run!" shouted someone else.

Pandemonium erupted as dozens of helpless onlookers noticed a bloody explosion of water near the pier and then watched with horror while an injured baby seal made its way onto the shore. The shark's tall fin was clearly visible as it suddenly turned away from the screaming crowd of people and headed back toward the open sea.

Sharks rarely attack people unless mistaking them for their usual prey of marine life, particularly seals. Surfers, boogie boarders and other water sports enthusiasts suffer about 60 percent of all shark attacks, true because sharks frequent the surf zone, where its warm waters provide a rich menu of fish. Usually, though, sharks prefer to feed after twilight, prompting most public beaches to close between dusk and dawn. Signs are typically posted warning swimmers not to swim with an open wound, as sharks can smell a drop of blood from up to three miles away. When sharks do decide to attack people, they typically tend to target lone individuals that have strayed too far from shore. Shiny jewelry can also be mistaken for shimmering fish scales by a hungry shark.

Carolyn sadly watched as the lifeguard used someone's boogie board to perform a mercy killing on the unfortunate baby seal.

"There really was nothing they could have done for it," opined Mr. Bennett, grateful that things were beginning to settle down.

"It was beyond being helped," agreed Susan.

"Oh, how horrible!" Carolyn's mother shook her head with dismay. "At least they could have tried!"

Swimmers, surfers and boogie boarders were ordered to remain out of the water for the rest of that day. A purple flag warning went into effect, which indicated dangerous marine life in the area. Thankfully, no beach-goers had been injured because the lifeguard had been swift to follow proper protocol.

"I think we should just stay up here on the boardwalk as we head back," suggested Mr. Bennett. "We don't need to go down there."

"Are you thinking of that Chinese food place we saw earlier?" questioned Mrs. Bennett. "We do have to walk right past it on our way back to the car. Let's eat there."

"How can any of you think of food at a time like this?" Carolyn was clearly bothered by the baby seal incident.

Despite the recent tragedy beneath the pier at the far end of the boardwalk, many seagulls, pelicans, sea otters and even baby seals were already making their way back to the structure where local fishermen had resumed their fishing activities.

"Oh, look!" pointed out Susan as they passed a small dress shop. The stunning formal evening gown displayed in the shop's front window was a full-length, baby blue masterpiece! It was made of soft cotton and polyester, which was all the rage in 1972, and fit the mannequin precisely in all the right places. Matching baby blue lace woven into floral designs was sewn around its main bottom ruffle and its form-fitting bodice. The deep rounded neckline was suggestive but yet modest at the same time, bordered with a hanging row of ruffles that matched the hanging ruffles on its long puffy sleeves.

Carolyn became transfixed as she stood staring at the gorgeous dress. If only Lenny could see her in that!

"Come on, I'm hungry," urged Mr. Bennett.

"That would be perfect for Carolyn to wear to the Harvest Festival Prom," mentioned Susan. "It's in just three more weeks."

"It is a beautiful dress," admired Mrs. Bennett. "And she really doesn't have anything appropriate to wear to a formal."

"No," replied Mr. Bennett with finality as he continued his way toward the Chinese restaurant he had seen earlier.

Carolyn and her mother remained at the store window, gazing at the dress for several more minutes while Susan followed after Mr. Bennett. "Hey," Susan remarked as she grabbed Carolyn's father by the arm to get him to stop.

"Yes?" replied Mr. Bennett as he removed his arm from her grasp and stopped to wait for Carolyn and her mother to catch up.

"If you buy that dress for Carolyn," proposed Susan, "I'll make sure she goes to the prom with Jim Otterman, and not Lenny."

"I'm listening," prompted Mr. Bennett.

"Well," described Susan, "Jim Otterman is smart and handsome, with distinguished red hair like you. Jim gets straight A's in all his classes, and his parents have so much money he doesn't even have to work. He's in my biology class."

"What does he do with his free time, then, if he doesn't work?" questioned Carolyn's father, suddenly interested in knowing more about Jim Otterman.

"He takes photography and aviation classes," revealed Susan. "Someday he plans to take over his father's multi-million-dollar mortgage brokering firm."

"Just how do you know he would even ask Carolyn to the prom?" Carolyn's father was skeptical.

"Trust me." Susan smiled mischievously. "If you buy Carolyn that dress, I'll make sure of it."

"What's in it for you?" pressed Mr. Bennett suspiciously.

"There's another dress in there that caught my eye, too," grinned Susan. "And, Carolyn will never know we had this conversation. What do you say?"

Mr. Bennett stood studying Susan carefully for several moments before nodding affirmatively. Just as Carolyn and her mother arrived, he gave Susan a wink and one of his sly smiles.

"What was that all about?" pressed Carolyn.

"Trust me," grinned Susan.

It was almost ten o'clock that night when Susan and Carolyn were dropped off in front of their dormitory by Carolyn's parents. Miss Dixon had been waiting for them in her office, where the hall monitor instructed them to report upon their arrival. Mr. and Mrs. Bennett had already said their brief farewells to Carolyn and Susan, and were on their way home. They still had the long four-hour drive back to their valley home ahead so had been anxious to be on their way.

"I hope they'll be all right," worried Carolyn as she and Susan walked down the hallway toward Miss Dixon's apartment.

"I'm sure they'll be fine," assured Miss Dixon, who had already opened her door and overheard Carolyn's remark. "Parents or not, they had no right to keep you out this late! You've already missed your first day on the job at the daisy patch, so you absolutely must be there tomorrow. The foreman was quite upset by your absence."

"Didn't you make arrangements for us to be out today?" asked Carolyn curiously as she and Susan sat down on the Dean's overstuffed couch. Each of them was still holding a large plastic gift bag from the small dress shop on the boardwalk. The beautiful formals inside each bag were clearly visible.

"Mr. Rosario was the one who spoke with them," advised the Dean as she noticed the bright yellow teddy bear Carolyn was holding.

"Looks like you girls had quite a day." Miss Dixon smiled and nodded at their bags.

"We sure did," smiled Susan in return.

"Well, the party's over now and tomorrow you'll both be at your jobs, bright and early. Especially you, young lady!" Miss Dixon turned her attention to Carolyn.

"What I don't understand is why they would be so upset if Mr. Rosario made arrangements for me to be out?" Carolyn wanted to know. Something about the whole thing seemed odd to her.

"Apparently they did not understand the arrangement," informed the Dean. "All I know is that you will be in jeopardy of losing your job unless you are there tomorrow."

"I'll tell you what happened," speculated Susan. "Mr. Rosario speaks Castilian Spanish, just like they do in the old country. None of the Spanish-speaking people around here can understand him. Believe me, I tried to have a conversation with him in Spanish once, and we were barely able to communicate. It's no wonder he's sending those kids out to learn what he can't even teach them himself."

"You don't say?" Miss Dixon was quite interested in finding out what Susan had just revealed to her.

"Well, just be there," advised the Dean. "I'm sure it will be okay. If it's not, there's an opening over in squash."

"I'll be there," promised Carolyn, not desirous of working in the squash fields.

"How are we going to see to get ready for bed?" questioned Susan as she and Carolyn got up to leave the Dean's office. Many of their things from the move had not yet been put away and were still strewn throughout the room.

"Here." Miss Dixon handed Susan a battery operated camping lantern. "You can return it to me in the morning."

Susan and Carolyn raised their eyebrows with surprise.

"You bet," grinned Susan as she tried it out to be sure it worked.

"Don't stay up too late," cautioned the Dean. "I'll be keeping an eye on that window of yours. If I see that light on after 10:30...."

"You won't," interrupted Susan. "I promise."

"Good night girls." Miss Dixon sighed deeply as she watched them leave.

"You haven't asked Carolyn to the prom yet?" questioned Mrs. Vandevere. "Lenny, you can't just wait until the last minute to invite a girl to the prom."

"It's my parents," began Lenny.

"What about them?" pressed Linda Vandevere.

"My father was pretty upset when your husband – I mean, Dean Vandevere – called him on the phone that night," mentioned Lenny.

Mr. Vandevere and his gorgeous dark haired wife Linda resided in the Dean's apartment of the boys' dormitory. Nearly every boy in the school had a crush on her, some less secretly than others, but of course she was strictly off limits and deeply in love with her handsome husband, the Dean of Boys. Linda was small, dainty and pleasant but clearly unaware of the effect her innocent smile had on

127

the young men under her husband's charge. Occasionally some of the boys would come to her and seek out her advice or even confide in her, as she was known as someone who could be trusted.

Dean Vandevere was in his early thirties, worked out every day, and was well built and evenly tanned. He smiled often and had a dark brown handlebar mustache, but his sun bleached hair threatened at any time to violate the campus hair length policy. It was his wife Linda who made sure he remembered to get his hair trimmed when needed, so he could set a proper example for the boys.

"My husband called your father?" Linda Vandevere was surprised.

"That was the night Pete and I came back late from being on the beach with Susan and Carolyn," revealed Lenny.

"Really?" Linda Vandevere raised an eyebrow.

"You can't tell anyone else!" pleaded Lenny. "Carolyn and Susan have no idea how much trouble Pete or I got into, and I'd like to keep it that way. We were both on cleanup duty in the boys' dormitory showers and restrooms for an entire week!"

"Surely Susan and Carolyn must have been grounded, too?" queried Linda.

"No, I don't think so," replied Lenny. "But, they were moved to a new room up on the second floor."

"Probably so they couldn't sneak out at night again," snickered Mrs. Vandevere, suddenly amused by the situation.

"It's not funny!" Lenny was serious and wondered if confiding in Linda Vandevere had been a mistake.

"Hey, I'm sorry," apologized the Dean's wife. "What about Dean Dixon? Does she know about it?"

"Of course she would! She would have to know whatever Dean Vandevere knows," assumed Lenny. "Why would Dean Dixon choose to just let them think they got away with it?"

"That's a good question," mused Linda Vandevere.

"Well, I don't understand it, either, but she must have her reasons," rationalized Lenny.

"Maybe Miss Dixon still hopes one of them will come forward and admit what they did?" Linda Vandevere was merely speculating.

"What makes you think that?" frowned Lenny.

"From what I've heard," explained Linda, "that's the way she operates. I've never heard of anyone pulling the wool over that lady's eyes. She seems to know about everything."

"Maybe she just listens in on the rooms?" deduced Lenny. "That would make sense if she's as devious as people say she is."

"Good thing your Dean's not like that," reminded Linda Vandevere with a twinkle in her eyes.

"Maybe so, but your husband's no dummy," opined Lenny. "You know how Pete and I are both on the track team?"

Linda merely nodded.

"Well, Pete went and told him some lame story that night about us having to do extra laps, no matter how long it took us, and that was why we'd come back late." Lenny shook his head with frustration.

"Your Dean didn't buy it?" guessed Linda. She was well aware of her husband's ability to discern when any of his boys were trying to mislead him in some way.

"No," responded Lenny. "I think the campfire smoke on our clothes was a dead giveaway."

"You should have stopped at the gym for a shower," grinned Linda. "Why didn't you?"

"We did," responded Lenny. "We even changed into our gym uniforms. But, clever Pete decided to bring up our smoke-covered clothes so he could wash them. He couldn't even wait until the next day!"

"That was when Dean Vandevere called your father?" assumed Linda Vandevere.

"Yes, and not only that, then he made me talk to him, too," answered Lenny. "I've never known him to be that upset, not ever!"

"Well, there's nothing you can do about that right now, but you can go ask Carolyn to the prom," encouraged Mrs. Vandevere.

Relieved to see Lenny at breakfast, Carolyn rushed over to sit with him as usual but stopped short when she noticed Linda Shaver seated across from him. They were so deeply involved in conversation that neither of them noticed her.

Carolyn had wanted nothing more than to tell Lenny about the new blue dress her parents had bought her to wear to the Harvest Festival Prom, and how nice it would look with a baby blue corsage. Now, Lenny was probably asking Linda to the prom instead!

No longer hungry, Carolyn hurriedly exited and left her uneaten breakfast at the food return area, grabbing only a banana to eat on her way to the daisy patch.

Lenny thought of Linda Shaver as a sister, someone he could confide in and tell anything to. That irrational fear of doing or saying the wrong thing that he often felt when he was with Carolyn seemed to evaporate when he was Linda. Lenny had just finished telling her about his conversation with Linda Vandevere.

"Was your father really that upset the night Dean Vandevere made you call him?" Linda wanted to know.

"I told him everything," answered Lenny. "Even the part about Carolyn and me holding hands on the beach as we watched the sunset."

"Wow!" Linda felt as if she had been shot down in flames.

Even though Linda Shaver was merely tutoring Lenny and knew he was smitten with Carolyn, Linda secretly wondered what she might be able to do to change that. How could Lenny not notice how she felt about him?

"You knew that our family lived in Watts during all those riots before we moved to Ocean Bay?" Lenny became quite serious.

"No, I had no idea you were from there." Linda became somber. "As I recall, the riots were in 1965, only seven years ago. What a horrible thing that was!"

"Indeed." Lenny shook his head sadly. "My Aunt Jennie was one of those killed during the race riots there. She was in one of the cars they blew up."

"How horrible!" Linda was so overcome by emotion that tears began to escape down her beautiful cheeks. If it were allowed, she would have reached over to put a comforting hand on Lenny's arm.

"That was when Pete came to live with us," continued Lenny.

"What about Pete's father, or his brothers and sisters?" asked Linda. It seemed odd that Pete wouldn't want to stay with them.

"Pete's father died in a construction accident when he was in the first grade, leaving Aunt Jennie to raise him alone. Pete's an only child, just like me. Now, my parents are his parents, too, and he's especially close to my mom. You see, Jennie was her twin sister." Lenny shrugged his shoulders.

130

"No wonder you two are so close," recognized Linda. "You really are like brothers."

"Well, when my dad found out that Carolyn is white, he came unglued." Lenny suddenly felt uncomfortable, especially since Linda was white, too. "He forbade me to ever see her again."

"But yet you have," reminded Linda. "You must really care about her deeply."

"I do!" Lenny was clearly frustrated. "I just don't know how to ask her out. I get so nervous every time I'm around her that I just don't know what to say."

"I can tell she cares about you, too," consoled Linda.

"Tell me then, just how can I possibly tell Carolyn that my own father has forbidden me to see her because she's white?" demanded Lenny. "Not only that, Carolyn's own father wouldn't even come inside to see her when he saw me and Pete sitting at the table. Just why do you think that was?"

"Never mind any of that," advised Linda. "You need to just go ahead and ask her, and I would do it soon, before somebody else does."

"Hey!" called Jim Otterman as he saw Carolyn walking toward the daisy patch. "Wait up."

"I can't," replied Carolyn. "It's my first day at a new job and I can't be late."

"May I at least walk with you, then?" asked Jim as he hurried to keep pace with her.

"Suit yourself," agreed Carolyn without slowing.

"My name is Jim Otterman, by the way. I don't think we've been properly introduced." The red headed, freckle-faced young man had been anxious to introduce himself to Carolyn for some time now.

"Nice to meet you," nodded Carolyn without returning his smile.

"Your roommate Susan is in my biology class," explained Jim. "I asked her if you had a date to the Harvest Festival Prom yet, but she said I should ask you."

Carolyn came to a sudden stop to turn and study Jim Otterman, almost as if he were a new strain of bacteria. "And you came all the way out here to find me and ask me this?"

"Well, yes," grinned Jim sheepishly. "Susan did mention that you might be out this way today."

"Did she?" sighed Carolyn with irritation as she resumed her trek to the daisy patch. "Don't you have a job or a class or somewhere else you need to be?"

"Actually, no," answered Jim. "I don't have a job. My parents decided I should take aviation and photography instead, when I'm not in my other classes, of course. I'm a senior, so I have classes in the morning, but my first class today isn't until 10:00."

"How nice for you." Carolyn was being flippant.

"It has its advantages," responded Jim, unfazed.

"Then I suppose you're a straight A student, too?" Carolyn was clearly irritated by Jim Otterman and his persistence.

"Well, yeah, I guess I am," verified Jim. He tried his best to appear humble about it, but Jim had a cocky and conceited arrogance about him that no amount of effort on his part could conceal.

Nevertheless, Jim Otterman was barely five feet eight inches tall, skinny and gangly looking, with slouched bony shoulders. It was obvious from Jim's posture that he made no effort whatever to stand up straight. And, while Jim clearly did not get out much, his fair skin was partially sunburned, especially around his freckled ears and face. Jim's eyes appeared larger than they were due to his thick, oversized glasses with round black rims that clashed horribly with his light complexion. Worst of all was the greasy looking hair tonic Jim wore to keep his curly red hair combed into place.

"Looks like we're here," pointed out Carolyn with obvious relief, anxious to rid herself of Jim Otterman once and for all.

"Actually," added Jim with a confident smirk, "I also just happen to be on a field assignment for the school's yearbook committee and have been commissioned to take an assortment of photographs for the upcoming yearbook."

Jim then pulled off and slid his backpack onto one arm. While holding it by the shoulder strap on that arm, Jim unzipped the backpack with his free hand and pulled out an expensive camera. "Perhaps I could get a couple pictures of you picking daisies today?"

"Whatever for?" questioned Carolyn, more annoyed than ever.

"Oh, it'll be a series documenting the work-study program that we have here at Oceanview Academy. Parents love that kind of stuff," rambled Jim. "Helps 'em feel like they're getting their money's worth."

"I need to go get my money's worth now," Carolyn smiled an insincere smile.

Jim thought that was quite funny and began to laugh. "I'll be around."

"Of that, I have no doubt," muttered Carolyn as she turned away from Jim Otterman and approached what appeared to be the foreman of the daisy patch.

"¡Hola!" greeted Carolyn, waiting politely to be acknowledged.

The foreman and other workers appeared at first to be ignoring her completely.

"Sólo ignorarla," laughed one young woman. "Tal vez ella te sólo se cansa de esperar y simplemente desaparece."

"Es no hay manera de tratarla," scolded the older woman beside her. "Aquí es de la clase del Sr. Rosario, para mejorar sus habilidades para hablar."

Carolyn immediately recognized the name "Mr. Rosario" and nodded affirmatively. "¡Sí, estoy en la clase del Sr. Rosario!"

"Bueno, solo no se pare, entonces," chuckled the foreman. "Dar a la joven unos guantes, un par de tijeras y un cubo de agua para poner sus margaritas."

"Sí, señor," nodded the older woman, hurrying to comply. Maggie Grenzaro was only 54 years old, but the constant exposure to harsh working conditions made her appear much older than she was.

After grabbing a pair of gloves, a set of clippers and a bucket of water for Carolyn to put her daisies in, Maggie approached Carolyn with a sincere smile and handed them to her. "Estas son para que su uso."

"Estos son para...," Carolyn paused, trying to remember the word for daisy. "La margaritas?"

"Sí, margaritas," smiled the woman. "Mi nombre es Maggie," she added, pointing to herself.

"Hola, Maggie," acknowledged Carolyn.

"Y es Albert Tumalez," indicated Maggie as she nodded her head in his direction.

"Eso es correcto," Albert was condescending. "Soy el Sr. Tumalez, gringa. Ahora, manos a la obra!"

Several of the other workers merely laughed and snickered at his remark, while one of the men smiled at Carolyn in a way that made her most uncomfortable. It was as if he were undressing her with his eyes! Carolyn began to wonder whether she was safe working there, and obviously did not understand why the foreman had treated her as he had.

"Ven conmigo," indicated Maggie sympathetically as she took Carolyn by the hand and quickly led her to another area of the daisy patch, just far enough to be out of the foreman's hearing range.

"No dejes que te molesten," advised Maggie. "Quedarse conmigo, y estarás bien."

Carolyn waited, hoping that the woman would demonstrate for her what she expected.

Maggie then pointed at her own gloved hands and then at Carolyn's hands and said, "el guante."

"El guante," repeated Carolyn.

"Ponte," indicated Maggie as she took one of her own gloves off and then put it back on again.

Carolyn quickly put on the gloves provided for her and waited for Maggie to continue.

"Tijeras de poda para las flores," indicated Maggie as she held up her clippers and then pointed to the pair Carolyn had placed on the ground beside her bucket of water.

"Tijeras de poda para las flores," nodded Carolyn as she picked them up.

"Ahora, vamos a utilizar las tenazas para cortar las margaritas," continued Maggie. "Así."

Maggie then reached gently with one hand to steady one of the daisy blossoms and held it still while she used the clippers in her other hand to cut it. "Los tallos deben ser lo suficientemente largos para caber bien en un vaso, generalmente cerca de 8 a 12 pulgadas de largo."

Carolyn merely stared at Maggie with bewilderment.

Maggie then tried another approach. Gently holding another daisy bloom, she counted, "Un." Maggie then tenderly placed the daisy into the bucket of water.

Carolyn did likewise, counting "un" as she placed her daisy into the bucket of water provided.

"Bien," nodded Maggie. "Ahora, vamos a hacer otro."

"Dos," indicated Maggie as she picked yet another daisy and carefully placed it in her bucket, repeating the Spanish counting word aloud for each one until reaching an even dozen.

Maggie then pointed one at a time to each of the flowers in her bucket, speaking the numbers slowly and clearly for Carolyn so she would understand. "Uno, dos, tres, cuatro, cinco, seis, siete, ocho, nueve, diez, once y doce."

"Sí," grinned Carolyn, understanding what was expected, and repeating each of the counting words aloud as she picked each of the twelve daisies required to achieve a dozen.

"Excelente," praised Maggie. "Ahora, tenemos que recoger todas las margaritas en esta fila."

Carolyn furled her brow and sighed deeply. This was going to be more challenging than she had imagined.

Maggie then waved her hand over the bucket and indicated, "una docena."

"¿Una docena de incluso?" nodded Carolyn.

"Ahora seleccionamos mucho decenas," revealed Maggie, waving her free hand toward the lengthy row of unharvested daisies. "Seguir adelante."

Carolyn and Maggie then proceeded to harvest daisies together in silence until their buckets were filled to capacity.

"Debemos asegurarnos de no llenar el cubo demasiado," mentioned Maggie. "De lo contrario, serán aplastadas las margaritas. Además, no debemos romper cualquiera de los tallos."

Carolyn just could not understand.

Maggie took one of the flowers, broke the stem to demonstrate, and then shook her head in the negative. "No debemos romper los tallos."

Carolyn then nodded and repeated, "¿No romper los tallos?"

"Sí," chuckled Maggie. "No romper los tallos."

"¿Por qué usted perder el tiempo con esos niños?" criticized the younger woman as she approached. "¡Ninguno de ellas se va a usar después de que se fuera de la escuela, de todos modos!"

"¡Se quemó!" said Carolyn, believing that she was using a Spanish slang term her Spanish instructor had taught them that meant "burned 'em good." It was her intent to try and lighten the mood. Unfortunately, the term was from an antiquated Castilian dialect that none of them would have understood anyway, even had she pronounced it correctly.

"¿Qué dijo ella?" the younger woman suddenly laughed.

"Suena como que dijo algo sobre quema margaritas," laughed Mr. Tumalez as he arrived to bring them each a new bucket of water and retrieve the buckets filled with daisies.

Carolyn had lightened the mood all right, realizing at once that she had become a cheap source of entertainment for the Spanish-speaking group of daisy pickers.

"¡Usted no se quema cualquiera de mis margaritas, señorita!" Mr. Tumalez appeared quite serious for a moment and then broke into hysterical laughter. Several of the others joined in the hilarity, making what sounded like several crude or socially unacceptable remarks.

"Está caliente aquí," Carolyn suddenly mentioned. "Tráeme un vaso de agua, por favor."

"Usted puede obtener su propia maldita agua potable," informed the foreman, obviously having understood Carolyn's last remark.

"Al menos ella sabe cómo pedir un vaso de agua," smirked the younger woman.

"Well, let me tell you this in plain English!" Carolyn suddenly shouted at all of them as she threw down the clippers and turned to the foreman. "I quit! And, in case you don't understand, that means Lo dejé. ¡Que te vaya bien!"

Carolyn then turned to give a glaring glance of disapproval at the one lewd man, in particular, before storming away from the daisy patch. She was not going to work there with these people any longer, and that was that!

"Oh, Carolyn, what am I going to tell your father?" muttered the Dean. She and Carolyn were seated in her office. Surprisingly, Carolyn had come directly to her, without bothering to wait for an invitation.

"Perhaps you should tell him the truth!" blurted Carolyn. She was obviously quite upset. "Maybe you should tell him how you sent a poor defenseless girl out there alone to work with a vulgar bunch of people that made her fearful for her own safety!"

"What did they do or say to you?" Miss Dixon was concerned.

"Most of them were nothing but a bunch of bullies!" maintained Carolyn. "And, even though I couldn't understand a word they said, I most certainly got their meaning!"

"Why do you say they were vulgar?" questioned the Dean, extremely concerned about the accusation.

Tears erupted and freely flowed down Carolyn's cheeks as she described the one lecherous looking man, in particular, and how he had gawked at her with wanton desire, practically raping her with his eyes. Carolyn then went on to describe how the others had laughed and pointed at her, intentionally treating her with rudeness and disrespect.

"Is that when you left to come here?" asked the Dean, clearly unhappy about what had occurred.

"No," responded Carolyn as Miss Dixon offered her a box of tissues. After wiping her eyes and blowing her hose, Carolyn continued, "There was one older woman who tried to protect me from them."

"Protect you?" Miss Dixon was frowning.

"Yes," sniffed Carolyn. The tears were still flowing. "She took me by the hand and led me away from them, to a safer part of the daisy patch, and then tried to show me what they wanted me to do."

"Which was?" prompted the Dean with a raised eyebrow.

"Well, she spoke simple sentences to me, mostly counting words, and showed me how to cut and put the daisies into a bucket full of water," described Carolyn.

"Just how long were you there?" queried Miss Dixon.

"About three hours, I think," guessed Carolyn. "Then when it got hot, I asked them if I could get some water to drink, but the foreman started swearing at me. I'm positive one of the words he used was a swear word. I don't want to repeat it."

"Indeed!" Miss Dixon was not happy.

"That was when several of them started making lewd comments about me, laughing and pointing, that kind of thing. Especially that one man!" Carolyn's tears erupted anew.

"Did any of them touch you or hurt you physically in any way?" delved the Dean. She needed to find out before making some necessary phone calls about the situation.

"No," responded Carolyn as she blew her nose again. "But, that was when I threw down the clippers and told them I quit!"

"And that was when you came here?" deduced Miss Dixon.

"Yes, ma'am," nodded Carolyn, whose eyes were now red and swollen from crying. "Please don't make me go back! Please don't!"

"Don't worry, you will not be going back to the daisy patch," assured the Dean. "And they will be hearing from me, of that you can be certain! Right now, I'd venture to say the daisy patch will no longer be one of the job opportunities offered here at Oceanview Academy."

"Thank you," sniffed Carolyn, whose tears were beginning to subside.

"However," sighed the Dean, "you will still need to work somewhere until we can get you back into the lumber mill."

Carolyn silently waited to learn what job opportunity she was going to be sentenced to in the interim.

"There is one opening in squash," mentioned Miss Dixon, thinking aloud. "And, one in the dairy, but that's it."

"I don't think I could possibly get up early enough to work at the diary," replied Carolyn.

"Squash it is, then," pronounced Miss Dixon. "I'll call them today to make the arrangements. Plan to be there at nine o'clock in the morning. You may want to bring a hat, too, if you have one."

Carolyn had put on sunscreen before going to the daisy patch, but was fair complexioned and realized the Dean was right. She would need to find a hat she could wear.

"Here," Miss Dixon suddenly got up, grabbed a straw hat from a peg on the wall in her office and handed it to Carolyn. "You may keep it until your squash assignment is over."

"Why, thank you!" smiled Carolyn. Perhaps the Dean wasn't so bad after all. Maybe Susan was wrong about her.

Not wanting anyone in the cafeteria to see her red swollen eyes at dinner, Carolyn went straight to her room. She needed to get caught up on some of her homework, anyway.

"Hey!" it was Veronica at the door. "May we come in?"

"Sure," responded Carolyn, surprised to see both Joyce and Veronica enter the room carrying a tray full of food.

"You need to eat something," grinned Veronica as she set the tray down on the small desk beside Carolyn's books.

"Thank you!" Carolyn was grateful for their thoughtfulness.

"So, are you going to show us the new dress?" prompted Joyce.

"Susan told us about it at dinner," grinned Veronica. "Lenny seemed quite interested, too."

"Lenny was there at dinner?" Carolyn was surprised. Lenny normally ate dinner in his room, so he could study his chemistry assignments.

"Linda Shaver was not there," mentioned Joyce, as if reading her mind. "Lenny did seem to be looking for someone though."

"He did?" Carolyn frowned.

"Lenny was looking for you, silly!" Veronica playfully slapped Carolyn on the arm. "So, what happened? You look like you've been crying."

"Well, yeah, I have," admitted Carolyn. "I didn't want Lenny to see me looking like this."

"Okay, I want to see the dress," reminded Joyce. "She can tell us what happened while she tries it on."

"Sure," shrugged Carolyn, though stopping to sample a spoonful of the chili on her dinner tray first. "This is good! Thanks again."

"You'd do the same for us," smiled Veronica.

Carolyn then proceeded to share with Joyce and Veronica the details of the incident at the daisy patch while she undressed and put on the stunning new baby blue formal.

"Oh, it's gorgeous!" gasped Joyce. "Lenny will be speechless."

"And I thought he already was!" Carolyn was being mordant.

Joyce and Veronica understood exactly what she meant and just nodded. Lenny was well known for saying very little.

"My father was like that," reminisced Veronica. "Never would say a thing, unless my mother forced him to."

"Not my dad," informed Joyce. "All of us kept wondering if he'd ever shut up."

Veronica Jensen had only one sister and had come from a home where levity and frivolity were discouraged. Her father was a serious, hard-working accountant while her mother was a stay-at-home mom. Veronica had worked hard after school each day to save enough money to come to Oceanview Academy. When realizing she was serious about it, Veronica's parents finally had consented, provided she be willing to work every spare moment to help pay for the extravagance. Veronica, however, soon realized that it was boogie boarding and fun-loving friends to spend her free time with that would be her priority. Joyce, Susan and Carolyn were a most welcome change from Veronica's boring home life back in Los Angeles.

Joyce Troglite, on the other hand, had come from a rather large family back east. Joyce's father was often away from home for weeks at a time, lecturing and teaching self-improvement seminars to work groups from various organizations whose workers had been mandated by their employers to participate. Joyce's mother and five sisters were heavily involved in sporting activities, community projects and church functions, leaving little time to hike or explore the wilderness as Joyce preferred. When learning of the scenic campus at Oceanview Academy and the isolated location it enjoyed, Joyce jumped at the opportunity to escape her hectic home life. After meeting Veronica and learning how exhilarating it could be to catch and ride a surging ocean wave toward the shoreline, boogie boarding had quickly become one of Joyce's greatest loves in life.

"Lenny has asked you to the prom?" assumed Joyce.

"Not yet," confirmed Carolyn sadly.

"You've got to be kidding!" Veronica was stunned. "Why not?"

"Then Lenny's a fool," commented Susan from the doorway as she silently entered the room. "Oh my goodness! Look at you! Turn around, Carolyn. That has got to be the prettiest dress I've ever seen!"

Susan handed Carolyn a large hand mirror from the dresser so Carolyn could see what she looked like from behind. Susan had managed to persuade her parents to have several full sized wall mirrors delivered to her, and had used them to cover one entire wall of their dormitory room. Susan used the mirrors regularly while getting ready in the morning. Carolyn soon began to appreciate the advantage of seeing more than the tiny mirror over their small sink allowed. Sadly, the complete lack of countertop or cabinet surface around the sink had made it necessary for Susan and Carolyn to mount two small shelves on the wall beneath it, using scrap wood and leftover screws from the lumber mill.

Joyce and Veronica had long since returned to their rooms, the electricity had been turned off for the night, and Susan and Carolyn were in their beds. Too excited to go to sleep just yet, they discussed what type of shoes they would wear with their new formals. The prom was going to be held in the cafeteria, and not in the gymnasium, so shoes would be needed for the occasion.

"Did you see that?" questioned Susan as she suddenly got up and looked out the window. "There's a light on down there!"

"It's just the lamp post," assumed Carolyn.

"No, someone's either got a flashlight or a lantern of some kind. It keeps moving around." Susan ducked down and then surreptitiously peeked up over the edge of the windowsill.

Carolyn then got up and stealthily came over to where Susan was before cautiously poking her head up to get a look at what was outside. "It can't be! That looks like Miss Dixon and that nephew of hers. What are they doing?"

"They're unloading boxes from his ratty old pickup truck and carrying them into her apartment!" realized Susan. "Lots and lots of 'em! And we both know she's got a lantern!"

"Look at the way they're nervously glancing around," noticed Carolyn. "It's as if they want to make sure no one sees them."

"Duck!" cautioned Susan as she grabbed Carolyn by the arm to pull her down.

"You don't think they saw us, do you?" whispered Carolyn, suddenly concerned.

"I don't think so," answered Susan, "but we need to be more careful from now on."

"Well, at least we know the Dean's not listening in on us at the moment," chuckled Carolyn sardonically. "And just when we thought it was safe to trust her!"

7. Room with a View

"**W**ow! Look at you!" Susan was truly impressed by what she saw. "Just like a new penny!"

"Ray?" Carolyn was also astonished by the transformation.

Ray Dixon had obviously showered and changed into spotlessly clean blue jeans with a bright white t-shirt and a new looking plaid shirt before coming to Ms. Neilson's home for his six o'clock dinner invite.

"New boots, too!" grinned Susan as she held the door open and stood aside so Ray could enter.

"Hello again," nodded Ray as he took off his ten-gallon cowboy hat and brought forward a bouquet of freshly cut daisies from behind his back that he handed to Susan.

"Thank you!" smiled Susan as she took the flowers from him and deeply breathed in the fragrance. "You didn't have to do that."

"My pleasure," nodded Ray as he stepped inside. The snakeskin boots Ray wore had steel tips like his other ones, but were spotlessly clean and in excellent condition.

"Hope you like spaghetti," mentioned Carolyn as she took Ray's hat from him and hung it on a peg by the door.

"Do we have a vase anywhere?" questioned Susan as she handed the bouquet of daisies to Carolyn and headed for the kitchen.

"Daisies?" Carolyn seemed troubled for a moment. "I thought they shut those people down."

"Those Spanish-speaking people are long gone," chuckled Ray. He was well aware of Carolyn's three-hour stint at the daisy patch forty-four years ago. "They have a florist on campus now, and nearly all the daisy pickers speak English these days."

"Here's a vase," called Susan from the kitchen as she filled it with water. "Here, give me those."

"Smells wonderful!" grinned Ray as he inhaled the delicious smelling dinner that awaited him. Not only had Ray managed to scrub off most of the grease from his hands, but had also shaved and somehow found time to visit a barber for a fresh buzz cut. His graying hair was no longer overgrown or raggedy looking. Ray then reached into the front pocket of his western shirt, took out and put on his thick, horn-rimmed glasses.

"How in the world did you ever find time to visit a barber this afternoon?" questioned Carolyn. She assumed Ray had driven all the way into Ocean Bluff and back.

"They've got a hair shop right here on campus now, too," informed Ray. "I figured since I was headed over this way anyhow, I'd just come early and stop by for a trim."

"Very nice," approved Susan as she carefully arranged the vase full of daisies and placed them on the table. "Too bad there wasn't anything like that around here back in 1972."

"Mrs. Jorgensen ran a small beauty salon before she moved here with her husband, but got bored doing nothing all day while her husband was busy being Dean of Boys," described Ray. "So, the school decided to let her set up shop right here on campus."

"They do have a need for it," acknowledged Susan.

"There's a lot of changes around here," agreed Carolyn. "I was just surprised to see some of the kids walking around holding hands!"

"By the way, I love your pickup truck!" complimented Susan as she glanced outside at the new looking vehicle. "Don't tell me ... it's a Dodge. It is a new Dodge Ram, right?"

"You didn't think I'd be driving over here in the old one, did you?" laughed Ray as he followed Susan to the table and waited for an invitation to sit down.

"What year is it?" asked Carolyn as she brought and set a pitcher of water on the table.

"Oh, let me see," reflected Ray. "I think it's a 2014. I'd have to look. I usually get a new one every couple of years."

"Must be nice," mentioned Carolyn as she studied the table to make sure everything was in place.

"Please, sit down," invited Susan with a motion of her hand as she pulled out a chair for herself.

"Allow me," offered Ray as he hurried over to push in Susan's chair for her.

"Hope you don't mind if I bless the food?" mentioned Carolyn as she sat down and folded her hands for prayer.

"Please do!" requested Ray as he sat down, folded his arms and bowed his head for the prayer.

Susan merely nodded with approval and did likewise.

"Dear Father in Heaven," began Carolyn. "We thank you for this food and pray that you will bless it, that it will nourish and strengthen our bodies, and help us that we can be healthy and well. We are grateful for the opportunity we have to be here, to renew old acquaintances, and for our new friend Ray. Please be with all of us as we endeavor to try and find out what happened to Joyce Troglite and Veronica Jensen forty-three years ago, and that you will protect and keep us safe now as we do. We ask these blessings and favors humbly in the name of thy son Jesus Christ. Amen."

"Amen!" repeated Ray and Susan together.

"Everything looks great!" approved Ray as he unfolded the paper napkin by his plate and tucked it onto the front of his shirt like a bib. After putting several helpings of salad onto his plate, Ray dished up a healthy serving of spaghetti and grabbed a large chunk of garlic bread from the serving plate beside him.

"Parmesan?" smiled Susan.

"Absolutely!" Ray swiftly took the can from her and sprinkled it generously over everything on his entire plate.

"Salad dressing?" offered Carolyn as she set two choices near Ray's plate.

"My favorite," informed Ray as he grabbed the ranch dressing and squeezed a good sized blob of it onto his salad.

Carolyn quietly put some of the sesame ginger vinaigrette dressing on her salad before handing it to Susan, who did likewise.

"Bon appetite!" grinned Susan as she delicately wound a long strand of spaghetti around her fork before eating.

"You two are gonna starve," chuckled Ray when he noticed how little either of them had put on their plates.

"Gotta watch our girlish figures," advised Carolyn as she poured water into each of their glasses from the pitcher.

"You must work out?" assumed Susan. How could Ray possibly eat like that and still maintain such a hard, muscular physique, especially at his age! Susan blushed when Ray caught her checking him out.

"If you call delivering or picking up produce, dairy, bakery or other supplies, and lifting heavy boxes of ice cream working out, then I suppose I do," acknowledged Ray as he took a bite of garlic bread and continued to talk with his mouth full. "Not to mention all-purpose fix-it guy and handyman."

"Do you still deliver lumber to the mill?" asked Carolyn.

"The mill?" Ray gave Carolyn a curious glance. "That's been gone for twenty years now."

"The lumber mill's not there anymore?" Carolyn was astounded.

"Wow!" Susan was flabbergasted.

"Too much of a liability issue," recalled Ray. "School almost went under after a class action lawsuit filed by some parents following a rather serious incident there."

"How horrible!" frowned Susan.

"Turned it into a manufacturing plant for surfboards," continued Ray as he stabbed a large piece of tomato with his fork and quickly devoured it. "Good salad, by the way."

"I thought they outlawed any kind of water sports after Steve Fredrickson was killed by that shark!" Carolyn was indignant.

"Time goes by, people forget," sighed Ray as he gulped down some water. "That Jensen kid goes out there almost every day now."

"Boogie boarding," nodded Susan. "Ted said that was one of his passions. That was when I had everyone in my class stand up to introduce themselves during my first day teaching. You know, where they're from, what job they do here at the school, and what their future career goal is. Ted Jensen, of course, went on to mention that when he's not busy plowing crops, he can usually be found boogie boarding down on the beach, and hopes someday to be a world-class surfer."

"That was the day you found out Ann Roth is his girlfriend, and she thought you might be a threat of some kind," grinned Carolyn.

"You never know." Ray winked at Susan.

Susan then rewarded him with one of her naughty laughs.

"So, tell me about yourselves?" Ray was still looking at Susan.

Susan then proceeded to tell him of her long time career teaching mostly third and fourth graders at an elementary school up in Ocean Bay, from which she was now retired.

"What made you decide to come here?" asked Ray.

After a moment of silence, Susan finally answered. "Carolyn and I both want to find out what happened to our friends all those years ago. This just seemed like the right opportunity."

"Indeed," commented Carolyn.

"Not only that," continued Susan, "my ex ran off with some floozy he met at an AA meeting! Can you believe it?"

"Ouch!" responded Ray.

"And, my divorce won't be final for two more months, so I just needed to get away," added Susan.

"Wow!" Ray was surprised. "May I say, your ex is a fool."

"Thanks," blushed Susan.

Even Carolyn could not help but notice the undeniable attraction between Susan and Ray, despite the fact that there was fourteen years' difference in their ages. Peculiar, since Ray had been such a mystery to both of them for so long.

"I'd like to know something," interjected Carolyn.

Pulling his gaze away from Susan, Ray turned to Carolyn and waited for her question.

"What in the world was in all those boxes you and Miss Dixon were unloading from your ratty old pickup truck that night back in 1972?" Carolyn wanted to know.

"That's right!" realized Susan, suddenly curious. "And the two of you were looking around to make sure no one was watching you!"

"While you were fumbling around with that lantern," added Carolyn. "We were watching you from our room up on the second floor that night, and have always wondered about it."

Ray suddenly began to laugh so hard he nearly choked on his spaghetti. When he finally stopped coughing, Ray shook his head. "You 'demon girls' never cease to amaze me!"

"Well?" pressed Carolyn.

"Strawberries," revealed Ray. "Lots and lots of 'em."

"Stolen?" Susan became serious.

"Is that what you girls have thought of me all these years? That I'm nothing more than an ex-convict and now I'm a strawberry thief, too?" Ray erupted into new laughter and stomped the heel of his right snakeskin boot on the floor while he slapped his knees with glee. "Seriously?"

Susan and Carolyn patiently waited for Ray to continue, but were obviously embarrassed.

"Okay. I can see I need to clear a few things up. After I finished my last tour of duty, I came here," recounted Ray. "I was stationed in Okinawa in 1968 but then sent to Vietnam when the war broke out in 1969 where I did recon work in the jungle territory near Laos."

"I'm so sorry!" apologized Carolyn.

"That's all right," assured Ray. "It was in the spring of 1971 when I was honorably discharged, and finally got to come home. And of course, you already know about my step dad Mark Killingham and his sister, Cathy Dixon."

Ray took another bite of food before continuing. "When I worked in produce – which I still do, by the way – I noticed that a lot of the fruits and vegetables were going to waste."

"That's true," confirmed Carolyn. "When I worked in squash, the foreman took over half the squash in my bucket and just threw it down on the ground at the end of that row. He said it was no good because it was either a half inch too big or too small for the crates they would pack them in for market. What a waste that was!"

"Exactly," nodded Ray. "And, when Cat learned what was going on, she'd have me go and glean the throwbacks so they wouldn't just sit there and rot. Most of the things we were able to save went to a local food bank where homeless or starving families could benefit from them. The strawberries, as I recall, became some of the best jam I ever ate. There's nothing like fresh strawberry jam over vanilla ice cream."

"Strawberries?" chuckled Susan, shaking her head.

"They have a cannery on campus now, too," revealed Ray. "It was Cat's idea. All the food that was considered irregular in size or shape is now taken to the cannery and put up by the students who work there. Pretty hard work, too!"

"I'd rather work in a lumber mill," snorted Susan.

"So, back to the strawberry loading," persisted Carolyn. "Why were you and Miss Dixon glancing around like that?

"Well, my aunt just happened to have a cat she wasn't supposed to have," confessed Ray. "The school had a strict no pet policy for the Deans and students alike. They still do, actually. So, she technically was breaking the rules by having one."

"She was looking for her cat?" realized Carolyn, feeling foolish for imagining that Dean Dixon and her nephew Ray had been involved in a fencing operation for stolen merchandise.

"Well, you know how cats are." Ray shook his head. "My aunt was beside herself, trying to find the stupid thing before someone saw it or could find out that she had one. It must have slipped out when we were carrying in all those boxes of strawberries."

Susan began to smile.

"Did she ever find it?" Carolyn sincerely wanted to know.

"Oh yeah, she did," grinned Ray. "Now, it's your turn. Tell me about yourself, Ms. Carolyn."

"I used to call her Carolina la Gata because she loves cats so much," chuckled Susan.

"Another cat lover?" Ray raised an eyebrow, sighed deeply, and took a big bite of salad, chasing it down with a long drink of water.

"Well," began Carolyn, "I've been married for 33 years now, and have worked for 26 of them as a Legal Secretary."

"Impressive," commented Ray.

"And she loves cats!" interjected Susan. "Tell him how many you have. Twenty, was it?"

"No, of course not!" responded Carolyn. "I've only got two of them living in my house."

"And in your yard?" grinned Susan.

"Maybe half a dozen or so," admitted Carolyn. "But, they're all neutered, current on their shots, and very well taken care of."

"She's got igloos for them all over her yard," described Susan.

"I only have five igloos," clarified Carolyn. "And I change out and wash the fleece blankets inside them every single week."

"How often do you feed them?" asked Ray. "Who's feeding them now while you're here?"

"My wonderful husband is taking care of them in my absence," replied Carolyn. "And they are fed twice each day."

"Definitely a keeper!" nodded Susan. "Her husband."

"I figured as much," grinned Ray, amazed at how unchanged Susan and Carolyn really were from the way he remembered his aunt describing them.

"Actually," mentioned Carolyn as she pulled out her cellphone, "I have a photo of the covered feeding station my hubby built for them. It protects their food from the weather, rain or shine."

Ray and Susan looked on with interest as Carolyn scrolled through picture after picture of the various cats in her feral cat colony until finally reaching the photo of the covered feeding station.

"Those are some lucky cats," commented Ray. "The colony we have over at the dairy is lucky to get a bag sliced open and thrown onto a plywood-covered pallet each morning."

"You have a feral cat colony over at the dairy?" Carolyn was immediately interested.

"It's been there for years," answered Ray. "You might even remember some of their ancestors from back in 1972."

"Oh, my goodness!" realized Carolyn. "I do remember those cats. There was a Siamese one that was especially friendly."

"Indeed there was," confirmed Ray.

"Has anybody ever tried to capture any of them to get them neutered?" quizzed Carolyn.

"Not that I know of," responded Ray.

"How many are there?" pressed Carolyn, suddenly realizing that her stay here might involve more than she had bargained for.

"Ann Roth would know," assumed Ray. "She's always over there fooling around with those animals. Trouble is, if they get 'em all fixed, what happens when there's no more cats around and the rat population gets out of control?"

"Let me show you something," suggested Carolyn as she proceeded to pull up a website on her phone. "Here it is. The website for the Feral Phoenix Foundation where I volunteered for over twenty years. Listen to this. It says that female cats can reproduce up to three times a year, and their kittens, if they survive, will become feral without early contact with people. That would be during the critical human handling period, which is the first eight weeks of life. And, cats can become pregnant as early as five months of age. In fact, a breeding pair of cats can produce around 15 kittens per year, assuming they have only two litters. That means that they can exponentially produce as many as 420,000 offspring over a seven-year period of time!"

"Oh my God!" exclaimed Susan. "That can't be right."

"Oh, I promise you, it is," assured Carolyn. "But, cats tend to congregate around a food source."

"There's always food at the dairy," realized Ray.

"Precisely!" exclaimed Carolyn. "So, when cats are trapped and removed from an area, new cats will move in to take advantage of the food source. So I don't think you have anything to worry about."

"Sounds like your rat population will always be in peril," grinned Susan.

"Trap-Neuter-Return, known as TNR, is practiced by various animal rescue groups all over the country," elaborated Carolyn. "It's where the caregivers who are feeding feral cats trap them in humane traps and then bring them to a spay/neuter clinic to get them fixed. Most of the cats are returned to the caregivers who then release them back into the colonies they came from, but adoptable cats and kittens are placed into kind and loving homes whenever possible."

"I don't think I've ever seen anyone so passionate about cats since my aunt was alive," commented Ray as he got up to take his empty plate to the sink but then frowned as he glanced outside.

Susan quickly got up and came over to see what he was looking at. "Hey, someone's out there," whispered Susan as she quickly untied and lowered the makeshift sheet on the kitchen window.

"And it's getting dark," realized Ray.

"Oh no, the door knob!" remembered Carolyn. "We were going to see if you could install it for us."

"That's right! We bought a new door knob kit when we were in town today because Carolyn saw somebody out there in the fog last night," explained Susan. "I must admit I wasn't entirely convinced, but there's definitely someone out there now!"

"No worries, I've got a tool kit in the truck. I'll be right back. It shouldn't take more than five minutes to install," promised Ray.

Carolyn quickly cleared the table and began to wash the dishes while Susan went outside to sit on the front porch and watch as Ray installed the locking door knob.

"Wow!" exclaimed Susan when she saw Ray return from his pickup truck with a huge, bright red metal tool box that he plopped down onto the front porch with a thud. "That thing almost needs wheels!"

"I like to be prepared." Ray smiled mysteriously. His comment was meant to be taken any way Susan cared to interpret it.

"Seriously, though," quizzed Susan, "what if they come back?

Ray momentarily paused and stepped up onto the top of his tool box with just his right foot, and only long enough to lean forward and pull up that pant leg so Susan could see the handle of a 45 revolver protruding from the matching snakeskin boot holster Ray had fastened to his snakeskin boot. "Like I said."

"The man's prepared," agreed Carolyn as she joined them in time to notice Ray's weapon.

"You can count on it." With a nod of assurance, Ray quickly pulled his pant leg back down over his loaded revolver and snakeskin boot holster before removing his foot from the tool box lid so he could open it.

"My husband's like that, too," pondered Carolyn. "Lots of tools and guns. But personally, I have no use for guns. They're just too dangerous."

"Not in the hands of a highly trained expert," Susan smiled at Ray flirtatiously. "We're actually very lucky he's here."

"Indeed we are," agreed Carolyn as she sat down beside Susan.

"Even with the door lock, are you sure you ladies will be safe here?" worried Ray. "Perhaps I should keep watch. Just for tonight."

"Where would you sleep? In your truck?" Carolyn was being slightly sarcastic.

"Why not?" Ray shrugged his shoulders. "I've slept in worse."

"I'll bet you have," realized Susan, still taking in the fact that Ray had been in Vietnam. "Is that why you never married?"

Ray silently finished assembling and installing the new door knob. After testing to be sure they both worked, Ray handed the new keys to Susan and Carolyn before he sat down to answer Susan's question. Susan was flushed with embarrassment, convinced she had blown it by asking something too personal so soon.

"We could use some Irish coffee about now," sighed Ray.

"Too bad we don't have any," apologized Susan. Then turning to Carolyn she asked, "Do we have any coffee at all?"

"Never drink the stuff," replied Carolyn.

"That's okay," Ray studied Susan for a moment. "Let me see. Why did I never marry? That's a good question. So, I'll do my best to try and give you a good answer."

"Forty, or rather, forty-four years ago, Ms. Eggersol lived right here in this very house. And, as you already know, Virginia Eggersol was the English Literature instructor at Oceanview Academy back in 1972." Ray's expression took on a faraway look as he thought of her.

"Ginny. That's what I used to call her," added Ray as his eyes began to slightly water. "She never did marry, either."

"I take it you knew her quite well?" deduced Carolyn.

"Oh, yes, I knew Ginny quite well," confirmed Ray.

"I knew her too," mentioned Carolyn. "Sometimes I'd come here to her house for special tutoring after class. Ms. Eggersol was actually one of the few teachers who really cared about her students, and wanted to see them succeed in life."

"You used to be able to see the ocean from here," reminisced Ray. "Now, all views of it are blocked by all those cypress, eucalyptus and other trees over there along the cliffs."

"How come you didn't marry her, then?" pressed Susan. It was obvious to her what Ray was leading up to.

"We were engaged, all right," admitted Ray. "For five years."

"What happened?" urged Carolyn, also anxious to find out.

"It was foggy that night," recalled Ray. "Ginny had gone out to the looney bin to visit that Roth kid."

"Jon Roth?" Susan was surprised.

"Birdboy," muttered Carolyn as she nodded her head.

"Ginny was also a counselor of sorts," added Ray. "She minored in abnormal psychology before she went into English Literature. Anyway, for whatever reason, Ginny took quite an interest in the Roth boy. She was actually starting to get through to him. Times being what they were, and even though she wasn't family, the people over there at the looney bin would let her talk to him."

"And?" prompted Susan anxiously.

"Ms. Eggersol was quite close with Principal Roth and his wife," Carolyn suddenly recalled. "Maybe she had their permission. I just never realized at the time that Birdboy was their son."

"Don't ever call him that," cautioned Ray.

"Yeah, we found that out the hard way when we were at the cafeteria this morning," recounted Carolyn.

"You should have seen him," interjected Susan. "One moment he was friendly and glad to see us again after all these years, and the next moment he became enraged when Carolyn mentioned how everyone used to call him Birdboy."

Ray shook his head with amazement.

"The way Jon Roth acted after that and the evil look he had in his eyes sure made me uncomfortable!" assured Carolyn.

"Jon even slammed his fist on the table and told Carolyn not to EVER call him that again!" described Susan. "Everyone in the cafeteria stopped to see what would happen next, but then Ann came over and suddenly everything was just fine again. It was all rather odd."

152

"So, why was Birdboy, or rather, Jon Roth institutionalized?" questioned Carolyn as she turned to Ray Dixon for an explanation. "And just what did happen to Ms. Eggersol? Did he have anything to do with it?"

"Oh, nothing like that," assured Ray. "It was after Ginny left the looney bin that night and was on her way home. The fog was really thick, too, and you know how narrow and windy that road is ...."

Ray broke off in mid-sentence and swallowed hard before continuing. "She was hit by a drunk driver. Both vehicles went over the edge, and both drivers were killed when their cars landed on the jagged boulders below. That was in 1976."

Susan got up and came over to sit beside Ray, tenderly putting one arm around him as she wiped an unbidden tear from his cheek with the other. "I'm so sorry!"

"It's not your fault." Ray tried to force a smile of assurance.

"What about her family?" Carolyn wanted to know.

"Ginny's parents were killed in a plane crash several years before that," recalled Ray. "The plane was found a few days later and many of the bodies were eventually recovered and identified."

"But not her parents?" deduced Susan.

"No, not them," confirmed Ray.

"That would explain why Ms. Eggersol's furniture is still here," guessed Carolyn. "There must not have been anyone to claim it at the time. I did think some of the furniture looked familiar."

"The house actually sat vacant for two years," reflected Ray. "Then out of the blue, Edith Roth unexpectedly stopped by the trailer park for an ice cream cone one afternoon and gave me a small box with all of Ginny's personal papers inside. It's still back at my place."

"Did you ever go through it?" asked Carolyn. "To see if there was anything in there about Jon Roth?"

"Perhaps I should go through that box again," realized Ray. "Tomorrow when your class is finished, Susan, why don't you two come over? I owe you a meal, anyway."

"You don't have to do that," objected Susan.

"I insist," urged Ray as he smiled flirtatiously at Susan.

"Can we bring anything?" inquired Carolyn, also anxious to find out if there were any clues they needed to find inside the box.

"Just yourselves," replied Ray.

"Ms. Neilson actually got a pretty good deal, then," commented Carolyn. "A furnished place to stay, with everything already here."

"And here we are, just three houses away from Jon Roth and his family," sighed Susan.

"And it was YOU who accepted his invitation for us to come to his house for a barbecue luncheon on Sunday!" Carolyn was certainly not looking forward to it. "And just how did he already know we were staying here at Ms. Neilson's house, anyway?"

"Especially when we hadn't even mentioned it to him yet?" comprehended Susan.

"Jon Roth did do a good job of acting surprised when he saw us, though," recalled Carolyn.

"Maybe Ann told her father about us being here," speculated Susan. "She must have! There's no other way he could have known."

"You're not actually going over there on Sunday, are you?" Ray was genuinely concerned for their safety.

"We kind of have to now." Susan grimaced. "Besides, if Ann Roth is in any kind of danger from him, we do need to learn more about it and make sure nothing happens to her."

"As I told you before," reminded Ray, "my aunt and I always suspected that Jon Roth had something to do with the disappearance of those girls, but just couldn't prove anything. It's just too risky for the two of you to go over there alone!"

"Susan's right, though, we do have to go over there," pointed out Carolyn. "Two bodies and all their stuff wouldn't just disappear into thin air, ocean or not. Someone would have found those boogie boards, eventually. And no self-respecting shark would be caught dead eating a boogie board!" Carolyn's feeble attempt at humor to lighten the mood went over like a lead balloon.

"Most sharks would never bother a human, either," interjected Ray.

"Maybe a baby seal, though," recalled Susan. "Remember that day we were at the boardwalk with your folks?"

"Oh, that was horrible!" Carolyn shuddered at the memory.

"They should have at least done something to try and help the poor little thing," opined Susan.

"That stupid lifeguard! He actually used someone's boogie board to club an injured baby seal to death, right in front of everyone!" Carolyn was still angered by the very memory of it.

"Still, that shark really did do quite a number on the baby seal," remembered Susan. "There was blood everywhere."

"There probably was nothing else they could have done for it," assumed Ray. He would probably have done the same thing.

"You have no idea who you're talking to here," Susan informed Ray as she nodded toward Carolyn. "Carolyn also volunteers at some wildlife center."

Ray smiled as he rolled his eyes and shook his head. Carolyn reminded him so much of his aunt!

"It's true, I do that, too." Carolyn shrugged her shoulders. "The Central Valley Wildlife Center is a place where people can bring sick, injured or orphaned wildlife for emergency treatment. Most survivors are eventually released back into the wild. The unreleasable ones with permanent disabilities can become special ambassadors who travel with their handlers to wildlife seminars where they help educate the public about their responsibility toward these animals and their environment."

"Oh, my God!" laughed Susan. "A regular Dr. Doolittle."

"You and Ann should get along quite well," grinned Ray. Perhaps this was just the shoo-in Susan and Carolyn needed to befriend Jon Roth's daughter without him becoming suspicious of the real reason for them being there.

The following day after class, Susan had little trouble persuading Ann Roth to accompany them on a brief field trip to the Ocean Bluff Mental Institution. As it turned out, Ann was as anxious as Susan and Carolyn were to learn more about Jon Roth.

Ann Roth's straight dark hair gleamed in the afternoon sunlight. Ann was seated in the back seat of Susan and Carolyn's rental car, deep in thought. Susan drove slowly and carefully toward the Ocean Bluff Mental Institution while Carolyn and Ann admired the breathtaking scenery in silence. The tragic story of Virginia Eggersol's demise along this very road after being hit by a drunk driver had given Susan a whole new respect for the dangerous, windy road they were traveling. In spite of everything, it was an enjoyable drive. The sprawling ocean view below them was frequently framed by eucalyptus and aging cypress trees growing along the windswept cliffs as they passed. Gently interspersed between some of them was a hearty mat of creeping succulent ice plants with hot pink blooms. Occasional junipers and creeping cypress shrubs also grew there at impossible angles, caused by constant exposure to excessive wind.

Susan was somewhat concerned what Ray might think if they showed up late for their dinner date with him, but this was necessary. Besides, it was only four o'clock so they should have plenty of time.

Susan glanced in the rearview mirror and could not help but notice again how much Ann looked like her father and grandfather. It was uncanny! Ann's pale skin almost made her seem unhealthy, yet at the same time Ann possessed an inner glow of innocence. Ann's long bony fingers were neatly folded on her lap.

"Ann? Are you all right?" asked Susan.

Ann carefully adjusted the glasses on her long hooked nose and gingerly pushed an unwanted strand of her straight dark hair away from them before replying. "Yeah, I'm fine."

"Are you sure your parents won't mind you coming with us?" questioned Carolyn, truly concerned by the fact that neither of them had personally bothered to ask them.

"I'm not due back home for another two hours," assured Ann. "This is when I normally go out to the dairy to feed the cats, anyway."

"You said Ted is feeding them for you today?" asked Carolyn.

"He certainly is," smiled Ann.

"You don't have to do this," reminded Susan as she rounded the next hairpin turn and slowly drove through the huge wrought iron gates that led onto the grounds of Ocean Bluff Mental Institution.

"I know," assured Ann. "But, I have more of a right than anyone to know why my father was really here, and am just as anxious as you are to find out what happened to your friends."

Carolyn glanced at the large two-story brick building with its white spiraled steeples and whimsical clock tower. Despite its true purpose, one could not help but be awed by the inspirational grounds surrounding Ocean Bluff Mental Institution.

"It really is beautiful here," admired Ann, not having been here previously. "It's just like a huge park with all the trees, flowers and pathways everywhere! And look at all those white benches along the walkways where you can just sit and enjoy the view as you listen to the sounds of the ocean below!"

Susan pulled the white Dodge Dart around the circular entrance drive before coming to a halt in front of its main entrance.

"Here we are," indicated Susan as she opened the car door, climbed out, and then opened Ann's door for her.

"Thanks," nodded Ann as she got out and followed Susan and Carolyn toward the intimidating building.

Ann then paused on the front steps long enough to read the large metal plaque centered over its ornate entry doors that read: "When the waves reach to our heads we begin to listen to anything; no advice is too contemptible for us; no person too insignificant for us to be willing to listen." by Johann Peter Lange - 1872.

"That's quite a saying," appreciated Ann as she watched Carolyn lift the huge brass lion-head door knocker and let it fall against the huge brass plate beneath it.

Suddenly, an elderly woman with white hair, thick horn-rimmed glasses, and a white knee-length nurse's uniform answered the door. It was the same woman who had answered the door upon their last visit. "Oh, it's you again. And who's this?"

"I'm Ann Roth," informed Ann. "I'm here to find out what you might know about my father. His name is Jon Roth."

"Good heavens!" whispered the woman with surprise. Her intense blue eyes carefully scrutinized Ann Roth with curiosity and amazement. "Don't just stand there! Come in."

The woman quickly grabbed Ann by the right hand and began leading her to the small sitting room where Susan and Carolyn had previously been made to wait on the antique Queen Anne style couch for their fruitless interview with Nurse Redden.

"You really shouldn't be here!" cautioned the older woman, nervously glancing around to be sure they were alone. "If Nurse Redden finds you here ...."

"Helen, go to your room," instructed Nurse Redden from the doorway to the sitting room. None of them had heard her coming.

"Helen's a patient here?" questioned Susan with surprise.

"Indeed she is," confirmed Nurse Redden without smiling as she folded her arms and waited for Helen to leave.

"But I thought ...," began Susan.

"I know what you thought," interrupted Nurse Redden. "Helen likes people to think she works here. No harm in letting her think so, I suppose. So, why have you come back?"

"You told us that only blood relatives are entitled to see your files," reminded Carolyn, refusing to be intimidated by the rude woman. "This is Jon Roth's daughter, Ann."

"That's right! And I'm here to see my father's file," demanded Ann, clearly irritated by the way Nurse Redden was treating them.

"Can't help you," snapped Nurse Redden.

"I AM his daughter, and I can prove it!" retorted Ann as she pulled out a copy of her birth certificate, unfolded it, and held it open for Nurse Redden to see.

Without unfolding her arms and only casually glancing at the paper, Nurse Redden informed them with finality, "No minors will be permitted to review the records without written consent from a blood relative in their immediate family who is over eighteen years of age, absent an order from the court, that is."

Susan, Carolyn and Ann were all stunned and stared at Nurse Redden with amazement and disbelief.

"As I told you before, perhaps you should ask Jon Roth anything you want to know about him." Nurse Redden tilted her head slightly back out of habit to see them more clearly through her bifocals as she placed her hands on her hips and shook her head.

"Helen's been here for a long time, hasn't she?" quizzed Carolyn, suddenly changing the subject. "Perhaps we could chat with her?"

"I don't think so," sneered Nurse Redden triumphantly. Clearly, this particular trip had been a waste of their time.

During their return trip to Oceanview Academy, Susan finally spoke as she glanced in the rearview mirror at Ann. "Have you thought of asking your mother if she knows anything?"

"I've thought about it," replied Ann. "But, I'm really not sure if she does know about it, so I would hate to bring it up, just in case."

"You mean you actually don't know whether or not your mother knows her husband was in a mental institution?" clarified Carolyn.

"That's about the size of it," confirmed Ann.

"How did you find out?" pressed Carolyn, curious to know.

"From a file I came across in the administration office," revealed Ann nervously. "Actually, it's a confidential file and I wasn't even supposed to look inside."

158

"So you waited until no one was around to have a look?" assumed Susan with a knowing smile.

"Oh, please!" begged Ann. "You can't tell anyone! Not only would I lose my job, but there's no telling what my father would do."

"If he found out you looked at a forbidden file, or if he found out it was about him?" grilled Carolyn.

"Either one." Ann swallowed uncomfortably.

"Just what did the office file have to say about him?" continued Carolyn, hoping to learn what they could.

"All it really says is that he was committed to the Ocean Bluff Mental Institution in the spring of 1973, immediately following a tragic incident at the beach," recalled Ann.

"That's it?" frowned Susan.

"I'm afraid so," replied Ann. "It doesn't even say why! But, that made me curious to find out whether it was around the same time that Steve Fredrickson died from that shark attack, or when Veronica Jensen and Joyce Troglite disappeared."

"Steve Fredrickson died on March 23, 1973," reminded Susan.

"Yes, indeed," muttered Carolyn sadly.

"That's what I found out," replied Ann. "Unfortunately, the records don't give an exact date on when Jon Roth was actually committed. Try as I might, I just couldn't find anything else about when or why. All it indicated was that it was in the spring of 1973."

"There's got to be something else," opined Carolyn.

"I even looked in the sealed portion of the record," admitted Ann. "Wait a minute! It did say he was released in March of 1983 after a ten-year commitment!"

"If that's true, then March of 1973 would have had to be when they put him away," deduced Carolyn.

"We just need to find out the exact day then," mused Ann.

"And why they put him there, too," reminded Susan. "I didn't want to say anything before, but what if you or your mother are in danger of some kind?"

"That's a very good question," considered Ann. "What I don't understand is how the school could have hired him to be the theology instructor, if he really is dangerous. Surely there must be someone who knows what it was he actually did."

"Forty-three years is a long time," reminded Carolyn. "Some of the people that were here back then aren't even alive anymore."

"Like Dean Dixon, for example," mentioned Susan as she drove through the main entrance gate to Oceanview Academy. "Perhaps you should duck down. Just in case your father is out and about."

"Good idea," agreed Ann as she unbuckled her seatbelt and quickly laid down on the seat.

"How 'bout this," proposed Susan, "between now and Sunday when we come over for the barbecue, maybe you could try and look around at home to see if you can find anything else?"

"Like paperwork," suggested Carolyn.

"Yes, like paperwork or hidden files that your parents might have there at home," described Susan.

"There is a bomb shelter in the back," mentioned Ann. "That's the only place I haven't looked already."

"A bomb shelter!" exclaimed Susan. "I thought they quit making those back in the 60's."

"They did," replied Ann. "My grandpa, the one you knew as Principal Roth, had it built back in 1963. At least that's what they tell me. It supposedly has a back entrance that connects to one of those underground bunker tunnels that are all over the campus."

"Have you ever seen which one it leads to?" questioned Susan, suddenly quite interested.

"No, I haven't," responded Ann. "That's my dad's private man cave where he goes to be alone, grade papers, that kind of thing. It's strictly off limits, even to my mother or me, without an invitation."

"I don't think she should even try going down there alone," advised Carolyn. "Perhaps Sunday one of us could keep her parents occupied while the other one goes down there with her?"

"A diversion tactic," recognized Ann. "Not a bad idea!"

"We're here," advised Susan as she pulled to a stop in front of Ms. Neilson's house. "I think you should just get out here, instead of me trying to drop you off over at your house."

"I agree!" approved Ann as she stealthily got out of the white Dodge Dart and glanced around to be sure no one was watching.

"It's already five o'clock!" noticed Susan as she watched Ann scurry off in the direction of her parents' home. "We'd better get over to Ray's before he thinks we stood him up!"

"Weren't you going to change into your jeans first?" asked Carolyn, hoping to do so herself.

160

"There's not time," decided Susan.

"Let's at least grab our sweaters," suggested Carolyn. "Even in late spring, it still gets cold, damp and foggy around here at night."

"At least this house doesn't have one of those horrible steam heaters! Remember how we used to hear them clanking at night?" chuckled Susan as she unlocked the door to Ms. Neilson's house and went inside to grab her sweater.

"And to think I almost knocked 'twice on the pipes'!" smirked Carolyn as she dashed in after Susan.

"What?" Susan did not get it at first.

"You know, the night I 'knocked three times on the ceiling'?" reminded Carolyn with an irrepressible grin as she sung the words in the phrase to the tune it was from. "When we were crawling under the girls' dorm that night?"

Susan and Carolyn immediately broke into hysterical laughter as they changed into more comfortable shoes, used the restroom and grabbed their sweaters.

"Oh, I was going to try and stop by the store for the ingredients to make Irish coffee, so we could take it all with us!" mentioned Susan, realizing she'd forgotten completely about it until this very moment.

"Kinda late now," smiled Carolyn as she continued to reflect upon the incident forty-four years ago when the girls' dormitory had been put on demon alert in 1972.

"We'd better get going then," replied Susan as they quickly made their departure.

It was only five thirty in the afternoon and sunset not expected for two more hours. Still, deep shadows danced across the overgrown gravel road that led down to Silver Creek Trailer Park, mostly due to the dense coastal forest surrounding it. Susan scowled as she slowed enough to avoid the many deep ruts on each successive switchback of the steep narrow road. Upon finally reaching the sandy beachfront below where the rundown trailer park store awaited them, Susan and Carolyn both breathed a sigh of relief. "Ray really needs to do something about that road!" opined Susan.

"Why? He's already got a four-wheel drive pickup truck," grinned Carolyn.

"You're the one driving us out of here tonight!" advised Susan. She could not even fathom trying to negotiate such a road in the dark.

The worn out hinge on the old store's rickety wooden sign was squeaking almost as loudly as the sign itself was banging against the weathered post beside it. In fact, the entire structure was in desperate need of a new paintjob. Susan slowed to a stop in front of the Silver Creek Trailer Park Store and then shut off the engine of the new rental car. Neither Ray nor his pickup truck were anywhere in sight.

"Maybe he gave up on us," teased Carolyn. "He did say to come over after your class was over, and that was at three."

"He'll be back," assured Susan.

"Well, at least we brought our sweaters," remarked Carolyn as a blustery blast of wind blew unwanted sand onto the hood of the white Dodge Dart. "Maybe we should just wait in here."

"Look!" noticed Susan. "There's a note on the door!"

"All right," agreed Carolyn after a pleading look from Susan. "I'll go see what it says."

Susan waited anxiously as Carolyn retrieved the note and began to study it. Finally, unable to stand it any longer, Susan got out of the car and came over to where Carolyn was. "Well? What does it say?"

"He'll be up at the house, waiting for us," responded Carolyn.

"Let me see that," commanded Susan as she grabbed the note from Carolyn. "Up at the house?"

"He clearly isn't at the abandoned trailer over there on the end," laughed Carolyn. "Or here in the store, either. The light's not even on."

"What house?" Susan was puzzled and began to study their surroundings more carefully.

"Over there," indicated Carolyn. "It looks like an ivy-covered driveway gate, at the edge of the forest."

Susan and Carolyn gingerly walked over to the gate, which proved indeed to be a swinging wrought iron driveway gate covered with a thick layer of unkempt ivy.

"How does it open?" wondered Susan aloud.

"Just pull the latch up and out," came Ray's voice over an intercom box nestled from view near the gate. It was so well hidden within a thicket of foliage growing around it that the intercom box was invisible to anyone not knowing it was there. This particular intercom

162

box just happened to be mounted inside a slightly larger, weather-proof containment case attached to the trunk of the same tree on which the swinging gate's main hinges were attached. In fact, it was the same type of intercom system used by Dean Dixon in the girls' dormitory over at Oceanview Academy back in 1972 where announcements could be made and two-way communication possible only when the person attending the main box at the other end would activate it.

Susan looked on with interest as Carolyn finally managed to locate and undo the tricky latch. Carolyn then carefully grabbed the long swinging driveway gate and pushed it the rest of the way open. The uphill road that loomed beyond it was just as challenging as the one on which they had already driven down to get where they were.

"You've got to be kidding!" exclaimed Carolyn.

"You're driving!" informed Susan as they headed back to the white Dodge Dart.

"You can do it," came the sound of Ray's voice behind them from the hidden intercom. He sounded amused.

"That's an awfully steep road," worried Carolyn.

"Good thing we have all-wheel drive, then!" laughed Susan.

"We do?" Carolyn was surprised.

"Of course we do," assured Susan with a mischievous grin. "The new 2016 Dodge Dart comes with it. At least that's what the guy at the rental place told me."

"Well, let's just hope he's right," replied Carolyn as she got back into the car in and started it up.

Although the road turned out to be much easier to negotiate than either of them anticipated, the all-wheel drive certainly did come in handy. Next to the road was a treacherous drop-off where the rocky shoreline could be seen below. The only thing standing between the road and the abrupt downward slope on its edge was a three-foot high, black wrought iron fence. The continuous metal chain threaded through large eyelet holes at the top of each post dangled loosely between each one. "We're definitely leaving here before dark!" advised Carolyn as they made the trek.

Susan and Carolyn were both surprised when the road suddenly leveled out and led directly up to an unusually shaped white structure with bright red trim. The building itself was octagonal in shape and approximately thirty feet in diameter. A long pointed tower projected upward at least sixty feet from its center that was only about fifteen feet in diameter at the very top, but entirely round. Randomly placed windows could be seen spiraling their way up its exterior, obviously to provide natural lighting to as many interior locations as possible. An octagonal shaped lookout tower at the very top had large picture windows on all sides, except for a single arched exit door that led to an exterior catwalk and encircled the entire upper tower at that level. The catwalk was about three feet wide, could only be accessed through the arched exit door, and was protected by a sturdy wrought iron railing that had been painted entirely white. The tower's conical shaped roof came to a perfect point on top and was covered entirely with bright red ceramic tiles. At ground level was a covered entryway, also covered with bright red ceramic tiles, beneath which Ray Dixon was standing and smiling at them. The cement porch and steps leading up to it were painted bright red, to match the ceramic tiles, and a large brass bell mounted beside the front door was graced with a long brass chain with which to ring it.

"It's a lighthouse!" exclaimed Susan as they approached and came to a stop in front of it.

"Isn't this one of the buildings we saw from the beach when we were down there with Lenny and Pete that night?" questioned Carolyn.

"Yeah, I believe it is," realized Susan. "And we thought they were just vacation homes."

"You can't really tell it's a lighthouse from the beach, though," reminded Carolyn. "The forest blocks it from view on that side."

"It was a lighthouse once," informed Ray as he opened the car door on Susan's side. The faded tattoos of naked women on his well-tanned but muscular arms did not look quite so leathery in the soft evening light. Susan rewarded him with one of her promising smiles and took his hand as she got out of the car.

Susan was wearing the elegant pair of sterling silver earring posts with dolphins on them that her brother Damien had given her when he was still alive. The loose fitting baby blue blouse she wore had elbow length sleeves sporting button looped cuffs. Only visible when she leaned forward, the cleavage on her excellent shape did not go unnoticed by Ray. Susan blushed slightly when she noticed him appreciating her.

"Welcome to my humble abode, ladies," greeted Ray as he flirted shamelessly with Susan.

164

"You actually live here?" asked Carolyn.

"Yes, I do," smiled Ray as he hurried over to assist Carolyn as she got out of the car, as well. "It was originally built in 1872 by the first Killinghams to come here from Ireland."

"That would have been fifteen years before the Ocean Bluff Mental Institution was built in 1887," calculated Carolyn.

"That sounds right," agreed Ray as he led them up the steps and held open the front door for them.

"This place is incredible!" Susan was truly impressed.

"You live here alone?" questioned Carolyn as she stopped to examine a large brass name plate mounted by the entrance bell and read it aloud. "Killingham."

"This is where I grew up," revealed Ray proudly, still waiting for them to come inside.

"What are those freestanding structures over there?" indicated Carolyn with a nod of her head at two smaller buildings nearby. Both were white like the lighthouse with bright red tiled roofs and matching red trim, but were scarcely bigger than walk-in tool sheds and were located several yards away from the main structure.

"Well, let's see. The first building has a commercial grade heat pump with stand-by generator inside," indicated Ray as he folded his arms. "It's actually a turbine generator unit designed to help convert kinetic energy into electricity, and has an exhaust compression system that deals mostly with converting the exhaust into electric power."

"Very ingenious," nodded Carolyn, well aware that Ray was drastically simplifying the explanation for their benefit.

"The next building houses a diesel powered backup generator, but hasn't been actively used since 1961, other than to start it up periodically to make sure it still works," described Ray.

"Where do you keep all your maintenance and handyman tools, then?" questioned Susan with a big smile.

"Down at the Silver Creek Trailer Park behind the ice cream shop, where I keep all my old car parts and other miscellaneous stuff." Ray was quite hungry and wanted them to hurry up and come inside.

"Old car parts?" Susan furled her brow.

"My hobby, when I have time for it," grinned Ray. "That's what you gals caught me doing yesterday."

"Restoring old cars?" realized Susan. "Okay, yeah."

"How in the world do you ever manage to keep all this up by yourself?" grilled Carolyn.

"You ladies sure ask a lot of questions," laughed Ray as he nodded for them to come inside.

"Oh, that smells wonderful!" noticed Susan as the delicious aroma of roasting meat suddenly wafted throughout the open door.

"Was your step-dad's family here while the military base was next door?" interrogated Carolyn as they stepped inside.

"The military actually took over this place, too, during World War II, and used it as a defensive seaside outpost. It was often used to send light signals by Morse code to ally vessels at sea." Ray shook his head.

"They made your family leave?" Susan was indignant about it.

"Yes, ma'am," confirmed Ray. "That was when the Killingham family set up shop over there where the trailer park used to be. At first it was just supposed to be temporary, until the military people left. Then, it became a lucrative business venture, especially with the ice cream shop. People love ice cream! So, they decided to branch out and set up the second ice cream shop in town."

"But the Killingham family still moved back over here to live after the military people left?" asked Susan.

"They did indeed," chuckled Ray as he started for the spiral staircase that led upstairs.

"Wait! What's down here?" persisted Carolyn as she headed the other direction and peeked through an interior archway that led into the octagonal shaped first-story level of the building.

"All right, quick walk-through," agreed Ray. "Then we need to get upstairs after that. I'm starving! Follow me."

Carolyn and Susan tailed Ray with interest as he escorted them through the large commercial kitchen, laundry room, walk-in pantry and shower area on the ground floor level of his home. Susan and Carolyn exchanged a frown when they saw the large military style shower.

"That's just like the shower at the girls' dormitory!" snorted Carolyn with disgust.

"Why would they put one here?" demanded Susan.

"It was installed by the military when they were here," grinned Ray, well aware of how the girls felt about the huge shower stall in the girls' dormitory.

"You should have seen my mother's face when she first saw the shower room over there," laughed Carolyn. "It was my first day there, when my parents dropped me off. Then, when my mother went to use the restroom, she noticed the shower area and thought it must still be under construction."

"Remember that time I turned on the wrong handle and gave Veronica an icy cold blast of water while she was rinsing off her hair?" recalled Susan.

"It is hard to tell which handle activates which of the multiple shower heads pointing out in every direction from a single water dispensing pole," agreed Ray as he walked over to the wrought iron spiral staircase that wound its way up the central tower of his home. "Okay, can we eat now?"

Ray began ascending the spiral staircase but paused about a third of the way up and nodded toward a moon-shaped guest room that had been built just off the staircase at that level.

"The Daisy Room?" questioned Carolyn with a smile as she read the name plate hanging on the room's door.

"Look!" Susan was at the opposite room. "The Violet Room."

"There are two rooms on each of the four levels," informed Ray as he continued upward. You ladies are more than welcome to stay in any one of the eight guestrooms here, if you like."

"We really can't stay that long after dinner. I'll need to get back and prepare my history class lesson for tomorrow," mentioned Susan.

"You may want to reconsider," suggested Ray. "At least until we know what's lurking in the forest over by Ms. Neilson's house and that it's safe over there. But, that's entirely up to you. Just think about it, won't you?"

"Look at the beautiful hardwood floors and the Queen Anne furniture in those rooms!" appreciated Carolyn.

"The bed quilts and matching throw rugs were all made by hand," revealed Ray proudly. "And so were the wooden rocking chairs and seat cushions. All made by Killinghams."

"Where are the restrooms located?" asked Carolyn, seriously considering Ray's offer to stay there in order to avoid driving on the treacherous road after dark. Carolyn foresaw no way they would be able to eat fast enough to make a polite exit in time.

"There's one toilet at each level, each shared by the two guest rooms on that level," informed Ray. "Each room does have its own sink, but – as you know – the showers are all downstairs."

Susan had assumed until now that Ray must be quite wealthy.

"Just last year I had to sell off the big house over on the next parcel to the school," mentioned Ray as they reached another set of guest rooms, about half-way up the tower. "Gotta pay those taxes somehow."

"Who lives in the big house now?" frowned Susan, unable to conceal her disappointment. She was actually beginning to consider Ray as a future prospect, especially if he was successful financially.

"Nobody," replied Ray with a shrug of his shoulders. "The school just uses it as a rented guest house for parents when they come here to visit their kids. Comes in real handy on graduation weekend."

"Who used to live over there in the big house when they first built all this?" quizzed Susan.

"Servants, mostly," smiled Ray as he started up the final leg of the spiral staircase. "There was a butler, a maid, a nanny, a gardener, a cook, and even a tutor for the children. From what I was told, the original Killingham family named each of their eight daughters after various flowers, and each of these guest rooms is named after its original occupant."

"Each room has its own window," noticed Susan, beginning to wonder if Carolyn might not be right about taking Ray up on his offer to stay there for the night.

"That really does smell amazing!" complimented Carolyn as they finally reached the lookout tower room but then became speechless when she saw the fascinating room.

Susan also stood motionless, as if glued to the spot, and stared with amazement at the highly shellacked, natural wood siding that covered all eight of the octagonal room's four-foot high surrounding walls and the interior of its conical shaped ceiling above them. Resting above each four-foot wall was a large viewing window made of bullet-proof glass that extended upward to the room's fifteen-foot high ceiling above. "Wow! And just look at the table!"

"Right here is where the main lighthouse lamp used to be, when this was used as a lighthouse," informed Ray as he motioned toward the perfectly round wooden table in the center of the room. The table was surrounded entirely by a perfectly round wooden bench, both of them made from the same highly shellacked yellow pinewood that covered the inner ceiling and walls. The table was set for three with Liberty Blue Wedgwood China, highly polished vintage silverware on white cloth napkins, lead crystal drinking glasses etched with delicate ivy designs, and a huge Bohemian glass vase overlaid in cobalt blue, filled with fresh cut long-stemmed daisies.

"It was my step-dad's idea to have the table put here to fill up this space after the lighthouse was decommissioned by the military at the end of World War II," explained Ray.

"Why would they decommission it?" Susan was curious.

"Because you can't have a lighthouse without proper approval," sighed Ray. "A valid permit is required to be in compliance with federal regulations, and since they're the ones who voided the permit and decommissioned the lighthouse in the first place, it hardly seems likely they might change their minds."

"How sad," remarked Susan.

"Not only that, there's a complete set of installation, validation and operational protocols, as well as on-site inspection requirements that are necessary to be sure the system complies both electronically and procedurally with federal code. Besides, you'd need the right kind of lamp, and those were pretty hard to come by in those days. Still are, in fact," described Ray. "The special type of compound lens used by a lighthouse lamp is also extremely expensive. It's not like you can just go pick one up at the hardware store. They have to be custom made."

"What did happen to its lamp?" quizzed Carolyn.

"It was confiscated by the military and taken to another lighthouse somewhere else where they needed it. Guess they figured they'd invested too much time and money into the thing to leave it behind, and after all, possession is nine tenths of the law." Ray sadly shook his head.

"They actually stole the lighthouse lamp from your family when they left?" Susan could not believe what she was hearing.

"That's about the size of it," confirmed Ray. "That was also when my step-dad decided to install the Tiffany chandelier hanging above us. Every lighthouse should have a great light, don't you think?"

"It's beautiful!" Carolyn knew that some Tiffany lamps were worth anywhere from twenty to thirty thousand dollars, though most of the more common models usually sold for only a few hundred dollars.

Still, the Tiffany chandelier hanging above them did bear a striking resemblance to one Carolyn had recently seen on Antiques Roadshow that had sold for around forty-three thousand dollars!

Ray pulled back the bench so Susan and Carolyn could sit down before retrieving the large crockpot. The wooden countertop where the crockpot sat and the small red ceramic sink beside it extended across two of the room's eight walls. Ray carefully unplugged the large crockpot and put on a pair of cooking gloves before carrying it to the table. Ray then carefully placed the crockpot on a red tile trivet, removed its hot lid, and put a large serving fork inside. "I hope you like meat and potatoes."

Carolyn was intrigued by the ingenious use of space in the lookout tower room. Beneath the counter and sink, where the crockpot had been, was a series of wooden cupboards and some open shelves filled with dishes and various cooking tools in small wooden boxes with handles on them. On the next wall was a small red refrigerator. Beside it was a bright red, hard plastic trash receptacle with swinging lid, where the very edge of a trash can liner could barely be seen protruding.

Two more of the eight four-foot walls were filled entirely with shelves of rare and valuable looking old books. The catwalk access door faced due west on the ocean-side wall. The final two walls were located on either side of the catwalk access door wall, and had bench seats built right into them from the same highly shellacked knotty pinewood veneer that adorned the rest of the lookout tower room. Bright red seat cushions placed on the bench seats bore a striking resemblance to the chaise lounge cushions once manufactured at the lumber mill to accompany its popular patio furniture kits.

"Have you actually read all these books?" asked Carolyn as Ray joined them at the table.

"Most of them," responded Ray after he quickly blessed the food so they could eat.

"This is almost like eating at the Space Needle Restaurant up in Seattle," grinned Susan. "Except better!"

"Way better!" smiled Carolyn. "You can literally see everything for miles from up here."

The sound of ocean waves could be heard crashing against the craggy shoreline below, interrupted occasionally by cries from a lone seagull as it circled overhead in search of small prey below near the shoreline. It was almost mesmerizing to watch the panoramic scene sprawled out below and around them, complete with brilliant tentacles of color moving across the water's surface while the setting sun slowly made its way toward the ocean horizon.

"I can't believe you did all this, just for us," said Susan.

"It seems like I left the rolls down in the kitchen, though," apologized Ray.

"This is plenty," assured Susan as she took a bite of pork loin. It was so tender that the meat literally melted in her mouth. "Oh, this is by far the best pork roast I've ever eaten!"

"If you don't mind my asking," prefaced Carolyn, "have you looked into the possibility of getting a conservation easement for this place?"

"A what?" Ray furled his brow.

"A conservation easement," repeated Carolyn as she took another bite of the delicious meat. "Getting one could qualify you for significant tax benefits."

"How significant?" Ray was interested at once. The thought of having to sell off what little was left of the Killingham family empire was something he had been trying not to think of just yet. Still, unless he thought of something soon, it could happen as soon as next year.

"Well," continued Carolyn, "I could not help but notice that you do have seagulls living and nesting in the cliffs along here."

"What's that got to do with it?" Susan interjected, clearly puzzled by Carolyn's line of thought.

"Seagulls were put on the endangered species list a few years back when their numbers began declining to dangerously low levels," informed Carolyn. "You see, they are migratory birds, and must nest in specific areas that are environmentally fragile, like this one."

"A conservation easement?" prompted Ray.

"Conservation easements are designed to help protect land for future generations while enabling owners to retain many of their private property rights, including the right to live on and maintain the use of their land as it exists at the time of the arrangement," explained Carolyn.

Ray and Susan continued to eat as they waited for Carolyn to elaborate. Clearly, neither of them had ever heard of such a thing.

"For example," mentioned Carolyn, "the wildlife center where I volunteer was able to qualify for some sort of special tax benefit under Section 501(c)(3) of the Internal Revenue Code after registering with the IRS and the Secretary of State. There is usually an initial fee as well as annual dues, and there are certain requirements that must be met."

"That doesn't sound very helpful," frowned Ray.

"Perhaps so, but if you could find some organization already classified under the 501(c)(3) umbrella who would be willing to enter into a conservation easement with you," described Carolyn, "then perhaps the organization itself would be willing to be responsible for the brunt of the financial burden."

"What organization would even be willing to do that for me, and why?" Ray was perplexed.

"The seagulls!" beamed Carolyn as she pulled out her cellphone and began searching for something. "Here it is! The Migratory Bird Convention Act of 1916 was designed to protect and manage migratory bird species who nest in environmentally fragile habitats in both Canada and the United States. It was revised in 1994 to include waterfowl, cranes, seabirds, loons, grebes, herons, egrets, shorebirds – including gulls and terns – and several other endangered species of birds."

"Of course!" nodded Susan. "All he needs to do is find some type of bird rescue group who would be interested in helping to protect the seagulls who nest here. That might actually work!"

"You would still be able to live here and enjoy your property," reminded Carolyn. "You just wouldn't be able to subdivide or build anything else here without permission from the group who holds the easement. And, a conservation easement is legally binding not only to you, but to your heirs or anyone to whom the property might ever be sold in the future."

"Wouldn't that lower the property's value on the open market?" questioned Ray.

"Of course it would, if you were planning to sell the place," confirmed Carolyn. "But, you would need to go through an attorney and fill out all the proper paperwork, and could stipulate to anything the other party is willing to include in the agreement."

"Huh," mumbled Ray as he took another bite of meat and slowly chewed it. "Oh, my little demon girls! It's absolutely brilliant! And I think I know just the organization to hit up for it, too."

172

"Who?" asked Carolyn. She was curious to know what wildlife organizations existed in that area. She had not heard of any.

"Do you hear that?" Susan suddenly asked as she got up and walked over to the catwalk's door. "Look! Somebody's down there on the beach calling for help!"

Ray immediately got up to join Susan by the catwalk door before opening it and going outside. "Be careful! It's a long way down."

Susan and Carolyn immediately joined Ray on the catwalk so they could get a better look at who might be down on the beach shouting for assistance. Both were glad they had brought their sweaters with them, as it was quite windy.

"It's Ann!" recognized Carolyn.

"We need to get down there, right now!" directed Susan as she hurried back inside.

"Wait!" called Ray as he watched his guests leave and begin rapidly descending the spiral staircase.

"Oh, heck!" muttered Ray as he followed after them.

"Do you think anyone heard us?" questioned Ted as he started to hobble over to where Ann was kneeling near the injured seagull.

"I saw some people up there in the lighthouse," replied Ann.

"Don't get too close to it," cautioned Ted as he sat back down to get the weight off of his injured ankle. "It could be dangerous."

"It's got a broken wing!" argued Ann. "We can't just leave it here like this, especially with the sun going down."

"Well, that's not our only problem," pointed out Ted. "Today is boys' beach! How are you going to explain both of us being down here together?"

"I do live right up there in the faculty housing area," replied Ann. "When I went outside to empty the trash for my dad, I just happened to hear someone shouting for help down here."

"Okay," sighed Ted, "that sounds reasonable."

"What about your ankle?" questioned Ann. "Can you stand on it at all?"

"Not very well," admitted Ted. "But I think it's just sprained."

"Hey!" shouted Susan as she and Carolyn started across the sand towards Ann.

Upon seeing the injured seagull, Carolyn immediately grabbed Susan by the arm and motioned for her to stop where she was. Carolyn then placed her index finger to her lips to indicate silence. The injured seagull was clearly agitated, nervously flapping its good wing and starting to hop away. At least there was no sign of blood anywhere.

"Look! It's Ms. Rives!" recognized Ted with relief.

"Susan?" smiled Ann as she turned to look. "And Carolyn!"

"Give me your sweater!" Carolyn commanded Susan. She then cautiously approached to get a better look at the injured bird. Carolyn again put her index finger to her lips and indicated for Ann and Ted to be quiet. They both nodded that they understood.

"It's cold out here," whispered Susan, unwilling to part with her sweater. "You're not using my sweater on that thing! Use your own!"

"I think it has a broken wing," whispered Ann as Carolyn kneeled beside her on the sand to observe the injured seagull. It was Carolyn's hope that kneeling and reducing her height would make her seem less threatening to the nervous bird.

"Did you see what happened?" questioned Carolyn in hushed tones as she quickly evaluated the situation to determine the best course of action. Something would have to be done immediately to restrain the bird before their window of opportunity was gone.

"It was fighting with another seagull over a fish or something when they both crashed into the side of the bluffs," revealed Ted as he tried to get up and hobble closer.

Carolyn noticed at once that the bird was distracted by Ted and used the opportunity to her advantage. Expertly tossing her sweater over the seagull's head to prevent it from seeing what she was doing, Carolyn moved in from behind to gently but firmly straddle the bird with her legs. Not waiting to be pecked by the dangerous bird, Carolyn swiftly reached under the sweater and successfully secured the bird's beak with her hands.

"Seagulls really can be very dangerous when they're injured," whispered Carolyn, "especially if they feel trapped or threatened in some way. I really should be wearing leather gloves and protective eyewear, not just regular glasses. Kind of late now, though. I just don't know how much longer I can hold this thing! The trick is to hold the patient firmly enough to prevent further struggling yet loosely enough to avoid additional injury to the bird or the rescuer, and this bird is extremely strong!"

"What can we do?" asked Ann.

Ray had just arrived on the scene and was out of breath but could see at once what was going on and just shook his head. Was there no end to the troublesome situations Susan and Carolyn always seemed to get themselves into?

"We need something to put the seagull in, for starters, and the sooner the better!" directed Carolyn as she paused to maintain her grasp on the struggling patient. "The bird needs to be kept quiet and still. We need a mid-sized pet carrier or even one of those plastic Tupperware tubs with a lid to put it in, one about two feet square in size. A clean towel to put inside for the bird to rest on would be good, too, and then all we'll need to do is cut some holes in the lid so it can breathe. Leather gloves and protective eyewear wouldn't hurt anything, either, for whoever assists me while we transfer it to the container. I would suggest we hurry!"

"I have some leather welding gloves and a pocket knife for the lid," mentioned Ray as he struggled to catch his breath. "And I'm pretty sure I do have one of those tubs, too."

"Excellent! And the gloves and the plastic tub should both be fairly clean," cautioned Carolyn. "Not covered with axle grease, or anything like that."

"Okay," nodded Ray. "I can do that."

"And some protective eyewear, if you have it," reminded Carolyn. "Just a pair of safety glasses will do, but the most important thing is that tub to put the bird in, and quickly, please!"

"I better go help him," suggested Susan.

"I'll stay here and help Carolyn with the bird," informed Ann.

"And a first aid kit for me?" called Ted as he rubbed his swollen ankle. "If you have one handy."

"My cellphone's in my pocket," advised Carolyn. "We need to find someone locally who has experience handling marine birds. Someone who can give it the medical attention it needs, and tonight. What was the name of that Marine Biology professor again?"

"John Murray! He's also a Veterinarian!" replied Ann excitedly but was unable to obtain a signal on Carolyn's cellphone.

"Ray's got a satellite phone," advised Ted when he noticed the problem. "You can still catch him if you hurry."

"I'll be right back," advised Ann as she ran after Susan and Ray to borrow his phone. "Wait! We need your satellite phone!"

"Here you are," offered Ray with a smile as he paused to retrieve it from his left boot before handing it to Ann. "Unlike Carolyn's cellphone, this one works everywhere."

"Thank you!" nodded Ann with appreciation. "Now all we need is Professor Murray's phone number so we can call him. I think I have it up at the house."

"No need. It's on speed dial," informed Ray as he and Susan turned to leave again. "Just press number four and the pound sign."

"Wow! A weapon in one boot and a satellite phone in the other?" flirted Susan as she grabbed Ray's hand to hold it while they headed back for his place.

"As I mentioned before, I do come prepared," beamed Ray while he flirted openly with Susan.

"Does John Murray have anything to do with the organization you were planning to hit up for the conservation easement?" questioned Susan innocently as she slipped her arm through Ray's.

"As a matter of fact, he does," responded Ray. He decided to make no effort whatsoever to discourage Susan's advances. After all, she was getting a divorce and it would be final in just two more months.

"What makes you think he might be interested in helping with something like that?" delved Susan, curious to find out.

"Well, not only is John Murray the Marine Biology professor over at Oceanview Academy, but he also belongs to some bird rescue group based out of Ocean Bay," replied Ray thoughtfully.

"Ocean Bay? Not the Ocean Bay Bird Conservancy?" grilled Susan with interest. She had heard of it.

"As a matter of fact, yes," replied Ray with a sly look at Susan. She was so beautiful in the evening light! Ray tried to envision himself pulling her close so he could kiss her full on the mouth. Did he dare? Her crooked smile was enticing and seemed almost impossible to resist.

Susan glanced at Ray in time to see the look on his face as they hurried along in the sand together. She was not unaware of the effect she frequently had on men and boys alike, and enjoyed the power it gave her to influence them as needed when necessary.

"What do you plan to do when Ms. Neilson comes back?" asked Ray, anxious to know Susan's future plans.

"I don't know," shrugged Susan. "I haven't really given it much thought. Being retired, I can probably do pretty much whatever I want."

"Oh yeah?" smirked Ray as he pulled her closer and put his arm around her to allegedly shield her from the brisk onslaught of ocean breeze assaulting them.

"Thanks!" Susan smiled sweetly. "A mere sweater is no match for this kind of weather."

"I do have an extra coat you can borrow back at the house," offered Ray. "Remind me when we get there. We should probably get one for Carolyn, too."

"Ray?"

"Yes?"

"Tell me more about Vietnam," encouraged Susan.

"I really don't like to talk about it," reminded Ray. The memory of his experiences there were just too painful to talk about.

"Then tell me this," Susan changed her approach, "was there ever anyone else special in your life besides Ginny? Someone over there, perhaps? Do you know whether there are any little rays of sunshine running around someplace?"

"Rays of sunshine?" Ray raised a provocative eyebrow and laughed with amusement. "Are you asking me if I know whether I have any children anywhere?"

"I was just curious," admitted Susan.

"I really don't know," confessed Ray. "There could be."

"There could be?" Susan pulled away and stopped to give Ray a surprised look. She attempted to appear shocked but really wasn't.

"Did you think I was a virgin?" teased Ray as he reached over and pulled her close again.

"We'd better hurry up and get that stuff," suggested Susan with an elusive smile as she wriggled free from his grasp.

"Indeed," agreed Ray as he studied Susan more carefully. He still was unsure whether she was just playing him for a fool or was genuinely interested.

"I am looking forward to going through that box with you later tonight, by the way," reminded Susan. Her remark was meant to be taken any way Ray cared to construe it, and he knew it.

Ray merely nodded and smiled knowingly as they continued toward his storage shed in silence.

John Murray was only thirty-three years old but had already managed in his short life to become an oceanographer, a marine biologist and a veterinarian before beginning his stint as instructor at Oceanview Academy five years ago.

His young wife Jeon had been a foreign exchange student at the Ocean Bay Institute of Marine Biology while John was serving his residency there. Even though Jeon was twelve years younger than John, it had been love at first sight, and they had been married two months to the day after their first encounter. They had no children yet.

Pleasant but serious and business-like, John's other main love in life was helping to rehabilitate endangered species of marine life. In fact, that had been one of his reasons for accepting the position here at Oceanview Academy in the first place. Needless to say, the phone call from Ann had spurred John into immediate action and he was now racing toward the section of beach she had described to him over the phone just minutes before.

"Over here!" called Ann when she saw him, trying to speak softly to avoid upsetting the injured seagull again.

Upon seeing the injured seagull, John Murray suddenly slowed his pace and continued his approach in a stealthier manner. "We need to keep it quiet," whispered Professor Murray. He was well aware of the fact that the bird might injure itself further if any of them made any sudden moves, but was relieved to see no sign of blood anywhere.

Though short and slightly overweight, John Murray was still a strikingly handsome young man and many of his female students had serious crushes on him. Ann was no exception and gazed at Professor Murray with unconcealed admiration as he approached. John slowly set down a small duffle bag to remove and don a pair of leather bird handling gloves. John then put on a pair of protective eyeglasses and pulled out a large beach towel.

"Do we have something to put our patient in?" questioned the Professor. It was twilight already and they really needed to get the bird to safety as quickly as possible. He would most likely have to make the two hour drive up to Ocean Bay tonight, as the school had not yet seen fit to equip him with the type of x-ray equipment that would be needed to properly diagnose the bird's injuries. The break would need to be properly set and splinted as soon as possible.

"Here they are," indicated Carolyn with a sigh of relief as she noticed Ray and Susan approaching. Ray was carrying a plastic Tupperware tub. Sitting on top of it was the lid into which large holes had already been cut, and inside was a clean towel, a pair of welding gloves and a pair of safety glasses. Susan was carrying the first aid kit.

"Ray," greeted the professor.

"John," smiled Ray as he set down the plastic tub.

"I'm gonna need someone else to spot me when I take the bird from you," John indicated to Carolyn, even though he did not yet know her name. "These birds are incredibly strong."

"Tell me about it!" sighed Carolyn, relieved that she was about to be freed from her struggling burden.

Ray rapidly put on the welding gloves and safety glasses he had brought with him while Ann spread out the towel in the tub and then stood ready with the tub's lid in hand.

"On my mark," said John. "One, two, three!"

"Stand back," Professor Murray instructed Ann as he quickly and efficiently placed his large beach towel over the injured seagull before securing his hold on it so Carolyn could let go. Ray then assisted John as they swiftly but gently placed the seagull into the towel-lined tub before carefully removing the beach towel that had been wrapped around it.

The injured seagull immediately became upset and tried to flap its wings, including the one that appeared to be broken, but was unable to succeed in the safety of the confined space. The seagull then tried in vain to peck repeatedly at Professor Murray's arms but was unsuccessful due to the thick leather gloves that he wore. After squawking quite loudly at first, the seagull finally calmed down and seemed to resign itself to the situation when John grabbed the lid from Ann and secured it onto the top of the tub.

"John, this is Susan Rives, the substitute history class teacher," introduced Ray. "You already know Ted and Ann."

"And this is my friend Carolyn," mentioned Susan.

"Nice to meet you both," acknowledged John Murray before turning his focus on Ray. "We need to get this bird up to the Ocean Bay Bird Conservancy tonight."

"You can't take care of it here?" asked Ray. He was anxious to return with Susan and Carolyn to the rest of their uneaten meal.

"We just don't have the proper equipment here at the school," apologized Professor Murray. "I keep hoping they'll spring for it, though. Maybe something like this might finally convince them."

"It would be nice to see the school take more of an interest in the wildlife here," agreed Ray. It appeared as if an opportunity might be presenting itself for him to chat with John Murray about the possibility of establishing a conservation easement. "We can put the tub in the back of my pickup truck. I have some tie-downs we can use to strap it in."

"Looks like we're going for a ride, then," realized John Murray. "Let me just call my wife first to let her know. We probably should strap down the beach towel on top of it, too, for protection from the wind."

John had a satellite phone, as well. In fact, most of the staff at Oceanview Academy did, as there were just too many dead zones in the area for cell phones to be of much use unless one just happened to be directly in the faculty housing area or at the top of Ray Dixon's lighthouse home.

While John Murray was on the phone with his wife, Susan took advantage of the opportunity to lean close and whisper to Ray, "Be sure and talk to him about one of those conservation easements."

"You read my mind," replied Ray.

"You ladies may take Ann and Ted to the lighthouse for now," advised Professor Murray. "My wife will let everyone know where they are. Ted shouldn't try and walk all the way back to the boys' dorm on that ankle, and Ann shouldn't be walking home in the dark, either. It's all good. No one will be in trouble."

Ann suddenly felt a sense of panic at the thought that her father might be coming to the lighthouse to get her. She really would rather walk home on her own. Yet, it really wasn't safe for her to be wandering around after dark, and she knew it.

Ted, on the other hand, was quite relieved and anxious for the opportunity to spend more time with Ann.

"We'd better wrap your ankle first," advised Susan as she began wrapping Ted Jensen's injured ankle with the ace bandage from her first aid kit. Susan and Ann then helped Ted get up and supported his weight from either side as they began their trek to the lighthouse.

Carolyn quickly grabbed John Murray's duffle bag, the first aid kit, and whatever else had been left lying on the beach during the unexpected bird rescue.

Ray and John were already half-way to the pickup truck with their patient, carrying the tub together from either side, but already it was getting dark.

"Have you had a chance to find out anything else about what we discussed earlier?" Susan mentioned to Ann, trying to seem nonchalant about it.

"It's all right, Ted already knows that we're trying to find out about why my father was in the mental institution," revealed Ann so Susan could feel free to talk in front of him.

"And I don't care if he is your father," remarked Ted as he winced with pain from his injured ankle while trying to negotiate the sandy surface of the beach. "If Jon Roth had anything to do at all with the disappearance of my Aunt Veronica, so help me...."

"Your aunt?" Susan suddenly cut Ted off.

"Veronica Jensen was my dad's older sister," informed Ted.

"Veronica only had one sister," mentioned Carolyn suspiciously from behind them. "She didn't have any brothers."

"My dad wasn't born until their parents were in their forties," explained Ted as he turned his head to glance back at Carolyn. "I never actually knew my aunt. But, I did grow up hearing about her and how her disappearance had ruined everyone's life. None of them ever got over it."

"Neither did we," informed Carolyn sadly. "That's one reason we're here. To try and find out what really happened to Veronica Jensen and Joyce Troglite."

"That's what Ann tells me," informed Ted.

"One thing that Ted and I have in common is that our parents were all in their forties before they had us," explained Ann.

"Huh," mumbled Susan. She already knew that Jon Roth would have been forty-four years old when he fathered Ann.

"Do your parents still live in Nevada?" interrogated Carolyn, challenging Ted to see if he really was who he said he was.

"My dad's family never lived in Nevada," scowled Ted. "The only place they've ever lived is in Los Angeles."

"I knew that," smiled Carolyn with satisfaction. "Just testing to be sure you are who you say you are."

"Okay, then," nodded Ted, surprised by Carolyn's tactic.

"I'm sure glad you're on our side," chuckled Ann, grateful for Susan and Carolyn's help. Ann had wanted all her life to find out the truth about her parents and had suspected for some time that something was seriously amiss with Jon Roth.

They had finally reached the lighthouse. John and Ray had already secured the Tupperware tub containing the injured seagull into the back of Ray's pickup truck with the beach towel on top and were getting ready to leave. "Here's an extra key," flirted Ray as he handed it to Susan.

"So soon?" teased Susan.

"And here's my phone number, too," added Ray as he handed her one of his old faded business cards from the trailer park. "It's still the same number. You should be able to reach us with your cellphone from here, if anything comes up."

"Okay, thanks," replied Susan as she unexpectedly gave Ray a hug. "Be careful!"

"I always am," flirted Ray, unavoidably aroused by Susan's close contact. "I'm looking forward to going through that box of things with you ladies upon my return."

The others exchanged curious looks after Susan and Ray's surprising display of affection but chose not to comment on it.

"You might want this," realized Carolyn as she pulled Ray's satellite phone from the duffel bag and handed it to him.

"Oh yeah, thanks!" nodded Ray.

"And this is yours," indicated Carolyn as she handed the duffel bag itself to John after removing Susan's first aid kit from it.

Susan, Carolyn, Ann and Ted watched Ray and John drive away before entering the lighthouse.

"Why in the world are we going this way?" questioned John when Ray started down the narrow road leading from his lighthouse home to the old trailer park next door. "Wouldn't it be a lot faster to just take the other road?"

"Perhaps, but I think I left my wallet at the trailer park, and my driver's license is in it," explained Ray sheepishly. "You see, when Susan and I were down there getting the tub, we stopped to cut holes in the lid. That was when I took out my wallet so I could get to my pocket knife. Don't worry, I know right where it is."

"Guess that means you're driving without a license, then?" razzed John with an amused look.

"Just don't tell anyone," grinned Ray as he pulled the truck to a stop, put it into park, and got out to unlatch and pull open the long swinging driveway gate covered with ivy.

Ray had not yet bothered to tell Susan or Carolyn about the easier route that led directly from his lighthouse over to the old servants' quarters and then continued on until it joined up with the road behind Jon Roth's residence. Ray feared that if Susan or Carolyn went that way, they might be seen by Jon Roth. That, in turn, might prompt Jon Roth to wonder why they had been at the lighthouse in the first place.

After quickly retrieving his wallet from where he had left it, Ray returned to the truck. Ray then held up the wallet for John to see before putting it back into his pocket and informed, "Got it!"

John Murray merely smiled and nodded as Ray got back into the pickup truck and started the engine again.

"So," began John Murray after a few moments of silence, "what's the story between you and Susan? Isn't she only here for a few more weeks?"

"That's quite a long story," replied Ray as he continued up the narrow gravel road that led from his dilapidated beachfront trailer park to the main road above.

"We've got a two-hour drive ahead of us," reminded John.

"Do you want the forty-four-year version, or just the two-day version?" teased Ray.

"You've known her for forty-four years?" John was surprised.

"Actually, I met her once forty-four years ago," clarified Ray. "She was in my aunt's office at the time, with Carolyn. That was in 1972. Apparently, both of them were called in to see Dean Dixon on more than one occasion back in those days."

"Oh, I see," laughed John. "Two of her favorites, then? I didn't realize both of them had gone to school here."

"Something like that," smirked Ray.

"You and Susan certainly do seem to be hitting it off quite well these days," prompted John Murray. He was anxious to find out more.

"Say, John, not to change the subject, but I've been meaning to ask you about something," prefaced Ray.

"Sure," John shrugged his shoulders.

"Well, you know how I had to sell off the old servants' quarters last year in order to pay my taxes?" began Ray.

"No, I didn't realize you were in financial difficulty," admitted John. "Most people around here probably assumed – like I did – that you just didn't need or want so much property to maintain all by yourself anymore, what with you getting up in years and all."

"That was partially true," agreed Ray, "but not the only reason. And it hasn't been that long since the trailer park went out of business, along with both ice cream shops. And now, there's just not enough coming in anymore."

"What about the other ice cream business over at the school, and the jobs you do over there?" questioned John.

"What little I make as a handy-man, doing deliveries and making ice cream for the school just isn't enough," explained Ray. "By next year, I'll probably be forced to put my entire property up for sale, including the lighthouse. I just can't bring in enough to pay all these taxes anymore."

"Wow! I had no idea," replied John Murray, sadly shaking his head. "Sure wish I could help you."

"Perhaps you can," responded Ray. "Carolyn was telling me earlier today about how someone with a conservation easement can qualify for substantial tax breaks. Is that true?"

"Oh my!" sighed John Murray. "That's a very complicated subject, and probably one best answered by an attorney."

"You do know something about marine birds," reminded Ray as he pulled onto the main road. "Like this seagull here, that we have in the back."

"Yeah?" John waited to see what Ray would say next.

"Carolyn found an endangered species list on the internet earlier tonight that listed seagulls, and she even showed it to me. She then suggested that I find out whether it might qualify my property for one of those conservation easements. The website we were looking at even described how seagulls will only nest in certain types of places, and from what it described, this certainly sounds like one of them."

John was silent for several moments before answering. "You do know, of course, that you can't believe everything you read on the internet? Carolyn's heart is definitely in the right place, though, that much is certain. However, while seagulls are a 'protected' species because they are wild birds, they are not actually considered to be an 'endangered' species."

"There's a difference?" scowled Ray.

"Oh, absolutely. An endangered species - not merely a protected species - would need to be present on a particular parcel of land in order to qualify it for a conservation tag, which is not necessarily the same as a conservation easement," described John. "There really is no one-size fits all conservation tag or easement for any given situation. Each arrangement is individual and unique, set up by the landowners and their attorneys to address the specific circumstances involved for those parties and their properties."

"That all sounds rather complicated," mumbled Ray. His hopes of an easy solution to his financial worries seemed in peril.

"Besides," added John, "you probably wouldn't want to become a non-profit organization yourself, as there's a requirement that two-thirds of your income would need to come from public support versus private funding. That's not for someone like you."

"Oh, well," sighed Ray. "It did sound too good to be true."

"However," grinned Professor Murray, "you DO happen to have an endangered species nesting on your property."

Ray gave John a sideways glance. "Well, what is it?"

"Let me explain first," prefaced John. "The Waterfowl Habitat Program, for example, has incentives where it sometimes provides landowners with not only tax breaks but even payments for adhering to practices that help maintain natural food sources and breeding areas for endangered species of birds on their land."

"Yes?" Ray was becoming impatient.

"Snowy Plovers and Lesser Terns are both on the endangered species list," informed John Murray, "and both of them just happen to be nesting on your beach!"

"Really?" Ray slowly began to smile again.

"The Western Snowy Plover has been federally listed as threatened since 1993, and is a species of special concern. The other imperiled bird nesting on your beach is the Lesser Tern, and it has been on both state and federal endangered species lists since 1971 and 1970, respectively."

"You don't say!" beamed Ray as he nodded his head.

"Just make sure you see an actual lawyer who specializes in these types of things," advised John. "It's a very complicated area of law and not even all attorneys understand it."

Neither Ted nor Ann had eaten, so Susan and Carolyn offered them some of the delicious pork roast and potatoes from Ray's crockpot. It had been a difficult climb up the spiral staircase for Ted with his ankle like it was, but the delicious aroma had kept him going.

"I suppose we should save some for Ray," chuckled Susan as she took another bite.

Ann was just grateful she had been able to feed the feral cat colony over by the dairy first before the seagull incident, but said nothing about it. Other people would usually not understand.

Carolyn's hair was still wet from the unplanned shower she had taken in Ray's military style shower, and the extra pair of men's pajamas she had managed to locate and change into hung loosely on her tall, slender frame. Carolyn sincerely hoped her own clothes, which were currently washing in Ray's commercial washing machine, would not be damaged, especially since the skirt was made of rayon. Still, one could never be too careful in cleaning up after the handling of wildlife, to avoid the possibility of contracting a zoonotic illness such as Escherichia coli (also known as E.coli) or some other form of drug resistant bacterium. It was always better to be safe than sorry.

"That was delicious!" approved Ted. He was seated on one of the bench seats by the catwalk door with his ankle propped up on its red cushion. Ted also had a bag of ice on his ankle that Carolyn had managed to locate and bring up from the commercial kitchen below, down on the first floor following her shower.

"We were hoping to try and get into that bomb shelter on Sunday when you guys come over for lunch," indicated Ann, though still nervous about the possibility of getting caught by her father.

"Oh! I forgot to tell you about the box Ray has here," responded Susan. "We were planning on going through it tonight."

"What box?" asked Ann, her curiosity piqued.

"You knew that Ray was engaged to Ms. Eggersol?" questioned Carolyn. "She used to be the English Literature instructor here at Oceanview Academy."

"I might have heard that, I'm not sure," mused Ann.

"Well, back in 1976, when Virginia Eggersol's car was hit by a drunk driver one foggy night, she plunged to her death on the jagged boulders below," described Carolyn.

"How horrible!" exclaimed Ann.

"That was when she was on her way back from the mental institution after paying a visit to young Jon Roth," added Susan.

Ann Roth was speechless.

"Ray said Ginny minored in abnormal psychology before going into English Literature, so she would go out to the mental institution to visit Jon Roth on a regular basis," continued Carolyn.

"Ray also said that even though Ginny wasn't a part of Jon's family, the people over there would still let her talk to him for hours, and that she kept notes of it all in her journal," recalled Susan.

"The journal she had with her was undoubtedly destroyed in the crash, but we're hoping her other notes are all still in that box," deduced Carolyn. "And we'd like very much to see them."

"Where is it then?" pressed Ann, anxious to see the box.

"We don't know," replied Susan. "Ray has it stashed around here somewhere, though. He was just about to show it to us when you started shouting for help down there on the beach."

"That figures!" muttered Ted.

"How did Ray ever get the box?" pressed Ann.

"He said that Edith Roth brought it over to him after Ginny's death, and thought he should have it," revealed Carolyn.

"My grandmother gave it to him?" Ann was astounded. "And just how did she get it?"

"We don't actually know," replied Susan.

"Perhaps she felt the box was safer here than over at your house?" speculated Carolyn.

"Do you hear something?" questioned Ted.

"What do you mean?" replied Ann with a worried expression on her face.

"I heard it, too," verified Susan. "Someone's trying to unlock the door down there."

"Call Ray right now," commanded Carolyn with urgency. "And ask him whether anyone else besides you has a key to this place!"

Susan hurriedly pulled out the tattered business card Ray had given her before his departure and began dialing the number on her cellphone. It rang only twice before Ray answered.

"Hello?" greeted Ray, though he was certain it was Susan.

"Ray, there's someone trying to break in," whispered Susan. "Who else has a key to the place?"

"Where are you right now?" questioned Ray, suddenly concerned.

"We're in the tower room, with Ted and Ann," replied Susan.

"Are there any cars outside?" asked Ray.

"We can't see without going out onto the catwalk, and didn't want to risk it, just in case it's someone that shouldn't see us here," explained Susan.

"Go to the Daisy Room," directed Ray. "It's the only room with a view of the entrance. You should be able to see who it is from there. If not, you need to hang up and call Dean Jorgensen. You'll find a campus phone directory on a bulletin board in the pantry."

"Okay, I'm on my way down to the Daisy Room," indicated Susan as she hurried from the tower room and began descending the spiral staircase.

"Stay here with Ted," Carolyn directed Ann before following after Susan.

"Where are you guys right now, anyway?" asked Susan as she made her way down the stairs.

"We're almost to Ocean Bay," revealed Ray.

"Just ten minutes away," added John in the background.

"All right, we're in the Daisy Room," informed Susan.

"Leave the lights off so whoever it is won't see you when you look out the window," instructed Ray, fearful for their safety and frustrated not to be there when they needed him most.

"It's so dark and foggy out there, I can't tell who it is," described Susan.

"Is there a vehicle out there with them?" probed Ray.

"No, there's not," replied Susan.

"Then one of you needs to get down to the first floor and turn on the porchlight. There's a switch just inside the door. The other one of you should then be able to see who it is from the Daisy Room," guessed Ray.

Carolyn nodded for Susan to stay where she was and raced from the Daisy Room, swiftly descending the remaining steps to the first floor. Upon finding the switch, she quickly flipped it on.

Just at that moment, a vehicle began slowing to a stop in front of the lighthouse door, causing the shadowy figure on the front porch to flee for cover.

"Well?" pressed Carolyn as she returned to the Daisy Room to learn what Susan had seen.

"Someone just pulled up in a car," explained Susan. "The person at the door saw them and made a run for it. They're gone now. There was no way to see who they were. I couldn't even tell whether it was a man or a woman."

Just then the front bell began to ring, startling Susan and Carolyn so badly that they jumped with fright. Susan glanced back out the window again and noticed that Jon Roth was standing on the front porch. "It's Jon Roth!"

"You ladies be careful!" cautioned Ray. "I want you to hang up right now and call Dean Jorgensen before you answer the door or let him in, do you hear me?"

"We'll be okay," assured Susan. "Trust me!"

8. Home Leave

Despite Carolyn's every effort to avoid him, Jim Otterman just seemed to be everywhere. Even worse, Linda Shaver appeared to be simultaneously stalking Lenny Owens at every turn. It was almost as if the two of them were in collaboration to try and prevent Lenny and Carolyn from being alone together. Carolyn wanted nothing more at that moment than for Lenny to ask her to the Harvest Festival Prom, and dreamed of wearing the stunning baby blue evening gown her parents had bought for the event.

In fact, Carolyn could hardly wait for Lenny Owens to see her in the baby blue masterpiece. Perhaps then Lenny might finally work up the courage to ask her to go steady with him. Right now, Carolyn would settle for Lenny just working up the courage to ask her to be his date for the Harvest Festival Prom, and fervently hoped that he would do it soon. Meanwhile, it was imperative that Jim Otterman and Linda Shaver be stopped from interfering!

"What's wrong?" asked Veronica as Carolyn sat down at her table. She could not help but notice how downcast Carolyn was.

"Hey, cheer up!" encouraged Susan as she and Joyce joined them for breakfast.

"Lenny still hasn't asked me yet," revealed Carolyn.

"What's wrong with him?" frowned Joyce. "The guy has to be just plain stupid not to see how crazy you are about him!"

"And what's not to like, right?" winked Susan.

"Maybe Lenny prefers Linda Shaver," replied Carolyn with a frown. "No matter where Lenny goes, there she is."

"Then it sounds like you'd better make more of an effort to get there first," suggested Veronica with sly grin.

"Every time I try to go anywhere near Lenny, that stupid Jim Otterman shows up out of nowhere!" complained Carolyn. "Jim absolutely will not take a hint and will not go away."

"Sounds like he's quite determined," laughed Veronica.

"Have you just come out and told Jim you're not interested?" questioned Joyce.

"The direct approach, I like it," approved Susan as she devoured another bite of fake bacon.

"Yes, I have!" replied Carolyn. She was not very hungry at the moment. Just the very thought of Jim Otterman and his greasy red hair had caused her to lose her appetite.

"Maybe there's something I can do?" suggested Susan. "Jim's in my biology class. Would you like me to talk to him?"

"And that's another thing," Carolyn angrily turned to Susan, "Jim told me that YOU suggested he should ask me to the Harvest Festival Prom! How could you do that?"

"Wait just a minute!" argued Susan. "That's not true."

"I'm listening," fumed Carolyn.

"We'll see you guys later," indicated Veronica as she and Joyce quickly got up to leave. Clearly, Susan and Carolyn needed some privacy to resolve their dispute.

"Look here," persisted Susan, "this is what happened. Jim asked me whether or not you had a date to the prom yet."

"And so naturally you told him I didn't?" snapped Carolyn.

"No, not at all," persisted Susan.

"Then just where did Jim get the idea that YOU suggested he ask me then?" demanded Carolyn.

"What I did tell him was that I didn't know whether or not you actually had a date to the prom," clarified Susan. "And that you were the one he should be asking about it, not me!"

"Jim obviously interpreted that to mean he should ask me to the prom, then," realized Carolyn, finally starting to calm down.

"Hey, I never suggested that Jim be your date, or that he even ask you to the prom!" assured Susan. "But, I'll be more than happy to tell the little creep to leave you alone when I see him in class today. Would you like me to toss a match on that greasy red hair of his and light him on fire for you?"

"What? No, of course not!" chuckled Carolyn. "He might explode! You wouldn't want to end up burning down the entire school. You are kidding, right?"

"Of course, silly!" Susan and Carolyn then began to laugh most heartily.

"Hey, I have an idea," proposed Susan. "Maybe what you need is a day or two away from this place. A change of scenery."

"What do you have in mind?" questioned Carolyn.

"Have you used up your home leave for the semester yet?" asked Susan anxiously.

"My parents can't afford any extra trips," admitted Carolyn sadly. She would have liked nothing more than to go home for an extra weekend visit so she could see some of her friends from back home, and especially her pet cat Socky, but that would not be possible this time. In fact, Carolyn would most likely need to work through Christmas break to make up for the lack of income during her stint in the produce department.

"You should come with me to my house!" invited Susan. "I'm going there this weekend."

"I don't know," hesitated Carolyn. "What if Lenny was planning on asking me to the prom sometime this weekend? Besides, I could never afford it."

"My parents will come and get us and then bring us back. It won't cost you anything! All you need is your parents' permission, and you can call them tonight. Besides, the prom is still another week away," reminded Susan. "Lenny will ask you by the end of next week, if he's going to."

"And if he doesn't?" countered Carolyn.

"Then at least you won't have to see Jim Otterman for two entire days," tempted Susan. "Guaranteed."

"That would be nice to get away from Jim Otterman," agreed Carolyn. The very thought of Jim Otterman made Carolyn shudder. Not only was Jim barely five feet eight inches tall, skinny and gangly looking, with slouched bony shoulders, but it was obvious from Jim's posture that he never even tried to stand up straight. Not only that, Carolyn would never consider going to the prom with someone shorter than she was! Worst of all, Jim's greasy red hair and sunburned freckled face would clash as badly with her baby blue evening dress as they did with the round black rims on his thick oversized glasses!

"Maybe by then Jim will have asked someone else to the prom," reasoned Susan.

"Or Lenny might have asked Linda Shaver by then," feared Carolyn, still worried about it.

"Oh, come on!" persisted Susan. "It'll be fun. Absence makes the heart grow fonder. Lenny will ask you next week. He just has to."

"All right," Carolyn finally agreed. "I'll call my parents tonight and see what they say."

The next morning found Susan and Carolyn waiting on the front steps of the girls' dormitory with their suitcases, waiting for Susan's parents to arrive.

"Come on, let's go!" urged Susan as she grabbed her suitcase and headed for a bright yellow sports car that had just pulled up out front.

"Wait just a minute!" hesitated Carolyn. "That can't possibly be your parents. Who is it?"

"We need to hurry before anybody notices it isn't them," advised Susan, anxious to be on their way.

"I'm not going anywhere until you tell me who that is," insisted Carolyn. The handsome young man driving the bright yellow sports car appeared to be about 28 years of age, and his dark, shoulder length hair was in clear violation of the school's hair length policy for men.

"That's Jorge," whispered Susan. "He's a neighbor."

"A neighbor?" doubted Carolyn.

"My dad's car is in the shop right now," added Susan. "So, Jorge offered to come and pick us up. Come, where's your sense of adventure?"

"We are going to your parents' house for the weekend, then?" clarified Carolyn.

"Absolutely!" Susan was serious and Carolyn could detect no sign of deception on her part. "We just don't want anyone to be upset because we had to get there another way, that's all. Unless, of course, you'd rather stay here and take your chances with Jim Otterman?"

"Let's go," agreed Carolyn. She needed no further persuasion.

"Jorge!" acknowledged Susan as she threw her suitcase into the tiny trunk. "Thanks so much for coming! This is Carolyn."

"My pleasure," Jorge flirted shamelessly with both of them, his Italian heritage unmistakable.

"You'll probably need to keep your suitcase on the seat beside you in the back," Jorge apologized to Carolyn as he closed the trunk and got back into the tiny car.

"It is a pretty small trunk," agreed Susan with a grin.

Carolyn merely nodded as she climbed into the small back seat with her huge suitcase. "Nice to meet you, Jorge."

"Likewise," responded Jorge as he winked at Carolyn in the rearview mirror before starting up and revving the loud engine.

"Jorge!" laughed Susan. "Someone might notice us!"

"Not for long," grinned Jorge as he put the car into gear and took off at a rapid speed.

Carolyn tried in vain to duck down to avoid being seen by curious onlookers, but the space available was insufficient.

"I'll have you ladies out of here in no time," promised Jorge as he sped out onto the main road.

"I hope no one saw us," mentioned Carolyn nervously.

"No one did," assured Susan. "Dean Dixon's car wasn't even there when we left."

"Are you sure?" questioned Carolyn hopefully.

"Absolutely," responded Susan. "Trust me!"

Located only two hours north of Oceanview Academy, the huge metropolis of Ocean Bay had been built around a natural harbor section of the coastline. Sailing ships, yachts, barges and oceangoing vessels of every kind could be seen along its bustling docks and busy piers. Shops and merchants were everywhere.

Bright red trolley cars filled with people were expertly guided by an overhead cable support system down various tracks in the center of Ocean Bay's busiest streets. The clanging sound of trolley bells announced each passenger stop.

"Wow! I didn't realize it was this big," admitted Carolyn as she attempted to take it all in.

"Ocean Bay, Population 296,007," read Susan as they passed by a sign near its entrance.

Carolyn gaped with amazement at the variety of towering skyscrapers, the busy traffic and the never-ending horde of pedestrians dashing all at once in every direction imaginable.

"Is it always this busy?" Carolyn finally asked.

"It's one of those cities that never sleeps," replied Susan proudly. "Never a dull moment and always something to do."

"Should we drive up to the top of Zigzag Hill before I take you ladies home?" grinned Jorge. He was anxious to show off the street racing technology and expert maneuvering capabilities of his little yellow sports car.

"Your parents might be worried if we don't get there pretty soon," cautioned Carolyn.

"They know we're with Jorge," smiled Susan. "We're good."

Zigzag Hill had originally been designed to make it easier for its many residents to traverse the steep 29% grade on which it was built, which was definitely too steep for most vehicles. Its one-way series of sharp hairpin turns meandered back and forth down a less-steep grade of only 7% that was manageable at a slow pace.

"Speed limit five miles per hour?" read Carolyn. "We're not going down that road are we?"

"We most definitely are!" smirked Susan, anxious to see the look on Carolyn's face as they did.

"Ten miles an hour is a must!" insisted Jorge as he geared down to begin the wild descent.

Susan had purposely unbuckled her seatbelt to make the ride more enjoyable and squealed with glee at each hairpin turn as she was literally bounced from her seat.

"Undo your seatbelt! Live a little!" encouraged Susan.

"No way!" persisted Carolyn.

The picturesque homes built down the side of zigzag hill were constructed in freestanding colonial style architecture, while most of the homes in the meandering hillside area below it were whimsical looking three-story homes.

"Those are called Painted Ladies," indicated Susan. "Even though they are all connected, each one is owned by a different family and painted a different color."

"How do they get gardening supplies to their back yards?" questioned Carolyn. "Do they have to carry those things through their houses, or is there an alley? And just why are they all built so close together?"

"Those are good questions," agreed Jorge. "I can answer the last one. With the buildings supporting one another, there's less chance of them toppling to the ground during a major earthquake. At least that's what they say."

"Earthquake?" Carolyn's face took on a worried expression.

"Relax, it's been over sixty years since the last significant event," assured Jorge.

"Oh, that makes me feel better already," replied Carolyn unconvincingly.

"And, there is a narrow alley back there, but not too many people would even want to plant a garden where the sun is always blocked by the tall buildings," described Susan. "Some of the wealthier homes do have small courtyards in front with room for a small garden, though."

"Everything seems so crowded," considered Carolyn. "I think I'd rather live out in the country, if I had to choose."

"Wouldn't we all!" chuckled Jorge as he pulled up in front of one of the Painted Lady homes and came to a stop.

"Here we are," announced Susan. "This is where my parents live with my little brother Damien."

The Rives home was painted white with dark green trim, while the homes on its right side were painted pastel pink, pale green, light blue, lavender and yellow. The homes on its other side were beige, yellow, gray and mauve, respectively. Each had trim painted in a contrasting yet complimentary color for that particular house.

"They are cheerful," approved Carolyn, pleased by the various color combinations used throughout the block.

Jorge rapidly unloaded their luggage and was on his way, even before Susan's mother could open the front door to welcome them. "Susan!" exclaimed the woman as she rushed forward to embrace her daughter before kissing her several times on each cheek. "How are you? Oh, my baby girl!"

"I'm great!" replied Susan as she struggled to free herself from her mother's tight grasp. "And this is my friend Carolyn. Jorge had to get to work so he couldn't stay." Her mother merely nodded with understanding and then turned her attention to Carolyn.

"Carolyn!" beamed Mrs. Rives. "We're so glad to have you here! Susan's told us so much about you in her letters."

Carolyn was surprised when Mrs. Rives suddenly gave her a hug, as well, and then stood back to hold her face between her hands so she could get a better look at her. "Welcome to our home!"

"Well, don't just stand there!" came a man's voice from inside. "Come on in! I'd like to meet her, too."

"That's my dad," smiled Susan as she picked up her suitcase and walked up the remaining steps to the front door before going inside where Mr. Rives was seated in an overstuffed recliner waiting for them to enter. A large console television set connected to a rabbit-eared antenna system leading to the roof above was sitting in front of him. It was tuned to a polo game he had been watching.

"Dad hurt his back the other day," explained a handsome young man about fifteen years of age that was descending the home's main staircase. "He was in a little fender bender. And, I'm her brother Damien." Damien politely shook hands with Carolyn before grabbing and taking both suitcases upstairs.

"Very nice to meet you," called Carolyn as she watched Damien disappear with her suitcase. "And Mr. Rives?" added Carolyn politely as she went over to shake hands with him, as well.

"Dinner is ready," announced Susan's mother. "Damien, come back down here and take your father's dinner tray to him, please."

"The rest of us will eat in here at the table," invited Mrs. Rives.

"Yes, mother," replied Damien as he came back downstairs to comply. "You two can stay in my room."

"Why will we be staying in Damien's room?" questioned Susan as she pulled out a chair to sit down at the table. "Is there something wrong with my room?"

"Storage," called Mr. Rives from his chair.

"Storage?" repeated Susan with a worried look on her face. She started to get back up.

"After dinner," directed her mother as she grabbed Susan's arm to stop her so she would sit back down.

"Where will Damien sleep?" asked Susan. She clearly was upset by the arrangement.

"On the couch," grinned Damien as he sat at the table. "We have one of those fold-out couches," he explained for Carolyn's benefit. "I'll be comfortable enough."

"Perhaps we should sleep on the couch," suggested Carolyn. "We wouldn't want you to give up your room."

"It's not a problem," smiled Damien.

After a delicious meal of salad, eggplant parmesan and homemade rolls, Susan and Carolyn helped Mrs. Rives with the dishes. When everything was cleaned up and put away in the kitchen, Susan and Carolyn quickly retired to the room upstairs that would be theirs for the weekend.

"At least we're closer to the bathroom from here," noted Susan. "And you're gonna love the shower!"

"Why? Does it have multiple heads?" smiled Carolyn.

"No, but it has one big head. And it's placed high enough up to accommodate a ten-foot person," grinned Susan.

"Why so high?" asked Carolyn.

"Because whoever installed it was probably too cheap to put in an extender," laughed Susan. "At least it's an individual stall."

"Just what are we going to do while we're here?" Carolyn finally asked. She hoped they would not be confined to watching television with Mr. Rives for the rest of the weekend.

"What would you like to do?" Susan had a mischievous smile.

"We probably won't be able to go anywhere, with your dad's car in the shop," reminded Carolyn.

"Oh ye of little faith," smirked Susan.

"What do you have up your sleeve?" pressed Carolyn.

"Okay, here's what we're going to do," whispered Susan, to make sure no one could overhear. "Jorge is going to take us to the park tomorrow. Damien will probably come along."

"The park?" pressed Carolyn.

"There's boats to rent, carnival rides, trails through the forest, ducks to feed, and even a museum," described Susan.

"I do like museums," Carolyn nodded with approval.

"There's also a conservatory with educational science exhibits, and a gift shop," continued Susan.

"That all sounds like lots of fun, but won't it cost money to do all that stuff?" questioned Carolyn.

"That's why I had Jorge come and get us," revealed Susan. "My dad thinks we came here on the bus. He sent me the money for our bus tickets, but I kept it. Now we have the money to use while we're here."

"You told me your parents were coming to get us," reminded Carolyn. She was not happy about having been misled.

"They were, until my dad had his accident," justified Susan.

"I guess I should thank him for the bus ticket, then," muttered Carolyn, concerned with the way Susan had deceived her parents.

"Yeah, you probably should," agreed Susan.

Carolyn frowned and shook her head with disapproval, no longer excited about their trip to the park the next day.

"Hey, it will be fun," urged Susan.

"So, how long has Jorge been your boyfriend?" asked Carolyn. "I take it he's not actually your neighbor."

"Forever," laughed Susan.

"And your parents are okay with you having a good-looking boyfriend like that who is almost thirty years old?" quizzed Carolyn.

"My parents are from Nicaragua," revealed Susan. "It's kind of like the old country, as far as some of their customs go. When prearranged marriages are not possible, then an acceptable prospect is considered the next best thing. Most parents are usually in favor of it. It's a thing of family honor. Nobody wants a daughter without any prospects that will end up as an old maid. That would be thought of as a continuing financial burden upon the parents and is usually frowned upon by the entire community."

"Wow!" Carolyn was astonished. "So, how is Jorge an acceptable prospect? Are you betrothed to him?"

"No, of course not!" Susan began laughing. "We're just good friends."

"Then how is he a prospect?" pressed Carolyn.

"Well, it's our parents who consider us as prospects for one another," chuckled Susan. "That way, we're free to come and go as we please, and with their blessing."

"So, your parents think you and Jorge are betrothed, then?" grilled Carolyn.

"Sort of," admitted Susan with a shrug of her shoulders.

"Would you really ever marry him?" questioned Carolyn.

"Who knows. Anything's possible. Jorge comes from a wealthy Italian family that owns a winery on the other side of the city," revealed Susan. "Extremely wealthy."

"How does Jorge feel about your arrangement?" interrogated Carolyn. She still found it difficult to comprehend.

"He's good with it," assured Susan. "We have a fairly open relationship."

"What does that mean?" Carolyn was puzzled.

"We each go out with other people, if we feel so inclined," explained Susan with a crooked smile. "Don't worry, our parents have no idea!"

"I wouldn't want that kind of relationship with someone," commented Carolyn.

"Don't knock it until you've tried it," Susan raised an eyebrow and grinned. "You should never limit your options."

"I don't think Lenny would want that kind of relationship, either," mentioned Carolyn.

"Lenny's an idiot," replied Susan. "Just look at you! You're a smart, beautiful and highly desirable young lady who's crazy about him. There's no excuse for him putting you off like this! And, he's not the only fish in the sea, you know!"

"But seriously, what if Lenny doesn't ask me to the Harvest Festival Prom?" fretted Carolyn, still concerned about being away for the weekend.

"My dear Carolina la Gata," smiled Susan. "Either Lenny will ask you or he won't. There are other guys besides Lenny Owens or Jim Otterman. Trust me!"

"Lenny is the only one I'm interested in," maintained Carolyn. "You just don't understand."

"Oh, I understand, all right," countered Susan. "Remember all the trouble Pete and I went to, just to get you two alone together down on the beach? And then all you two did was hold hands! Really?"

"I know!" sighed Carolyn, not wanting to admit that Susan might be right. Perhaps Lenny just wasn't as interested in her as he had led her to believe.

"You will have a good time tomorrow with Damien," promised Susan. "He can be your date for the day, and he's a lot of fun."

"Damien?" frowned Carolyn. "He's shorter than you! And, he's only fifteen years old."

"He's actually the same size as me when I don't have my heels on," corrected Susan. "Besides, you and I are only sixteen years old, so we're only one year older than him."

"Say, why do you call me Carolina la Gata?" asked Carolyn. It was time to try and change the subject.

"Because you are like a cat, and because you love them so much," grinned Susan. "Someday you will probably be an old lady with fourteen cats in your house."

"I doubt it," replied Carolyn, certain she would never want more than two.

"Did you ever get around to asking Lenny if he likes cats?" questioned Susan with a sly grin.

Carolyn suddenly became serious. "No, I didn't!"

"Well, if he doesn't like cats, then he's not for you," chuckled Susan. "Better go to sleep now. You're gonna need it tomorrow."

Carolyn lay awake for hours, long after Susan was sound asleep. Try as she might, Carolyn could not easily fall asleep and thought of little else but the tall, dark and handsome young man named Lenny Owens. Just why was he so important to her? Perhaps Lenny

200

really was an idiot, after all. Carolyn would find out by the end of next week. One thing was certain, though. Whether Lenny asked her to the Harvest Festival Prom or not, there was NO WAY she would go to it with Jim Otterman! She would miss it entirely rather than be subjected to such humiliation.

"Which is your favorite?" asked Damien as he and Carolyn followed after Jorge and Susan. They had been at the zoo since it opened at 9:00 that morning and it was nearly time for lunch already.

"The lions," replied Carolyn matter-of-factly.

"Of course they are!" grinned Susan as she glanced over her shoulder at Carolyn and Damien. "Mine, too! No self-respecting Leo would answer otherwise."

"You're a Leo, too?" chuckled Damien as he grinned at Carolyn. "No wonder!"

"What's that supposed to mean?" questioned Carolyn, unsure if it was a compliment or a criticism.

"Oh, my Carolina la Gata!" sighed Susan. "Since we could hardly tear you away from the lion exhibit, the morning is nearly gone now and there's barely enough time left to go on the rides."

"What about the museum?" asked Carolyn. She had really been looking forward to seeing it. "It's only open until 4:00, but the rides are all open until midnight."

"Carolyn's right, we can go on the rides any time," Jorge reminded Susan. He was under strict orders from Susan not to reveal their evening plans to Carolyn just yet, but at least would try to get Carolyn out of going on the rides if the museum was her preference.

"But, there is enough time to go on a boat ride before lunch," suggested Damien. "They rent them by the hour."

Ocean Bay Park's huge central lake was lined with boat docks at one end that rented small rowboats, pedal boats, and even electric boats, for a nominal price. Sprawling lawns bordered by meandering, flower lined walkways and inviting park benches surrounded the eastern side of the lake. A dense forest of tall evergreens with thick foliage beneath it met the lake on its opposite shore, where several couples were enjoying leisurely picnic lunches on its narrow sandy beach. Tall cattails with water lilies growing around them hugged the lake's southern shore, where a family of ducks was busy floating around and occasionally surface diving into the water to forage for food. Being omnivores, the ducks would mostly eat a combination of aquatic plants, small fish and insects, but would also spend a good deal of time begging for handouts from many of the park's two-legged visitors. Partial to grains and seeds, the ducks would also eat pieces of bread and other tidbits that were offered.

"Yeah, that's a great idea!" agreed Jorge. "After that, we can all have lunch at the conservatory on our way over to the museum."

"Look here," directed Damien as he stopped to read a sign by the boat rental shack. "It says their boats are simply the safest on the market and are the most non-tipping, self-bailing, unsinkable boats available anywhere."

Damien was striking in his appearance. While his Nicaraguan heritage was obvious in his features, he was also fair complexioned. That was not the only thing he shared in common with his older sister Susan. Despite his diminutive size, Damien was equipped with an alluring smile that most women found irresistible, and flirtatious hazel brown eyes. Carolyn, however, seemed virtually immune to Damien's charming personality and flirtatious ways. Damien had never encountered anyone quite like her and soon decided that it would be a personal dare to see if he could win Carolyn over. Naturally, Damien had no way of knowing about Lenny Owens or that he was foremost on Carolyn's mind.

"If there's a way to sink one of those boats, Susan will no doubt find it," teased Jorge.

"Oh yeah?" responded Susan, who took Jorge's remark as a challenge. "Come on, Carolyn. We're going for a boat ride!"

"The rowboats are the least expensive," noticed Carolyn. She was far more concerned at the moment with the rapid depletion of their meager funds than with the possibility that Susan might actually succeed in sinking one of the rental boats.

"On me," smiled Jorge as he whipped out his wallet and handed Susan a twenty-dollar bill. "It's only ten dollars for an hour, even if you do come back sooner."

"And the pedal boats are fifteen dollars an hour?" questioned Susan as she studied the sign again. "A rowboat will do."

"What about you and Damien?" questioned Carolyn. "Aren't you guys going to come with us?"

"We'll just watch," flirted Damien, anxious to see whether Susan would be successful in her attempts to sink the tiny rowboat once it was out in the middle.

Susan flirted shamelessly with the boat tender as she handed him the twenty-dollar bill from Jorge, and then grinned at him like a Cheshire cat while he nervously fumbled to pull out and hand her a ten-dollar bill in change. Susan often had that effect upon men and thoroughly enjoyed it.

Susan then hurried down the wooden boat dock to the nearest rowboat and climbed inside. "Come on!"

The boat tender mindlessly handed a set of boat oars to Carolyn without taking his eyes off of Susan the entire time.

"Thanks," mumbled Carolyn as she grabbed the oars out of his hands and hurried after Susan.

"You row the boat while I rock it," directed Susan with a mischievous smile as Carolyn untied the small rowboat from its dock to climb inside.

"You are kidding, of course?" snickered Carolyn as she tossed in the boat's mooring line, climbed in, sat down, positioned the oars, and began to row.

"Hey, where's your life jackets?" called Damien.

"They're okay," chuckled Jorge. "We're right here."

Susan then laughed with merriment as she placed one hand on either side of the boat, and began leaning from side to side in a rhythmic manner. In no time, the small boat began rocking from side to side along with her.

"Susan!" objected Carolyn. "What are you doing?"

Susan suddenly began singing a popular song of the day about rocking the boat and then did her very best to try and get the small rowboat to rock even more than it already was! Jorge and Damien were seated on a bench feeding ducks while they watched, unable to keep from laughing when they saw what Susan was trying to do.

"Are you crazy?" shouted Carolyn. "Stop it!"

Susan merely ignored Carolyn and continued singing and doing her utmost to try and tip the tiny boat over.

"I know the sign claimed their boats are unsinkable, but this is ridiculous!" screamed Carolyn. "You'd better stop right now, or this boat ride is officially over! I have no intention of falling into that slimy green water and getting my clothes all wet!"

Susan began to laugh uncontrollably, thoroughly amused by the expression on Carolyn's face.

"All right, that's it, then!" pronounced Carolyn. "We're going back right now!"

It became quite difficult for Carolyn to row the boat with Susan persistently rocking it. Still, Susan continued to sing and howled with glee while she observed Carolyn's efforts. Nevertheless, Carolyn managed somehow to make it back to shore in record time. Jorge and Damien were both laughing so hard they could hardly breathe. Even the boat tender was amused by the whole affair, and watched anxiously to see what would happen. Part of him hoped that the attractive singing girl would succeed in swamping the small rowboat so he might have an opportunity to swim out and rescue her.

"Let's get out of here!" insisted Carolyn, thoroughly embarrassed by the entire situation.

"Did you see the look on that guy's face?" howled Damien. "That was great!"

"Who, the boat tender?" laughed Susan, trying to appear demure about it. "You didn't really think I'd tip the boat over did you?"

"We're just lucky you didn't succeed!" snapped Carolyn, still quite upset by the close call.

"I don't believe for one minute that she would have done it," smiled Jorge. "Madam Susan would never want to go swimming in that green slimy water."

"Exactly!" smirked Susan. "I was just trying to help cheer you up, Miss Carolina la Gata. You know, to get your mind off of old what's his name?"

"What's his name?" questioned Damien, curious to find out, though no one bothered to tell him.

"I guess you probably wouldn't have wanted to go swimming in there any more than I would have," realized Carolyn, finally starting to see the humor in it.

Though Carolyn tried her best not to laugh along with them, the merriment was just too contagious and soon all four of them were laughing uncontrollably as they made their way to the conservatory where they planned to eat lunch at its lush garden restaurant.

Susan suddenly put her arm through Jorge's and rested her head on his upper arm while they walked toward the restaurant.

"Shall we?" offered Damien as he held out his arm to Carolyn.

"After you," smiled Carolyn as she motioned for Damien to go ahead. She had no intention of bending down to lock arms with a guy that was only five feet five inches tall!

"Hey, come on!" urged Susan as she grabbed Carolyn's arm to try and pull her back up. "You've been looking at that same painting for almost twenty minutes already! There's three more floors to see before the museum closes and it's already after three o'clock."

"You go ahead," indicated Carolyn. She was spellbound by the huge Renaissance style oil painting and was sitting on a marble bench in front of the masterpiece to study it more closely.

"It does have a lot of detail," noticed Damien as he sat down beside Carolyn.

"Nice use of color, too," approved Jorge as he sat down on the other side of Carolyn.

"You guys!" Susan sighed with frustration.

"No, really," commented Jorge. "Take a look at this painting. The bright red jacket with tails on it that he's wearing really draws your eye to the guy kneeling at the young maiden's feet. And nice contrast with the green foliage in the background. They must be in an English garden somewhere."

"But see how she's shoving him away with one arm and clinging to her mother with the other?" snickered Susan. She had come closer to get a better look at the painting herself and was standing behind the bench with her hands on her hips, looking over the tops of their heads at it.

"I like his pony tail," remarked Damien. "It shows that he took the time to get cleaned up before he went to see her. How often do you ever see a clean shaven guy with a pony tail?"

"Jorge is clean shaven, and could probably manage to get his hair into a pony tail if he tried," teased Susan.

"I kind of like it hanging down, the way it is," chuckled Jorge as he ran one hand through his dark wavy, shoulder length hair.

"Just look at the stunning baby blue gown the young woman has on," pointed out Carolyn, transfixed by the resemblance it had to the very dress her parents had purchased for her to wear to the upcoming Harvest Festival Prom next weekend.

Susan suddenly nodded with understanding. No wonder Carolyn was so drawn to the painting. "I like the elegant yellow gown her mother has on. It bears a remarkable similarity to the one Carolyn's father bought for ME to wear to the prom next weekend."

"I was wondering when you'd notice," smiled Carolyn.

"Perhaps it's a sign!" speculated Jorge as he gave Susan a sidelong glance and a sly wink.

"I like the low necklines they wore back then," grinned Damien. "Very nice!"

"Oh, you!" chided Susan as she playfully slapped her little brother on the arm. "We really do need to get going if we are going to see anything else. The Egyptian display is up on the third floor."

"I really would like to see that, too," realized Carolyn as she got up to follow after Susan.

"After that, we'll be going to Jorge's house for dinner," revealed Susan with a mysterious grin.

"We just had lunch at the conservatory only two hours ago," reminded Carolyn. "And thank you very much, Jorge, for the delicious cobb salad. I've never had anything quite like it."

"My pleasure," nodded Jorge.

Not only was Jorge twenty-eight years of age, but he was also six feet two inches tall. His Italian features, dark shoulder length hair, handsome face and tall trim physique were frequently noticed by those around him. So, in spite of their difference in age and size, Jorge and Susan did make a striking couple.

"Jorge's mother is a fantastic cook!" informed Susan. "She's been slaving all day to make us an authentic Italian dinner for tonight."

"Really?" Carolyn was surprised. She had assumed they would be returning to Susan's house for dinner that night. In fact, Carolyn was certain she had overheard Susan's mother telling Damien that she would be making home-made lasagna for the occasion.

As if reading her thoughts, Damien whispered, "We can always have the lasagna later. Susan called our mother a little while ago to let her know we'd be eating at Jorge's house tonight."

"You knew I was there on the staircase this morning?" questioned Carolyn as she turned to give Damien a curious glance.

"Of course," smirked Damien. "You'd be surprised what I know, for a fifteen-year-old, that is."

Carolyn silently wondered if Damien had overheard the conversation between her and Susan the night before, but decided to say nothing more about it.

Jorge's bright yellow sports car slowed as it reached the very outskirts of Ocean Bay. A meandering hillside district of expensive villas with spacious yards could be seen below. These were definitely not Painted Ladies and most certainly were not connected. It was clearly a neighborhood for the very well-to-do. The winding road they were ascending began to climb through a hillside vineyard to an extravagant villa and matching winery at the very top. Views of the entire city and the bayside harbor below were unparalleled. The outlines of various boats and ships were reflected in the bay water below against the setting sun.

The entire west-facing slope on the steep hill had long since been denuded of its ancient old growth forest, to make room for the various varieties of grapes in the huge vineyard now growing down its side. What was left of the tall conifers and other deciduous trees surrounding them remained only on the east facing slope in the background.

"Moranga Vineyards," read the arched wooden sign. Its hand crafted lettering had been etched into the wooden sign with a special burning tool. The sign itself was carefully mounted on top of an arch shaped opening in a wrought iron trellis to which well-manicured grape vines clung.

"He's Jorge Moranga, by the way," Susan mentioned to Carolyn with a nod of her head as they drove through the opening.

Jorge rolled his eyes and shook his head in response.

"It's not Jorge's fault his parents happen to own the most prestigious parcel of land in Ocean Bay," added Susan for effect.

"Not to mention the winery!" grinned Damien.

"Well, we won't have time for a tour of the winery tonight anyway, not if we're gonna make it out of here in time for the concert," reminded Jorge. He had forgotten completely about his promise to keep Susan's evening plans a secret until she was ready to reveal them.

"Jorge!" chided Susan. "It was going to be a surprise!"

"A concert?" questioned Carolyn with concern. "I didn't bring a dress with me at all! What would I wear?"

"Relax," advised Damien. "It's not that kind of a concert."

"What kind of a concert is it?" puzzled Carolyn as Jorge pulled up in front of the hilltop villa where he lived with his parents.

"Welcome to our humble home," grinned Jorge as he got out and opened Carolyn's door first before going around the small yellow sports car to open Susan's door for her.

The sand colored brickwork on the villa and winery were identical in shape, size and layout pattern, as were their red tile roofs. A fifty-foot long corridor connecting the winery to the house was held up by wrought iron posts, and the corridor's roof of red tiles matched those on the villa and winery exactly. On either side of the connecting walkway was a waist-high wrought iron trellis on which more of the highly manicured grape vines were trained to grow, with access openings on either side at intermittent locations that led to connecting walkways into a huge rose garden where two white marble benches were strategically placed to enjoy it. An aging sundial stood in the midst of the rose garden that had been brought over from the old country when the Moranga family had first come to Ocean Bay three generations earlier. A solitary oak tree had been left near the garden benches to provide shade when necessary on hot sunny days.

Behind the winery was a large parking area, where its full-time staff would park on weekdays when the winery was actually open. It included ample room for visitors as well as seasonal workers and additional staff during harvest season, which was currently underway. Several partially filled wooden boxes of grapes could be seen stacked near the various rows of grapes that were currently being picked, where workers would resume harvesting on Monday morning. Jorge had tried in vain to persuade his parents to keep the winery doors open on weekends during this critical time, especially on the production end of it, but had met with such resistance that he'd finally given up.

The front entryway courtyard of the villa itself was surrounded by a four-foot high wrought iron fence on which yet another variety of carefully maintained grape vines grew. A marble fountain in the middle of the courtyard was graced with a half nude maiden holding a large decanter from which water actually flowed out and into the pool below her. The water would then recycle itself back up through the statue and into the container for another round. Carefully placed accent lights were mounted at ground level around the base of the statue that pointed to it from three different angles. The lights themselves were equipped with automatic sensors that would come on when they detected an insufficient level of light. Since it was dusk already, the lights just happened to come on as they approached.

Carolyn was speechless as she followed Jorge, Susan and Damien through the courtyard and into the Moranga home.

"Jorge?" called his mother from the next room.

"Mama!" answered Jorge. "Sei pronta per noi?"

A short, pleasantly plump Italian woman suddenly emerged from the kitchen and approached.

"She only knows enough English to get by," explained Jorge to Carolyn. "But, she often understands more than she lets on."

"Quanto tempo è necessario prima che sia necessario fretta fuori di nuovo?" asked Mrs. Moranga.

"Mama wants to know how long we have before we have to take off again, to go to the concert," translated Jorge.

"That's what I'd like to know," interjected Carolyn. "And, Damien was just about to tell me what kind of a concert it is when we pulled up out front."

Susan shook her head ever so slightly and gave Jorge a warning glance.

"I think Madam Susan wants that part to be a surprise, too," smiled Jorge. "Please, follow me."

"Attendere! Potete andare svegliare tuo padre e lui ruota in qui, per favore?" asked Mrs. Moranga, with a pleading look as she put her hands on her son's arm and looked up at him. "È diventata dificile per lui per far funzionare la sedia a rotelle da se stesso."

"Mama would like all of you to follow her to the kitchen while I go get Papa," directed Jorge.

"Why does he have to go get him?" Carolyn whispered to Susan. "What's wrong with him?"

"He's just really old," replied Susan matter-of-factly. "He's been in a wheelchair for as long as I can remember."

"Isn't he almost a hundred?" asked Damien.

"I think he is," confirmed Susan as they followed after Jorge's mother to the kitchen. "And he speaks no English at all."

The surprising old world simplicity of the villa's inner sanctum was an unexpected contrast to its lavish exterior grounds and modern entryway. The well maintained antique furniture and hardwood floors made the visitors feel as if they just had stepped back in time. There was no television, no phone, no microwave, nor any other modern appliances anywhere that they could see. All interior lighting was accomplished exclusively with oil lamps and candles. The wood burning Wedgwood stove in the adjoining kitchen sat beside a freestanding, solid wood prep table where Mrs. Moranga had just placed a homemade loaf of whole wheat bread to cool.

"It smells wonderful!" smiled Susan as she nodded toward the delicious smelling bread.

"Grazie!" beamed Jorge's mama.

"What does she do for a refrigerator?" inquired Carolyn, worried that some of the food might be unsafe to eat.

"The refrigerator is out in the winery," informed Jorge as he entered the kitchen with his Papa and pushed his wheelchair up to the large wooden dining table near an exterior window. "Modern contrivances just upset Papa, anyway, so we've tried to do everything we can to make him feel like he's still in the old county."

"But he's so senile he doesn't know the difference!" Susan laughed but immediately became serious after a disapproving glance from Jorge.

"È vero, lui non ricordo nemmeno chi lui è la metà del tempo." Mrs. Moranga merely shrugged her shoulders and shook her head. "Non preoccuparti."

"I'm so sorry," apologized Susan. She had forgotten that Jorge's Mama often understood everything that was being said, even though she was unable to speak much English in return.

"Nice view," noticed Carolyn as she glanced out the picture window by the dining table and realized she could see the entire bay below. "Just look at all the lights down there, that's amazing!"

"Le insalate e il burro sono fuori in cantina," indicated Jorge's Mama. "Si può andare da loro, per favore?"

"Mama would like me to go get the salad, butter and other perishable items from the refrigerator," grinned Jorge. "Everything's over at the winery. Damien, would you and Carolyn like to come help me carry it all back?"

"I'll stay and help Mama set the table," offered Susan.

"Grazie!" smiled Jorge's Mama as she walked over to an antique hutch, opened its front doors, removed a small stack of dishes, and handed them to Susan.

"My parents did not have me until they were pretty well up in years," explained Jorge as he walked with Damien and Carolyn over to the winery.

"Do you have any brothers and sisters?" questioned Carolyn.

"I'm it," grinned Jorge as they entered the modern looking facility.

"Wow!" marveled Carolyn as she noticed the drastic contrast between the winery and the villa they had just come from.

"I oversee the winery and the grounds, while Mama maintains the villa," grinned Jorge. "Just the inside, of course."

"You oversee all of this and the winery, too?" questioned Carolyn with amazement.

"With lots of help," chuckled Jorge. "Everything is delegated. We employ a full-time staff of permanent employees that includes an office manager, a production manager, a wine grower, an official taster, a public relations and sales representative, a marketing manager, and an assistant manager who is responsible for coordinating tours and maintaining the tasting room for guests."

"Isn't it harvest season right now?" inquired Carolyn. She suddenly recalled seeing the various half picked wooden boxes of grapes down by the vineyard. "Where is everyone? Wouldn't you normally be open during the weekends this time of year?"

"Yes, it is harvest season," verified Jorge with a deep sigh. "However, my parents insist that the place be shut down on the weekends so its employees can spend time with their families. That's the way Papa said it's always been and will be, for as long as he's alive. And Papa doesn't take very well to change."

"Is your Papa really almost a hundred?" asked Damien.

"He'll be ninety-eight this year," replied Jorge as he opened the modern refrigerator, removed and handed a huge ceramic bowl of fresh salad to Carolyn. It was actually quite heavy.

"How old is your mother?" quizzed Carolyn as she took the bowl from him. "She seems quite a bit younger."

"Oh, she is," chuckled Jorge as he handed a ceramic butter dish and an unmarked glass bottle of salad dressing to Damien. "Women marry quite young in the old country. Mama was only twelve."

Damien and Carolyn both looked shocked by the revelation.

"They tell me Papa was about my age when he whisked her away," added Jorge. "Naturally, they both were relieved when Susan and I told them we were betrothed. Especially since they have no one else to follow in their footsteps or to keep the winery going."

"But you're not actually betrothed, are you?" pressed Carolyn as Jorge picked up a huge platter of deviled eggs, olives, pickles and slices of celery filled with peanut butter.

"You never know," Jorge smiled a crooked grin. "Perhaps someday we could be."

Jorge, Damien and Carolyn walked in silence down the covered walkway from the winery to the main villa as they carried the perishable food items inside and to the large family dining table.

"Mangiamo, muoio di fame!" directed Jorge's Papa. "Vieni su, sedersi!"

While they had been gone, Susan and Mrs. Moranga had finished setting the table with plates, silverware, water glasses, cloth napkins, and serving spoons that sat ready to use in the huge salad and other new arrivals to the table. The homemade whole wheat bread had been sliced and was sitting in an oblong ceramic bread dish, covered with a cloth napkin to keep it warm. In the center of the table was a whole baked chicken on a ceramic platter that had been slowly cooked in the wood burning stove to perfection. None of the ceramic serving dishes had any designs on them but all appeared to be handcrafted and were simple beige in color.

"Dobbiamo modo preghiera prima!" insisted Mrs. Moranga.

"She wants us to pray first," interpreted Jorge.

"Si prega," indicated Mr. Moranga as he motioned at Jorge. "In modo che io possa capire che si."

"Okay," agreed Jorge. "Caro Signore, grazie per questo cibo che stiamo per prendere. Siamo grati per la vostra bontà e questa volta abbiamo insieme. Amen."

"Amen!" smiled Jorge's aging father as he grabbed a piece of bread and began eating it as if he were famished.

"Non vuoi un po' di burro?" questioned his wife. "È stato appena fatto oggi."

"Mama, non va bene per lui, comunque," pointed out Jorge. "Lascialo."

Jorge then turned to the others to repeat what had been said in English so they could understand. "She's trying to get him to eat the butter. She says she just made it today. I told her it's not good for him, to just leave him be."

"She makes her own butter, too?" Carolyn raised an eyebrow.

"Sì, lo faccio," Mrs. Moranga confirmed with pride as she handed the butter dish to Carolyn.

"Chi è la tua amica?" asked Mr. Moranga as he nodded at Carolyn, curious to know more about her.

"Carolyn e Susan erano coinquilini, quando essi sono state alla scuola," replied Jorge. "I told him you were roommates when you used to be in school."

"When we used to be in school?" queried Susan.

"Yes, back when you used to be in school," Jorge repeated again. "You know, before we became betrothed?"

"Oh yes," smiled Susan, suddenly nodding with understanding. Naturally Jorge could not mention to his parents that she and Carolyn were currently roommates in a boarding school two hours away.

"Susan era una graziosa sposa," reminisced Mr. Moranga, believing that his demented memory of Jorge and Susan's wedding was real. "Vieni qui, mia figlia e dare tua papà un abbraccio prima di andare. Mama mi dice che si andante ad un concerto? Mi unisco a voi, ma per questa stupida sedia a rotelle!"

"Papa wants you to give him a hug," Jorge indicated to Susan. "And he knows we need to get going pretty quickly in order to make it in time to the concert and only wishes he were not in a wheelchair so he could come with us."

"Aren't we going to sample any of the wine while we're here?" urged Damien.

"No, I'm afraid not," smiled Jorge, clearly amused by Damien's suggestion.

"Why not?" persisted Damien.

"Perché sei troppo giovane!" informed Mrs. Moranga.

"She's right, I'm afraid," grinned Jorge. "You are too young. The last thing I need tonight is to get arrested for contributing to the delinquency of three minors!"

"Who's a minor?" demanded Damien jokingly.

"You are, stupid!" reminded Susan as she popped him on the back of his head with her hand.

"So are you!" retorted Damien with a mock frown.

"Immagino sia stato vale la pena di provare, eh?" laughed Jorge's Mama, well aware of everything that had been said.

"Mama says it was worth a try," laughed Jorge.

"None for me, thanks!" remarked Carolyn as she wrinkled up her nose. "Even if I were of age, I'd never wanna drink something that smells like that!" Carolyn had smelled the odor of wine before when walking past an outdoor beer garden at the fair one year, and had found the odor most offensive.

"È sicuro che sembrano essere godendo la tua insalata," smiled Jorge's Mama as she watched Carolyn eating her salad. "In particolare il vino rosso vinaigrette dressing."

"Mama says she's glad you are enjoying the salad," translated Jorge. "Especially the red wine dressing."

"You're kidding?" Carolyn was stunned.

"Don't worry, we won't tell anyone," razzed Susan.

"You don't feel any different, do you?" poked Damien.

"No, of course not!" Carolyn was indignant at first but then smiled, quickly seeing the humor in it.

"Contento che ti è piaciuta," nodded Mrs. Moranga. "Abbiamo sicuramente non vorrebbe mio figlio per essere arrestato per il recupero dei minori in stato di ebbrezza."

"Qui, qui!" agreed Mr. Moranga as he raised his glass of water and then took a drink.

The others then lifted their glasses and did likewise.

After finishing the rest of her meal, Susan finally got up and came over to give Jorge's father a big hug. "I wish we didn't have to leave so soon."

"Questa è la mia ragazza!" beamed Mr. Moranga.

"Perhaps he could come with us," suggested Carolyn, who was just consuming the remainder of her salad, including the delicious dressing. "It might do him some good to get out once in a while."

"Ah, not for this kind of concert," commented Susan. "It's outdoors and would be much too chilly for him at his age."

"Egli probabilmente addormentarsi prima ancora arrivati," added Jorge's Mama with a grin.

"She understands everything we say, and agrees that it would definitely be too chilly for him at his age," chuckled Jorge with amusement. "Thank you for a lovely meal, Mama."

"Sei il benvenuto, mio figlio," responded Mrs. Moranga as she gave Jorge a warm hug. Then, turning to Susan, Carolyn and Damien, Jorge's mother spoke in English, "Please return soon!"

214

"Thanks, we will," agreed Susan as she hugged each of Jorge's parents before heading for the door.

"Thank you," smiled Carolyn as she hugged each of them, as well, before following after Susan.

"Arrivederci," nodded Damien before leaving.

"Ciao," bid Jorge as he hugged each of his parents before leaving. "Meravigliosa pasta, Mama. Tornerò più tardi stasera per ripulire i piatti, Mama. Basta lasciare loro per me."

Meanwhile, back at Oceanview Academy, Lenny and his cousin Pete were just finishing up a dinner of fake hamburger and fries. "I sure hope they serve something better than this at the prom next week," said Pete.

"You and me both," agreed Lenny.

"Hey, it's the red headed wonder himself," pointed out Pete sarcastically as he saw Jim Otterman getting up from a nearby table.

"We'd better get back to our room before curfew," urged Lenny, not anxious to run into the likes of Jim Otterman. Lenny was well aware of Jim's attempts to try and force his attentions upon Carolyn, but was in no mood to confront him about it right then.

"I guess you're right. Carolyn or Susan would have shown up by now if they were planning to be here," nodded Pete.

"Come to think of it, I didn't see them this morning or last night, either," realized Lenny. "I wonder what's going on?"

"What if they got themselves into trouble again?" asked Pete.

"I sure hope not," replied Lenny. He was beginning to worry about why he had not seen them.

Lenny had remained at the cafeteria until closing time in the hope that Carolyn might show up for the evening meal so he could have the opportunity to finally ask her to the prom.

"Actually, you never know what kind of trouble Susan or Carolyn could get themselves into," came the voice of Jim Otterman from behind them as he stopped by their table on his way to the tray return area. "There's all sorts of things to do up in Ocean Bay."

"Hold it! Just what do you mean by that?" demanded Pete suspiciously as he grabbed the back of Jim Otterman's jacket to prevent him from leaving and easily pulled him back.

Luckily for Pete, any remaining cafeteria workers were currently in the back washing dishes. Everyone else had already left and returned to their respective dormitories for the night.

Lenny glanced quickly toward the kitchen door to be sure no one in the back had noticed what was going on out in the dining area.

"Well?" pressed Pete. He maintained his grasp on Jim's jacket while he waited for him to respond.

"Susan told me. She's in my biology class," grinned Jim smugly. "She just happened to mention that she and Carolyn would be staying with her parents this weekend."

"Just why would she tell the likes of you?" demanded Lenny, suddenly interested in what Jim might know.

"Susan tells me lots of things," smirked Jim. "Like the fact that Carolyn doesn't have a date for the prom yet."

"Really? Are you sure about that?" Lenny slowly stood for the express purpose of intimidating Jim Otterman while he glared down at him with disgust. Lenny, of course, was six feet five inches tall, while slouchy Jim Otterman appeared shorter than the five feet eight inches he was due to his poor posture. If Jim was afraid, he didn't show it.

"I take it they didn't tell you they were going to be gone for the weekend?" sneered Jim. "You should have seen the good-looking, long haired Italian guy who picked them up yesterday afternoon in a bright yellow sports car! Right in front of the girls' dorm, too! Good thing Dean Dixon wasn't around when they left. Sure would be a shame if she ever found out."

"Was that a threat?" interjected Pete, who still had a grip on Jim's jacket. Pete was more than ready to slam Jim Otterman's face into his tray at that point, even if Lenny wouldn't.

"Guess that depends on how you wanna take it," replied Jim with an even grin.

"One of these days...," muttered Lenny as he scowled at Jim while clenching and unclenching his fists.

"One of these days, what?" scoffed Jim. "You might ask Carolyn to the prom? Seems to me like you would have done that already if you were going to."

Pete, who still had a decent hold on Jim Otterman's jacket, unexpectedly grabbed Jim's tray with his other hand and set it down on the table before he suddenly yanked Jim close. Pete had pulled Jim Otterman so close, in fact, that their noses were nearly touching.

216

"What are you gonna do? Beat me up?" Jim put on a good front and tried to appear unconcerned, but his fear was beginning to show. Fortunately for both Lenny and Pete, the cafeteria workers were still in the back, and no one had yet come out.

"He's not even worth it," cautioned Lenny, who gently but firmly removed Pete's hand from Jim's jacket. Lenny then shook his head ever so slightly with disapproval at Pete.

"I think you'd better leave now," Lenny advised Jim as he picked up and handed his tray back to him.

"Carolyn will be going to the prom with me!" sneered Jim Otterman as he swaggered away. "You just wait and see."

"You certainly aren't gonna let him get away with that, are you?" demanded Pete. He was angry now and wanted nothing more than to teach Jim Otterman a good lesson!

"This isn't the right time or place for it," advised Lenny as he watched Jim Otterman leave. "Have you forgotten how angry Dad was after the beach incident?"

"He was pretty upset," agreed Pete.

"I'm not even supposed to see Carolyn again, or have anything more to do with her, as far as he's concerned," reminded Lenny. "The last thing I need is you causing some big scene that's going to get us into trouble again! Dean Vandevere would call him for sure."

"Hey, I'm sorry, man," apologized Pete. "I wasn't thinking."

"Well, think about this," added Lenny as he picked up his tray to leave, "Dad already threatened to pull the plug on our tuition if we did anything else after the beach incident."

"No one saw anything," assured Pete as he snatched up his tray to leave. "They're all still in the back."

"Good thing, too! You do realize, don't you, that they don't offer the kind of classes I need back home to get me into pre-med?" interrogated Lenny as they walked toward the tray return area.

"Not in our neighborhood," recognized Pete. "Plus, Carolyn wouldn't be there, either."

"Well, it really would have been nice to know they were going away for the weekend," remarked Lenny as they reached the tray return area. "That way, I could have been finishing up my chemistry assignment instead of waiting around here all evening for nothing!" Lenny was also irritated by the fact that Jim Otterman had known that Susan and Carolyn would be out of town when he hadn't.

"They'll have to be back by Monday for their jobs," reminded Pete. "Perhaps Carolyn just didn't have a chance to tell you first."

"So, after all this, what if Carolyn really doesn't want to go to the Harvest Festival Prom with me?" questioned Lenny.

"Oh, she does," grinned Pete. "Trust me, she does!"

"You don't think Jim Otterman would try to blackmail her into going to the prom with him, do you?" worried Lenny as he and Pete exited the cafeteria and headed toward the boys' dormitory.

"Because of the sports car thing?" pondered Pete. "It's hard to say what Jim Otterman might do, but you just need to make sure you ask her first."

"That's the plan," advised Lenny.

"What we need is some leverage," decided Pete.

"Leverage?" frowned Lenny.

"We get something on him," recommended Pete. "Then, he can't say anything about the sports car."

"Good luck with that!" snorted Lenny as they reached the boys' dormitory and began climbing its steps.

Jorge Moranga had just dropped Susan, Carolyn and Damien off at the front steps to the Ocean Bay Coliseum and had gone to park his small yellow sports car.

"I told you it was outdoors!" grinned Susan.

"But, this looks like a rock concert!" Carolyn was indignant about it. "We can't go in there!"

"Sure we can," laughed Susan as they waited for Jorge.

"It'll be fun!" promised Damien. He was looking forward to seeing the Doobie Brothers, a new rock group that was making their first appearance in the Ocean Bay area.

Located just past the eastern edge of the city, the open air Ocean Bay Coliseum boasted a seating capacity of over 12,000 people. Open year round, the staggered seating areas surrounding it were equipped with huge awnings to keep spectators protected from rain and sun alike. Musical concerts and theatrical performances were normally conducted during dry weather, like now. Still, the onset of fall brought with it increased wind during the evening hours.

Built in a natural meadow at the edge of a rugged mountain range beyond it, the Ocean Bay Coliseum and its large parking area were surrounded almost exclusively by an old growth forest.

Naturally, no views could be had from there of the ocean or the bay from which the city of Ocean Bay had derived its name.

Two tall Corinthian style columns with highly ornate capitals depicting acanthus leaves stood on either side of the Ocean Bay Coliseum's huge entrance gate, intended to give it a Roman look. A small windowed ticket booth was located in the very center of its entryway, decorated on top with several strategically placed acanthus leaves matching those on the capitals of the columns nearby. The opening on one side of the booth was reserved for incoming human traffic only, while the opposite opening was used exclusively for those exiting the facility. There were, of course, emergency exits placed wherever necessary as required by law throughout the stadium.

"We already have tickets," informed Susan, "but we still better get in line so we can get in before it starts."

"There's certainly a lot of people in line already." Carolyn shook her head with disapproval at the motley looking bunch.

"Good thing you didn't wear your new blue evening gown!" pointed out Susan with a crooked smile.

Carolyn merely glared at Susan with disapproval. Perhaps coming here had been a mistake, after all. "We could get in all kinds of trouble if anyone found out we went to a rock concert!"

"Hey, my parents are fine with it," promised Susan. "You'll enjoy it. Trust me!"

That old familiar phrase was quickly losing its veracity with Carolyn, who rolled her eyes at hearing it, yet again. "Trust you?"

"She does say that a lot, doesn't she?" grinned Jorge as he joined them.

"If your parents are fine with us being here, then why aren't they with us?" challenged Carolyn.

"My dad hates rock music," replied Susan with a grin.

"You got that right!" chuckled Damien as all of them got into line to wait for their turn to enter.

Carolyn and Susan were each dressed in bell bottom blue jeans and wore tall platform style sandals. Carolyn wore a red pullover top with a matching black cotton blazer that had red cuffs and a red collar. Susan had on a light blue satin blazer over a white silk top, one she would never have gotten away with wearing at Oceanview Academy because it was cut way too low in the front. Carolyn's purse was made entirely of hand tooled leather that had leather fringe dangling from its bottom edge, while Susan's purse was made of blue denim that had strips of blue denim hanging from its covering flap.

Fringe was quite popular in 1972. In fact, many of the other concertgoers were also wearing fringe, some in the form of leather jackets with fringe dangling from their sleeves and bodices, and others with fringe hanging down from the tops of high heeled gogo boots. Some of the women wore miniskirts. Nearly everyone there wore blue jeans and would have been considered in blatant violation of Oceanview Academy's strict dress code policy against them. Some concert attendees wore skintight black leather pants.

Most of the men and boys there wore their hair shoulder length or longer, many of them pulled back into ponytails. Some had bandanas tied around their foreheads to keep stray hairs out of their faces. Jorge and Damien each wore blue jeans and black leather jackets with fringe over dark colored t-shirts.

"Are you sure you ladies will be warm enough? Those blazers don't look very warm," commented Jorge.

"If we're not, then we may just borrow your nice warm jackets," teased Susan.

Their reserved seats turned out to be in the second row, right in the front center section. Jorge had connections, of course, and made sure their seats were the best available.

Once the band began playing, the music became so loud that the vibrations of it could be felt in the very ground beneath their feet! Even worse, a cloud of sweet smelling smoke suddenly seemed to envelop the entire audience as many of its members lit up and began to smoke what looked like hand-rolled cigarettes.

Carolyn's headache became unbearable from the loud noise and her eyes began to burn from the continuous cloud of smoke. "I don't feel well," Carolyn shouted so Susan could hear her.

"What?" yelled Susan, even though she was right next to her.

"I need to get some fresh air!" screamed Carolyn, right in Susan's ear. "A pair of ear plugs wouldn't hurt anything, either!"

"Right after this next song," promised Susan.

"Listen to the music," smiled Jorge as he stood to applaud.

"Kind of hard not to do!" shouted Carolyn, unsure if Jorge could even hear her.

"That's the name of the song," explained Damien as he, too, stood to applaud. *"Listen to the Music."*

220

"I am listening to the music!" replied Carolyn.

"*Listen to the Music* is the name of the song," chuckled Susan, who also had stood to clap. "This is the one where the drummer tosses out maracas to the crowd."

"Maracas?" Carolyn had never heard of them.

"Souvenirs!" clarified Susan. "You'll have a better chance of snagging some if you stand up."

Realizing that everyone else was already standing, Carolyn finally stood up. Unexpectedly, the drummer - who was occasionally tossing maracas out to the audience - made eye contact with Carolyn and smiled flirtatiously. Carolyn glanced behind her to make sure he wasn't looking at someone else. Amused by her reaction, the drummer suddenly tossed the maracas to Carolyn.

"Get 'em!" screamed Susan. "Get 'em!"

Carolyn leaped up and attempted to grab at least one of the maracas, but the couple behind her had been standing on their seats and nearly knocked Carolyn down when they snatched them away.

"Hey!" hollered Susan as she turned around to confront them but immediately changed her mind upon seeing them. They were a rather rough looking pair, and thankfully Susan had sense to realize it.

"I did have my hand on one of the maracas," Carolyn informed Susan, "but that guy behind me just grabbed it away."

"Better let him keep it. Maybe the drummer will throw another pair this way," hoped Susan.

The song ended without any more maracas being tossed to the crowd. The drummer then smiled and shrugged his shoulders at Carolyn as he reached down to pick up a small empty box by his feet and tipped it to show that nothing else was inside.

"That's it then," realized Carolyn. "Can we please go to the ladies' room now?"

"Yeah, I have to go, too," agreed Susan. Susan then let Jorge know that she and Carolyn were planning to use the restroom.

"Let's all go," agreed Jorge. "Come on!"

Damien glanced up and saw Jorge leaving with Carolyn and Susan, so he got up to follow them.

"Whew!" Carolyn took a deep breath and then slowly let it out when they reached the opposite end of the coliseum where the restrooms were located near its entrance. "At least there's not as much smoke over here!"

"Plus, it's just way too loud where we were," added Susan. "The music's still loud from here."

"Where's Damien?" questioned Jorge as he arrived at their location. They all glanced in every possible direction, but Damien was nowhere to be seen.

"Let's use the restroom and then meet back here," suggested Susan. "That's probably where he is right now, anyway."

"Okay," agreed Jorge, though he had a bad feeling about it.

After meeting back at their agreed upon rendezvous point, Damien was still nowhere to be seen.

"We've got to find him!" Susan became frantic. "If we're not home by midnight, my dad will kill us!"

"I doubt he'd actually kill you," assured Jorge, "but we do need to find Damien."

"Hey, Jorge!" greeted a tall young man dressed entirely in matching beige leather decorated with beads and fringe. He was about thirty years old, thin, and had a strip of beige leather tied around his forehead to prevent his long blonde hair from falling into his face.

"Steve!" recognized Jorge. "How the heck are you?"

The two men briefly embraced and slapped one another on the back. "And who do we have here?" Steve flirted with Susan.

"This is Susan, my fiancé," informed Jorge with a smug look.

"Wow! Okay, then," nodded Steve. "And who's this?"

"This is her friend, Carolyn," introduced Jorge. "Right now, though, we seem to have misplaced Susan's brother Damien."

"Have you tried the beer garden?" asked Steve.

"Beer garden?" scowled Susan.

"Down on the other side of the podium in the middle," indicated Steve.

"Damien wouldn't be down there," objected Susan.

"It's the only place we haven't looked," advised Jorge.

"We just have to be home by midnight!" reminded Susan.

"Curfew?" teased Steve.

"Actually, yes," confirmed Susan. She was in no mood to play games. "If we're not home by midnight, my dad will lock us out."

"He wouldn't do that, would he?" questioned Carolyn.

"I'm afraid he might," agreed Jorge. "To teach her a lesson. Susan's father is very strict about curfew."

"Never fear, Steve is here," advised Jorge's friend Steve. "Where do you live? I can take you ladies home and then come back to help Jorge find, ah, what's his name?"

"Damien," reminded Susan.

"Hey, I do have to be back by the time they finish up," explained Steve. "I'm a roadie for the band. But, if you don't mind leaving early, there should be just enough time to get you there and be back to help Jorge look for Damien. Provided, of course, that you live somewhere in the city."

Jorge turned to Susan. "Do you mind?"

"Ah, sure, why not," agreed Susan. "Yeah, we live over in the Painted Lady district."

"I know right where that is. This way, ladies," indicated Steve as he bowed and motioned with one arm for them to go first.

"How well does Jorge know this guy?" Carolyn whispered to Susan as they began to walk toward the exit door leading to the parking lot.

"I have no idea," shrugged Susan.

"Is this where you're gonna tell me to trust you?" Carolyn was being sarcastic.

"Probably not this time," responded Susan. "But, I'm sure it will be okay. Jorge wouldn't let us go with this guy if he wasn't sure about him."

"Wait here, while I get my wheels," directed Steve. "I'll be right back."

"What time is it, anyway?" questioned Carolyn.

"Just a little after ten o'clock," replied Susan after checking her wristwatch. "We've got plenty of time."

"Maybe we should just call your parents now and let them know what's going on," suggested Carolyn. "It's not your fault he wandered off. I'm sure they would understand."

"You definitely don't know my dad," responded Susan. "It's best we do it this way. Trust me on that!"

Carolyn turned in time to see Steve pull up in a modified golf cart with a high powered racing engine and stared at it with disbelief.

"Ladies, your chariot awaits," grinned Steve. "Susan, is it?"

"Yeah," nodded Susan.

"Would you like to sit on the front seat by me, or on the back with your friend?" asked Steve.

"Definitely in the front," chose Susan. "I like to see where I'm going." The seats in the back were butted up back-against-back to the front seats and faced toward the rear, making it nearly impossible for whoever sat in them to see where they were headed without turning their head to see.

"At least I'll be able to see anyone who might be after us," commented Carolyn.

Steve thought that was quite funny and laughed. "Wait until you see what she can do!" Steve then revved up the engine and took off.

There were no seatbelts on the golf cart, though seat belts were generally not required in 1972 anyway. Thankfully, there were side handles for Carolyn to hang onto as they drove up the steep winding road that led back to the city of Ocean Bay.

"Look at all this traffic!" fretted Susan as they became trapped in a traffic jam that had brought the entire flow of traffic to a complete standstill. By now, Carolyn had already removed her sandals and was holding onto them with one hand, just to make sure they didn't fall off onto the road behind them.

"There seems to be some kind of an accident up there," noticed Carolyn as she turned and saw the lights from several emergency vehicles in the distance ahead of them.

"Not a problem," informed Steve as he suddenly turned his wheel and drove up onto the sidewalk beside them.

"What are you doing?" questioned Susan with alarm.

"Hang on!" advised Steve as he began negotiating the sidewalk, frequently sounding the loud air horn installed on his modified golf cart as needed. "We'll get you there in time!"

Frightened pedestrians could be seen leaping out of the way, but the shocked looks on their faces after Steve had passed were best seen from Carolyn's vantage point. Occasional sidewalk tables with chairs were bumped out of the way unintentionally, along with public trash receptacles beside them. Thankfully, no one appeared to be too seriously hurt that had been in the oncoming path of Steve's modified golf cart. Susan suddenly realized they were only a few blocks from her parents' home.

"Right over there!" indicated Susan.

"That's not it," mentioned Carolyn, thinking Susan might be confused in all the excitement.

"That's my house," pointed out Susan as they neared a peculiar looking church building. "My father's the preacher there."

"Oh, I see," nodded Steve. "No wonder he's so strict."

Carolyn started again to say something but saw Susan's warning glance. She realized at once that Susan was using the church story as an excuse to get away from Steve as quickly as possible. Not only that, Susan did not want someone like Steve to know where she actually lived. Just in case.

Once Steve had dropped them off, Susan and Carolyn quickly ran toward the old church.

"They're actually open?" questioned Carolyn as she sat on the building's front steps to put her sandals back on. "What kind of church is open this time of night? The writing looks oriental."

"I have no idea, but we'd better get inside before he decides to come back," instructed Susan as they waved goodbye to Steve and watched him drive off in his modified golf cart.

Originally built in 1900, the gothic style building they were about to enter had once been used by a local Protestant sect as its main place of worship. It was now being used by another group entirely. The entire three-story structure was painted bright red with black trim. Attached, but set back from it, was a Painted Lady style residence that was also painted red with black trim. Small black gargoyles sat menacingly around the base of the cathedral's tall spiraled steeples.

"I don't think we should go in there," advised Carolyn upon seeing the gargoyles.

"Greetings," came a voice from the front door. Neither of them had heard it open. The gentleman standing there wore bell bottom blue jeans with a brightly colored tie-dyed t-shirt and had a bright yellow strip of cloth tied around his forehead. His long black hair was neatly braided in back and came nearly to his waist. His beard was also quite long, braided into matching pigtails, and was almost as long as his hair. Though impossible to determine his nationality, he appeared to be an Asian American.

"Please, come in," encouraged the aging hippy, who wore no shoes. "You can leave your shoes over there."

"Actually, I just put 'em back on," explained Carolyn, not anxious to take her sandals off again.

"No shoes," insisted the hippy, almost apologetically.

"Thanks," nodded Susan as she took off her sandals and placed them on a shelf near the door where at least twenty other pairs of sandals and shoes already sat.

"Fine, all right," agreed Carolyn with a shrug of her shoulders as she did likewise.

"Nearly everyone is meditating already," indicated the hippy. "Are you hungry?" The hippy picked up a platter of brownies and offered them to Carolyn and Susan.

Carolyn had not realized until this very moment how very hungry she had suddenly become and started to reach for one.

"Hold it!" commanded Susan as she grabbed Carolyn's forearm to prevent her from taking one of the brownies. "It's probably laced with something."

"Of course it is!" laughed the hippy.

Grateful for Susan's intervention, Carolyn merely shook her head in the negative and said, "No thanks."

"Your choice," grinned the hippy as he set the brownies back down. "Just help yourself if you change your mind."

There was yet another chamber beyond the one in which they were currently standing, separated from it by continuous long rows of brightly colored beads that hung down to the floor.

Mediterranean looking wall hangings covered nearly every visible square inch of wall surface, while brightly colored squares of cloth hung from strings extended across the room's high vaulted ceiling above them. Most of the flags were adorned with images of birds, flowers or fish and had oriental looking writing on them. Burning candles and incense burners with smoke actively coming out of them were sitting on small tables in various corners of the room, much too close to the flammable looking wall hangings for Carolyn's comfort. She tried to put the possibility of disaster out of her mind.

The sound of chanting could be heard in the background, beyond the curtain of brightly colored beads. Carolyn could hear the words "Nam-myoho-renge-kyo" being repeated over and over again by those in the other room.

"There's something very wrong with these people," Carolyn whispered to Susan.

"Or very right," responded the hippy, who had easily overheard. "Depends upon your point of view, doesn't it? Tell me, do

226

you know how each of your seven Chakras might be influencing your health or even your life force?"

"Chakras?" repeated Carolyn.

"Each of us has the power within us at any given moment to overcome whatever problem or difficulty we may encounter in life," described the hippy. "By meditating on the magnitude of life's inherent possibilities, each of us can bring our Chakras into alignment with the very powers of the universe. Look, they are all around us!"

"Oh yeah, so they are," responded Susan as she urgently tugged at Carolyn's sleeve. "We need to leave. Now."

"Do you think Steve's gone by now?" whispered Carolyn.

"Even if he's not, we'd be better off taking our chances with him," replied Susan as she dashed over to the shoe rack, grabbed her sandals, and ran outside without stopping to put them on.

Carolyn did likewise, regretting the decision to take them off when she felt the cold hard sidewalk on her feet as she followed after Susan. They ran for nearly a block before stopping to sit on a bench at a bus stop to put their sandals back on again.

"I'm freezing!" mentioned Carolyn.

"Me, too, Ms. Carolina la Gata," empathized Susan. "But, it's only a few more blocks until my parents' house. We can do it."

"Do you see those guys over there?" questioned Carolyn as she noticed some unsavory looking characters on the opposite side of the street headed in the same direction they were.

"Yeah, come on," directed Susan.

"Who are they?" Carolyn had a very bad feeling about them, as all of them were dressed in black pants and jackets with black caps, and their features were completely indistinguishable in the dark.

"Probably some of the local gang members," muttered Susan. "This isn't the best of neighborhoods."

"Are we in any kind of danger?" quizzed Carolyn, clearly worried about their safety.

"You never know," answered Susan. "There's at least one or two murders in the park over there each week."

"Murders? You are kidding me, right?" Carolyn was truly afraid and wished she were safe in her room at Oceanview Academy.

"I wish I were," mumbled Susan as she began to walk a little faster. "What time is it?"

"It's a little after eleven thirty," informed Carolyn after glancing at her wristwatch in the dim light of the street lamp they were currently passing.

Both Susan and Carolyn noticed at once that the pace of the three dark figures on the opposite side of the street seemed to increase incrementally to match their own.

"Should we make a run for it?" whispered Carolyn.

"Not yet," maintained Susan. "We need to get a little closer first. We'd never be able to run all that way in these sandals!"

"Are there any other churches or places like that between here and there?" prompted Carolyn.

"That was it," replied Susan. "And we don't want those thugs seeing where we go when we get there, either!"

"Wake up!" Pete came over to Lenny's bed to shake him. "You all right? You were shouting for Carolyn in your sleep."

"Oh, my gosh!" sighed Lenny as he sat up. "I was having a horrible dream. Susan and Carolyn were in some sort of danger."

"It was just a dream," chuckled Pete. "Go back to sleep!"

Lenny was drenched with sweat, which was not customary for him. Perhaps he was coming down with an illness of some sort. "I'm sure you must be right. It was just a dream," mumbled Lenny unconvincingly.

"They're probably eatin' pizza and watching television right now," assured Pete.

"Still, that dream was so real," persisted Lenny. "I dreamed that they were running down a dark alley, and that someone was after them. I couldn't actually see their faces, though."

"Then how do you know it was Susan or Carolyn?" razzed Pete. "If you couldn't see their faces...."

"I did see them!" Lenny cut him off. "It was the faces of the people after them that I couldn't see."

"Hey, even if you're right, and you did have some psychic revelation of some sort, what could you possibly do about it now, anyway?" questioned Pete.

"Not a darn thing," muttered Lenny as he laid back down and put his hands behind his head. "Go to sleep."

"Good night!" chuckled Pete. "Make sure you ask her to the prom when she gets back tomorrow."

228

"Indeed," agreed Lenny as he lay awake, worried that something really might be wrong. Perhaps there was some way he could convince his parents to accept Carolyn, despite the incident at the beach. And the fact that she was white should not make any difference! Lenny wanted nothing more than for things to work out between him and Carolyn and was frustrated with himself for waiting for so long to ask her to the prom.

"I know you're still awake," whispered Pete.

"Can't sleep," answered Lenny.

"Hey, if it's Jim Otterman you're thinking of, I'll be more than happy to help you get him alone somewhere," offered Pete with a mischievous laugh. "I'll even help you beat him up!"

"Good night!" replied Lenny with finality.

"What in the world are you girls doing?" demanded Mrs. Rives as she entered the kitchen and found Susan and Carolyn eating the last of her lasagna. "That was for our lunch tomorrow!"

"We were starving," muttered Susan between bites as she and Carolyn continued to devour the delicious lasagna.

"Of that I have no doubt!" snapped Susan's mother. "It's well after midnight! Where have you girls been? Fortunately for you, your father fell asleep while he was waiting for you to return. He's still asleep in his chair by the door. Perhaps I should go wake him?"

"Oh, please don't do that!" begged Susan as she took a big drink of milk to wash down the lasagna.

"Just how did you get in here, anyway?" demanded Mrs. Rives. "I suppose you climbed through all the neighbors' yards to come in through the back, so your father wouldn't see you come in late again? You'd better hope none of the neighbors saw you!"

"We were going to come in through the front," volunteered Carolyn, "but some guys were chasing us down the street and we didn't want them to know which house we were going to. That's why we came in through the back instead."

"Is this true?" questioned Mrs. Rives as she turned to Susan.

"Yes, ma'am," assured Susan. "We didn't have quite enough cab fare, so the driver dropped us off over by the cathedral."

"That's over twelve blocks away!" scolded Susan's mother. "What were you girls thinking? You know what kind of a neighborhood this is! It's not safe out there, especially for two young girls wandering around alone at night! Thank God you're safe!"

"Did Damien make it home okay?" Susan suddenly asked with genuine concern. "We wanted to stay and help Jorge look for him after he wandered off at the concert, but Jorge insisted that we come home when we did so we wouldn't be late."

"Oh, girls!" Mrs. Rives shook her head with dismay. "Yes, Damien is safe. He's asleep in his room. According to Jorge, Damien got food poisoning from Mrs. Moranga's cooking! At least your father bought it, anyway. I'm glad to see her cooking didn't have the same effect on the rest of you."

"Oh mother, I'm so sorry that we caused you any worry!" Susan got up, embraced her mother, and began to sob.

"All right, all right!" Mrs. Rives gently pushed her daughter away. "Go get those clothes off right now. I think we can get them washed and dried by morning. Your brother's clothes should be done washing by now."

"Won't Mr. Rives be able to hear the washing machine if you start it so late?" worried Carolyn.

"The washer is down in the basement," explained Susan. "You can't really hear it from here, anyway. My father never goes downstairs if he can help it. It's just too hard on his knees."

"Hurry up," instructed Susan's mother. "We'll tell him tomorrow that the taxi dropped you off before curfew, but we just didn't have the heart to wake him."

"Works for me!" agreed Susan. "Thanks, Mom!"

Susan and Carolyn slept until nearly noon that day, exhausted from the previous day.

"Girls? It's almost time for lunch!" Mrs. Rives gently knocked on the door to their room. "Girls?"

"Come in," mumbled Susan as she stretched and yawned.

"Here are your clothes." Susan's mother quickly handed the pile of clean, neatly folded clothing to Susan. "I had to wait until your father went out to bring them back up."

"Thanks!" yawned Susan as she took the clothes from her mother and tossed them on the bed. "Where'd he go, anyway?"

"Actually, your father got a call from the auto shop. They said his car is ready," revealed Mrs. Rives. "Don't say anything, though.

230

He was hoping to surprise you. Jorge came by this morning to take him over there. Looks like you won't have to take the bus, after all."

Carolyn breathed a deep sigh of relief upon hearing the good news. She was not anxious to take the bus as mentioned previously.

"I thought Jorge was driving us back," mentioned Susan.

"Jorge has his big show at the art gallery this afternoon," reminded Susan's mother. "You wouldn't want him to miss it."

"You never mentioned that Jorge is an artist, too," remarked Carolyn. "What kind of art?"

"Pottery, sculptures, that kind of thing," listed Susan. "The fountain at his parents' house is one of his pieces."

"Really?" Carolyn was quite impressed.

"They stole my angel!" hollered Mr. Rives as he came in the front door and angrily slammed it behind him.

"His angel?" questioned Carolyn. "One of Jorge's, too?"

"It's not that kind of an angel," explained Susan.

"What do you mean they stole your angel?" called Susan's mother as she rushed down to console him. "Where did this happen?"

"After they were done working on it, they parked it out on the street!" fumed Mr. Rives. "Who parks a Rolls Royce out on the street in that neighborhood? Tell me that? Of course they stole the angel!"

"The angel?" Carolyn was still confused.

"The hood ornament on a Rolls Royce is called The Spirit of Ecstasy," explained Susan. "Some people call it the Lady of Ecstasy. My dad just calls it his angel."

"I've never seen one," admitted Carolyn.

"It looks just like an angel," confirmed Mrs. Rives. "He has always been very proud of it."

"I will not be seen driving around in my car without the angel," informed Mr. Rives with finality. "You'll have to take the bus back."

Susan's father then pulled out his wallet, took out two twenty dollar bills, and handed them to Susan. "I'm sorry for falling asleep before you got in last night. Thankfully you all made it home safely before curfew."

"No problem," responded Susan as she gave him a big hug and snatched the money from him. "Thanks!"

"Jorge is already waiting out front to take you to the bus station," added Mr. Rives. "You should have enough left over after buying your bus tickets to pick up a couple of sandwiches somewhere. Seems as if someone ate all the lasagna last night, anyway."

Susan and Carolyn exchanged a guilty smile.

"Hurry up, then." Mrs. Rives clapped her hands. "Go get your things. Don't make Jorge late for his art show. He really should try to get there by noon, or as soon thereafter as he can."

"What time does the bus leave?" inquired Carolyn.

"Who knows," replied Susan's father. "Just take the next one, whenever it is."

"How will we get from the bus station in Ocean Bluff out to the school?" quizzed Carolyn.

"Can't you just call someone from the school to come out and pick you up when you get there?" asked Susan's mother.

"Yeah, we can do that," agreed Susan without hesitation.

"We can?" Carolyn was not so sure. Carolyn was also unsure why Susan had not just gone ahead and told her mother the truth about Steve and his modified golf cart, instead of making up some story about running out of cab fare. After all, Mrs. Rives had been quite willing to cover for them regarding what she did know.

"Chop, chop!" urged Susan's father.

Susan and Carolyn raced upstairs, hurriedly got dressed and tossed their belongings into the two large suitcases.

"Good thing we had a shower last night!" mentioned Carolyn. She clearly was unhappy about having to start a new day without one.

"We can always have a shower when we get there," reminded Susan. "Come on, let's go!"

Susan and Carolyn bid Mr. and Mrs. Rives farewell before racing outside to climb into the small yellow sports car. Damien was with Jorge waiting for them.

"Jorge! Thanks for taking us," greeted Susan. "Whoa! There's no way we're all gonna fit with the suitcases, too!"

"I could sit on someone's lap," Damien grinned at Carolyn.

"Or they could sit on yours!" suggested Susan.

"Do you mind?" Damien asked Carolyn, almost flirtatiously.

"Sure, why not?" acquiesced Carolyn.

After they had all climbed into the tiny yellow sports car with the two huge suitcases, even though one suitcase was inside the trunk, Carolyn was reminded of an old photograph she had once seen where a group of students crammed themselves into a phone booth.

232

Susan's parents stood on the steps of their home and waved farewell to them as they drove away.

Once they were at the bus station, Jorge and Damien helped carry Susan and Carolyn's large suitcases up to the baggage window.

"That will be five dollars extra for each oversized piece of luggage," informed the man at the window. "And, you'll need to check them in. Anything that big will need to go down below."

"How much is the fare?" questioned Susan.

"That will be sixty dollars," replied the Ticketmaster.

"Sixty dollars!" exclaimed Susan. "For two one-way bus tickets? That can't be right!"

"Oh, I see. Only two of you are going, and only one way?" verified the man. "Well, the round trip tickets were fifteen dollars each, which is why I thought it would be sixty dollars for all four of you. And, let's see, oh yes, the one-way tickets are seven dollars and fifty cents each, so it would be fifteen dollars for two one-way tickets, plus the excess baggage charge of five dollars each, bringing it to a total of twenty-five dollars."

Susan pulled out a twenty-dollar bill, and then a five-dollar bill, and laid them both down on the counter.

"Oh, wait! There's tax, too," continued the Ticketmaster. "Let's see, tax on twenty-five dollars at a rate of 2.5% would be, oh dear. Hang on."

Susan placed one hand on her hip and rolled her eyes while she drummed the fingers of her other hand on the counter where the twenty-five dollars were still waiting.

The poor Ticketmaster made several unsuccessful attempts to try and figure out what the sales tax might be on his small, battery operated calculator, but was clearly flustered.

"Here," offered Susan as she slapped a one-dollar bill down on top of the other two bills. "You can keep the change as a tip."

"Gee, thanks!" beamed the Ticketmaster with relief.

Carolyn was suddenly reminded of a clever quip her father might have used in this particular situation, about the Ticketmaster not being the sharpest tack in the box.

The Ticketmaster slowly picked up and placed each of the two suitcases onto a rolling baggage cart before returning to his counter to prepare the two one-way tickets from Ocean Bay to Ocean Bluff. It seemed to take forever for him to record the information in his handwritten ledger before finally handing the tickets over to Susan.

"So, what time does the bus leave?" asked Carolyn.

"It doesn't say," scowled Susan as she studied one of the tickets. "That's a good question."

"Right up there," indicated the Ticketmaster as he pointed to a handwritten chalkboard mounted on the wall above him. "Bus to Ocean Bluff leaves at two o'clock."

"I wish I could stay and have lunch with you," mentioned Jorge, "but I've got to get back to the gallery. People are probably arriving there now."

"Hey, thanks for a nice weekend," Carolyn smiled at Jorge. "And for putting up with me."

"Oh, that reminds me!" Jorge suddenly pulled a small white cardboard box from his jacket pocket. "This is for you."

"From all of us," added Damien with a flirtatious grin.

"To remember your big weekend in Ocean Bay," supplemented Susan with a mysterious smile.

"What is it?" asked Carolyn, surprised by the gesture.

"Open it and see," suggested Jorge.

Carolyn carefully untied the gold ribbon tied around it, opened the lid of the little box, and gaped with awe at what was inside.

"Well? Do you like it?" Susan demanded to know.

"Oh! It's absolutely beautiful!" Carolyn felt tears begin to form in the corners of her eyes.

It was an expensive ceramic brooch with a miniature replica on it of the huge oil painting the four of them had seen in the art gallery the previous day. Carolyn stared with awe at the tiny scene that captured the dashing young man in his bright red jacket with tails who was kneeling at the young maiden's feet, at the stunning blue gown she had on, at the beautiful yellow gown her mother had on, and especially how the young maiden was clinging to her mother with one hand and pushing the young man away with the other.

"It's perfect! Thank you so much, all of you!" Carolyn gave each of them a hug and then carefully replaced the lid and ribbon on the precious box before putting it inside her purse.

"There's only one thing wrong with it," pointed out Susan.

"What's that?" questioned Carolyn. It seemed flawless to her.

"The young man in the picture has RED hair!" Susan flashed a crooked smile at Carolyn.

"That's not funny!" Carolyn couldn't help but chuckle. She knew full well that Susan was alluding to the fact that Jim Otterman had red hair and then added, "At least she's pushing him away!"

They both laughed heartily but didn't bother to explain their inside joke to Jorge or Damien.

"Well, this is it then," Susan gave Jorge a hug and romantic kiss on the lips. "Until we meet again."

"Indeed," grinned Jorge with a knowing smile.

Carolyn merely smiled and nodded at Jorge and Damien before following Susan toward a stale sandwich machine at the bus station.

"We can't eat this!" Susan decided at first glance. "There's a cafeteria across the street. Let's go over there."

"Do we have enough?" questioned Carolyn. "We just spent over half of what your father gave us on the tickets. Plus sales tax."

"Yep," acknowledged Susan. "Still, cafeteria food should be reasonable enough. If we keep it under five dollars each, then we'll still have five dollars left."

After a leisurely lunch of cornbread and chili, Susan and Carolyn returned to the bus station.

"It's still just one o'clock," sighed Susan.

"And the bus leaves at two?" confirmed Carolyn.

"Hang on, I'll be right back," directed Susan. "I see someone I know over there. Wait here."

Carolyn was puzzled by Susan's request but patiently waited as Susan went over to chat with a handsome young man about thirty years of age that was just picking up his suitcase from the baggage return area.

Susan then raced over to the Ticketmaster and could be seen handing him their bus tickets.

Carolyn became concerned, so she quickly got up and went over to the ticket counter and asked Susan, "What are you doing?"

"Here you are, ma'am," indicated the Ticketmaster as he handed Susan twenty-five dollars.

"That was twenty-six dollars," reminded Susan.

"You did say I could keep the tip," insisted the Ticketmaster.

"Okay, that's fine," agreed Susan as she quickly folded the bills and put them into the small front pocket of her blue jeans.

"Excuse me," prompted Carolyn as she grabbed Susan's arm. "Just how are we planning to get back?"

"With Mike," informed Susan with a sly look as she walked over to the rolling baggage cart and grabbed her suitcase. "Come on!"

Carolyn noticed that the bus driver was just getting ready to take the rolling baggage cart over to the bus and begin loading suitcases onto it for the next departure, which would have been theirs.

"Who's Mike?" questioned Carolyn suspiciously as she retrieved her large suitcase, just in the nick of time before the bus driver rolled the baggage cart away.

"A friend," replied Susan mysteriously. "Mike just happens to be driving to Ocean Bluff."

"When?" frowned Carolyn.

"Right now!" smirked Susan. "And, we still have our twenty-five dollars! How 'bout that?"

Carolyn followed Susan over to a small blue Pinto hatchback where Susan's friend Mike helped them load their suitcases into the back. Thankfully, both of their suitcases fit, even though Mike's own luggage was inside already. At least there was more room in the Pinto than there had been in Jorge's small yellow sports car.

Once they were settled inside Mike's small blue Pinto, he started the engine and began to drive out of the parking lot toward the main highway. After stopping at a stop sign, Mike turned where indicated by a sign that read, "Ocean Bluff, 122 miles."

"We should be there in just a couple of hours," informed Mike. "Sorry I can't take you all the way to that school of yours, but I'll be headed inland from Ocean Bluff. I've got an important business meeting in Ashton at six o'clock and can't be late for it."

"Thanks for taking us as far as you are," grinned Susan.

"I'm Carolyn, by the way," indicated Carolyn. It seemed strange to her that Susan's friend Mike had not even bothered to ask for her name, nor had Susan taken the time to introduce them.

"Nice to meet you," nodded Mike as he quickly glanced at Carolyn in his rearview mirror.

Susan had chosen to sit in the front passenger seat, so Carolyn had taken the seat in the back.

"Have you known each other long?" questioned Carolyn. She was curious why Susan had said nothing about Mike before.

"Oh, for about five minutes," chuckled Mike. "We just met."

Carolyn suddenly realized the seriousness of their situation and glowered at Susan with disapproval. How dare Susan make a decision like this on her own for both of them, and to ask for a ride with a complete stranger! Carolyn became sullen and quiet as she reflected upon the events of the past two days. From the very onset of the weekend, when Jorge had picked them up instead of Susan's parents, Carolyn should have listened to her own inner voice of warning!

Susan and Mike continued to engage in meaningless conversation about the weather, sports, and even the stock market. Uninterested in the mindless chatter and too upset to feel like joining in, Carolyn ignored them completely and stared out the back window of the small blue Pinto at the windswept ocean cliffs overgrown with aging cypress trees and at the huge ocean beyond that as they made their way toward Ocean Bluff. Carolyn thought about their wild ride down Ocean Bay's main downtown sidewalk with crazy roadie Steve following the rock concert, and of the looks on the faces of frightened pedestrians who had leapt from harm's way. Worse still was their dangerous flight on foot from the dark hooded strangers outside that peculiar temple of chanting people! How terrifying it had been to be chased by them for all those blocks, down one dark alley after another in the dangerous neighborhood where Susan's parents lived! Just how had things gotten so out of control, anyway?

"Carolyn?" called Susan. "Earth to Carolyn!"

"What?" muttered Carolyn.

"You're not still upset with me are you?" chuckled Susan, mostly for Mike's benefit.

"What do you think?" responded Carolyn as she folded her arms and looked away again, without smiling.

"You can probably get a cab out to the school from Ocean Bluff," recommended Mike. "Or call someone from there to come out and get you. It would probably be the safest thing to do."

"We intend to," assured Carolyn as she glared at Susan.

"After all," added Mike, "not everyone's as nice as I am."

"Hey, we do appreciate the ride," mentioned Carolyn.

"Not a problem," nodded Mike with a polite smile.

Incredibly, Carolyn had actually nodded off to sleep during their drive back to Ocean Bluff and had to be wakened by Susan upon their arrival. She was still exhausted from their weekend.

After helping Susan and Carolyn remove their suitcases from his small blue Pinto, Mike bid them good journey and resumed his drive alone to the City of Ashton for his important business meeting.

"I'd like my half of that money now," requested Carolyn.

"No way!" responded Susan as she walked over to the curb, put one hand on her hip, and stuck out her thumb with the other hand. "You can thank me later! There's no way I'm gonna let you blow the rest of our money on a cab when we can just hitchhike and get a ride for free! Besides, if nobody stops, we can just walk. It's not that far."

Carolyn grabbed Susan's arm and held it, glaring at her with finality as she informed, "First of all, it's a half hour drive! And more importantly, we are NOT hitchhiking! You keep calling it our money, so I would like my half of it, please!"

"Possession is nine tenths of the law!" smirked Susan as she wriggled her arm free from Carolyn's grasp and put her thumb back out again. "And here comes our ride now!"

"Well, I'm not letting you do something stupid like getting us killed," persisted Carolyn as the potential ride drove past without stopping. "I'm calling the school."

"Ah, no, you're not," determined Susan. "Besides, the only phone booth is inside that bus station and it's closed right now."

Carolyn walked over to the thick glass door of the bus station and tested its locked door in vain. The row of rotary dial pay phones inside were visible from outside. "Perhaps they're always closed on Sundays here," surmised Carolyn. "I wonder if the bus just drops people off, even if the station is closed."

"Very likely," guessed Susan. "So, you see, there's no way we can call anyone from here anyway."

"Wait! There's a phone booth over there on the corner," noticed Carolyn. "All I need is a dime, please?"

"All right, here, suit yourself," offered Susan as she handed Carolyn a twenty-dollar bill. "Bills are all I have. Good luck getting change somewhere."

"You don't even have a dime?" questioned Carolyn.

"No change at all," sighed Susan.

"What are we going to do?" fretted Carolyn as she looked around to see if anything else might be open. "Even Kay's Diner and Patty's Pancake House are closed!"

"And the gas station, too," pointed out Susan. "The whole place is like a ghost town! There aren't even any houses around here. Hey, remember those horrible pancakes we had when we ate at Patty's Pancake House with your parents?"

"Yeah, I do," nodded Carolyn. "And I'm so hungry right now, I'd gladly eat one, too!"

"Okay, here comes another prospect," indicated Susan. "Let's not blow it this time."

"Hey, chicas!" flirted a creepy looking brown skinned man about forty years of age as he rolled down his darkly tinted window and slowed to a stop in his lowered Chevy Impala. "Need a ride?"

Carolyn recognized the voice immediately. "Oh, my God! It's the man from the daisy patch!"

"Are you sure?" whispered Susan, realizing at once that it would be unsafe to ride with him.

"Hey, I know you!" the man looked Carolyn up and down with a lustful expression on his face as he slowly licked his lips.

Carolyn glared at him with abject disgust and motioned for him to leave, pointing toward the highway as she did. "Sólo lárgate. Ya no quiero hablar contigo!"

"Muy bien! Sigan en eso!" nodded the horrible man as he popped an 8-track tape into his dashboard quad player and turned up the volume. The song "Low Rider" began to play. With one last menacing grin, he then flicked a switch to activate the hydraulic pumps and valves on his modified vehicle and made it "jump" several times before slowly driving away.

"Seriously?" Carolyn looked at Susan and shook her head.

"I'm afraid I agree with you on that," acknowledged Susan. "That guy was nothing but trouble! How horrible he was!"

"Guess we'd better get started walking then," suggested Carolyn. "Morning will be here before you know it."

"Hey, I'm so sorry! This was a really stupid thing to do," apologized Susan. Carolyn studied her for a moment before replying.

"You really mean it?" Carolyn was skeptical.

"Well, I'm not gonna tell you to trust me," began Susan, "but I do see what looks like our last best chance before dark."

Carolyn turned in time to see a rickety old pickup truck approaching. It was being driven by an older gentleman, definitely over fifty years of age.

"Come on, put your thumb out!" urged Susan. "He looks all right. We don't want to end up walking back in the dark past that looney bin up there on the hill! Some of 'em are free to come and go from there as they please, did you know that?"

"No, I hadn't heard that." Carolyn needed no further convincing and finally put her thumb out, just as the old pickup truck neared and slowed to a stop.

"You ladies shouldn't be out here like this!" advised the man. "It isn't safe. Where you headed, anyway?"

"Oceanview Academy," revealed Susan with a pleading look.

"Get in," motioned the man. "Name's Killingham. I run the ice cream shop over there."

"Thank you so much!" acknowledged Susan as she hoisted her heavy suitcase into the back of his pickup truck.

"You girls look familiar," mentioned the man as Susan opened the passenger door to get in.

"I'm Susan, and this is my friend Carolyn, but I don't think we've ever met," replied Susan as she sat down beside him.

Carolyn merely nodded and forced herself to produce a cordial smile while she heaved her oversized suitcase into the back of the pickup truck beside Susan's. "We do appreciate it!"

"Not a problem," replied the man as he put his rickety old pickup truck back into gear. Carolyn barely managed to slam the passenger door shut before the aging pickup truck jolted forward.

"What's in the back?" questioned Carolyn. She was curious about the numerous ten-gallon canisters with matching lids she had noticed in the back of the pickup truck, beside their suitcases.

"Ice cream," answered the man as he turned onto the narrow stretch of highway that wound along the windswept bluff tops toward Oceanview Academy. "You ladies are fortunate I happened along."

"We sure are," agreed Susan as she moved her knees to one side while Mr. Killingham shifted his truck into a lower gear for the ascent up the steepest part of the hill where Ocean Bluff Mental Institution was located.

"Creepy place," indicated the man. "I've heard some pretty unbelievable stories about what goes on in there."

240

Carolyn and Susan exchanged a look of concern. What if Mr. Killingham was one of the patients from there who was free to come and go as he chose? There was an awkward moment of silence as they approached and then passed by the institution.

"You making a delivery somewhere?" questioned Susan loudly, to make sure he could hear her, particularly since he was clearly over fifty and up in years.

"Yep," nodded the man. "Ice cream."

"Uh huh," nodded Susan. "That's what you were saying earlier. Where are you taking all that ice cream?"

"Some of it to Oceanview Academy," informed the man. "Those kids sure do go through the stuff. Can barely keep up on the orders. The rest is for my other shop, down there at the Silver Creek Trailer Park store."

"Really?" Carolyn was interested at once.

Susan and Carolyn exchanged a meaningful glance. That was where the man had seen them before!

The ice cream served at Oceanview Academy's cafeteria was one of the few things there that Carolyn really enjoyed. "Do you provide all their ice cream for them, then?"

"Sure do," verified the man quite proudly.

"It's quite good," mentioned Carolyn before Susan jabbed her in the side with an elbow.

Susan then leaned over and whispered so only Carolyn could hear. "You don't need to tell him we go to school there! The last thing we need is him telling someone he saw us out here hitchhiking!"

"Who am I gonna tell?" laughed Mr. Killingham, whose hearing was much sharper than Susan expected. "Your secret is safe with me. Let's just get you girls safely back to your dormitory."

"Thanks," responded Susan, rather sheepishly. There was more to this older gentleman than met the eye, and she sincerely hoped he would keep their confidence.

Lenny Owens had been anxiously waiting at the cafeteria, hoping for Carolyn to get back in time for dinner so he could finally ask her to the prom. Lenny had waited as long as time would allow and was walking back to the boys' dormitory by himself when he just happened to see the aging gentleman in the rickety old pickup truck drop Susan and Carolyn off out in front of the girls' dormitory. Lenny considered going over to see Carolyn right then and there, but knew he had barely enough time to get back to the boys' dormitory before curfew. He would have to wait until breakfast to ask Carolyn then.

The curfew for both dormitories was at six o'clock sharp, but individual room curfew was not until eight o'clock. That left the students free to wander about their respective dormitories to visit with friends, do their laundry or take showers. Once inside their rooms at eight o'clock, the students then had one hour to do everything else they needed to accomplish in their rooms before the electricity went off for the night. Lenny took full advantage of what little time was left to complete his chemistry assignment before lights out.

Wednesday arrived with all the swiftness of an eastern wind before a harsh winter storm. Still, Lenny had not yet managed to isolate or invite Carolyn to the Harvest Festival Prom.

Carolyn had become despondent by circumstances surrounding her during the past two days. She was now getting ready to head down to the beach. Perhaps watching Joyce and Veronica practice their boogie boarding was just what she needed to get her mind off her troubles. And she sincerely hoped Jim Otterman would not show up during her walk across campus to get there! Avoiding him lately had become more of a challenge than she cared to deal with at the moment.

"Carolyn?" came the voice of Dean Dixon on the intercom box to her dormitory room.

Carolyn breathed in deeply and then suddenly let it out before acknowledging. "Yes, Ms. Dixon, what is it?"

"May I see you in my office, please?"

"Sure, I'll be right there," replied Carolyn, suddenly roused from her dejected mood.

Carolyn worried about what Ms. Dixon could possibly want. Had the ice cream man betrayed their confidence? Had someone finally told Ms. Dixon about the bright yellow sports car they had been seen leaving in? Surely something would have resulted from it sooner than this! Such thoughts raced through Carolyn's head as she walked the length of the long second floor hallway, descended the split-level staircase, and then headed down the first floor hallway. Upon arriving at Ms. Dixon's apartment, Carolyn paused to say a silent prayer for help before knocking on the door.

"Come in," responded Dean Dixon from inside.

Carolyn swallowed hard before reaching for and turning the door knob. After slowly opening the door to Ms. Dixon's apartment, Carolyn nervously walked inside and waited for Ms. Dixon to acknowledge her. The Dean was busy writing something that seemed important in a small notebook on the coffee table in front of her.

"Sit down," indicated Ms. Dixon, as she finished writing.

Carolyn quickly located and fixed her attention on the all-too-familiar bare spot on Dean Dixon's carpet.

"Okay, then," began Ms. Dixon. "You're probably wondering why I wanted to see you."

"The thought had crossed my mind," replied Carolyn nervously as she glanced up at Dean Dixon's unyielding scrutiny.

"How is your new job at the mill coming along?" questioned the Dean. "Is everything going okay for you there?"

"Yeah, fine," mumbled Carolyn with a shrug of her shoulders. "And it sure beats working in squash!"

"Or in the daisy patch, I'll bet," smiled Dean Dixon.

Carolyn then looked up at Ms. Dixon with a questioning look. What did Dean Dixon really want?

"I understand you had an incident yesterday where you severed the tip of your finger," described the Dean. "And that the Supervisor there at the lumber mill had to drive you all the way over to the Ocean Bluff Emergency Clinic to have it sewn back on?"

Carolyn merely nodded.

"You know, that is the kind of thing I normally would like to know about when it happens, rather than finding out after the fact," scolded the Dean, though not too harshly.

"Well, I was kind of bleeding all over the place at the time," described Carolyn as she glanced down at the bandage on her left hand. "The lead worker actually fainted when I showed it to her, so that's why I had to go find the Supervisor. I didn't mean to get so much blood on everything! I told them they could take the cost of the ruined chaise lounge cushions out of my paycheck if they needed to."

"That's what I understand. Tell me how it happened?" requested Ms. Dixon, but more gently.

"Well, you know those thread cutting rings they have us wear?" asked Carolyn. "You know, so we don't have to stop all the time to pick up and grab a pair of scissors?"

"Those must be kept pretty sharp," assumed the Dean.

"Trust me, they are!" verified Carolyn with an ironic smile.

"Were you trying to hurry too fast to make rate when it happened?" pressed Ms. Dixon.

Carolyn shook her head in the negative and waited a moment before replying to the Dean's question. "Remember that beautiful blue dress my parents bought me for the prom?"

"Yes," nodded the Dean. "As I recall, they also bought a yellow one for Susan."

"Yes, ma'am," responded Carolyn. "That's the one."

"And that has to do with this, how?" Dean Dixon was puzzled.

"Well," continued Carolyn, "I tried the dress on when I got back, just to make sure everything was okay with it, especially with the prom coming up so soon."

"And?" prompted the Dean.

"It was so tight I couldn't even zip it shut!" Carolyn suddenly burst into tears. "I should have known eating all that Italian food up at Susan's was a mistake!"

Unable to help herself, Cathy Dixon began laughing and shaking her head with amusement.

"It's not funny!" snapped Carolyn. "I've been fasting ever since! I've just got to lose enough weight to wear that blue dress again for the prom!"

"You are serious?" Dean Dixon was no longer humored.

"Well, I was getting a bit light headed and almost passed out while I was working at the mill yesterday. That's how I ended up cutting off the tip of my finger. It wasn't because I was being careless!" Carolyn was defensive about it.

"Oh, Carolyn!" muttered the Dean. "You're a growing girl, blossoming into a beautiful young woman! It's normal for someone your age to have growth spurts like this."

"Oh really?" challenged Carolyn. "Like it was normal for me to grow fourteen inches and go through three entire dress sizes when I was in the eighth grade? I should be finished having growth spurts by now, don't you think? Someone as short as you couldn't possibly know what it's like to be at least a foot taller than every single guy in your entire class!"

"You're right," agreed Ms. Dixon, who was only five feet five inches herself. "That's something I couldn't possibly understand. But, what I do understand is that I cannot stand by and let you do this

244

to yourself, young lady. You've absolutely got to eat something, or you won't be any good to anybody, especially yourself."

Carolyn remained silent and began to stare at the bare spot in the carpet again. Just then, Dean Dixon's phone rang.

At first, Carolyn paid little attention to the conversation Ms. Dixon was having until she heard the words, "saw them where?"

"I see," nodded the Dean as she gave Carolyn a troubled glance. "They did, did they? When was this? Sunday afternoon? No, you did the right thing. I appreciate you letting me know."

After a deep sigh of frustration, the Dean picked her phone back up and called the front desk. "Diana? Please send someone to find Susan. Yes, Susan Rives. Have her report to my office at once!"

"Wait here," instructed the Dean. Her entire demeanor had changed following the phone call. Carolyn was certain that her worst fears were about to be realized, and that she and Susan were about to be in horrible trouble.

After a few moments, Cathy Dixon returned with a small plate containing two oatmeal cookies and a glass of milk, and handed them to Carolyn. "I want you to eat these, right now," instructed the Dean.

"I can't eat something like that!" argued Carolyn. "It will undo everything I've been through already."

"That's what I'm hoping for," replied the Dean. "I'll tell you what. After we get done with another matter that involves Susan, you can go get your blue dress and try it on for me. I might know a way to help you alter it so you can still wear it, though I can't promise anything without seeing you in it first. Is that a deal?"

"You would do that for me?" Carolyn was baffled.

"Just eat those cookies before Susan gets here, please," requested Ms. Dixon. "Otherwise, I'll have to give her some, too!"

Carolyn quickly ate the delicious cookies and washed them down with the glass of milk. She hadn't realized how hungry she actually was until that very moment.

"Good girl," nodded the Dean as she whisked away the empty plate and glass before answering the knock at her door.

"Ms. Dixon," acknowledged Susan as she entered the Dean's apartment and sat down on the couch beside Carolyn. "You know, Carolyn might be excused from her job for the rest of the week after her accident, but that doesn't mean I'm excused from my job!"

"I've already had Diana call them for me," informed the Dean. "Your job is the last thing you need to worry about right now."

Susan gave Carolyn a suspicious look and mouthed the words, "Did you tell her?"

Carolyn merely shook her head in the negative and waited nervously for the Dean to begin.

"Oh girls!" Ms. Dixon shook her head with dismay. "Just when I think there's nothing else that can surprise me, you always manage to do just that!"

"What did we do this time?" Susan asked coyly.

Ms. Dixon folded her arms, closed her eyes and shook her head before responding. "I don't even want to know about the guy in the bright yellow sports car that nearly everyone on campus saw you leave with on Friday afternoon. I already know that you were with your parents this past weekend, and that would fall under their purview."

"Indeed," smirked Susan, just a little too smugly.

Carolyn, on the other hand, was extremely nervous about the entire situation, and it showed.

"Nor is it my business what family activities you and your parents enjoyed together while you were there," added the Dean. "However, I did get a call from the theology instructor, just a little while ago, that concerns me greatly."

"Professor Rattusrisum?" scoffed Susan.

"Professor Rattusrisum's mother was unexpectedly rushed to the hospital this past weekend, with a brain aneurism," informed Ms. Dixon. "Without surgery to repair it, someone with a brain aneurysm could end up having a stroke or permanent brain damage."

"How horrible!" exclaimed Carolyn. "How did they know that's what was wrong with her?"

"Well, I'm not a doctor," clarified Ms. Dixon, "but it's my understanding that some of the symptoms include severe headaches, blurred vision, changes in speech, and even neck pain."

Susan became somber and waited for the Dean to continue.

"Anyway, it was late Sunday afternoon when the Rattusrisums were passing through Ocean Bluff, on their way to Ocean Bay," added Ms. Dixon. "That was when they happened to notice a young girl hitchhiking the other direction, and realized it was Susan! They also noticed that the other girl was clearly opposed to the idea and refused to participate, and that girl was Carolyn!"

"Professor Rattusrisum saw us hitchhiking?" Susan was flabbergasted.

"No," corrected the Dean. "He saw YOU hitchhiking, Ms. Susan. That was when he decided to stop at the first available phone booth to call his friend Mark Killingham."

"Mr. Killingham?" repeated Carolyn with surprise.

"Yes, Mr. Killingham," verified the Dean. "The man who owns the ice cream shop there in town. The Rattusrisums needed to hurry to get to the hospital in Ocean Bay before they began surgery on his mother. So, naturally they didn't have time to stop and bring you all the way back here. Thankfully, Mr. Killingham agreed to go pick you up and bring you along when he came out here to deliver the ice cream he was planning to bring over the next day, anyway."

"So, he made a special trip, just for us?" snickered Susan.

"Yes, he did!" scolded the Dean, upset about Susan's attitude. Cathy Dixon decided against telling them that Mark Killingham was actually the widower of her late sister Linda. That was something the girls did not need to know.

"Hey, Cat!" came a man's voice from behind her. It was her thirty-year-old nephew, Ray Dixon. That was something Susan and Carolyn didn't need to know, either.

"Oh, I didn't realize you had company," grinned Ray Dixon when he saw Susan and Carolyn sitting on his aunt's couch. Susan, in particular caught his fancy, even if she was just a teenage girl. So, Ray decided to make her day and deliberately shot her a flirtatious grin. However, it did not have the desired effect upon Susan.

Susan frowned with disapproval at Ray Dixon's crewcut and thick, horn-rimmed glasses, and basically at Ray in his entirety.

Carolyn wrinkled her nose with disgust at the foul smell of body odor and sweat emanating from Ray Dixon's muddy white t-shirt and grease covered blue jeans.

"Oh, Ray, hello!" beamed Dean Dixon. "You can just leave it over there in the kitchen."

Susan and Carolyn both watched with piqued interest as Ray Dixon brought in and set down a mysterious looking wooden crate on Dean Dixon's kitchen counter in the next room, flexing his huge muscular, tattoo covered arms as he did so.

"Technically, there's nothing in the rule book to cover a situation like this," admitted Dean Dixon.

"What now?" questioned Susan.

"Now, I would like the two of you to promise me nothing like this will EVER happen again!" requested Ms. Dixon.

"Absolutely, it won't!" promised Carolyn without hesitation.

"And if it does?" queried Susan.

Dean Dixon glared at Susan with disapproval and returned her even stare until Susan finally acquiesced and nodded with agreement. "Okay! Never again, I promise!"

"Good! And I want you to make sure that Carolyn eats something, every single day, whether she likes it or not," added the Dean. "Can you do that for me?"

"She told you about the dress?" chuckled Susan with a snicker.

Ignoring Susan's snide remark, Dean Dixon added, "Finally, I want both of you to be at that prom, whether anyone asks you or not. Agreed? You can still have an enjoyable time."

"Sure." Susan shrugged her shoulders. "I was planning to go stag anyway."

"You were?" Carolyn was surprised.

"And so can you!" assured Ms. Dixon.

Carolyn, however, was unconvinced, and had no intention of going to the Harvest Festival Prom without Lenny Owens as her date.

9. La Mariposa

Jon Roth rang the front bell again and was becoming more impatient by the moment. Glancing upward, Jon just happened to notice Susan Rives peering at him from the second level window of the lighthouse above him.

"He saw me!" panicked Susan, suddenly ducking down and nearly screaming when she noticed Ann Roth unexpectedly standing directly behind her.

"Sorry," apologized Ann. "I just had to see what was going on down here."

"We'd better call Dean Jorgensen before we answer the door," advised Susan.

"Not a bad idea," agreed Ann. She was well aware of her father's temper and had no idea how he would react to all of them being there together at the lighthouse like they were.

Down on the first floor, Carolyn had rushed to Ray's laundry room to check on her clothes. They had finished washing but were still soaking wet. And so was her hair! She most certainly could not be seen answering the front door in Ray's pajamas!

"Isn't there anything else you could put on before we answer the door?" questioned Susan, who had come downstairs with Ann.

"We called Dean Jorgensen already," advised Ann. "Ted's still up in the tower room."

"Maybe you should just turn the water on in the shower room and then hide around the corner," Susan suggested to Carolyn.

"Very devious," grinned Ann. "I like it!"

"Okay, then," agreed Carolyn. "I'll just be over here if you need me for anything."

Susan did her best to appear confident and unafraid when she opened the front door to confront Jon Roth. Ann, who was standing beside her, tried to do the same.

"Jon Roth!" greeted Susan with a smile that was just a bit too enthusiastic to be convincing.

"Dad!" smiled Ann. "Thanks so much for coming for me!"

"I was worried when I got that call from Jeon Murray," informed Jon Roth. "She said Ray and her husband had to take an injured seagull up to Ocean Bay?"

"That's right," confirmed Susan. "Please, come in!"

"It is getting late," replied Jon. "I really should be getting Ann home now."

"Oh, certainly," answered Susan with relief.

"Where's your friend Carolyn?" Jon suddenly asked, glancing behind Susan with suspicion.

"She needed to take a shower after handling the seagull," volunteered Ann.

Jon Roth could clearly hear the sound of a shower in the background and appeared satisfied that all was in order. "Oh yes," added Jon Roth. "Jeon also mentioned that the Jensen boy had sprained his ankle?"

"Ah, yes," verified Susan. "He's in the other room with ice on it. In fact, Dean Jorgensen is on his way over here right now to pick him up and take him back to the boys' dorm."

"I see," nodded Jon Roth, as he turned to leave.

Ann exchanged a glance of reprieve with Susan as she followed after her father. "We'll look forward to having you join us on Sunday for the barbecue," called Ann.

"I'm looking forward to it," bid Susan.

"Indeed," grinned Jon Roth. There seemed to be a sinister undertone to his smirk, something undefinable that made Susan shudder inside.

Susan watched with surprise as Jon Roth's dark green 1961 Ford Fairlane started up and headed towards the old servants' quarters, instead of down the steep road that she and Carolyn had traversed to get to the lighthouse in the first place.

"Just look at that car!" exclaimed Susan. "It's in good shape and all, but I think it's the very same car his parents used to drive."

"Why is he going that way?" questioned Carolyn as she came out of hiding to stand beside Susan.

"Look!" pointed Susan. "The road keeps on going, right past the old servants' quarters, toward the school. See how the lights on his car are still headed in that direction, before disappearing into the fog?"

"Huh. I wonder how come Ray never mentioned the back route to us?" wondered Carolyn aloud.

"That's a good question," pondered Susan as she shut the door. "And I certainly intend to ask him about it!"

"Do you think whoever else was out there walked over from the school, then?" speculated Carolyn.

"It would make sense," reasoned Susan. She was perturbed with Ray for not telling them about the back way to get there.

"What are we going to do if that prowler decides to come back, now that Jon Roth is gone?" pressed Carolyn.

"We just won't open the door!" replied Susan.

"I hear another vehicle approaching," mentioned Carolyn.

"It's probably Dean Jorgensen," guessed Susan. "You'd better go turn the shower back on and hide again."

Instead, Carolyn quickly raced up to the tower room to let Ted Jensen know that the Dean of Boys was pulling up out front.

Ted had dozed off and had actually begun to snore, so he was startled when Carolyn gently shook his arm to wake him.

After watching Dean Jorgensen drive off with Ted Jensen safely inside the backseat of his deep blue 2014 Ford Transit Connect Wagon, Carolyn and Susan quickly shut and locked the front door of Ray's lighthouse again. Carolyn most certainly could not leave without her own clothes, which were still in the clothes dryer. Also, they had no idea how much longer it would be until Ray's return. Perhaps two more hours, at least.

"Do you think we're safe here?" asked Carolyn.

"Probably safer than we would be over at Ms. Neilson's house," replied Susan. "That's on ground level, right within walking distance of the Roth residence. Plus, the fog is still rolling in! At least over here, we're up on the second floor, and have a pretty good view from that one window."

"Do you trust Ray Dixon?" quizzed Carolyn. "Enough to spend the night?"

Susan thought seriously about it for a moment before responding. "Yes, I think I do."

"Very well, then," agreed Carolyn. "Let's hope you're right. The Daisy Room's mine."

"I want the Daisy Room," teased Susan with a crooked grin. "I always did like a room with a view."

"Okay, fine," conceded Carolyn. "I'll take the Violet Room."

It was well past midnight when Ray Dixon and John Murray finally returned from the Ocean Bay Bird Conservancy, where the injured seagull would receive proper care by wildlife volunteers who frequented the center and would look in on it each day.

"I can just walk home from here," offered John, suddenly realizing that he had come on foot from his house when rushing to the beach after Ann Roth's phone call earlier.

"Nothin' doing!" insisted Ray. "Look how late it is! Plus, see how foggy it is? And, this feels like one of those times it might rain!"

"It rarely rains when it's foggy," reminded John.

"Still, this feels like one of those times that it could," persisted Ray. "I remember over in Vietnam, especially along the coastline, there were times when it would rain like there was no tomorrow, even when it was foggy. Sometimes, you'd even see thunderstorms while all that was going on!"

"I guess that can happen when cold water currents meet the warmer air above them, and create a dense fog near a mountain range of some sort," conceded John.

"Like here?" nodded Ray.

"Exactly! What we're talking about here is an orographic lift," described Professor Murray.

"A what?" frowned Ray.

"Because we are situated along a coastal mountain range here, marine breezes can sometimes force moist air up into an orographic lift," explained the Professor. "That happens when the air mass gains altitude and cools down adiabatically."

"Say, what?" Ray shook his head and smiled.

"An adiabatic process is one that occurs when there's no transfer of heat or matter between a thermodynamic system and its environment," elaborated John Murray, delighted for an opportunity to show off his knowledge. "Anyway, that can raise the humidity to 100% and create rain clouds. In other words, the orographic effect."

"My aunt used to do origami," chuckled Ray.

"Not origami," chided John teasingly. "Orographic. That's when it would start to rain. In fact, if the air on the very top of the troposphere is cold enough when it rises to meet it, you could even see a thunderstorm."

"Thank you Professor Murray, for the weather lesson!" grinned Ray, almost sarcastically.

252

Too tired to banter further, John simply shrugged his shoulders and got back inside Ray's pickup truck. "Let's go, then. You know, you really ought to tell Susan and Carolyn about the back road over here from the school."

"I will," assured Ray. "First thing tomorrow. I'm sure they're probably asleep already. You know what, let me just pop in and make sure they're okay first. I'll be right back."

Ray quietly unlocked the front door of his lighthouse and went inside. Satisfied that Susan and Carolyn were safe after seeing them asleep in the Daisy and Violet Rooms, Ray tiptoed back downstairs, went outside, quietly closed the front door, and got back into his pickup truck to take John Murray home. "Sound asleep."

Half-way to John Murray's home, Ray began to wonder whether he had remembered to lock the door to the lighthouse again, but didn't want to worry John unnecessarily so said nothing about it. The weather lesson had been enough.

After dropping John Murray off at his residence and thanking him for his help, Ray Dixon started to turn around to go back the way he had come but then suddenly changed his mind.

If the dark hooded figure that Susan and Carolyn had seen earlier was still lurking in the vicinity of the lighthouse, Ray's vehicle would only frighten them off again when he returned. In order to catch them in the act so he could discover who had been prowling, the element of surprise would be required. The incoming fog should help with that. But, if it rained before he could find and follow their trail, the opportunity might be lost. There was no time to lose.

Ray drove his pickup truck across campus, out the main gate, and down onto the treacherous switchback road that led to Silver Creek Trailer Park. Driving when the fog was thick created its own set of challenges, especially at night. After emerging from the dense coastal forest and parking in front of his rundown beachfront store, Ray quickly turned off the truck's lights and engine. After waiting for his eyes to adjust to the darkness, Ray covertly opened the door of his pickup truck and climbed out, being careful to close the door again as silently as possible.

It had been several years since Ray's tour of duty in Vietnam, but some things had become second nature for him. One of Ray's many skills during his military service had included trekking in enemy territory, and often in the jungle at night.

In full stealth mode, Ray carefully approached and stepped over his foliage covered swinging gate, rather than to try and open it. He did not wish to chance having a squeaky gate hinge give away his position, just in case the prowler might still be nearby.

Ray also wondered if the dark hooded figure he had seen outside Ms. Neilson's home the previous evening was the same prowler seen by Susan and Carolyn just a short while ago. He tried again to recall whether or not he had relocked the lighthouse door.

After pausing to listen to his surroundings for several moments longer before continuing, Ray walked cautiously in his steel-tipped snakeskin cowboy boots to avoid twisting an ankle in the foggy darkness, or unintentionally stepping too close to the dangerous drop-off beside the road he was traversing. The fog made it difficult, but Ray was barely able to make out the continuous metal chain threaded through large eyelet holes at the top of each wrought iron fence post along the steep road's outer edge.

Ray stopped again when he reached the top where the road leveled out near the lighthouse entrance, to listen for any unusual sounds and to try and survey his surroundings. Nothing seemed out of the ordinary, and the fog seemed less dense immediately around the lighthouse itself. Ray froze when the motion activated security lights on either side of his lighthouse entrance unexpectedly came on. The front door of the lighthouse was slowly opening! Someone in a dark hooded cape stealthily emerged from the lighthouse and began slinking down the road toward the old servants' quarters. Ray would either need to charge forward immediately to overtake and grab them, or hang back so he could follow from a discrete distance.

Despite the fact that Ray was in excellent physical condition for his age, he was seventy-four years old. Ray knew he had no chance of overtaking the prowler before they could get away, so he chose instead to follow. Swiftly secreting himself in the dense coastal forest nearby, just out of sensor range of the security lights, Ray waited until he felt it was safe to continue. He could not risk giving away his position to the fleeing intruder, so checking on Susan and Carolyn would need to wait.

Droplets of rain suddenly began to hit Ray in the face, making it more difficult than ever to see through his thick glasses as the water droplets accumulated on their lenses. John and his origami, thought Ray. Or, whatever it was called. Any footprints or other signs left behind by the prowler would be washed away by morning if it kept raining! Ray needed to follow them now, before the trail was lost.

The wind had begun to pick up, as well. It was going to be quite a storm. Early spring storms could be brutal at times, especially in March, but catching up with the prowler was Ray's first priority at that moment. An opening in the fog ahead near the old servants' quarters momentarily revealed the dark hooded figure passing by it. From the person's size and mannerisms as they moved, Ray suspected that it might be a woman. If only he could see their face! Ray quickly headed in that direction, making sure to stay near the inner edge of the road so his presence might be camouflaged by the dense forest beside the connecting road.

Finally reaching the old servants' quarters, Ray paused to get his bearings. Wasting no time, Ray took out a handkerchief to wipe the water from his glasses, but the dark hooded figure had vanished. Using the lighted keypad of his satellite phone, Ray spotted a fresh set of tracks in the mud and began to follow them for several yards. From the smaller size of the indentations, Ray was fairly certain that the perpetrator was a woman. Either that, or a man with very small feet. The tracks seemed at first to be leading toward the Roth residence, but then veered off the road and into the forest. The impressions suddenly became deeper, as if the person had started to run.

Without hesitation, Ray followed the weakening trail into the forest and followed it for as long as he was able. An occasional broken twig, and even a small piece of black fabric stuck on the branches of a thorny bush, indicated that he was still on track. Then, unexpectedly, Ray found himself standing beside a dense thicket of blackberry vines that were already exhibiting early spring buds, yet were overgrown with old dead canes from the previous season. The blackberry plants were clearly not being maintained by anyone.

Ray studied the blackberry thicket for several moments before noticing a faint foot path on the ground that led around it. Ray wiped the rain from his glasses and face again with his handkerchief and finally rung it out before putting it back in his pocket. The hackles on the back of Ray's neck began to stand on end, no doubt from a chilly gust of wind. Ray paused to remove the revolver from his boot holster before continuing. The lighted keypad on his satellite phone had dimmed considerably and soon would be of no use at all.

Behind the blackberry thicket was a gated opening to an underground bunker tunnel! Ray had thought he was familiar with the various underground bunker tunnels that honeycombed the entire campus area, but was truly surprised to see a bunker tunnel this far out. Could it be connected to the other tunnel system?

Ray recognized that the footprints leading into the bunker itself would not be disturbed by the rain, and that it would be necessary to return tomorrow when it was light out to continue his pursuit. The faint light on his satellite phone's keypad suddenly went dark. It was time to hurry back and check on Susan and Carolyn.

Back at the lighthouse, Ray quickly did an exterior perimeter sweep of the entire compound before heading for the front porch of the lighthouse itself. Ray shook his head with dismay when he tried the front door and found it unlocked. Ray cautiously stepped inside, closed the front door, and locked it behind him. He then pulled out his revolver before proceeding to search the interior of the lighthouse from the ground up.

Nothing seemed out of place anywhere on the first floor. Susan and Carolyn were sound asleep in the Daisy and Violet Rooms, and the sound of their steady breathing assured him they were alive. Ray continued his ascent up the spiral staircase, checking each of the other guest rooms, but everything was in place. Finally putting his revolver away, Ray headed for the tower room to make sure any leftover food had been put away. In fact, he had become quite hungry by then and thought of making himself a sandwich.

Ray shook his head with dismay when he entered the tower room. It was obvious that the books on his book shelf had each been pulled out, one by one, and put back in place at topsy-turvy angles. Susan or Carolyn would never leave the room in such a disarray, but clearly someone had been searching for something.

"Oh no!" muttered Ray. "The box!" There it was, sitting on the table, wide open. Ginny's journal was no longer inside!

Ray quickly looked around the tower room to see whether the journal had been thrown onto the floor or possibly left somewhere else, but nothing else in the tower room had been touched and the journal was gone! Only the book shelves had been targeted.

Ray was so stunned by what he saw that he had to sit down for a moment. How could something like this happen, especially now?

"Ray?" it was Susan. She had wakened and followed him to the tower room. "Oh my God! What happened in here? Why are all the books like that? Is that the box?"

"Yes," confirmed Ray. "Oh, thank God you're all right!" Ray got up and came over to Susan to give her a hug. He had not realized until that very moment just how important Susan had become to him during the past two days.

Susan hugged Ray back, but then pulled away when she noticed how wet he was, and how muddy his boots were. "What happened to you?" Like Carolyn, Susan had found and was wearing a clean pair of Ray's pajamas.

"It's a long story," answered Ray.

"Good thing we have all night," mentioned Carolyn from the doorway. Her stealthy arrival was second nature, especially after dealing with feral cats and other wildlife for so many years.

"I do have to teach class tomorrow," reminded Susan with a deep sigh. She had not even bothered to read her own assignment yet, and was going to try and bluff her way through it by giving them a choice between a pop quiz or an essay writing contest.

"Where is your truck?" questioned Carolyn. She had already gone to the Daisy Room's window to look outside after noticing Susan was no longer asleep in bed. The only vehicle parked out front was the white Dodge Dart rental car that she and Susan had arrived in.

"I left my truck down at the trailer park after taking John home," explained Ray. "So I could have the element of surprise if that prowler came back. And it's a good thing I did, too. Just as I got up here, I saw someone wearing a dark hooded cloak coming out the front door and followed them."

"What?" Carolyn could not believe it.

"Don't worry, I don't think they saw me! At least not right away," added Ray.

"Did you see where they went?" questioned Susan.

"I followed whoever it was past the old servants' quarters and down to an unkempt blackberry thicket half-way between there and the Roth house," described Ray. "There's a dirt road from here that extends all the way to the campus and comes out behind the Roth place. I didn't tell you about it before, because I didn't want you driving past the Roth house or end up putting them on alert that you were coming over here."

"That makes sense," approved Susan.

"The prowler managed to elude me after passing the old servants' quarters," continued Ray. "But, when I picked up their trail again, the tracks led me to a gated bunker tunnel opening behind the blackberry thicket. That was when the battery on my satellite phone gave out. I was using it as a flashlight."

"Wow!" Susan was amazed by Ray's story.

"Did you check to see if it was locked while you were there?" pressed Carolyn.

"We can do that when we go back in the morning," replied Ray. "It was just too dark to do us any good tonight."

"I can go there with you while Susan is in class," offered Carolyn, anxious to find out where the mysterious bunker tunnel opening would lead.

"Not without me, you're not!" objected Susan. "Class isn't until two o'clock in the afternoon tomorrow, anyway. I think we should all go."

"That's interesting," commented Carolyn as she approached and took a closer look at the open box on the table. "It's one of those faux books made to look like a real one."

"My parents used to have one of those," recalled Susan. "It's actually a very clever place to hide valuables in plain sight. Most people seeing it on the shelf would just assume it's a regular book."

The front of Ray Dixon's faux book was decorated with hand painted butterflies, while its exterior spine was embossed to appear as if it was an old atlas.

"Whoever came in here knew exactly what they were looking for, and where to find it," noted Carolyn.

"And they just happened to have had a key to get in here," guessed Susan.

"I just don't understand it," muttered Ray. "The only other person besides you that I've ever given a key to was Ginny."

"Obviously not the same key you gave me?" inquired Susan with a raised eyebrow.

"I sincerely wish it were," lamented Ray as he thought of Ginny and her tragic demise. "I'd always just assumed that the key had been with her when she died in that needless crash."

258

"Who went through all the things at her house after that?" questioned Carolyn. "Didn't you say it was Edith Roth who brought you Ginny's journal? Could she possibly have found and kept the key to the lighthouse for some reason?"

"I can't imagine why she would," scowled Ray. "None of this makes any sense."

"You did lock the door downstairs when you came back, didn't you?" Carolyn suddenly asked.

"Of course! I checked the entire building, inside and out before coming in and locking the door," assured Ray. "Whoever it was obviously got what they came for, though, so I don't think they'll be back."

Ray then began to rifle through the remaining contents of the faux box to see what was left and paused to pick up and study an old photograph.

"May I see that?" asked Susan as she gingerly grabbed the photo away from Ray. "Carolyn, look at this!"

Carolyn leaned closer to have a look at the photograph Susan was holding. "It's that man from the ice cream shop in town! The one who gave us a ride back to the school after that weekend with your parents up at Ocean Bay."

"Mr. Killingham, wasn't it?" Susan suddenly made the connection. "Oh, my God! This was your step dad?"

"Mark Killingham himself," confirmed Ray with a touch of sadness. "Sure do miss the old guy."

"Seems like he was older than that," reflected Susan. "Are you sure this was him?"

"My step dad was only fifty-three years old in 1972," chuckled Ray. "Even younger than you are now."

"But, you were thirty years old at the time," calculated Susan with a mischievous grin. "And I still remember the way you looked at me the day we first met, when we were in Ms. Dixon's office."

"As I recall, neither of you was overly impressed with me at the time," recounted Ray.

"Well, we were only sixteen-years-old back then," grinned Susan with a crooked smile as she flirted with Ray.

"And, we really didn't know you yet," added Carolyn.

"That's right," chuckled Ray. "That was back when you thought I was nothing more than an ex-convict and a strawberry thief."

All three of them shared a moment of laughter over Ray's comment. Truly, they had known nothing about him back then.

Carolyn suddenly reached over and picked up a familiar looking piece of paper from the faux box. It was the last thing still inside. Recognition swept over her as she studied it.

"What is it?" questioned Susan when she noticed Carolyn's odd behavior. "You look like you've seen a ghost."

"La Mariposa!" exclaimed Carolyn. "It was the poem I wrote when I was in Ms. Eggersol's English Literature class!"

"Ginny only saved things that were extremely special to her," mentioned Ray. "And out of the hundreds of students she had over the years, there were less than a handful of poems Ginny ever bothered to keep. But, I do seem to remember that one being her favorite."

"You should read it to us," suggested Susan.

"Yes, you should," agreed Ray. "I'd like to hear it, too."

"Well, let me go get my glasses, then," agreed Carolyn. "I'll be right back."

After going downstairs to retrieve her glasses from the night stand in the Violet Room, Carolyn returned to the tower room to read her poem:

La Mariposa

There was a little butterfly
who came to gaze at me.
He landed on my notebook,
then he climbed upon my key.

And as I sat there looking
deep into his eyes,
I knew it was the handiwork
of God, and no disguise.

But then the wind among the trees,
just as I hoped he'd stay,
caused him to be frightened,
and he flew away.

- by Carolyn Bennett

"That's nice," remarked Susan. "I always did think you should become a writer. You've got real talent."

"Maybe Carolyn should write a book someday about all the adventures you two had," laughed Ray. "The 'Little Demon Girls'!"

"Wait!" submitted Susan. "What about 'Demons in the Dorm at Oceanview Academy'?"

"I couldn't very well write an entire book just about that." Carolyn smiled with amusement.

"That's right," agreed Susan. "You'd have to say something about the 'nam-myoho-renge-kyo' people, too!"

"The what?" Ray was unable to follow the conversation.

"Some sect of chanting people we came across up in Ocean Bay," described Carolyn. "Right before running for our lives from three thugs that were chasing us up and down alleys at night in one of the most dangerous neighborhoods in the entire city!"

"Not to mention climbing over fences and through seven back yards to finally get away," reminded Susan.

"Good thing those Rottweilers were asleep," grinned Carolyn.

"Trouble just seems to follow you two, doesn't it?" teased Ray. "I can't wait to read the book!"

"I think it should have Susan's picture on the cover," decided Carolyn. "Don't you?"

"Not without yours, too!" insisted Susan.

"Definitely, both of you should be on the cover," snickered Ray as he nodded his head with delight.

"Agreed," promised Carolyn with a devious twinkle in her eyes. Perhaps someday she really would write such a book!

"So, what now?" questioned Susan as she motioned toward the disheveled bookshelf.

"We go over there in the morning and find out what's inside that bunker behind the blackberry thicket," proposed Ray.

"You know, I'm pretty sure our prowler must have been a woman," opined Carolyn. "No man would take the time to put each of those books back on the shelf while they were looking for that journal. Ann will sure be disappointed, too!"

"I think she's right about it being a woman," advised Ray.

"I'm not so sure," differed Susan. "We can't really be sure of anything at this point."

"The person I followed earlier was about five feet eight inches tall," recalled Ray. "Not only that, the movements and mannerisms were more like that of a woman. Plus, the tracks I found were much too small to be that of a man."

"Well, it couldn't have been Ann," mentioned Carolyn. "She was in here with us the first time that prowler tried to get in. And so was Ted."

"And we know it wasn't Birdboy," added Susan. "I watched the prowler take off when Jon Roth pulled up in his nifty old car."

Ray and Carolyn both snickered along with Susan at the mention of Jon Roth's classic 1961 Ford Fairlane.

"Just make sure you don't slip up and call him that when you go over there on Sunday," cautioned Ray.

"Don't you worry, I won't," promised Susan.

"Also, a woman would be more likely to take off and make a run for it, given the chance," pointed out Ray. "That's exactly what that person did. Whereas, a man would have been more likely to double back and confront me, or even sneak up from behind and clobber me over the head with something."

"You are still armed, aren't you?" inquired Susan.

"Absolutely," confirmed Ray as he lifted his muddy pant leg to show Susan the revolver he kept in his boot holster. "Do either of you know how to use a weapon?"

"Not me!" informed Susan.

"My husband had me shoot his shotgun once," mentioned Carolyn. "I was actually quite accurate. And, I did take handgun training once, back when I was thinking of becoming a police officer."

"Really?" Ray was surprised.

"Was that before or after you dropped out of law school?" razzed Susan.

"Before, actually," replied Carolyn. "Being a cop was just too dangerous, and becoming a lawyer was just too expensive."

"Hey, I do have a shotgun," revealed Ray. "It's yours to bring along in the morning, if you think you can handle it."

"If nothing else, I can club someone over the head with it, right?" responded Carolyn. "I'll see you two tomorrow. Just let me know if you need anything." Carolyn gave Susan a meaningful look.

262

"We will," promised Susan with a devious grin. Susan waited until Carolyn had left and then moved closer to Ray.

"I'd better get this gun cleaned up and dried off," stated Ray as he started to get up.

Susan reached over and grabbed Ray by the arm to pull him back down. "Perhaps we should get you out of these muddy clothes first. We don't want you getting sick on us."

Ray studied Susan for a long moment before replying. "You'd better not be playing me for a fool, young lady."

Susan slowly and deliberately began unbuttoning Ray's outer shirt. "There's no fool like an old fool."

"I'm serious!" cautioned Ray as he grabbed her hand to stop her from unbuttoning his shirt and then held it. "I really don't need any trouble right now."

"Whatever do you mean?" questioned Susan as she flirted with Ray. "Certainly you don't think I'm any trouble, do you?"

"Technically, you are still married," reminded Ray.

"The divorce will be final in just two more months," countered Susan. She then became serious and gently wiped a streak of mud from Ray's cheek. "What if that prowler does come back? I'd sure feel a whole lot better knowing you were here to protect me."

"What do you have in mind?" Ray felt himself drawn to Susan, and knew he would be powerless to resist her charms if he allowed himself to remain under her spell much longer.

"Perhaps there's some more of these pajamas somewhere?" Susan's gaze was inescapable. "For you."

Ray finally nodded with approval. "I'll tell you what. I'm going to go take a quick shower, and see if I can find another pair of pajamas – for me. I also need to get my satellite phone charged back up. We could end up needing it tomorrow, you never know."

"And then?" prompted Susan with a hopeful look.

"And then, I plan to go to sleep in the Rosemary Room," clarified Ray. "By myself. We all could use a good night's rest."

Susan gave Ray a disappointed look and hung her head with dejection as she slowly got up to leave.

"Wait!" requested Ray.

Susan silently remained standing where she was while she waited for Ray to speak.

"I want nothing more than for the two of us to get to know one another better," said Ray. "You have no idea what kind of effect you have on me, do you?"

Susan's alluring gaze pulled Ray right back into its power, and she smiled almost imperceptibly. Ray feared he might not escape the pull of her magnetism as easily this time.

"Even forty-four years ago," added Ray, "I was drawn to you in a way that I just can't explain."

"Perhaps you should try," encouraged Susan. Her smile increased its intensity as she slowly approached him again, but remained just out of reach.

"There are things about me you don't even know," warned Ray. "I think we should take it down a notch, and take our time."

"We all have our secrets," agreed Susan evenly. "But, there's really no hurry."

"You asked me yesterday to tell you more about Vietnam," recalled Ray, as he glanced at his watch. "Yes, it was yesterday."

"What time is it?" asked Susan.

"About half past midnight," replied Ray with a deep sigh. "But, if I don't tell you about it now, maybe I never will."

Susan slowly nodded. If Ray was willing to talk about it, she would let him. "I would like to know."

"You asked me if there was anyone special in my life over there," reminded Ray.

Susan nodded and came back over to sit by him as she patiently waited for Ray to continue.

"It was March 16, 1968," began Ray somberly. "My Lai was only one of the two hamlets of Sơn Mỹ village in Quảng Ngãi Province that was brutally massacred that day. That tragedy is generally known as the 'My Lai Massacre' here in America."

"I've heard of that!" exclaimed Susan. "That was where entire villages of innocent civilians were gunned down by a platoon of rogue American soldiers! That was horrible!"

"Indeed it was," agreed Ray. "Many of the women were gang-raped and some of their bodies mutilated beyond recognition before the welcome release of death. Twenty-six of those soldiers were charged with various crimes, including the murder of twenty-two villagers. But, only their platoon leader was actually convicted."

"You're kidding?" Susan was outraged.

264

"They gave him a life sentence," continued Ray, "but he served only three and a half years under house arrest."

"That's doesn't seem right," remarked Susan angrily.

"The woman carrying my unborn child was among the civilians that lived in that village," revealed Ray. His voice had become shaky. "You wouldn't even believe the red tape I went through before finally being allowed to come identify the body, especially since we were not technically married."

Susan put her arms around Ray to comfort him as she waited for him to continue.

"The day before it happened, I was unexpectedly deployed to participate in another mission over at Da Nang, which was about 70 kilometers north of Sơn Mỹ village," mumbled Ray. Tears were now streaming down his cheeks. "If only I'd been there to try and stop them! I'm sorry, but I just can't talk about this anymore."

Susan tenderly held Ray in her arms while the tears he'd held in check for years now flowed. "I'm so sorry! I promise, I will never ask you about it again."

"Not even Ginny knew about it," Ray finally was able to say as he battled to regain control. "She knew I struggled with post-traumatic stress on occasion, but never asked why."

"When was the last time it happened?" questioned Susan with concern. "And what should I do if it ever does again?"

"Probably just follow me around and keep an eye on me, and let it play out," described Ray. "If it gets too out of hand, you could always try slapping me across the face."

"I would probably do that anyway," grinned Susan, to lighten the mood. "If things got out of hand, that is."

"Don't worry, I've never been violent or tried to hurt anyone," assured Ray. "My dad told me once that I was trying to rescue a baby, but actually had the family dog wrapped in a little blanket and was carrying it through the forest to safety somewhere. But, that was thirty years ago, and also was the last time something like that happened."

"Oh Ray, I'm so sorry," apologized Susan.

"Well, on that happy note," prefaced Ray, "I think I should go take off these muddy clothes, take a shower, and see if there's any clean pajamas left."

"I'll tell you what," offered Susan. "You go take your shower while I find you some clean pajamas. I'll even make you a sandwich."

265

"What ever happened to all that roast, anyway?" asked Ray.

"Ted and Ann," smiled Susan. "And it was delicious!"

"Sure, you can make me a sandwich," nodded Ray as he got up to head back downstairs but then paused. "You do realize, of course, that when you're my age, I'll be almost ninety years old?"

"Actually, only eighty-eight," smiled Susan.

"Would that really be fair to you?" questioned Ray. He waited to see what her reaction would be.

"Why don't you let me decide that?" insisted Susan as she got up, walked over to Ray, put her arms around him, stood on her tiptoes, and then put one hand behind his head to pull it close while she seductively kissed him on the mouth. Ray was swiftly overcome with emotions he could no longer contain.

Ray passionately kissed Susan back for several moments, but then managed to pull away and headed for the spiral staircase leading downstairs. "I'll be looking forward to that sandwich!"

Susan was surprised but still managed to reward Ray with a seductive smile. "Me, too! Just tell me, what kind of sandwich do you have in mind?"

Susan's last remark was intended to be taken any way Ray cared to interpret it, and he knew it.

Ray swallowed uncomfortably for a moment but then smiled back at Susan in a flirtatious way. "Why don't you surprise me?"

"I'll do my best," Susan smiled a crooked smile. "Trust me!"

Morning sunlight streamed through the various lighthouse windows and woke Carolyn when it did. It seemed rather strange to Carolyn to actually sleep in, though most people would still consider six o'clock in the morning to be rather early. At home, Carolyn normally got up well before dawn each day to feed and care for her little colony of feral cats. Carolyn missed them terribly just now and wondered how her hubby was getting along with them. But, she missed him most of all, and wanted nothing more at that moment than to call and talk with him. Carolyn quickly decided to step outside to make her call so she wouldn't wake Susan or Ray before they were ready to get up for the day.

That was when Carolyn noticed Susan was no longer in her bed in the Daisy Room across from her! Carolyn tried to recall whether she had heard Susan come back downstairs after their visit with Ray in the tower room the night before, but couldn't. Uncertain now whether she should try and find either one of them or not, Carolyn stealthily headed downstairs to retrieve her clean clothes from the dryer. Her rayon skirt was ruined, though could be worn long enough for the return trip to Ms. Neilson's house for a change of clothes.

Susan would need a fresh change of clothes to wear, as well, so Carolyn made an executive decision. She would borrow the rental car keys from Susan's night stand and make a quick trip over to Ms. Neilson's house. Her plan was to return before they were awake.

Though Carolyn was still somewhat apprehensive about driving past the Roth residence, she knew there was no point in evading it now. Jon Roth already had seen them at the lighthouse the previous evening anyway. At least he had seen Susan, that is. But, Jon Roth was well aware that both of them had been there.

The dirt road was still somewhat muddy in places, but soon would dry. Too bad we didn't know about this way yesterday, thought Carolyn as she negotiated it in the new Dodge Dart rental car, whose white exterior was now spattered with dried dirt and fresh mud on top of that. It sure would have been much easier!

After passing by the old servants' quarters, Carolyn slowed when she saw a blackberry thicket off to one side of the road. Should she stop and get out to take a look?

No, it might be too dangerous. She would wait. That had to be the place, though! There were no other blackberry thickets anywhere in sight. Unable to stand it any longer, Carolyn pulled the car to a stop and slowly got out. She was careful not to let the car door slam, just in case anyone might be within hearing distance. After turning on the camera feature of her cellphone, Carolyn snapped two photos of the blackberry thicket from a distance and then two more close up. She then took a series of photos of the muddy indentations on the ground leading up to the gated bunker tunnel opening.

Carolyn was surprised to see that the iron-barred bunker tunnel gate had a combination padlock on it! All of the other bunker tunnel gates she had ever seen on campus had always been locked only with keyed padlocks. Carolyn carefully took numerous close-up photos of the combination lock itself from several different angles, and of the tracks on the floor just inside, beyond the iron bars. Nothing else of value could be seen near the opening, and the tunnel inside disappeared into the darkness beyond. They would definitely need flashlights and extra batteries when they returned!

The damp smell of hemlock and cypress trees permeated the air and the odor of fresh eucalyptus could be detected on the ocean breeze as it wafted inland. Seagulls cawed overhead, and the sound of ocean waves crashing against the shoreline resounded in the distance. Morning sunlight streamed through the thick coastal forest beside her. Sudden movement in the trees nearby caused Carolyn a moment of great concern. "Oh, hello there," Carolyn smiled with relief when she noticed a beautiful Siamese cat. Terrified at seeing an unfamiliar human, the animal quickly fled for cover.

Carolyn glanced around to be sure nothing else was watching her before rapidly returning to the dirty white Dodge Dart rental car. She hurriedly climbed inside, closed the door, started the engine back up, and slowly continued down the dirt road. Just as she rounded the bend ahead, there was the Roth house! It was less than fifty yards past the bunker tunnel gate! Carolyn wondered if the Siamese cat might belong to the Roth family. And, what if the bunker tunnel led to Jon Roth's mysterious bomb shelter? It certainly was not that far away. They would need to find out on Sunday when they went over there for that barbecue!

Unnerved to see Jon Roth standing on his back deck, drinking from a large coffee cup and reading his morning newspaper, Carolyn forced herself to nod and smile when they made eye contact while she drove past. He was wearing a green plaid bathrobe made of fleece and had on dark brown, fur lined slippers. If Birdboy wondered why Susan wasn't with her, he didn't seem to show it.

Perhaps it was only her imagination, but Jon Roth's smile seemed insincere and almost sinister! In fact, Jon Roth seemed creepier to Carolyn each time she had the misfortune of seeing him again. Would they be making a mistake in going over to his house for the barbecue on Sunday? Even so, there didn't appear to be much choice, not at this juncture, and not if they were going to get to the bottom of what had happened to Joyce and Veronica all those years ago. Carolyn knew at an instinctive level that this was where they would find the answers they sought, and that somehow Birdboy was involved! Would Ann and her mother continue to be safe there, and for how long?

Three houses down at Ms. Neilson's house, Carolyn pulled the mud spattered Dodge Dart rental car to a stop, opened the car door to get out, and then froze. Someone had broken in! The glass on the kitchen window had been smashed, and the front door left ajar! The hole in the window was large enough for someone smaller in size to easily climb through. There was no sign of tire tracks in the driveway, other than that of the 2016 Dodge Dart rental car.

Carolyn took a deep breath and then quickly let it out. Whoever had broken in would be long gone by now, anyway, so she may as well go inside and get what she came here for. It was nearly seven o'clock already! How had the time slipped by so quickly?

After again turning on the camera feature of her cellphone, Carolyn proceeded to systematically take a series of photographs all around the exterior of Ms. Neilson's house. Focusing at first on the ground outside the broken kitchen window, and then on the window itself, Carolyn then circled the entire perimeter of the small house again to search for any additional evidence. Nothing else seemed out of the ordinary. Carolyn then opened the front door with a small stick, and was careful not to touch any prints that might be on its knob.

Once inside, Carolyn noticed that absolutely nothing in the entire house appeared disturbed except for a solitary item. It was a lighthouse figurine that had been inside a glass curio cabinet in the living room. Perhaps there might be fingerprints on that! The lid of the lighthouse figurine lay beside it on the kitchen table, and the empty bottom half of it lay on its side. A small keyring with a label on it marked "lighthouse" sat beside it. If there had been a key on the keyring, it was missing now! Could it have been the missing key that had once belonged to Ginny? Just who was the prowler anyway, and how had the person known the key would be here? They must have come here first for the key before coming over to the lighthouse yesterday evening.

It would not be safe to leave their belongings at Ms. Neilson's home until after the broken kitchen window could be repaired, if then. At least at the lighthouse, Ray was armed and could protect them. Meanwhile, Carolyn would grab their things and head back.

"Where have you been?" demanded Susan. She and Ray were still dressed in his pajamas and appeared as though they had just gotten up. "You shouldn't have gone out there alone!"

"Someone broke in at Ms. Neilson's house, too," informed Carolyn. "I only went over there to get a few things so you could get dressed, but then just decided to grab it all after seeing the broken kitchen window."

"What?" Susan was flabbergasted.

"You may want to see the photos I just took," suggested Carolyn as she handed her cellphone to Susan.

Ray moved in beside Susan and put his arms around her while they looked at the photos together. Susan slowly advanced the photo frames on the cellphone.

"You went to the bunker gate, too?" questioned Ray with a raised eyebrow. "That wasn't very smart."

"Notice the combination padlock on it?" pointed out Carolyn. "All of the other bunker tunnel gates that I've seen around this campus are locked only with keyed padlocks."

"Looks like we'll need to find out the combination first before we can go in there," admitted Ray. "Or...," Ray broke off his thought.

"Or what?" pressed Susan.

"Or, we could bring along a pair of bolt cutters," suggested Ray. "Right now, that's probably our best option. We'll just need to make sure we're not caught."

"We'll need flashlights and extra batteries, too, before we even think about going inside that dark creepy tunnel," added Carolyn. "And, what if it leads to Jon Roth's bomb shelter?"

"Don't worry, I'll be armed," assured Ray. "You two should definitely stay here for the next few days. Carolyn's right, it's just not safe over there anymore. I'll be changing out the lock to the lighthouse door today and can have keys made for each of us."

"Works for me," agreed Susan as she gave Ray a suggestive smile. Ray blushed, ever so slightly.

"Hey, whatever you two have going on now is none of my business," assured Carolyn. "But, let's get one thing clear."

"What's that?" frowned Susan.

"I get the Daisy Room!" Carolyn slowly began to smile.

"Agreed," nodded Susan with a wicked grin as she handed Carolyn's cellphone back to her and then winked at Ray.

"Just how did the prowler know that key was in the lighthouse figurine at Ms. Neilson's house, anyway?" Carolyn suddenly asked.

"We may never know at this point," replied Ray, "but at least now we know how they got in here."

"And they sure won't be doing that again, either, will they?" tested Susan.

"Absolutely not," promised Ray as he gave Susan an assuring hug and a kiss on the cheek.

Sunday arrived like a bolt of lightning, and the barbecue at the Roth home was less than an hour away. The sun was out, though, and it seemed to be a perfect day for it. Ray and Susan held hands as they strolled beside Carolyn past the old servants' quarters.

"I just don't like the idea of you girls going in there without me," objected Ray.

"We've both got our cell phones with us," assured Susan.

"What if something happens where you need my help, and I can't get to you in time?" worried Ray.

"The code word can be Birdboy," suggested Susan. "If you get a text from either of us that says Birdboy, that means we're in trouble and need immediate assistance."

"Make sure you don't say it aloud!" cautioned Ray as they arrived at the blackberry thicket where Ray intended to hide so he could be close by but remain out of sight.

"What do you suppose really is beyond that solid iron blast door in there?" wondered Carolyn. "Too bad we only made it past the outer one with bars!"

It had been only two days since Ray used his bolt cutters to lop off the combination padlock on the bunker tunnel's outer gate. Unfortunately, the tunnel had led straight to a solid iron blast door only ten yards beyond that. Ray, Susan and Carolyn had all three tried in vain to pry it open, taking turns with a crowbar and a sledge hammer. Still, the iron blast door remained intact. In fact, it was the same type of impenetrable door that might be used on the back end of a bomb shelter to protect its occupants from any sort of nuclear fallout still lurking in the environment outside following a holocaust.

The only thing they still hadn't tried was explosives, as they had not wanted to alert Jon Roth of their efforts by making that amount of noise.

"You girls be careful!" bid Ray as he and Susan hugged farewell. "I'll just be right here if you need me, for anything at all."

"We'll be fine," promised Susan as she gave Ray a kiss on the cheek. "Trust me!"

Ray and Carolyn both rolled their eyes upon hearing Susan's infamous expression of "trust me."

"Come on!" Susan grabbed Carolyn by the arm and continued toward the Roth residence.

"What's your rush?" asked Carolyn. "We don't want to be too early! It might make us look over-anxious."

"Or, it might be a nice excuse to offer Ann or her mother any help they might need in getting everything ready," countered Susan.

"Okay, fine," agreed Carolyn. "Let's get on with it then."

Jon Roth was quite proud of his home and busy making sure that every last detail was enviously perfect before the arrival of his old nemeses. Susan and Carolyn had always troubled him, especially the concern that they someday might return to find out what had happened to Veronica and Joyce. And now, they were actually coming over to his home for lunch, like lambs to the slaughter! Figuratively speaking, of course. It seemed only fitting to serve them lamb burgers.

Jon had named his two most recent lambs Pete and Lenny, as a joke, knowing they would eventually be slaughtered and eaten, though he never would have imagined by whom. This was too good to be true! Jon chuckled to himself at the very thought of Carolyn eating a "Lenny Burger" and then learning the creature's name while consuming it. An irrepressible grin ensued.

"Dad, where are the paper towels?" questioned Ann. "Did you remember to get some more?"

"We can use cloth napkins today," replied Jon as he continued to smile. "After all, it isn't every day that we have such dear old friends over for a visit."

"It will be nice to see them again," replied Ann's mother rather distantly. She suddenly appeared to be deep in thought.

"Indeed," nodded Jon as he squirted some lighter fluid on his neatly arranged barbecue briquettes and then tossed a match onto them. Flames instantly leaped outward for several feet in every direction. Ann and her father both backed away immediately.

"Careful!" scolded Ann. "We both could have been burned!"

"Oh, I'm always careful," replied her father with a faraway look in his eyes that suddenly gave her an uncomfortable feeling.

272

Ann then turned to her mother and asked, "How well did you know Susan or Carolyn? You've never mentioned them."

"It's a very small world," answered Mrs. Roth uncomfortably before heading for the house.

"Let's use our best china today," called Jon Roth. He was well aware that his wife intended to use paper plates, plastic silverware and paper towels to minimize cleanup afterwards.

His wife paused at the door to the house without looking back at him, but finally nodded her head in agreement before going inside. This was getting to be ridiculous! She was exhausted already from cleaning house for the past three days, not to mention "helping" her husband scrub down and re-stain each of the three tiered levels of their large redwood deck almost entirely by herself! Mrs. Roth was especially thankful for the huge patio roof that covered most of it during the recent rain storm. Three rows of sky windows in the huge roof made it possible to look up and enjoy the old growth forest growing around the Roth home from nearly anywhere on the deck.

Mrs. Roth was also grateful that Ann had helped scrub off and re-stain the matching redwood patio furniture. Not only that, Ann had carefully cleaned the vintage chaise lounge cushions that went with them. The cheerful daisy pattern fabric on them consisted of yellow and white daisies over an olive green background. Jon Roth considered the patio furniture and their cushions to be treasured heirlooms, as both had been acquired from the old lumber mill. Jon would never forget his job at the lumber mill forty-three years ago when he was a student at Oceanview Academy!

"Mom?" called Ann as she came inside and found her mother in the kitchen. "Dad says he would like to use the crystal goblets, and real silverware, too."

"Of course he would!" muttered Mrs. Roth. She was nearly at her breaking point.

"Let me help," offered Ann.

"Thanks!" smiled her mother weakly as she handed Ann an empty serving tray to use for transporting the various items that would clearly be needed now.

"Dad is quite proud of the outdoor living space we have out there," reminded Ann. It was almost as if she could read her mother's mind. "I'm sure he just wants to show it off so he can make a good impression."

"I know," responded Mrs. Roth with a deep sigh of frustration.

"Actually, I'm surprised he just didn't go out and get new patio furniture," chuckled Ann as she carefully began placing her mother's crystal goblets on the serving tray.

"He'll never get rid of that patio furniture, believe me!" assured her mother. "It holds sentimental value for him. Just like that old car, and heaven only knows how he keeps it running!"

"Yeah, I suppose you're right," realized Ann.

"Is there room for the cloth napkins and the silverware?" questioned Mrs. Roth.

"That'll be another trip," answered Ann. "I'll be right back."

Ann had no sooner stepped outside than Jon Roth asked her, "Is the potato salad ready yet?"

"It's in the refrigerator, ready to go," assured Ann as she set down the tray of goblets and began transferring them to the table.

"We really should use the lace tablecloth," decided Jon Roth, unhappy with having the crystal goblets sitting directly on the redwood patio picnic table.

"Yes, sir," responded Ann as she hurried inside, leaving the half unloaded tray of goblets where they were.

Ann quickly hurried to the hall closet and retrieved the handmade white lace tablecloth that had been lovingly created by Edith Roth when she was alive.

"What are you doing with that?" demanded her mother. This was going too far!

Ann merely looked at her and shrugged her shoulders.

"All right, go on then," acquiesced Mrs. Roth. She certainly knew better than to do or say anything that might contradict or upset her husband in any way, especially with his temper.

Ann hurried back outside to spread the elegant lace tablecloth on her father's prized picnic table before resuming her task of setting out the crystal goblets. Mrs. Roth emerged from the house carrying a stack of china plates and left them on the end of the table for Ann to arrange. She then hurried back inside to retrieve the sterling silverware and a stack of cloth napkins. Jon Roth nodded with approval at their efforts. He wanted everything to be flawless.

The uppermost tier of the spacious deck was twenty-five feet wide and fifteen feet in length. It stepped down onto a slightly smaller second tier beneath it, and then down again onto a third and smallest tier beneath them both. All three sections were surrounded in their entirety by a continuous four-foot high slatted handrail. Built-in bench seats were located around the edges in each of the upper two sections.

The far edge of the lowest and smallest tier stepped down onto a well-manicured gravel foot path inlaid with large slate stepping stones. The path itself was bordered by a hearty mat of creeping succulent ice plants interspersed with sedums. The herbaceous evergreen ground cover would not bloom until early summer, but bright pink and yellow blossoms were expected. Several Hoary Manzanita bushes, however, were already blossoming. Some of them had pink blooms while others were white.

Gently curving for several yards through the old growth forest, the foot path connected with the dirt road that extended from behind the Roth house over to the old servants' quarters and lighthouse. Jon had used the path as an excuse to have several of the old growth trees removed to make room for it, and to enable limited views of the ocean beyond from his deck. Jon's other reason for having the trees removed was less known, but involved the careful placement of security cameras where the path and several other locations on his property could be monitored.

The monitoring station was located inside his bomb shelter where he could sit and watch, any time he wished. Jon Roth suddenly burst out laughing as he thought of how hard Ray, Susan and Carolyn had labored with their crowbar and sledge hammer to try and conquer his impregnable blast door. Jon slapped one hand on his thigh as he continued to howl with laughter.

"What's so funny, Dad?" questioned Ann with a cautious smile. She wanted in on the joke.

"This was such a great idea!" beamed Jon Roth as he suddenly hugged his daughter Ann and kissed her on the forehead. "It will be fun! I'm glad you thought of this."

"I'm glad you approve," responded Ann. Her father's behavior never ceased to puzzle or amaze her.

"Susan!" exclaimed Ann as she saw Carolyn and Susan coming up the path.

"You're early," greeted Jon Roth with a radiant smile.

"If there's anything we can do to help...," began Carolyn.

"Nonsense!" interrupted Jon. "You're our guests. Please, sit."

"Nice patio furniture. Surely these can't be from the lumber mill?" questioned Susan with surprise. "They still look like new."

"Indeed they are, and yes they do," smirked Jon, pleased that she had noticed.

Carolyn studied the Roth home with great interest. Even though the front of it was a charming cottage cove style circa 1950, the back portion of the home where the elaborate tiered deck was located was much newer by design. The entire dwelling was painted in brown, tan and other earthy colors that blended amazingly well with the forest surrounding it. But, the back portion of the Roth home reminded Carolyn greatly of a Frank Lloyd Wright home she had once visited.

"You have a beautiful place here," complimented Carolyn. She meant it and Jon Roth could tell.

"Thank you," smiled Jon Roth. Things could not be going better. Soon, they would be feasting on Lenny burgers. Jon tried to repress a huge grin at the very thought of it.

"Ted!" cried Ann as she rushed out to meet him. Dean Jorgensen had driven him over for the occasion, as Ted was still using crutches. Jon Roth's pleasant expression disappeared almost immediately as he watched Ted Jensen and his daughter embrace before she proceeded to help him up the walkway. Dean Jorgensen smiled and waved at Jon Roth and his family before driving away in his deep blue 2014 Ford Transit Connect Wagon.

"I didn't realize you were still coming," mumbled Jon Roth, though not meaning to be rude. "With your sprained ankle, that is."

"Wild horses couldn't keep me away," informed Ted as he gazed lovingly at Ann.

Jon Roth felt his blood pressure rise slightly when he saw the way his daughter Ann stared at Ted, with that same love-sick look.

"May I use your restroom?" Carolyn asked politely. Her true intent was to get a better look at the inside of the Roth residence and see if anything of interest might be there.

"Certainly," nodded Jon as he turned his attention to the barbecue coals. They were just now ready. "Ann, go see if your mother has the burgers ready for me to put on the grill yet."

"Be glad to," responded Ann.

Ted and Susan were seated on one of the bench seats where they watched Jon Roth poking at the coals to get them just as he wanted them while he waited for the meat.

Susan frowned as she saw Carolyn disappear into the Roth home by herself and checked to be sure her cellphone was on.

The interior of the Roth home still smelled of cleaners but was immaculate and spotless, including its plush white carpets and clean white walls. Carolyn debated on whether to remove her shoes, but decided against it. What if some unforeseen circumstances required her to make a hasty retreat? One could never tell about such things.

Carolyn could hear Ann and her mother in the kitchen, hurriedly grabbing the potato salad, chips and other food items they planned to take outside. Carolyn would offer to help them, just after using the restroom. No doubt it would be as clean as the rest of the home, judging by what she'd seen already.

Not only was the home "hospital clean" – an expression Carolyn had always used to describe the Bennett home after her own mother had cleaned it – but it was also very orderly and neat. Even the large framed family pictures hanging on the wall in the long hallway were exactly level, and appeared to be perfectly plumb. Carolyn paused to study the picture of Jon Roth's parents. His mother Edith had always been well thought of by the students at Oceanview Academy. Too bad the same could not be said for her son!

Deep in thought as she found and entered an immaculately clean restroom at the end of the hall, Carolyn went inside and closed the door. As she reached to lock its handle, Carolyn came face-to-face with a dark hooded cloak that was there drying on a hanger.

"Oh my gosh!" muttered Carolyn with disbelief as she stared at the cloak. It must belong to whomever had been lurking in the forest recently! And what was it doing here, of all places?

The hanger on which it hung dangled from a white ceramic wall hook mounted to the back of the door. Upon closer inspection, Carolyn felt and noticed that the thick wool fabric was still damp. Obviously, the cloak had recently been washed! A noticeable tear on the right sleeve of the cloak also caught Carolyn's attention.

Carolyn immediately took out and turned on her cellphone's camera. After snapping a couple choice shots of the cloak, including a close-up of the torn sleeve, Carolyn simultaneously broadcast the photos in a text message to both Susan and Ray that simply said, "Still wet, pockets empty."

Grateful that she had learned to use a smartphone the previous year, instead of the flip phone she had used before that, Carolyn glanced at the elegant marble counter top, solid brass faucet fixture, and lilac colored accent tiles. The bathroom also had lilac colored window and shower curtains, throw rugs and matching towels. A stunning round wall mirror was held up with expensive looking brass arms. How in the world could Jon Roth afford all of this on a teacher's salary?

Knowing she would soon be missed, Carolyn hurriedly searched the drawers, cupboards and medicine cabinet, but found absolutely nothing resembling Ginny's journal. Carolyn then used the restroom, washed her hands, brushed her hair and touched up her makeup before finally opening the bathroom door. Her plan was to slip into the large bedroom she had noticed next door to it, to see if anything suspicious might be visible.

Even more startling than coming face-to-face with the black cloak only moments before, was to open the bathroom door now and find Ann Roth's mother standing there! Carolyn gawked at Ann's mother in stunned silence for several moments.

"Sheree?" Carolyn finally managed to whisper.

"Carolyn?" muttered Mrs. Roth, who also was surprised.

"Sheree Wilkins?" questioned Carolyn, to be absolutely sure her eyes were not playing tricks on her.

"It's Sheree Roth now," replied Ann's mother with an almost expressionless gaze. Perhaps this was the opportunity Sheree had been praying for! But, would Carolyn of all people agree to help her? Could she be trusted? Sheree had to find out, but did not have time to stand on ceremony. It was no longer safe here, not for her or her daughter, and Sheree knew it. In fact, Sheree had finally decided only today that she could not risk staying here with Jon Roth any longer and must leave him, no matter what it took. Jon Roth was rapidly reverting to his Birdboy personality again, and Sheree feared the worst. Birdboy could be extremely dangerous and unpredictable, and would very soon need professional help once again. This window of opportunity to ask for outside assistance might not present itself again!

"Mother, you look as if you've seen a ghost," commented Ann as she joined them.

"Oh, I'm sorry," apologized Sheree. "Yes, of course! You are the Carolyn that Ann has been talking so much about. I just hadn't made the connection. I didn't realize it would actually be you!"

"Nor did I have any idea that Ann's mother would actually be you!" admitted Carolyn. She was genuinely dumbfounded by the irony of it all.

"It's nice that Ann has someone she can actually talk to about all those animals she seems to love so much," replied Sheree. "And please don't take this wrong, but the guest bathroom is over there, on the end. This one is private."

"Mother doesn't even let me use this restroom," mentioned Ann, to try and smooth things over.

"No, wait!" requested Carolyn as she held her free hand up in the stop position. "We're not doing this. We're not playing this game. We both know that I've seen the cloak already."

"What cloak?" demanded Ann as she turned to her mother.

Carolyn nodded toward the private bathroom's door and commanded, "Look inside."

Sheree appeared extremely nervous and anxiously glanced down the long hallway as her daughter went inside her private restroom and then saw the cloak.

"Just where did this cloak come from? Is it yours?" fumed Ann as she angrily approached her mother with both hands on her hips and awaited a response. "Well?"

"And where is the journal you took from the lighthouse?" pressed Carolyn. "Yes, we know you have it!"

"Oh, Carolyn, I'm so sorry! Please give me a chance to explain," begged Sheree in hushed tones. "Jon can never find out about any of this! Please come with me before he sees us, quickly!"

Carolyn hesitated and exchanged a surprised glance with Ann. Sheree started for the huge bedroom and urged, "Come on!"

Concerned about trusting Sheree too easily, especially after everything that had happened not only in the past but also during the past few days, Carolyn hung back. Carolyn would never have imagined that Mrs. Jon Roth and Sheree Wilkins were one and the same person, and yet they were! What if Sheree Roth turned out to be someone they should be concerned about, too? Who in their right mind would be lurking around the forest at night in a dark cloak and breaking into people's homes? It had been forty-three years, after all. Perhaps Sheree was as dangerous as her husband!

"Let's at least hear what she has to say?" pleaded Ann. "I think she's right; we can't let my father find us here like this!"

Finally, Carolyn nodded in agreement and cautiously followed after them. Sheree hastily led them through the bedroom and over to a walk-in closet whose sliding closet doors were entirely covered with mirrors from top to bottom. Sheree glanced behind them to be sure no one else had followed before opening the closet door. After quickly pushing the hanging clothes on the far left end over to one side, Sheree gingerly pressed a hidden button that triggered a secret door panel to slide open. "Follow me, and be sure to pull the clothes back before you close that closet door behind you!"

Once all three of them had passed through the secret escape door, Sheree pressed another button on the other side to make it close again. They were in an unexpectedly pleasant but small sitting room that overlooked the forest outside and was completely encased by large picture windows. "The glass is one-way," mentioned Sheree. "No one outside can see inside."

The entire room was about ten-foot square and contained only an oversized loveseat, area rug, and a small lamp stand with an adjustable reading lamp on it. The olive green fabric on the loveseat was decorated with darker green ivy leaf patterns on its soft plush surface. The pale yellow walls and burgundy colored area rug on its hardwood floor gave the room a comfortable feeling. Within the lamp stand was a small drawer and beneath it was a solitary shelf containing a small stack of popular magazines. The whole setup reminded Carolyn of the waiting room at some upscale doctor's office.

"Wow!" remarked Ann. "Does father know about this room?"

"Absolutely not!" assured Sheree. "In fact, this is the only room in the entire house where Jon hasn't installed hidden security cameras, microphones or both, and only because he knows nothing about it. The Roths actually did some major remodeling while their son was institutionalized for all those years. They had the bomb shelter installed inside that bunker tunnel, since the tunnel was already there anyway, and even had the blast doors put on either end of it. They also put in a generator, out by the greenhouse, and it can run everything in the house, including the bomb shelter, for up to a week."

"Impressive," remarked Carolyn.

"But, they never did tell Jon about this room," assured Sheree. "They wanted a place to retreat to if necessary after Jon's release, should he ever become dangerous again. Someplace he knew nothing about. It was Edith who finally told me about this room when she was still alive. She wanted me to have at least one safe place I could retreat to, if I ever needed it. She was well aware of her son's temper."

"What?" Ann was flabbergasted. "Back up for a moment. Did I hear you say there are cameras and microphones everywhere else? Even in my room? Are you sure?"

"I'm afraid so," apologized her mother. "And, the monitoring screens for them are all located in that precious bomb shelter of his."

"No wonder he doesn't want anyone else going in there," commented Carolyn as she shook her head.

"Jon would have seen you searching that restroom, had he not been out there on the patio," explained Sheree. "The only reason he didn't see my cloak was because I washed and hung it there when he was out someplace else, and made sure it was hanging on the back of the door to dry, out of the camera's eye."

"How can you live like this?" scowled Carolyn.

Sheree shrugged her shoulders and shook her head.

"So, father watches us go to the bathroom whenever he feels like it, too?" Ann was disgusted.

"I don't think he would do that," assured Sheree. "The purpose for the cameras was actually so they could keep an eye on both of us, following our releases from the institution, though Jon was actually released first, just a few weeks before I was. His parents were named as our legal custodians for a minimum of ten years after that, since we were already married anyway."

Ann and Carolyn both took a moment to process what Sheree was trying to explain.

"Does this mean I'm crazy, too?" Ann suddenly asked Carolyn. Carolyn slowly shook her head in the negative. "No, of course not!"

"See! This is exactly why I didn't want her to know!" Sheree was clearly frustrated by Ann's reaction.

"Listen to me," commanded Carolyn as she put her hands on Ann's shoulders and waited until she had her full attention. "Even though mental illness can sometimes be more common in people whose blood relatives have been diagnosed with something like that, it doesn't necessarily mean they're predestined to have it, too!"

"She's right!" agreed Sheree. "When I was pregnant with you, I was especially concerned about the subject and tried to learn everything I could about it. For example, did you know that there are only five major mental illnesses that are proven to be inherited? Those include depression, bipolar disorder, ADHD, schizophrenia and autism."

"Oh, great!" Ann rolled her eyes.

"But," elaborated Sheree, "only seventeen percent of the people who ever have those particular mental illnesses actually inherited them."

"Like heart disease or diabetes," added Carolyn. "Just because people in my family might happen to have those particular diseases doesn't necessarily mean that I will end up getting them, too."

"All it means," continued Sheree, "is that there could be a tendency toward it. Being aware of what to do and getting proper treatment or medication when needed is key to prevention."

"So, if Ted and I were to get married and have children," clarified Ann, "then there would only be a seventeen percent chance that they would become mentally ill at some point in their lives, is that what you're telling me?"

"That also means that there's an eighty-three percent chance that they won't!" countered Sheree.

"Still, it does seem surprising that they would actually let the two of you get married while you were still patients at the Ocean Bluff Mental Institution," opined Carolyn.

"That was only after we were both better and right before our release," revealed Sheree uncomfortably. "Initially, I was catatonic for two entire years, and it took me six more years after that to recover enough to be considered stable. I promise I will tell you both all about it when we have more time, but that's a very long story and we just don't have the time for it right now. We really need to get back."

Ann was clearly upset at not having been told any of this before, and was fighting back tears.

"Please don't cry!" pleaded Sheree as she gave Ann a hug.

"How did you know about the lighthouse key, anyway?" Carolyn suddenly asked.

"Edith was the one who told me about the lighthouse key and where to find it," revealed Sheree. "But, until you and Susan showed up there never seemed to be a reason to try and retrieve it."

"To break into Ms. Neilson's house?" asked Carolyn.

"Naturally!" confessed Sheree. "Edith also told me about the journal, and that Ray Dixon had it. Once I knew Ann was hanging around over there, it became imperative for me to try and get the journal out of there before Ann could see it."

"But, why?" asked Ann.

"Because I never wanted you to find out about my stay at the Ocean Bluff Mental Institution," replied Sheree nervously.

"Still, I had a right to know!" scolded Ann.

Sheree's lip began to quiver and tears welled up in her eyes. She removed her thick glasses to wipe them away with her sleeve.

"Here," offered Carolyn as she pulled a small packet of Kleenex from her purse and handed it to Sheree.

"Thank you," sniffed Sheree as she took it from her and proceeded to pull one out and use it.

"Sheree," began Carolyn, "I want you to know how sorry I am for what happened all those years ago with the clocks that night."

"Huh?" Ann had no idea what they were talking about.

"It wasn't you who hid them," replied Sheree. "I know that now. Ms. Dixon told me."

"Still, I should have done something to stop them," argued Carolyn. "And I didn't! I just let them do it."

"I'm guessing you were probably up the rest of that night trying to find and turn them all off?" Sheree smiled at the thought of it.

"Indeed I was," confirmed Carolyn, as she shook her head.

"Yet, you and Susan are still friends, even after all these years." It was more of a statement of the obvious than it was a question. Sheree studied Carolyn carefully. Would Carolyn be willing to help them get away from Jon Roth? Could she trust her?

"Carolyn and I were roommates," elaborated Sheree, for her daughter's sake.

"No kidding?" chuckled Ann with amazement. She sure hadn't seen that coming.

"However, Ms. Dixon, Edith and her sister Helen were the only real friends I ever had," claimed Sheree as she gave Carolyn a meaningful look.

"Helen from the mental institution?" quizzed Ann.

"You've been over there, too?" gasped Sheree.

"Susan and I took Ann over there one afternoon after school," explained Carolyn. "We were all trying to see what we could find out about Jon Roth."

"They wouldn't even let ME look at Dad's file," recalled Ann. "Nurse Redden said it was because I'm a minor and needed a blood relative over eighteen years old to come back and sign for me first. So, I was planning to see if you would. Believe me, none of us had any idea you were ever a patient there yourself! It's no wonder that old battle-axe looked at me the way she did!"

"Nurse Redden was definitely that!" agreed Sheree. "Oh, Ann, I wish you'd come to me sooner about this."

"So, about that journal?" reminded Carolyn. "If you already know we're looking for it, then I'm sure you also know why."

Sheree merely nodded her head in agreement.

"We're here to try and find out what happened to Joyce and Veronica all those years ago," added Carolyn, "and we suspect that your husband may have had something to do with it."

"I need to know, too," interjected Ann. "Father's behavior has become more and more peculiar than ever lately, and there's just something off about him."

"Even Susan and I are concerned for your safety," informed Carolyn. "If Jon Roth is as unstable as we suspect, it could be unsafe for either of you to remain here alone with him."

"I couldn't agree with you more," Sheree unexpectedly remarked. "I've been debating on whether to ask for your help, Carolyn. It really isn't safe here anymore, for either of us. Still, this is our home. And perhaps HE should be the one to leave!"

"You really think he would?" scoffed Ann. "There were some records I found over in the office at the school in a confidential file one afternoon. I knew I wasn't supposed to look at them, but when I saw father's name on the file, I just had to know what was inside."

"And?" prompted Sheree.

"All it really said was that Jon Roth was committed to the Ocean Bluff Mental Institution in the spring of 1973, immediately following a tragic incident at the beach," recalled Ann. "It didn't even say why!"

"There's actually a file there that says that?" Sheree was clearly alarmed. "Are there any files about me?"

"No, not that I saw," replied Ann. "But, I wasn't looking for anything with your name on it at the time."

"I wonder if Jon knows that file is there," worried Sheree.

"I doubt it," assured Ann. "If he did, it probably wouldn't still be there. But, finding it made me curious to find out whether it was around the same time that Steve Fredrickson died from that shark attack, or when Veronica Jensen and Joyce Troglite disappeared."

"That was on March 23, 1973," reminded Carolyn.

"Today is March 23rd!" realized Ann.

"Yes, indeed," muttered Carolyn sadly.

Sheree sadly nodded. She was well aware of the significance of this day, and how her husband was sometimes affected by it.

"There is no exact date on when father was actually committed in that file," recalled Ann. "And try as I might, I just couldn't find anything else about when or why. All it indicated was that it was in the spring of 1973."

"I had no idea you suspected anything," admitted Sheree as she reached for and opened a small drawer on the stand beside them. Inside was Ginny's journal! "Should something ever happen to me, everything I know is in there. I even made some entries of my own at the end of it."

Ann started to grab the journal, but Sheree pulled it away. "No! This is for Carolyn to read. If she feels you should know what is inside, I will leave it to her discretion. Right now, we are going to have to trust Carolyn to try and help us leave this place, but only if I can get us out of here in one piece first!"

Carolyn nodded her agreement as she reverently took the journal from Sheree and carefully put it inside her purse. Unknown to Ann or Sheree, Carolyn had stealthily snapped a photo of Sheree handing her the journal and had just texted it to Susan and Ray while putting the cellphone back inside her purse after "making room" for the journal.

"We need to get back out there right now!" fretted Sheree. "How long have we been in here?"

"Not long," assured Carolyn. "Just a few minutes."

"If Jon notices we're missing, that could set him off," feared Sheree. "Ever since his encounter with you and Susan in the cafeteria the other morning, things have not been the same."

"Everything sets him off," mumbled Ann. "Plus, I have a right to know what's in that journal, and why you were catatonic."

"In good time," promised Sheree, more tenderly.

"I'd just like to know what you can tell us about Joyce and Veronica," reminded Carolyn. "Do you know anything that could help us find out what happened to them? Did Jon do something to them?"

"I'll answer all your questions – both of you – but this just isn't the time for it," maintained Sheree. "I can't talk about it right now."

"Your mother's right," agreed Carolyn. "We do need to get back out there before we're missed."

"So, how do we know he won't be waiting by the closet door when we come back out of here?" asked Ann.

"Oh, I never go back that way," sniggered Sheree. "Not unless he's at class or I know without question that he's not at home. Besides, Jon has his own bedroom at the other end of the house, and his own closet. The only reason he would go into mine would be if he were searching for me."

"You have separate bedrooms?" Carolyn raised her eyebrows.

"We haven't slept together in years," assured Sheree proudly. "The only reason I even stayed here after my recovery – besides the fact that his parents were my legal guardians – was to make sure Ann was safe from that monster! But now, with his Birdboy personality emerging again, probably none of us is safe. I really had hoped that Birdboy was gone forever, and even believed it myself for a while, but I can see now that Jon Roth is a very sick man and needs professional help. Absolutely anything could set him off again."

Both Carolyn and Ann were speechless as they watched Sheree Roth bend down and carefully flip up the edge of the burgundy colored area rug. Beneath the rug was the outline of a trapdoor in the beautiful hardwood floor.

Sheree gingerly pressed against a small round indentation on one edge of the trapdoor, causing it to immediately release from the inside and open downward. Sheree hurriedly descended the short flight of wrought iron steps that led onto a hanging catwalk. The catwalk was suspended from the ceiling with wrought iron poles and enclosed on both sides by waist high handrails.

"Close the trapdoor behind you," directed Sheree. "Just push it up until the latch clicks into place."

286

"All rightie, then," agreed Carolyn as she motioned for Ann to go first and then followed.

Before closing the trapdoor above her, Carolyn covertly snapped a quick photo of the open trapdoor on her cellphone and texted it to Susan and Ray. Carolyn was startled when she realized Ann had been standing beside her the entire time.

"Aren't you going to say anything in your text?" asked Ann while she waited for Carolyn to close the trapdoor.

"A picture's worth a thousand words," replied Carolyn as she returned the cellphone to her purse, carefully checking to be sure the precious journal was still there. Carolyn was certainly glad she hadn't left her white tennis shoes by the Roths' patio door when coming inside to use the restroom!

The catwalk they were on seemed to go on forever, and the small recessed safety lights above them were so dim that they barely managed to stave off the pitch dark environment surrounding them.

"It sure feels cold and damp down here," complained Ann.

"It's supposed to be," replied Sheree. "That's how the military was able to preserve all their supplies when they kept them here."

"Seems like the moisture would have ruined it all and made it moldy or something," persisted Ann.

"Who knows, maybe it did," sighed Sheree. "We're almost to the back entrance of your father's beloved bomb shelter."

Carolyn could not help but notice a tinge of sarcasm in Sheree's voice, but was beginning to comprehend why Sheree had asked for her help and unexpectedly felt compassion for both Sheree and Ann. Carolyn made up her mind that very moment that she would indeed help rescue them from the clutches of Jon Roth.

Sheree finally reached a side gate to the catwalk that swung open and led down another flight of wrought iron stairs. Thankfully, it also had handrails.

"Where would the catwalk lead to, if we stayed on it?" questioned Ann.

"Through miles and miles of underground tunnels," described Sheree. "They lead to other bunker tunnel openings all over the campus, but most of them are locked from the outside with keyed padlocks, so there would be no way out."

"That would be a terrible predicament to be in," remarked Carolyn. "Seems like a person could easily get lost down here. too."

"Very possibly," agreed Sheree. "It's never a good idea to go exploring without a map and a good flashlight, that's for sure."

"Or a good pair of bolt cutters," added Carolyn.

"Have you ever explored any of them?" queried Ann as they finished descending the flight of stairs and reached the tunnel's floor.

"These tunnels? Only once," answered Sheree. "But I wasn't actually exploring at the time, so I don't remember much about it. The lights you see right here only extend as far as the Roth property above us, as nearly as I can tell. It gets pretty dark after that, and you'd definitely need a lantern or a flashlight to go any farther."

"That must be the bomb shelter?" assumed Carolyn when she noticed a solid iron blast door ahead of them, identical to the one she, Ray and Susan had spent three days trying to open from outside.

Sheree merely nodded and wasted no time locating a small round finger hole at the far right side of the door and stuck her index finger inside. Within moments, the thick door began rising upward.

"I would never have figured that out," marveled Carolyn as she and Ann followed Sheree inside.

"There's another opening mechanism just like it on the outside blast door you guys were trying to open with that crowbar and sledge hammer the other day," smiled Sheree as she inserted her finger into the interior door hole to activate the mechanism to make it close again. "Jon's been laughing about that ever since and just couldn't stand being the only one who knew about it."

"So he told you?" Carolyn was surprised.

"He never told me!" pointed out Ann.

"Wow!" chuckled Carolyn. "I think we tried everything short of dynamite on it, too."

"Or C-4?" added Ann with a grin. She would very much have enjoyed watching them try to open that door!

"Good heavens!" exclaimed Carolyn when she noticed the monitoring station in front of them. At least thirty closed circuit television monitors were simultaneously running, each with a different view of someplace inside the Roth home or on the outside grounds surrounding it.

"There's Susan and Ted," noticed Ann.

"But where's Jon Roth?" wondered Carolyn.

"That's a very good question," agreed Sheree as she urgently glanced at each of the various monitors.

"There he is!" spotted Ann.

Jon Roth could be seen carrying a crystal water pitcher filled with ice water from the house to the deck, where he proceeded to fill the crystal goblets before handing one to Susan and then one to Ted. The entire time, Jon kept glancing around, as if he were looking for someone, and did not appear very happy at the moment.

Then, unexpectedly, Jon looked directly at them! Of course, he did know where the hidden cameras were located that fed to the closed circuit television monitors they were watching, but did he suspect they were there watching him?

"What are we going to do?" fretted Ann. "He's probably already searched the house!"

"There's nothing we can do about that now," reminded Carolyn. "Perhaps it's time I sent a text to Ray."

Carolyn quickly pulled out her cellphone and took a "selfie" of herself with Sheree, Ann and the monitoring station in the background. Her message to Susan and Ray said, "Smile, you're both on camera!"

"Oh, look! There he is!" pointed out Ann. "There's Ray, by the outside blast door. He's reading your text now!"

"Where?" scowled Sheree. "I don't see him."

"He's pretty stealthy," replied Carolyn. "Look by the side, near the blackberry thicket."

"Okay, I see him now," said Sheree. "Ray's looking around now, like he's trying to find something."

"Indeed," nodded Carolyn.

"Text Ray to join us for lunch," suggested Ann. "Then when we get out there, I'll just tell father I forgot to mention it before."

"Which door do we open to get out of here?" queried Carolyn as she began preparing the text for Ray. She would definitely copy Susan on this one, too. Just in case.

"There's a third opening," revealed Sheree. "That's the one we'll need to use. It comes out in the greenhouse, by the generator. From there, it's just a brief stroll through the garden, where we've been all along. I just wanted to show you my begonias."

"That's right!" Ann liked the idea. "The pink ones, that are just starting to bloom."

"Works for me," approved Carolyn.

Carolyn suddenly noticed that the walls were lined with dozens of dark green hard plastic storage buckets. The five-gallon buckets were sealed with gamma lids and neatly labeled. The buckets contained dried wheat, dried beans, rice, lentils, soy beans, popcorn, split peas, and every sort of dried legume imaginable. All were arranged alphabetically with the labels facing exactly outward. In another area was a tilted can dispenser with every sort of canned food item known to man, also arranged in alphabetical order with the labels facing outward.

"There's enough food here to feed an army for a year!" exclaimed Carolyn.

"Oh, that's not all that's here," assured Sheree. "He's got everything. Medical supplies, toiletries, and anything else that might be needed to survive. See all those fifty-five gallon drums on that other wall? Those are all filled with drinking water."

"Actually, that's really not a bad idea," replied Carolyn. "My husband and I do have something similar to that of our own, but nothing this extensive and definitely not as well organized."

"Well, Jon's even got gas masks and chemical suits!" snickered Sheree. "Just tell me, who would want to live in a world where you'd need to wear that stuff to survive, anyway? Can you imagine being stuck with Jon Roth as the last man left alive on planet earth? Certainly not me! I've had enough!"

"Look over here!" called Ann from just ahead of them. "Outdoor gear! He's got backpacks, sleeping bags, tents, and all sorts of stuff. Even snow shoes!"

"And who would need snowshoes at the beach?" chuckled Sheree. "He really is nuts!"

Carolyn and Ann both laughed along with Sheree after her last remark. Sadly, they all knew how true it was.

That was when Carolyn noticed the huge gun cabinet with glass doors up ahead. Apparently, the glass doors were only intended to keep dust and other environmental factors from affecting the functionality of Jon Roth's arsenal of weapons, as the bomb shelter itself was already a secure facility.

"These all belong to your husband?" Carolyn became somber. "Why in the world would someone with a mental illness be allowed to have all these weapons?"

"He didn't get them while his parents were alive," replied Sheree. "And I definitely do not approve!"

Carolyn quickly snapped a photo of the entire collection. In it, the gun cabinet could easily be seen housing various rifles, handguns, revolvers, and even a machine gun and a rocket launcher! Carolyn then snapped a close-up of the glass covered shelves on which an unlimited supply of ammunition boxes could be seen in plain view.

Deciding not to alarm Susan, Carolyn sent the last two photos only to Ray with the words, "Be careful! Jon could be armed!"

"So, you mentioned there was a third way out of here?" reminded Carolyn. "This place really does give me the creeps."

"Amen to that," agreed Sheree. "Over here."

Sheree approached the gun cabinet, opened one of its glass doors, and pressed a button in the far right corner, right next to a 45 revolver.

"That looks just like the one Ray keeps in his boot holster," noticed Carolyn.

"He better have it loaded if he plans to pull it out," replied Sheree as she nodded toward a target paper hanging on the wall nearby. Repeated shots had previously been fired at the paper, leaving behind a plethora of holes directly in the bullseye zone!

The section of wall on which the hole ridden target paper hung suddenly rose upward. Sheree's beautiful pink begonias were definitely a sight for sore eyes! Carolyn and Ann followed her into the greenhouse without hesitation and were grateful to be free at last from the confines of Jon Roth's bomb shelter. Sheree quickly found and pressed another button - secreted beneath a relatively heavy but hollow frog figurine - which caused the wall to lower again behind them. The greenhouse side of the escape door was covered entirely by mirrors that gave the entire indoor garden area an aura of spaciousness.

"They're beautiful!" admired Carolyn as she approached the raised bed of perennials filled with pink, purple, yellow and red begonias. "Do you ever grow them outside?"

"Not this time of year," answered Sheree. "Most people just grow them indoors, anyway, since they don't do well when it's cold out. Begonias are usually native to tropical climates."

Carolyn could not help but notice that all of the other raised planter beds were filled with edible items such as tomatoes, squash, cucumbers, Swiss chard, onions, garlic, cilantro, basil, lettuce, kale, green beans, and even sweet potatoes. "Do you grow all of your own food here?"

"Most of it," responded Sheree proudly. "You didn't even see the pantry, did you?"

"It's a small room just off the kitchen where all of our oldest canned goods are kept so we can rotate and use them before they go bad," elaborated Ann. "We do our own canning, too."

"I've put up strawberry jam before," mentioned Carolyn, "but that's about it. It's just way too much of a mess to clean up for me, and it's actually cheaper just to buy it at the store, anyway."

"That's for sure," nodded Sheree. "But Jon always says it's not as much fun to buy it when you can make it yourself. Though I've never seen Jon help us out with all the fun we seem to keep having."

"We even grow our own meat," added Ann. "Unfortunately, I always get way too attached to them."

"Where are the animals?" Carolyn suddenly asked. She had not seen anything resembling a barn anywhere near the Roth home.

"The school lets us keep them over in a special area by the dairy, in exchange for our eggs." revealed Ann.

"You have chickens, too?" Carolyn was surprised.

"Several dozen of them," calculated Ann. "They're over by the dairy, too. I go over there every single day to feed and care for them, and to gather the eggs."

"Ann also feeds and cares for his lambs while she's there," remarked Sheree disapprovingly. "See what I mean? We're nothing more than free labor for that man! I can't remember Jon ever going over there to help with the care and maintenance of those animals himself, not ever!"

"Except when it's time to harvest them," reminded Ann with a grim expression.

"He slaughters them himself?" Carolyn's eyes became wide.

"Yes," verified Sheree. "And he enjoys it, too."

"Thankfully, he wants nothing to do with any of my cats," added Ann. "I also feed and care for the feral cat colony when I go over there each day."

"Tell me," questioned Carolyn, "just how can Jon Roth afford all of this on a teacher's salary? Do you guys purchase all the food for those animals, or does the school help out?"

"Jon can't really afford it with his salary, but yes, we do buy all the food," replied Sheree with a sigh of frustration. "He just gives the money to Ann and she usually purchases it. Professor Murray takes her into town each week to the feed store there."

"That still doesn't explain where your husband gets all his money," delved Carolyn. Something just didn't add up.

"Well," confessed Sheree, "there's actually a wall safe with untold amounts of money inside that Jon uses whenever he wants. It's located behind a secret panel in his clothes closet, but of course I have no idea it's there."

"Where did all that money come from?" quizzed Ann. "Do you think father might have robbed a bank or something?"

"No, nothing like that," assured Sheree. "The money actually belonged to his parents. They didn't believe in banks. Unfortunately, his inheritance is dwindling, and soon the money will run out."

"What will we do then?" Ann became concerned.

"It won't matter much," assured Sheree, "because we won't be here! We're going to get a whole new start somewhere else."

"You do have a rather nice setup here," mentioned Carolyn. "Perhaps if Jon were out of the picture, things might not be so bad. What if we were able to get him put back in the institution, where he could get the professional help he still needs? You could even go visit him if you wanted to."

"In a pig's eye!" spat Sheree.

"Even if we never went to go see him again, that does sound like the perfect solution!" opined Ann.

"Except for one thing," cautioned Sheree.

"That they might eventually let him out again?" feared Ann.

"Not just that," explained Sheree. "Every single year when it's time for the Psychiatric Assessment Review Board to do its annual evaluation of each patient, there would always be the possibility of Jon getting back out again. We would have to live in constant fear on a year-to-year basis. I couldn't live like that."

"Unless," interjected Carolyn, "they were to put him away for a capital offense. Then, even if he were found to be guilty but for insanity and got released again, it would most likely be back into an appropriate cell on death row in a prison somewhere. Especially if he gets a life sentence."

"I don't think that will be a problem, especially after I get done telling them what I know!" revealed Sheree with a firm nod.

"Perhaps Ray would let you two stay at the lighthouse for a while," recommended Carolyn. "He's got lots of extra rooms."

"That's a great idea!" agreed Ann.

"We'll have to see what Ray says first," reminded Sheree.

"Maybe we could get Ray to help us slaughter the rest of father's lambs?" suggested Ann. "We could get quite a bit for them at the meat market, and then pay Ray, too."

"I was actually thinking I might visit your father's closet before we leave," decided Sheree with a devious grin. "After all, I am legally entitled to half of everything that's here."

"I seriously doubt that Jon Roth has ever bothered to report any of his inheritance money for tax purposes," sniggered Carolyn. "So, it's doubtful he'd even try to report a loss on it."

"I like the way she thinks," smiled Ann as they finally exited the greenhouse.

"Ray!" called Carolyn when she noticed him walking up the dirt road toward them. Brilliant noon-day sunlight streamed through the forest around Ray, creating a halo-like phenomenon immediately around his person. Ray had already seen them in the greenhouse and had just been waiting for them to emerge.

"Got your invitation," grinned Ray. "And all your other interesting little tidbits, too. Good job!"

"Shall we have lunch?" Ann officially invited.

"Absolutely, I'm famished," accepted Ray as he accompanied Ann, Carolyn and Sheree toward the path leading onto Jon Roth's spacious redwood deck.

Susan leapt up and ran toward Ray when she saw him, and embraced him with relief. "Thank God you're here!" she whispered.

"Father, I forgot to mention that I invited Ray, too," remarked Ann. "I'll go get another place setting."

Before going inside, Ann paused to smile warmly at Ted, who immediately smiled back. The look of love and adoration in Ted's eyes when he looked at Ann was almost more than Jon Roth could bear. Again, Jon Roth could feel his blood pressure rising.

Sheree did her best to appear compliant, happy and thrilled to be there. After all, she did want her last March 23rd with Jon Roth to be something to celebrate.

The corners of Jon Roth's mouth turned upward in an almost sinister smile as he evenly studied his neighbor Ray. "Welcome! I'm glad you were able to join us."

"Me, too," smiled Ray as he pulled one arm away from Susan to warmly shake hands with Jon Roth. "We should do this more often, being neighbors and all. Get together for lunch, that is."

"Oh, absolutely," smirked Jon as he leered first at Ray and then at Susan. The game was definitely on! And, it was time for Lenny burgers! Jon grinned with glee as he went back over to his barbecue and began plating the perfectly done lamb burgers for his guests. "These will be the best burgers you've ever had. Trust me!"

10. The Darkroom

Lenny Owens had tried his best to find Carolyn alone so he could finally invite her to the Harvest Festival Prom, but never could seem to manage it. Why wasn't Carolyn coming to the cafeteria for her meals this week? Was she deliberately avoiding him?

"Hey, Lenny, how are you?" greeted Joyce as she approached with her breakfast tray. "Mind if we join you?"

"Not at all," smiled Lenny. "Please, sit down."

"So, did you ask her yet?" pressed Veronica as she sat down beside Joyce. "Did you ask Carolyn to the prom?"

"What do you think?" answered Lenny as he shook his head in the negative. "I actually think she's trying to avoid me or something."

"Nonsense!" replied Joyce. "All she ever talks about anymore is wishing that Lenny Owens would hurry up and ask her to the prom."

"Really?" Lenny seemed truly surprised. "That's not what Jim Otterman said.

"He's such a dweeb!" snorted Veronica. "I wouldn't listen to a thing Jim has to say. He even tried to ask ME to the prom. Eeew!"

"What'd you tell him?" grinned Lenny.

"Seriously?" snorted Veronica. "I'd probably go to the prom with Birdboy before I'd go with that little weasel!"

"Well, the Harvest Festival Prom is tomorrow night already," reminded Joyce. "It is November 3rd today, right?"

"All day," smiled Lenny.

"That gives you the rest of today then," reminded Joyce with a sly wink. "Better not put it off until the last minute."

"Very funny," replied Lenny. "What about you? Do you have a date yet?"

"Of course," answered Joyce as she tossed her head to get her shoulder length wavy brown hair out of the way so she could eat without it colliding with her fork as she did so.

Lenny could appreciate Joyce's rugged outdoorsy beauty, but she was just not his type. With the amount of sun Joyce was getting while boogie boarding so much, Joyce's skin would no doubt be leathery and wrinkled looking by the time she was thirty. Besides, Joyce was only five feet six inches tall, making her way too short for his liking.

"Just what is Birdboy's real name, anyway?" Joyce suddenly asked. "What do we really know about him?"

"No one seems to know his real name," replied Veronica.

"I think he's one of the faculty kids," mentioned Lenny. "I've never seen him at the boys' dorm."

"Interesting," mused Veronica. "Even the supervisor at the mill just calls him Birdboy, did you know that?"

"He doesn't seem to mind it," opined Joyce. "We all call him that. Oftentimes he will make a squawking noise when we do, just to be funny. He'll even flap his arms like wings once in a while."

"You really should find a third alternative," suggested Lenny. "There's something very off about that guy."

"Who? Birdboy or Jim Otterman?" chuckled Veronica.

"Either one," laughed Joyce.

"Nah, I think I'll just go stag," decided Veronica. "Susan's going stag, too. Who knows, maybe we'll meet someone there."

"Well, I do gotta get going," apologized Lenny as he got up. "Nice to see you ladies. Say hi to Carolyn for me, if you see her."

"We will," promised Veronica.

"Ask her today," called Joyce as Lenny was walking away with his tray. "I'm telling you!"

"Have you heard any more from your parents about whether they'll let you sign up for those flying lessons?" asked Veronica.

"Not yet," responded Joyce as she drank down the rest of her orange juice. "Just because I have a GPA of 3.8 or above, doesn't mean my tuition is paid in full, and that's usually a requirement."

"That sucks," opined Veronica.

"And," continued Joyce, "just because I sent them a letter doesn't mean I'm going to hear back anytime soon, either. My father's always out on the road somewhere putting on one of those stupid self-improvement seminars!"

In fact, Joyce's father was so busy traveling to the various self-improvement seminars he put on across the country, that it usually took him on the road for several weeks at a time. More often than not, his family had no idea where he was. Unless, of course, Mr. Troglite remembered to send or leave them with one of his lecturing brochures.

"That's awful!" remarked Veronica. "Of course, there's my dad, who never goes anywhere at all."

"He must go somewhere sometime," opined Joyce.

"Not really," replied Veronica. "He's self-employed and just works all the time."

"What was it he does?" Joyce couldn't recall off hand.

"He's an accountant," reminded Veronica. "All he ever does is work, especially at tax time. That's when he usually locks himself in his office and doesn't even come out for meals."

"He's gotta eat, doesn't he?" questioned Joyce.

"We usually take turns bringing food trays to him," explained Veronica. "My mother makes sure of that!"

Mrs. Jensen was one of those stay-at-home, penny-pinching moms of the mid-1950's who did not believe in women working outside the home. She waited upon her husband hand and foot if necessary to help further the success of his career, and made sure her two daughters did likewise. Levity or frivolity were discouraged in the Jensen home.

"In fact," continued Veronica, "it was when father found out about the work-study program here that he finally let me come. He said it would do me good to learn how to pay my own way in life."

"They don't help with your tuition?" Joyce was surprised.

"Not yet," confirmed Veronica.

"Do they know we go boogie boarding each afternoon?" grinned Joyce. "Maybe next time they're out, they can come watch you catch a wave and ride it in."

"My dad would never leave his business long enough to do that," replied Veronica. "It's doubtful they'll ever come up for a visit anyway. If they saw what a good time I was having, that would probably be the end of it. Becoming one with a surging ocean wave and riding it toward the shoreline is something my dad would never understand."

"What does he do for fun?" pressed Joyce.

"He doesn't," confirmed Veronica. "He even thought my job as a lifeguard this past summer was a waste of time."

"You were earning money!" pointed out Joyce.

"Apparently not enough," sniggered Veronica. "That was when he learned about the lumber mill job here and felt it could help teach me an alternative skill."

"Ouch!" laughed Joyce. "The one thing I've learned from working at the lumber mill is that I'd better stay in school and get a good education so I don't end up doing something like that for the rest of my life. Can you imagine doing that when you're thirty years old?"

"Or working with someone like Birdboy?" chuckled Veronica.

"I heard that!" came an unexpected voice from behind her. Veronica turned and saw that Birdboy was standing there holding a heavily laden food tray and then wrinkled her nose at it.

"May I join you ladies?" asked Birdboy politely.

Joyce and Veronica exchanged a look of disapproval and remained silent for a moment before responding.

"Please?" requested Birdboy.

"Suit yourself," agreed Joyce. She was clearly unhappy about being seen with Birdboy.

"I'm surprised to see you here in the cafeteria," said Veronica. "Don't you usually eat at home with your parents?"

"You don't even know who they are, do you?" taunted Birdboy with a smirking smile.

"Are we supposed to care?" retorted Veronica angrily.

"I was hoping one of you ladies might accompany me to the Harvest Festival Prom tomorrow night," announced Birdboy.

"I have a date!" snapped Joyce. Her response was just a little too swift for Birdboy's liking.

"How 'bout you?" Birdboy suggested to Veronica with a flirtatious smile that was just downright creepy.

"Have you tried Carolyn yet?" questioned Veronica. "I hear she doesn't have a date yet!" Veronica knew, of course, that Carolyn would never agree to go to the prom with the likes of Birdboy.

"Do you think she'd go with me?" Birdboy actually sounded hopeful about it.

"Why don't you ask her and find out?" sneered Joyce. "Oh, look at the time! We've got to hurry or we'll be late for work."

"You're right!" noticed Birdboy as he glanced at his oversized, out-of-style men's watch and then pushed his thick horn-rimmed glasses back up onto his nose. "Looks like we'd all better hurry. I'll walk you ladies down there."

Joyce and Veronica looked at each other with despair before rolling their eyes. They apparently had no choice in the matter.

Birdboy quickly grabbed a large breakfast roll and stuffed it into his mouth and began to chew as he hurried to take his uneaten breakfast to the tray return area. Before walking away, he also grabbed the two slices of fake bacon from his plate and stuffed them into his mouth, too.

Joyce and Veronica scowled with abject disapproval while they watched. Perhaps they could lose him if they made a run for it!

After racing from the central cafeteria doorway and descending its front steps, both of them were quickly disparaged by the realization that Birdboy was still close on their heels. In fact, he was still chewing what remnants of his breakfast he had quickly managed to stuff into his mouth before following after them.

"Don't you need to go brush your teeth or something?" asked Veronica.

Ignoring Veronica's remark completely, Birdboy then turned to Joyce and inquired, "So, who's your date to the prom?"

"One of the boys in my chemistry class," answered Joyce.

"Who?" insisted Birdboy with a mischievous grin. The half chewed food in his mouth was clearly visible and quite disgusting.

Stopping suddenly, Joyce turned to Birdboy and demanded, "Why should I tell you, anyway?"

"That's right!" interjected Veronica. "What business is it of yours who either of us goes to the prom with?"

"Gee whiz!" Birdboy shrugged his shoulders and tried to laugh it off. "I was just trying to be friendly."

"First of all," informed Veronica, "we're NOT your friends! Can't you take a hint? Go fly away somewhere, BIRDBOY!"

Jon Roth was well aware of the fact that neither of them knew his real name, but that was still no excuse for the derogatory way in which they had used the only name everyone did know him by. His face took on a serious and malevolent expression. The look in his eyes suddenly became cruel and faraway. "Someday, you will regret treating me like this."

Joyce and Veronica stared at Birdboy with disbelief as he turned and walked away without looking back.

"Eeew!" cried Joyce. She did not care whether Birdboy heard her or not.

"Double eeew!" exclaimed Veronica with a scowl on her face.

"Do you think we need to be worried about him now?" Joyce suddenly asked. "What do you think he meant by that?"

"What's he gonna do?" scoffed Veronica as they resumed their trek toward the lumber mill. "Maybe now, he'll just leave us alone."

"I hope you're right," responded Joyce. The malicious glare in Birdboy's eyes had made the hackles on the back of Joyce's neck stand up on end.

"Hey wait up!" called a voice from behind them. It was Steve Fredrickson.

"Steve!" responded Joyce with relief.

"Boy, are we glad to see you!" added Veronica.

"Birdboy giving you ladies a hard time?" grinned Steve as he caught up with them.

Steve Fredrickson was a senior, so he went to classes in the morning and didn't work until the afternoon. But, the class he was headed for just now took him in the same direction Joyce and Veronica were traveling on their way to the lumber mill.

"I know this is awkward, and I should have asked you earlier," apologized Steve as they all hurried along, "but I was wondering, Veronica, if you would go with me to the prom tomorrow night?"

Veronica's face lit up with delight and an irrepressible grin was all the answer Steve needed.

"Great! I'll be there to pick you up at five minutes before six tomorrow night," promised Steve.

It was only a five-minute walk from the girls' dormitory over to the cafeteria where the prom would be held. And, although the boys were ordinarily not allowed anywhere near the girls' dormitory at any time, prom night was an exception. The boys who had dates for the Harvest Festival Prom would be allowed to come on foot to pick up their dates at the front door and escort them over to the event.

"I'll be ready!" beamed Veronica.

"See ya then!" flirted Steve. "I gotta get to class now. You ladies have a great day, and don't let that Birdboy give you any guff."

Joyce and Veronica waited until Steve was just beyond hearing range to stop and let out a squeal of delight. They simultaneously grabbed one another's forearms as they did so and briefly hopped up and down with excitement before scurrying once again toward their jobs at the lumber mill.

"I can't believe it!" raved Veronica. "Steve Fredrickson is the most popular guy in school!"

"He's also senior class president," pointed out Joyce with a grin. "And, he goes boogie boarding every chance he gets. I'm surprised you haven't noticed him down on the beach. He's always down there."

"Well," blushed Veronica, "Actually, I have seen Steve boogie boarding. He's pretty good, too!"

"That's an understatement," grinned Joyce. She was well aware of the huge crush her friend Veronica had on Steve Fredrickson.

"Isn't Paul McCloskey his roommate?" asked Veronica.

"Paul?" Joyce feigned ignorance.

"You know, Paul McCloskey? The guy YOU are going to the prom with?" reminded Veronica. "You put him up to this, didn't you?"

"Well," smirked Joyce, "I might have happened to mention to Paul that my best friend Veronica still needed a date to the prom."

"That's quite okay with me," smiled Veronica. "Thanks!"

"Well, someone had to save you from the clutches of Birdboy," teased Joyce.

"You don't think he'll really try and ask Carolyn to the prom, do you?" Veronica was suddenly concerned about it. Their parting encounter with Birdboy continued to haunt her, especially the look in his eyes. Like Joyce, she had a bad feeling about him and feared that he somehow might try to get even with them for how they had treated him.

"No way," opined Joyce. "There's only one guy in the entire world that Carolyn's interested in. And it ain't Birdboy!"

Both Joyce and Veronica were still laughing with delight as they arrived at the lumber mill, just in time to clock in before being late. Unknown to them, Jon Roth had just clocked in and was still nearby, and had overheard them laughing after saying, "And it ain't Birdboy!" Jon Roth did not like that. Not at all. And, they weren't going to get away with it, either! He was still glaring at them with a venomous expression on his face as they finished clocking in and turned to go inside the lumber mill.

"Birdboy!" exclaimed Veronica. She was surprised to see him just standing there staring at her. She had nearly run right into him.

"Hey, we're really sorry about what happened earlier," Joyce quickly apologized to him.

"I'm sure you are," responded Jon Roth with an even glare. *But, not as sorry as you will be*, he thought to himself.

302

"We need to stay away from that one," whispered Veronica into Joyce's ear. "There's definitely something off about that guy."

"Way off," agreed Joyce as they headed for their workstations.

Dean Dixon had personally taken Carolyn into town the day before the prom, where a local seamstress was able to alter the stunning blue evening gown for Carolyn so she could actually wear it.

Although the bodice was made entirely of non-stretchable soft cotton, the main bottom ruffle and long puffy sleeves were entirely made of polyester. The matching baby blue lace woven into the gown's floral designs was sewn entirely around its main bottom ruffle and form-fitting bodice, but unfortunately was not stretchable. The deep rounded neckline was mildly suggestive but yet modest at the same time, though it offered no extra fabric for the seamstress to work with, either. The continuous row of ruffles hanging from the scooped neckline were also not an option. That left the long puffy polyester sleeves.

It had taken the entire afternoon for her to manage it, but the seamstress had carefully cut away a three-inch strip from each of the sleeves to use for the alteration. Although not as puffy afterwards, the sleeves still looked amazing, and hung as intended. The extra fabric was then used as an insert on either side of the bodice, enabling Carolyn to finally put on and zip up the dress again.

Still weak from the loss of blood during her recent finger injury at the mill, and from fasting for several days to try and fit into the stunning blue evening gown, Carolyn had nearly lost all desire to even go to the Harvest Festival Prom. Worst of all, she had missed being there on Friday while being in town having the dress altered, and along with it any possible opportunity Lenny Owens might have had to ask her as his date to the prom.

"What's wrong?" questioned Susan. "You look amazing!"

"Well, here I am. All dressed up and nowhere to go," frowned Carolyn as she studied herself in the full length wall mirrors of the dorm room she shared with Susan. Carolyn had even spent the last twelve hours in large hair curlers, hoping to put some body into her otherwise straight hair. Naturally she had avoided going anywhere, including the cafeteria, with curlers in her hair. Susan had spent over an hour helping Carolyn with her makeup, which was now much heavier than Carolyn usually wore it. The baby blue platform shoes

Susan had secretly obtained for Carolyn through a mail order catalog had arrived only yesterday, and matched Carolyn's dress perfectly.

"What are you talking about?" exclaimed Susan. "You look amazing, and you are going to that prom! Those shoes cost me twenty bucks, you know."

"I just can't! I don't even have a date," fretted Carolyn.

"Well, neither do I," reminded Susan. "There's nothing wrong with going stag to a high school prom. Lots of other kids will be there, too, that don't have dates. You'll see."

"Not anyone I know," replied Carolyn. "Except you, of course. And probably Sheree Wilkins."

Both Susan and Carolyn chuckled at the thought of Sheree Wilkins going to the prom by herself.

"Oh, who am I fooling?" Carolyn shook her head. "Even Sheree Wilkins probably has a date."

"With whom?" sniggered Susan. "Jim Otterman? I know, maybe Birdboy asked her to go with him."

"It's not funny," persisted Carolyn.

"What if Lenny's standing over there right now, waiting for YOU, Ms. Carolina la Gata?" tempted Susan. "Would you want some other girl without a date to get her clutches onto him?"

"No, I wouldn't," replied Carolyn. She suddenly wondered whether Linda Shaver had a date.

"Lenny will be there," assured Susan. "And once he sees you in this dress, look out! Wild horses wouldn't be able to keep him away, guaranteed. Trust me!"

"All right," Carolyn finally agreed. "Let's go."

The cafeteria lights were blazing brightly, and the faculty members who had volunteered to be chaperones at the Harvest Festival Prom were there in full force, as well. There would be no hiding in the shadows, either at the front door or inside. Not only was worldly music forbidden at Oceanview Academy, but dancing of any sort was also prohibited by its voluminous book of rules and regulations.

"Whoever heard of a prom without a band?" muttered Susan as they approached the cafeteria's front door.

"Or dancing?" added Carolyn.

Suddenly, military marching music could be heard from inside. It was an inferior quality recording of the school's band.

"Are you kidding me? I suppose this means we'll be doing the grand march at some point!" Susan was being sarcastic.

"Actually, we will be," informed Jim Otterman from where he stood at the doorway. Jim was wearing his hair without the usual greasy tonic, and had left his horrible looking glasses behind.

"I suppose you're in the band, too?" asked Susan.

"Yes, I am," smiled Jim proudly. "I'm one of the trumpets."

Carolyn and Susan both rolled their eyes and started for the cafeteria door, but Jim quickly stepped over to block them. "May I walk you ladies inside?"

"Here comes Birdboy," muttered Susan.

"With Sheree Wilkins!" noticed Carolyn with amazement.

Susan finally nodded her head in agreement and waited for Jim to open the door for them. Birdboy had asked Susan to the prom earlier that day, and had not taken kindly to her rejection, so she was now anxious to avoid him.

Interestingly, Carolyn was the only one of the four close friends that Birdboy had not tried to ask to the prom, but only because she had been nowhere to be found. Naturally, since Carolyn had been hiding in her dormitory room wearing hair curlers for most of the day.

Before going inside the cafeteria, Carolyn glanced around one more time to see whether Lenny Owens might be on his way over from the boys' dorm, but could not see him anywhere.

The lighting inside seemed much brighter than usual and took a moment to get used to. The smells of various food items wafted across the cafeteria's large dining area. Tonight only, plates filled with food would be brought out to the tables by various faculty members who had volunteered to serve it, instead of being served in the usual manner where students would go through line and select the food items desired.

"May I get you ladies some punch?" offered Jim. He was doing everything he could to make a good impression on Susan and Carolyn, and hoped with all his heart that Carolyn might somehow be persuaded to be his date for the evening.

"Sure," nodded Susan as she studied the room. She intended to find an excuse to make herself scarce at the first opportunity.

Carolyn was so busy searching for Lenny Owens that she had not even heard Jim offer to get them the punch.

All of the tables were arranged in one huge square, all facing inward, to make room for the grand march that would take place later that evening. The punch table was located over in a far corner of the room, frequented by boys who were filling up and taking glasses filled with punch back to their dates.

Some of those who had come stag were milling around next to the wall near the entrance, though most of them had finally managed to pair off and find a place to sit together at the large square of tables.

While Jim was away getting punch, Susan spotted Karl Branson, her blind date from the movie night earlier that year, and swiftly managed to become his date again for the Harvest Festival Prom.

The school's photography class instructor was over in another far corner of the room with a portable background screen set up for couples to pose in front of. Several couples were already in line, waiting to have their pictures taken together to memorialize the event.

Carolyn anxiously surveyed the room to see if Lenny Owens might be anywhere at all. Finally, there he was! Without hesitation, Carolyn made her way through the milling crowd of over two hundred students towards Lenny. Hopefully, Lenny would understand why she was late. Carolyn was quite anxious to spend the evening with him, and to see the expression on Lenny's face when he saw her in the stunning blue evening gown she now wore. Carolyn had not seen or spoken to Lenny in almost a week and truly missed their morning visits at breakfast each morning. Perhaps tonight Lenny would finally come out with it and ask her to go steady with him, as she had hoped for so long.

As Carolyn got closer to the tall, dark handsome young man named Lenny Owens, she stopped to stare with disbelief. Linda Shaver was standing beside him in a bright red dress! Clashing horribly with it was the baby blue corsage she wore. Had the baby blue corsage been intended for Carolyn? Had Lenny finally given it to Linda after thinking that Carolyn would not be there?

Tears began to well up in her eyes as Carolyn stood there, too overcome with emotion to move at first. It was at that very moment that Lenny Owens turned around and saw Carolyn in the stunning baby blue evening gown.

"Carolyn!" greeted Lenny with a beaming smile.

Linda Shaver noticed Carolyn at that same moment. The radiant smile on Linda's lovely face disappeared immediately. Almost without realizing it, Linda quickly slipped her arm through Lenny's as she stood there confronting her rival.

Understanding at once that Linda was indeed Lenny's date for the evening, Carolyn turned and fled from the cafeteria.

"Wait!" called Lenny as he wriggled his arm loose from Linda's grasp to run after Carolyn.

Hot tears of anger, frustration and embarrassment rolled down Carolyn's cheeks as she hurried outside and sped toward the girls' dormitory. Almost twisting her ankle as she ran, Carolyn paused only long enough to remove the baby blue platform shoes and then carried them the rest of the way.

Lenny stood by himself in front of the cafeteria, watching her as Carolyn disappeared into the girls' dorm. Why had he ever agreed to give Linda the corsage meant for Carolyn? Somehow, Linda had talked him into it, after convincing him Carolyn had no intention of being his date that night. Still, even if Carolyn hadn't shown up at all, Lenny knew in his heart that he should have saved the corsage for her. After all, Lenny had painstakingly obtained the baby blue corsage after learning from Joyce and Veronica of Carolyn's baby blue gown. Now, he had ruined everything! Would Carolyn ever speak to him again after this? Lenny knew he had hurt Carolyn deeply and had no idea what he could ever do to make it right.

Over at the girls' dormitory, Diana Berg watched with interest as first Carolyn and then Susan came back early from the prom. And Carolyn had been in tears! What was going on? Diana quickly notified Dean Dixon of the situation.

"There you are!" exclaimed Susan as she entered their dorm room. "I looked everywhere for you! What are you doing over here?"

Carolyn was lying face down on the bed, sobbing.

"Seriously?" chastised Susan. "Even Lenny Owens was looking for you! Lenny said he watched you come back over here, but couldn't follow you inside."

"What about Linda?" sniffed Carolyn.

"Lenny feels horrible," related Susan.

"Why would he give that corsage to Linda Shaver, then?" demanded Carolyn. "It clearly was not meant to be worn with that bright hussy-red dress!"

"You weren't exactly accessible this past week," reminded Susan. "Lenny came to every single meal, hoping you would be there. He even told Veronica and Joyce he was looking for you yesterday, to ask you to the prom, but you were in town getting your dress altered."

"Did they tell him that?" wondered Carolyn.

"I doubt it," replied Susan.

"Neither of them mentioned to me that Lenny asked where I was," mumbled Carolyn.

"You'd better quit crying, or you'll ruin your beautiful dress," cautioned Susan. "The alterations look great, by the way."

"Thanks," nodded Carolyn. "And thank you for the shoes, too! That was very thoughtful. Can you just unzip me now, please?"

"No! We should go back over there!" insisted Susan. "Lenny and Linda had a big fight, and she took off and threw the baby blue corsage in his face."

"So now he wants to give it to me?" sniffed Carolyn. "After Linda wore it? No thanks!"

"Look at yourself!" Susan was frustrated. "If you're not going back over there, I am, but I think you're making a mistake if you don't."

"How can I go back over there after crying like this?" demanded Carolyn. "Just look at me!"

"Suit yourself," answered Susan as she headed for the door. "Trust me, if you don't go back, you'll wish you had! And if you don't, I never want to hear about Lenny Owens again!"

Susan then stormed from their dormitory room and slammed the door behind her. Unknown to either of them, Dean Dixon had been listening in on the intercom speaker box, sadly shaking her head as she eavesdropped on their conversation.

Unable to unzip the stunning blue evening gown by herself, Carolyn knew she would need to find someone to help. Perhaps Karol Weeble was in her room? Carolyn hadn't seen her at the prom, and would have remembered it if she had. After all, someone weighing 374 pounds would be pretty hard to miss.

Too humiliated, embarrassed and ashamed to go back to the prom that night, Carolyn decided against it. It was more than she could bear. How could she face Lenny now?

Carolyn grabbed a tissue from the room's solitary night stand and dabbed her tear stained cheeks before blowing her nose. She would remove what makeup was left later.

After half running down the long second floor hallway, Carolyn quickly descended the split-level staircase, and then headed down the first floor hallway toward the east wing where she knew Karol Weeble's room was located. It was only because of the prom that the usual hall monitors were not present. Only Diana was on duty at the dorm's main entrance. Suddenly, it seemed to Carolyn like a lifetime ago that she and Susan had lived on the east wing of the first floor.

Carolyn rapidly knocked on Karol's dormitory room door, and heaved a sigh of relief when it slowly opened.

"Carolyn?" Karol was astonished to see her, but noticed at once that something was wrong. "Come in!"

After coming in and sitting down on the opposite twin bed, Carolyn related the events of the evening to Karol, who sadly shook her head. "I agree with Susan. All you need to do is fix your makeup and get back over there! Don't give up without a fight. If you do, Linda Shaver has already won."

"But how can I face Lenny now?" worried Carolyn. "I should never have run out like that!"

"Do you really want me to unzip you?" questioned Karol. "Last chance to change your mind."

"Unzip me," directed Carolyn.

"Want something to wear over that on your way back upstairs?" asked Karol. "I have a pup tent or two around here I could lend ya."

"That would be nice," accepted Carolyn. "Thanks!"

"Anything else?" questioned Karol as she pulled a giant-sized shirt from her drawer and tossed it to Carolyn. "Want me to go find Linda Shaver and punch her in the nose for you?"

"I wish!" sniggered Carolyn as she pulled Karol's giant-sized shirt over her head and then let it drop into place. "Seriously, there is something else you can do for me, if you don't mind."

"Name it," offered Karol.

"Would you mind bringing back some extra food for me tomorrow?" implored Carolyn. "It's going to be a day or two before I can work up the courage to go back over there again."

"To the cafeteria?" chuckled Karol. "Sure! I can do that. I'll even see if I can grab an extra loaf of bread or something, to tide you over. And maybe some peanut butter and jelly."

"That would be great!" replied Carolyn. Unbidden tears were still rolling down her cheeks, but she just could not help it. "At least tomorrow's Sunday, so I won't have to worry about getting my name on sick call to get out of classes or work."

"You've got it pretty bad, don't you?" Karol shook her head as she gave Carolyn an affectionate pat on the shoulder that nearly knocked her over. "Why heck, I can bring you food for the rest of the week if you like, just let me know."

"What can I do for you in return?" asked Carolyn.

"Wanna be my personal trainer?" Karol grinned mischievously. "I need to find a way to get into a dress like that!"

"It's a deal," smiled Carolyn. "Maybe tomorrow afternoon you'd like to come down to the beach with me? Joyce and Veronica will be boogie boarding. While we're there, we can take a quick jog up the beach and back."

"Definitely, I'll come and watch Joyce and Veronica do some boogie boarding," committed Karol. "But, just going there and back might need to be it for now. Until I get back in shape, of course."

Exactly one week had passed since the Harvest Festival Prom. The only places Carolyn had gone the entire time were directly to classes or work, and back to her room again. The only exception had been the two trips she had made with Karol Weeble to the beach to watch Joyce and Veronica boogie boarding.

Karol had brought Carolyn so much food, in fact, that it had not been necessary for Carolyn to go to the cafeteria at all since the prom.

"Carolyn?" came the voice of Dean Dixon on the intercom speaker box to her dormitory room.

It had been so long since she had heard the voice of Miss Dixon over the speaker box, that Carolyn had nearly forgotten about it. Fear suddenly enveloped her. What had she done now?

"Carolyn, are you there?" came the voice again.

310

"Yes, Miss Dixon," answered Carolyn. "Oh, and Susan's not here right now."

"Just you. Do you have a few minutes?" questioned the Dean. "Can you come down to my office?"

Carolyn swallowed hard before replying. "Yes, I'll be right there." Carolyn knew Dean Dixon would be disappointed in her if she found out about what had happened at the prom, especially after going to all that trouble to make it possible for her to wear the stunning blue evening gown for the occasion.

Carolyn sadly thought of Lenny Owens as she hurried to Dean Dixon's apartment, and wondered how she would ever be able to face him again. The night of the prom had been one of the most humiliating moments of her entire life thus far, and she had no one to blame but herself! How could she ever ask Lenny to forgive her?

It was even more degrading than the time her ninth grade boyfriend had shown up at her parents' home to pick her up for her first date. The young man's father had owned an ambulance company and decided as a joke to show up at the Bennett residence in an ambulance with the sirens blaring. Naturally, everyone in the entire neighborhood had come outside to see what was going on. If the young man's father had not been there as their chaperone, Carolyn would simply have fled back into the Bennett home and called it good.

Perhaps she was a coward? Carolyn suddenly wondered. Was that why she had run away from the prom last week? She could absolutely kick herself for it now!

"The door's open," came Dean Dixon's voice.

Carolyn had not even yet knocked! Did the Dean have a hidden camera somewhere? How had she known Carolyn was there already?

"Come in, Carolyn," invited Ms. Dixon.

After cautiously opening the Dean's door, Carolyn came in, sat down on the overstuffed couch, and began to stare at the familiar bare spot on Ms. Dixon's carpet.

"I have a confession to make," began the Dean.

Carolyn looked up at her with surprise.

"On the night of the prom," began Dean Dixon, "I received a message from Diana Berg that you had come rushing back from the prom in tears. Then, when she saw Susan come back after you – and I know that's what happened – she felt she should let me know."

"I take it she did?" guessed Carolyn uncomfortably.

"Eavesdropping is not something I normally like to do," clarified the Dean. "My original intent was to find out whether you were all right. That was when I activated the intercom to your room."

Carolyn knew immediately what Dean Dixon was going to say next and suddenly felt most uncomfortable.

"When I heard you and Susan arguing between yourselves," admitted the Dean, "I just didn't want to interrupt."

"But you kept listening?" clarified Carolyn.

"Yes, I listened to your conversation!" confessed Ms. Dixon. "Carolyn, I never thought I'd hear myself saying this, ever, but I agree with Susan. You totally blew it. I can't for the life of me understand why you didn't just turn around and go back over to the prom that night, especially after all you went through to fit into that blue dress!"

"Or all you did to help make it possible," reminded Carolyn as her lip began to quiver. "And I will repay you for it someday, too!"

Dean Dixon breathed in a deep breath and then quickly let it out. "Oh, Carolyn! What am I going to do with you?"

"How can I ever tell Lenny how sorry I am?" Carolyn suddenly burst into tears.

"Oh, not the tears again!" grimaced Ms. Dixon. "Here, I have something for you."

Carolyn wiped her cheeks with the backs of her hands and blew her nose on a tissue that Dean Dixon had just handed her. Carolyn then slowly reached for the oblong shaped box Ms. Dixon had placed on her coffee table.

"Linda Vandevere brought this over here a little while ago and said it was for you. She also indicated that it should be opened soon as possible," revealed the Dean. "Please, open it. I'd like to see what's inside myself."

Linda Vandevere was the wife of Dean Vandevere, the Dean of Boys, and on rare occasions would be sent by her husband to make special deliveries to the girls' dorm. This was such an occasion.

Carolyn's hands started to tremble after she removed the lid to the box. Inside was a perfectly fresh, baby blue corsage made of carnation blossoms and creeping baby's breath buds. Carolyn tenderly picked up the carnation to admire it and noticed a single piece of paper beneath it that she unfolded to read. It merely said, "I'm sorry!"

"All right," directed the Dean. "You can repay me, all right. And this is how you can do it. You can march right over to that cafeteria for dinner tonight, find Lenny Owens, and thank him for this corsage! In fact, I think you should wear it when you do. And then you can tell him how sorry you are for everything that happened at the prom that night, too. That is what you can do to repay me. Is it a deal?"

"I haven't been to the cafeteria since it happened," confessed Carolyn as she wiped her nose again.

"I know!" replied Ms. Dixon. "Karol Weeble finally had to tell me what she was doing with all that food. I told her if she didn't tell me, I would call her parents again."

"I'm sorry!" apologized Carolyn. "I didn't mean to get her into trouble. All she did was bring me some food so I wouldn't have to go back to the cafeteria just yet. I needed some more time."

"Well," continued the Dean, "just this morning, Karol was caught trying to abscond an entire loaf of bread from the cafeteria, along with some peanut butter and jelly. Naturally, the staff over there were concerned that Karol might be binge eating again, so they let me know."

"I don't think Karol would do that now." Carolyn was serious. "In exchange for bringing me the food, Karol asked me if I would be her personal trainer."

Dean Dixon stared at Carolyn with amazement and then began laughing quite heartily. It was several moments before she was able to speak again. Before long, Carolyn was laughing along with her.

"Oh, Carolyn!" Ms. Dixon was still grinning from ear to ear. "Please promise me you will go to the cafeteria TODAY and thank Lenny for the corsage. Can you do that?"

"Yes, ma'am," agreed Carolyn.

It was nearly dinner time and Carolyn knew she had no choice but to return to the cafeteria. She would need to wear just the right thing, especially with the new baby blue carnation corsage!

Just for fun, Carolyn actually tried the baby blue evening gown back on, but had no intention of wearing it now. No one else would be dressed in formal attire that night. It was just an ordinary day.

"Let me get a picture of you before you go over there," requested Susan as she zipped up Carolyn's dress.

"Oh, I can't wear this to dinner!" replied Carolyn. "I only wanted to see how the corsage looked with it."

"It's beautiful," assured Joyce as she grabbed Susan's camera and snapped a couple photos of Carolyn in the lovely gown.

"I think you should wear it tonight," encouraged Veronica.

"I'd look like a freak!" argued Carolyn. "No one else is wearing their formals now."

"We could all put our formals on and go over there with you," offered Susan with a mischievous smile.

"We could be trendsetters," smiled Joyce.

"Thanks, but what I really need is a baby blue pullover sweater, or something like that to wear it with," described Carolyn.

"Just make sure you bring it back in one piece," cautioned Susan as she pulled her favorite baby blue pullover sweater from her drawer and handed it to Carolyn.

As they finally entered the cafeteria together, Susan whispered to Carolyn, "The Dean called me in, too, you know."

"What?" Carolyn was flabbergasted. "Why?"

"To make sure you go through with it," Susan had a determined smirk on her face.

"There he is," pointed out Joyce.

"But he's with Linda Shaver?" noticed Veronica. "Why would he be with her, especially after everything that happened last week?"

"I'm going back," informed Carolyn as she turned to leave.

"No, you're not," insisted Susan as she grabbed Carolyn's upper arm and began leading her towards Lenny Owens.

Joyce grabbed Carolyn's other arm and Veronica took up the rear, just in case Carolyn decided to make a run for it.

"Perhaps I should take off the corsage first?" suggested Carolyn.

"Nothing doing," maintained Susan as they approached Lenny.

"Good evening, ladies," acknowledged Lenny. He seemed surprised to see Carolyn with them. "What's this?" questioned Lenny when he noticed the corsage Carolyn was wearing.

"It's from me," spoke up Linda Shaver. "I wanted to let Carolyn know how sorry I was for ruining the other one that had been meant for her. Dean Vandevere's wife is a friend of mine, so I had her deliver it."

Carolyn suddenly felt as if her knees would buckle. If Susan and Joyce had not been holding her up, she would probably be on the floor right now. "I thought the corsage was from Lenny," muttered Carolyn.

During an awkward moment of silence, Carolyn and Lenny gazed at one another with longing and desire. Carolyn felt herself blush beneath his penetrating gaze. Why had she ever run off like that? She wanted nothing more at that moment than to throw her arms around him and tell him how much she had missed him, but just couldn't bring herself to do it with the others present.

"I'm so sorry about the other night," apologized Carolyn as a tear escaped and ran down her cheek.

"Me, too," acknowledged Lenny as he focused his attention exclusively on Carolyn. If only they were alone! Lenny imagined what it might be like to take Carolyn in his arms and kiss her fully on the mouth. He had been such a jerk to let Linda Shaver talk him into being her date, and now Linda was under the impression they were going steady together. How was he ever going to get out of it so he could be free to hang out with Carolyn again?

"Thank you, Linda, for the corsage," Carolyn finally managed to say. "That was very thoughtful of you."

"My pleasure," smiled Linda, sweetly but triumphantly. Lenny Owens was now her boyfriend, and she intended to keep it that way.

It was finally March of 1973. Five months had passed since the unfortunate accident at the lumber mill where Carolyn unexpectedly sliced off one of her fingertips with a sharp thread cutting ring. The reattachment had been successful and she now had full use of it again. Carolyn's new assignment at the lumber mill was in the tufting area.

Outdoor all-weather tufted fabric chaise lounge cushions were one of the many items included with patio furniture kits sold by the lumber mill to its customers. Unlike the furniture itself, which required extensive assembly, the chaise lounge cushions came wrapped in plastic and ready for the customer to use. The desired fabric could be easily selected by the customer, since it was visible through the clear plastic wrapping in which it was shipped.

Multiple layers of selected fabrics were repeatedly cut in bulk by what resembled gigantic paper cutters. Their cutting blades were shaped into the exact size needed for each particular pattern piece. After being cut, large stacks of "seats" or "backs" or "full length" pattern pieces were rushed to the high powered sewing machine area where seamstresses would then sew them together. A six-inch opening would be left at one end so the assembled piece could be turned "right side out" before heading to the stuffing area. As Carolyn well knew, the seamstresses were allowed only two minutes and forty-five seconds to sew each full length chaise lounge cushion together. Failure to "make rate" often resulted in being transferred to another area of the lumber mill more suited for that particular employee's skill level.

Birdboy worked at the stuffing station. After the chaise lounge cushions were turned "right side out" again, Birdboy would then grab and hold each one up to a four-inch round plastic output pipe from which "stuffing" would be dispensed into them whenever he depressed a foot pedal. Like most jobs at the mill, stuffers were required to stand. Strong hands were needed to hold each cushion in place while filling it to prevent errant stuffing material from littering the area. When each cushion was properly filled with the correct amount of stuffing, Birdboy would then toss them onto a huge pile on the other side of his workstation where they would accumulate until sewn shut by someone else.

A special seamstress assigned to sew the chaise lounge cushions shut was expected to complete a minimum of six cushions per minute, but hopefully more. While doing so, a factory label would be inserted by hand into the seam that included the factory worker's official identification number, just in case something defective might later be found pertaining to that particular cushion.

After being sewn shut, the chaise lounge cushions were then sent to the tufting area where Carolyn worked. Tufters were allowed three minutes and fifty-five seconds in which to complete their task. There were usually four tufters working simultaneously, side by side, who would place the cushions that needed tufting on a work table in front of them that was made of heaving screening material.

Each tufter wore one of the sharp thread cutting rings, of which Carolyn was extremely mindful. Precut eighteen-inch strings would be individually threaded by hand through the large eye of a one-foot long hand sewing needle by the tufter. Small white half-inch "buttons" with round holes on their backs would then be placed on each threaded string by the tufter before stabbing the large hand sewing needle through a tiny pre-cut "hole" on the chaise lounge cushion's surface. It would then be pulled downward through the screened table beneath it and out through the bottom where it would be pulled free from the strings. The strings were then left hanging until all twelve pre-cut holes had been "set" with buttons.

As great as the concern of cutting off one's finger with the sharp thread cutting knife was the possibility of stabbing oneself in the leg with the large hand sewing needle when reaching down to grab and pull it through the cushion itself. After all twelve top-side buttons and their strings had been set onto the top side of the cushion, the tufter would then flip the entire cushion over by hand and "tie off" the threads sticking out from the bottom side. Thankfully, that side did not require use of the dangerous hand sewing needle. That was also when most of the tufters would temporarily remove their sharp thread cutting ring while "tying off" the buttons. Then, after putting their sharp thread cutting ring back on, they would slice away the remaining excess of string on all twelve bottom buttons. So, besides the danger of fingers getting in the way, many times the fabric around one of the already-tied buttons was inadvertently sliced open as well, ruining the entire chaise lounge cushion completely.

In no time, Carolyn learned the technique of pushing down on the fabric surrounding the back buttons before attempting to slice off the excess strings, and soon was "making rate" so she could avoid transfer to someplace even worse.

The tufted cushions would then be manually slid into plastic sleeves by a finisher person where each end of the plastic was then vacuum sealed before being placed into the correct box for that item. The boxes themselves were manufactured and printed at an outside location.

Birdboy's stuffing station just happened to be situated immediately behind the tufting tables where Carolyn worked with Veronica and Joyce. Susan still worked over in the stain department.

Another woman named Kira worked in tufting with Carolyn, Veronica and Joyce, but she was not a student. In fact, only a certain percentage of the mill workers were students. Many of them were local area residents that commuted to work from Ocean Bluff each day.

"Hey Birdboy!" called Veronica. "Slow down!" The pile of stuffed chaise lounge cushions was growing faster than the special seamstress seemed able to sew them shut. As a result, many of them were starting to fall toward the tufters, and sometimes stuffing would fall out and onto the workers, as well.

"Is it raining stuffing again?" smirked Birdboy. He was well aware how much Veronica hated it when his stuffed cushions fell from their huge pile into her standing room, and especially when the loose stuffing inside them spilled out and got into her hair.

"Yeah, slow down over there!" hollered Joyce, who had also gotten some of the stuffing into her hair, as well.

"Gotta make rate," snickered Birdboy. He had no intention of slowing down, either. Just knowing how much it bothered them prompted him to fill the cushions more swiftly. True, it was a rather mindless job, but at least it gave him a chance to be where he could continuously taunt Veronica and Joyce.

Carolyn was just as bothered by the stuffing falling out as her friends were, but usually said nothing about it. She was well aware that saying anything only made it worse and usually inspired Birdboy to go even faster.

Birdboy would often squawk when they said his name, and was cognizant of how much it bothered those around him. Frequently, when it was hot and the sweat was running down his smelly armpits, Birdboy would take joy in flapping his arms like the wings of a bird so the odor could waft its way down to where Veronica, Joyce and Carolyn were busy working. He especially loved the way Veronica wrinkled up her nose when the odor reached it.

The feelings of animosity continued to grow between Veronica and Birdboy at an exponential rate each passing day, and an unpleasant encounter between them appeared inevitable.

Carolyn often went for long walks by herself along the bluff tops after class that spring. After all, the bluffs were technically not in the forest nor actually on the beach itself, even though Dean Dixon seemed to think otherwise. Still, Carolyn was alone at the moment and didn't see how being there by herself could be so bad. March was a season of new life when flowers were blooming and the ocean breeze just seemed cleaner somehow. Seagulls loudly cawed overhead. Carolyn closed her eyes for a moment to just listen to the sound of the

318

surging ocean waves below. Breezy fingers of wind blew sensuously through her hair while delicate rays of sun kept them from feeling too cold.

Joyce sometimes accompanied Carolyn on these walks, but Joyce's first love was boogie boarding down on the beach with Veronica Jensen and Steve Fredrickson. Amazingly, no one had noticed or cared that either he or they were in violation of the girls' or boys' beach policy at least every other day.

Ever since the Harvest Festival Prom, Veronica and Steve had become inseparable and spent every available moment together boogie boarding down on the beach with Joyce. Steve had long since asked Veronica to go steady with him, and they were definitely an item. Future plans of marriage had even been discussed.

Slightly darker complexioned than Joyce, Veronica's dark waist length hair was kinky but not unduly frizzy. Her Polynesian heritage was noticeable, and her large, round, seductive brown eyes had turned many heads in her short life. Like Joyce, Veronica was muscular and well-tanned from her frequent visits to the beach.

Steve Fredrickson, though only one year older than Veronica and Joyce, was not nearly as experienced at boogie boarding as they were, at least not yet. But, with the frequency of his practice sessions, he had become every bit their equal in many skills, including "bottom turns" and "cut backs" and soon hoped to acquire the techniques necessary to complete 360° turns while riding a wave.

Steve's golden brown hair was dangerously close to being in violation of the boys' hair length policy, though no one from the faculty had yet challenged him about it. Steve was six feet tall, well built, handsome and reminded Carolyn of a popular actor she had once seen in a 1963 surfing movie. Steve was well liked by everyone on campus, both students and faculty, and had been unanimously elected as senior class president. His flirtatious green eyes were well known among the female students, though he was unpretentious about it. He also excelled in his studies and hoped one day to become a marine biologist.

Boogie boarding had not been widely practiced until 1970, so was a relatively new sport to the western world. Also known as body boards, boogie boards were originally an adaptation of the Polynesian "small board" or wood "plank" that was available on or near most beaches of the Polynesian islands. Floating the wooden board assisted the rider to stay afloat in the wave while swimming out to meet incoming ocean vessels so they could be properly welcomed to the island they were visiting. Eventually, those who practiced using the wooden planks discovered how they could get a better and higher ride on them by working their bodies with the energy and speed of a wave.

Tired of continuously transporting their swimsuits, zorries, towels and boogie boards to the beach each afternoon, Steve, Veronica and Joyce had found an ideal location to stash them. It was just inside one of the bunker tunnel openings that led out onto the beach. Sometimes it would flood during high tide, but a small ledge up near the top usually stayed dry. Wrought iron hand holds leading up the wall to the small ledge made it easy to climb for access.

As an added precaution, they would each put their towels inside large plastic Ziploc bags before stowing them inside a weather resistant tote. Though plastic Ziploc bags had been invented in 1959, they were not sold commercially until 1968 so were relatively new on the market in 1972 and therefore still quite expensive. Sturdy wrought iron stakes emerging from the bunker tunnel wall near its peak above the ledge provided a perfect place for them to securely tie off the strings on their tote bags. The boogie boards inside them were made of hydrodynamic foam that would cause the entire tote to float when inside it, should the water ever rise to that level. The secret location was also an ideal place to change in or out of their boogie boarding clothes.

All three of them were familiar with the basics of how to paddle to the highest point or crest of a breaking wave, and the great importance of pointing the nose of their boogie board in the desired direction of travel, obviously being the beach. And though most boogie boarders try not to think of it too much, it is right at that critical point of time when they are resting their hands or elbows near the outer edge of the board while trying to get ahead of the wave to "catch" it that they are most vulnerable. Shiny jewelry can also be mistaken for shimmering fish scales by a hungry shark, particularly like the expensive waterproof gold watch Steve Fredrickson often wore.

Though sharks rarely attack groups of swimmers that stay within close proximity of one another, they sometimes do decide to target lone individuals that have strayed too far from the shore by themselves. Being a student of marine biology, Steve Fredrickson was well aware of the fact that sharks can also smell a single drop of blood from up to three miles away, and of how important it was for surfers or body boarders to avoid the open water with even the smallest of cuts on their finger.

Steve was aware, too, that sharks prefer to feed after twilight and before dawn, so he felt relatively safe practicing his boogie boarding in the mid-afternoon sun. The downside to boogie boarding on a warm day, however, was that warm waters in surf zones also attract a rich menu of fish, including baby seals and other marine life upon which sharks customarily prefer to feed. Still, absolutely nothing could rival the feeling of one's body moving effortlessly toward the beach on a properly controlled boogie board after catching a wave.

Finally bored with watching her friends boogie boarding down below, Carolyn got up from the rock on which she was seated and continued her trek along the bluff tops.

"Hey there," called Jim Otterman from behind her as he hurried to catch up. He had noticed Carolyn walking the bluff tops earlier and hoped he might still find her there. "Mind if I walk with you?"

Carolyn was well aware of the huge crush Jim Otterman had on her and did not wish to do anything at all to encourage him. Susan had already mentioned to her that Jim had abandoned the use of hair tonic after learning that Carolyn found it disgusting. Susan had been the one to tell Jim that, of course. Apparently, Susan and Jim had been assigned to work together as lab partners in their biology class. Predictably, Jim would continue to ask Susan more and more questions about Carolyn each day. Just to shut Jim up, Susan would occasionally share some tidbit of information with him.

When Susan finally mentioned to Jim what she and Carolyn both thought of his creepy looking, black-framed horn-rimmed glasses, Jim switched almost immediately to contact lenses. Most recently, Jim had visited the school nurse and acquired a prescription of Tetracycline to help clear up the severe acne condition on his face. According to Susan, Jim was doing everything humanly possible to make himself more desirable so Carolyn would notice him. His posture was still hideous, though, and nothing short of stilts could bring his height up to an acceptable level, as far as Carolyn was concerned.

"Did I tell you that Bart Higbee got his pilot's license last week?" Jim suddenly asked.

"Who's Bart Higbee?" asked Carolyn, unsure why she was expected to know or even care.

"Bart's my roommate," replied Jim.

"Good for him," said Carolyn as they walked along.

"He plans to take me up for a flight over the beach later this afternoon," mentioned Jim. "His plane is a four-seater, too, and he said I could bring two other people along. I was thinking maybe you and Susan might like to go?"

"Me and Susan?" Carolyn was surprised.

"Yeah, but it's 3:30 now and Bart plans to take off at 5:00," clarified Jim. "I'm supposed to take an aerial photo of the campus for the upcoming yearbook, but it needs to be a late afternoon shot."

"Susan mentioned that you were taking flying lessons," advised Carolyn. "Can't you just go up anytime you want?"

"I am taking lessons," verified Jim. "I just don't have my pilot's license yet. And, if I miss out on this opportunity, it'll be too late."

"Too late for what?" prompted Carolyn.

"To count as extra credit for my photography class," revealed Jim. "It's a special assignment and it's due by Monday."

"And you waited until Friday?" Carolyn raised an eyebrow.

"I know, I shouldn't have waited until the last minute," agreed Jim, "but there's nothing I can do about that now. This is it."

"Well, Susan has classes right up until 5:00 today," revealed Carolyn. "I think she said she had to stay after to make up a test or something, from when she was out sick last week."

"What about you?" Jim tried not to appear too anxious.

Carolyn paused and looked at Jim for a moment. Even without the greasy hair tonic, Jim's distinct carrot red colored hair resembled the feathery crown of a South American bird known as the Crimson-crested Woodpecker. Carolyn suddenly smiled as she thought of the colorful bird Jim reminded her of.

"Does that mean yes?" asked Jim hopefully.

Carolyn took in a deep breath and quickly let it out. If she said yes, Jim might get the wrong idea, yet she really did want to go. The opportunity to ride in a plane above Oceanview Academy was a unique experience that might not present itself again.

322

"Bart's an excellent pilot," assured Jim. "He got a perfect score on his flight test."

"Wouldn't I need permission from my parents? Or the Dean?" Carolyn inquired.

"I have no idea," admitted Jim. "But, Bart would know. Why don't we go ask him?"

"I don't know," hesitated Carolyn. "I think it might be boys' beach today."

"Who cares?" replied Jim. "The hangar's not on the beach, anyway. Neither are the bluffs where we are now."

"I'm pretty sure the bluffs are considered a part of the beach. I remember Dean Dixon telling me that once," reflected Carolyn. "We really shouldn't be here, either, not alone like this."

"Bart will be with us on the flight, of course," assured Jim. "At least come meet him and see what you think. If you don't want to go up after that, then it's your decision."

Jim still had not answered her question about the permission issue. Was he deliberately evading it? Carolyn decided she would definitely ask Bart about it when they got there.

"All right," Carolyn finally agreed. "I'll come meet Bart. That doesn't mean I'll go on the flight with you, just that I'll think about it."

"Great!" beamed Jim as he politely bowed and motioned for Carolyn to go ahead of him on the narrow trail.

"One more thing," added Carolyn over her shoulder.

"I'm listening," replied Jim.

Carolyn suddenly stopped and turned around to face him. "Just so we're perfectly clear on the subject, you can never expect me to be anything more than your friend. I am still interested in someone else."

"Perhaps that could change?" Jim winked at her with a hopeful looking smile. He knew quite well who Carolyn was referring to, and Jim planned to do everything in his power to persuade her differently.

"I'm serious!" chided Carolyn. "If I even so much as think your intentions are romantic in any way, our friendship is over."

"Yes, ma'am," nodded Jim with his fingers crossed behind his back. "Agreed."

Carolyn studied Jim for several moments longer for any sign of deceit but finally was satisfied. "All right, let's go meet Bart Higbee."

It was a short, five-minute walk to the airplane hangar, yet Jim Otterman had somehow managed to convey so much useless trivia about himself during the one-sided conversation that Carolyn soon found herself irritated by Jim's incessant babbling.

"Do you always have so much to say?" she finally asked.

"I'm talking too much, aren't I?" realized Jim. "Sorry about that! It's just that we so rarely get to chat with one another."

"After everything Susan has told me about you already," chuckled Carolyn, "I may just know more than you think."

Jim suddenly frowned and appeared worried.

"Nothing bad!" promised Carolyn. The last thing she wanted to do right now was hurt Jim's feelings, especially when they hadn't even gone up for the plane ride yet. Hopefully, it would work out.

"Jim!" called Bart Higbee as he saw them coming.

"Bart," nodded Jim. "This is Susan's roommate, Carolyn."

"Hi!" smiled Carolyn in acknowledgment.

"Susan couldn't make it, then?" Bart seemed disappointed. His crush on Susan was no secret to his roommate Jim, though Bart had not mentioned it to anyone else. Still, Carolyn picked up on it immediately.

"Susan had to stay after class to make up a test, from when she was out sick last week," explained Carolyn.

Jim Otterman was barely five feet eight inches tall, skinny and gangly looking, with slouched bony shoulders. Bart Higbee, on the other hand, appeared much taller than Jim because of his better posture, despite the fact that both of them were the exact same height.

Both Jim and Bart were straight A students and from families of means, as were all aviation students at Oceanview Academy. Unlike Jim, Bart took his flying lessons quite seriously and had a natural aptitude for flying and also for airplane mechanics.

The Higbee Flying Services of Oahu had been in operation for three generations now, so Bart had been exposed to a professional flying environment from boyhood. His father often flew both airplanes and helicopters and usually was available for business 24 hours each day. Amazingly, the cruise ships which frequented the Hawaiian island chain produced as many customers interested in helicopter tours as it did inter-island taxi service flights for straggling cruise passengers left behind after failing to board their vessels in time.

Bart Higbee was of Polynesian heritage with a pleasant face and genuinely contagious smile. Anyone with Jim Otterman as a roommate would need to have a sense of humor, thought Carolyn.

"Where's my camera, anyway?" questioned Jim. He was anxious to show off his expensive new Hasselblad camera to Carolyn.

"Right where you left it, on the back left passenger seat," pointed out Bart.

"Well, let's get going, then," suggested Jim as he grabbed the empty wooden crate that was usually turned upside down to be used as a step on which to climb into the various student and school owned planes housed in the Oceanview Academy airplane hangar.

Bart Higbee's Piper Cherokee 180 was a four-seater single engine airplane with low wings, fixed landing gear, and a fixed pitch propeller, so it was simple to operate and easy to maintain. It was white on top with navy blue on its belly and wing bottoms. It also had a lighter blue racing stripe along the sides that curved upward into its tail section.

"Hold it!" commanded Bart with an amused look on his face. "We aren't going anywhere without doing a preflight inspection first."

"I thought you were taking care of that while I was out rounding up our passengers," replied Jim.

"Passenger," corrected Bart. "Besides, you did say you wanted to watch while I did the walk around?"

"Didn't we actually check everything out before I left?" Jim whispered to Bart.

"You wanna do this or not?" challenged Bart. "If you plan to be ready for your next exam, you need to be able to do this in your sleep."

Jim had failed his recent flight test, but didn't want Carolyn to know it.

"I thought you two were in the same flying class," mentioned Carolyn as she moved closer to get a better look at the little book Bart was holding.

"See," sniggered Bart. "Even our passenger is more interested in this than you are!"

"Well, we do need to get up there," persisted Jim. "We've only got so much time."

"Why would you need to check it all again, if you just did?" wondered Carolyn.

"You wanna tell her, or should I?" offered Bart as he opened his small book and made a notation of the date and time.

"All right," agreed Jim. "The reason he has to check it all again is to make sure absolutely nothing has happened in the interim that might alter the results of the inspection."

"For example?" pressed Bart.

"Well, a bird nest might be in the cowling or air intakes," explained Jim. "Or, there could be cracks in the spinner or nicks in the propeller."

"The nose bowl is another expression used for the spinner or cone covering the middle of the propeller," elaborated Bart, for Carolyn's benefit.

"It might be windy today," acquiesced Carolyn, "but I don't think I've seen many species of birds around here that would be capable of building a nest in just under an hour."

Bart Higbee laughed heartily. "She's got a point! But, it's still regulation. Now, this is what Jim and I will do. For a preflight inspection, we will walk around the entire craft. The reason a preflight should always start in the cockpit is that when you secure an airplane after flying there is a wire-like control lock that goes through holes in the control column that keeps the controls from moving in the wind and also has a flag attached that covers the throttle to remind you to remove it so you can wiggle the control surfaces and use the throttle."

"What if you were to start it somewhere else besides the cockpit?" asked Carolyn. "Can you ever do that?"

"Like anywhere we want?" interjected Jim with a flirtatious grin. His remark was meant to be humorous and to be taken any way Carolyn wished to interpret it.

Carolyn merely rolled her eyes and shook her head.

"I always start a preflight by reaching into the cockpit to make sure the throttle is closed, the magneto switches are off, and then turn on the master electrical switch before I check the fuel gauges and lower the flaps so as to be able to check the hinges and linkages," described Bart. "With the flaps up you can't see everything."

"Then, with the flaps extended, the inspection is done in a clockwise direction around the aircraft," articulated Jim, "until arriving once again at the starting point."

"What did you write in the little book?" questioned Carolyn.

"The date and time," replied Bart.

"That would be Friday, March 23, 1973, at 4:00 o'clock p.m.," grinned Jim.

"He even knows what day it is," teased Bart. "Seriously, though, I have a better idea. Jimbo, why don't you check to be sure you have some film in that expensive looking camera of yours while I finish up the preflight? That should make things go much faster."

"Jimbo?" snickered Carolyn.

"I hate it when he calls me that," mentioned Jim.

Bart just grinned and shrugged his shoulders in response.

"Maybe while you guys are doing all that, I should run up to the dorm and check with Miss Dixon. Just to make sure it's all right if I go up with you," suggested Carolyn.

"No need," revealed Bart. "The Deans have both given us their blessings already. That would include Susan, too, if she were here. Too bad she's busy."

"Are you certain I won't need a permission slip from my parents?" pressed Carolyn. She did not want to be in trouble with Dean Dixon again.

"Not for something like this," assured Bart. "Technically, we're not even leaving the campus, only going up for a quick flight above it."

"And, since it's for the upcoming school yearbook, it's actually a school-sponsored activity," reminded Jim.

Bart raised one eyebrow, shook his head and grinned.

"Okay," began Bart. "One thing that is done on a preflight inspection is to drain a small quantity of fuel from a fitting on the bottom of the wing to check for water in the fuel from condensation or contaminated fuel, and to check by the color that the proper fuel has been put in the tanks. Red is 87 octane, while blue is 100 LL."

"That means low lead," interjected Jim.

Bart and Carolyn both gave Jim a disparaging look at that point.

"Then," resumed Bart, "after inspecting the leading edge of the right wing at the fuselage junction, I work my way outward."

"Okay," nodded Carolyn.

"Then, at the wingtip here, I'm checking for security by giving it a shake." Bart then demonstrated. "The lower surfaces are checked after that."

Carolyn watched with great interest as Bart bent down to get a better look at the airplane's belly and wing bottoms, inspecting them as he went.

"Then, at the aileron," described Bart, "we look for any looseness by wiggling it forward and backward, and do the same thing with each flap."

"Do you do that with all the moving parts?" quizzed Carolyn.

"Absolutely," assured Bart.

"Ailerons are used to bank the aircraft," informed Jim. "A bank is a tilt to the left or right, whereas a roll is a complete rotation of the aircraft either to the left or right. Of course, if you were to perform a roll, you do initiate and stop it with the ailerons."

"In other words, an aileron is a hinged flight control surface usually forming part of the trailing edge of each wing of a fixed-wing aircraft," interjected Bart. "Ailerons are used in pairs to control the aircraft when it rolls."

"We're not actually going to be flying upside down or anything like that, are we?" quizzed Carolyn with alarm.

"Hardly," smiled Bart. "A Cherokee 180 is not equipped for inverted flight and with the wing airfoil it would be difficult to maintain level flight with no engine power."

"No engine power?" worried Carolyn.

"If I were to roll this plane 180 degrees to the right, for example," described Bart, "the engine would almost immediately stop."

"That would not be good." Jim was stating the obvious and again managed to elicit glances of disapproval from Bart and Carolyn.

"Actually," grinned Bart, "It depends on what angle we need to get for Jim's photos. Perhaps a steep banking turn at 90 degrees might be necessary."

Carolyn realized at once that Bart was teasing her. At least she certainly hoped so. Her mind then began to wander as Bart and Jim finished the preflight inspection, checking the plane over and marking off each item in Bart's little book.

"Hey, earth to Carolyn," chuckled Jim.

"Sorry," apologized Carolyn. "I was just thinking of what it would be like to go up there. That runway ends pretty suddenly on the far edge of that bluff over there. What if you aren't able to get the plane up into the air before you reach it?"

"Then we'd most likely sail over the edge and crash onto the boulders below it," laughed Bart.

"It's not funny!" scowled Carolyn. "Maybe this isn't such a good idea after all."

"Hold it," commanded Bart. "I'm sorry! I was just having some fun. Seriously, it's safer to fly in a plane like this than it ever would be to ride in a car. Statistics have shown that for every five million auto accidents in the United States alone, there are only about twenty accidents while flying."

"That's right," corroborated Jim. "The National Aviation Safety Council compiled a risk-of-dying table just last year, and they figured out that the odds of dying in a motor vehicle accident were about one in 98 for a lifetime. Whereas, the odds of being killed while flying were only one in 7,178."

"And that includes air taxis and private flights," added Bart. "Have you ever seen anyone inspect a car like this before getting in and driving away?"

"Actually, yes," replied Carolyn. "Every time my dad drives on a gravel road of any kind, he stops, gets out, and checks each and every tire for rocks. Then, he pulls forward six inches and repeats the process again, until he's finally satisfied that no remaining pieces of gravel are in his tires. That's what this reminds me of."

"Your dad sounds like a very practical man," surmised Jim.

"He was an airplane mechanic during the Korean war," revealed Carolyn. "Maybe that's where he gets it from."

"No doubt," smiled Bart as he resumed the inspection. "We're almost done here. One of the most important things is to make sure there are no birds, nests, or debris from nests of any kind inside any of the air inlets. And yes, we also need to check for any nicks, scratches or gouges on the propeller."

"Those would be caused by dirt or gravel on the runway," elaborated Jim.

"Now all we need to do is check the fluids, as we discussed earlier," added Bart.

"I'll clean the windows while he does that," offered Jim as he retrieved a soft rag from a plastic bag that Bart kept in the glove box.

"Don't forget the tires," teased Carolyn. She was reminded of a crew of service station attendants that would come out to work on the Bennett family car when getting gas at an old Texaco station when she was growing up. There would usually be at least four men, all dressed in white shirts with black bowties and caps, and each one would perform a different task, including tire check, oil check, and window washing.

"Actually, proper tire inflation is critical for proper takeoff," replied Jim. "On a Piper Cherokee 180 like this, the tire pressure should be 24 psi on all three wheels."

"Do you guys mind if I go ahead and get inside while you finish up?" asked Carolyn.

"Not as long as you don't mind climbing back out when we're done," answered Bart. "The rear passengers like Jim need to be seated first, and then the pilot next, and the front seat passenger gets in last."

"That's because there's only one door, and it's located on the right side of the airplane where the passenger sits," described Jim.

"I can see that!" snapped Carolyn. "I'll just wait."

"Actually, I think we're about done here," announced Bart.

Jim quickly climbed inside the back seat of the plane by his camera and buckled up his seatbelt and harness.

"The last person to get in will need to untie the mooring straps," explained Bart.

"Sure, I can do that," agreed Carolyn.

"I'm just kidding," chuckled Bart. "But, I would like you to hang onto this one while I untie the other two. Here, let me just retie it in a slip knot that you can quickly untie before climbing in."

Carolyn grabbed and held onto the stabilizing mooring strap indicated while Bart circled the plane and untied the other two. Now that the inspection was complete, things seemed to be moving rather rapidly. Bart climbed inside the plane and scooted over to the pilot's seat while Carolyn untied the final mooring strap and climbed in after him. The hatch door shut more easily than she expected.

"I didn't mean to slam it," apologized Carolyn.

"It's fine," assured Bart as he buckled up his seatbelt.

"Shall I read off the checklist?" asked Jim.

"Sure," nodded Bart.

"All circuit breakers in," began Jim.

"Check," responded Bart.

"Battery switch in the 'on' position?" continued Jim.

"Check," repeated Bart.

"Rotating beacon on," read Jim.

"Check," indicated Bart.

"Alternator switch is in 'off' position," added Jim.

"Check," muttered Bart.

"Auxiliary fuel pump is on?" questioned Jim.

"Pressure observed," verified Bart.

"Bart will now actuate the primer plunger three times," explained Jim, for Carolyn's benefit.

"Primer plunger is confirmed 'safe' in closed position," confirmed Bart. "Throttle is opened one quarter inch, and the mixture is full rich. Carburetor heat is in 'off' position."

"Window is open," informed Jim as he opened the window and yelled, "clear prop."

"That's to announce the starting of the motor," explained Bart.

"Bart will now turn the ignition key to start the motor," Jim described to Carolyn. "Once the propeller is turning and the motor is started, he then turns the key to the 'both' position."

"Oil pressure is observed to rise," verified Bart.

"If not, he would need to shut the motor back off," shouted Jim, to be heard above the noise of the engine starting.

"Alternator switch is in the 'on' position," called out Bart.

"Now we turn the radios on," smiled Jim.

"Seriously?" Carolyn felt as if she were about to take off in a rocket ship for outer space.

"It'll all be worth it, once we get up there," assured Jim.

"Directional gyro set," indicated Bart.

"The altimeter is set by field elevation or barometric pressure," described Jim.

"Vacuum gauge checked for proper pressure," added Bart.

"He's turning on the transponder to standby now," mentioned Jim. "That's a radio code used to identify us during our flight."

"Where's the radio tower?" questioned Carolyn.

"Well, we really don't have one this far out," answered Bart. "That's why we don't do any flying at night around here, and we have to keep a sharp lookout for other possible aircraft before we take off."

"And for flocks of birds, that type of thing," elaborated Jim.

"If we had a radio tower, now is when we would be informing them that we are rolling onto the active runway," informed Bart. "But, we are still going to turn on our landing beacons, and tune our transponder to 'alt' - that way, if we were to get lost, the nearest tower personnel would hopefully be able to spot us."

"Isn't that what Amelia Earhart would have done?" poked Carolyn with a wry smile.

"Most likely," countered Bart. "And, having our transponder in the 'alt' position would theoretically let them know our mixture is rich and our throttle is open to maximum rpm."

The small aircraft suddenly jolted as it took off down the runway and raced toward the finality of the precipice ahead. "We are going to accelerate to 75 mph before pulling back the yoke to rotate and climb," continued Bart.

"When he clears the end of the runway, the flaps are retracted and the airplane is trimmed for a cruise climb of 100 mph," added Jim.

"Are you sure we're gonna make it?" fretted Carolyn. She was not ready to die just yet, especially not like this!

"We'll be fine," assured Jim as he put a comforting hand on Carolyn's shoulder.

"This is where the tower operator would normally give us any last-minute instructions, restrictions or traffic information before wishing us a nice day," smiled Bart.

"Nice takeoff," complimented Jim.

"Thanks," nodded Bart. "And we would then give them our flight plan before wishing them a nice day in return."

"Wow! There's really a lot to it," appreciated Carolyn.

"Have you ever operated a camera like this before?" Jim suddenly asked, as he tried to show Carolyn his new Hasselblad.

"No, why?" Carolyn was busy trying to look out the plane's windows to see everything she could as they quickly flew past.

"Just in case the best shots happen to be on your side," replied Jim. "That way, I could just hand the camera over to you."

"I think you can handle it," declined Carolyn. She was not about to miss out on anything, just to take a few pictures for Jim.

"Fair enough," responded Jim.

"Hey, look!" Carolyn suddenly noticed that her friends were still down on the beach boogie boarding. She distinctly saw Joyce, Veronica and Steve Fredrickson.

"Is that a shark?" pointed out Jim. "Over by, ah, what's his name? Steve Fredrickson?"

"Oh my God, it is a shark!" recognized Carolyn. "Bart, can you fly back over there? Is there something we can do to warn them?"

332

"I can fly back over," replied Bart, "but the regulations require me to stay at least five hundred feet up."

"What about over the water?" persisted Carolyn. "Can you fly any lower out there? Maybe we can somehow scare that shark away?"

"Even over the water, it's five hundred feet," clarified Bart.

Bart had seen sharks near boogie boarders before, so he wasn't overly concerned about it now. Carolyn just wasn't accustomed to having a bird's-eye view of everything, thought Bart. What she needed was something genuine to worry about. "What about a better angle?"

Bart smiled a crooked smile as he unexpectedly banked his plane 90 degrees to the right and did a steep banking turn over the beach.

"Stop it!" screamed Carolyn.

"Or, we could climb up to a suitable altitude, reduce power and then dive to accelerate," offered Bart with an irrepressible grin as he proceeded to do so.

"Please make him stop!" pleaded Carolyn as she grabbed Jim's hand, which was still on her opposite shoulder.

"He'll probably wait until the last minute to pull up," laughed Jim. He was delighted to have Carolyn holding hands with him like she was.

Bart then pulled up and leveled off the plane before returning to upright position again. "Technically, we should be wearing life vests out here over the water like this."

"Hey, slow down and make another pass over the beach," directed Jim as he let go of Carolyn's hand. "That would make a nice shot with the three of them boogie boarding like that down there."

Carolyn suddenly noticed that Steve Fredrickson was struggling to escape from the upright fin of a shark, and had just seen Joyce and Veronica back on the beach running away from the water!

"Oh my God! Steve's being attacked by a shark right now! We've got to get down there so we can help!"

"She's right!" confirmed Jim with a worried expression.

"I'll have to land on the runway," explained Bart, suddenly becoming serious. "Sorry, Jimbo, we're gonna have to cut this short."

Jim was busy snapping photos as fast as he could of the scene below with his zoom lens. "Understandable."

"It seems like they'd let you go ahead and land on the beach, under the circumstances," opined Carolyn.

"We wouldn't do them much good if we crashed," replied Bart as he circled to position his flight path for a safe landing on the tricky bluff top runway.

"It wouldn't do us much good, either!" added Jim.

"Where did Joyce and Veronica go?" Carolyn suddenly asked. "Did you see where they went? Where are they?"

"The shark's gone, too!" exclaimed Jim. "You don't think it took them, do you?"

"No!" maintained Carolyn. "They definitely came back up onto the beach. I saw them!"

Carolyn and Jim watched helplessly from the plane while Steve Fredrickson weakly dragged himself onto the beach below. Even from their vantage point, it was obvious that his injuries were severe.

Bart knew he did not have time to circle back for a second attempt and was intently focused on safely landing his plane.

Carolyn did not realize she had been holding her breath until she felt the jolt of the small plane's wheels coming into contact with the ground on the small runway. "How long will it take to stop?"

"Hang on," cautioned Bart. "You can't just jump out while it's still moving."

Had it not been for Jim's restraining hand on Carolyn's shoulder, she most certainly would have flung the plane's door open and leaped out onto the ground. "Hurry! Make it stop!" she screamed.

"I'll go get help while Bart secures the plane," offered Jim. "Or, I can go down there and try to help Steve while you go for help."

"Is there a phone out here anywhere?" questioned Carolyn. "Can't we just call for someone?"

"There's no phone or control tower out here, either," regretted Bart. "I wish there were."

"Thanks for the ride, man," mentioned Jim as the plane finally came to a stop. Carolyn immediately flung open the door, leaped out, and began running for the trail which led down to the beach.

"Oh, hell!" muttered Bart as he shut off the plane's engine. "Just moor it down and we can do the post-flight later. Neither of you is probably trained in First Aid, anyway."

"Carolyn has to be," surmised Jim as he and Bart quickly tied down the plane. "I know she was in Mrs. Bovinae's Senior Lifesaving Class. First Aid is a prerequisite."

"We'd better hope it is!" added Bart as he reached under the front passenger seat for a first responder kit that he kept handy.

Bart and Jim then sprinted in the direction they had seen Carolyn headed, but were so far behind by now they couldn't even see her anymore. Carolyn was undoubtedly half-way down the treacherous trail which wound down to the beach below.

"I'll be back with help," advised Jim as he suddenly veered off in the direction of the dairy. The dairy was closer to their location than anywhere else Jim could think of that might have a phone or someone who could help.

Meanwhile, Bart scrambled down onto the steep trail and began negotiating it while trying not to drop his first responder kit. A hearty mat of creeping succulent ice plants with hot pink blooms lined the edge of the trail, though loose rocks could still be found on the trail itself. The damp smell of hemlock and cypress trees permeated the air and the odor of fresh eucalyptus could be detected on the ocean breeze as it wafted upward. Seagulls cawed overhead, and the sound of ocean waves crashing against the shoreline below became louder as Bart descended the trail.

When finally reaching the beach, Bart saw Carolyn kneeling beside Steve Fredrickson's lifeless body. Massive amounts of blood had pooled on the ground beside him, even on the sand. Carolyn looked up at Bart with her tearstained face and gently shook her head in the negative.

Unwilling to accept the obvious, Bart dashed over to where Steve was and checked his pulse.

"I gave him CPR already," advised Carolyn sadly. She had already ripped the shoulder strap from her purse and tried to apply a tourniquet to the upper part of Steve's injured right leg. The shark had mutilated it quite badly from the calf down. Steve had also sustained a series of shark bites on his right arm and hand, as well, and Carolyn had immediately ripped the legs from her jeans so she could use them to try and stop some of the bleeding there and on his leg. That was when Steve had finally lost consciousness and died.

"We're gonna try it again," informed Bart.

Bart and Carolyn were still working as a team, trying to perform CPR on the dead, lifeless body of Steve Fredrickson when Jim and the others arrived. In spite of everything they had both tried to do, Steve Fredrickson was gone.

"Where are Joyce and Veronica?" questioned Jim.

"I don't know," replied Carolyn sadly.

"There are some fresh tracks in the sand over here," called Jim.

"Let's spread out and see if we can find them," suggested Dean Vandevere.

Thankfully, Dean Vandevere had a walkie-talkie in his jeep and was at the dairy when Jim Otterman had dashed in looking for someone to help. Reinforcements were quickly called to come and were now spreading out to search the entire area for any sign of Joyce or Veronica.

Earlier that same day, on March 23, 1973, the noon whistle had just blown. The morning shift at the Oceanview Academy lumber mill had ended and it was finally time for lunch.

Veronica and Joyce each had only one class that afternoon and were looking forward to boogie boarding after that. Next week was spring break, so several of the usual classes had already completed their midterm exams and were in adjournment until after the break.

Relieved that they would also have the next week off from their tufting job at the mill, Veronica and Joyce wasted no time straightening up their workstations and tallying up their "rate count" sheets – which were kept by hand – so they could leave.

Life was good, especially for Joyce and Veronica, with an entire week of boogie boarding to look forward to! Neither of them had plans to travel home during spring break since Joyce's family lived on the east coast, and Veronica's family just could not afford an extra trip on their already strained budget. Both families would just have to wait until summer break to see them again.

Birdboy seemed oblivious to the fact that the lunch whistle had blown and continued pumping stuffing into the newly sewn chaise lounge cushions that had accumulated at his feet.

"Hey Birdboy!" called Veronica. "Time to fly away and go have some lunch now!"

"Oh, leave him be," laughed Joyce. "If Birdboy wants to work off the clock to get caught up on his rate count, that's his business. We certainly won't tell!"

"Come on, I'm starving," urged Carolyn. "We still need to go all the way up to the dorm to change out of our jeans before we can go to the cafeteria, or we won't have time for lunch before our class."

All three of them were in Ms. Eggersol's English Literature class together, but only Carolyn seemed to enjoy it.

"I can't believe Susan decided to take Advanced Composition class instead," remarked Joyce. "English Literature is bad enough!"

"Hey, Veronica," called Birdboy as he tossed several handfuls of stuffing into her workstation, where she had just finished sweeping.

"You creep!" shouted Veronica.

"You forgot to sweep over there, too!" laughed Birdboy with glee as he tossed yet more stuffing in her direction.

Veronica suddenly grabbed her cleanup broom and rushed over to where Birdboy was. She then began smacking him on the back and shoulders with the bristles of her cleanup broom. "Stop it, you freak!"

"Who are you calling a freak?" demanded Jon Roth as he howled with laughter and ducked to evade the swipes from her broom.

Then, unexpectedly, Jon Roth became deadly serious, grabbed ahold of Veronica's broom handle and refused to let go, even though Veronica was also still holding onto it, as well. Jon Roth's nostrils flared with deeply repressed rage as he stood there and glared at Veronica in an evil and threatening manner that truly frightened her.

Carolyn debated on whether or not to get involved but then offered, "Shall I go get the supervisor?"

"Come on Birdboy, please let go of the broom," urged Joyce as she approached them and also grabbed onto the broom handle.

Joyce, Veronica and Birdboy all three stood there glaring at one another and clutching Veronica's cleanup broom for an eternal moment while Carolyn watched with astonishment.

"Fine! Have your old broom!" shouted Jon Roth as he suddenly shoved it away with all his might and then let go.

Joyce and Veronica were propelled backward onto the stack of freshly tufted chaise lounge cushions behind them, so neither was injured, and both were still holding onto the broom when they landed.

Birdboy then climbed onto Joyce's tufting table, stood up tall, flapped his arms like a bird with his elbows bent, and began squawking quite loudly. Any remaining workers at the mill who had not yet left for lunch stopped to watch the spectacle.

"Birdboy is about to fly away and go have lunch!" hollered Jon Roth. He then flapped his bent arms like wings once again, bent his knees as if he were on a diving board, and leaped face-first onto the huge stack of freshly tufted chaise lounge cushions below, squawking as he did so. The cushions on which Birdboy landed were made from a cheerful fabric with an olive green background that had yellow and white daisies all over it. It was one of Jon Roth's favorite designs.

"He's absolutely nuts!" exclaimed Joyce.

"We'll see who's nuts," promised Jon Roth as he slowly got up, brushed the excess stuffing from his arms and legs, and slowly sauntered away. "Yes, we'll definitely see about that."

"Is there a problem here?" demanded Benny Gomez, the shift supervisor. He had arrived at the scene just in time to witness Birdboy's swan dive onto the huge pile of chaise lounge cushions.

Susan Rives had just finished rinsing off and putting away her brushes and cleaning up her workstation in the stain department, and had also managed to get there in time to witness Birdboy's infamous swan dive onto the pile of chaise lounge cushions.

"Did you see the way he looked at us?" asked Joyce. "There's something wrong with that guy!"

"What did you girls say to him?" questioned Mr. Gomez.

"Only that it was time for lunch," mentioned Veronica.

"That's the way it happened," corroborated Carolyn. "They had just gotten done sweeping up when Birdboy went nuts and starting throwing stuffing at them."

"Why would he do that?" quizzed Veronica.

"Did you see the wild stare in his eyes?" added Joyce. "It was almost like he was someone else for a moment."

"I always knew Birdboy was off his rocker," commented Susan.

"Well, Birdboy was definitely a bubble off plumb today!" assured Veronica. "There's no way I'll work here anymore with that creep lurking around behind us! I just won't do it!"

"Are either of you hurt?" inquired Mr. Gomez. The last thing he wanted to do was fill out an accident report when it was already time for lunch! Unlike these students, Benny would be expected to return to his post for the afternoon shift.

338

"We're fine," promised Joyce. "Just shaken up. But, I won't work with Birdboy again, either. No way!"

"None of you will have to," agreed Mr. Gomez. "Birdboy, or whatever his name really is – who knows – is fired! I'll have to go look up his contact info in the office file and then give his parents a call."

"Who are his parents, anyway?" queried Joyce.

"I don't know off hand, but that's not important. I've got it written down somewhere, and they definitely will be hearing from me," assured Benny Gomez.

"I wonder if his parents know he's like this?" wondered Carolyn. "And whether he's dangerous or not?"

Carolyn then grabbed her cleanup broom and began re-sweeping the tufting station.

"I think Birdboy is the Roth kid," Susan whispered to Veronica, so no one else could hear.

"Really?" Veronica seemed surprised.

"But I'm not sure," added Susan. "I just remember them calling out that name for roll once in my history class, and I think it was him."

Carolyn was too busy helping Joyce re-sweep the tufting area to overhear the conversation between Susan and Veronica about Birdboy's possible identity.

"Hey, ladies, don't worry about cleaning all this up again," offered Benny. "Just leave the rest of it. I know it wasn't your fault. And don't worry about Birdboy, either. He absolutely will not be working here again!"

"What if Birdboy decides to come back here sometime or tries to retaliate?" asked Joyce.

"Just let him try," smirked Benny Gomez. He had never liked Birdboy, anyway, and would welcome an opportunity to teach the punk a good lesson. Benny Gomez was well aware of the fact that Birdboy would occasionally toss stuffing at the tufters, as he had seen him doing it on more than one occasion. Benny also found it curious that none of them had ever reported it. Still, whatever the reason, there was no excuse for anything like this!

Jon Roth was deep in thought as he trudged his way across campus to have lunch at home. Edith Roth would have a sandwich and a glass of milk waiting for her son's lunch each day, but usually the sandwiches were made with some horrible fake meat substitute and tasted rather like cardboard to Jon. Not that he wasn't grateful, but he just couldn't bear the thought of eating one more of his mother's fake meat sandwiches at the moment.

"Jon!" called Sheree Wilkins. "Wait up!"

"Sheree?" Jon smiled when he saw her.

Ever since the Harvest Festival Prom, Jon Roth and Sheree had become good friends. In fact, she was his only friend, and right now he sure could use one.

"Do you have any more classes today?" asked Sheree.

"No, I'm done until after spring break," replied Jon.

"Me, too!" beamed Sheree.

"Wanna come over for lunch?" offered Jon. If there was a fake sandwich waiting for him – and he was certain there would be – he could just give it to Sheree and then make himself a peanut butter and jelly sandwich instead.

Sheree appeared hesitant.

"My mother will be there," assured Jon.

"In that case, sure!" agreed Sheree. She had often heard Jon talk about his parents' home but had never actually visited it.

"They are just getting ready to build a patio onto the back," mentioned Jon, "so there's a pallet of lumber stacked in the driveway."

"That's okay," smiled Sheree. "Just because I don't work at the mill doesn't mean I haven't seen lumber before."

Jon was deep in thought as they walked in silence toward the faculty housing area. Sheree didn't mind, though. She was just happy to have someone to hang out with who didn't judge her, and accepted her the way she was. That meant everything to her.

While it was true that Sheree wore hideous horn-rimmed glasses, thought Jon, so did he. And, while her coke-bottle eyeglasses were so thick they made Sheree's eyes appear like large insect eyes, so were his. At least he didn't have an acne problem like Sheree did, but in time that would no doubt clear up. In fact, her pale alabaster skin would someday be quite beautiful, imagined Jon.

And, even though Sheree's buck teeth were firmly attached to an unsightly orthodontic headgear device that wrapped around her head, in time her teeth would no doubt be straight and beautiful. Jon tried to imagine what Sheree might look like when all that was behind her.

Jon also tried to imagine what Sheree would look like someday after she filled out and was no longer flat chested or knock-kneed anymore. Perhaps she would even outgrow the need for all that hardware, including the flat shoes with thick braces on them, and the special brace on her back. Jon was well aware that Sheree had been in a severe car accident during which her back had been broken, and that it had been several months before Sheree was able to walk again.

Right now, Sheree's clothes were out of style and hung on her like nothing more than a plain brown sack. Still, being with Sheree actually made Jon Roth feel ruggedly handsome and good-looking in comparison, and he needed desperately to feel that way. Especially after the way his morning had gone. Jon Roth was sick and tired of popular girls like Joyce and Veronica feeling as if they had some right to continuously demean him both in school and at work.

"A penny for your thoughts," Sheree finally said.

Jon smiled warmly at Sheree and then took her hand in his to hold as they continued walking along.

"Won't we get into trouble?" worried Sheree. No boy had ever held her hand before and she was nervous about it, especially knowing that it was against the school rules.

"I doubt it," smiled Jon.

"I just wouldn't want anything to happen where we wouldn't get to see each other anymore," mentioned Sheree.

"Nothing's gonna happen," promised Jon. "I don't think we have anything to worry about."

Jon did enjoy Sheree's company, and she wasn't too bad to be around, as long as he didn't have to look directly at her for very long. Walking along side-by-side was the perfect opportunity to do just that.

"After lunch, I'll show you my father's bomb shelter if you like," offered Jon. Perhaps while they were in there he could shut off the lights and even try to kiss her. With his eyes closed, he could imagine that she was just about anyone, perhaps some movie star. Jon grinned as he thought of it. Would Sheree kiss him back? There was only one way to find out. He would, of course need to convince her to temporarily remove the orthodontic headgear device that wrapped around her head.

Veronica and Joyce were already at the beach and had just finished changing into their swimsuits.

Steve Fredrickson had just enough time to join them for a couple hours of boogie boarding before heading back up for his last class. He still had a mid-term to take for his German class.

"Steve!" called Veronica. "There you are!"

Steve rushed up to Veronica, pulled her close, and gave her a passionate kiss of greeting.

Joyce cleared her throat to remind them she was there. "Good thing no one else is around, or you two would be expelled from school!"

They all laughed heartily. No one else ever came down to the beach when they were boogie boarding, except Carolyn or Susan.

"Where are Susan and Carolyn?" asked Steve.

"Carolyn's up there on the bluffs," pointed out Veronica.

"Oh yeah, there she is!" nodded Steve as he waved at her.

Carolyn noticed Steve, Joyce and Veronica waving at her and waved back.

"Carolyn hasn't been the same since that Harvest Festival Prom last fall," mentioned Joyce. "That thing with Lenny and Linda Shaver was just too much for her."

"She's gotta get over it sometime," replied Steve. "You guys need to get her down here for some boogie boarding."

"Carolyn won't go into the water," informed Veronica.

"She's afraid of sharks," laughed Joyce.

"What about Susan?" questioned Steve. "Maybe you could get her to come out with us."

"Susan feels the same way," revealed Joyce, "but right now she's making up one of the exams she missed last week."

"That's no fun," grinned Steve. "Come on! Surf's up."

The three of them raced toward the water, threw down and climbed onto their boogie boards, and then began paddling toward the open sea.

"Here comes a wave!" noticed Veronica. She was anxious to catch it, and to feel herself become one with the sheer pleasure of being propelled toward the shore on her boogie board. Perhaps she would try a 360° turn again today. They were getting easier lately.

The next hour went by rather quickly, yet Joyce, Steve and Veronica never seemed to tire of boogie boarding. It seemed to be their greatest joy in life. Carolyn had disappeared from the bluffs above, and had they looked, they would have seen her walking along the bluff tops with Jim Otterman toward the small airplane hangar nearby.

After finally managing to master a 360° turn while riding a wave, Steve Fredrickson beamed with delight. He now knew it could be done! He would need to be in class in less than half an hour but felt he had enough time to catch just one more wave. He wanted to see if he could do the 360° consistently, and that it had not just been a fluke.

Right at that moment, a small, single engine plane flew by overhead, making it difficult to hear much of anything.

"Shark!" hollered Joyce. "Over there, by Steve!"

"Where?" shouted Veronica.

"Get out of the water!" screamed Joyce. "Hurry!"

Steve was just about to catch his final wave for the day when he noticed Joyce and Veronica frantically making their way toward the beach. Too late, Steve noticed the fin of a shark as it unexpectedly attacked him. The horrific pain of its teeth as the creature bit down on his leg was unimaginable. Steve desperately began striking the shark's face with his right fist while clinging to his boogie board with his other hand so he would have a way to float back to shore again. He was farther out than anticipated and knew getting back would not be easy, especially with the injuries he was sustaining.

Just then, the small plane made another pass over the beach. It was someone showing off, thought Steve, as he saw the plane roll 90 degrees to the right before doing a steep banking turn over the beach!

The shark suddenly let go of Steve's leg. Seizing the opportunity to escape, Steve began using his right arm to paddle. His right leg was useless at this point. The bright gold watch on his right wrist flashed in the brilliant sunlight. Without warning, the shark circled back and bit down on the watch, most likely mistaking it for some shimmering fish scales.

Steve was unaware of the agonizing cries he had made during his struggle. The water had become shallow enough that he was able to stand on his good leg. Steve then used his good left hand to smack the shark on the head with his boogie board, as hard as he could, finally driving the creature away.

The small plane above was now doing a nosedive and coming directly for him! What was wrong with that pilot? Why was he doing this? Was the plane going to crash right on top of him? At the last moment, the plane veered upward again and climbed back up for one last pass over the beach before circling around to land over on the bluffs.

Steve became dizzy and collapsed, but had somehow managed to drag himself to shore. Where were Joyce and Veronica? Steve looked around but they were nowhere to be seen. What had happened to them? "Help!" he shouted. "Please, someone help!"

Unsure how long he had been there alone on the beach, Steve was vaguely aware that someone was finally there. He could feel a tourniquet being put around his injured leg. Opening his eyes for only a moment, Steve could see Carolyn trying to help him. Steve tried to say thank you but was only able to mouth the words before slipping back into the unconsciousness of death.

Steve then felt as if he were floating and glanced down at the beach below him. Carolyn was there alone by herself, trying to stop the bleeding wounds on his lifeless body. Why weren't Joyce and Veronica with her? What had happened to them?

Earlier that same day at the Roth residence on March 23, 1973, Jon Roth and Sheree Wilkins had finished an enjoyable lunch.

"What time is it?" questioned Sheree.

"It's just a little after one o'clock," informed Jon after glancing at his wristwatch. "We've got all afternoon."

"Won't you have some ice cream, too?" offered Edith Roth. She had never known her son to turn down the delicious ice cream she was able to get from the Silver Creek Trailer Park Store.

"Maybe tonight," replied Jon. "Sheree and I are going berry picking, over by the bunker."

Sheree, of course, did not like to eat ice cream in front of other people because of the problems it created with her orthodontic headgear, and Jon wished to spare her the embarrassment. Eating the sandwich had been enough of a challenge for Sheree as it was.

"Okay, maybe later then?" asked Edith.

"Perhaps," replied Jon absentmindedly. He considered whether or not he should mention to his mother that he planned to show Sheree the bomb shelter, but then decided against it. Jon also contemplated telling either Sheree or his mother about the incident at the mill that morning but decided against that, too.

"If you have any extra berries, could you bring me some?" inquired Edith Roth with a smirk as she handed her son a small plastic bucket. She was well aware of the fact that there were positively no berries ready to be picked in the month of March.

"Absolutely!" agreed Jon as he took the bucket from her and handed it to Sheree.

Edith was pleased that her son had finally found a young lady that was interested in him, despite her appearance. Perhaps true beauty did come from inside, and that was what mattered most, anyway.

"Thanks for the delicious lunch," smiled Sheree as they started to leave. Sheree was self-conscious about whether or not any pieces of food might still be clinging to her orthodontic headgear. "May I use your restroom first?"

"Down the hall to your right," indicated Edith Roth.

Sheree carefully set the plastic bucket down on a nearby lamp stand and hurried down the hall to use the restroom and to check her braces for any visible pieces of food.

"I like her," commented Edith. "She seems like a very nice young lady. Just make sure you don't do anything the two of you will regret later on."

"Yes, she is very nice," agreed Jon rather distantly. His mind was still on the incident at the lumber mill, and he was greatly troubled by it. "And, I would never do anything to dishonor her, mother, I promise."

"I believe you." Edith Roth smiled with relief as she gave her son a warm hug and kiss on the cheek. "Just be home by six. We're having pot roast."

"I'll be here," beamed Jon. Pot roast was one of his favorites, and it was rare that his mother served real meat in the Roth household, so he wouldn't think of missing it.

"Okay," smiled Sheree as she returned and picked up the bucket.

"I have some old clothes you kids might want to change into first," suggested Edith with a droll smile. "For the berry picking."

"We'll be careful," promised Jon as he gave Sheree a sly wink. "We won't be picking that many berries, anyway."

Sheree suddenly flushed with embarrassment, but she did her best to try and act normal when they departed.

"This way," indicated Jon as he led Sheree around the Roth residence, and down a small dirt foot path.

Gently curving for several yards through the old growth forest, the foot path finally connected with a dirt road that extended from behind the Roth house over to the old servants' quarters and lighthouse on the adjoining property next door.

"It's so beautiful back here!" admired Sheree. "These cottage cove style homes are really lovely, too!"

"Perhaps someday you and I could have a home like this?" proposed Jon with a twinkle in his eyes. He wanted to see how Sheree would react.

Sheree blushed again, not sure how to respond. Was Jon just toying with her, or was he genuinely interested in pursuing a future relationship with her? And why? Why would any man be interested in someone that looked like her? What did he really want from her?

"Not right away, of course," assured Jon with a wry smile. "Just someday, if we're still together when the time comes."

Sheree slowly looked up at Jon and tried to smile, but tears were streaming down her cheeks.

"Hey, don't cry," bid Jon as he stepped close enough to tenderly wipe the tears from her cheeks with the back of his free hand. "I didn't mean to upset you."

"I'm not upset," assured Sheree as she finally managed to smile.

"Look," nodded Jon. "We're here."

"Blackberries!" grinned Sheree. "But, they don't look like they'll be ripe for several more months."

"Probably not until late summer," agreed Jon.

"Your mother must have known that when she handed you the bucket," deduced Sheree. She was suddenly suspicious.

"I think she knew I just wanted a chance to be alone with you for a while," admitted Jon. "And, to show you this."

Sheree watched with great interest as Jon walked around behind the blackberry thicket and indicated for her to follow. Sheree was indeed surprised when they came face-to-face with an iron-barred bunker tunnel gate that had a combination padlock on it!

Jon adeptly unlocked the combination padlock and easily pulled open the gate. Several yards farther on was a blast door inside the bunker tunnel opening.

"I don't think we should be here," objected Sheree.

"Nonsense! This is my family's very own bomb shelter," explained Jon as he nimbly placed his index finger inside a small hole on the right side of the doorjamb around the blast door and activated the opening mechanism inside.

Sheree stared with amazement as the blast door rose upward and then with awe at the bomb shelter's interior, which was gently lit by recessed lights throughout.

"Everything one might need to survive for an indefinite period of time," mentioned Jon proudly. "My father had it built back in 1963."

"Wasn't that just after the Cuban Missile Crisis?" asked Sheree.

"The Cuban Missile Crisis was actually in October of 1962," clarified Jon. "But, lots of people began putting in bomb shelters right after that. Most people were just installing them underground, so having our own bunker tunnel to put one in was perfect."

"I'd heard that the military had tunnels like this all over the campus," admitted Sheree, "but I just hadn't seen one until now."

"You don't get out much, do you?" teased Jon.

"Well, not really," confessed Sheree.

"The bunker tunnels are indeed all over the campus," confirmed Jon. "Most of the openings to them are used to store tractors and farm equipment for the school, but rumor has it that all of them are connected by underground passageways. One even leads out onto the beach."

"You haven't been down there, have you?" questioned Sheree.

"Actually, yes," replied Jon. "All it takes is a good flashlight and an adventurous spirit."

"I'm not that adventurous," informed Sheree.

"Nonsense," insisted Jon as he grabbed two heavy duty flashlights and handed one to Sheree.

"This is definitely not a good idea," objected Sheree.

"Sure it is," differed Jon as he secured the outer gate and blast door they had just come through.

"What are you doing?" Sheree became alarmed. "We're trapped in here now!"

"Not really," chuckled Jon as he opened the interior blast door that led to the interior tunnel system. "There is a series of catwalks in

347

here, probably in case the tide comes in too far, and it's easy walking all the way."

"But, it's boys' beach today," reminded Sheree.

"No one will know we're even there," assured Jon. "Trust me!"

"Wait!" called Sheree as Jon headed into the tunnel, climbed up a set of wrought iron steps, and onto the catwalk above.

"Just put your finger inside that hole on the right side of the blast door when you come out," instructed Jon from where he waited for her. "I wouldn't take you there if it wasn't safe. It'll be fun."

Sheree was hesitant at first but finally acquiesced herself to the situation. After all, Jon would be with her and he was familiar with the tunnels. What could possibly go wrong?

"That's it," encouraged Jon as he watched Sheree close the interior blast door behind her.

Sheree quickly turned on the flashlight Jon had handed her before climbing the steps after him.

"How far is it?" she suddenly asked.

"Not that far," promised Jon as he started out ahead of her on the catwalk, forcing her to walk as fast as she could to keep pace with him.

"I don't think I can walk that fast with these braces on my feet," informed Sheree. She had fallen farther behind with every step, yet Jon had not bothered to look back or check to see whether or not Sheree was keeping up with him. "Jon?"

Irritated at having to pause for Sheree, Jon finally stopped. He gave no indication to Sheree that he minded waiting, but she seemed to sense it and was struggling her best to hurry.

"Can't you just take those things off?" Jon suddenly asked.

"Not really," answered Sheree. "My back is still healing from the surgery I had last year, so I need to keep the braces on my shoes whenever I walk very far. At least they're not as much trouble to get off and on as this stupid back brace! You know what, maybe I should just go back. I'm holding you up."

"Nonsense!" objected Jon. "I'm such an idiot! I just wasn't thinking. In fact, I'd forgotten all about your braces."

Sheree slowly nodded and then smiled. It was nice to know that Jon saw her for herself, and had actually forgotten about her braces! That meant a lot to her.

348

"In fact," added Jon, "I'm happy to carry you if you need me to. Just let me know if you get to feeling like this is too much for you."

"I'll be fine," assured Sheree. "I just need to take it a little slower. But, you don't necessarily have to wait for me. I'm bound to catch up eventually."

Jon studied Sheree in the dim lighting. Without all the braces, she actually wasn't all that bad. And, they were just temporary, anyway. When Sheree caught up to him, Jon reached out and took her free hand to hold as they continued.

The dim recessed lighting above them suddenly ended and nothing but darkness lay ahead.

"How come the lights don't go any farther?" questioned Sheree.

"They only go as far as the edge of my parents' property," described Jon. "Right now, we're directly under the mailbox."

"Okay, that makes sense," nodded Sheree. "I know exactly where we are now. Good thing for the flashlights!"

"Indeed," agreed Jon.

"It sure is cold in here," mentioned Sheree.

"It's supposed to be a constant 58 degrees," informed Jon, "but the moisture does make it feel colder. If you listen, you should be able to hear the sound of water dripping here and there."

Sheree quietly listened for several minutes but heard nothing. Then, after walking along in silence for nearly half an hour while holding hands with Jon, Sheree finally began to hear the sound of ocean waves pounding against the outer wall of the bunker tunnel opening they were approaching.

"That's the beach you hear," smiled Jon Roth as he suddenly pulled Sheree close and hugged her. "Do you mind if I kiss you? Is it allowed to take this one off?"

Sheree blushed deeply as Jon gently reached for and carefully took off her head brace.

"Are you sure about this?" questioned Sheree as he handed it to her. She could feel her heart pounding in her chest and swallowed hard.

Jon closed his eyes and bent down slightly to kiss Sheree tenderly on the lips. True, her headgear was temporarily out of the way, but the wire dental braces professionally affixed to her teeth precluded any possibility of trying to French kiss her just yet.

Sheree was so overcome by emotion from Jon's kiss that she suddenly pulled away and began to cry.

"Sheree, you'll be so beautiful someday when all these braces are gone," predicted Jon as he pulled her close again and put his free hand under her chin to get her to look up at him. "The other guys have no idea what they're missing out on."

Sheree flushed so deeply with embarrassment that she could feel a warmness on her face. Then, as she glanced away, the welcome relief of daylight unexpectedly flooded through an opening up ahead. "Look! We must be near where it opens onto the beach!"

"Yes, we are," grinned Jon. "Come on!"

Sheree watched with great interest as they approached another iron-barred bunker tunnel gate. Jon let go of Sheree's hand, removed a key from his front shirt pocket, and unlocked the padlock keeping it secure. "Where did you get that key?"

"From my dad's desk drawer," confessed Jon with a wink.

"Someone's out there!" Sheree suddenly noticed. "What if they see us here together?"

"It's just Joyce and Veronica," snorted Jon. "And their popular friend Steve, of course. They come down here together and go boogie boarding nearly every single day."

"All three of them?" Sheree found it hard to believe.

"And here come two of my greatest admirers now," sneered Birdboy sarcastically as he watched Joyce and Veronica running into the bunker tunnel opening, directly towards them.

It had been only three short hours since Steve's tragic death on the beach, yet it seemed like a lifetime ago. The search for Joyce and Veronica had been suspended until daybreak the following day.

Carolyn was just getting ready to go take a shower, but paused to glance out the second floor dormitory window at the Dean's apartment below. Though it was doubtful that Dean Dixon's nephew Ray had anything to do with Joyce and Veronica's disappearance, one could not be absolutely certain. It would behoove her and Susan to continue their ever vigilant watch of the comings and goings down at the Dean's apartment, just in case. Was Ray Dixon somehow involved? Or the Dean? And if so, why? Still, Ms. Dixon just didn't fit the profile of someone who might try and harm someone. Her nephew Ray, on the other hand, was said to be an ex-convict, and no one seemed to know for certain when or for what he might have been incarcerated. They would need to try and find out more about Ray Dixon, particularly his whereabouts between 4:30 and 5:00 o'clock p.m. on March 23, 1973.

Carolyn's ruined blue jeans were covered with blood and missing both legs. Had the Sheriff not asked her to save them as evidence, Carolyn would already have thrown them away. She was now wearing only her bathrobe.

Carolyn was roused from her thoughts when the door to their dormitory room opened and Susan came inside.

After finishing her make-up test earlier that day, Susan had gone down to the beach to join her friends, but instead had arrived just in time to watch the Sheriff car pull away with Carolyn inside.

Susan was horrified to learn what had happened, and quickly volunteered to remain on the beach with the search party until operations were suspended for the day.

"Carolyn? Are you all right?" Susan ran over and hugged her friend Carolyn. "I'm so sorry I wasn't there! Perhaps I could have done something to help?"

"I didn't get there in time, either," sniffed Carolyn as the tears again began to well up in her eyes.

"But, you were there! And you did everything you could!" reminded Susan sadly. "Mr. Vandevere told me how you and Bart tried to save Steve's life."

"They wouldn't even let me help look for Joyce or Veronica!" mentioned Carolyn angrily as she shook her head.

The Sheriff had insisted on driving Carolyn back up to the girls' dormitory so she could change from the bloody clothing she had worn while trying to save Steve Fredrickson's life, and so she could clean up, but most of all to protect her from being mobbed with questions from bystanders. He wanted Carolyn to have as little contact as possible with the other students until after her deposition the following morning. That was the soonest that an official court reporter could manage to be there.

"Did they find any other signs of them in the bunker tunnel?" Carolyn anxiously asked.

"No," confirmed Susan sadly. "It's like they literally vanished into thin air. There were some tracks leading right up to that locked gate – the one with the iron bars on it - but no one seemed to have a key."

"Are you kidding me?" fumed Carolyn. "Surely they must've had cutting tools or something they could have used on it?"

"One guy had a hacksaw, but didn't get very far," replied Susan.

"Well, it was definitely Joyce and Veronica's tracks leading into that cave," persisted Carolyn. "Bart, Jim and I all saw them down there with Steve. They both came running out of the water right when Steve was attacked by that shark!"

"You SAW it happen?" Susan was flabbergasted.

"Yes!" informed Carolyn. "I was up in an airplane with Bart Higbee and Jim Otterman at the time."

"Seriously?" Susan couldn't believe it.

"They even managed to get permission from the Dean ahead of time for you and me to go up with 'em," revealed Carolyn. "Except, you were unavailable because you were taking your test."

"Wow!" muttered Susan.

"Anyway, we were flying directly over the beach when the shark attacked Steve down below, and we all saw it!" described Carolyn. "Jim even took an entire series of aerial photos of the whole area with his camera, right while it was happening."

"Good heavens!" exclaimed Susan.

"Tomorrow after both of our depositions are over, Jim said I can go with him over to the darkroom and watch while he develops the pictures," mentioned Carolyn. "Perhaps we'll see something else in the photos that we just didn't notice today."

"That's probably not all he hopes will develop!" warned Susan.

"Jim won't try anything," believed Carolyn.

"Don't be so sure," cautioned Susan. "That kid has it bad for you. You're all he talks about!"

"Oh, my God!" added Susan when she noticed the bloody pile of clothing on the floor in one corner of their room. "I'm getting rid of those things this very minute!"

"You can't," informed Carolyn. "The Sheriff asked me to save them for him. He's coming by for them tomorrow when they get here with the court reporter. At least my deposition is scheduled first. I'm just anxious to get it over with."

"Then the very least I can do is get a plastic bag from Ms. Dixon to put 'em in for now! Maybe she can keep them in her refrigerator overnight." suggested Susan.

"That's a good idea, thanks!" nodded Carolyn. "I'm gonna go take a shower now."

"Are you sure you're all right?" pressed Susan.

"I will be," promised Carolyn with a weak smile.

"Better hurry then," suggested Susan. "See what time it is? It's 8:30 already and the lights go off at 9:00."

"That's okay," mumbled Carolyn. "At least they do leave the lights on in the restroom and shower areas at night."

"It'll be dark when you get back in here, though," cautioned Susan. "But, I still have that extra flashlight."

"Thanks, I'll need it," Carolyn forced a smile. "Besides, I really don't think anyone will try and stop me from washing off all this blood, no matter what time it is. Trust me!"

Saturday morning dawned brightly on March 24, 1973. Even the usual morning fog had failed to make an appearance. Yet, Lenny Owens had been at the track since dawn, running to be alone so he could think. Lenny had finally mustered up the courage to break it off with Linda Shaver at dinner the previous evening. Strange, since he and Linda had never really been going together in the first place, at least as far as Lenny was concerned. But, that was all water under the bridge now. It was finally time to man up about things, and Lenny was going to start by finding Carolyn and talking to her about their relationship that very day! Lenny hoped with all his heart that Carolyn still felt the same way about him as he still felt about her. Of course it wouldn't be easy, but Lenny would find a way to make his parents understand, especially his dad.

"There you are!" called Pete, who had just arrived. "I didn't see you at breakfast."

"I'm not hungry," answered Lenny as he ran by.

"Hey, hold up!" hollered Pete.

When Lenny refused to comply, Pete waited for Lenny to make another circuit and then joined him on the track.

"You'll ruin your good shoes," cautioned Lenny.

"I'm trying to have a serious conversation with you!" informed Pete as he struggled to keep up.

Lenny merely kept on running without reply.

"Will you please stop for a minute?" implored Pete. "Did you know that Steve Fredrickson died on the beach yesterday afternoon? He died from his injuries after being attacked by a shark."

Still, there was no response from Lenny.

"What in the blazes is wrong with you?" shouted Pete as he grabbed Lenny's arm to try and get him to stop. "Did you hear what I said? Steve Fredrickson died in Carolyn's arms, by the way."

Lenny frowned and suddenly came to a stop.

Pete stopped too, and bent over to put his hands on his knees as he gasped for air. "I thought that would get your attention."

"You could have come up with something better than that!" scoffed Lenny as he resumed his running.

"Seriously?" hollered Pete from where he was.

Once Lenny had circled the entire track again, Pete seized the opportunity to run beside him so they could continue their conversation.

"Since you managed to ditch out of worship service this morning, you missed the big announcement," added Pete.

Lenny finally stopped moving forward but continued running in place as he waited for Pete to catch back up to where he was.

"What big announcement?" asked Lenny.

"That there's going to be a general assembly at four o'clock in the gymnasium this afternoon," revealed Pete.

"What for?" quizzed Lenny.

"I told you already!" Pete was frustrated. "About Steve Fredrickson! Bart Higbee filled me in on some of the details at breakfast this morning, but I'm sure they'll tell everyone else more about it at the assembly," described Pete.

"You're serious, aren't you?" realized Lenny.

"You think I'd put myself through all of this just for kicks?" snapped Pete.

Lenny finally quit running in place and began walking. Even then, it was difficult for Pete to keep up with his long-legged cousin.

"That's really horrible about Steve. He sure was a nice guy," mentioned Lenny.

"Bart told me that he and Carolyn were giving CPR to Steve when he died, but Steve had lost so much blood already that they just couldn't save him," revealed Pete. "Steve literally died in Carolyn's arms yesterday. Apparently, she took it pretty hard."

Lenny came to a complete stop, faced his cousin, and grabbed his upper arms. "Why in the world was Carolyn on the beach with Bart Higbee in the first place? Wasn't it boys' beach yesterday?"

Pete took a deep breath before continuing. "Bart said he was flying Carolyn and Jim Otterman over the beach when they just happened to look down and notice Steve being attacked by the shark. Bart said he landed the plane right away after that so they could all hurry down to the beach to try and help."

Pete now had Lenny's undivided attention. "Why was Carolyn flying with Jim Otterman? It figures that Bart would be the one to help her with the CPR! Jim Otterman probably doesn't even know how!"

"Jim is Bart's roommate," reminded Pete. "Bart said Jim just needed a pilot to take him up for some aerial yearbook photos of the campus. But why Carolyn was with them, I have no idea."

"That little weasel!" scowled Lenny.

"Well, then do something about it!" snapped Pete. "Don't just let that little weasel move in on her. You know he'll never quit trying, not as long as he thinks he has a chance."

"I just don't get it," muttered Lenny. "Carolyn told me herself that she can't stand Jim Otterman."

"Then why don't you be man enough to go and ask her what's really going on?" challenged Pete. "I'm sick and tired of watching you stand by and fret about it when you're not even willing to go and talk to her. And, Carolyn's just as bad as you are! No wonder your personality profiles matched up for that blind date last fall. You two are just alike."

"I think you're right," recognized Lenny.

"Good!" responded Pete. "You know, if ever there were a time to go offer Carolyn some moral support, this would definitely be it!"

"Did you see Carolyn at breakfast this morning?" asked Lenny.

"No," replied Pete. "Bart said she's down in the Administration Building right now with the Sheriff and some Court Reporter, having her deposition taken."

"You don't say." Lenny raised an eyebrow and finally let go of Pete's arms.

"Jim and Bart were being deposed, too," added Pete.

"How's Veronica taking all this?" Lenny suddenly asked. "Especially the news about Steve?"

Pete became very serious and hesitated.

"Well?" pressed Lenny.

"Joyce and Veronica were boogie boarding with Steve when he was attacked by the shark," revealed Pete. "But, by the time Carolyn and Bart got down there to help, Joyce and Veronica were long gone."

"Gone?" questioned Lenny.

"Vanished," clarified Pete. "Jim was the one who went for help. After that, there was a search party out there until dark last night looking for them, and they're back out there again right now. I was actually coming to see if you wanted to go down there with me and join them. I think they could use all the help they can get."

"Let's go!" agreed Lenny without hesitation.

"Aren't you going to at least change out of your track shoes and PE clothes first?" asked Pete.

"Heck no," replied Lenny. "These will be just the thing for climbing around on the rocks down there. You should probably go get your track shoes on, too!"

"That's okay. At least there are no classes today," sighed Pete. "Maybe after the general assembly at 4:00 they can get more people to come join in the search."

"What could have happened to them?" mused Lenny. "Joyce and Veronica are both excellent swimmers."

"Bart said there were tracks in the sand that led into a bunker tunnel opening," described Pete. "They went right up to and beyond an iron-barred gate with a big padlock on it."

"And they couldn't get it open?" Lenny furled his brow.

"They probably have by now," responded Pete. "Hey, look over there!"

Lenny turned his head just in time to see Carolyn with Jim Otterman as they disappeared around the far end of the Administration Building together.

"It's right on the way to the beach," mentioned Pete as he nodded his head in the direction Jim and Carolyn were headed.

"Indeed it is," agreed Lenny. He needed no further persuasion to follow after them.

"Hey, wait for me!" called Pete as he hurried to keep pace with his six-feet-five-inch cousin.

"That rotten little red-headed weasel!" mumbled Lenny.

Neither Jim nor Carolyn had seen Pete or Lenny behind them as they hurried toward the Art Building where the photography studio was located. Jim had promised the Sheriff copies of any and all pictures taken the previous day during their flight over the beach. Jim had even taken close-up photos of Steve Fredrickson's lifeless body and of the tracks in the sand leading into the bunker tunnel opening.

"The little weasel's even got a key!" pointed out Pete as they watched Jim Otterman nimbly unlock the front door to the Art Building.

"They probably give one to all the kids taking photography," assumed Lenny. "What we need to do is get up there and stop that door from closing before it locks behind them. I don't trust Jim alone with her, not for a single minute."

"Carolyn must know what he's like by now," opined Pete.

"I doubt it," rebutted Lenny. "Come on!"

Waiting until Jim and Carolyn had just disappeared around a corner, Lenny rushed up barely in time to stick his foot in the front door to the Art Building before it could close and lock.

"Nice," grinned Pete.

"After you," motioned Lenny as he grabbed and pulled the door back open. "I'm not going in there alone."

"If you thought we got in trouble for going down to the beach that time with Carolyn and Susan," reminded Pete, "that will seem like nothing if we get caught doing this!"

"I doubt Jim Otterman would want to get himself into trouble along with us," surmised Lenny. "After all, there's no way he should be in here with Carolyn by himself anyway. We're just here to keep him honest."

"What if they do have permission to be here?" persisted Pete.

"Not alone, they wouldn't," rebutted Lenny.

"Maybe Jim took some pictures of what happened yesterday," speculated Pete. "He is carrying one of those big fancy cameras."

"The only reason he'd be bringing it here would be to develop some pictures," guessed Lenny.

"That's probably not all he hopes will develop, once he gets Carolyn alone in that darkroom!" smirked Pete.

"Not if we get there first," fumed Lenny.

"This place is sure bigger than it looks from the outside," noticed Pete. "It's almost like a rat maze."

"There they are!" spotted Lenny. "That way."

As Pete and Lenny rounded the next hall corner, they found themselves in yet another long hallway. Jim and Carolyn were nowhere in sight. There were various doors along the hallway, all closed.

"Which one?" questioned Pete. "They could have gone into any one of those rooms."

"Then we check 'em all," responded Lenny.

On the small pony wall at the end of the hall was a doorframe. Actually a big picture frame, the doorframe was mounted right onto the pony wall over a full-sized mirror. It was intended to give the illusion of a doorway leading into another hall, but instead reflected the hallway behind them. Above it was a plaque that read, "Hall of Memories."

Lenny stood in front of the mirror studying himself for a moment as he stood there beside his cousin. Were they really doing the right thing? How would Carolyn react to them following her like this? The last thing Lenny wanted to do was blow it with her now!

The long hallway behind them seemed to stretch on into infinity. Stunning photographs taken by various art students were hanging on its walls. The name of each photographer was engraved on a small name tag beside the framed masterpiece.

"These are really quite good," appreciated Pete. The photo he was looking at was of a small cluster of cypress trees along the bluff tops overlooking the ocean beyond.

Lenny frowned as he noticed a series of photos by Jim Otterman.

"Oh, look!" pointed out Pete. "There's Carolyn at the daisy patch. And here she is picking squash. And here's one of her tufting at the mill. He's even got one of her serving food in the boys' food line at the cafeteria back when the school year first began. Looks like Jim's been following Carolyn around for months."

"That little weasel," mumbled Lenny.

"Kind of reminds you of one of those murder mystery movies where they have some psychopath that fixates on his victim and puts a whole series of pictures of them up on a wall somewhere," teased Pete.

"What if Jim Otterman really is some kind of a psychopath?" scowled Lenny.

"Psychopaths don't usually display their work in a public forum like this," chuckled Pete. "Usually their pictures are off in a creepy closet somewhere, or someplace where no one else can see them."

"We're too late," realized Lenny as he saw a RED light come on above one of the doors.

"Are these all darkrooms?" wondered Pete as he opened one of the doors and looked inside. "This one is definitely a darkroom."

"This one, too," informed Lenny after looking inside another of the rooms. "They're all darkrooms."

"And now Jim Otterman has Carolyn right where he wants her, right inside in his own private darkroom," teased Pete.

Lenny's nostrils flared with anger as he started for the door that was obviously to Jim Otterman's darkroom.

"Wait!" cautioned Pete. "What if Jim's developing film from the photos he took yesterday? They might be very important. What if he took pictures of the body? Or of the tracks leading into the tunnel?"

Lenny unexpectedly slammed the palm of his right hand against the wall with frustration. "Just how long does it usually take to develop a picture in one of those darkrooms, anyway?"

"I have no idea." Pete shrugged his shoulders. "I guess it might depend on how many pictures there are. Jim does take a lot of them."

"Come on," urged Lenny after taking a deep breath and rapidly letting it out. "Let's go help out with the search. Carolyn has a right to make up her own mind. Jim didn't exactly force her to come down here with him. We both saw her come in here of her own free will."

"Are you trying to convince me, or just yourself of that?" Pete gave Lenny a wry look.

"This was a terrible idea," admitted Lenny without answering Pete's question. "Let's get out of here before we really do get into trouble again. That's the last thing we need."

Just after Pete and Lenny had exited the Art Department building and were again headed toward the beach, Dean Vandevere's jeep slowed down and pulled up beside them.

"I've been looking for you two," he announced.

Pete and Lenny exchanged a worried glance but came over to Dean Vandevere's jeep to see what he wanted.

"Get in," directed the Dean. He was not smiling.

Were they in trouble? worried Lenny. Had someone seen them prowling around in the Art Department? What would he tell his father when they called him?

"I got a phone call last night," informed Dean Vandevere as they slowly drove toward the boys' dormitory. "It was from your dad."

Lenny and Pete exchanged a look of bewilderment. Was something wrong at home?

"I'm sorry, Lenny, but it's your mother," revealed the Dean. It was almost as if he could read their thoughts.

"What's wrong with her?" questioned Lenny with alarm.

"She's had a heart attack," replied the Dean. "She's in the hospital's special cardiac unit up in Ocean Bay right now. They don't know how much longer she has, but your father asked that both of you return home immediately."

"But ....," Lenny stopped in mid-sentence.

"Your father was quite worried about how he could afford enough for both of you to make the trip, but I finally convinced him to let me lend you the money," mentioned the Dean. "He's a proud man. Said he wasn't about to start taking charity from anyone."

"Never has, never will," mumbled Lenny and Pete in unison, as if reciting a frequently heard saying from their childhood.

"Old man Killingham will be stopping by the school with an ice cream delivery later today, and agreed to take you both to the bus station over in Ocean Bluff," described the Dean. "This should be enough for your tickets." Dean Vandevere unexpectedly pulled an envelope from his pocket with one hand and offered it to Lenny.

"What about the return trip?" pressed Lenny as he hesitantly accepted the envelope. "How are we supposed to get back again?"

"You should have enough in there for two round trip tickets," reassured the Dean.

"Okay, thanks!" Lenny nodded with obvious relief.

360

"I also mentioned to your father that there is a special grant fund available to help existing worthy students like you, when unexpected hardship circumstances such as this arise," elaborated Dean Vandevere. "I certainly think this qualifies."

"What kind of a grant?" asked Lenny. Unless he could finish up his junior year at Oceanview Academy, there would be no chance of him getting into medical school, as the particular chemistry class he needed was not offered at Ocean Bay High.

"The benefactor has chosen to remain anonymous, but I'm well aware that you plan to go to medical school someday," acknowledged the Dean. Again, it was as if the Dean could read his thoughts. "At the very least, this grant should make it possible for both you and Pete to come back here and finish out your junior year. After that, who knows."

"Do we have to do something else to apply for it?" quizzed Pete. "And does it really apply to both of us?"

"It should, and there's nothing else you need to do," assured the Dean as they pulled up in front of the boys' dormitory and came to a stop. "Of course it will require approval from the school board, but I don't see a problem. You guys have kept your noses clean since that incident on the beach last fall. You're both excellent students, and in good standing. I think you can count on it. Trust me!"

Meanwhile, over in Jim Otterman's personal darkroom, Carolyn watched with great interest while Jim got everything ready.

"Why do you need so many different solutions?" questioned Carolyn. "How long will this take?"

"Just watch," instructed Jim. "The chemicals here are actually arranged in a consecutive order. First is the developer. It changes the chemical structure of the emulsion on the paper to create the dark areas on a photo. The second tray is a bath solution that is used to stop the developing process and prevent the image from getting any darker than you want it. The third tray is called a fixer."

"A fixer?" repeated Carolyn.

"Yes," confirmed Jim. "It fixes the image onto the paper and makes it light safe after thirty seconds."

"So, if a person were to open the door to the darkroom after all the pictures have made it up to that point, then would they all be safe?" quizzed Carolyn.

"Supposedly," replied Jim. "But, you wouldn't want to cut it too close. It's always better to be safe than sorry. Anyway, the fourth tray is a water wash where the picture is rinsed off to remove any excess chemicals."

"I never realized there was so much to it," admitted Carolyn.

"Okay, let's get started." Jim smiled at Carolyn, careful not to appear too flirtatious just yet. "Now that the darkroom door is shut, and the red light is on – which indicates to anyone outside that we are in the process of developing film and that the door must not be opened – we can safely remove the film from the camera."

Carolyn moved closer to see whether or not she could see any images on the film as Jim removed it from his Hasselblad camera.

"You won't see anything on the film just yet," informed Jim. "The negative goes shiny side up, which is the top of the curl, and upside down in the negative carrier."

Carolyn did not understand at all but nodded anyway.

"We then open the enlarger head by turning the knob on the left," demonstrated Jim. "The negative carrier then goes downward at a twenty-degree angle and should fit snugly into the grooves for it."

Carolyn's mind began to wander as Jim proceeded to elaborate in great detail all the steps involved in composing and focusing the negative, preparing a test strip, and finally developing the pictures. It was then that Carolyn suddenly noticed Jim's tribute wall to her. Literally hundreds of photos of Carolyn were mounted on the walls of Jim's darkroom!

"Why do you have all those pictures of ME in here?" questioned Carolyn with trepidation. A feeling of claustrophobia and panic began to overtake her. It suddenly became difficult for her to breathe.

"Because you are my favorite subject," flirted Jim.

"Finish what you're doing with those photos!" directed Carolyn.

"Of course," smiled Jim. He had no intention of hurrying, either.

"How many pictures are there on that roll?" demanded Carolyn.

"I have no idea," smirked Jim. He knew, of course, but wasn't going to tell Carolyn that.

"Why are you doing this to me?" snapped Carolyn.

"Just what is it you think I'm doing to you?" laughed Jim. "Can't you see that I'm busy developing a roll of film at the moment?"

"Well, hurry up, then!" commanded Carolyn. "I plan to go help them search for Joyce and Veronica, and the sooner the better!"

"They've got plenty of other people down there already," assured Jim. "And I know it's terrible what happened to Steve, but you did everything you could. What we need to do now is focus on developing these pictures so we can see if there was anything else going on down there."

"Okay," agreed Carolyn cautiously. It was definitely Carolyn's intention to make a run for it at the first available opportunity. In fact, she was keeping a careful watch for that magic moment when all the photos would reach the final wash tray so she could leave.

How could she have allowed herself to be lured into this situation in the first place? Was she over-reacting? Had Jim been stalking her from the very beginning? Carolyn then noticed a photo taken of her with her parents on her very first day at Oceanview Academy! Things were worse than she had imagined.

"Please remind me again how long each step takes," asked Carolyn. "What was it, ah, one minute for the developer?"

"Very good," beamed Jim.

"And thirty seconds in that next tray?" questioned Carolyn.

"No less than that," verified Jim.

"And another minute for the fixer?" grilled Carolyn.

"Very good," nodded Jim. "You were paying attention."

"Then three minutes or longer for the final wash," recalled Carolyn, "but no less than that or else they might turn yellow?"

"You're a quick student," praised Jim. "Then, when you hang them all up to dry using special tongs, you need to be careful not to touch any of them together. Otherwise, you might never be able to get them apart again." Jim then seemed to undress Carolyn with his eyes.

Jim's innuendo was not lost on Carolyn, and she fervently hoped he would not try touching her inappropriately!

If only she had listened to Susan and gone back to the cafeteria that night during the Harvest Festival Prom. Somehow, if she ever got out of this, Carolyn planned to go find Lenny and talk to him about their relationship. It was time she finally told Lenny how she felt, and she was not going to let anything or anyone stand in her way this time. The only thing to fear was fear itself. At least that's what Susan always said. And right now, she was going to need all the courage she had.

"They're all done," whispered Jim as he slipped his arms around her. "Do you know how beautiful you are?"

"Remember what I told you on the bluffs yesterday afternoon?" asked Carolyn.

"That was a long time ago," replied Jim as he began kissing her on the back of the neck.

"Stop it!" commanded Carolyn as she slapped Jim across the face and stepped away from him. "I told you that if I even so much as thought your intentions were romantic in any way, that our friendship would be over! Does that ring a bell?"

"Oh, come on, you didn't really mean it," flirted Jim as he reached for her.

"Get your hands off of me!" screamed Carolyn as she jabbed her knee into Jim's groin area. "And since these are ready, I'll just take them to the Sheriff myself!"

Carolyn then snatched the entire photo drying rack by its base and started for the door. It was the short round carousel type on a tripod.

"Wait!" called Jim. He was doubled over in pain. "You should give them at least three more minutes!"

"Give me one good reason why I should even believe you?" demanded Carolyn as she began ripping pictures of herself off Jim's tribute wall with her free hand. "Just how much longer do you want me here, anyway? In three minutes, I should be able to clear off every single one of these walls!"

"You can go!" acquiesced Jim. He was just now able to stand again. "The photos should be fine."

"You'd better hope so!" snapped Carolyn. "And you'd better hope you haven't ruined any chances I might have with Lenny, either! 'Cause if you did, I'm coming back and ripping down the rest of your little picture collection! Do you hear me?"

"Well, I can always print more!" retorted Jim as he watched Carolyn turn to leave.

Carolyn paused at the doorway and then turned to glare at Jim. "Perhaps the School Board might be interested in coming to see the walls in your darkroom here? Either you leave me alone from now on, or I will let them know about it. Trust me!"

364

11. Missing Link

"**B**efore we eat, let's have a word of prayer," insisted Jon Roth. "Ray, would you like to offer it?"

"I'd be happy to," agreed Ray. Waiting a moment for everyone to bow their heads, Ray then prayed. "Dear Lord, for what we are about to partake, make us truly grateful. Amen."

"Short and sweet, I like it!" approved Jon Roth as he grabbed a pair of tongs and finished plating the perfectly done lamb burgers for his guests. "There's nothing like a good lamb burger."

"Thanks for having us over," mentioned Carolyn, to be polite.

"Yes, thank you," added Susan uncomfortably.

"Dad, did you know that Carolyn and Mom were roommates when they went to school here together?" Ann suddenly asked. "Small world, isn't it?"

"Indeed," replied Jon Roth. The smile had disappeared from his face and his eyes narrowed as he studied Carolyn more closely.

"That was only for a short time, though," interjected Sheree.

"Awkward," Susan whispered to Ray.

"Not as awkward as this," replied Ray in hushed tones as he gently pulled Susan a few feet away so he could covertly show her the photo on his satellite phone of Jon Roth's gun cabinet.

Susan's mouth involuntarily dropped open with disbelief as she studied the huge assortment of rifles, handguns, revolvers, and even a machine gun and a rocket launcher!

"Where is this? Did Carolyn send it?" asked Susan.

Ray nodded affirmatively. "This is the Roth Family bomb shelter, and yes it's from Carolyn."

"What if Birdboy is armed?" realized Susan with alarm.

"There's always that possibility," surmised Ray as he advanced to the next message on his phone so Susan could see it, too. It was a close-up of the glass covered shelves in Jon Roth's gun cabinet on which vast quantities of new looking ammunition boxes could easily be seen. The message merely read, "Be careful! Jon could be armed!"

Susan exchanged a look of concern with Ray. "Seriously, what if he is armed and dangerous?"

"Then it's a darn good thing I am, too," reminded Ray as he swiftly unclipped the gun holster from his snakeskin boot and reattached it to the side of his waist belt, using Susan to block Jon's view.

"Perhaps you two have something you'd like to share with the rest of us?" questioned Jon Roth as he placed the platter of grilled lamb burgers on the elegantly set picnic table.

"Oh, it's nothing," assured Ray with a forced smile. "Susan was wanting me to do some work on her car sometime tomorrow, and we were just looking up the price of auto parts."

"They're absolutely through the roof," informed Susan.

"Well, I'm sure you won't find a better mechanic," mentioned Jon Roth as he motioned for them to join the others who were now seated at the elaborately set picnic table.

"It isn't every day that we get to use our best dinnerware," mentioned Ann as she squeezed some catsup onto her lamb burger. "Dad wanted everything to be just perfect today."

"Today's a very special day," replied Jon as he piled some potato salad onto his plate and then passed the serving bowl to Ray, who was seated beside him.

Naturally, Jon Roth was seated at the head of the table, and his wife Sheree at the opposite end. Ray, Susan and Carolyn were seated on his right, while Ann and Ted were seated on his left. Ted had his injured leg propped up on the bench beside him.

"Did my daughter happen to mention that we grow our own meat?" Jon Roth asked of no one in particular.

"Ah, actually, she did," replied Carolyn. "That must be a lot of work for her to take care of an entire feral cat colony and then all of your chickens and lambs on top of that."

"It's good for her," answered Jon with an even smile as he reached for and grabbed a handful of potato chips. "Keeps her out of trouble. Lord only knows how much she could get into around here."

"Dad's just afraid I'll spend too much time with Ted," explained Ann to the others while she spooned a huge blob of mustard on top of her catsup.

"Well, you are my daughter," reminded Jon Roth, "and your mother and I only want what's best for you."

"Ted plans to be a world-class surfer someday," revealed Ann.

"Is there something wrong with Ted, that he can't speak for himself?" jabbed Jon Roth.

"I can speak for myself," advised Ted.

366

"Please do," offered Jon Roth as he finished putting the last of his chosen condiments onto his oversized lamb burger. "I'm all ears."

"Well, what I actually would like is to be a farmer," elaborated Ted. "One who just happens to be a world-class surfer, as well."

Everyone but Jon Roth chuckled at Ted's remark.

"I didn't know you could surf on a boogie board," replied Jon.

"Technically, you can't, but you also can," answered Ted. "It just takes lots of practice, but as you can see, I'm out of commission for a while until my ankle heals up."

"Good for the soul," smirked Jon Roth.

"Didn't your Aunt Veronica used to practice a lot, too?" Ann innocently asked.

"Yes, she did," replied Ted. "Right on that very beach. My grandparents told me once that boogie boarding was one of the greatest loves in her life, besides Steve Fredrickson, of course."

Jon Roth's glass suddenly began to slip from his hand and some of the water inside sloshed out onto his plate. Amazingly, he was able to catch it in mid-air and prevent it from continuing its descent.

"Your aunt?" questioned Jon Roth as he glared at Ted. How had he never made the connection before? Of course! Ted Jensen had those same sultry brown eyes, even though he was fairer-complexioned.

"Veronica Jensen was my dad's older sister," informed Ted with an almost imperceptible smile of triumph. Ted had waited a long time to reveal his true identity to Jon Roth and to see how he would react.

Susan and Carolyn silently exchanged apprehensive looks with Ray and Sheree. Even Ann was beginning to be concerned at this point. Why was Ted deliberately trying to provoke Jon Roth? Didn't Ted know how dangerous her father could be?

"My dad wasn't born until his parents were in their forties," explained Ted. "I never actually knew my Aunt Veronica. But, I did grow up hearing about how she disappeared while boogie boarding one afternoon. That was one of the reasons I came to school here, so I could try and find out what happened to her."

"You don't say?" replied Birdboy with a malevolent gaze.

"One thing that Ted and I have in common is that our parents were all in their forties before they had us," explained Ann, to try and steer the conversation in a different direction.

"How quaint," acknowledged Birdboy with flared nostrils.

Sheree seemed to sense the sudden shift in her husband's personality and was gravely worried about it. If Birdboy were allowed to take control, then Jon Roth could very well disappear forever. Still, Jon Roth was also a cruel tyrant in his own right, and Sheree had already made up her mind to leave him anyway. In fact, the emergence of Birdboy would not change her mind one way or the other, but could possibly put all of them in serious danger, and that was the last thing she wanted right now.

"How are the lamb burgers?" Birdboy suddenly asked with a mischievous smile.

"Why? Is there something wrong with them?" frowned Susan.

"Heavens no!" grinned Birdboy. "Lenny and Pete were raised with the greatest of care."

"Lenny and Pete?" repeated Carolyn. She had not yet taken a bite of her lamb burger and wasn't about to now!

"Last year we slaughtered Pete," explained Jon Roth, who was struggling to regain control of himself. "This year it was Lenny."

"These are supposed to be Lenny burgers," chuckled Ann as she took another bite. She obviously had no idea that the names her father had chosen for his lambs had any significance.

"Lenny burgers?" scowled Susan as she slowly spat out the contents of her mouth into one of the cloth napkins before taking a big drink of water.

"You think you're pretty funny, don't you?" Carolyn suddenly challenged. "Naming your lambs after our some of our friends?"

"Next year it will be Joyce and Veronica," chuckled Jon Roth. "I hear female lambs are even more tender than their male counterparts."

"That's it!" snapped Carolyn. "We're leaving! Thank you Sheree and Ann for your hospitality. And, of course, I'm sure that BIRDBOY is well aware that today is the anniversary of Joyce and Veronica's disappearance from that beach down there!"

"You named the lambs after their friends?" Ann was shocked to think that her father could do such a thing. True, he did have a warped sense of humor, but this really was over the top.

"Thanks for the lunch," nodded Ray as he stood up to escort Carolyn and Susan back to the lighthouse.

"We're coming, too," announced Sheree. "That is, if you'll have us. I understand you have plenty of extra rooms over there?"

"You're not going anywhere!" informed Birdboy as he deliberately stood to be more intimidating. The cruel expression on his face was noticed by everyone.

"We don't want any trouble," advised Ray Dixon as he pulled up his shirt and tucked it behind his gun holster, revealing his 45 revolver to Jon. "Sheree, Ann and Ted are welcome to come with us."

"Can you wait just a couple of minutes while I go grab a few things?" implored Sheree. "Ann, please come with me. We'll be right back, I promise!"

"You'll never get away with this!" threatened Birdboy as he watched Sheree and Ann disappear into the house.

"We all know about your bomb shelter," advised Carolyn, to keep Birdboy off balance.

"So, they told you about that, too, did they?" fumed Birdboy.

"Aren't these the same chaise lounge cushions you guys used to make at the lumber mill?" mentioned Susan. She could see what Carolyn was trying to do and hoped to help if she could.

"In fact, they ARE some of the chaise lounge cushions we made when we used to work at the lumber mill," replied Birdboy. "I've always loved the cheerful yellow and white daisies over an olive green background."

"We're ready," announced Sheree as she and Ann emerged from the house. Each of them was carrying a large suitcase.

"That was really fast," commented Birdboy suspiciously. "It's almost like you had them packed already and were just waiting for the right moment to leave."

"Irregardless," replied Sheree calmly, "we're leaving. Goodbye Jon Roth, or Birdboy, or whoever you think you are. It is my sincere hope that our departure might inspire you to resume your prescribed medication. Perhaps you may recall the Clozapine you agreed to continue taking when they finally cleared you for release from the Ocean Bluff Mental Institution?"

Turning to the others, Sheree then added, "Did any of you know that Clozapine was first developed in 1961? The first clinical trials took place in 1972, and their remarkable success with Jon Roth in 1973 was one of the reasons the medication was finally approved as a recommended treatment for treatable patients with schizophrenia."

"How dare you!" spat Birdboy as he started toward Sheree.

"Don't make me use this, Jon," advised Ray as he drew his revolver, cocked the hammer, and carefully leveled it at Birdboy.

"I'm sure the school will be very interested in knowing how you quit taking your medication five years ago, and completely discontinued your therapy sessions over at the Institution," threatened Sheree.

"I don't know who you think you are, but you're certainly not the woman I married," fumed Birdboy.

"Why, thank you," smiled Sheree so calmly that it enraged him even more. "You're right. The frightened, insecure little girl wearing all those corrective braces and who was afraid of her own shadow just doesn't exist anymore."

"You were nothing but a useless catatonic for months after that day on the beach!" shouted Birdboy. "You were a patient at the institution, too, you know! And it was only my love and support that got you through all those dark times and gave you the strength to go on and the will to get better. Without me, you'd probably still be there!"

"Ann already knows that both of you were patients there," interjected Carolyn. "But at least Sheree has chosen to better herself, and to try and stay well!"

"This is none of your business!" bellowed Birdboy.

"Don't even think about it," threatened Ray Dixon.

"Well, I'm your daughter," reminded Ann, "and it certainly is my business! Yes, I've known for years that you were a schizophrenic and a possible danger to us. But it was because mother loves you so much that she convinced me to endure your constant mood swings and outbursts of abnormal behavior! I did not even find out until earlier today that she had been a patient there, too, but frankly it doesn't matter. Like Carolyn said, at least Mother has chosen to better herself, and done everything in her power to try and stay well!"

"Is this true?" Jon Roth had tears oozing from his eyes as he pathetically looked at Sheree.

"Truer than I'd care to admit," answered Sheree rather coldly. Part of Sheree sincerely wished she were still able to feel sympathy for her husband, but it just wasn't there anymore.

"You haven't heard the last from me!" hollered Birdboy as he took in the sight of his family standing by Susan Rives and Carolyn Bennett with their suitcases. "You will regret this! Trust me!"

"I'm counting on it," snickered Sheree as she picked up her suitcase and walked away without looking back.

Waiting until the others were well on their way, Ray finally released the hammer on his revolver but continued to hold it as he followed after them. Jon Roth then watched them leave in silence.

When they finally reached the lighthouse entrance, Ray glanced behind them to make sure they were not being followed before returning the 45 revolver to its holster.

"Susan?" Ray approached and hugged her tightly.

"What are we going to do?" asked Susan.

"Can you please take Sheree, Ann and Ted inside and get them settled?" asked Ray. "I need you to stay there with them and keep everyone safe."

"What if Birdboy comes over here?" questioned Susan.

"Just keep the door locked," advised Ray. "And, we've all got our phones."

"What about me?" queried Carolyn.

"I need your quick reflexes," revealed Ray. "You're with me."

"I'm not even armed," reminded Carolyn.

"I know just where we can remedy that," smirked Ray.

"You can't go back over there without me," warned Sheree. "The ammunition next to Jon's gun cabinet is booby trapped, if that's what you have in mind. And, there might be other things that only I would know. You need me."

"He's probably got it rigged with C-4," guessed Ray.

"Would you know how to safely disarm it if he did?" grilled Susan. Now that Ray finally had come into her life, she did not want to lose him like this!

"We'll be fine," assured Ray. "Sheree's with us."

"You're not going back?" Ann grabbed her mother by the arm.

"This is something I must do," replied Sheree. "I need you to stay here with Susan and Ted. Can you do that for me, please?"

Ann finally nodded but clearly was unhappy about it.

Carolyn pulled Ginny's journal from her purse and handed it to Ann. "Perhaps you'd like something to read while you wait for us?"

"You are coming back, aren't you?" asked Ann with alarm.

"We certainly hope so," responded Carolyn. "But, just in case, you must keep it safe. This little book may very well become the missing link in a long chain of evidence, and could possibly help us find out what happened to Joyce and Veronica that day."

"Carolyn's right," confirmed Sheree. "Jon Roth must never get his hands on that journal! If something happens to me, that little book will be your last best hope of getting him put away for good."

"Then I'll guard it with my life," promised Ann as she took and clutched the little book to her chest.

"Don't worry, Jon Roth is definitely NOT getting into this lighthouse!" promised Susan. "Trust me!"

"What if Birdboy gets to the bunker before us?" posed Carolyn.

"Then I'd suggest we hurry," recommended Ray.

Ray, Carolyn and Sheree walked in silence past the old servants' quarters and over to the blackberry thicket. Ray then put his finger to his lips to indicate silence.

"If Jon's in there, he'll see us coming," whispered Sheree.

"Where's the camera?" questioned Ray.

"Up there!" pointed out Sheree.

Ray quickly located an appropriate sized tree limb from the ground and used it to redirect the lens of Jon Roth's surveillance camera toward the ceiling. Ray then commanded, "Hurry, open the gate!"

Sheree dashed over to the six-digit combination lock on the iron-barred gate and rapidly keyed in the code. "March 23, 1973 is the date to remember, and 03/23/73 is the code for this lock," advised Sheree.

"Unbelievable!" muttered Carolyn as she and Ray followed Sheree into the bunker tunnel entrance.

Sheree then hurried over to the small round finger hole at the far right side of the blast door and stuck her index finger inside. Within moments, the thick door began rising upward.

"Truly unbelievable!" chuckled Ray as he thought of the three days he had spent with Susan and Carolyn trying to break through it.

"Jon got such a kick out of watching you guys try to open this door with that crowbar and sledge hammer the other day, that he actually brought me in here to watch," Sheree revealed to Ray.

372

"At least we know Jon's not in here now," mentioned Carolyn.

"Are there any other monitoring stations like this?" quizzed Ray.

"Not that I know of," replied Sheree.

"Keep a lookout," Ray instructed Carolyn as he stealthily approached the gun cabinet. "And there's the ammunition, of course. Is there a high-beam flashlight around here that I can use?"

"Absolutely," answered Sheree as she grabbed one and handed it to Ray Dixon. "We all should have one," she added as she grabbed two more of the high-beam flashlights and handed one to Carolyn. "It's extremely dark in those tunnels, and that's the only other place Jon would be right now."

"Why is that?" inquired Ray as he methodically located and disconnected the power source for the C-4 wired to Jon Roth's stockpile of ammunition.

"Because Birdboy goes down there every year on March 23rd to visit their graves," revealed Sheree.

"Joyce and Veronica really are buried in those tunnels, then?" grilled Carolyn.

"Yes, they are," Sheree sadly confirmed.

"Do you think you are strong enough by now to share with us what really happened that day?" encouraged Carolyn. The last thing they needed was to have Sheree break down and become catatonic again, as she would become useless to them after that.

"Don't worry," assured Sheree. "Unlike Jon, I DO take my medication, and have learned to recognize when I'm beginning to feel strange. The closest thing I can think of to describe it would be how a patient with post-traumatic stress disorder would react. If you think I'm acting odd, just stay with me until it plays itself out. Try to interact and talk with me if you can."

Carolyn took in a deep breath and let it back out again. "I wasn't trying to eavesdrop the other night, Ray, but I did overhear you telling Susan about your tour in Vietnam and that you have PTSD."

"Good thing we both have you along, then, isn't it?" Ray gave Carolyn a wry grin as he handed her a shotgun. "It's already loaded."

"My husband has a shotgun just like this," approved Carolyn. "I see the safety is on."

"And here's some .00 buckshot," offered Ray.

"Excellent," responded Carolyn as she grabbed the handful of extra shotgun shells and stuffed them into her shoulder bag.

"Does this blast door open the same way as the other one?" asked Ray as he approached it.

"What if Jon is on the other side, just waiting for us?" Sheree suddenly became apprehensive.

"Sheree, I know you can do this," encouraged Carolyn as she temporarily shouldered the shotgun and then put her free hand on Sheree's upper arm. "Ray and I are both with you, you're not alone. There's nothing to fear but fear itself." Carolyn then unshouldered the shotgun and nodded at Sheree.

"Okay," agreed Sheree as she approached the blast door and inserted her index finger into the locking mechanism beside it.

Both Ray and Carolyn stood with their weapons at the ready as the thick blast door slowly opened upward.

Meanwhile, back at the lighthouse, Susan had just finished hauling Sheree's huge suitcase to the Lilly Room. Susan then directed Ann to put her luggage in the Heather Room across from it. Ted was already waiting for them up in the tower room with his leg propped up on the bench seat beside him.

"The Daisy and Violet Rooms where Carolyn and I are staying are just one floor down," reminded Susan.

"Where will Ted stay?" questioned Ann.

"For now, until we can get Ted safely back to the boys' dormitory, probably up in the Lavender Room across from Ray," guessed Susan. "Ray sleeps in the Rosemary Room, immediately below the tower room, up at the top. That way, Ted won't have far to go to get there, if it turns out he needs to stay here."

"Have you and Ray slept together yet?" Ann unexpectedly asked. "You two seem to be quite friendly now."

Susan blushed deeply. "That's none of your business, young lady! And, that's something you shouldn't even be thinking about yet."

"Were you a virgin when you were my age?" pressed Ann with a raised eyebrow and a crooked grin.

"We are not having this conversation," advised Susan with finality. "Why don't you go check on Ted while I see what there is to eat around this place?"

"Since we never got to finish our lunch?" nodded Ann. "Sure."

"And I will be right up!" cautioned Susan. "I'd like to know what's in that journal, too!"

Birdboy had not failed once since his release from the Ocean Bluff Mental Institution to make an annual pilgrimage to the makeshift burial site where Joyce and Veronica now were. Though disappointed that his barbecue had not gone as hoped, he was not about to let that interfere with what now needed to be done. His secret was no longer safe and any trace of the bodies would need to be moved.

"What about Sheree?" questioned Jon Roth.

"You're better off without her," snapped Birdboy, as he argued with his other self.

"Perhaps Sheree's right," proposed Jon. "If I were to take my medication again and get the help I needed...."

"You'd what?" interrupted Birdboy. "You'd get better again just to become the groveling little househusband you've always been?"

"What do you know about it?" bellowed Jon Roth. Even though Birdboy was actually a part of him, he wished fervently at this moment that Birdboy were a separate entity so he could punch him in the face!

"I know plenty," smirked Birdboy. "I know how Joyce and Veronica always taunted you and made fun of you."

"That was all your fault!" accused Jon Roth.

"But, I'm you!" Birdboy began laughing an evil laugh.

"Not for long, not if I can help it!" threatened Jon Roth. "Somehow I'm going to make my wife and daughter know how sorry I am for everything that has happened, and get the help I need to get rid of you once and for all!"

"You'll never get rid of me," persisted Birdboy.

"Where was it again?" mumbled Jon Roth. He felt sure the gravesite was near but always had such a hard time finding it each year.

"You won't find their grave without me!" howled Birdboy in a menacing manner.

"Stop it!" thundered Jon Roth. "Just stop it! I don't need your help finding them, either!"

Several yards away, Ray, Carolyn and Sheree were silently trailing Jon Roth, easily able to overhear his conversation with himself.

Tears began to flow down Sheree's cheeks as she listened.

Carolyn noticed at once and put a reassuring hand on Sheree's shoulder. "You are stronger than you think, Sheree. You can do this."

"Jon?" called Sheree. The sound of her voice echoed through the tunnel more loudly than intended.

"It's Sheree!" warned Birdboy. "Quick, hide!"

"You're nothing but a coward!" Jon Roth accused his alter personality. "You hide!"

"Are you all right?" questioned Sheree as she cautiously approached, not knowing whether she was facing Jon Roth or Birdboy.

"What are they doing here?" demanded Jon Roth. "I see you've managed to help yourself to my weapons locker without getting blown to bits. Perhaps it's for the best if you do just go ahead and shoot me. I really don't think I can go on like this anyway."

"Jon?" repeated Sheree, more cautiously this time.

"Yes, it's me," confirmed her husband. "Jon Roth."

"We need to know where Joyce and Veronica are buried," prompted Carolyn. "Even after all these years, their families still need closure. Please, Jon, if there's any part of you that Birdboy hasn't destroyed yet, won't you just tell us where they are?"

"I can show you where they are," revealed Sheree.

"But how?" mumbled Jon Roth.

"It was right over there," motioned Sheree. "See where the light is coming in from outside?"

"That's where the tracks led in here from the beach that day!" recognized Carolyn as she ran over to the iron-barred gate.

"And here is the key that opens it," offered Sheree.

"Where did you get that?" Jon Roth was flabbergasted. He had searched for the key for years!

"I picked it up that same day it happened," revealed Sheree. "I even had it with me when I arrived at the Ocean Bluff Mental Institution. Each time the staff tried to take it away from me to treat all my injuries, I apparently became highly agitated, despite my catatonic condition."

"And you remember all that?" questioned Carolyn.

"I didn't at first," answered Sheree. "But, it was Helen who finally reminded me of everything, and who was kind enough to put the key onto this chain for me so I could wear it around my neck."

"Wouldn't the chain be considered a security risk at a place like that?" questioned Ray.

"Definitely," corroborated Jon Roth. "Especially for someone catatonic like she was. Patients like that could easily become suicidal, or even violent and dangerous."

"No one ever knew I had the key but Helen," informed Sheree.

Jon truly had never realized that the neck chain Sheree wore was attached to a key. In fact, the few times they had been intimate after finally getting married, Sheree had refused to take off her top. Jon always knew that Sheree was self-conscious about being flat chested so he had never pressed the matter, nor had he ever noticed the key.

Carolyn immediately took the key from Sheree and tried it in the lock, without success.

"They probably cut the other lock off when they were still searching for Joyce and Veronica," guessed Ray.

"Would the Sheriff who removed it have taken the other lock with him as evidence?" wondered Carolyn aloud.

"Most likely," answered Ray.

"If he did, and if this key fits that other lock, then this could very well be a smoking gun," mentioned Carolyn with excitement.

"A smoking gun?" questioned Sheree.

"A piece of evidence that is actually a missing link in the chain of custody," described Carolyn. "It's a legal term. For example, there were also some aerial photos of Joyce and Veronica running into this tunnel, right at the very same moment that Steve Fredrickson was being attacked by that shark."

"How would you know that?" challenged Jon Roth.

"Because I was there in the plane that flew overhead when Jim Otterman took those photos, and because I was with Jim Otterman in the darkroom when he developed them, and finally, because it was me who personally took the photos from Jim and gave them to the Sheriff working this case! That is referred to as chain of custody. Each piece of evidence must be tracked, along with each person who handled it."

"Like this key?" Sheree nodded with understanding.

"Precisely," confirmed Carolyn.

"So, the fact that I watched Jon Roth open the original lock on that gate with this key before Joyce and Veronica came running inside," added Sheree, "and then personally picked the key up off the ground after it was dropped, and have had the key in my constant possession ever since, would that be like a documented chain of custody?"

"You got it," smiled Carolyn.

"But how?" Jon could not believe what he was hearing.

"Please show us where they are," requested Carolyn.

"Are we going to have to carry them out of here?" Sheree began to panic at the very thought.

"Heavens, no!" assured Carolyn. "The Sheriff will have to come back here with the new key and open this gate from the other side."

"Very well," agreed Sheree. "Unless Jon has moved them, we should find them right over there."

"Let's think about this first," insisted Jon Roth. "They've been here for a very long time. Do we really have the right to disturb them now? Perhaps we should just leave them where they are."

Carolyn suddenly took a step toward Jon Roth and motioned with her shotgun - still held in the ready position - in the direction Sheree had indicated. Ray's weapon was carefully trained on Jon.

"Jon," began Carolyn. "We still do not know what actually occurred here. For all we know, you murdered them in cold blood after brutally beating them to death."

"But, that's not what happened!" insisted Jon Roth.

"He's right," corroborated Sheree. "It was an accident. A tragic, horrible accident, but an accident nonetheless."

"Then you should have nothing to worry about," replied Ray.

March 23, 1973

Joyce, Steve and Veronica had been boogie boarding for over an hour, enthralled with the exhilarating adrenaline rush of catching and riding one perfect wave after another. The conditions seemed to be perfect. Steve Fredrickson finally managed to master his first 360° turn while riding a wave, and beamed with delight. He now knew it could be done! Steve still had another half hour before he needed to be in class, so he decided to catch just one last wave. He wanted to see if he could do the 360° consistently, and that it had not just been a fluke.

Right at that moment, a small, single engine plane flew by overhead, making it difficult to hear much of anything.

"Shark!" hollered Joyce. "Over there, by Steve!"

"Where?" shouted Veronica.

"Get out of the water!" screamed Joyce. "Hurry!"

Steve was just about to catch his final wave for the day when he noticed Joyce and Veronica frantically making their way toward the beach. Too late, Steve noticed the fin of a shark as it unexpectedly attacked him.

"Get the bungee cords from that ledge!" called Veronica. "We can string them together, toss it out, and try to hook his boogie board, and then pull him in. There's no way we can go out there with that shark still so close!"

Veronica was an experienced lifeguard and knew what she was doing. Speed was of the essence, and they needed to get Steve away from the shark and out of the water just as soon as humanly possible! Both she and Joyce had taken Advanced First Aid and hoped that the first aid kit they had with them on the ledge would be adequate. Even if Veronica had to sew Steve up herself, she would do it!

"Perhaps it won't come up where it's shallow?" hoped Joyce.

"Come on, let's get the stuff from the ledge and see what's there that we can use!" instructed Veronica. "Maybe we can tie the towels together, too."

Both Joyce and Veronica winced as they heard Steve's desperate screams of agony. Just then, the small plane flew by overhead again, abruptly drowning out the sound of Steve's final cries for help.

"Dear God!" muttered Veronica as she raced inside the bunker tunnel opening and climbed the wrought iron rungs on its wall that led up to the ledge where their belongings were stashed.

"Look!" pointed out Joyce from where she stood below the ledge. "It's Birdboy and Sheree Wilkins! And the gate is open!"

"We don't have time to worry about them right now," advised Veronica as she hurriedly tossed everything on the ledge to Joyce and began climbing down.

"Well, what's this?" smirked Birdboy as he suddenly grabbed Veronica's boogie board from the ground and held it high above his head out of reach.

"Give it back!" demanded Veronica as she finished climbing down and began rummaging through their things for the bungee cords.

"Ah, that looks interesting," added Birdboy as he suddenly grabbed one end of the bungee cord Veronica was holding and began pulling on it.

"Let go, you moron!" screamed Veronica. "Steve is out there being attacked by a shark right now, and he needs our help!"

"Seriously?" Birdboy laughed with glee. "You can come up with something better than that, can't you?"

"She's not kidding, Birdboy!" snapped Joyce as she shoved him with all her might, grabbed onto the bungee cord, and tried to get it away from him. "Let go of it!"

"Jon, they're not kidding!" shouted Sheree when she finally noticed Steve Fredrickson dragging his mortally wounded body onto the beach outside. "He'll bleed to death if you don't let them help him!"

"I'm not falling for that!" taunted Birdboy as he suddenly shoved both Joyce and Veronica out of his way, and then closed and locked the iron-barred gate with his key.

"Jon, please!" begged Sheree. "Steve will die without their help!" Sheree suddenly tried to grab the key from Jon. Just as she did, Birdboy shoved her down onto the ground as hard as he could. The key miraculously landed right beside her, unseen by anyone else but Sheree.

Sheree's ankle brace loudly snapped as it broke, but had prevented her ankle from actually breaking along with it. She now had a sprained ankle, water on the knee, and hairline fracture to her right hip. Sheree's head brace had fallen into a nearby crevice and her glasses had been smashed when she landed on them. Though unable to see very clearly, Sheree spotted the key when a gleam of sunlight hit it just the right way. Sheree quickly grabbed the key and tightly clutched it in her hand. Her efforts to try and stand were to no avail, so she began crawling toward the gate. The pain from her injuries was unimaginable!

"Get away from me, you freak!" commanded Veronica as Birdboy started toward her again.

Birdboy was still holding onto the bungee cord and boogie board. Unexpectedly, he hooked the bungee cord onto it and began swinging it around and around, over his head like a propeller. "Perhaps it's time to see how high Birdboy can really fly?"

"Birdboy, what are you doing?" questioned Joyce.

"He's nuts!" screamed Veronica.

"I'll show you who's nuts!" bellowed Birdboy as he swung the boogie board toward Veronica with all his might and hit her with it.

Veronica screamed with terror as her wet feet slipped on the slimy surface where she stood.

"Veronica!" cried Joyce as she helplessly watched her friend fall backward and hit her head against the hard wall.

The sound of Veronica's neck breaking upon impact could be heard throughout the cave.

"Jon, no!" sobbed Sheree. Immobilized by terror, she suddenly found herself unable to move. Sheree tried with all her might to make her pain-ridden body respond to the commands her mind was attempting to give it, but she just could not make it move! Her fists were tightly clenched, the right one secretly holding Jon's gate key.

"You'll never get away with this!" shouted Joyce as she got up and began to run deeper into the tunnel.

Birdboy began loudly squawking and flapping his arms like wings as he took off after Joyce.

"Help!" hollered Joyce as loud as she could. "Someone, please help!" The sound of the small plane flying by outside could be heard one final time as it approached the tiny bluff top runway, preventing her cries for help from being heard.

Sheree kept thinking, "Help! Someone help!" But, the words were inaudible to anyone but her and spoken only in her mind.

Joyce was an excellent runner and managed to outdistance Birdboy for several yards, but he was much taller and his longer legs soon had the advantage as he overtook her.

"You're not going anywhere!" menaced Birdboy as he grabbed Joyce's arm and suddenly wrapped the bungee cord around her wrists. "I'm not going to prison for the rest of my life, just because your stupid friend Veronica is a klutz!"

"Birdboy, please?" begged Joyce. "Don't do this!"

"Come on!" directed Birdboy. "You still don't even know my real name, do you?"

"Sheree just called you Jon," realized Joyce. "Is that your real name? Jon?" Joyce tested the bungee cords to see if she could manage to loosen them. If necessary, she would wrap them around Birdboy's neck and strangle him if she had to, in order to escape!

"What are you going to do?" Jon Roth suddenly asked himself.

"You're the one who did this!" pointed out Birdboy. "You figure it out!"

"Jon, please?" pleaded Joyce. "Is that who you are?"

"Jon Roth might be willing to try and help you escape," smirked Birdboy, "but not me!"

Joyce could clearly see that Birdboy had multiple personalities, and was extremely afraid. "Are you Edith Roth's son, Jon?"

"My mother has nothing to do with this!" screamed Birdboy as he shoved Joyce down with all his might.

Joyce's head hit the ground with tremendous force, and her skull did crack, but still she remained conscious and continued to struggle.

"Jon, why?" wept Joyce as she tried in vain to loosen the bungee cords binding her hands.

"Shut up!" commanded Birdboy as he roughly grabbed Joyce by one arm and began dragging her toward a small recess in the tunnel wall nearby. Joyce finally lost consciousness and suddenly collapsed into a lifeless heap at Birdboy's feet.

Sheree watched in silent terror as Birdboy dragged first Joyce and then Veronica into the small recess area of the tunnel wall. It had originally been used as an ammunition locker by the military when armored tanks were also housed there. One by one, Jon dragged every loose boulder and rock he could find over to the opening and managed to conceal it completely from view.

"Sheree!" called Jon Roth as he tenderly rushed to her side to check her injuries. "Are you all right?"

Sheree wanted to tell Jon Roth to just go away and leave her alone, but was unable to utter a sound. Her breathing became shallow and rapid as he picked her up and began to carry her. Was he planning to bury her alive, as well? What would he do with her?

March 23, 2016

Over in the lighthouse, Susan, Ann and Ted had just finished eating lunch and were ready to begin reading the journal.

"Should we read the entries my mother made at the end first?" questioned Ann.

"No," replied Susan. "I think we should take it in order, just like it is. Ted?"

"I vote for taking it in order," agreed Ted. "Let's read Ginny's entries first."

"Very well, then," nodded Susan as she opened the little book on the table in front of them and then slid it over to Ann.

"Ginny says here that both my parents were taken to the Ocean Bluff Mental Institution on March 24, 1973. Could that be right?" wondered Ann. "Why weren't they taken there on the 23rd?"

"Let me see that," directed Susan as she took back the journal. "Ginny goes on to describe how Jon picked up Sheree and carried her through the tunnels, all the way back to his parents' house, the day Joyce and Veronica disappeared. It was his mother Edith who called for an ambulance the following day. That's when Jon and Sheree were both taken over to the Ocean Bluff Mental Institution."

"Didn't you say Sheree had been catatonic?" questioned Ted. "It seems odd that Edith would have waited to get help for her."

"Grandma was the school nurse," reminded Ann. "Perhaps she tried to take care of Sheree herself first before bothering anyone else."

"I remember when that ambulance was called out!" interjected Susan. "Kids who saw the ambulance were talking about it for weeks, how Birdboy was finally taken away to the looney bin, but nobody ever knew for sure why they took him. There was quite a bit of speculation about it, though!"

"Carolyn and I both saw Birdboy take a flying leap off a tufting table at the lumber mill the previous day, but Carolyn never realized he was actually the Roth boy," continued Susan. "The few of us who did know his real name was Jon Roth figured they took him away because of the incident at the lumber mill, and that alone would have been enough! But, absolutely nobody knew that Sheree had been taken away, too!"

"How did you know my dad's real name?" questioned Ann.

"He was in my biology class," revealed Susan. "Whenever the teacher took roll and called out for Jon Roth, Birdboy would answer. So, it obviously had to be him."

"That's incredible!" marveled Ted.

Susan, Ann and Ted spent the next two hours studying the little journal, each waiting for the others to catch up before turning to the next page. Thankfully, Ginny's penmanship was impeccable and easy to read. It almost looked as if she had used a ruler on which to write.

"Ginny indicates here that patients with catatonia sometimes experience loss of motor skills or can exhibit constant hyperactive motor activity," read Ann. "She then goes on to say that catatonic patients can even hold rigid poses for hours while they ignore any external stimuli."

"That's pretty creepy," mentioned Ted.

"Ginny concludes that entry by describing how patients who exhibit the constant type of hyperactive motor activity can sometimes suffer from complete exhaustion if not treated."

"Wait, there's more on the next page," noticed Susan. "It goes on and on about how they can sometimes copycat movements or repeat meaningless phrases that someone says to them."

"Ginny then describes the many faces of schizophrenia, and says there are several different types," read Ann. "She says here that my mom suffered from Kahlbaum syndrome, which is the motionless type."

"It almost sounds like she was in shock," assessed Ted. "Perhaps what she saw was so traumatic that she had post-traumatic stress disorder, or something like that. I read somewhere that PTSD is actually one of the many faces of schizophrenia."

"Just when did you read that?" quizzed Ann.

"When I learned that your father might have it," replied Ted. "I also did some research to find out whether something like that could be inherited. In case we ever decide to have children."

"We don't dare," responded Ann sadly. "Perhaps we can adopt, though. Then we wouldn't have to worry about it."

"Hey, you two," interjected Susan. "I just tried to text Ray, and then Carolyn, and there's no response."

"Maybe because they're in those tunnels," guessed Ted.

"Hey, let's see what my mom had to say at the end, after all the stuff Ginny wrote. We can always come back to this part," suggested

Ann. She was extremely anxious to find out what Sheree had written at the end of Ginny's journal.

"Sheree says it all started on March 23, 1973," began Susan.

"We already know that!" said Ann.

"Sheree and Jon Roth were very much in love," added Susan. "They had just shared their first kiss."

"Seriously?" Ann was impatient.

"If you'd let me finish," replied Susan.

"Yes, please, let her finish," instructed Ted. He was as anxious as anyone to find out what had happened to his Aunt Veronica and her best friend Joyce Troglite on the beach that day.

Back in the cave, Sheree meticulously described to Carolyn and Ray what she could recall of the tragedy all those years ago.

Carolyn and Ray kept a vigilant watch with their weapons trained on Jon Roth as they listened.

Jon was still tall but had not been thin for years, and struggled greatly to remove the main rocks and boulders that stood as a testament to his evil deed. Breathing heavily and sweating profusely, Jon took a moment to wipe his forehead with his sleeve.

"Did anyone think to bring any water along?" asked Jon Roth.

"Obviously, you didn't!" observed Ray as he pulled a small flask from his left rear pocket, removed the lid – which was held to it by a small chain – and took a drink.

Ray then handed the flask to Carolyn. "Water?"

"Thanks!" smiled Carolyn as she took the flask from Ray, wiped the rim with her blouse, and took a refreshing drink.

Carolyn then passed the flask to Sheree, who smirked at Jon while she gulped down some water before handing it back to Ray.

"Do you want me to finish moving these rocks or not?" asked Jon. "I have a bad back and don't even know if I'll be able to walk back after all this."

"You should have thought of that back in 1973!" snapped Sheree. She had absolutely no sympathy for Jon Roth whatever.

"One small sip," decided Ray. "Agreed?"

Jon nodded his consent and then waited for Ray to toss him the flask. Jon immediately began guzzling what he could from the flask.

"That's enough!" cautioned Ray as he cocked the hammer on his revolver, and carefully leveled it at Birdboy's groin. "You drink any more, and you'll wish you had a bullet-proof cup on!"

Jon stopped drinking from the flask, put the lid back on, and suddenly tossed it back to Ray. Ray maintained his ready stance and allowed the flask to land on the ground. "All right, then," mumbled Jon as he resumed his task of moving the boulders.

Sheree gingerly picked up the flask for Ray and then paused. "Another missing link, I believe. Look down there!" Sheree was staring at a wide crack next to where the flask had landed.

Carolyn kept her shotgun in ready position but moved over to where Sheree was and shined her flashlight at the place. It actually was a shallow crevice, several inches wide, in which Sheree's head brace still sat where it had landed back in 1973. Beside that were remnants of the broken eyeglasses she had landed on when she fell.

"We need to mark this spot so it's easy to find when we can get the Sheriff out here," informed Carolyn.

"Let's build a small rock pointer by it," suggested Sheree.

"Excellent idea," agreed Carolyn as she handed the shotgun to Sheree to hold while she grabbed several small rocks that Jon had already discarded on a pile nearby and neatly stacked them beside the small crevice. Carolyn then snapped a photo of the entire area with her cellphone, including a photo of Jon Roth trying to remove a large boulder. Carolyn then retrieved the shotgun from Sheree, who was greatly relieved to be rid of it.

Jon Roth grunted and groaned as he struggled to loosen yet more of the large rocks so he could roll them aside, but suddenly stopped. "Did anyone feel that?"

"I didn't feel anything," advised Carolyn suspiciously.

"There it is again!" exclaimed Jon with alarm.

"I felt that!" assured Carolyn as she began moving toward the iron-barred gate.

"Me, too," informed Ray. "Everyone over to the gate. You, too, Jon. Let's go."

"It's an earthquake!" shouted Sheree with alarm.

"We'll be all right," promised Carolyn as she came back for Sheree and took her by the arm. "I won't let anything happen to you."

"Don't make promises you might not be able to keep," advised Sheree as she accompanied Carolyn over to the gate.

"If only we had the right key," fretted Sheree.

All at once, violent tremors began shaking the entire tunnel system. Several cave-ins could be heard from deep within the underground passageways adjoining the one where they were. The earth movement continued for about two minutes. The magnitude of the quake felt like it was about a four on the Richter scale.

Jon had rushed over to hold Sheree up, not wanting her to fall onto the slippery damp floor.

"I'm fine," informed Sheree as she wriggled to free herself from his grasp and grabbed onto the iron gate bars to support herself.

"I have no right to ask you this ...," began Jon.

"You're right, you don't!" snapped Sheree as she cut him off.

"Forgive me for everything that I've put you through, Sheree, please!" begged Jon Roth. He was now on his knees beside her and had tears streaming down his face.

Sheree looked down at him and took a deep breath of air that she quickly let out before replying. "Look, I know it wasn't you who did all this. I'm well aware that it was Birdboy."

"I truly thought he was gone," sniveled Jon Roth.

"Perhaps you should consider getting help and taking your medicine again," suggested Sheree. "After we get out of here, that is." Sheree did still love Jon Roth and she felt her resolve weakening, but was determined to maintain a stoic front for his benefit. If she caved in to him now, Jon might never be prompted to get the treatment he needed.

"Even with the medicine, Birdboy was never really gone," admitted Jon Roth. "It was because of the anemia from the Clozapine that I finally quit taking it, not because I didn't want to get better. I even tried two or three other medications first, including Clonazepam, but it made things even worse. That's when the diabetes first kicked in."

"Why didn't you just tell me this?" asked Sheree.

"I've tried to, for years," replied Jon, "but I know now that I can never be free from Birdboy, no matter what I do, nor can I allow him to hurt anyone else, ever again."

Just then, an aftershock of lesser magnitude and shorter duration could be felt. Lasting only a minute or so, the quake was still enough to cause more damage. Another tunnel collapse could be heard from somewhere within the passages nearby.

"We sure can't go back that way," decided Ray as he pulled out his satellite phone and tried again to get a signal. Perhaps at the bunker tunnel entrance that might be possible.

While Ray was distracted with his phone, Jon Roth suddenly bolted toward him, grabbed the revolver, and shoved Ray away with amazing speed and alacrity. Jon swiftly cocked the hammer and then jammed the gun's muzzle against the bottom of his own chin.

"Sheree, I love you with all my heart," pledged Jon Roth. "Please tell Ann that I love her, too."

"Jon, you don't have to do this," warned Ray. How could he have let his guard down like that?

"He's right, Jon," interjected Carolyn. "Let us get you the help you need. Please don't do this!"

"Don't do this!" mocked Birdboy, who was suddenly taking control again.

"You will NEVER hurt anyone again!" screamed Jon Roth as he argued with himself. "I won't let you!"

"You won't do it," challenged Birdboy with a haughty laugh. "You're not man enough to pull the trigger."

"Forgive me, Sheree," pleaded Jon Roth. "I just don't see how I have a choice. I won't let Birdboy hurt you or Ann, or anyone else, ever again! Please take care of Ann!" Jon Roth then pulled the trigger.

A third, but even smaller earthquake shook the ground as he did, lasting only about thirty seconds and definitely less than two points on the Richter scale.

"JON!" screamed Sheree. "Jon!" Sheree then slowly sat down where she was. Tears were streaming down her cheeks.

"Don't you go catatonic on us!" commanded Carolyn as she knelt beside her. "Sheree?" Carolyn then gently tapped the sides of Sheree's cheeks with the palm of her hand.

"Here, you hang onto this," instructed Carolyn as she handed the shotgun to Ray. "You're gonna need to leave your revolver where it is for the Sheriff to see, so you might want this instead."

"Thanks," nodded Ray as he took the shotgun from Carolyn and shouldered it. It was doubtful he would be needing it now, anyway.

"How about you, Ray?" questioned Carolyn. "Are YOU all right? Ray?"

388

"Yeah," confirmed Ray. "I'm fine."

"So, does either of you know when high tide is?" Carolyn suddenly asked. Her question captured Ray and Sheree's attention immediately.

Sheree pointedly avoided looking at the area where Jon Roth's splattered remains lie nearby and focused on Carolyn. "Ebb tides are usually in the mid-afternoon. That means the tide is all the way out. That was also why Joyce and Veronica would do most of their boogie boarding when the water was like it is now," described Sheree.

"Good, that makes sense," replied Carolyn. "And we know they kept their stuff on that ledge out there to keep it dry when the tide came in, so hopefully the water level won't get any higher than that."

"Too bad the ledge is on the other side of the gate," mentioned Sheree. "That would have been a good place to climb up to."

"Hey, I got a signal," advised Ray excitedly. "Let's get a group selfie and I'll send it to Susan to let her know we're all right."

"Sure, why not?" agreed Carolyn as she and Sheree stood beside him for the picture. The photo showed them standing together with the iron-barred gate behind them. Beyond that could be seen the beach and ocean background beyond, reflecting the late afternoon sun.

Ray immediately texted the photo to Susan with a message that said, "Gate locked, please send Sheriff before high tide, we're trapped."

"When is high tide?" asked Carolyn.

"Usually the tide comes back in around sundown, but doesn't reach high point until 9:30 or 10:00 at night up here," revealed Sheree.

"At least it's at low ebb right now," observed Ray.

"That gives us a little time," noted Carolyn. "Hey Ray, would you mind taking some key photos of all this on your satellite phone?"

"I can do that," agreed Ray.

"Good, because I just can't get a signal in here to send any of the photos I just took with my cellphone," described Carolyn. "Perhaps then you can send them to Susan to share with the Sheriff. Then, at least he'll know what he's up against and can come here prepared."

Ray quickly snapped several photos of Jon Roth's dead body, including two close-ups showing the revolver still in Jon's hand by his mangled bloody head.

Sheree let out an involuntary sob and began crying again. "I never even had a chance to tell Jon I forgave him!"

"Then you can make it up to him now by being strong for Ann's sake," mentioned Carolyn. "She's going to need you now more than ever, especially when she finds out about all of this."

"Please tell Susan not to let Ann see those photos!" begged Sheree. "Just put that it's for the Sheriff's eyes only."

"I can do that," agreed Ray as he sent the photos of Jon's body. His message simply read, "Jon Roth suicide - for Sheriff's eyes only."

Ray suddenly noticed that the skeletal remains of Joyce and Veronica were now showing, along with their boogie boards and other belongings. "I think I should photograph and text them everything else I can, before the tide comes in. We really don't know how long it will take them to contact the Sheriff or for him to get here."

Frightened by the earthquakes, Susan, Ann and Ted sat quietly in the lighthouse watching the setting sun and contemplating what they had just learned from the little journal.

"I sure hope they're all right, too," worried Susan. "They should have called us by now."

"We never did read the last half of Ginny's entries," reminded Ted. "We only read the first half before skipping to the part written by Sheree at the end."

"What time is it?" questioned Susan.

"About four o'clock," advised Ann.

"Okay, let's take a look at it now, while we're waiting for them to call," agreed Susan as she flipped through the little journal until reaching the place where they had left off.

"Here is where Ginny mentions Helen," noticed Ann. "That must be the nurse from the institution that turned out to be a patient."

"It has to be," agreed Susan.

"What?" Ted seemed surprised.

"Oh, I don't believe this," muttered Ann, who became quiet after reading the next page. "It says here that not only were Helen and Edith sisters – they were identical twin sisters!"

"Was Edith mentally ill, too, then?" questioned Ted, who was over on the bench seat with his throbbing ankle propped up. He could no longer sit at the table where Susan and Ann were.

"I don't think she was," replied Ann. "At least not as far as anyone knew. But sadly, Jon Roth, Sr. did not know about the mental illness in Edith's family when he married her."

"Poor guy," commented Susan.

"By the time he found out," continued Ann, "Edith was already pregnant with my dad."

"When did they first realize their son had inherited his mother's family illness?" questioned Ted with great interest.

"Right about the same time he realized who her family was," answered Ann. "As far as they knew, Jon was only four years old when he had his first episode as Birdboy. That was when he tried to jump off the roof of their garage wearing a cape and had roofing shingles tied to his arms like wings."

"That had to be tough." Ted shook his head sympathetically.

"Borden?" Susan's eyes suddenly became wide with surprise. "It says here that Helen and Edith's maiden name was Borden."

"Borden?" repeated Ted with a puzzled expression. "Does that have some significance?"

"You've never heard of Lizzie Borden?" quizzed Susan.

"No," replied Ted and Ann together.

"Well," began Susan, "Lizzie Borden was tried but finally acquitted for the hatchet murders of her father and step-mom. That was back in Massachusetts in 1892. The family who adopted her illegitimate son came out west on a wagon train after that."

"There are probably lots of Bordens," pointed out Ted.

"Let me see that," requested Ann. After studying the journal more carefully, Ann then handed the book to Ted as she mentioned, "Ginny has Helen and Edith's entire family tree drawn up here. It shows the complete family line, all the way from Lizzie's illegitimate son Jon down to Edith and Helen. Apparently the real father never stepped forward, so Jon Borden took on and kept his mother's maiden name after learning his true identity."

"Unless that was his true identity," mumbled Susan. "I heard somewhere once that Lizzie Borden's father was also the father of her illegitimate child. But, I might be mistaken. I'd have to look it up."

"How did Jon Borden ever find out he was adopted, then?" questioned Ted.

"It doesn't say," replied Ann. "Maybe he saw it in someone's journal, or found the adoption papers somewhere. Who knows."

"Well, that's not all it shows here in her journal," noticed Ted. "Helen had a daughter, too. Her name was Virginia Borden, and it has Ginny Eggersol written in parentheses beside it."

Ann hurried over to sit by Ted so she could see what he was looking at. "That's not possible. Ginny Eggersol's parents were killed in a plane crash several years before she died."

"That's right!" recalled Susan. "Ray told Carolyn and me about it at dinner the other night. He also mentioned that Ginny Eggersol died in 1976. She was on her way back from the mental institution late one foggy night when a drunk driver ran her off the road, and both cars crashed into the rocks below, killing both of them instantly."

"How horrible!" exclaimed Ann.

"Ginny mentions here that she learned of her adoption when she was twelve years old," added Ted as he read some more from the little book. "She had found the paperwork in her father's desk and pressed the issue until the Eggersols finally let her know about Helen."

"Wow!" marveled Ann. "That would make Helen Borden my dad's aunt. I wonder who Ginny's real father was, then?"

"Looks like he never stepped forward, either," noted Susan. "And, patients at mental institutions often are required to relinquish custody of their babies so they can be put up for adoption by good families, but usually the children are never told about it."

"It seems they would have a right to know," argued Ann. "Especially in cases where they might someday want to have children of their own!"

"Maybe that's how Ginny was able to get in to see Jon Roth at the looney bin like she did," speculated Ted.

"Since she was family!" recognized Ann. "Wow!"

"It certainly is a small world," commented Susan. "Well, I don't see any other entries in here."

"I'm definitely having my tubes tied before Ted and I get married," announced Ann. "Like you said, we can always adopt."

"Just don't tell 'em you're descended from Lizzie Borden!" chuckled Susan.

"No kidding!" grinned Ted as he shook his head.

"Oh, my God!" Susan suddenly exclaimed.

"What is it?" pressed Ann.

"I've had my cellphone on vibrate all this time," replied Susan, "so we never heard it when Ray called!"

"Are they all right?" asked Ann.

Susan's face became pale as she saw the texts and photos from Ray Dixon. She swallowed hard before answering. "Ray, Carolyn and Sheree are fine. Excuse me, I've got to call the Sheriff right now."

12. Amazing Grace

Lenny quietly sat by his mother's bedside, watching her sleep. Minnie Owens was finally resting comfortably – for now – but only because she was heavily sedated. The doctors had done all they could for her, so now it was just a matter of time. Minnie was not expected to make it through the night.

The heart rate monitor attached to her chest steadily beeped, almost in time with the continuous rhythmic dripping sound of the IV leading to Minnie's fragile hand. Even the noise of her labored breathing seemed to echo throughout the austere hospital room.

Lenny had been brought up in a family where "real men" did not routinely show their emotions, and especially did not cry. Tears were slowly trickling down Lenny's cheeks as he watched his mother slipping away. He loved her with all his heart, and could not accept the fact that she soon would be gone forever. Or, would he really see her again someday up in heaven? If only Lenny could be certain.

Lenny thought of his Aunt Jennie, who had been killed during the 1965 race riots in Watts, and then of his Uncle Bill, who had been killed shortly before that in 1962 during a meaningless construction accident when Pete had been in the first grade. How had Pete endured losing both of his parents so early in life?

Jennie was Minnie's twin sister and best friend, so there had been no question about Pete coming to live with the Owens family after his mother's death. Pete had since become like a brother to Lenny and thought of his parents as if they were his own.

Lenny was suddenly grateful that his father and Pete had gone to get something to eat down in the hospital cafeteria and were not there to see him cry. Still, he could not help it! What would he do when they returned? Lenny would need to quickly dry his cheeks and slip out to go get his own dinner, hopefully before they had time to notice his tears.

Carolyn had made him cry once! Did she even know it? Would Lenny ever get the chance to tell Carolyn how he felt about her? No one else had ever had that effect on Lenny, and it frightened him to think that anyone could.

"Lenny?" Minnie Owens had opened her eyes and saw the tears on her son's cheeks.

"I'm right here, mom," responded Lenny as he pulled his chair as close to the clunky hospital bed as possible. Lenny then took her fragile hand in his. He was afraid to squeeze it too tightly, or that he might accidentally bump the IV in her hand, or one of the many various tubes and cords connected to her.

Minnie weakly squeezed her son's hand and whispered, "I love you, Lenny, and am so proud of you!"

"I love you too, mom," responded Lenny as more unbidden tears escaped the corners of his watery eyes.

"Better not let your father see you crying," advised his mother with a gentle smile. "You know how he gets."

"Is there anything I can do for you?" offered Lenny. He felt so helpless and wanted to do whatever he could to make his dying mother more comfortable.

"There is one thing you can do for me," responded Minnie Owens, with obvious effort.

"Name it," prompted Lenny.

"Promise me you'll stay in that school, so you can become a doctor like you've always dreamed of?" requested his mother.

Lenny thought of Carolyn right then, and how his father had threatened to take him out of Oceanview Academy if Lenny so much as dared to see "that white girl" again! How could Lenny's father be so unreasonable? What could it possibly matter that Carolyn was white, anyway? Mixed couples were not that unusual anymore.

"Promise me?" pressed his mother, with pleading eyes.

"I promise," Lenny finally agreed.

"I'm so proud of you! You'll make a wonderful doctor," replied his mother as she unexpectedly took her last breath and died. The instruments surrounding her bed began beeping loudly, and the on-duty nurse came rushing into the room.

"I'm sorry, but you'll need to wait out in the hall," instructed the nurse. "I can't let you be in here right now."

A voice overhead repeated the words, "Code Blue in 23A, Code Blue in 23A, all available staff to 23A, Code Blue."

Lenny was numb with shock and grief, but all he could do was sit there and stare at the lifeless body of his precious mother.

"Come on, son." It was his dad, who had just returned with Pete. "Let's give them room to work." Mr. Owens gently separated

Lenny's hand from that of his mother. Lenny hadn't even realized he was still holding her hand.

As Lenny stood to accompany his father out into the hall, he could see that tears were on his father's cheeks, too. Once they were in the waiting area, Mr. Owens tightly hugged his son Lenny and began to sob inconsolable tears of grief. Not knowing what else to do, Pete put his arms around both of them and allowed his own tears to flow.

"Mr. Owens?" It was the doctor.

"Yes, Sir?" responded Lenny's father, who immediately pulled away from his boys to remove a white handkerchief from his back pocket. Mr. Owens then wiped his eyes and face, blew his nose, and returned the handkerchief to his pocket before finally turning around.

"I'm so sorry," consoled the physician, who managed to let a tear of his own escape. The doctor then put a reassuring hand on Mr. Owens' shoulder for a moment before walking away.

Susan and Carolyn were unusually quiet as they searched through their wardrobes for something appropriate to change into for Steve Fredrickson's funeral.

"I don't have anything black to wear at all," realized Susan.

"Neither do I," admitted Carolyn. "Strange, isn't it?"

"What's strange about wanting to wear black to a funeral?" puzzled Susan.

"Sure, we know that Steve is gone, and we should wear black for him," qualified Carolyn, "but we also know that Joyce and Veronica could still be alive. What are we doing getting dressed to go to a funeral for them, anyway? We should be out looking for them!"

"I couldn't agree with you more," responded Susan.

"It's almost as if they don't believe me," commented Carolyn, "about the tracks heading toward the cave instead of away from it!"

"Too bad Jim didn't take better photos of those tracks," snorted Susan. "That was quite a disappointment!"

"To say the least!" agreed Carolyn.

"At least they have the testimony of you three who actually saw the tracks," reminded Susan.

"Actually, Jim finally told 'em he wasn't sure which way the tracks were headed," revealed Carolyn.

"You've got to be kidding?" Susan was surprised.

396

"And Bart just couldn't remember," added Carolyn somberly.

"Are you truly positive about which way the tracks were headed?" pressed Susan.

"Of course I am!" snapped Carolyn. "I'd stake my life on it!"

"Well, it does seem like their bodies would have washed up somewhere by now, if they really were out there in the ocean someplace," surmised Susan. "Unless the shark took them out so far and so deep that they won't wash up for years."

"Both of them?" doubted Carolyn. "And taken by a single shark, at the same time? Seriously?"

"Maybe he had friends," suggested Susan as she shrugged her shoulders. "I don't know."

"The photographs clearly show only ONE shark," persisted Carolyn. "And all three of us saw it when we were flying over the beach that day! That's about the only thing our depositions did agree on. And on how Steve died, of course!"

"Calm down!" suggested Susan. "I do believe you!"

"Just how long do you think someone could survive in those tunnels without any food or water?" wondered Carolyn aloud.

"Probably three days without water," opined Susan.

"I agree," said Carolyn. "Which means that unless they did find a water source in there, they're probably dead by now. But, the point is, we really do not know! And, if they are dead, we need to find them."

"Hey, Jesus went for 40 days without food or water when he was fasting in the wilderness," reminded Susan.

Carolyn merely rolled her eyes and shook her head.

"What?" demanded Susan. "It says so in the Bible!"

"I know," apologized Carolyn. "It's just that going to their funeral when we don't even know if they're actually dead seems wrong somehow."

"Still, we do need to go to the funeral for Steve's sake," persisted Susan. "His family will be there, and will want to meet the brave young lady who tried to save him and was there for him when he died."

Carolyn suddenly burst into tears. "I just can't! Don't you understand? Watching him die like that was more than anyone should have to endure. It was horrible! I've already said my goodbyes to

Steve, right there on the beach! Please don't ask me to go through anymore!"

"My dear Carolina la Gata," consoled Susan as she put an arm around Carolyn and let her cry. "Sometimes we need to do things we don't think we can, but we still need to do them anyway. The only thing to fear is fear itself."

It was April 11, 1973, at two o'clock in the afternoon. Cars were parked bumper-to-bumper alongside every available road on campus at Oceanview Academy. Still more of them were parked in front of the faculty homes over near the bluffs, and even alongside the various crop fields. Over thirteen hundred people, including friends, classmates, faculty and family members had assembled for the memorial service of Steve Fredrickson, Veronica Jensen and Joyce Troglite.

Steve's parents were missionaries in South Africa so had not been able to get there any sooner. The search for Joyce and Veronica had been publicly abandoned on April 7, 1973, so both were officially listed as missing and presumed dead.

All of the folding chairs available, in addition to chairs from both the cafeteria and some of the classrooms, were set up on both sides of the freshly mowed lawn area that separated the dormitories from the administration building downhill below it. Arrivals were still entering the makeshift seating areas, accessing them from the gently sloping cement walkway whose wide steps wound their way downhill, straight through the very center of the expansive lawn area. Both sides of the walkway were lined by a hearty mat of creeping succulent ice plants with hot pink blooms that guests were carefully stepping over to get to their seats. The outer edges of both planting beds were accented with golden yellow coreopsis, lavender and sedum plants where they met the edges of the expansive lawn on either side.

Noisy seagulls circled overhead as they made their way toward the beach beyond. The pungent odors of cypress and eucalyptus trees that grew in abundance along the windswept cliffs nearby wafted toward the massive collection of folding chairs now filled with weeping guests. The usual morning fog was gone and brilliant rays of sun could be seen streaming through the coastal forest along the bluffs nearby. The sound of ocean waves in the background blended melodically into the hum of voices as people waited for the service to begin.

The chairs were all arranged facing west, toward the back door of the administration building below them for logistical reasons. Even farther uphill and behind the vast assortment of folding chairs were the front steps to the cafeteria.

Jon Roth, Sr. had set up his portable pulpit on the rear steps of the administration building so the long extension cord needed for his microphone could reach to the nearest electrical outlet inside. One of the thick glass doors to the administration building had been propped slightly open with a rubber doorstop to make room for the electrical cord. Being the school principal, the task of conducting the funeral service had fallen upon him. Still troubled by the recent commitment of his son Jon to the Ocean Bluff Mental Institution, Principal Roth found it difficult to gather his thoughts for the funeral service he was about to conduct.

What had happened between their son Jon and Sheree Wilkins on March 23rd? How ironic that it had been the very same day of Steve Fredrickson's death and also the disappearance of Joyce Troglite and Veronica Jensen. Were the events somehow connected? He certainly hoped not! Thankfully, the fact that Sheree Wilkins had been secretly taken away had not been made public, and hopefully could be kept quiet. It was bad enough that several of the students had seen Jon Jr. being taken away by the men in white coats that next afternoon. Edith Roth, who sat beside her husband, was having similar thoughts.

Susan and Carolyn were dressed in brightly colored clothing that sharply contrasted with the drab, dark apparel worn by most guests in attendance at the funeral service. Susan wore a bright red blouse and matching red high heeled platform shoes whose long shoe laces were woven back and forth around her ankle before being tied into neat bows on top. The bright red and yellow floral pattern in Susan's skirt contrasted well with equally brilliant green leaflet designs over a black background. Just to make sure that she and Carolyn were in compliance with the school's dress code, each of them had knelt on the ground in their dormitory room and measured to be sure their skirts were no shorter than two inches above the floor. Both of them were wearing their makeup as heavy as they dared without getting into trouble, though Carolyn was concerned that her eye makeup would run when she cried.

Carolyn's orange and tan striped skirt and matching top were form fitting but made of stretchable polyester. Both the skirt and top had stripes that ran diagonally downward from each side and met exactly in the front and back centers of the outfit. An orange band of ribbing that exactly matched the orange stripes was worn outside but pulled down over the top of the skirt. The tan suede platform shoes Carolyn wore accentuated her tallness, something Susan had advised her to be proud of. That way people could look up to her. Still, she felt uncomfortable in the outfit and felt that it drew unnecessary attention to herself, especially considering the occasion.

Some of those present stared at both Susan and Carolyn with disapproval, though most really didn't care.

"I don't see Lenny or Pete anywhere," Carolyn whispered to Susan as they began their descent down the walkway. "I haven't seen either of them since the day Steve died. Where do you think they could be? Do you see them anywhere?"

"Let's sit up here in the back," suggested Susan.

"Hello, girls," greeted Ms. Dixon from behind them. "The families have requested that you two join them down in the front. They are all quite anxious to meet you."

Susan nodded but urgently began looking for a solitary seat near the back where she could sit by herself.

"Both of you," insisted the Dean, as she gently grasped Susan by the arm to stop her. "After all, you two were Joyce and Veronica's closest friends. And, the Fredricksons are especially anxious to meet Carolyn. They have seats reserved for both of you down in the front."

"Yes, ma'am," Carolyn nervously agreed.

"Come on, girls, everyone's waiting for you."

Music could suddenly be heard from behind them. Three sets of bagpipes were being played by musicians that had been brought in for the occasion. Overlooking the crowd, they were located up on the cafeteria steps. The haunting melody of Amazing Grace brought instant silence to the congregation, and elicited many tears from those present. Susan and Carolyn uneasily made their way to the front with Dean Dixon and quickly sat down.

Why weren't Lenny or Pete at the service? wondered Carolyn as she again studied the vast crowd to try and find them.

After a lengthy opening prayer by his wife Edith, Principal Roth got up to address the congregation. His rambling remarks went virtually unheard by Carolyn, who was busy thinking of Joyce and Veronica. The moment this was over, she planned to change her clothes, go down to the beach, and look for them again. True, she had been down there every single day since the search was called off, but she wasn't about to give up on them. Joyce and Veronica were down there somewhere and Carolyn was going to find them!

"You're not going back down there again today, are you?" whispered Susan.

Carolyn remained silent but nodded her head in the affirmative.

"Not without me, you're not!" advised Susan.

Dean Dixon put her hand on Susan's shoulder to indicate silence. Susan merely nodded in acquiescence.

The closing prayer was said by Professor Rattusrisum. While he prayed, Carolyn wondered whether his mother had ever recovered from her brain aneurism surgery, or whatever it was, and then of how things might have been different had Professor Rattusrisum not seen Susan or her hitchhiking that day in Ocean Bluff. His attitude toward both of them had been condescending ever since, which was unfortunate as he had been one of Carolyn's favorite teachers prior to that.

"Amen," said the Professor, at long last.

"Please wait until your row is dismissed before you leave," reminded Edith Roth after quickly grabbing the microphone. "The students who have parents here may join them up in the cafeteria if they wish. The rest of you please return to your respective dormitories. Your dinner will be brought to you there. We just don't have room for so many people in the cafeteria all at once."

Carolyn and Susan exchanged a look of disappointment, realizing they would not be able to go to the beach as planned. It did not go unnoticed by Mr. Fredrickson, who assumed they were disappointed about not eating in the cafeteria.

"Won't you girls please join us?" invited Mr. Fredrickson. "I'm Steve Fredrickson, Sr."

"And I'm Nancy." Mrs. Fredrickson introduced herself. "We'd be very honored to have both of you join us for dinner."

"We'd like to come along, too, if you don't mind," mentioned Mrs. Jensen.

"Absolutely!" agreed Mrs. Fredrickson.

"I'm Veronica's mother, by the way," she explained for Carolyn and Susan's benefit, as she and the other parents had already had a chance to get acquainted prior to the funeral service.

"Where's Mr. Jensen?" asked Carolyn.

"My husband was unable to come, but sends his regards," apologized Mrs. Jensen. "Veronica spoke highly of both of you in her letters so we feel as if we know you already."

"And I'm Lila," mentioned the girl with her. "I'm Veronica's sister." Lila looked so much like Veronica, in fact, that it was overwhelming for Carolyn and Susan to even look at her.

"We do look a lot alike," added Lila, cognizant of the effect her appearance had made. "Veronica may have mentioned that our dad is an accountant, and with April 15th being only four days off, he really couldn't get away."

"She did mention that," revealed Susan.

"And we're Joyce's parents," Mrs. Troglite introduced herself to both Susan and Carolyn.

"I understand you were there when all this happened?" questioned Mr. Troglite as he shook Carolyn's hand.

Carolyn studied him for a moment. He did look like a lecturer, but was far more direct than even Joyce had described him. "Actually, I was only nearby at the time. Until it was too late to be of much help, that is." Tears began to stream down Carolyn's cheeks.

"Dale Troglite, please!" chastised his wife. "At least introduce yourself before you start interrogating the poor girl!"

"It's okay," assured Carolyn. "You all have a right to know what happened down there."

"Unfortunately," added Susan, "even we don't know exactly what did happen down there. That's what we're hoping to find out."

"Touché," replied Dale Troglite. "Oh, these are our other five daughters. Their names each begin with a J."

"I'm Jennifer," mentioned the oldest girl among them. "I'm fifteen years old."

"And I'm Josephine," said the next girl. "I'm fourteen."

"Jasmine," nodded yet another girl. She seemed more serious than the other two. "My thirteenth birthday is next week."

"Jasmine and Joyce were very close," interjected their mother, "so this has been particularly hard on her."

"My name is Juliana, and I'm only twelve," the next sister introduced herself.

"And I'm the baby of the family," stated the final child. "My name is Jessica and I'll be in the ninth grade next year."

"Jessica's actually only eleven, but did so well on her SAT test that she'll be skipping a couple of grades," bragged Dale Troglite.

"So, you're in the sixth grade now?" questioned Susan.

"I am," replied Jessica.

"Won't that be rather difficult for a twelve-year-old to be thrown into a class of fourteen-year-olds?" quizzed Susan as she turned to Mr. Troglite.

"You must be the one that plans to be a school teacher someday," interjected Mrs. Jensen. "Veronica mentioned that in one of her letters."

"Why don't we all head up to the cafeteria?" suggested Mrs. Fredrickson.

"Just look at that line!" noticed Mr. Fredrickson. "Hey, I have an idea. While we're waiting, why don't we all go down to the beach so Carolyn and Susan can show us where it happened."

"That's not a bad idea," agreed his wife. "I'd like to see."

"That's fine with me," said Mrs. Jensen. Lila merely nodded.

"That is a good idea!" approved Dale Troglite. "I'm sure we've all read the deposition transcripts, but we would like to see the place for ourselves. Let's go!"

It was obvious that Mrs. Troglite and her daughters were accustomed to having Dale Troglite make their decisions for them.

"That is okay with you, isn't it?" inquired Mr. Fredrickson.

"Sure, that's fine," replied Mrs. Troglite. "You girls wouldn't mind going down to the beach for a few minutes, would you?"

"I definitely would like to go," informed Jasmine. The other sisters merely nodded their agreement.

Everyone then turned to Carolyn and Susan, who both seemed startled by the families' unexpected eagerness to go to the beach.

"We don't exactly have the right shoes for it," pointed out Carolyn. "Or the right clothes."

"We can just take our shoes off when we get there," suggested Dale Troglite. "Is that okay with everyone?"

Everyone merely shrugged their shoulders, obviously not too concerned about it.

"Perhaps we should wait until tomorrow morning before going down there," recommended Susan. "That way it will still be early enough in the day for the Sheriff to go there with us. And, tomorrow is only Thursday, so the Sheriff's office should be open at the regular time."

"What's that got to do with it?" frowned Dale Troglite.

"The Sheriff would need to unlock the iron-barred gate for us," revealed Carolyn. "That's the place where Joyce and Veronica's tracks led to."

"Then that's exactly the place we want to see," replied Joyce's father. "I'm sure the Sheriff thinks he did a proper search of the bunker tunnel it mentions in your deposition, but I think I'd like to see it for myself, even if the outside is all we get to see today. We definitely will go back again in the morning."

"Wouldn't anyone else around here have a key to it?" questioned Mr. Fredrickson. He suddenly seemed as anxious as Mr. Troglite to investigate the area beyond the gate.

"The Sheriff and his search party had to cut the other lock off the following day," described Susan. "No one had a key to the original lock – at least not that we know of – so the new lock was put on by him. No one else has a key, that we know of."

"What if they are still in there somewhere?" asked Veronica's mother. "And, what if they're still alive?"

"It's been nineteen days," pointed out her daughter Lila.

"Nothing has washed up on the beach anywhere around the place," informed Carolyn. "I've been down there every single day to check."

"My husband's right," agreed Mrs. Troglite. "We do need to get in there so we can see for ourselves."

"It would be too late to get the Sheriff out here today, though," Carolyn agreed with Susan. "It's already four o'clock, and their office probably closes at five. Besides, it takes half an hour to drive out here from Ocean Bluff where the Sheriff's office is located, just one way."

"Well, there's still nothing to stop us from seeing the beach around it, is there?" asked Nancy Fredrickson. "I really would like to see the place where my son died."

"Of course," agreed Carolyn. "Follow me."

404

And so it was that Carolyn and Susan found themselves walking to the beach that afternoon with the families of Steve Fredrickson, Veronica Jensen and Joyce Troglite.

Half-way down the steep rocky access road that cut through the coastal forest down to the beach below, nearly everyone in the group had already managed to remove and were carrying their shoes.

"Ouch!" complained Jasmine when she stepped down on a sharp pebble. "When do we get to the soft sand?"

"Soon," assured Carolyn.

"You'll need to watch for rocks, too," advised Susan as she noticed a run in her pantyhose. "These are toast."

"Mine, too," Carolyn whispered to Susan. "Buck up!"

"That's too bad about your other friend's mother," mentioned Nancy Fredrickson. "I know he wanted to be here."

"What friend's mother?" quizzed Carolyn.

"What was his name, dear?" asked Mrs. Fredrickson.

"Leonard?" guessed Steve Sr.

"Lenny," realized Nancy. "That's what it was."

"Lenny Owens?" grilled Carolyn.

"Yes, that was it," confirmed Nancy.

"No, I hadn't heard anything about it," responded Carolyn with a worried expression on her face. "What about his mother?"

"Dean Vandevere got a phone call about it while we were there in his office last night," described Nancy. "Apparently she died."

"How?" pressed Carolyn.

Susan gently jabbed Carolyn in the side with her elbow and shook her head.

Carolyn merely gave Susan an irritated look in response and asked again, "How did it happen?"

"He didn't tell us," replied Nancy Fredrickson.

"Perhaps his wife Linda might know something?" suggested Mr. Fredrickson.

No wonder Pete and Lenny had not been there for the funeral service today, realized Carolyn. They were undoubtedly busy attending one for their own mother – and she was like a mother to both of them from what Lenny had told her. If only Carolyn were able to console Lenny somehow during his time of grief and let him know how sorry she was to hear of his loss. She would definitely be paying Linda Vandevere a visit!

"We're here," informed Susan. "Carolyn?"

"Sorry," apologized Carolyn. "I was just thinking."

"If this is too much to ask of you," began Nancy Fredrickson, "we'll certainly understand."

"I'll be fine," responded Carolyn. "Okay then, up there on the bluff is where I sat watching them boogie board down here."

Everyone looked up to see where she was pointing.

"They came down here nearly every day to boogie board, right after their last class," mentioned Carolyn. "The ledge just inside that bunker tunnel opening is where they kept their things, so they wouldn't have to haul it all back and forth each day."

"What things?" asked Dale Troglite.

"Swimsuits, zorries, boogie boards, towels, that sort of thing," described Susan.

"Where did their stuff go?" queried Mrs. Troglite. "No shark would have taken all that!"

"That was my thought," replied Carolyn.

"Let her finish," urged Steve Fredrickson, Sr.

"Jim Otterman is one of the photography students, and his roommate Bart Higbee is a pilot," elaborated Carolyn. "They had permission to take Susan and me up for a flight while they took some photos for the upcoming yearbook."

"Except I was busy taking a make-up test for one of my classes at the time," interjected Susan, "so I wasn't with them."

"It was while we were flying over the beach that we saw the shark swimming toward Steve," related Carolyn. "He didn't even see it at first, but Joyce and Veronica sure must have."

"Why do you say that?" quizzed Dale Troglite.

"Because of the way they scrambled from the water and began running up here," replied Carolyn. "Veronica was not only an excellent swimmer, but she was an experienced lifeguard. I was in her senior lifesaving class. My guess is that she intended to grab whatever she could from that ledge to try and rescue Steve with it."

"Like what?" frowned Steve Fredrickson, Sr.

"Perhaps bungee cords tied together and hooked onto one of the boogie boards," assumed Carolyn. "They could have easily tossed it out to Steve and then pulled him in, even if he weren't able to swim on his own after being attacked like he was."

"Perhaps that's what they tried to do?" suggested Nancy.

406

"That's what we just don't know," replied Carolyn. "I had Bart land the plane just as fast as he could – and it seemed like it took him forever, though I'm sure he did his best. Once the plane was landed, I threw open the door, leaped out, and raced down here as fast as I could, down that other trail right there. I would have brought you all that way, but it's pretty steep, so I thought the access road would be safer."

"What about the guys you were with?" pressed Steve.

"Jim ran for help while Bart tied down his plane and followed after me with his medical kit," answered Carolyn. "Bart didn't even stop to do his post-flight inspection. He just came right down here."

"That really is a pretty big deal for a pilot," recognized Mr. Fredrickson. He was a pilot himself.

"What happened when you first got here?" urged Nancy.

Carolyn grew quiet and her face took on a distant expression. Tears began to flow down her cheeks again. Everyone patiently waited for her to continue.

"Steve was slowly dragging himself onto the beach," related Carolyn. "His injuries were horrible! Blood was everywhere."

"That was when Carolyn ripped the pant legs off her favorite pair of jeans to use as bandages," added Susan.

"Yes," confirmed Carolyn. "One on his right forearm, and the other on his right leg. I also tore the strap from my purse and tried to make it as tight as I could to try and stop the bleeding, and used it as a tourniquet with a small stick I found here on the beach."

"Did Bart help you with that?" asked Nancy. Being a nurse, she knew how difficult it was and how much strength it took to properly apply a tourniquet. "From the photo in the file, it looked like you did an excellent job with the tourniquet."

"That was when Steve passed," whispered Carolyn, as if she were reliving the moment. She did not seem to hear Nancy's question about the tourniquet.

"The report said you both gave him CPR," reminded Steve, Sr.

"We did," replied Carolyn. "Bart got here right as Steve died, but we gave him CPR anyway, just in case there was any way to bring him back. We continued for at least fifteen minutes or more, and were still giving him CPR when Dean Vandevere got here with Jim."

"Carolyn had blood all over her face, arms and legs," described Susan. "She was literally covered with it!"

"The Sheriff had me save all my clothes for their evidence locker," added Carolyn.

"They made her go back up to the dormitory at that point," added Susan. "To change and shower."

Nancy Fredrickson suddenly threw her arms around Carolyn and began sobbing. Steve Sr. hugged both of them and cried, too. "Thank you for what you did for our boy! We know you did all you could."

The others remained silent for several moments, listening to the sound of ocean waves against the shoreline. A lone seagull loudly cawed overhead as it flew by and heavily dropped a clam shell onto the hard surface of a large rock below. Gentle rays of sunlight reflected against the moist shell as it fell open. The seagull then circled and landed to devour its prey.

"It is beautiful here," recognized Mrs. Jensen. "I can see why Veronica loved it so much."

"After the Sheriff took Carolyn back up to the dormitory, the rest of us searched all along here until dark that day," described Susan.

"Even in the tunnel?" questioned Dale Troglite.

"Everywhere but there," replied Susan. "The Sheriff and his men were the only ones allowed inside, just in case it might be too dangerous, and because they weren't sure what might be in there. But, everyone who could came back down here the next day, and the day after that, and every day - until the search was finally called off."

"And some of us still come down here each day," added Carolyn.

"You never tried to sneak inside that tunnel anyway, just to have a look?" asked Jasmine.

"The Sheriff had someone guarding it every moment, and would lock it up at night," answered Susan. "I even snuck down here one night with that very intention."

Carolyn gave Susan a baffled look. Susan had certainly never mentioned anything to her about coming down here at night!

"Yes, we're definitely going to see the Sheriff," announced Dale Troglite, "first thing tomorrow morning."

"Yes, we are," added Steve, Sr. as he pulled away from his wife and Carolyn to approach Dale Troglite. "And if there is anything in there, we'll find it."

It was Sunday morning, April 29, 1973. The exhaustive search that Steve and Dale had made of the bunker opening and all adjoining tunnels beyond it had been fruitless. The Fredricksons were now back in South Africa, continuing their mission there. Mrs. Troglite and her daughters had safely returned to their home back east, while Dale Troglite had resumed his scheduled lecturing tour somewhere in the midwest. Mrs. Jensen and her daughter Lila were at their home in Los Angeles, but still held out hope that Susan or Carolyn might someday find Veronica for them. That hope was all they had left.

"The Bennetts are here," advised Dean Dixon's voice on the intercom to Susan and Carolyn's dormitory room.

"This should be interesting," chuckled Susan as she grabbed her huge suitcase and began shoving it toward the door, making it scoot across the floor.

"You really should get a luggage cart for that," recommended Carolyn with a smile.

"What I really could use is one of those new rolling suitcases! They just came out with 'em last year," replied Susan. "Have you seen one yet? My mother showed me hers when I went home for Christmas. My dad always likes to get her the latest new gadgets for Christmas each year. The year before that he got her a trash compactor."

"He did seem like the practical type," joked Carolyn. "Everyone should have a Rolls Royce parked in their garage."

"Well, what can I say?" smirked Susan.

Unfortunately, neither Susan nor Carolyn happened to have one of the new rolling type suitcases so were forced to struggle with what they had. "You'd better not get any ideas about hitchhiking again!" cautioned Carolyn.

"No one would ever pick us up with these huge suitcases, anyway," laughed Susan. "Hey, are you sure they'll fit in your dad's car? Is he still driving that white Dodge Dart?"

"What do you think?" replied Carolyn.

Susan merely laughed in response.

Carolyn and Susan then decided to have a race, to see who could push their suitcase down the long dormitory hallway the fastest. Due to the considerably smaller size of her suitcase, Carolyn made it first.

"How are we gonna get 'em downstairs?" questioned Susan.

"One step at a time," smirked Carolyn. It would be fun watching Susan struggle to get her gigantic suitcase down the steep staircase.

When they did finally reach the lobby downstairs, Susan and Carolyn came face-to-face with Mr. and Mrs. Bennett.

"Mom!" exclaimed Carolyn as she ran over to give her mother a big hug. "Dad," acknowledged Carolyn. Both of them merely nodded at one another.

Susan couldn't help but notice that the relationship between Mr. Bennett and his daughter was rather formal, especially compared to the spontaneous closeness that Carolyn enjoyed with her mother.

"This should be interesting, indeed," muttered Susan to herself.

"Here, let me help you with that," offered Mr. Bennett as he took Susan's suitcase and carried it outside. He then placed it into the trunk of his white Dodge Dart. It filled the entire trunk.

"What about Carolyn's suitcase?" questioned Mrs. Bennett.

"Too bad you don't have one of those luggage racks on top," commented Susan with a crooked smile.

"Perhaps they could put it on the backseat in-between them?" suggested Carolyn's mother. "It's small enough that it might just fit."

Mr. Bennett suddenly grinned at the thought of Carolyn and Susan forced to ride for four long hours with the tall suitcase between them. "I believe your mother's right. Let's give it a try."

Much to Carolyn's relief, the suitcase did fit and she would not have to leave it behind.

After everyone was seated and the doors all locked, Mr. Bennett started the engine and slowly pulled away in his white Dodge Dart.

"Thanks for inviting me to come along," mentioned Susan as she glanced at Mr. Bennett's face in the rearview mirror. She would be spending the next two days with Carolyn and her parents at their home in the valley.

"Someone's gotta keep an eye on you two," responded Mr. Bennett with a twinkle in his eyes. Those who knew him well soon realized that was how he smiled.

Susan and Carolyn quickly realized that by pushing the suitcase slightly forward, they were able to open up a two-inch space through which they could see one another as they traveled along.

"So, how are those tires?" razzed Susan.

410

"Rock-free," assured Mr. Bennett.

"Does your dad always drive this slow?" whispered Susan through the narrow space behind the suitcase.

"Always," responded Carolyn. "And he almost never stops for restroom breaks."

"That's right," recalled Susan.

"Hope you remembered to go before we left," chuckled Carolyn.

"Have you girls eaten breakfast?" Mr. Bennett suddenly asked.

"No, we haven't," answered Susan. She and Carolyn both hoped he was not planning to stop at Patty's Pancake House again!

Carolyn's father rather enjoyed taking scenic detours so he could avoid driving on major thoroughfares, whenever possible. Today he planned to do just that. According to the map Mr. Bennett had studied earlier, the alternate route would take them right past a popular cattle ranch restaurant that advertised an elaborate smorgasbord brunch.

"Where are we going?" Susan suddenly questioned. "Isn't the highway back there?"

"Another way," answered Mr. Bennett with that twinkle in his eyes again. "There's a really nice restaurant this way."

"That's not the Swedish place, is it?" questioned Mrs. Bennett.

"You'll see," assured Mr. Bennett. He was not about to give away the surprise.

Naturally, the detour took them over a barren mountain range, and through a particularly narrow stretch where it wound alongside a towering mountain range on one side and a treacherous drop-off on the other. No turnouts could be seen for miles, but there really wasn't room for one on that type of a road.

Traffic finally began to back up behind Mr. Bennett's slowly traveling vehicle. "We really should try to find a place to pull over," recommended Carolyn's mother. "There's more than five cars behind us already."

"Where would you suggest I pull over?" Mr. Bennett suddenly questioned. "It's not like there's somewhere to do it along here!"

"Calm down," urged Carolyn's mother. "I'm sure they can see that. There's bound to be a place soon."

It was more than thirty minutes longer before Mr. Bennett finally found and pulled into an acceptable turnout. Car after car drove by and honked at him, many of them shouting obscenities out their windows as they did. Eventually, a highway patrol officer pulled in behind them and came to a stop. Additional cars were still making their way past the white Dodge Dart.

Mr. Bennett turned off his engine, rolled down his window, and waited for the officer to approach.

"Is your dad wanted for something?" whispered Susan, through the narrow space behind the suitcase.

"Not that I know of," replied Carolyn. She was truly grateful to be on the side of the car shielded from view behind the suitcase. Susan, on the other hand, was on the other side where all the angry drivers were passing by and glaring at everyone else inside the vehicle. Thankfully, the obscenities had ceased now that the highway patrol officer was present, though a few of the drivers still managed to show their middle finger to the white Dodge Dart from behind the officer's back.

"May I see your driver's license, Sir?" asked the officer.

Mr. Bennett slowly reached into his back pocket, removed his wallet, took out his driver's license, and handed it to the officer.

"Will you please step out of the vehicle, Sir?" instructed the patrol officer.

Mr. Bennett slowly opened his door and climbed from the vehicle, waiting to hear what else the policeman had to say.

"Better close your door, Sir," recommended the officer.

"We're not gonna have to get out, too, are we?" panicked Susan. It was bad enough that all the angry drivers passing them could see her face through the back passenger window!

Carolyn merely held her finger to her lips to indicate silence. She wanted to overhear what the officer had to say, if she could, and slowly rolled down her window to make that possible.

"Mr. Bennett, are you aware of the speed limit here?" questioned the highway patrol officer.

"Probably about 35 miles per hour," guessed Mr. Bennett. It had been quite a few miles since the last speed sign and he really didn't recall what had been posted.

"The speed limit here is 55 miles per hour, Sir," informed the highway patrol officer.

Mr. Bennett merely nodded.

412

"Are you aware that any car having more than five vehicles behind it is required to pull into the first available turnout to let them pass?" pressed the officer.

"Yes, Sir," responded Mr. Bennett.

"The problem here," explained the officer, "is that you had about 120 angry vehicles behind you. That was when I stopped counting. And there were at least five other places you could have pulled off the road before this."

"I didn't see any," indicated Mr. Bennett.

"Well, they were there," advised the officer. "I must say, this is the first time I've ever given someone a moving violation for IMPEDING TRAFFIC." The officer tried to suppress a smile as he pulled out his tablet and began writing. "But, you give me no choice."

"I'm not signing that!" announced Mr. Bennett.

"In that case," suggested the officer as he pulled out a pair of handcuffs, "I can certainly take you in. Naturally, since it is a Sunday, the courthouse is closed, so you would be spending the night in jail."

Mr. Bennett was clearly quite angry but said nothing more.

"The choice is yours, Sir," explained the officer. "You can sign the ticket now and appear later on your own recognizance, if that's how you choose to respond to this – as opposed to merely paying the fine – or I can arrest you and take you to jail now. What's it gonna be?"

Without comment, Mr. Bennett grabbed the pen and tablet from the officer and signed the citation before handing them back to him.

The highway patrol officer fought to suppress a grin as he ripped off the ticket and handed it to Mr. Bennett. "Have a nice day, Mr. Bennett. And please, try and keep up with the flow of traffic."

Mr. Bennett merely nodded as he folded the ticket and put it into his polo shirt pocket before climbing back into the white Dodge Dart.

"Oh, my God!" Susan only mouthed the words to Carolyn through the narrow opening behind the suitcase. "How embarrassing!"

It was almost lunch by the time the Bennett family car reached Morris Ranch, a popular cattle ranch restaurant that Carolyn's father had seen advertised earlier that day while en route to Oceanview Academy to pick up his daughter and her friend Susan.

"Hey look!" pointed out Susan as Carolyn's father pulled into the parking lot. "There's our friend, Mr. Highway Patrolman."

The officer had already gotten out of his patrol car and was headed toward the restaurant door, most likely for lunch.

Mr. Bennett slowly cruised the parking lot, searching for a space. The only spot available just happened to be right next to the highway patrol car.

"Better make sure it's not a handicap space," razzed Susan. "You wouldn't want him to give you another ticket."

Carolyn gave Susan a reproving glance through the crack behind the suitcase and silently mouthed the words, "Really?"

"Maybe we should find another place to eat," advised Carolyn's mother. She appeared worried.

"Just where did you have in mind?" questioned Mr. Bennett as he pulled into the spot.

There had not been any other establishments whatsoever along the desolate but well-traveled shortcut Mr. Bennett had chosen to take.

"Maybe there's something up ahead?" suggested Carolyn's mother rather sheepishly.

"I doubt it," replied Mr. Bennett as he shut off the engine.

"We really are out in the middle of nowhere, aren't we?" chuckled Susan.

"We can certainly wait until tonight to eat, if that's what you'd prefer," proposed Carolyn's father.

"This looks good to me!" Carolyn spoke up. "I'm famished!" Carolyn also had to use the restroom and knew her father would not be likely to stop again until reaching their destination.

The City of Ashton where the Bennett family lived was located in a desert region still two hours ahead. The Morris Ranch restaurant was located about half-way between the City of Ashton and Oceanview Academy, and was the only place to get food or gas for a hundred miles in either direction.

"You're not the one all those people saw sitting back here, either!" whispered Susan to Carolyn through the narrow space behind the suitcase.

"Wanna sit on this side of the suitcase after our breakfast?" suggested Carolyn.

414

"I'm sure we'll all feel better after we've had something to eat," mentioned Carolyn's mother. She was well aware that everyone was cranky because they had not eaten yet that day.

"Hopefully nobody will come along and key your door or slash your tires," remarked Susan.

"Why would you say that?" frowned Mr. Bennett.

"Who do you think all these other cars belong to, anyway?" asked Susan as she motioned toward the other cars in the parking lot. "These are all the people who were honking and cursing at you as they drove past you back there!"

"Susan may be right," waffled Carolyn's mother.

"Well, it's a good thing we're parked beside Mr. Highway Patrolman then, isn't it?" retorted Carolyn's father as he opened his door to get out.

Carolyn was stunned by the bold manner in which Susan had bantered with her father, something she would never have dared to do!

"Besides," added Mr. Bennett as the four of them approached the restaurant door, "we have just as much right to eat here as anyone else. And, if Mr. Highway patrolman doesn't help us out – should we need it – I can be sure to mention that to the Judge, too, when I show up to contest his traffic ticket!"

"What if he tries to get all 120 of the other drivers as witnesses?" teased Susan as they walked inside. "What if he's in there now getting their names so they can testify?"

"I seriously doubt it," snickered Mr. Bennett.

"Hello," greeted a hostess with the name Cyndi on her badge.

"Table for four," indicated Carolyn's father.

"Your name, Sir?" quizzed Cyndi.

"Bennett," answered Carolyn's father.

The Highway Patrolman who had given Mr. Bennett the ticket earlier was almost done loading up his plate in the smorgasbord line when he heard the name Bennett and immediately turned to look.

"Hello again," greeted the officer with a smirk on his face as he walked past the Bennett group on his way to a table nearby.

Several of the other customers then recognized the man with the bright orange hair that had been stopped by the officer earlier.

"Oh, God!" muttered Susan. "Now they all know who we are!"

"And no suitcase to hide behind," added Carolyn.

"The sooner we eat, then, the sooner we can be on our way," prompted Carolyn's father as he handed each of them a plate.

"Thanks," mumbled Susan as she took the plate from him and grabbed a tray and some silverware. Carolyn did likewise.

Susan and Carolyn rapidly loaded whatever looked quick and easy to eat onto their plates and began to look for a table.

"There's one right over here," called Mr. Bennett.

It was right next to the Highway Patrolman's small table, the kind intended for solitary customers eating alone, and was on the end, right next to the family section where Mr. Bennett had already pulled out a chair and was sitting down.

Carolyn and Susan exchanged a look of dismay. It seemed as if Mr. Bennett was enjoying their predicament.

"I just can't seem to get away from you Mr. Bennett, can I?" grinned the officer as he watched Carolyn's father and his party sit down at the table beside him.

"Guess you're just not fast enough," joked Mr. Bennett, which was rare for him.

"Indeed," nodded the officer as he slapped a ten-dollar bill on the counter by his check and suddenly left.

"He's checking out your car," noticed Carolyn's mother, who could easily see the parking lot outside through the large picture windows on the restaurant from where she sat.

"Maybe he's checking for rocks in your tires," smiled Susan.

"Good," acknowledged Carolyn's father. "He's welcome to keep any he finds."

"So, how's Socky?" Carolyn suddenly asked, to change the subject. Socky was her seven-year-old lilac-point Siamese cat. Carolyn missed Socky terribly and was anxious to see her again.

"Socky's doing just fine," beamed Mrs. Bennett. She, too, was glad to see the subject change directions.

"So, how's Jim Otterman doing?" asked Carolyn's father.

Carolyn nearly knocked over her orange juice upon hearing the question, and steadied the glass just in time. "What do you mean?"

"Your boyfriend, Jim Otterman," clarified Mr. Bennett. "That is the boy you went to the prom with, wasn't it?"

"Jim Otterman?" repeated Carolyn, with a questioning look at Susan. "Last I saw him, he seemed just fine."

"I mentioned to your father that you were planning on going to the prom with Jim," explained Susan. "When he bought us the dresses."

"I see," nodded Carolyn. She could see the smug smile on her father's face but chose to ignore it, for now. Carolyn would definitely be having a word with Susan about this!

"Are you all right, dear?" asked Carolyn's mother.

"I'll be fine now that I've eaten," promised Carolyn. "I'm just not used to waiting until almost noon to eat breakfast."

"I knew I should have brought a picnic basket along," fretted Carolyn's mother.

"We're good now," assured Susan.

Susan never had told Carolyn about her conversation with Mr. Bennett at the Boardwalk, or how she had promised to make sure Carolyn went to the prom with Jim Otterman – instead of Lenny Owens – in exchange for him buying the prom dresses for both of them. Now, was Mr. Bennett about to throw Susan under the bus? And how would she ever explain it to Carolyn?

"Perhaps we should visit the ladies' room before we leave," recommended Carolyn. She needed to isolate Susan so she could speak with her alone about the Jim Otterman situation.

"That's a good idea," recognized Mrs. Bennett. "I think I'll join you. It'll be at least two more hours until we get to Ashton, and maybe more the way your father drives."

"You don't think he'll be checking his tires again before we leave, do you?" joked Susan.

"He might, you never know," replied Carolyn's mother.

Mrs. Bennett walked with Susan and Carolyn to the ladies' restroom and offered to let them go first. Carolyn, however, insisted that her mother go first instead. That way, she still might have an opportunity to talk with Susan alone.

Once Carolyn's mother had finished using the restroom and washed her hands, she said, "I'll meet you two at the car."

Carolyn then blocked Susan's way to prevent her from leaving, too. "I'd like a word with you before we go back out there."

"I can explain," responded Susan.

"This better be good," fumed Carolyn. "Jim Otterman?"

"It was the only way I could get your father to agree to buy us the dresses," explained Susan. "He made me promise I'd find you someone else to go to the prom with so you wouldn't be going out with 'that black kid' anymore – his words, not mine."

"And how did my dad just happen to know about the name Jim Otterman?" grilled Carolyn. "He certainly didn't come up with the name Jim Otterman out of thin air, not unless someone else told him about it, and that someone obviously was you!"

"I may have mentioned to him that I knew of someone else who was interested in you, someone named Jim Otterman," admitted Susan.

"So, let me get this straight," began Carolyn. "You talked my father into buying those dresses for us in exchange for agreeing to make sure I went to the prom with Jim Otterman instead of Lenny Owens?"

"Not exactly," argued Susan.

"Oh, I think that's exactly how it was," differed Carolyn. "In fact, all that information you fed Jim Otterman about me in your Biology class was deliberate, wasn't it? No wonder poor Jim thought he had a chance with me! And it was all so you could help my dad to keep me and Lenny apart! What were you thinking?"

"I'm so sorry," apologized Susan. "I had no idea it would come to any of this."

"And it wasn't bad enough that the entire school thought I was going out with the little creep," continued Carolyn. "Now, even my parents think Jim Otterman is my boyfriend! How dare you!"

"Are you girls all right in here?" questioned Mrs. Bennett, who had come back into the ladies' restroom to find out what was taking Carolyn and Susan so long. "Your father is in the car with the engine running. Let's go."

Carolyn and Susan silently followed Mrs. Bennett to the white Dodge Dart in the parking lot and got inside. Neither of them said a single word for the remainder of the journey.

It was obvious to Carolyn's parents that something was amiss between them, but they had no idea what it could be.

The City of Ashton was surrounded by crops at every border, particularly grapes and oranges, but also almonds, cotton, peaches, corn and cantaloupes. Like an oasis in the midst of an otherwise dry prairie land, the agricultural opportunities in Ashton had originally drawn immigrants from as far away as Russia, Germany, Japan and Armenia.

Irrigation canals dating back to 1875 skirted and crisscrossed the entire area, most of them lined with palms, eucalyptus and other drought resistant trees. But, it was the Central Valley Railroad Company who had first staked its claim upon the barren valley plains in 1872. Chinese railroad workers became a common sight by 1875. Russian and German cattle ranchers, as well as Japanese farmers, also made an impact upon the newly established agricultural community.

By 1900, the City of Ashton had managed to draw in over 12,000 residents. Many renowned wine cellars established and maintained by skillful Armenian vineyard keepers and wine masters had sprung into existence almost overnight. By 1956, the construction industry was in full swing, and just barely getting started. By 1970, the City of Ashton was home to more than 400,000 people, a major university, the best zoo for miles around, and every other amenity expected in a city its size.

Unlike the crowded metropolis of Ocean Bay, most homes in Ashton were single story dwellings with half acre yards surrounding them, allowing for a comfortable distance between each home.

Susan marveled at the immense vastness of Ashton, especially the lush landscaping in each yard, particularly in such an otherwise desert-like environment.

"Don't they ever run out of water here?" Susan finally asked.

"That's what all the canals are for," informed Mr. Bennett. He was proud of his hometown heritage, and was directly descended from some of its original pioneer inhabitants.

"How long does it take to drive across a town this size?" questioned Susan.

"Depends on whether you're on a major thoroughfare or in one of the neighborhoods," replied Mr. Bennett.

"How far until we get to your house?" Susan decided to be direct. She needed desperately to use the restroom again. Carolyn certainly had been right about her father not stopping, no matter how many hints were given by his passengers.

"Would you like a quick tour of the city first?" offered Carolyn's father. "There's actually quite a lot to see."

"Maybe we could do that later," suggested Carolyn's mother. "I'm sure everyone else is anxious to get there and stretch their legs."

Mr. Bennett merely nodded and drove until reaching a relatively new tract home development of upper middle-class homes.

"This is known as Little Armenia," informed Mr. Bennett.

"Most of our neighbors are actually from Armenia," volunteered Carolyn, for Susan's benefit.

"Ar-what?" questioned Susan.

"Armenia," interjected Mr. Bennett.

"It's over by Turkey, near Russia," elaborated Carolyn. "Three of my best friends are Armenian. Rosy, Anny and Dani Sumarian live right over there, across the street."

Susan merely nodded as Carolyn's father slowed down to pull into the cement driveway leading onto his property.

"There's their grandpa now," pointed out Carolyn. "He speaks nothing but Armenian, and mostly just walks up and down the sidewalk each day, to the end of the block and back. He's almost a hundred."

"That's rather odd," commented Susan as Mr. Bennett shut off the engine to his white Dodge Dart.

"Not really," interjected Carolyn's mother. "The poor man was in a Russian prison camp before coming here, so having the freedom to come and go is probably what keeps him going."

"And this must be your house here?" approved Susan as all of them got out of the car in front of the mauve colored home with burgundy trim. It was in immaculate condition, as was its well-kept yard.

"I can't believe how big the yards are!" exclaimed Susan.

"Most of the homes up in Ocean Bay don't even have yards," recalled Carolyn.

"Not very many," smiled Susan. "None with yards big enough to have lawns or gardens like this in them."

"Վերադարձեք այստեղ!" shouted a middle-aged Armenian woman next door, who was chasing a lively Cocker Spaniel dog across her front yard with a broom.

"That's Mrs. Atasgarian," advised Mr. Bennett with a twinkle in his eyes. "She's always chasing that stupid mutt out of her yard."

"Ոնզի, գնացեք ձեր շուն! Դա գնացել է դեպի հարեւանի կրկին," screamed Mrs. Sumarian from across the street.

"She's probably calling for Rosy to come out and get her dog again," snickered Carolyn. "That thing's always getting out."

420

"And one of these days it's going to dig enough holes to knock down someone's fence," guessed Carolyn's father. "Maybe then they'll take the leash law seriously, once Code Enforcement pays them a visit."

"Որտեղ է Ռոզի?" hollered Mrs. Sumarian.

"I got it, Mama," answered a handsome young Armenian boy, about thirteen years of age. "Look! Carolyn's back!"

The Bennett family smiled and waved at their neighbors from across the street.

"Rosy and Anny are both gone to Armenian Camp this week," called Dani as he retrieved the runaway dog. "Who's your friend?"

"This is Susan," called Carolyn.

"Hello!" Susan rewarded Dani with one of her flirtatious smiles, something which was clearly not appreciated by his mother.

"Yeah, yeah," nodded his mother. "Բարեւ!"

"What did she say?" questioned Susan.

"She says hello!" grinned Dani as he flirted back with Susan. The exchange did not go unnoticed by Carolyn's father.

"Dani's mother understands English flawlessly," explained Carolyn as they removed their suitcases from the car and began carrying them toward the Bennett home.

"She just can't speak it," added Mr. Bennett with a twinkle in his eyes. Having Susan here should prove interesting, to say the least.

"It must be a lot of work to keep all this up," assumed Susan as they entered the Bennett home.

"Especially mowing the lawns," commented Carolyn. "My room is the last one on the right, down the hall."

The 2,300 square foot, single story home was neat and clean inside, as well. So much so, in fact, that it did not have that "lived in" look that so many homes often have. Absolutely nothing was out of place, and the smell of cleaners distinct.

"We'll have dinner at six," advised Carolyn's mother.

"Can we do anything to help?" offered Susan.

"Your job will be to clean up afterwards," informed Mr. Bennett with a slight grin. "You girls go relax and make yourselves at home."

"Thanks," smiled Susan.

"That's the living room over there, just past the kitchen," indicated Carolyn as she struggled to pick up and carry her suitcase.

Susan bent down to get a better grip on her gigantic suitcase from the side so she could scoot it down the long hallway.

"I wouldn't recommend scooting it," cautioned Carolyn.

"That's right," confirmed Carolyn's father from behind them. "I'm very particular about my hardwood floors."

"You wouldn't happen to have a dolly or a luggage cart, would you?" asked Susan.

Without further comment, Carolyn's father picked up Susan's suitcase and carried it to the end of the hall.

"Okay, then," grinned Susan.

"The room on the right is mine," indicated Carolyn as she carried her suitcase down the long hall.

"The other one's theirs?" questioned Susan as she nodded at the room immediately across the hall from Carolyn's room.

"It is," replied Carolyn.

"No sneaking out in the middle of the night for you!" whispered Susan with a crooked smile.

"The floor creaks in some places, too," informed Carolyn.

"Dead giveaway, every time," chuckled Susan as she and Carolyn carried their suitcases into Carolyn's room and plopped them onto her queen size bed.

"We're both sleeping in here?" quizzed Susan.

"Unless you'd like to sleep on the sliding Chesterfield couch out in the living room," suggested Carolyn.

"Is it comfortable?" pressed Susan.

"It belonged to my great grandmother, and folds down sideways into a bed," described Carolyn. "And no, it is not very comfortable. In fact, it's about as hard as a rock, unless you're lucky enough to find yourself sleeping on one of the springs."

"We can't both sleep in the same bed in here," objected Susan. "Look how small it is!"

"It's a queen size bed," pointed out Carolyn.

"What about that other room, the one next to this one?" queried Susan. "Isn't that a guest room?"

"My father uses it as a den," revealed Carolyn uncomfortably. "Actually, it's more like a home office of sorts."

"Your dad has a business at home, too?" Susan was surprised.

"No, it's just where he does his bills and stuff," clarified Carolyn. "Or, calls me in to sit down and get lectured, whenever he feels the need for it. Kind of like going to Dean Dixon's office, but not as pleasant."

"How could that be possible?" snickered Susan as she opened her suitcase and pulled out something more comfortable to change into.

Carolyn quickly closed the door to her bedroom, in case her father should come back down the hall while Susan was changing. "That's also where my dad keeps all his belts."

"His belts?" frowned Susan. "Why would he keep them in there? Oh my God! He doesn't beat you with them, does he?"

"Not very often," answered Carolyn with a somber expression.

"No wonder you're not comfortable joking around with your dad," realized Susan. "I had no idea."

Carolyn's father had already left to go outside and water his huge yard, and could be seen through Carolyn's bedroom window. "That's usually my job, when I'm here."

"Mowing and watering, too?" probed Susan.

"And pulling weeds, or whatever else they decide needs to be done," elaborated Carolyn. "When I'm not in here studying."

"Is that your cat out there?" pointed out Susan as she saw a beautiful lilac-point Siamese cat stretching and yawning out in the back yard, making her way toward the house. "Your dad just tried to squirt it with the hose!"

"Socky!" exclaimed Carolyn. "Come on, I'll show you the yard now. And you can meet her."

Susan hurried after Carolyn as she raced down the hall, through the spacious living room, and into the sprawling back yard.

Carolyn darted over to pick up and hug her beloved pet Socky, and showered her with kisses.

Startled by her absentee human's unexpected appearance, the animal struggled to get away, jumped back down, and made a beeline for the house.

"Socky! Come back!" called Carolyn as she chased after her.

"She'll be waiting for you," assured Mr. Bennett as he handed the running garden hose to Carolyn and then headed for the house.

"Looks like you've got your work cut out for you," grinned Susan as she headed for a comfortable looking hammock on the long, covered deck which extended the entire length of the home.

"I've already done the bottle brush plants, but everything else still needs to be watered," mentioned Mr. Bennett as he opened the door to go back inside. Socky chose that moment to dash inside, as well.

The back yard alone was about 75 feet long and also just as wide, with a huge mulberry tree in the middle of it. "Is that your tree house?" asked Susan.

"It was," admitted Carolyn. The tree house itself was nothing more than a few old bed boards nailed together in the crux of the tree's upper branches. "There used to be a thick rope hanging down with knots tied every eighteen inches, to climb up on."

"What kind of tree is that one over there?" inquired Susan.

"The tall one with the white flowers and bean pods on it?" chuckled Carolyn. "We call it the bean tree. The other really tall tree beyond it is a Ponderosa pine."

Once Carolyn was done watering the big trees in the middle of her parents' sprawling lawn, she proceeded to water the row of oleander bushes at the rear of the big yard. There were twelve of them, all in bloom, some pink and some white.

"You're so lucky to have a yard like this!" admired Susan. "It's like having your very own park."

"And being the groundskeeper, too!" added Carolyn.

Opposite the bottle brush plants was a row of rhododendron bushes, interspaced with tulips, daffodils and other bulbs that were just now coming into bloom. Surrounding part of the spacious covered deck - where Susan was busy lounging in the swinging hammock - was a series of trellises on which grew jasmine, wisteria and honeysuckle vines. Near the back, just in front of the oleander bushes was a huge cement slab into which was mounted a permanent clothesline.

Though the first electric clothes dryer had been available to the public since 1938, Mr. Bennett was somewhat of a utilitarian and prided himself in having his family do some things the old fashioned way. An automatic dishwasher was yet another modern convenience lacking in the Bennett home. Hence, the grin on Mr. Bennett's face earlier when informing Susan that she would be cleaning up after dinner.

"How come your dad doesn't just get some automatic sprinklers installed?" questioned Susan as she watched Carolyn roll up and put away the hose.

"Because he doesn't think they're necessary," replied Carolyn as she sat down to rest on a chaise lounge beside the hammock.

"Hey, I'm really sorry about what happened earlier," mentioned Susan. "I had no right to make a deal with your dad like that, and I don't blame you for being angry with me."

"Hey, you did what you thought you had to do at the time," admitted Carolyn. "And, it's probably the only way he would have bought the dresses for us anyway."

"Have you tried it on recently?" grinned Susan. "Just to see if it still fits?"

"I never want to wear that dress again!" assured Carolyn. "Too many bad memories associated with it."

"Understandable," said Susan. "Say, I wonder how Lenny and Pete are doing by now?"

"Hopefully we'll get a chance to find out when we get back," anticipated Carolyn. "It sure would have been nice to know why Lenny and Pete weren't at the funeral that day, before finding out after the fact from the visiting families!"

"I know," agreed Susan. "What did your parents say when you told them about Steve dying on the beach like that?"

"I haven't," replied Carolyn. "Nor do I intend to."

"But, why?" pressed Susan. "They would be proud of how you handled everything."

"My dad would somehow use it as an excuse to keep me from going back," believed Carolyn. "He'd triumphantly tell me how dangerous it proves the school really is, and I'd probably never get to see Lenny again!"

"That's ridiculous!" objected Susan.

"Shhh! Here he comes," warned Carolyn. "My dad always likes to come out and admire the yard about this time of day, right before he goes in for dinner."

Susan and Carolyn watched while Mr. Bennett proceeded to inspect his yard, proudly admiring everything.

Suddenly, a commotion could be heard coming from the front yard on the other side of the house. "Sounds like Rosy's dog is loose again," guessed Carolyn.

"Maybe Dani might come over to get it again?" smiled Susan hopefully.

"Susan! He's only thirteen years old!" chastened Carolyn.

"Most women end up marrying men an average of two years younger than they are, did you know that?" informed Susan.

Just then, Carolyn's mother walked up. "That's true, Carolyn's father is two years younger than me."

"See!" smirked Susan triumphantly.

"Dinner's ready!" called Mrs. Bennett, loudly enough for her husband to hear.

Before Mr. Bennett had a chance to respond, Mrs. Atasgarian could be heard screaming in Armenian while Rosy Sumarian's dog raced through her yard and successfully made it to the back. Swatting repeatedly at the animal with her broom, Mrs. Atasgarian somehow managed to miss and hit the fence instead.

Already loosened by previous dog-digging attempts, the fence had been on the verge of collapse for some time. Mr. Bennett helplessly watched as the entire south side of his backyard fence fell to the ground with a mighty crash, smashing most of his bottle brush plants when it did. "Get that filthy mutt out of here!" shouted Mr. Bennett.

Mrs. Atasgarian then hollered back at him in Armenian.

"Oh, shut up!" commanded Mr. Bennett.

Susan and Carolyn began laughing uncontrollably as the dog found its way into the Bennett yard and began racing back and forth, circling and barking viciously at Carolyn's dad. Mr. Bennett and the dog clearly had a history. Even Carolyn's mother began laughing.

Mr. Bennett furiously marched to his garage and brought out his flat blade shovel. Seeming to sense Mr. Bennett's evil intentions toward it, the dog quickly let out one last parting bark before zooming from the yard and then back out into the front.

The dog was so upset that even Dani had been unable to grab it in time to prevent it from racing up the street. Carolyn and Susan followed her parents to the front yard.

"Carolyn!" called Dani. "Can you help me go look for her?"

"Sure," agreed Carolyn. "Let me get my bike."

Carolyn hurried to the garage to get her new Schwinn racing bike, that she had ridden only twice before leaving for Oceanview Academy last fall.

"Mom, have you seen my bike?" questioned Carolyn. "And, can Susan borrow yours? We need to help Dani get the dog back."

"We were going to tell you about your bike at dinner tonight," hesitated Mrs. Bennett.

"What about my bike?" demanded Carolyn. "He sold it, didn't he? He sold my brand new bike!"

"No, he didn't sell it, sweetheart," continued Mrs. Bennett. "Your father just forgot to close the garage door one night, so someone came along and stole it. We made a police report the very next day."

"What?" Carolyn could not believe what she was hearing. "And you never even bothered to tell me about it?"

"They stole our bikes, too," added Carolyn's mother. "I'm so sorry we didn't tell you sooner, but your daddy wanted to wait until he could tell you about it in person."

"I sure hope it's not true what they say about things happening in threes," piped in Susan with an amused grin.

Susan and Carolyn were both exhausted and still asleep the following morning when the noise outside began. Socky was asleep on the queen sized bed in-between them.

"What in the hell was that?" demanded Susan.

Carolyn got up and raced over to her bedroom window, pulled back the thick curtains, and looked outside. "Wow!"

"What is it?" pressed Susan as she got up and came over to the window to see what Carolyn was looking at.

"Looks like an entire construction crew out there working on the fence," noted Carolyn. "I count five guys."

"This should be interesting," Susan grinned a crooked smile. "We need to get showered and dressed."

"Sounds like my dad is already in the shower," mentioned Carolyn.

"Where's your other bathroom?" persisted Susan. "And I need to use it right now!"

"I'm afraid that's the only one," regretted Carolyn.

"What? There's only ONE restroom, and your dad's in there taking a shower?" Susan shook her head. "What are we going to do? It's not like we can go out and take a tinkle somewhere in the yard with all those hot looking construction guys running around back there!"

"We have an old coffee can in the garage," offered Carolyn. "My Grandma Bennett has me bring it along when we go camping, to use in the middle of the night as a pee pot."

"A pee pot?" Susan began laughing uncontrollably. "Don't make me laugh right now!"

"I'll be right back," informed Carolyn. "I'm going for the can."

Carolyn raced for the garage, retrieved the old coffee can, and returned to her bedroom. "Here! At least they didn't steal that, too!"

"Even bike thieves have to pee sometimes," roared Susan as she took the can from Carolyn and proceeded to use it. "I hope you brought some toilet paper, too!"

Carolyn took a deep breath and raced again from the room, this time to a hall closet where the extra toilet paper rolls were kept. Fortunately, they were still kept there.

After they had both finally showered and gotten dressed, Carolyn's dad regrettably informed them that they would not be going to the park as planned.

"Now what?" Susan wanted to know.

"He won't leave, not with the construction going on," answered Carolyn. "We could go for a walk around the neighborhood, and see if we can help Dani find Rosy's dog."

"Oh, boy!" Susan rolled her eyes.

"Perhaps when my mom gets home from work later, we can get her to take us to the mall," suggested Carolyn.

"I think we should play a little game," decided Susan. "Do you have a phone in your room?"

"Actually, I do," revealed Carolyn as she opened a small pink cupboard in the corner of her room and brought out a pink princess phone. "My dad made me buy it myself, and it's just an extension line, but it's a phone."

"Do you have a phone book handy?" questioned Susan.

"I'll be right back," replied Carolyn.

Once Carolyn had returned with the Bennett family phone book, which Mr. Bennett normally kept in a particular drawer in the kitchen beneath the old rotary dial wall phone, Susan took the book from her and set it down on the bed.

"What do you have in mind?" wondered Carolyn.

"Let's start in the D section," selected Susan.

"Why there?" inquired Carolyn.

"D is for dare," smirked Susan with a mischievous look. "You pick a number, any number, and dial it for me. I'll do the talking."

"Oh, Susan, I don't think we should be doing this," resisted Carolyn. "What if it's someone we know?"

"Then we just hang up!" chuckled Susan. "Go ahead, dial."

Carolyn then began dialing one of the phone numbers on the rotary dial princess phone. "Is it ringing?"

"It is," replied Susan.

"Hello?" came a man's voice at the other end.

Susan then tried to sound sophisticated and advised the man, "I know who you are, and I saw what you did."

"Really?" laughed the man before hanging up.

"He sounded annoyed," revealed Susan.

"Let's not do this," implored Carolyn. "I don't have a good feeling about it."

"What else are we gonna do around here?" shrugged Susan. "Go play with Dani? Hey, that might not be such a bad idea."

"All right, here's another number," indicated Carolyn. "It says the person's name is D. Dixon."

"Oooh! Just like in Dean Dixon," howled Susan. "Maybe it's one of her relatives."

Carolyn quickly dialed the number, but was not happy about it. The phone began ringing. An older woman answered. "Hello?"

"Yes, is this D. Dixon?" inquired Susan in a serious voice.

"Yes?" the older woman sounded frail. Susan was holding the phone in such a way that she and Carolyn could both hear the other party. "Who is this?"

Susan quickly hung up and then burst into laughter. "Let me dial one, and you can do the talking."

"No!" objected Carolyn. "This was your idea."

"Just one more, and then we can go help Dani find his dog," promised Susan. "Okay?"

"Very well," Carolyn finally agreed. "Just one."

Susan slowly perused the phone book until coming to a John Dick. "Let's call Mr. Dick."

"You're terrible," advised Carolyn, who was hardly able to hold back the laughter now herself.

Susan slowly and deliberately dialed the number, waited for it to begin ringing, and handed the phone to Carolyn.

"Hello?" came a man's voice. He sounded like a man in his mid-twenties. "Can I help you?"

"John?" questioned Carolyn.

"Yes, this is John," replied the voice. "Who is this?"

"You don't remember me?" responded Carolyn.

Susan was rolling on the floor with laughter, holding her hand over her own mouth to keep from making any sound.

"How can I remember you if you don't tell me who you are?" bantered the man on the other end of the line.

"This is Susan," informed Carolyn.

Susan's eyes got wide and her mouth dropped open. She could not believe that Carolyn had actually used her real name!

"Susan who?" pressed the man.

"From last night," advised Carolyn.

"At the store?" responded the man.

"Yes," answered Carolyn.

"What did he say?" whispered Susan as she came close to listen in on the conversation.

"Do your parents know what you girls are doing?" the man suddenly asked, with an amused chuckle.

Carolyn immediately hung up the phone.

"Why did you hang up?" demanded Susan.

"He knew what we were doing," countered Carolyn.

"Call him back!" urged Susan.

"No," replied Carolyn. "I'll tell you what, if you still want to call him later when we get back, we can call him then."

"All right," acquiesced Susan.

"I'm going over to help Dani find that dog," informed Carolyn. "Come on, it will be fun. Perhaps you'll get to meet some of the construction crew when we go out there."

Susan slowly began to smile. "Okay, let's go."

Dani Sumarian peeked through the front curtains of his parents' house and grinned with delight when he saw Carolyn and her friend Susan approaching the front door.

Dani had known Carolyn since 1962 when the Bennett family first moved onto their street. Dani had only been three years old at the time. His sisters Rosy and Anny were Carolyn's very best friends, so she had spent many hours at the Sumarian home over the years.

Next week was Dani's fourteenth birthday, and perhaps now Carolyn would finally notice him in the way he had always hoped. True, her friend Susan was quite attractive, but she simply was not Carolyn, and Dani had been secretly in love with Carolyn from afar for as long as he could remember.

"I'm not sure if this is such a good idea," Carolyn suddenly hesitated, "but I know how important Rosy's dog is to her."

"Well, it was your idea to come over here," reminded Susan.

"It's just that I usually don't come over here unless Rosy or Anny is around," clarified Carolyn.

"Why?" frowned Susan.

Carolyn blushed deeply and then explained, "It's Dani. He's had a crush on me for years."

"Nothing wrong with that," teased Susan. "Dani's not a bad looking kid for his age, either."

"I just don't want to lead him on, or give Dani the wrong idea," explained Carolyn. "You know, give him false hope, or encourage him in any way. Then, he'll never get the hint."

"So?" snickered Susan. "You'll be gone again after tomorrow anyway. What difference does it make?"

They had reached the Sumarians' front porch, so Carolyn whispered, "Dani often just stands out here and stares at our house, but only when I'm in the kitchen doing the dishes each night where he can see me through the window."

"A regular peeping Dani?" chuckled Susan.

"Shhh!" cautioned Carolyn as the door suddenly opened without them bothering to knock.

"Carolyn!" acknowledged Dani with an adoring smile. "And Susan, was it?"

"Did you ever find Rosy's dog?" asked Carolyn.

"Finally, yes," reported Dani. "Won't you come in?" He seemed far too anxious for Carolyn's liking.

"We'd be delighted," accepted Susan, before Carolyn could decline. Susan then followed Dani inside.

"Ինչպես զեղեցիկ եք տիկնայք կարող է գալ ավելի է ասել բարեւ," greeted Dani's grandfather from the couch. He had just gotten back from one of his daily walks up and down the street.

"Grandpa would like to know if you can stay for lunch," lied Dani. He knew his Grandpa could not understand a word of English, and that neither Carolyn nor Susan would know the difference.

"Mama?" called Dani in English. "Grandpa has invited Carolyn and her friend Susan to stay for lunch."

"Համոզված եք, որ?" questioned Mrs. Sumarian suspiciously as she came into the front room wiping her hands on an apron that she was wearing. "Կամ էլ դուք պարզապես կատարել է, որ մինչեւ փորձեք եւ ստանալ նրանց մնալ?" This would not be the first time Dani had stretched the truth in order to persuade the Bennett girl to hang around. Not only that, Dani's mother was not certain that she approved of Susan, either. Susan seemed even more forward than most American girls, and even those were bad enough.

"He did," assured Dani uncomfortably.

Turning to her father-in-law, Mrs. Sumarian then questioned, "Արդյոք դուք հրավիրում այդ աղջիկներին է մնալ Ընդմիշում?"

"Yes, lunch," replied Mr. Sumarian in broken English. Even though he could say yes or no, and repeat some words, that was the extent of his American vocabulary. Still, despite what everyone believed, he actually understood more than he let on.

"Very well," replied Mrs. Sumarian. "Please stay for lunch."

Grandpa Sumarian was well aware of Dani's infatuation with Carolyn. After all, she was a beautiful girl, and he saw no harm in helping to further Dani's cause.

"Այստեղ, դուք կարող եք տեղադրել թիթեղները է սեղանի վրա," instructed Dani's mother as she grabbed a stack of plates from her cupboard and shoved them at her son.

"Thanks, Mama," smiled Dani triumphantly as he gave her a kiss on the cheek.

"He's got it as bad for you as Jim Otterman does," whispered Susan so only Carolyn could hear.

"Ya think?" responded Carolyn sarcastically.

"We're having stuffed grape leaves," described Dani as he set the plates down around the table.

"Dolma," corrected his mother.

"That's what they call it in Armenian," clarified Dani.

"And do not forget it," smiled Mrs. Sumarian as she put a huge platter of dolma onto the table next to a large bowl of pita bread.

432

"Papa, ճաշ պատրաստ է," called Mrs. Sumarian.

"Where's your dad?" Susan suddenly asked.

"At work," replied Dani matter-of-factly.

"Office job," mentioned Mrs. Sumarian.

"It smells wonderful," commented Susan as all of them sat down at the kitchen table for lunch.

"Pray," commanded Dani's mother.

"Yes, Mama," agreed Dani.

Before Dani had a chance to do so, Grandpa Sumarian suddenly said "Amen" in English and then began eating.

Mrs. Sumarian took a deep breath and suddenly let it out before shaking her head. "He's old."

"Amen," grinned Susan as she, too, began to eat.

"Amen, amen, whatever," mumbled Dani's mother. "Eat! Eat!" She then indicated for the rest of them to go ahead.

"This is delicious!" praised Susan as she sampled the dolma. "What's in it?"

"Grapes," muttered Grandpa Sumarian as he waved his hand toward the back yard.

"That's where the grape leaves come from," explained Dani.

"So you DO understand some English, don't you?" realized Susan as she flirted with Dani's grandpa.

Grandpa Sumarian merely nodded and winked back at Susan.

Dani's mother, on the other hand, appeared as if she were about to reprimand them both.

Like Dani's mother, Carolyn frowned at the exchange between Susan and Grandpa Sumarian, but Dani merely laughed.

"Rice and meat inside," described Mrs. Sumarian. "Lamb."

"The pita bread is wonderful, too," complimented Carolyn.

"Homemade," added Mrs. Sumarian.

"More water?" offered Dani as he picked up a glass decanter full of water and prepared to pour some into Susan's glass.

"Just water, huh?" joked Susan.

"No strong drink for children in this house!" advised Dani's mother indignantly. Then, turning to Dani, she instructed, "Երբ մենք արդեն կերել, ես ուզում եմ, որ նրանք գնացել, որպեսզի դուք կարող եք անել ձեր գործերը!"

"Yes, Mama," agreed Dani reluctantly. "She says I must go do my chores after this."

"We need to be getting back, anyway," realized Carolyn. "Thank you again for the delicious lunch."

"You welcome," smiled Dani's mother. "Dani, get grape leaves, they take home, for dolma."

Dani needed no further encouragement and quickly volunteered. "I'll get the cutters. Come on!"

"Dani wants us to follow him out back so he can pick some grape leaves for us to take home," Carolyn explained to Susan.

"Thank you again!" Susan smiled and nodded at both Mrs. Sumarian and her father-in-law before following Carolyn and Dani into the huge back yard. More than half of it was filled with row after row of grape vines.

"The grapes themselves won't be ready until fall," apologized Dani, "but the leaves are good any time."

"That's good to know," replied Susan.

While Dani was busy getting his cutters from the shed and harvesting a small basket of grape leaves, Susan mentioned to Carolyn, "There's something I need to tell you."

"What?" asked Carolyn.

"When you were in the shower this morning, I called Jorge," revealed Susan. "He should be here by 3:30 or so."

"Today? My dad will have a fit when he sees that bright yellow sports car!" fretted Carolyn. "Not to mention Jorge!"

"It's not that I'm not having a nice time here," added Susan, "but I just can't sleep another night on that hard mattress! Not only that, your dad spends more time in the bathroom than I do! What if I have to use the restroom again while he's in there? I'm not using that dirty old pee pot thing again! Besides, this may be the last chance that Jorge and I will have to be together until June. Please try to understand."

Carolyn was stunned. "You're leaving today?"

"You know there's not adequate room in your dad's car for both of our suitcases," continued Susan. "Do you really want to ride like that again, cramped up behind your suitcase for four long hours?"

"But Susan, we haven't even gone out to see the farm animals at the college yet," reminded Carolyn. "My mom already made special arrangements, and the guy is going to meet us out there at four o'clock. What do I tell her?"

"Why don't we have Jorge take us out there first before he and I head back to Ocean Bay?" suggested Susan. "We should have time."

"My dad would never let me ride in that car," argued Carolyn. "Not if he knew about it!"

"Probably not, but it never hurts to ask!" chuckled Susan as she bent down to pet the Sumarian dog. "I think he likes me better than your dad does!"

"Here you are," offered Dani with a big smile as he handed the basket of grape leaves to Carolyn. "You can bring the basket back anytime, there's no hurry."

"Thank you, Dani," accepted Carolyn. "We'll see you later."

Dani then watched as Carolyn and Susan departed through the side gate, making sure to close it behind them to keep the dog from escaping again. He wished they could have stayed longer.

Carolyn's mother arrived at home by three o'clock. She had been able to get off work a few minutes early and was anxious to take Susan and Carolyn out to visit the farm animals that were kept in the Department of Animal Sciences and Agricultural Education at Ashton University where she worked as a secretary in the business office. The Department Head could not meet them there at four o'clock as hoped due to an unexpected family emergency, but had agreed to let them come out to look around on their own.

Hopefully Susan would enjoy seeing the various animals as much as Carolyn always did, especially the babies.

Just as Mrs. Bennett brought the white Dodge Dart to a stop in the Bennetts' driveway, a bright yellow sports car suddenly screeched to a stop out front. Carolyn's mother was quite surprised to see the tall, well-built Italian man climb from the tiny vehicle and approach her. "Mrs. Bennett?"

"Yes," confirmed Carolyn's mother rather cautiously.

"I'm Susan's friend, Jorge Moranga," announced Jorge as he smiled and shook Mrs. Bennett's hand.

Mrs. Bennett merely stood there studying him for a moment, not knowing what to think.

"From Ocean Bay," added Jorge. "Susan's parents sent me here to bring her home. Unexpected family emergency."

"Hello, I'm Carolyn's father," greeted Mr. Bennett from behind them. Neither Jorge nor Mrs. Bennett had noticed him approach. "You must be the young man Susan's father said would be coming here to pick her up?"

"Yes, Sir," responded Jorge. "Nice to meet you."

"What kind of emergency?" questioned Carolyn's mother. "What's happened?"

"It's her grandfather," replied Jorge. "He's not doing very well and would like everyone in the family to be there. They don't expect him to last too much longer."

"Oh, I see," nodded Carolyn's mother. "I'm so sorry. Won't you please come in?"

Mr. Bennett gazed with disapproval at the bright yellow sports car, and then at Jorge, before finally shaking his hand. He then acknowledged, "Jorge."

Jorge responded, "Mr. Bennett."

The two men then walked toward the Bennett home together in silence, following after Carolyn's mother.

"What do you think they said to each other?" worried Carolyn from where she and Susan were peeking out the bedroom curtains in her parents' room, which was on the front side of the house.

"I don't know, but they're coming this way," pointed out Susan.

"We're not supposed to be here in my parents' room," panicked Carolyn. "Come on, let's get out of here!"

Just as Carolyn's parents and Jorge entered the front door, Mr. Bennett turned to Carolyn's mother and instructed, "Would you please phone Susan's parents to let them know Jorge has safely arrived to pick her up? We don't want them to worry."

"Oh, certainly," agreed Mrs. Bennett.

It did not even occur to her that Carolyn's father had doubts about whether or not it was actually Mr. Rives he had spoken with on the phone earlier, but the purpose of his request was not lost on Carolyn, Susan or Jorge.

"Let's sit down," invited Mr. Bennett, who headed for his formal living room and then motioned for them to sit on the antique Chesterfield couch.

"Oh, my!" exclaimed Susan as she sat down. "I think I just sat on one of those springs Carolyn was telling me about."

"Couches do have springs," smirked Mr. Bennett as he sat in his relaxing recliner across from them.

Carolyn and Jorge had also managed to sit in less than desirable locations on the hard couch but said nothing.

Just then, Carolyn's mother entered the room and advised, "Susan's mother says hello to everyone, and was delighted to know Jorge had a safe trip."

Susan let out a visible sigh of relief. Thankfully, her mother had been the one to answer the phone and corroborate Jorge's story.

"She'll look forward to seeing Susan and Jorge later on tonight, whenever they get there," continued Mrs. Bennett, "and for them to just take their time and be safe."

Mr. Bennett finally seemed satisfied and nodded with approval.

"Oh, before I forget," interjected Carolyn's mother. "The man at the Department of Animal Sciences and Agricultural Education who was going to meet us there at four o'clock will not be able to join us, but said for us to feel free to come out and look around."

"Did you still want to go out there?" Carolyn asked Susan.

"I was looking forward to it," mentioned Susan. "Maybe Jorge can drive us out there. Do we have enough time?"

"What kind of place is it?" questioned Jorge.

"Oh, it's part of the school where I work," explained Carolyn's mother. "They offer various courses in agriculture, animal science, pre-veterinary medicine, livestock and dairy science. The animal science courses have farm labs where the students are required to actually care for the animals. They have cows, chickens, horses, sheep and even pigs out there. The baby animals are especially cute this time of year."

"Hey, I can run 'em out there," volunteered Jorge. "I think I'd like to see the animals, too!"

"That's a great idea!" agreed Carolyn's mother. "And I can have dinner ready by the time you all get back."

"Sounds like a plan," approved Susan with a smile that was just a bit too mischievous for Mr. Bennett's liking.

"Oh, thank you!" beamed Carolyn as they stood up to leave.

"Hold it!" commanded Carolyn's father.

Carolyn and Susan exchanged a worried glance with Jorge.

"My daughter is not riding in that bright yellow death trap you have out there," advised Mr. Bennett as he stood up and reached into his pocket for his keys. "But, if she promises me to be careful, Carolyn may drive you out there."

Carolyn was stunned but quickly recovered when she felt her father's car keys in her outstretched hand. "Thank YOU!" Carolyn unexpectedly gave her father a hug.

"Just be careful," stipulated Mr. Bennett. "No one drives but you, and that's the only place you will go – just there and back again – understood?"

"Absolutely," promised Carolyn. "And I'll even check the tires for rocks afterwards."

"I know you will," replied her father with that twinkle in his eyes that indicated a hint of a smile behind them.

"Rocks?" whispered Jorge.

"Later," advised Susan. "I'll tell you all about it."

"Let's go!" smiled Carolyn as she left with Susan and Jorge to drive out to Ashton University in her father's white Dodge Dart.

Once all of them were inside the vehicle, Carolyn started the engine and slowly started backing out of the driveway.

"Is there something wrong with it?" teased Jorge.

"She has to go really slow while her father is watching," snickered Susan.

"Oh, okay," grinned Jorge from the back seat.

Once Carolyn was out on the street, she put the white Dodge Dart into drive and began creeping down the street in it.

"At least it's automatic," laughed Susan. "Are you sure you can really drive this thing?"

"Hey, look over there!" pointed out Jorge. "What's that old lady doing with a shotgun? Did you see that?"

"That's Mrs. Minasian," answered Carolyn with a smile. "She always sits out on the porch in her rocker with it."

"With the shotgun?" doubted Susan.

"Absolutely," assured Carolyn.

"Has she ever shot anyone with it?" asked Jorge.

"Actually, yes," confirmed Carolyn as she reached the end of the block and pulled out onto a major thoroughfare. "That's a long story."

"I'm all ears," encouraged Jorge. "At this rate, it will probably take us a long time just to get there."

Carolyn then sped up, ever so slightly, but made sure she was under the posted speed limit.

"Several years ago," began Carolyn, "there was a big black cat in our neighborhood. It had killed several people's pets, including one of mine. Kelly was a beautiful Siamese kitten and I was standing right next to her when it happened. The big black cat that did it just sprang out of nowhere, grabbed her in its jaws, and took off. I chased them for two blocks before that monster finally dropped her lifeless body on the ground and took off." Carolyn had tears rolling down her cheeks as she related the tale.

"How horrible!" exclaimed Susan.

"So, what happened to the big black cat?" prompted Jorge.

"Well, one day it finally killed someone's Doberman Pinscher dog," recalled Carolyn, "and even tried to attack a small child."

"Just how big was that cat?" pressed Susan.

"Pretty big," replied Carolyn. "Someone must have had it as an exotic pet that finally escaped, but it looked like a small jaguar to me."

"A jaguar?" doubted Susan.

"I've heard of people with exotic pets getting loose," mentioned Jorge. "It can happen."

"My dad said it looked like a black leopard to him," added Carolyn as she came to a stop for a signal light.

"Actually, they do look a lot alike," mentioned Jorge. "I saw a special on it recently. Black jaguars are more muscular than black leopards, and have slightly shorter tails, but they are roughly the same size and it would take an expert to tell them apart."

"Well, it definitely was one or the other," assured Carolyn. "Anyway, my dad finally managed to chase it into an enclosed patio we used to have with his big flat blade shovel."

"You don't have an enclosed patio," interrupted Susan.

"Not anymore," replied Carolyn. "My dad had to tear it down to make room for the patio that's there now. The other one was only half the size of it, and was built around that same outdoor barbecue."

"That is a nice barbecue," said Susan. "Even has a chimney."

"Let her finish about the black cat," urged Jorge.

"When animal control finally got there," resumed Carolyn, "it was sunset." The light turned green just then and Carolyn began to drive again. "The entire neighborhood was gathered. Everyone wanted to watch them take that monster away."

"Including Mrs. Minasian?" asked Jorge.

"Especially her," replied Carolyn. "The big black cat not only killed her cat, but mutilated its entire litter of kittens. There was nothing left but little body parts strewn all over her front porch."

"Oh, my God!" exclaimed Susan. "That's horrible!"

"In other words," restated Carolyn, "it killed for sport, not because it needed to. That animal took sheer pleasure in killing things."

"Did they finally put it in a zoo?" pressed Susan.

"Hardly. We all just helplessly watched while it poked its head out from the top of our chimney – it actually managed to climb up the chimney from the inside – and its evil yellow eyes reflected against the last rays of sun before it jumped out and took off," described Carolyn.

"You mean that thing's still out there, just roaming the neighborhood?" quizzed Susan with alarm.

"Not anymore," replied Carolyn as she approached the turnoff to Ashton University. "Mrs. Minasian eventually shot and killed it, right there in her own front yard. She had waited for it for weeks."

"Then why is she still out there with the shotgun?" asked Jorge.

"Because she's convinced that it may have bred and that its offspring are still out there," described Carolyn. "And she plans to pick them off, one by one, if and when any of them ever dare to show up."

"Good thing you have Mrs. Minasian looking out for everyone in your neighborhood!" smiled Jorge.

"There's the Department of Animal Sciences and Agricultural Education," read Carolyn from the sign on the building as she pulled in and carefully parked her father's white Dodge Dart.

"Oooh, look how muddy it is over there!" objected Susan.

"They probably just watered everything," realized Carolyn.

"Why would they water the dirt?" puzzled Susan.

"To keep the dust down," answered Carolyn. "Besides, the pigs really do love to wallow in the mud. It helps cool them down, especially when it gets hot out here in the summertime."

"Well, I have no intention of wallowing in the mud and pig poop, thank you very much!" Susan was indignant.

"Fine!" retorted Carolyn as she started the car back up. "I guess I can always come back out here tomorrow, by myself."

"What if you just drive around the outside of the pens?" suggested Jorge. "We can probably see most of the animals from the car. That way we won't have to get all that mud on our shoes."

"Only if you two will help me wash the car before we go back," stipulated Carolyn. "And check the tires for rocks."

"Okay, it's a deal," agreed Susan.

Carolyn drove first past the horse barn, where several young foals and their mothers were sectioned off in individual paddocks. Some of them were busy nursing. "They let them out into that pasture over there during the morning, but usually bring them in about the time classes end each day. Most of them are probably in their stalls in the barn right now. I think my mom said the pasture is about sixty acres."

"Oh, look at that," noticed Susan. "That's clever. Each paddock has its own private entrance where the horses can come and go from their stalls in the barn as they please."

"Who cares for them on the weekends?" asked Jorge.

"Faculty, staff or student volunteers," replied Carolyn. "From what I understand, the students are on a rotating schedule. The ones signed up for the class are required to volunteer at least one weekend each month."

"That sounds fair," approved Susan.

Carolyn then drove over to the chicken area, but it appeared to be empty. "They're probably all inside."

"With the chicks?" questioned Susan.

"Actually," clarified Carolyn, "some of the chicks are left with their mothers, but others are raised separately. It depends on what they plan to do with them."

"Too bad we can't get inside to see them," regretted Jorge.

"Then we'd still have to get our feet muddy," reminded Susan. "It's probably better this way."

"And over there are the lambs," pointed out Carolyn. "I think they usually just leave them out there in the pasture, but nowhere I can drive very close to."

"That's okay," replied Susan. "So, what's left? Pigs?"

"Baby pigs are cute," agreed Jorge.

"I actually do see some of the pigs out in their pens right now," noticed Carolyn. "And the babies are with them!"

"Oh, drive over there!" insisted Susan. "They're adorable! Jorge, look at the baby pigs!"

"The really young ones are probably inside the barn with their mothers," clarified Carolyn. "The ones out here are just learning to self-feed, but still need to be with their mothers for a while yet."

"Can't you get any closer?" pressed Susan.

"There's a road alongside the feeding pens," indicated Jorge. "We could drive up right next to them."

"And YOU are washing this car afterwards?" verified Carolyn.

"Absolutely!" agreed Jorge.

"Very well," conceded Carolyn.

The road was somewhat muddy but negotiable, so Carolyn slowly and carefully turned onto it.

"Better not stop," cautioned Jorge.

"That's right," chuckled Susan. "You sure wouldn't wanna get stuck along here!"

"What's that noise?" Carolyn suddenly asked.

"Some guy in a tractor coming up behind us," answered Susan.

"At least he's on the other side of that little ditch," observed Carolyn from the rearview mirror, "but he's sure awful close to it!"

"Actually, he's hanging over it, and he doesn't even see you!" warned Jorge. "If that tractor keeps coming like it is, it will take out the entire driver's side of your dad's car when it pins us up against that row of pig feeders!"

"There's absolutely no way to turn around and he's gaining on us!" panicked Carolyn.

"Better step on it!" urged Susan.

"This dirt road keeps getting narrower and narrower," noticed Carolyn. "Oh, no! It leads right up to that closed barn door up ahead, and there's a big padlock on it!"

"What now?" demanded Susan. "Can't you just back out?"

"You're gonna have to back out of here," advised Jorge. "There's no way to turn around."

"That guy still doesn't see us," fretted Carolyn. "Jorge, can you get out and try to wave your arms over your head, and at least get him to stop? The feed dispensing tube from his tractor to the pig feeders is hanging right over this dirt road, and it's gonna take out the top of my dad's car about the same time it takes out the side, unless we can get him to stop! Susan, you'd better duck down, there's no way you'll be able to open your door. We're too close to the pig feeders."

"She's right!" exclaimed Susan. "Jorge, hurry! Go! Get out there right now! Go! Go! Go!"

Jorge quickly got out of the white Dodge Dart and began hopping up and down, yelling and waving his arms back and forth above his head, screaming "Stop! Stop!"

Carolyn honked her horn, as well, but the noise from the tractor was far too loud for it - or Susan's and Carolyn's screams - to be heard.

Not expecting to see someone's car along the muddy access road that surrounded the pigpens, the tractor driver was caught unaware. Nevertheless, he managed to stop the tractor just in time. Stopped only inches from the white Dodge Dart, the man suddenly began to laugh.

"What in the world are you folks doing in here?" asked the man.

"Looking at pigs!" shouted Susan from the passenger window.

"I can see that!" grinned the man. "So, how do you folks plan to get out of here? I don't even have a key to the barn ahead of you."

"That's a good question," replied Carolyn. "Is there any way you can back up?"

"There's no reverse on this thing," advised the tractor driver. "I wish there were. You're going to have to back up."

"Not with that feeder tube in the way," objected Carolyn.

"That, I can do," agreed the man as he pressed a button to automatically raise the feeder tube. "But, I can't back up."

"The tractor's flush with the ditch on the other side," observed Jorge. "And there's only a couple of inches to spare on your side."

"What am I going to do?" fretted Carolyn.

"You can do this!" encouraged Susan. "You have to do this! There's no other way out."

Jorge and the tractor driver began to call out directions to Carolyn as she ever so slowly backed up.

"You have two inches on this side between the car and the pig feeders," called Jorge. The ditch itself was only six inches wide.

"She won't make it on this side," cautioned the tractor driver, "unless she goes over at least one inch your way. Otherwise, she'll hit the side of the tractor, because it hangs out over the ditch on that side."

Carolyn turned the wheel minutely, held her breath, and gently pressed the gas pedal again.

"That's it," said Jorge. "Now, straighten it out."

"Put it back where you had it," instructed Susan.

"Keep coming," urged Jorge. "You're half way there."

"Looks like you're stuck between a ditch and a pig feeder," laughed Susan. "Literally!"

Carolyn paused to give Susan a glaring look.

"It is pretty funny when you think about it," snickered Susan. "Someday you'll look back on this and see the humor in it."

"Well, today's not that day," fumed Carolyn.

"Keep coming!" hollered Jorge. "Just a few more inches to go."

"She's okay now," advised the tractor driver. "You're clear of the tractor, at least."

"You still have twenty feet or so to back up," estimated Jorge as he opened the back door to get back inside.

"Hold it!" objected Carolyn. "Absolutely not. You're going to need to rinse off your feet somewhere first. You can't get in here with all that mud on your feet."

"She's right," snickered Susan.

Jorge took in a deep breath and then quickly let it out as he slammed the car door shut and began walking through the mud toward the access road behind them.

"Jorge doesn't get mad very often," mentioned Susan, "but I think he's not too happy right now. Those new dress shoes he had on are pretty much ruined."

"Better the shoes than my dad's car!" pointed out Carolyn as she continued slowly backing down the muddy road. "Plus, we're still gonna have to wash it before we can go back!"

"Where?" queried Susan.

"I guess we'll have to find someplace," replied Carolyn.

After what seemed an eternity, the white Dodge Dart was finally backed up enough to be on the main dirt road again.

"What if I take my shoes off and then hold them outside the window while you try and find a place to wash the car?" questioned

444

Jorge as he walked along beside the car. "That way I could at least sit down inside the car."

"That should work," agreed Carolyn as she took the car out of reverse and put it back into drive, but kept her foot on the brake so Jorge could get back in.

Jorge then carefully opened the car door, sat down, rolled down the window on his side, and removed his shoes. He then carefully closed the door and held his muddy shoes outside through the open window as Carolyn drove away in search of someplace to wash the muddy vehicle.

"Over there!" pointed out Susan. "They are watering the lawn over by that building, and they're using a hose. We can just unhook it to wash the car."

"Thank goodness!" sighed Carolyn as she carefully pulled onto the lawn. "Good thing nobody's here to see this. They don't even like people walking on these lawns."

"What they don't know won't hurt 'em," smiled Susan.

Jorge tossed his shoes out of the way and onto the lawn before opening his door and getting out.

Carolyn shut off the engine before she and Susan emerged from the mud-covered Dodge Dart.

"Oh, Carolyn!" Susan suddenly exclaimed. "Look at this!"

Carolyn quickly came over to the passenger side of the vehicle to see what Susan was looking at. The chrome strip at the top of the rocker panel had somehow caught on the edge of the pig feeders – unknown to any of them at the time – and pulled loose from the car.

"That's not good," muttered Jorge.

"Can't you just snap that end back on?" inquired Susan.

"We probably should rinse the mud off first," recommended Carolyn. "If any mud got underneath it, my dad would know."

"I'll kink up the hose while you unscrew it," called Jorge as he ran over to the hose nearby. Unfortunately, the faucet itself was key operated and could not be shut off by just anyone.

Carolyn immediately raced over and tried to unscrew the hose from the automatic watering device. "It won't come off!"

"Here, you come kink up the hose while I unscrew it," proposed Jorge. He then dropped the hose, but Carolyn had not yet gotten far enough away from the sprinkler and was thoroughly drenched.

"Thanks!" muttered Carolyn.

"It'll dry," laughed Susan.

"Maybe you'd like to come help?" suggested Jorge.

"You two are doing just fine," grinned Susan as she got back into the car to wait.

Carolyn then kinked up the hose the best she was able while Jorge finally managed to unscrew the sprinkler, but not without getting drenched in the process.

After they had thoroughly rinsed off the white Dodge Dart and tossed the running hose out onto the lawn, Carolyn and Jorge inspected the damage to the chrome strip more carefully.

"There's a clip missing," mentioned Jorge. "It's going to need something to hold it on."

"I got this!" called Susan. "There's got to be something we can use in this glove box."

"My dad keeps his glove box orderly, too," advised Carolyn. "Make sure you put everything back exactly like it was, or he will notice that something is out of place."

"There's a rubber band and a paperclip," described Susan. "Absolutely nothing else we could use."

"You can have my shoelaces," offered Jorge. "Let me just go rinse them off. I still have to rinse off my shoes."

"This is terrible!" worried Carolyn. "It's already six thirty, and my parents eat at six. They're gonna know something happened."

"So, we had a good time looking at the animals and lost track of the time," laughed Susan. "That's all they need to know."

After several attempts between the three of them, Jorge somehow managed to get the chrome strip at the top of the rocker panel to stay in place.

"Will it hold?" quizzed Carolyn anxiously.

Jorge tested it with his hands, and it held. Susan and Carolyn each tested it, as well.

"Hey look, you guys are both pretty much dry now," laughed Susan. "Won't you get wet again hooking the sprinkler back up?"

Jorge and Carolyn both gave Susan an irritated look but did not respond as all of them climbed back into the white Dodge Dart to head for the Bennett home. It was already quarter before seven.

Back at Oceanview Academy, Pete and Lenny had finally returned from an extended leave of absence for both family and financial reasons. At first, it did not appear possible that they would ever be able to return to Oceanview Academy, and that Lenny's dream of becoming a doctor stood in peril. Still, he kept up on his studies, just in case.

Lenny eventually told his father that Minnie's last words to him before she died had been, "I'm so proud of you! You'll make a wonderful doctor." That was more than Mr. Owens could bear, and was what ultimately prompted him to contact Dean Vandevere about the possible grant Lenny and Pete had both described.

True to his word, Dean Vandevere went before the school board and obtained approval for both Pete and Lenny to receive a stipend from the special grant fund created for worthy students who qualified. Pete had been a stretch, but Lenny was an easy sell, and ultimately it was unanimous that both of them be allowed to finish out their junior year tuition free at Oceanview Academy. Naturally, they were requested to keep that fact in strict confidence from the other students.

Duty bound to meet everyone's expectations of him, Lenny began studying harder than he ever had, paying particular attention to the chemistry class that would be necessary if he were to qualify for medical school.

Linda Shaver was delighted to see Lenny back, but soon realized that he still had no interest in continuing their friendship. The only girl Lenny wanted was Carolyn, and that situation was hopeless. Lenny's father had made him solemnly promise never to see Carolyn again, as a condition of allowing Pete and Lenny to accept the stipend.

"Wanna go down and do a few laps on the track?" asked Pete.

"I can't," declined Lenny. "I still have to finish my assignment in biology class."

"I thought you weren't going to take that class," mentioned Pete. "Don't you have enough to handle as it is?"

"I plan to keep my promise to Mama," informed Lenny.

"Hey," said Pete as he put his hand on Lenny's shoulder. "Wouldn't she want you to be happy, too?"

Lenny didn't answer. He knew what Pete was alluding to, but pretended to continue studying.

"What about Carolyn?" Pete finally came out and asked. "Don't you think you ought to tell her why you can't see her again? It would be the gentlemanly thing to do."

"I plan to," Lenny finally replied.

"How will you ever get the chance if you stay here in this room all the time?" asked Pete. "It isn't healthy. You need to get out once in a while! Besides, doing a few laps will help you study better."

All at once, Lenny pounded his fist on the table. "It just isn't fair! Why did I ever promise such a thing?"

"To become a doctor?" guessed Pete.

Lenny suddenly grabbed his chemistry book and threw it across the room as hard as he could, causing the book's binding to snap when it crashed against the opposite wall. Several important pages fluttered out and onto the floor.

"Come on!" urged Pete. "That'll all be here waiting for you when you get back."

Without further comment, Lenny calmly changed into his track clothes and followed Pete down to the track.

Meanwhile, over in Ashton, Carolyn's father was particularly anxious about the late return of his daughter Carolyn and her friends Susan and Jorge. Had he made a mistake in allowing them to drive out to the University with the family car? Would Carolyn remember to check the tires of his white Dodge Dart for rocks?

"There he is," pointed out Susan as they approached. "He's out front watering the yard."

"He's probably been watering it since six o'clock!" muttered Carolyn.

"Good thing it's only seven o'clock now," informed Jorge.

"Oh no!" realized Carolyn.

"What?" demanded Susan.

"I forgot to check the tires for rocks," regretted Carolyn.

"Tell him you wanted to make sure you got 'em all, just in case you picked up any more on the way home, and decided to do it here," suggested Susan.

"That's not bad," smiled Jorge.

"Let's just hope that chrome strip holds up," reminded Carolyn.

"Indeed," muttered Jorge. He did not want to be there when it finally worked its way loose again, and it inevitably would.

"Carolyn, where have you been?" called her mother as she came out to meet them at the car.

"We just lost track of the time," apologized Susan. "It's my fault we're late. I wanted to see the baby pigs, too, while we were there."

"Well, dinner's ready," advised Mrs. Bennett.

Carolyn's father could be seen turning off and rolling up the hose before he approached. "You're late."

"It took them longer than they thought to see the baby pigs," explained Mrs. Bennett to her husband. "I'm sure they still have time for a quick meal before they take off, don't you?"

"Absolutely," smiled Jorge.

"If you leave now, that'll put you in Ocean Bay at midnight," described Mr. Bennett.

"That sounds about right," agreed Jorge as he followed Susan, Carolyn and Mrs. Bennett into the Bennett home.

"We really should eat fast, though," Jorge whispered to Susan. "I'm more worried about that chrome strip than I am about getting home late. I wouldn't take any bets on how long it will hold."

"Point taken," replied Susan in hushed tones.

"So, did you get to see all of the other animals, too?" asked Mrs. Bennett as she quickly dished up the corn-on-the-cob that she had been keeping warm in a huge pot of hot water on the stove.

"Let me help with that," offered Jorge as he took the platter of corn from Carolyn's mother and carried it over to the kitchen table.

"I see we're having fake hot dogs, too," noticed Susan.

"They're not so bad," assured Mr. Bennett with a twinkle in his eyes. He already knew that Susan loathed eating fake meat as much as he did.

Carolyn's mother quickly brought a plate of hot dog buns over to the table and set them down next to a bottle of catsup, and jars of pickle relish and mustard.

"Thank you for dinner," mentioned Susan as they all sat down, had prayer, and began to eat.

"Aren't you going to eat?" questioned Carolyn, when she noticed her father wasn't joining them.

"Your daddy couldn't wait," explained Mrs. Bennett, "so he ate while we were waiting for you."

"Did you check the tires for rocks?" asked Carolyn's father.

"We wanted to wait until we got here to do it," explained Carolyn, "just in case there were any more."

"I'll take care of it," decided Mr. Bennett. "You enjoy your dinner." In actuality, Carolyn's father wanted an excuse to inspect his vehicle more carefully, to make sure everything was shipshape.

"Eat faster," Susan mumbled to Jorge, even with her mouth full.

"No kidding," replied Jorge.

"Susan's suitcase is already here by the door," advised Carolyn's mother. "Your daddy knew how much trouble she had with it earlier."

"That was thoughtful," acknowledged Susan. "Thanks."

"You did have everything packed, didn't you?" asked Carolyn. She was upset that her father had taken the liberty of moving Susan's suitcase in her absence.

"If I didn't, you can bring it with you when you come back tomorrow," advised Susan. "I'm not worried about it."

What Susan and Jorge were worried about at the moment was whether or not they would be successful in finishing their meal in time to leave before the chrome strip at the top of the rocker panel decided to come unfastened again.

Carolyn's mother rambled on about the various animals at the University while the rest of them ate in silence, nervously watching Mr. Bennett inspect his vehicle.

"Looks like the tires checked out okay," nodded Carolyn.

"He may not be done yet. You never know with him," chuckled Mrs. Bennett.

"Doesn't he usually start it back up and drive forward a few inches at a time as he does?" recalled Susan.

"Not if there weren't any rocks on the first inspection," clarified Carolyn. She was quite familiar with the routine.

Susan smiled with relief and was just about to excuse herself when suddenly they could see the chrome strip at the top of the rocker panel snap loose with a boing, right in front of Mr. Bennett.

"At least it missed him," Susan suddenly laughed at the look on Mr. Bennett's face. "Jorge, I think that's our cue to leave now."

Mr. Bennett's face became several shades pinker than it already was as he slowly turned to glare at them through the kitchen window from outside.

"He looks pretty upset," observed Jorge.

"Oh, Carolyn, what happened to that strip on the car door?" quizzed Mrs. Bennett.

"There's a good explanation for that," replied Carolyn.

Her father had come in just at that moment and had heard her remark. "It had better be a good one, too!"

"We need to get going," advised Jorge rather nervously.

"No one's going anywhere until someone tells me exactly what happened to my car!" shouted Carolyn's father. He was so upset, in fact, that he almost seemed as if he were about to have a stroke.

"Looks like things really do happen in threes," joked Susan.

"Sit!" commanded Mr. Bennett.

Susan immediately sat back down, as did Jorge.

"Did anyone else besides my daughter drive that car?" pressed Mr. Bennett. "I want the truth!"

"No, Sir," assured Jorge.

"Absolutely not," corroborated Susan.

"Is that true?" interrogated Carolyn's father as he turned to her.

"I'm the only one who drove the car," confirmed Carolyn.

"You obviously drove too close to some sort of farm equipment out there," deduced Mr. Bennett. "There's bright yellow paint on the outer tip of the chrome strip at the top of the rocker panel."

"There is?" Carolyn was surprised. How had they not seen it?

"And then you tried to hide what you did by reattaching it with a rubber band, a paper clip and some dirty old shoe laces?" Mr. Bennett actually smiled at that point, but it was more of a sardonic grin. He then shook his head.

"That was all we had available," added Carolyn.

"Why didn't you just come and tell me what happened?" grilled Carolyn's father. "At least I have the proper tools here to fix it!"

"Because maybe your daughter is afraid of you and didn't know how you would react!" blurted Susan, sorry at once for doing so.

"Afraid of me?" Carolyn's father seemed troubled.

"It truly was an accident, Sir," informed Jorge.

"You two may leave now," invited Mr. Bennett. "Carolyn can tell me all about it after you go. After all, you've got a five-hour drive ahead of you. I suggest you get started."

Jorge quickly got up, thanked Mrs. Bennett for the meal, grabbed Susan's large suitcase, and hurried toward the bright yellow sports car out front. Susan was right on his heels, and did not even bother to look back when they left.

"Oh, Carolyn," muttered her father, after Carolyn had finished relating the particulars to him of their encounter with the tractor that day and how his car had nearly met with an untimely end between it and the row of pig feeders beside it.

All at once, Carolyn's mother began to laugh. "It is pretty funny, when you think about it!"

Try as he might, Mr. Bennett could not fight off the urge to smile. If only he had been there to see it for himself. "Carolyn, you must promise me nothing like this will ever happen again."

"I promise," agreed Carolyn. "I will never drive any type of vehicle whatsoever anywhere near a pigpen again, not ever! That's not an experience I wish to repeat. It was pretty scary."

"I think she's learned her lesson," persuaded Carolyn's mother.

"Just how do you plan to reimburse me for this?" Carolyn's father suddenly asked.

"Just how were you planning to reimburse me for my new bicycle that got stolen when you neglected to shut the garage door that night?" countered Carolyn.

"She's got a good point," recognized Mrs. Bennett.

"I'll tell you what," agreed Mr. Bennett. "We'll call it even."

"You mean it?" replied Carolyn cautiously. Usually her father's agreements had some sort of condition attached to them.

"Just promise me you will not get into any more trouble," clarified Mr. Bennett. "And that you won't let that Susan talk you into anything else. There's only one month left until school's out for the summer. Can you do that for me?"

"Trust me, I'll do my best," replied Carolyn.

The last month of school sped by quickly and graduation was the following weekend. Frustrated by the fact that Lenny had been avoiding her, Carolyn finally mentioned it to Susan.

"Did you see the flyer posted down in the administration building yesterday?" asked Carolyn as she and Susan made their way to the cafeteria for breakfast.

"No, what did it say?" questioned Susan.

"That the juniors will be marching in first when the seniors graduate next week – in pairs!" described Carolyn.

"So?" shrugged Susan.

"In pairs!" repeated Carolyn. "It also said that the junior girls will be asking the junior boys of their choice to march with them."

"You're not still thinking of Lenny are you?" grinned Susan.

"Well, I was hoping to see him at breakfast this morning so I could ask him," revealed Carolyn.

"Oh, my dear Carolina la Gata," Susan sadly shook her head.

"What's that supposed to mean?" demanded Carolyn.

"What it means," explained Susan, "is that there are some things I haven't told you."

"Like what?" frowned Carolyn as they entered the cafeteria and made their way to the food line.

"Wait until we get to the table, and I'll tell you then," suggested Susan. "There are things you don't know."

"Lenny's over there by himself at that table on the other side, and I'm going over there right now!" informed Carolyn.

"Hold it!" instructed Susan as she pulled Carolyn out of the food line and into a corner of the entryway.

"This better be good," fumed Carolyn.

"When Lenny's mother died last March, his father made him swear that he would not have anything else to do with you," began Susan. "And that if he did, he would not let him come back here."

"That's nothing new," replied Carolyn.

"Lenny's promise to his dying mother was that he would do whatever it took to become a doctor someday," added Susan.

"Did Lenny tell you this?" Carolyn suddenly became suspicious.

"Pete did," admitted Susan. "I went to him after we got back from your parents' house that weekend."

"You mean after I got back from my parents' house by myself," corrected Carolyn.

"Whatever," mumbled Susan. "When I saw Pete at break one day at work, when you were out sick, he and I sat down and talked."

"And he told you all this in one short ten-minute break?" doubted Carolyn.

"He did," assured Susan. "And he also told me how much Lenny still cares for you, and how it has broken his heart that things had to turn out like this. There's not a day that goes by that he doesn't think of you, and how he wishes it could be different."

"Well, he sure has a strange way of showing it!" responded Carolyn. "I'm going over there anyway. Excuse me."

Lenny had just finished his breakfast and was preparing to leave. He thought sadly of the enjoyable breakfasts he had once shared with Carolyn and wished with all his heart that she were here with him now.

"Lenny?" Carolyn timidly whispered.

"Carolyn!" smiled Lenny when he looked up and saw her. The change in his countenance was miraculous and did not go unnoticed by Jim Otterman, who was seated at another table nearby. In fact, it was the first time Lenny had smiled in months. "Please, sit down."

"Are you sure?" Carolyn hesitated. She did not want to get Lenny into trouble.

"I've missed you so much!" informed Lenny as he rushed over to pull Carolyn's chair out for her before sitting back down. "Not a day goes by that I haven't thought of you."

"Me, too," admitted Carolyn.

"If only things could have been different for us," regretted Lenny. "There's so much I need to tell you."

"Please do," urged Carolyn.

"There were certain promises I had to make to my father, just so he would let me come back here," revealed Lenny nervously.

Carolyn merely nodded. "That you wouldn't see me anymore?"

"I'm so sorry!" apologized Lenny as he returned Carolyn's longing gaze with equal intensity.

"Will you march with me at the graduation ceremony this next weekend?" blurted Carolyn.

"I will," beamed Lenny, without hesitation.

"Won't your father be there?" reminded Carolyn.

"Well, the year's over anyway," pointed out Lenny as he reached over and put his hand on Carolyn's. "There's not much he can do about it now, is there?"

"Are you still planning to go to medical school?" asked Carolyn.

"It was my mother's dying wish," replied Lenny sadly. "She made me promise her. The very last words out of her mouth were, 'I'm so proud of you! You'll make a wonderful doctor.'"

"I'm proud of you, too," added Carolyn as she and Lenny maintained their visual exchange of longing and desire. Just then, unbidden tears escaped the corners of her eyes, but she did not look away and continued to let Lenny hold her hand. How she longed to have Lenny take her into his arms at that moment!

Neither of them noticed that Jim Otterman had been intently scrutinizing them from nearby, or that Jim had finally grabbed up his tray before angrily storming from the cafeteria in frustration.

"Bart told me what you went through on the beach that day, that must have been awful for you!" mentioned Lenny.

"It was," agreed Carolyn, visibly shaken by the memory of it.

"Everyone knows that you and Bart did everything you could to save Steve Fredrickson," reminded Lenny.

Carolyn sadly nodded in acknowledgement.

"If only I could have been here for you," regretted Lenny. "I can't even put into words how bad I feel about missing their funeral."

"You were kind of busy with a funeral of your own at the time," reminded Carolyn. "And all I wanted to do was to be there for you!"

"Perhaps when I finish medical school someday, our paths will cross again," hoped Lenny. "Meanwhile, this last week is all we have right now. I just can't make any promises about the future, not with things the way they are with my dad."

"Then, let's make the most of the time we have left," suggested Carolyn, though startled when Lenny suddenly let go of her hand. Fortunately, he had done so just in the nick of time to avoid being seen by Professor Rattusrisum. The last thing Lenny and Carolyn needed right now would be to get put on "social" for the rest of the week.

When students were caught holding hands at Oceanview Academy, they were customarily put on "all boy" and "all girl" social status for the rest of that week. The girl would not be allowed to speak to any members of the male sex for an entire week, with the exception of teachers during open class period. Likewise, the young man in turn was not allowed to speak to any member of the female sex for the rest of that week, particularly the one with whom he had been caught. Further incursions usually led to suspension or expulsion from school.

"That was close!" remarked Carolyn.

"We'll just have to be more careful," grinned Lenny. "I would like to see as much of you as I possibly can this week."

The last week of school was like a blur, but Lenny and Carolyn managed to eat every single meal together that entire time, even with final exams going on.

Graduation arrived like a harbinger of fate, a cruel reminder to both Lenny and Carolyn that time waits for no one.

Carolyn and Lenny silently stood together in a long line of juniors, waiting for their cue to march down the long aisle surrounded on either side by family members and guests attending the graduation. The juniors would then seat themselves up in the front, immediately behind the section reserved for the graduating seniors who would march in immediately after them.

The junior girls wore pastel pink satin dresses for the occasion, while the junior boys wore burgundy pants, jackets and matching bowties with pastel pink shirts.

Pete had been asked by an attractive girl named Nan to march with her for the ceremony, and they were standing directly behind Lenny and Carolyn. Pete suddenly cleared his throat to get their attention. "Go!" whispered Pete.

Carolyn slipped her arm through Lenny's as they began marching down the graduation aisle. Both of them wished they could make their last day together last forever.

The ceremony was being held in the school's gymnasium, though most of the guests had been allowed to wear their shoes after sufficiently wiping them off at the door. The floors would need to be refinished at the conclusion of the school year, anyway.

Carolyn suddenly noticed an angry looking black man in the audience glaring at them. She knew at once that it must be Lenny's father. Was he really as unreasonable as her own father was about the unimportant difference between them?

Lenny noticed him, too, and whispered, "That's my dad."

Carolyn merely nodded. All eyes were on the juniors as they continued their way to the front of the gymnasium. As they got to the front, the couples would part. The girls then sat on the north side of the aisle while the boys sat opposite them on the other side.

They would not even be allowed to sit together! Carolyn and Lenny squeezed each other's hand when they reached the front and then parted to sit on their respective sides of the room.

The ceremony seemed to take forever but suddenly became unbearable for Carolyn when Principal Roth began recounting the horrible tragedy on the beach that year, mentioning how much Steve Fredrickson, Veronica Jensen and Joyce Troglite would be missed by everyone. Tears flowed freely throughout the congregation.

Relieved that her own parents would not be there until the following day to pick her up and take her home for the summer, Carolyn hoped she would have the opportunity to meet Lenny's father. Perhaps once they met, he might change his mind about her.

Finally, the names of the individual seniors were being called to come up and receive their diplomas! The seniors had chosen black and white as their class colors, which Lenny and Carolyn both found rather intriguing under the circumstances. The senior girls wore white silk gowns with matching mortarboards, and the senior boys wore all black. The tassels on them were black and white, together.

Professor Rattusrisum was then called upon to say closing prayer, which was unusually brief for him. The moment "amen" was spoken, the entire senior class removed and threw their mortarboards into the air and shouted, "Amen!"

Suddenly feeling lost and alone in the swirling mass of excited people, Carolyn looked in vain to try and find Lenny. Where was he? It took nearly twenty minutes for Carolyn to extricate herself from the crowd and make her way outside. Where was Lenny?

Finally spotting Mr. Owens with Lenny and Pete near the boys' dormitory, Carolyn hurried toward them. An older van parked in front of the boys' dorm was already packed with Lenny and Pete's belongings and they were just opening the doors to get inside! Was Lenny planning to leave without even bothering to say goodbye? Not caring how undignified it might appear to anyone watching, Carolyn suddenly yanked off her shoes and broke into a full-out run. "Lenny!"

"Wait, dad," instructed Lenny, refusing to get into the van just yet. Lenny then waved to let Carolyn know he had seen her and would wait for her to get there.

"For what?" snapped his father. "You won't be seeing her again anyway!"

"Then at least let me say goodbye to her," persisted Lenny.

"Get in this van right now!" urged Mr. Owens. "I won't have any son of mine make a spectacle of himself with some white girl!"

"Carolyn!" called Lenny.

"You'll regret this," threatened Mr. Owens.

"I already do," replied Lenny. "Besides, you've already made it perfectly clear that I won't be coming back here next year, anyway."

"You're not about to let Lenny break his promise to Minnie, are you?" reminded Pete, who was on Lenny's side in the matter.

"That's enough from you!" cautioned Mr. Owens.

"She's really a nice girl," persisted Pete. "You haven't even met Carolyn yet. I think you'd like her."

"Well, Dad, now's your opportunity to finally meet her," informed Lenny as Carolyn arrived at the van, breathless and gasping for air.

"No!" muttered Mr. Owens, who stubbornly remained in the driver's seat of his van waiting to leave.

Pete then got back out, circled around, and opened the driver's side door to the van while Lenny and Carolyn approached.

"Dad, this is Carolyn," introduced Lenny.

Mr. Owens studied Carolyn carefully. He could understand at once why his son was so taken with her. But, a white girl? Why?

"I'm very pleased to meet you, Sir," Carolyn smiled sweetly as she extended her hand to Lenny's father.

"Nice to meet you, too," Mr. Owens finally replied, though he would not shake her hand. His attitude toward Carolyn had softened considerably, but his decision about her continuing her relationship with his son was final.

Lenny then pulled Carolyn aside to say his farewells to her. He unexpectedly put his arms around Carolyn's waist and pulled her close. Carolyn's knees felt as if they would buckle beneath her when Lenny's body pressed against hers. Lenny's deep desire for her was obvious.

Pete put a restraining hand on Mr. Owens' shoulder while he climbed back into the back seat of the van behind him. Realizing that it was pointless to try and stop his son Lenny from making a fool of himself, Mr. Owens finally slammed shut the driver's side door to his van, folded his arms, and waited in silence. Pete then shut his door, too, but more softly.

"I've enjoyed every minute of our time together," smiled Lenny as he gazed into Carolyn's eyes.

"Me, too," Carolyn smiled back with unconcealed longing.

"I hope God gives you what you deserve in life," mentioned Lenny. "I'll always love you."

Carolyn then closed her eyes, expecting Lenny to kiss her on the mouth, and was surprised when he kissed her on the cheek instead. Tears flowed down her cheeks as she hugged Lenny goodbye.

Lenny could not hide his sadness as he pulled away, climbed into the old van and closed the door. He and Pete both waved at Carolyn as it drove away. Mr. Owens was clearly upset, but said nothing else and certainly did not look back!

Would she and Lenny ever cross paths again? wondered Carolyn as she watched the van disappear from view. Why hadn't she told Lenny that she would always love him, too, while he was here? It was probably too late. Tears streamed down Carolyn's face as she wandered across the campus, toward the beach. She needed to be alone right now.

Carolyn began to think of her friends Joyce and Veronica, and of Steve Fredrickson. Would she ever be able to find out what had really happened to them? Carolyn knew it could not have been a shark. Was Ray Dixon somehow involved, or was it something even more sinister?

No matter how long it took, Carolyn promised herself, she would figure it out, even if it took her the rest of her life!

13. Final Disposition

Incoming tidewater had continued its trek until finally reaching the iron-barred gate of the bunker tunnel entrance behind which Ray, Carolyn and Sheree were helplessly trapped. The series of earthquakes had subsided, but the sound of angry waves could easily be heard above the unrelenting wind. The last rays of sun had disappeared, leaving only the purple twilight with which to see. Sheree and Carolyn's flashlights had been crushed beneath the pile of small boulders beside them, and Ray's dying flashlight batteries would soon be worthless, right along with the battery in his satellite phone.

"It seems like someone should have been here by now," said Sheree. She was starting to shake from the cold.

Carolyn, too, was beginning to shiver. "It's so cold in here!"

"I don't want you ladies to think I'm getting fresh or anything," quantified Ray, "but it looks to me like both of you are exhibiting the first signs of hypothermia. We need to huddle together for warmth right now, especially with the sun gone, as it's only going to get colder."

"What happens when the water gets over here?" questioned Sheree. "How high do you think it will get?"

"See that line of residue on the wall up there?" pointed out Ray.

"That's above our heads!" exclaimed Sheree.

"Sheree, can you swim?" questioned Ray. "I know Carolyn had lifesaving class with Susan, once upon a time."

"Not really," admitted Sheree, embarrassed by her shortcoming.

"Well, let's just hope they get here before it comes to that," remarked Carolyn.

"We need to keep each other talking about something," interjected Ray, "anything, just to make sure we remain conscious and alert until the rescuers arrive. And they will!"

"They really are taking their time," mumbled Sheree.

"That water will be on our feet in less than ten minutes, from my calculations," announced Carolyn. "Do we have anything to eat?"

"I don't have anything," admitted Ray. "Just a pack of gum."

"Me, neither," added Sheree.

"And we drank the rest of Ray's water," evaluated Carolyn.

"That's about the size of it," agreed Ray.

"I know I should have mentioned this earlier," revealed Carolyn, "but I'm worried about my blood sugar dropping. I can feel it."

"You're not a diabetic are you?" grilled Ray.

"I'm afraid so," admitted Carolyn. "Type two, but strictly diet and exercise controlled. I don't need any medication for it."

"At least there's that," Ray sighed with relief.

"Even that can be serious, though," opined Sheree. "Jon had type two diabetes."

Ray suddenly found and pulled a pack of gum from his pocket and handed it to Carolyn. "It's not much, but it's yours."

"It's sugar free," noticed Carolyn with a wry grin.

"I'll take some," said Sheree as she took a piece of it from Carolyn and popped it into her mouth.

"It's almost so dark now, that we won't even be able to see when the water gets here," pointed out Carolyn. "Even with your flashlight."

"We could climb up onto that pile of rocks," suggested Ray.

The bloody remains of Jon Roth were strewn across the rock pile, and the idea of having to go over there was repulsive to all of them.

"As a last resort, of course," qualified Ray.

"Well, we need to do something now, if we're gonna do it, before it's too dark to see," recommended Carolyn.

"Are you thinking what I am?" proposed Ray.

"Yeah, probably," responded Carolyn with a deep sigh.

"What are you guys talking about?" Sheree was perplexed.

"Jon had a flashlight," reminded Carolyn.

Sheree scowled. "But, it's underneath his body somewhere!"

"He had protein bars in his pocket, too, if I'm not mistaken," described Carolyn.

"You can't be serious!" objected Sheree.

"Would you rather wait until the water gets there and ruins both the flashlight and the protein bars?" grilled Carolyn.

"She's right," agreed Ray. "And hopefully we won't be reduced to eventually eating him!"

"What?" exclaimed Sheree with horror.

"I'm with Sheree on that one," announced Carolyn. "Personally, I'd rather die than have a single bite of second-hand Lenny burgers!"

Sheree stared at Carolyn with disbelief but then suddenly began shaking her head and laughing. "Me, too!"

"Well, I never was much for second-hand Lenny burgers myself," chuckled Ray with a sardonic grin.

"Seriously, that water is going to be on him in less than five minutes," reminded Carolyn.

"I can't help," advised Sheree, "but you should hurry."

Ray and Carolyn then approached the lifeless body of Jon Roth.

"On three," said Ray.

Carolyn merely nodded as she grabbed the bloody sleeve of Jon's shirt.

"One, two, three," counted Ray as he and Carolyn suddenly rolled the corpse over onto its back.

Carolyn fought back the urge to vomit as she quickly reached into Jon's front shirt pocket to remove the two protein bars.

"This one's half open and has blood inside," observed Carolyn with a grimace as she started to toss it away.

"I'll take that," insisted Ray. "Just in case we need it later."

"The other one has blood on the wrapper, but it's water proof and can be rinsed off before I open it," evaluated Carolyn.

"The flashlight's ruined," noticed Ray. "It was right under him when he fell on it."

Carolyn quickly walked over to the advancing tidewater and rinsed off the outer wrapper of the protein bar.

Ray seized the opportunity, as well, to rinse off any remaining blood from the half eaten protein bar.

"Too bad he didn't have any water, too," commented Sheree.

"Last chance to decide where we hole up in the dark," pressed Ray. "Here, where the water won't get us for at least ten more minutes, or over where Sheree is and the water is already at her feet."

"What about in there, with them?" Carolyn suddenly noticed.

"With Joyce and Veronica?" realized Sheree.

"That is up at least three feet higher than this," calculated Ray. "As long as there aren't any more earthquakes, that might not be a bad idea. It could buy us just enough time until they get here. They should be here soon."

Without further comment, the three of them quickly made their way over what was left of Jon Roth and into the makeshift cairn where Joyce and Veronica had been entombed exactly 43 years ago that day, on March 23, 1973.

"At least he's finally at peace now," commented Sheree. "He never had any, you know."

"Probably not, after what he did to them," responded Carolyn as she reverently glanced at Joyce's skeleton. "This one must be Joyce, because her hands are still bound together behind her back with this bungee cord."

"There's a bungee cord still there?" questioned Ray.

"Look!" noticed Carolyn. "There's one of the boogie boards! Right behind her!"

"It's old and weathered, but I'll bet it still floats," surmised Ray.

"This end of the bungee cord is hooked into the boogie board already. So, we could use the boogie board to hang onto when the water gets up this far, and then hook the other end of the bungee cord onto the top of that gate," realized Carolyn. "Oh Joyce, thank you!"

Carolyn carefully removed the bungee cord from the fragile skeleton's wrists. Ray then held the skeleton away from the wall while Carolyn pulled out the boogie board.

Sheree began to feel sick and suddenly threw up. "I'm sorry!"

"I think we all feel like that," assessed Carolyn as she quickly unwrapped the protein bar and broke off a piece for Sheree, and another piece for Ray, before devouring the remainder of it herself.

"We should be good now," opined Ray.

"That's the last of the flashlight, then," noted Carolyn as it went dark and left them huddled together beside the skeletons of Joyce and Veronica.

The Ocean Bluff station house normally doubled as both a fire station and a police department, but severe damage from the series of earthquakes earlier that afternoon had necessitated its evacuation.

Thankfully, the town's only store, gas station and post office remained unscathed, along with the town's entrance sign which indicated a population of 317 people. The recreation hall that doubled as a church on Sundays and as a senior center during the week, had been commandeered and was now being used as a command center by the police and fire departments until other arrangements could be made. A huge makeshift divider composed of freestanding cubicle sections was arranged across the middle. Much to the delight of the law enforcement and firemen alike, Kay's Diner and Patty's Pancake House were right next door and across the street, respectively.

Chief Otterman – who was also the town's Mayor - had just finished consuming a large cup of coffee and a piece of strawberry rhubarb pie with a scoop of vanilla ice cream on top. It wasn't often anymore that Killingham ice cream was still available at Kay's Diner. Especially since it all had to be brought from Oceanview Academy now.

Jim debated on whether or not to return to the makeshift police station tonight, or just wait until morning, but finally followed a prompting to check in on things just one last time before going home for the night. Besides, he really should power down his computer. Jim was deep in thought as he laid a twenty-dollar bill on the table by his check. That was what Jim always paid for anything he ordered, even if it was just a cup of coffee, and insisted upon leaving the change as a tip. Kay often wondered how someone on a policeman's salary could afford such extravagance, but kept it to herself. Even the combined salary of Mayor and Chief of Police in a town like Ocean Bluff was meager and came from a very limited budget. Naturally, none of Jim's friends or acquaintances in Ocean Bluff was aware of his true financial circumstances, nor did they need to know.

Jim was an only child whose parents had been killed while on winter holiday in Switzerland back in 2004. They had been skiing in the Alps when an unexpected avalanche had buried them alive, along with several other unfortunate vacationers. It had taken weeks for all the bodies to be safely recovered, and his parents had been among the last to be found.

Being the sole heir to his father's multi-million-dollar brokerage firm was not a responsibility Jim took lightly, so he had hired an entire regiment of well-paid employees to run it for him. Thankfully, it was only necessary to visit the home office once or twice each year. Jim hated big cities, and would only travel there by plane. Jim's personal aircraft was nothing more than a single engine Piper Cherokee 180 that seated four, but it met his needs. It was not

464

much unlike the one his former roommate Bart Higbee had owned back in 1973.

Guilt-ridden by the fact that he had not corroborated Carolyn's testimony at her deposition on the morning of March 24, 1973 – the morning following the tragic death of Steve Fredrickson on the beach – Jim Otterman had sought for years to make it right.

Jim had studied a variety of subjects in college, including pre-medicine, chemistry, marine biology, geology and even anthropology, but ultimately decided upon law enforcement. The digitally enhanced copies of Jim's crime scene photos from that day on the beach in 1973 clearly revealed that Veronica Jensen's and Joyce Troglite's tracks in the sand led *into* the bunker tunnel opening! Why hadn't he seen that before, and why had he second-guessed himself at the time?

Jim entered the makeshift station house, walked over to and sat down at the card table currently being used as his desk. Jim wearily opened a tattered file on the middle of it. Because of their similarities, the Jensen and Troglite cases had finally been consolidated – the tragic cold cases that no one else believed would ever be solved. At the close of each day for over forty years, Jim had taken a few moments to glance through the file again and scrutinize every possible detail.

Jim Otterman had also spent countless hours during the past two years exploring the entire tunnel system beneath Oceanview Academy on his own, using rare old plat maps from the town library. After a sizable donation to the Ocean Bluff Library, Jim had finally been able to convince the town librarian to part with the plat maps, and to keep the details of his donation confidential. The library's new annex had been constructed shortly thereafter, followed by another anonymous donation of considerable size.

Jim knew that the "anonymous" benefactor would soon need to provide the rundown little town of Ocean Bluff with a new fire station and police department! That was okay, thought Jim, as long as he was able to continue his quest. Money really was no object to Jim and meant very little to him without the one thing in his life that he had wanted most - a woman he knew he could never have. Jim had never bothered to get married or have a family, and Kay from Kay's Diner had been his only other romantic interest, short-lived though it had been. Once Kay learned of Jim's continued obsession with Carolyn, a former schoolmate that he would probably never see again, she had cut off the relationship.

"Ready to close it down for the night?" came a voice from the other side of the freestanding cubicle dividers. It was Ralph Edson, the Fire Chief. "That wind is really picking up out there."

"At least we shouldn't have any fog tonight," replied Jim.

"Between your guys and mine, all the houses have been checked and appear to be undamaged," informed Ralph. "Looks like the station house was our only casualty here in Ocean Bluff."

"It was an old building," shrugged Jim.

"You don't seem too worried about it," noticed Ralph.

"Not as worried as I am about that earthquake," replied Jim.

"The bunker tunnel thing again?" Ralph raised an eyebrow and shook his head. "You've been through every inch of those tunnels, and you're a geologist! Even the kids' fathers and scores of other searchers went through that place back then. Those girls were shark bait. If they were in that tunnel, someone would have found them by now."

"But they are in there!" exclaimed Jim as he pounded his fist on the card table, almost making it collapse.

"Okay, maybe they are," conceded Ralph. "Perhaps tomorrow we can go out there and see if that quake turned up anything new. Or even do a flyover."

"I plan to go out there at first light," indicated Jim.

"I'll be here," promised Ralph. "My wife's been keeping dinner for me and it's starting to get dark."

"I'll lock up," replied Jim. "Say, did you check the landline?"

"Nobody uses that anymore," chuckled Ralph. "Everyone in town has satellite phones, including us."

"I'm gonna head back over to the station house and see if I can find that message machine," Jim suddenly decided.

"You can't go through that mess by yourself!" objected Ralph. "Besides, it's starting to rain out there."

"All the more reason to find it now, before the thing gets wet," persisted Jim. "I can't explain it, but I just have a feeling that I need to check the message line."

"Come on, let's go," urged Ralph. "The sooner we find it and put your mind at ease, the sooner I can get home for dinner."

After locking the door to the senior center, Jim and Ralph made their way toward the remains of their station house.

"Don't you think it's rather odd that today's earthquake would happen at precisely 4:23 p.m. on March 23, 2016?" questioned Jim.

"What do you mean?" frowned Ralph.

"Think about it," urged Jim. "It was at precisely 4:23 p.m. on March 23, 1973, that Joyce and Veronica were seen running into that bunker tunnel, and that was the last time anyone ever saw them again!"

"When you were flying over the beach that day with Carolyn and Bart," recounted Ralph. He had heard it all before.

"I think it's a sign of some kind," informed Jim as they arrived at the pile of rubble.

"Hey, there's your message machine, right there!" noticed Ralph with surprise. "What are the odds of that?"

Jim hurried over to the antiquated message machine and checked to see if it was still plugged in. Naturally, it was not.

"I'm taking this back to the senior center to see if there's anything on it," described Jim.

"You'll probably need this," assumed Ralph as he picked up the message machine's cord and began coiling it into a bundle to take with them. "It actually looks undamaged."

A sudden onslaught of rain began coming down, prompting the two men to quickly run for cover under the awning at the entrance to Kay's Diner. "We could just go in here, and get a cup of coffee," suggested Ralph.

"I already had one," revealed Jim. "But, nothing's stopping you. The strawberry rhubarb pie's pretty good today, too. In fact, Kay's even got some of that Killingham ice cream right now."

"After you," motioned Ralph as he held the door open for Jim.

Jim quickly raced over to the counter with the message machine, carefully set it down, and waited for Kay to notice him.

"Yes?" greeted Kay suspiciously.

"I need to plug this in so I can listen to it while Ralph has a helping of that ice cream and pie," advised Jim.

"And a cup of coffee, too, please," added Ralph.

Kay merely motioned for Jim to come behind the counter to plug in his machine while she went to fill Ralph's order.

"Did you check the messages on your satellite phone?" quizzed Ralph with a grin.

"I did," assured Jim in a serious tone. "Okay, here goes."

No one else was in Kay's Diner but the three of them, so Kay suddenly decided to stop what she was doing and came over to listen in. Jim then pressed the playback button.

"Help!" came a woman's frantic voice. "Help! Is anyone there? Please pick up if you are! Hello?"

The dial tone could then be heard.

"Who was that?" demanded Jim. "That voice! It sounded so familiar, but I just can't place it."

The next message suddenly began playing. "Help! Is anyone there yet? If you get this message, please call Ray Dixon at the lighthouse right away." The woman then slowly repeated the number before hanging up.

"That's Ray's number all right," recognized Ralph.

When he was able to get a day off, Ralph sometimes went over to help Ray work on the old truck he was rebuilding, so was quite familiar with Ray's number.

"Are you sure?" quizzed Jim. After quickly dialing Ray's number on his own satellite phone, a recording came on that indicated the phone was either out of service or had been disconnected.

"Let me try it on mine," insisted Ralph. Ralph quickly dialed Ray's number on his satellite phone, but got the same message Jim had just gotten.

"That's not possible," muttered Jim. "Ray never goes anywhere without that phone, and he always keeps it charged!"

"Maybe something happened to him during the storm?" speculated Ralph. "We didn't go to the lighthouse. We were planning on checking out Ray's place tomorrow when we go out to the school."

"My deputies are all gone for the night," pointed out Jim, "so I'm officially deputizing you as my assistant for the night. Let's go!"

Kay smiled as she handed Ralph a piece of pie and a cup of coffee that she had already put in containers to go.

"Thanks!" smiled Jim as he slapped another twenty-dollar-bill onto the counter before Ralph could get out his wallet.

Ralph and Kay exchanged a curious look but said nothing. Now was not the time to press Jim about his seemingly unending supply of spending money.

"I'm an idiot!" Jim suddenly said. "The number that woman gave was for Ray's satellite phone, yet she said she was calling from the lighthouse."

"She sure did," recognized Ralph as he tried to take a sip of coffee but realized at once it was too hot and he was going to have to wait. "Isn't there a caller ID on that thing? Maybe she was calling from another phone but just gave you that number?"

"But why?" frowned Jim as he raced back over to the counter where his message machine still sat.

Rewinding the tape to the most recent message, Jim pressed the play button again. "Help! Is anyone there yet? If you get this message, please call Ray Dixon at the lighthouse right away." The woman then slowly repeated the number before hanging up.

"Here it is!" recalled Jim. "The caller ID button. I wasn't sure if it even had one."

"Have you ever used it before?" asked Kay surreptitiously.

"And you have?" questioned Jim.

"I have one just like it in the back," revealed Kay. She then unceremoniously pressed an unexpected combination of buttons on the device to bring up a small display panel.

"That's not the same number," noticed Jim immediately and began dialing it.

After only one ring, a woman's voice answered. "Ray? Is that you? Are you guys all right?"

"This is the Sheriff," informed Jim. "Your number was on the caller ID here at the station."

Kay gave Jim a disapproving look and mouthed the words, "Really?" Ralph merely shrugged his shoulders.

"Thank God!" replied Susan. "I'm a friend of Ray Dixon's and am waiting for him at the lighthouse, but he and two other people are trapped behind a locked gate down on the beach."

"And the tide's coming in right now, too!" mentioned Ted in the background.

"May I send you some photos that they sent me that show where they are?" questioned the woman. "Are you using a smartphone?"

"Actually, it's a satellite phone, but yes, it works pretty much like a smartphone," replied Jim. He then gave her the number.

"Okay, got it," informed Susan. "I'll send them to you right now." She then hung up, waited a moment, and proceeded to send the series of photos to the Sheriff.

Ann stealthily came up behind Susan to watch as she began texting the photos to the Sheriff. When the photo of Jon Roth's bloody corpse came up, Ann let out a gasp of surprise.

Susan immediately tried to cover the display on her phone. "Oh, no! I'm so sorry! Your mother did not want you to see these."

"Kind of late now," replied Ann.

Ted immediately got up and came over to the table so he could see for himself. "Can you back up and start from the beginning?"

"Let me finish sending these to the Sheriff first," replied Susan.

"Thank God my mother and I will no longer have to live in constant fear like we were!" Ann suddenly remarked.

"Is that Joyce and Veronica?" Ted became excited when he saw the photos of the skeletons. "Why in the world would you keep these from us?"

"I'm going down there right now," announced Ann. "The sun is going down and there's no way the Sheriff will get there in time."

"She's right," agreed Ted. "That tide has them waist deep right about now, and it's only gonna get worse."

"Didn't Carolyn mention she was a type two diabetic?" recalled Ann. "Just like my dad used to be. Do we know if they had any food with them?"

"This is exactly why I didn't show you two the photos just yet," responded Susan as she finished sending them all to the Sheriff. "We're waiting for the Sheriff. It's just too dangerous for us to try and go down there ourselves. Here, you look at the pictures while I go downstairs to use the restroom. I'll be right back!"

Ted then took Susan's smartphone from her and began looking through the photos as Ann sat beside him and looked on.

"I'm sorry to say this, but Jon Roth was a monster," opined Ted, "and I'm truly glad we're finally rid of him!"

"Me, too," added Ann, though with a tinge of sadness. "He must have finally felt some remorse for what he did, though, to take his own life like that. See how the gun is still in his hand in that photo?"

Meanwhile, over at Kay's Diner, Jim Otterman sat down to look at the series of photos that had been sent to him.

"This says these are from a Susan Rives!" he suddenly noticed. "Of course! That's where I've heard that voice before!"

470

"I suppose she's someone else you went to school with?" asked Kay, rather snidely. Kay was still bitter over their breakup, even though she had been the one to cut it off.

"As a matter of fact, yes!" answered Jim. "She was Carolyn's roommate."

"Of course she was," sniggered Kay as she rolled her eyes.

"And also my lab partner in biology class," added Jim evenly.

"Oh, my goodness!" muttered Ralph as he saw the first photo on the phone. Jim had not yet glanced at it. "Are you seeing this?"

Jim then turned to study the first photo and saw Ray Dixon and Sheree Roth with – it couldn't be – with Carolyn Bennett! Jim stared at the photo with disbelief. The photo showed the three of them by the infamous iron-barred gate. Jim was quite familiar with the place in the photo and knew exactly where they were!

The message read, "Gate locked, please send Sheriff before high tide, we're trapped."

"This photo had to be taken at least two hours ago!" realized Jim angrily. "See how the late afternoon sun is reflecting off the ocean water in the background behind them?"

"There's nothing left but twilight out there now," reminded Ralph. "That kid in the background was saying something about the tiding coming in, too."

"Of course it is!" snapped Jim as he advanced to the next photo.

"Eeew!" grimaced Kay when she saw the photo of Jon Roth's bloody corpse. "How horrible! Why would he do such a thing to himself?"

Jim immediately recognized the distinctive gold watch on Jon Roth's hand in the photo, where it still held the gun Jon Roth had used to end his own life. There was no question in Jim's mind that the photo was of Jon Roth.

"Remarkable," mumbled Jim, not sure now what to think.

"That's one word for it," agreed Ralph. Neither of them had ever really liked Jon Roth and knew of no one else who had.

Jim stood to leave as he advanced to the next photo but then sat back down again. "Son of a gun! I don't believe this!"

Ralph and Kay both stared at the photo of the two skeletons with astonishment. Both of them were well aware of Jim Otterman's lifelong quest to solve what had come to be known as The Oceanview

Matter – the consolidated cold case files of Joyce Troglite and Veronica Jensen.

"Do you think it's really them?" questioned Ralph.

"Absolutely it is!" assured Jim. "This photo even shows their boogie boards and a pile of other stuff, probably rotten beach towels and clothing items."

"I wonder what Jon Roth actually did do to those poor girls?" Kay suddenly pondered. "That guy always did give me the creeps!"

"Me, too," agreed Ralph. "Everyone around here thought it was kind of odd that the school hired him to be their theology instructor."

"They say he was locked up over there in that looney bin for a spell, too," recalled Kay. She made it a point to eavesdrop on customer conversations whenever possible, and always tried to keep abreast of the latest gossip.

"Jon obviously couldn't live with what he'd done," deduced Jim. "I've actually suspected him for a couple of years now, but just couldn't prove anything. I even followed him into those tunnels one afternoon, sure that he would lead me to something, but I think he knew I was trailing him and went another way."

"Hey, I'm sorry I doubted you," apologized Ralph.

"Kay, can you please call the lighthouse and let Susan know we're on our way to unlock the bunker tunnel gate down on the beach?" requested Jim. "Tell her I've got the key, and not to worry. I definitely know where they are!"

"The tidewater is probably several feet deep there already," cautioned Ralph.

"Then we'd better get going," recommended Jim as he got up and headed for the door.

Ralph had just finished eating his pie and quickly began gulping down the rest of his coffee.

"After you call Susan, please call the Coast Guard and have them meet us there," added Jim. "We're gonna need life-flight."

"You're kidding, right?" Kay gave Jim a doubtful look.

"Now!" commanded Jim. "And tell them to send medical help for at least three people. No one ever uses that airstrip at night, but it does have low intensity runway edge lights for emergencies and I'll make sure they're on. They shouldn't have any trouble finding the place after that. The bunker tunnel is about a hundred yards north of the airstrip, but it's down on the beach so they'll need ropes and rappelling gear to get down there! And floodlights, too!"

"Nobody's gonna fly out there in this kind of weather," argued Kay. "Not even the Coast Guard!"

"They damn well better!" barked Jim. "I don't care what they have to do to get someone down there or what it costs! And if they give you any guff about it, have 'em look me up. I'm good for it!"

"Landing a helicopter on the runway actually might be safer than trying to get that close to shore at night by boat during high tide in a storm like this one!" said Ralph. "Let's just hope Ray, Sheree and Carolyn are all still alive when they get there."

"Oh, and try to call John Murray, after that," added Jim. "Just in case he can get to those runway edge lights before we do!"

Kay was speechless for a moment as she watched Jim and Ralph race out the door of her rundown diner. She then quickly made the calls that Jim had requested.

Back at the lighthouse, Susan Rives slowly climbed the spiral staircase, deep in thought. She would need to call the Sheriff again, just to be sure he had gotten her text messages okay and had seen the photos. Susan also wanted to verify that help was on the way.

As she reached the tower room, Susan suddenly noticed that Ann Roth was not there. "Where is she?"

"I couldn't stop her," informed Ted.

"How could you just let her go out there by herself?" demanded Susan. "Look at that wind! Can't you see those waves out there?"

"At least eight foot swells," estimated Ted.

"This is serious!" shouted Susan. "Don't you even care that Ann's out there by herself?"

"Of course I care," replied Ted as he readjusted his sprained ankle into a more comfortable position on the bench seat beside him.

Susan breathed in deeply and then suddenly let it back out. "It's dark, it's windy, and it's even starting to rain! Ann is a sixteen-year-old girl who thinks she is invincible, and whose father just shot himself in the head! Ann may try to put on a tough front, but anyone in her situation would be emotionally compromised after something like that!"

"Ann's mother is still alive and trapped inside that bunker tunnel on the beach, with tidewater coming in," reminded Ted. "Nothing could have stopped Ann from going down there."

Ted then picked up Susan's smartphone and unexpectedly began dialing someone's number.

"Just who are you trying to call?" Susan suddenly asked. "We need to keep that line free in case the Sheriff calls us back!"

"Ann asked me to keep trying to reach John Murray's wife, Jeon, so she could go feed the animals at the dairy for her," explained Ted. "None of them have eaten yet tonight."

"The cats?" Susan raised both eyebrows and shook her head. "She's as bad as Carolyn about those stupid cats!"

"Not just the cats," smiled Ted. "The lambs, the chickens, or whatever else Ann feeds over there each day. It's a tremendous responsibility and Ann takes it very seriously."

"I know she does," answered Susan more softly. "I'm just worried about all of them right now."

"Especially Ray?" inquired Ted with a mischievous grin.

"So, what if I am?" Susan gave Ted a crooked smile.

"Nothing wrong with that," replied Ted. "Especially at your age. You two both deserve whatever happiness you can still get."

"Because we each have one foot in the grave?" sniggered Susan.

"I didn't mean it like that," countered Ted. "You know, being older and all, but each of you getting a second chance at happiness."

"Or a third," added Susan, "but then who's counting?"

"What was my Aunt Veronica really like?" inquired Ted. "Was she as rebellious and strong-willed as my mom and grandparents always made her out to be?"

"Well, she did have a mind of her own," recalled Susan. "I remember her saying her father was a serious, hard-working accountant, and that any kind of levity or frivolity were discouraged in their home."

"That sounds like Grandpa Jensen, all right," agreed Ted.

"He was so hard-working, in fact," added Susan, "that he was too busy to come here for Veronica's funeral service. Her mother and sister came here without him."

"I remember Grandma Jensen saying that," nodded Ted sadly.

"Veronica had worked for an entire summer as a lifeguard after school every day to earn enough money to come here," remembered Susan. "That was the only way she was able to get your grandpa to finally agree to let her come here."

"Didn't she work in the lumber mill?" quizzed Ted.

"She did," confirmed Susan. "Veronica and Joyce both worked in tufting, along with Carolyn."

"Wasn't that where they would put the buttons in chaise lounge cushions?" inquired Ted.

"Yes, it was," replied Susan as her eyes took on a faraway expression. "And the tufting area was right next to the stuffing station, where Jon Roth worked."

Ted frowned as he thought of Jon Roth.

"Of course, we all called him Birdboy back then," continued Susan. "Most of us didn't even know his real name at the time."

"So, they knew each other, then?" delved Ted.

"They knew each other, all right," answered Susan, "but they certainly weren't friends. In fact, there was an incident between them at their workstation that day. Birdboy ended up getting fired over it."

"The same day that Joyce and Veronica first went missing?" questioned Ted.

"Yes indeed," verified Susan. "Birdboy had been throwing stuffing at them while they were trying to work, and Veronica got mad and kept asking him to stop."

"And?" pressed Ted, anxious to learn more.

"Veronica was trying to sweep up the mess in her work area when Birdboy came up and tried to grab her broom," described Susan. "That's what everyone said happened, though I didn't get there until right after, so I didn't actually see it."

"Why would he grab her broom?" frowned Ted. "That doesn't make any sense."

"I don't know, but apparently Joyce got involved at that point, trying to help Veronica get the broom away from him," continued Susan. "That was when Birdboy shoved Joyce and Veronica out of his way, as hard as he could, with the broom, and propelled them backward onto a stack of freshly tufted chaise lounge cushions. Thankfully, neither of them was injured, at least not then."

"What a jerk!" opined Ted.

"That was when I got there, just in time to see Birdboy climb up onto one of the tufting tables. He began flapping his arms like a bird and squawking like a vulture," elaborated Susan. "Right before he took a flying leap and landed on another pile of chaise lounge cushions."

"Wow! The guy really was nuts!" assessed Ted.

"That was the last most of us ever saw of Birdboy for a very long time," added Susan. "It was the very next day when the men in white coats showed up at his parents' house to take Jon Roth away to the looney bin."

"They should have just kept him there!" replied Ted.

"Well, if they had, you wouldn't have Ann Roth in your life," reminded Susan with a mischievous grin.

"That is true," acknowledged Ted.

"Veronica spent every free moment she had down there on that beach, boogie boarding with Joyce and Steve," described Susan. "They would all talk about the sheer ecstasy of catching and riding waves."

"My Aunt Veronica really was a lot like me," realized Ted. "You know, sometimes when I'm boogie boarding – when my ankle's not sprained, of course – it's almost like I can feel Veronica out there with me. And, there really is no way to describe the sheer joy of being propelled toward the shore by a power greater than yourself, but at the same time being in complete control of it. Does that make any sense?"

"Yeah, as long as that power doesn't happen to be a shark," qualified Susan.

"You really should try it sometime," smiled Ted.

"No thanks," responded Susan. "Too dangerous! Carolyn and I used to go down there all the time to watch, though. They did all those fancy maneuvers, bottom turning and cutting back, and even those revolving jumps."

"That would be 'bottom turns' and 'cut backs' but doing 360° turns while riding the wave is something that even I have yet to master!" marveled Ted. "I didn't realize Veronica was that good. That's impressive!"

"You know, you could have a nice future with Ann," pointed out Susan. "Don't be in any hurry to end up like Steve Fredrickson. It wasn't pretty, believe me!"

Both Susan and Ted became quiet, each lost in their own thoughts for several minutes.

Ted then grabbed Susan's smartphone and advised, "I'm calling the Sheriff to see what's going on. We should have heard something from him by now."

"No, I'm calling the Sheriff," corrected Susan as she grabbed her smartphone back from Ted. Susan then looked through her call log for the Sheriff's number before pressing the small phone icon on her display to dial it.

"Make sure he knows about Ann being out there by herself, too," reminded Ted. "I sure hope she's all right."

"Exactly what I had in mind," revealed Susan.

After only one ring, a man's voice answered, "Sheriff."

"This is Ray's friend Susan," she began. "I wanted to be sure you got the photos we texted you, and that someone is on their way out there to help them."

Jim considered revealing his true identity to Susan right then, but decided he would much rather enjoy the look of surprise on her face later when she finally saw him and realized who he was. Her caller ID had listed her as Susan Rives when calling him earlier, while his caller ID had only indicated to her that he was the Sheriff.

"We're on our way out there now, Ma'am," replied the Sheriff in a professional tone.

"Also," added Susan, "there's a sixteen-year-old girl out there named Ann Roth, and she's out there by herself. She saw the same photos we texted you, before we had a chance to stop her."

"That's not good," replied the Sheriff. "Is anyone else with you there now at the lighthouse, Ma'am?"

"Ted Jensen is here, but has a sprained ankle," described Susan. "And, I promised Ray I'd stay here with Ted and Ann."

"Ann does have a mind of her own," replied the Sheriff with a smile to his voice.

"Who is this?" Susan suddenly demanded. "I know that voice!"

"Just stay put and I'll get back to you when everyone is safe," instructed the Sheriff, without answering her question. Jim then ended the call without hesitating for Susan to say anything else, and then put his satellite phone back into his front uniform shirt pocket.

"What are you smiling about?" delved Ralph, but Jim chose not to answer him.

The patrol vehicle Jim and Ralph were in was a forest green 2016 Wrangler Unlimited 75th Anniversary Edition with hard top, all-wheel drive, built-in winch and light bar on top. Relentless wind riveted through the row of cypress trees beside them as Jim drove along the narrow, winding, two-lane stretch of road from Ocean Bluff out to Oceanview Academy. Heavy rain made it almost impossible to see in the increasing darkness, even with the windshield wipers on high.

"Maybe you should turn on your light bar," suggested Ralph. "We don't wanna end up going over that cliff!"

"No, we don't," agreed Jim as he switched on the emergency light bar mounted on top of their patrol vehicle.

"What did Susan say, anyway?" pressed Ralph.

"That Ann Roth is out there somewhere by herself," revealed Jim. "Headed where we are. Keep an eye out for her."

"Why on earth would they let her go out there alone in weather like this?" wondered Ralph. "You're the only one with a key to that place, how was she planning to get inside?"

"Well, there are other keys running around," clarified Jim, "but this is the only one that fits the new lock."

Jim slowed down upon seeing the entrance arch to Oceanview Academy and steered the patrol car beneath it.

"Do you think the Coast Guard is there yet?" queried Ralph.

"Quit asking me stupid questions!" requested Jim.

"Why is that a stupid question?" persisted Ralph.

"Because without the runway edge lights turned on, they would have no way of seeing where to land," described Jim.

"Maybe Ann got here before us and turned them on already?" speculated Ralph. "Or even John Murray?"

"Ralph?"

"What?"

"Shut up, please!" insisted Jim.

Jim was worried about Ray, Sheree and especially Carolyn, and was in no mood for Ralph's incessant babbling at the moment.

Ralph merely nodded and began looking outside the window on his side, using his flashlight to search for anything out of the ordinary, including Ann.

"Stop!" commanded Ralph.

Jim immediately slammed on his brakes. A mid-sized cedar tree had come uprooted and fallen across the road. Jim had barely managed to stop in time. "That was close! Thanks, Ralph!"

Back in the bunker tunnel, Ray finally succeeded in getting Carolyn positioned on top of one of the boogie boards and Sheree on the other. Learning to maintain their balance was another matter, as they had only sound to go by in judging when the next surging onslaught of water might approach to try and unseat them from the boogie boards.

"It's so dark in here," complained Sheree.

"And cold!" added Carolyn.

Ray did not respond.

"Ray?" prompted Carolyn. "Are you all right?"

Still, Ray did not answer.

"Where is he?" panicked Sheree. "Ray?"

"Give me your hand," requested Carolyn, carefully reaching out until finding it. "Let's make sure we don't get separated again."

"Ray?" called Sheree. "Where is he?"

"Ray?" hollered Carolyn. "Let's each try to feel for him, to see if he's floating in the water someplace."

"What if something else is floating in the water?" feared Sheree. "Would any sharks be able to get in here? What if they smell all that blood from Jon's body?"

"Eeew!" muttered Carolyn after inadvertently grabbing one of the skeletons. "I just grabbed either Joyce or Veronica, but I'm not sure which one."

"Ray?" screamed Sheree. "This is hopeless! We're going to die in here!"

All at once something emerged from the water beside them and took a deep breath of air. Sheree screamed with fright while Carolyn froze with fear.

"Anybody hungry?" questioned Ray from the darkness.

"Where were you?" demanded Carolyn. "We both thought something had happened to you!"

"Please don't do that again," requested Sheree. "My heart is still pounding with fright."

"I felt something moving by my feet and dove down to see what it was," elaborated Ray.

"Why were you down there for so long?" pressed Sheree.

"Used my knife to kill it before bringing it up," replied Ray.

"Just how long were you down there, anyway?" asked Carolyn.

"At least three minutes," guessed Ray.

"How'd you ever learn to do that?" inquired Sheree.

"In Vietnam," revealed Ray. "Here, this is raw but it will keep us alive. We all should eat some."

Ray handed a piece of raw fish to Sheree, who cautiously sampled it. "What kind of fish is it?"

"Could be a baby shark," mentioned Ray. "It's kind of hard to tell, but I'm pretty sure that's what it is. From the size of it and how it feels, I'd say it's a Black Tip Reef Shark."

"A baby shark?" Carolyn became alarmed, suddenly thinking of her day on the beach with Steve Fredrickson and of his fatal shark bite injuries. "What about its parents? Could they be in here, too?"

"Relax, you girls are both safe, just as long as you stay up on those boogie boards," assured Ray. "Besides, shark moms don't stick around to provide protection for their young, anyway. Shark pups are always left to feed and fend for themselves."

"What about you?" questioned Sheree. "What if there's any more of them in here?"

"Oh, they wouldn't want a tough old bird like me," replied Ray. "Besides, they usually go for the feet first, and I've got my boots on."

"If something happens to you, we don't stand a chance," pointed out Sheree.

"Nothing's gonna happen to me," promised Ray. "As you may recall, there's only three inches between the bars on that gate, so nothing big enough to be much of a threat can get through. Eat or be eaten, right?"

"I'm allergic to most seafood," informed Carolyn. "Having low blood sugar is like a walk in the park compared to anaphylaxis. I've eaten salmon without any problems, but never shark."

"You need to keep your protein level up," recommended Ray, "especially being a diabetic. It's either that or the half eaten protein bar that was in Jon Roth's pocket when he shot himself."

480

"Okay," Carolyn finally agreed. "I guess the worst it can do is kill me, right?"

Bart Higbee was now semi-retired from his lifelong career of inspecting and maintaining commercial airliners and propulsion systems for orbiting spacecraft. Though offered an opportunity to take up residency at an orbiting space station recently - to assist with the many ongoing maintenance challenges there - Bart had chosen instead to remain earthside near his family.

Bored with an abundance of spare time on his hands, Bart often volunteered to pilot small planes during humanitarian aid missions of mercy to third world countries, and most recently as a rescue helicopter pilot for a local branch of the Coast Guard.

Bart had been chosen for this particular mission because of his unmatched piloting skills in unusually dangerous weather conditions. Not only that, Bart had recently participated in a successful night hoist rescue operation involving a group of stranded mountain climbers on the vertical face of a treacherous cliff.

"There it is, sir!" pointed out his co-pilot, Mike Larsen. "The runway edge lights are on, but I can't seem to get any radio signal."

"Not surprising out here," replied Bart. He was all too familiar with the remote airstrip at Oceanview Academy where he had once attended school and first learned to fly.

Bart then noticed someone signaling them from below with a handheld flashlight being waved back and forth over their head, about a hundred yards north of the airstrip. It was Ann Roth standing on the bluff top trail, immediately above where Bart knew it led to the infamous bunker tunnel opening below it. Bart frowned as he thought of that day on the beach 43 years ago, and how horribly Steve Fredrickson had died. Bart knew from experience that sharks often did return to the scene of previous hunts, though it was normally juvenile sharks that sought shelter in small caves during inclement weather conditions like this.

"Shouldn't we be landing over on that air strip?" asked Mike.

"We won't be landing just yet," replied Bart, as he steered the helicopter past the young woman with the flashlight and then hovered over the beach above the bunker tunnel entrance. "Shine your floodlight down there on that opening beneath the cliff."

Mike Larsen immediately shined a floodlight at the partially submerged bunker tunnel entrance below them. "Who is that guy trying to climb down that trail in this kind of weather? He must be crazy!"

"It can't be!" Bart shook his head. "That guy bears a strong resemblance to my old roommate, Jim Otterman. Looks like he's trying to get down to the locked gate where those people are trapped. He's got a Sheriff uniform on, too. Interesting."

"He'll be swept away!" feared Mike.

Bart grabbed his bullhorn and shouted, "Stop! Remain where you are! Let us handle this."

"I've got the *only* key to that gate!" shouted Jim, though unheard above the loud humming whir of the helicopter above him. "Just keep your floodlight on!"

"What's he trying to tell us?" quizzed Mike. "He's still heading down there. Tell him again to stop!"

"He won't stop. Finish suiting up," instructed Bart. "You're gonna need to tie yourself off up here and repel down there to get him. I don't dare let loose of these controls, not in this wind!"

Already dressed in a wetsuit in anticipation of a possible water rescue, Mike needed only to put on his fins, gloves and headgear before proceeding with the rescue.

Jim Otterman had finally reached the iron-barred gate and was hanging onto it with one hand to keep from being swept away.

"Jim Otterman?" questioned the man who had repelled down to assist. "I'm going to need to tie you off and haul you up."

"Where's your rescue basket?" hollered Jim. "There's still three people in there!"

"Sir, there is no rescue basket, and no life-flight coming, not in this weather," explained Mike Larsen. "We're it. And I'm going to have to haul each of you up individually, starting with you."

"I've got the only key to that gate!" yelled Jim.

"Hand it over," instructed the man. "I think I'm a little better equipped for diving than you are."

"Don't drop it!" cautioned Jim as he took out and handed the precious key to the stranger.

"Just hang on and stay where you are, Sir," replied the man as he dove down with the key, quickly finding and unlocking the gate with the combined aid of his head lamp and the helicopter's floodlight.

Almost losing his grip on the gate as it swung outward, Jim Otterman somehow managed to avoid being pulled out to sea by an outgoing surge of tidewater.

The highest tide would not occur until 9:38 p.m. when the water would reach a depth of about nine feet inside the bunker tunnel. Fortunately, it was only 7:30 p.m. but already the water was more than six feet deep. Mike Larsen then used the head lamp on his diving helmet to quickly locate Ray Dixon, Sheree Roth and Carolyn Bennett-Hunter.

"You first!" ordered Mike as he grabbed Ray by the arm and began pulling him toward the gate.

"They go before me," insisted Ray.

"No, Sir," differed Mike. "They're up out of the water, and you're not, so that makes you my first priority, especially with these shark pups in here. Good thing you have those boots on!"

"Just go," insisted Sheree, "so he can come back for us!"

"Oh, my God!" screamed Carolyn when she noticed several small baby sharks circling in the water beneath them in the rays of the floodlight. Several of them could clearly be seen feeding on the submerged corpse of Jon Roth.

Sheree suddenly made a face. "I think I'm going to be sick!"

"Jon may have just saved our lives," realized Carolyn, "but now that the gate is open, who knows what else can get in here!"

"Please hurry, Ray, just go!" shouted Sheree.

Even though the floodlight made it possible to see, Sheree and Carolyn continued to hang onto one another for support, and to stabilize the boogie boards on which they were huddled as they waited.

Mike Larsen quickly tied off and hauled Ray Dixon up to the waiting helicopter, and then Jim Otterman, before returning for Sheree Roth and finally Carolyn Bennett-Hunter. Mike concluded his rescue rappelling sequence by making one last trip down to close and secure the iron-barred gate with a zip tie to prevent the evidence behind it from being washed away before morning when the Sheriff and his men could return at low tide to process the crime scene.

"Carolyn," acknowledged Bart Higbee with a welcoming smile.

"Bart! How are you?" beamed Carolyn.

"Apparently better off than you right now," chuckled Bart as he changed gears and piloted the helicopter up and toward the runway.

Carolyn sat down by Sheree and Ray to huddle for warmth. Unexpectedly, someone behind Carolyn wrapped a dry blanket around her and pulled her close. Assuming at first that it was a Coast Guard medic, Carolyn made no effort to push the person away.

"Hey, I'll take one of those," requested Ray.

"Me, too," added Sheree.

"Here you are," came a familiar voice from behind her as Carolyn saw blankets being handed to Sheree and Ray from the very edge of her peripheral vision.

Carolyn slowly turned around, stunned to see Jim Otterman sitting there with his arms around her! He was drenched, too, and older looking than she had remembered him, but staring at her with that same familiar longing gaze.

"Have some water," offered Jim as he picked up and handed Carolyn an unopened bottle of water.

"I guess you two know each other?" assumed Ray. "I'll take one of those waters, too, if you don't mind."

"Me, too!" said Sheree as she studied Jim with disapproval.

Jim unceremoniously grabbed and handed bottles of water to Ray and then Sheree before returning his attention to Carolyn.

"I must look pretty bad right now," guessed Carolyn. The situation was awkward at best and Carolyn knew she needed to distance herself from Jim Otterman's proximity at the first possible opportunity.

"She's a type two diabetic," advised Ray, irritated by the way Jim Otterman was ogling Carolyn. Couldn't Jim see the wedding ring on her hand? "What have you got for Carolyn and the rest of us to eat?"

Jim immediately opened a duffle bag full of emergency food and other supplies and handed each of them a protein bar.

"We can leave you here on the runway, or take you somewhere else," offered Bart as he set the helicopter down on the runway but left it running. "It's your call, Jim."

Ralph Edson and Ann Roth raced toward the helicopter.

"That's Ralph Edson, the Ocean Bluff Fire Chief," revealed Jim Otterman from where he sat behind Carolyn. "The rest of our men had already gone home for the night, so I deputized Ralph to come over here with me. It was quite a big day with that earthquake and all. But, we wanted to make sure we got over here before highest tide."

"Who called the Coast Guard?" questioned Ray.

"Some woman named Kay," Bart answered for him.

"Ah yes, Kay's Diner," nodded Ray knowingly. "I'm sure the entire town of Ocean Bluff knows all about this by now."

"Probably," agreed Jim. "Kay even saw the photos Susan texted over to us."

Ray just shook his head in response. He had dated Kay himself for a short time several years ago, but had quickly tired of having the entire town of Ocean Bluff know his business.

"Hey Jim," acknowledged Ralph as he poked his head inside the helicopter's open door. "I finally managed to get that cedar tree off the road with your winch."

"Excellent!" approved Jim. "Then we can take everyone back in the Jeep. Ray, Sheree and Carolyn can ride in the back seat."

"Mom!" screamed Ann as she ran up to the helicopter and climbed inside. Sheree and Ann then embraced.

"And Ann can ride in the front with us," added Jim.

"What in the world are you doing out here like this?" demanded Sheree. "Where are Susan and Ted?"

"Back at the lighthouse," replied Ann sheepishly. "Plus, I had to get Jeon and John Murray to help me feed all the animals. They're still over there now. I couldn't reach them by phone, probably because of the weather."

"Oh Ann, what am I going to do with you?" asked Sheree.

"Not only that," continued Ann. "When I saw the photos, and knew you were in danger, I just had to come. John lent me his flashlight so I could help signal the helicopter pilot when he got here."

"Wait a minute! Did you actually see the photos of your father, too?" questioned Sheree with alarm.

"It's okay, Mom," assured Ann. "Yes, I saw the photos."

"Ann!" Sheree choked back a sob as she pulled her daughter close again to give her a comforting hug.

"Hey, at least we'll never have to live in fear again," pointed out Ann as she pulled away just far enough to look at her mother's face. "And, hopefully Jon Roth finally felt some remorse for what he did to those poor girls all those years ago!"

Sheree stared at Ann with a tinge of sadness. "Jon Roth was still your father, and he did love you, Ann."

"I know," assured Ann as a stray tear finally managed to escape the corner of one eye.

"Thanks for coming, Bart," acknowledged Jim. "It was good to see you again. Please let me know what Ocean Bluff owes you guys."

"Consider this one on the house," advised Bart. "I've waited for 43 years to finally know what happened to Joyce and Veronica, and to see this matter resolved!"

"The next low tide is at 4:15 a.m. in the morning," revealed Jim. "The entire Ocean Bluff Police Department will be down there gathering up all the evidence, including the skeletal remains of Joyce and Veronica, and whatever's left of Jon Roth. You're welcome to join us if you like."

"As much as I'd like to," responded Bart, "we need to get back. We have another rescue still ahead of us tonight."

"You're kidding?" frowned Mike Larsen.

"Yes, I'm kidding!" grinned Bart. "Seriously, we're on Coast Guard time now with this helicopter and need to get it back."

"Let's not wait another 43 years to see one another again," suggested Jim as he and the others climbed from the running helicopter and made their way toward the waiting patrol vehicle. "Otherwise, we both might be dead by then."

Mike Larsen quickly closed the helicopter door and strapped himself back into the co-pilot chair.

"Touché!" nodded Bart as he put the helicopter back in gear and took off. Perhaps now the haunting dreams of Steve Fredrickson dying on the beach could finally be put behind him.

Jim, Ralph, Sheree, Ann, Ray and Carolyn paused to watch as Bart Higbee and his co-pilot Mike Larsen flew away and disappeared into the stormy night sky.

"Let's get into the Jeep!" urged Jim.

"You guys are all wet," pointed out Ralph.

"That's what usually happens when it rains like this," replied Jim. "Hey, we forgot to give Bart back his blankets!"

"I doubt he cares," interjected Ray as he and the others climbed into Jim Otterman's patrol vehicle.

"Since all five members of your Police Department will be down here tomorrow morning," commented Ralph, "I'll make sure the

Fire Department finishes poking through the rubble of our station house."

"The station house is gone?" quizzed Ray as he shut the Jeep door after getting in. "What about all your case files?"

"The Oceanview Matter is right here with me," indicated Jim as he opened his glove box to reveal a tattered looking file inside.

"Jim's been carrying that thing around with him for over forty years," mentioned Ralph. "He rarely goes anywhere without it!"

"It's the consolidated cold case files for Veronica Jensen and Joyce Troglite," described Jim as he shut the glove box, started the engine, and began driving. "Unfortunately, the rest of my files were at the station house. And we'll definitely have to build a new one."

"Why don't we just head over to the lighthouse," suggested Ray. "I've got enough rooms for everyone. That way you guys can get a good night's rest and an early start without having to drive all the way back over from Ocean Bluff. You can call your men from there, too."

"What about our wet clothes?" wondered Jim.

"I do have washing machines," informed Ray.

"And extra pajamas," added Carolyn with a smile. She was glad that she and Susan had retrieved their suitcases from Ms. Neilson's house and would have their own pajamas to wear tonight.

"Jim can stay at the lighthouse if he wants to, but I just can't," declined Ralph. "I need to get back home. My wife's probably worried sick by now. Not only that, the station house in Ocean Bluff is where I plan to be in the morning."

"How will I get back to Ocean Bluff?" questioned Jim as he turned onto the access road leading behind the Roth house.

"I'm sure one of your men might be willing to give you a ride back tomorrow," teased Ralph. "They'll probably be coming back out here with your Jeep when they do, anyway. Or, you could fly back. Don't you still have your little plane over there at the school's air strip?"

"Not in this weather," assured Jim as he pulled to a stop in front of the lighthouse. "But, I think I will take Ray up on his offer to stay here tonight. That will make it easier for me to get closing statements from all of you, so I can finally close my file."

"Surely you don't plan on interrogating all of us tonight, do you?" frowned Carolyn.

"Not everyone," replied Jim with an insinuating glance.

Susan had tried in vain to study the next history lesson for her class, or to keep her mind occupied while waiting to hear from Ray Dixon. But, at least she had been successful in reaching Dean Jorgensen by phone and convincing him to spearhead a school-wide closure of Oceanview Academy for the following day.

After receiving the photos Ms. Rives had texted him, Dean Jorgensen had immediately sent them to Dean Barringer, the Dean of Girls, and also to Principal Glazier. A general assembly for the entire student body was called at once, where it was announced to everyone that the long missing remains of two former students had finally been located in one of the bunker tunnels and that classes would be suspended the following day in their memory and as a tribute to them. It would also be mentioned that Jon Roth had died during the process, but it would not be revealed how. That was not something the students needed to know, nor was it something they wanted the general public to know, either. The school's reputation needed to be protected. Recruitments for a new theology instructor would begin at once.

Most of the students attending Oceanview Academy in 2016 knew nothing about the 1973 disappearance of Joyce Troglite or Veronica Jensen, or of the tragedy involving Steve Fredrickson. Dean Jorgensen, Dean Barringer and Principal Glazier unanimously agreed during an informal staff meeting that all students should be reminded again of the potential dangers associated with boogie boarding. Perhaps some of the many students who were currently boogie boarding after class each day could be made more aware of the growing shark problem, as well. None of them wanted to see another tragedy like the one involving Steve Fredrickson, that much was certain.

Ted Jensen was already asleep in the Lavender Room, across from the Rosemary Room where Ray Dixon normally slept, immediately below the tower room of the lighthouse. Dean Jorgensen understood that Ted Jensen would not wish to be bothered by needless questions from the other students just yet, so had given his consent for Ted Jensen to remain at the lighthouse for a couple of days until things settled down, provided that Ray Dixon would be there. It would be totally inappropriate for a male student to be left alone with one of the female teachers for an extended period of time. Susan had assured Dean Jorgensen that Ray Dixon had been located and was en route to the lighthouse as they spoke. Naturally, Susan hoped it was true!

Susan was exhausted and debating on whether to change into her pajamas for the night when she suddenly heard a vehicle outside. She ran at once to the Daisy Room so she could look outside and see who it was. "It was the Sheriff!" Susan then hurried from the Daisy Room and downstairs to the front door.

Anxious to know that everyone was okay, Susan excitedly flung open the lighthouse door but then stood there in shock after getting a good look at the Sheriff.

"Susan?" grinned Jim Otterman as he tipped his wet hat and nodded in acknowledgment.

Susan continued to stand there for several moments longer before she was able to speak again. "Jim? Jim Otterman!"

"I told you she'd recognize me," smiled the Sheriff.

"Ray!" exclaimed Susan when she saw him approaching from behind the others and raced past all of them - including Jim - to embrace Ray. It did not matter that he was soaking wet. She was just glad to see him and to know that he was safe.

It was Jim's turn to be astonished when he saw Ray and Susan embrace and begin passionately kissing, as if no one else were there.

"All rightie, then," smirked Jim.

"Please, come in," Carolyn invited the others, well aware that Ray and Susan might be awhile.

"The showers are over there," indicated Ann. "The women get to go first!"

"It shouldn't take 'em too long," hoped Ray as he finally approached with Susan on his arm. "It's one of those group shower stalls like they have over at the school."

"Really?" smirked Jim. "Maybe there's room for all of us."

"Cool your jets, Jimbo," advised Ray. "We'll get our turn soon enough."

"Hey, everyone!" greeted Ted, who had hobbled downstairs to see what was going on. "The Dean gave me permission to stay here for a couple of days, by the way, if that's okay with you."

"That's fine," nodded Ray. "I think I'll set out some sandwich stuff while they're in there, too. I'm starved!"

"I'll help you," offered Jim.

"I'll watch," advised Ted as he pulled up a chair at the downstairs kitchen table and put his leg on the chair beside him.

"Nice setup you got here," mentioned Jim as he began spreading mustard on slice after slice of whole wheat bread that Ray had laid out on the food prep island.

"For as long as it lasts," replied Ray sadly.

"What do you mean?" questioned Jim. "That Susan is quite a number, and she's absolutely crazy about you! Have you thought about asking her to stay on permanently?"

Ray shook his head and tried not to smile.

"Oh, come on, I can tell!" urged Jim as he slapped a slice of ham onto each of the sandwiches they were constructing.

Ray sighed deeply before responding. "I have an appointment to see a lawyer next week about getting some type of easement for this place, but it may be a long haul."

"What kind of an easement?" probed Jim as he began slicing a tomato and placing the slices of it on the sandwiches.

"Tell him about the seagull!" encouraged Ted.

"Well, Carolyn helped Ann and Ted rescue a seagull a few days ago," revealed Ray. "So, while John Murray and I were driving it up to the Ocean Bay Bird Conservancy - where they can care for it and rehabilitate it until it's ready to be released again back into the wild again – John was describing to me some of the types of situations where people can get conservation tags or easements to help them reduce their tax obligations when they happen to have endangered or protected species living or nesting on their land."

"Things aren't that bad for you, are they?" joked Jim.

"I'm afraid so," admitted Ray.

"Sure wish I could do something to help," replied Jim thoughtfully. "This lighthouse has been in your family since the 1800's, if I remember correctly."

"1872," clarified Ray as he finished rinsing off several pieces of lettuce and spread them out on a paper towel to drain.

"Probably only the seagulls can save him now," interjected Ted. "They're on the protected species list."

"Even better," recalled Ray, "John Murray was saying that Snowy Plovers and Lesser Terns are on the endangered species list, and some of them nest right here on this beach, too!"

490

"Really?" Jim slowly began to smile.

"He also advised me to make sure I see a lawyer who specializes in these types of things," advised Ray, "and that it's a very complicated area of law that not all attorneys understand."

"Then there's always hope," reminded Jim as he began placing the pieces of freshly drained lettuce on the sandwiches.

"Probably not unless some anonymous wealthy benefactor were to come along and make a sizable donation to the cause," sniggered Ray. "Otherwise, I probably will lose this lighthouse, the Silver Creek Trailer Park, and all the land they're standing on, too."

"Ray already sold off the old servants' quarters last year in order to pay his taxes," informed Ted.

"Oh yeah," recalled Jim. "I heard about that. The school rents it out to parents when they come to visit their kids here at the school. Not a very profitable use for it."

"Does everyone know about this?" frowned Ray.

"Susan told me about it," smiled Ted. "She actually holds out high hopes that you and she can get that second chance at happiness, once her divorce is final."

"Really?" smirked Jim.

"It's not like it sounds!" snapped Ray.

"You certainly will need a miracle in order to offer an attractive amount of financial security to a woman like Susan," agreed Jim.

"I guess I'll just have to wait and see what that lawyer can do for me," replied Ray.

"Hey, you guys!" called Ann as she and the other women entered the downstairs kitchen in bathrobes.

"Those sandwiches look great!" noticed Carolyn. "Mind if I bless the food so we can eat?"

"Please do!" indicated Ray. "Be sure and thank the good Lord for our safe rescue tonight, too!"

"Amen!" agreed Sheree.

Carolyn then blessed the food before they all ate, making sure to express everyone's deepest gratitude for their safe rescue.

Unable to sleep any longer, Carolyn had gotten up and was slowly ascending the spiral staircase to the tower room of the lighthouse. The first rays of morning sun were visible, and the water was calm.

"Usually there's fog this time of day," came a voice from behind her. It was Jim Otterman.

"Mind if I join you?" asked Jim hopefully.

"I suppose you plan to depose me before I've even had my breakfast?" presumed Carolyn. "Hey, I'm sorry, but I was just too tired last night. I hope you understand."

"No problem," smiled Jim. "I think everyone needed a good night's rest. It was a hard day for all of us."

"What time will you be going down to the beach?" inquired Carolyn as she and Jim entered the tower room and sat down at the round table in the middle of it. She was trying to speak in whispers, to avoid waking any of the others just yet.

"Actually, I was thinking of having my Deputies take care of it," revealed Jim, "since I still need to take everyone's depositions over here at the lighthouse."

"You wouldn't want to miss out on gathering up all that evidence from two separate crime scenes," pointed out Carolyn.

"Two?" frowned Jim.

"One from 1973 and the other one from yesterday," clarified Carolyn with an even smile.

"The evidence from both of them has been so compromised at this point, that it really doesn't make any difference who goes down there to gather everything up," replied Jim.

"Probably true," agreed Carolyn. "I know one thing for certain, and that's that I never want to set foot in that bunker tunnel again!"

"Demolition experts are going to seal off the rest of those tunnels later this week," informed Jim. "I plan to call them today."

"That's a good idea," nodded Carolyn.

"Are you happy?" Jim suddenly asked.

"What do you mean?" Carolyn became suspicious of Jim's motives for asking her such a question.

"I mean, are you truly happy with your life now?" explained Jim.

Carolyn studied Jim carefully before answering. "Yes, I am. I've been married for 33 years to a man who loves me with all his heart, and I'm still absolutely crazy about him."

"Are you?" pressed Jim.

"Yes, I am," frowned Carolyn. "Why?"

"I know this sounds crazy," mentioned Jim rather sheepishly, "but even after all these years, I still care for you, and I've never gotten over you, Carolyn. Can you blame me for wanting to know that you are truly happy now?"

"You're really serious, aren't you?" realized Carolyn. "What about your wife and family now?"

"I never married," informed Jim.

Carolyn felt a sudden rush of panic at what Jim might say next, but had to know. Jim merely looked at her for a few moments without saying anything at all.

"I suppose you still have your darkroom full of photos?" quizzed Carolyn, sorry at once for asking.

"Actually, no," assured Jim. "Would you believe me if I told you that I have my own satellite surveillance system now?"

"You're not kidding, are you?" realized Carolyn. "Does this mean you've been spying on me with it?"

"Just making sure you're okay," assured Jim.

Carolyn appeared skeptical.

"For example," mentioned Jim, "I know that you have a long haired orange cat who loves to help you pull weeds in your yard."

"I don't believe it!" Carolyn was flabbergasted. "You really have been spying on me!"

"You have several other cats, too," added Jim. "At least six of them, maybe more. Three of them are black, though I don't think you're a witch or anything. They certainly seem to worship you."

"Your family really did have a lot of money," acknowledged Carolyn. "As I recall, you never even had to work when you went to school here. But, a satellite surveillance system? How in the world did you ever talk them into giving you the money for something like that? You certainly wouldn't be able to afford it on a Sheriff's salary!"

"Actually, my parents were killed during an avalanche over in Switzerland when they were skiing in the Alps," elaborated Jim. "It was in 2004."

"I'm sorry," replied Carolyn.

"Not only did they leave me with a sizable fortune, but also my dad's business," continued Jim. "I hire people to run it for me these days, but still have to show up once or twice a year for board meetings."

"Nobody around here knows anything at all about your money, do they?" Carolyn suddenly deduced.

"Just you," answered Jim seriously. "And I certainly hope you won't tell 'em. It's better this way."

"Would you arrest me for trying to bribe an officer if I tried to make a bargain with you?" Carolyn asked with a mischievous grin.

"What kind of a bargain?" posed Jim.

"The kind that would buy my silence," answered Carolyn with a devious look in her eyes.

"No, I won't arrest you," promised Jim. "Whatever you want, just name it. It's yours."

"Anything, huh?" clarified Carolyn.

"Absolutely anything," agreed Jim. "As long as it would make you happy. Just ask."

"Okay," agreed Carolyn. "This is what I envision for this place. Picture if you will a lighthouse bed and breakfast, run by Ray and Susan Killingham. The kind of place wealthy people will pay big money to come and see."

"What would they do when they get here?" Jim decided to play along with Carolyn's idea to see what else she had in mind.

"Well, they could possibly play golf on what could become the Silver Creek Golf Course over there – and that little store could be refurbished and used as a golf shop where guests could buy or rent golf clubs, equipment, clothing, gear, accessories, and even golf carts," elaborated Carolyn.

"That would be a nice setting for it, too," smiled Jim.

"Naturally, Ray would need to somehow obtain a conservation easement of some kind, as well," continued Carolyn, "to protect seagulls, Snowy Plovers, Lesser Terns and other endangered species of birds who happen to do their nesting right here on this beach."

"Bird watchers might want to come and stay here, too, then?" Jim had an amused look on his face.

"You may not know this," divulged Carolyn, "but unless Ray is able to get that easement, he's in danger of losing all of this, and along with it his chances of providing a good life for Susan."

"I'm already aware of that," admitted Jim, more seriously. "What else?"

"Well," thought Carolyn, "I'd like to see Sheree Roth and her daughter Ann be able to trade the Roth House straight across for the old servants' quarters next door. Someone with a big mortgage brokerage firm should be able to manage that."

"What would they do with it?" Jim seemed perplexed.

"The old servants' quarters could be a part of the same bed and breakfast company that runs the one here at the lighthouse, a place for overflow rooms when there are more guests than the lighthouse can manage," pictured Carolyn. "And Sheree is an excellent cook, by the way. Every good bed and breakfast needs one of those!"

"Really?" nodded Jim.

"There's no way Sheree or Ann can be expected to go back to that house where they lived with Jon," clarified Carolyn, "not after everything that happened over there."

"Who would live at the Roth House?" prodded Jim.

"Well, since it was built by a famous architect," reasoned Carolyn, "it could become one of those touring homes, the kind that people like to walk through and see. That could be an added attraction to the people who come and stay here at the bed and breakfast."

"That's actually not a bad idea," recognized Jim.

"Did you know that Sheree and I were roommates, before Susan?" questioned Carolyn.

"I may have heard something like that," admitted Jim.

"Thankfully, I've had the opportunity since coming here to tell Sheree how horrible I feel for how we treated her back then," confessed Carolyn. "Sheree truly is a lovely person, and deserves to find someone decent that she can spend the rest of her life with."

"Me?" Jim was stunned by what Carolyn was leading up to.

"Why not?" countered Carolyn. "Sheree loves it here as much as you do, Jim, and definitely could use some consoling about now."

Jim studied Carolyn for several moments and then shrugged his shoulders. "Would that make YOU happy, Carolyn?"

"Yes, it would," assured Carolyn. "Sheree has so much to offer someone, and should have someone who will give her the kindness and love she so desperately needs."

"Why would she ever have married someone like Jon Roth?" Jim wanted to know.

"Sheree was very insecure back then," recalled Carolyn. "She wore braces, glasses, and thought of herself as unattractive."

"She's really quite pretty now," admitted Jim.

"Yes, she is!" smiled Carolyn.

"And what makes you so sure she would be interested in someone like me?" countered Jim.

"You know," mentioned Carolyn, "Jon Roth was the only guy that even gave Sheree a second glance, and that tyrant truly had her convinced that no one else could possibly ever want her."

"Why would he do such a thing?" frowned Jim.

"Because Jon Roth was a monster!" snapped Carolyn. "And not one of us who saw him shoot himself in the head yesterday feel badly about it, either, not even Sheree! That's the extreme to which he had finally pushed her. In fact, yesterday at lunch, Sheree had already told Jon she was leaving him for good. Sheree had no idea where she would go, or what she would do, but only knew she couldn't take it anymore."

"Perhaps I should be writing this down," suggested Jim, "so I don't have to take your deposition later on."

"This particular conversation is private," insisted Carolyn. "But, I'll be happy to repeat whatever is pertinent later on at my deposition."

"Fair enough," nodded Jim. "So, do you think Jon Roth shot himself because of Sheree leaving him?"

"Jon Roth was a very sick man," replied Carolyn. "In his own way, I believe he loved Sheree and his daughter Ann. But, he also knew that the only way to protect them from Birdboy was to end his own life."

"But, he was Birdboy," reminded Jim.

"That's what I thought, too," replied Carolyn, "until we heard him arguing with himself there in that tunnel. And it was a very heated argument at that."

"Fascinating," mused Jim. "It's too bad there isn't any documentation on him, from the mental institution. That would go a long way to answering any unsolved questions about the whole thing."

"Wait here, I'll be right back," instructed Carolyn. "I have something for you."

Jim considered the suggestions Carolyn had made while he waited for her to return, which she promptly did.

"This is Ginny Eggersol's journal," informed Carolyn as she sat down with the little book. "Sheree and Ann said I should keep it. But, like them, I've already read it and really have no use for it now."

"What does it say?" asked Jim as he reached for it.

"Not so fast," Carolyn smiled coyly. "What about the things I've mentioned, as the price of my silence, do we have a deal?"

"I can't promise Sheree would even give me the time of day," advised Jim.

"What if you had a unique insight into why she was institutionalized and why she's well now?" proposed Carolyn.

"Is that what's in the little book?" questioned Jim.

"That, and much, much more," assured Carolyn. "For example, the entire Jon Roth story, which you can read for yourself."

"Really?" Jim was more than intrigued.

"But," stipulated Carolyn, "no one must ever know you have this book, including Sheree and Ann, or that you have read it, and especially where you got it from!"

"What if there is information in there that I am forced to include in the case file?" worried Jim.

"I assure you," promised Carolyn, "that you already have everything you need – or will have after you depose the three of us – to close that file for good. The information in this journal will become moot and unnecessary. Besides, there's sensitive information in the book about Jon's ancestry that you wouldn't want made public, as it could besmirch your future step-daughter's good name."

"Now I'm really intrigued," admitted Jim, "but I would have to read it first before I could promise something like that."

"Then you may just have to arrest me for withholding information from a law enforcement officer," teased Carolyn. "Because there's no way I'm giving you this book without your promise."

"Carolyn!" Jim was clearly frustrated.

"There's even an additional entry at the very end of it, personally made by Sheree," added Carolyn. "It tells of her experience with Jon Roth, Joyce and Veronica in the tunnels back on March 23, 1973, and describes everything that happened to them that day. Wouldn't you like to know the whole story?"

"I suppose I do have everything I need already to close the case," admitted Jim.

"Besides," continued Carolyn, "Ann needs an acceptable father figure she can look up to."

"Someone like me?" smiled Jim.

"Not just someone like you," corrected Carolyn. "It needs to be you! If you can manage it, that is."

"I almost feel like I'm making a deal with the devil," chuckled Jim. "Okay, everything you want, you got it, insofar as the people involved will cooperate. I can't make any of them go along with any of this, especially if I can't tell them about it."

"I have a feeling you can be quite persuasive," grinned Carolyn.

"As can you!" flirted Jim. "All right, it's a deal."

Jim reached out to shake hands with Carolyn, so she reached out to shake hands with him when Jim unexpectedly took her hand in his and brought it to his lips and kissed it.

"What are you doing?" objected Carolyn as she quickly pulled her hand away.

"Saying goodbye," replied Jim, most seriously. "Or, would you rather I just kiss you on the cheek, like Lenny did that day?"

Carolyn was clearly shaken to the core. "How do you know about that? I've never told a soul about it! Not even Susan."

"I was there," answered Jim. "After we marched the seniors up for their graduation that day, everything became chaotic with all those people trying to make their way out of the building. That was when I saw you trying to find Lenny. You looked everywhere for him."

"And you followed me?" questioned Carolyn with surprise.

"I did," confessed Jim. "I watched the entire thing. I even followed you down to the beach after Lenny's dad drove them away. Pete and Lenny both looked back. Mr. Owens never did."

Carolyn's eyes began to water as she thought of the experience.

"You didn't appear to want company after that," recalled Jim, "so I left you to your thoughts. I could tell you were hurting, though."

"You have no idea," mumbled Carolyn.

"Oh, I think I do," assured Jim rather dejectedly. The look of melancholy on Jim's face was telling and Carolyn perceived at once that he was referring to her.

"After you left," added Jim, "I went over to sit on a log on the beach and noticed the initials LO and CB on it. At first I was going to change the L to a J before I carved a heart around it," recounted Jim.

498

"But, I knew it would upset you if you ever came back and saw the J and would know it had been me, so I left it."

"It was *you* who drew that heart around those initials?" Carolyn was quite surprised. "I saw the heart when I was down there with Susan, just last week."

"Guilty," admitted Jim with a shrug of his shoulders.

"We both just assumed it was Lenny who came back and carved the heart around those initials," admitted Carolyn.

"You sound disappointed," said Jim.

Carolyn breathed in a deep breath and then quickly let it out.

"Do you ever wonder what happened to him?" tempted Jim.

"To Lenny?" frowned Carolyn.

"Believe it or not, you're not the only one I keep tabs on with my satellite surveillance equipment," described Jim with an even smile.

"Why would you do such a thing?" pressed Carolyn.

"So that someday if you ever wanted to know how Lenny was, I would be able to tell you," replied Jim.

Carolyn merely shook her head with disbelief.

"Didn't you ever wonder if he actually became a doctor like he'd planned?" inquired Jim with a raised eyebrow. "Or if he married? Or what he's doing now?"

"Well, you obviously want to tell me," consented Carolyn. "Let's have it."

Jim nodded and smiled quite smugly before starting. "Okay then, Lenny Owens did graduate with a Bachelor's degree in Biochemistry after completing pre-medicine. Most of his job positions have been in supervisory or management capacities, and he currently...."

"Stop!" interrupted Carolyn. "I don't want to know."

"Are you sure?" urged Jim. "Lenny also participated in varsity basketball and fencing. En guard!"

"Fencing?" doubted Carolyn.

"Trust me!" assured Jim. "Fencing."

"Don't you want to know if he's married, or has a family?" questioned Jim.

"All I really want to know is whether Lenny is happy," replied Carolyn. "It would be nice to know that Lenny is as happy as I am."

"Are you?" persisted Jim.

"I've already told you that," reminded Carolyn, "and yes, I'm very happy."

"Then I'm happy for you," replied Jim, "and I'm sure Lenny would be, too."

"You're not going to answer my question about whether Lenny is happy, are you?" realized Carolyn.

"How would I know?" shrugged Jim. "Only Lenny could tell you something like that."

Carolyn slowly nodded as she got up to gaze out the lighthouse window and watch the first rays of morning sunlight. After several moments, she came back over to where Jim was and sat back down.

Carolyn rewarded Jim with a compassionate smile before she unexpectedly gave him a hug and a kiss on the cheek. "Thank you for saving my life. I'll never forget you, either," added Carolyn as she handed Jim the little journal.

Unbidden tears escaped from Jim's eyes as he watched Carolyn get up and leave the tower room to head back downstairs. Thankfully, the others were still asleep!

Susan and Carolyn had just finished eating breakfast, and had decided to go for an early walk on the beach. It was hard to believe that just hours ago, such stormy conditions had prevailed themselves upon the now peaceful scene. Not a cloud could be seen in the sky. There was very little breeze, either. A stray seagull could be heard cawing as it flew by overhead. Even the ocean water was as calm as glass, save for some small delicate waves slowly approaching the shore. The sound of them was almost a whisper. Morning high tide would reach its zenith at 10:00 a.m. but seemed in no hurry to do so as it had the previous night. Nature itself seemed to be celebrating the discovery and final release of Joyce Troglite's and Veronica Jensen's remains from the dismal bunker tunnel where they had been unjustly entombed for all those years against their will.

"There they go," noticed Susan as she watched Jim Otterman's Deputies make their way down the beach with evidence collection bags. "I wonder where Jim is?"

"He plans to finish taking Ray's and Sheree's depositions here at the lighthouse before he does anything else," informed Carolyn.

"Jim sure took your deposition rather early this morning," commented Susan as she and Carolyn arrived at the weather beaten log where the initials LO and CB were carved.

"Indeed," acknowledged Carolyn as she brushed off some errant sand before sitting down on the log.

"I saw Jim try to kiss your hand," confessed Susan, "before you pulled it away."

Carolyn merely nodded but clearly had nothing else to say about it. Susan then sat down, too.

"Oh, come on!" urged Susan. "What else were you two up there talking about for so long? And don't tell me that him trying to kiss your hand was part of his interrogation!"

"Nothing, and everything, depending upon your point of view," replied Carolyn rather distantly.

"That's rather cryptic," pointed out Susan.

"I just needed to convince Jim that I'm truly happy now, with my life," Carolyn finally explained. "It was the only way to steer him in a new direction." Carolyn then gave Susan a mischievous wink.

"Just what's that supposed to mean?" scowled Susan.

"Well," began Carolyn, "one thing I've learned from working with feral cats and other wild animals is that they usually won't take 'no' for an answer."

"Like Jim?" grinned Susan.

"Exactly like Jim," chuckled Carolyn. "Take our cat Henry, for example. He incessantly scratches the furniture, gnaws on the edges of books, unrolls toilet paper, or pretty much does whatever he wants. We can tell him 'no' all day long, and even whack him with a newspaper, but it does absolutely no good whatsoever."

"Have you ever tried whacking Jim with a newspaper?" laughed Susan as she slapped her hand on her knee.

"The point is," continued Carolyn, "that the only thing that really works in situations like that is re-direction."

"Re-direction?" quizzed Susan with a worried look on her face.

"Not you!" laughed Carolyn. "I'm talking about Sheree."

"Oh!" Susan sighed with obvious relief. "I see. That actually makes sense, when you think about it. If Jim were to somehow become interested in Sheree, then perhaps he'll finally forget about you."

"That's the general idea," confirmed Carolyn.

"So, how do you plan on getting that to happen?" quizzed Susan.

"We'll just have to see," smiled Carolyn mysteriously.

"Is that what you and Jim were talking about for so long?" Susan suddenly asked, anxious to be in on it.

"Perhaps," Carolyn replied.

"Okay, don't tell me, then," responded Susan.

"The rest is up to Jim," Carolyn finally divulged. "And Sheree."

"That makes sense," agreed Susan. "Say, how's Janette doing these days, anyway?"

"Janette from Ashton?" clarified Carolyn. "She actually was planning on coming out here with me, but couldn't get time off work."

"Maybe she can still make it up here?" suggested Susan. "Now that the Oceanview Matter has been solved, it could be a really fun time for her. When was it that you and Janette came up to Ocean Bay for a visit, anyway?"

"Let me see," pondered Carolyn. "I think it was around 1979, give or take a year or two. I know it was before I got married."

"Remember when Jorge took us all up zigzag mountain in his little yellow car so we could hear Janette scream when he drove us back down?" described Susan.

"She wasn't the only one," reminded Carolyn.

"Janette was definitely screaming louder than you!" Susan smiled at the memory. "We never did get a chance to take your hubby up there the time he came out, though, did we? What year was it when you and he came for a visit? Wasn't it about 1985?"

"I think it was," believed Carolyn. "And that really was the last time you and I ever saw each other until now. I just can't believe how quickly time passes by!"

"Let's keep in better touch from now on," suggested Susan as she gave her friend Carolyn a hug.

"We will," promised Carolyn as she hugged Susan back.

"You're going back now, aren't you?" guessed Susan.

"I have to! As much as I'd like to stay a little longer," Carolyn finally said, "it's time I was getting back home. I can't even begin to tell you everything my hubby is going through feeding all those animals for me right now. And I miss him so much!"

"I'll bet he misses you, too!" Susan smiled a crooked smile.

502

"Hey, you still have two weeks of vacation left," pointed out Susan. "What are you gonna do with all that time on your hands? Maybe we could try and find Lenny?" proposed Susan.

"I don't think that's such a good idea," declined Carolyn.

"You already know where Lenny is, don't you?" accused Susan with a suspicious grin.

"Not exactly," smirked Carolyn.

"Is that what you and Jim were talking about?" guessed Susan. "Being in law enforcement, Jim could probably find anybody he wants."

"I imagine so," Carolyn smiled mysteriously.

"You're not gonna tell me, are you?" pouted Susan.

"If I knew where Lenny was, I would tell you," replied Carolyn. Susan did not need to know that Carolyn could have learned Lenny's location from Jim, had she really wanted to. "Besides, I'm happily married now."

"It would be fun to know whatever happened to Lenny, though," speculated Susan. "We could always look him up on the internet and see what's there. I've always wondered whether Lenny ever became a doctor or not."

· "It was his mother's dying wish," reminded Carolyn rather wistfully. "Lenny wasn't the type to give up on his dreams."

"It does seem rather odd that Lenny never bothered to look you up again," mused Susan. "Perhaps Lenny was an idiot, after all."

"Actually, I did see Lenny one other time," admitted Carolyn.

"Where?" demanded Susan as she suddenly grabbed Carolyn's arm and waited for the details.

"It must have been about 1979," recalled Carolyn. "I was at a camp meeting session with two of my nieces."

Camp meeting was originally an American phenomenon of frontier Christianity, with strong roots in traditional practices of certain protestant churches from Scotland that later immigrated to the United States. Modern-day protestant groups still held annual gatherings to commemorate the camp meeting practice within the Oceanview area. Such gatherings were, of course, held during the summer months during favorable weather. Just as in frontier times - when people with primitive means of transportation would camp out in tents at or near the revival site - modern-day camp meeting patrons would try as much as possible to duplicate the event by actually camping in tents. Even the stirring revival meetings would be held in a giant tent, with fellow believers remaining at the site for several days and enjoying spiritual renewal and comradery with one another.

"And?" pressed Susan.

"They were ages four and six at the time, and one of them needed to use the restroom," described Carolyn. "The meeting was just too long for them to sit through the entire thing."

"And that's when you saw Lenny?" persisted Susan.

"Not at first," answered Carolyn. She actually enjoyed keeping Susan in suspense. "Anyway, I was holding their hands to make sure they didn't get lost in such a huge crowd of people."

"You certainly wouldn't want that," agreed Susan.

"We were just walking up a hill near the outside edge of the campground, almost to the restroom," continued Carolyn, "when I looked up and saw Lenny just standing there, staring at me."

"What did he do?" asked Susan.

"Lenny seemed really happy to see me," described Carolyn.

"He didn't even come over and give you a hug or anything?" frowned Susan. "Certainly he could see your hands were full with two little girls to hang onto! Lenny didn't think they were yours, did he?"

"No, he didn't," assured Carolyn. "I told him they were my nieces. I even introduced them to him. But, you're right. It wasn't like I could let go of the girls' hands, either, and one of them was fidgeting terribly, ready to wet her pants at any moment. She was hopping up and down, holding herself, that kind of thing."

"You should have just let her!" chastised Susan.

"Well, Lenny could see that I needed to get her to the restroom pretty quickly," replied Carolyn, "so our conversation was brief."

"What else did you guys say?" quizzed Susan.

"I asked him if he had ever gone to med school, and how everything was going for him," recounted Carolyn.

"And?" Susan's fingers were almost ready to cut off the circulation in Carolyn's arm at that point.

"Do you mind?" chuckled Carolyn as she shook Susan's hand loose from her arm.

"Sorry!" laughed Susan. "Well?"

"Lenny told me that yes, he was going to med school and that becoming a doctor was certainly the plan," revealed Carolyn.

"How come you never mentioned any of this before?" demanded Susan. "You've been here nearly a week already!"

"It's not like we haven't been involved in one life-threatening situation after another, either!" reminded Carolyn.

"True, but we certainly do make a great team, don't we?" asked Susan with a sly grin.

"Yeah, we do," agreed Carolyn.

"So, was that all Lenny had to say for himself?" grilled Susan.

"I'm afraid so." Carolyn shrugged her shoulders.

"Didn't he ask you anything at all about YOU?" wondered Susan. "Surely he wanted to know how you were?"

"He did," replied Carolyn, "and I told him I was doing okay."

"That's just sad!" exclaimed Susan. "And what then?"

"Then, he just turned around and walked away," concluded Carolyn. "Lenny did have on a rather nice suit and tie that day, and he even still had the afro."

"I wonder when Lenny came back here to carve the heart around those initials, then?" delved Susan. "You saw him when he left with his dad, and the heart wasn't here then, so he had to have come back later."

Carolyn considered telling Susan that it had actually been Jim who had carved the heart onto the log around the initials but decided against it. What was the point? That would just lead into a conversation about Jim and other questions Carolyn didn't feel like answering.

"Well, at least he bothered to write," commented Susan.

"Excuse me?" replied Carolyn with surprise. "What are you talking about?"

"Lenny," clarified Susan. "At least that's what he said the time I ran into him."

"Wait a minute!" responded Carolyn. "When was that?"

"Oh, let's see," pondered Susan. "Probably around 1975."

"Are you serious?" Carolyn was flabbergasted. "You spoke with Lenny in 1975? Was that before or after that time Karlin, Eula and Stacia came with me to visit you for the weekend?"

"Definitely after," recalled Susan. "You guys came down during spring break, but it wasn't until later that year – probably in September – that I saw Lenny."

"Just exactly where did you see him?" pressed Carolyn.

"At some sandwich shop during lunch," answered Susan.

"Was he alone?" grilled Carolyn.

"Actually, he was," confirmed Susan. "We were in line waiting to place our orders."

"And that's when he told you he had written to me?" questioned Carolyn. She could not believe Susan had never mentioned it!

"That's what he said," replied Susan.

"But, I NEVER received any letter from Lenny!" revealed Carolyn. "Are you sure?"

"Absolutely," verified Susan. "Lenny even asked if I'd seen you and how you were."

"And you didn't think I would want to know about this?" Carolyn was clearly irritated.

"Didn't your dad confiscate one of MY letters to you once?" reminded Susan.

"Oh my God!" realized Carolyn. "That's right! Yes, he did. I do remember that. It was the time you called and told me you'd written, and then later that same day I just happened to find your letter inside his desk drawer when I was looking for a paperclip!"

"Your dad never did like me," commented Susan.

"He never liked Lenny much, either!" fumed Carolyn.

"I wonder what Lenny would have said in his letter to you?" pondered Susan.

"Obviously, I'll never know," muttered Carolyn rather distantly. "My dad probably just threw it in the incinerator."

"Seriously? Why would your dad do something like that?" asked Susan. "What if there were letters from other people that he intercepted, too, that you never even knew about? How would you have known?"

Carolyn breathed in deeply and then quickly exhaled. "Well, it's not like I can very well ask him about it now. My father died twelve years ago!"

"Maybe your dad thought he was protecting you, in his own way, of course," surmised Susan with a shrug of her shoulders.

"That's still no excuse for taking someone else's mail!" Carolyn was absolutely livid.

"Can't you just stay a few more days?" urged Susan. "Might do you some good."

506

"Actually, I was thinking that I need some time to recover from my 'vacation at the beach' before I return to work!" sniggered Carolyn. "I think I'm more of a mountain person, anyway. Maybe I'll go do some hiking up in a lush, old growth forest somewhere."

"Oh, I think I could get used to living at the beach," pondered Susan as she glanced up at the lighthouse.

"Maybe you should," suggested Carolyn. "Ray's actually a pretty decent guy. I think you should give him a chance."

"It's hard to believe we thought he was an ex-con and a strawberry thief!" laughed Susan.

"You two are good for each other," pointed out Carolyn. "I think you should settle down here. Maybe you could turn the place into a bed and breakfast."

"What about my house in Ocean Bay?" questioned Susan.

"Your daughter and her kids already live there," reminded Carolyn. "Sell it to her! Just make sure she signs something where it has to stay in the family, if it's important to you. Then, if she ever decides to leave, it would revert back to you."

"That's not a bad idea," acknowledged Susan.

"I'll bet your grandkids would love to come visit Grandma Killingham in her magical lighthouse by the sea," grinned Carolyn.

"I'll bet they would," agreed Susan.

"I didn't happen to see anyone in the Violet Room last night, either," Carolyn gave Susan meaningful glance.

"What can I say?" blushed Susan.

"Do I finally get to be your maid of honor?" probed Carolyn.

"Absolutely!" nodded Susan. "Of course, that means you will need to come back down here."

"I wouldn't miss it for the world," assured Carolyn.

"Perhaps while you're here we can find some other mischief to get into?" added Susan with a crooked smile.

"We'll see," replied Carolyn, rather patronizingly.

"Hey, do you ever hear from Eula or Stacia, or your other friends from when you went to college at Powell Mountain University?" queried Susan.

"Oh yes, the co-ed parochial boarding college up on the hill in the middle of nowhere," reflected Carolyn. "Not to be confused with the co-ed parochial boarding academy here on the beach in the middle of nowhere. That certainly made this place look like a walk in the park!"

"Remember when you and Janette were at my place in Ocean Bay and you were telling us about the couple that were run down and killed up at Powell Lake?" pressed Susan.

"Yes, and that was pretty sad," replied Carolyn. "It was a love triangle between a student couple from the school and a local lumberman who worked at the forest camp up there. But, he finally did confess and went to prison for it, for the rest of his life."

"As he should have!" opined Susan. "Say, did they ever find out what happened to Karlin? I sure liked her."

"They never did find her body, so no, we don't know for sure what happened to her," clarified Carolyn. "Karlin was not only my roommate, but also a very dear friend, and there's no way she would have just taken off like that. Something had to have happened to her. We just don't know what it was. There were several theories about it, but no one was ever able to prove anything."

"Weren't there rumors of other people that disappeared up there, too?" pressed Susan. "Right about that same time?"

"I don't think they ever found any of them, either," recalled Carolyn. "But, I really don't think the lumberman was responsible for Karlin or the other disappearances. That was an entirely separate matter and would have had nothing to do with the couple he ran down."

"Why not? How can you be so sure?" pressed Susan.

"Well," added Carolyn, "because students have actually been disappearing up there for years. Some as far back as 1956. And, the lumberman was only in his twenties when we knew him back in 1975. He just wasn't that kind of a guy."

"You *knew* him?" Susan was surprised.

"Actually, yes," revealed Carolyn. "That school was about an hour away from the nearest town, so Karlin and I would sometimes catch a ride with Woody into town. At least that's what we called him. Woody the Woodcutter. But, I'm not even sure if that was actually his real name. We were stunned when we found out about that couple he ran down, though. He didn't seem capable of something like that."

"Oh, my God!" exclaimed Susan. "You're lucky you didn't disappear, too! But, it is rather strange that at least three of your friends have disappeared under mysterious circumstances, don't you think?"

"You're still here!" reminded Carolyn with a raised eyebrow.

"Indeed," nodded Susan. "Lucky for me that things only happen in threes! So, what made you come here first, to find Joyce and Veronica?"

"Probably because they disappeared first," replied Carolyn.

"Do you ever plan to try and find out what happened to Karlin?" questioned Susan.

"Haven't we been through enough already?" asked Carolyn. "We really are lucky to be alive after what we went through finding Joyce and Veronica."

"I'll bet Karlin's family would love to find out what happened to her, too," pointed out Susan. "Surely you must have some ideas about it?"

"I might have," admitted Carolyn, "but it would be just too dangerous. I don't think we should tempt fate beyond what we have already."

"Well, if you ever change your mind, count me in," pledged Susan. "If Karlin is meant to be found, we will find her. Trust me!"

14. Epilogue

Seven years had come and gone since the final disposition of the Oceanview Matter, and it was finally 2023. The tiny town of Ocean Bluff had grown from a size of 317 residents to a population of 7,423. Not only did the anonymous donations of an extremely generous benefactor manage to improve the curbside appeal of Ocean Bluff as a whole, but also made it possible for other improvements to be made to its outlying areas nearby. In fact, Ocean Bluff had finally succeeded in becoming a highly sought after vacation destination.

Mayor Otterman and his wife Sheree lived at the newly refurbished annex building, located within a short walking distance of the Killingham Lighthouse Bed and Breakfast, just north of Oceanview Academy. The annex building was what the old servants' quarters had come to be called, and served as overflow accommodations for guests of the Killingham Lighthouse Bed and Breakfast when its other rooms were already booked to capacity.

The south half of the annex served as a private residence for Jim Otterman and his wife Sheree, with its own separate entrance. The north half of the annex had undergone extensive upgrades just the previous year to bring it up to code and make its accommodations ready for guests. An interior door that led from the north to the south half of the annex was situated near a small office in the middle where Sheree Otterman kept track of its books and room reservations.

Sheree was also responsible for periodically retrieving cash from a donation box situated at the entrance to the Roth House nearby where she had once lived while married to her late husband Jon, and for general maintenance and upkeep of the edifice as needed. Any guests wishing to make donations using the latest voice-activated smartwatches were welcome to do so, which made it easier for Sheree than having to deal with actual cash anyway. Most smartwatches in 2023 were voice-activated and capable of independent Internet access on their own, making the unsafe distraction of handheld models far less desirable.

Preferring the "old way" of doing things wherever possible, however, Sheree still used her handheld satellite phone and kept it with her when tending to the small vegetable and begonia garden in the old greenhouse. Self-guided tours of the historic Roth House were not only quite popular with guests staying at the Killingham Lighthouse Bed and Breakfast, but also among other tourists stopping by to see it while in the area for the annual Oceanview Festival. Unknown to most guests, the donation box situated at the entrance to the Roth House remained under constant video surveillance from a monitoring station in the bunker nearby. This particular bunker had once been Jon Roth's bomb shelter, and was the only remaining bunker or tunnel in the surrounding area that remained. Demolition experts hired by Jim Otterman back in 2016 following the recovery of Joyce Troglite's and Veronica Jensen's remains had spent weeks sealing off and eliminating the rest of them.

Highly paid security guards working in the Roth House bunker station kept a constant eye on not only the Roth House but also on the entire lighthouse and golf course area for their employer, Jim Otterman. Donations made were slated to help children and adults receiving mental health treatment by a non-profit outreach program based out of the Ocean Bluff Mental Institution. Highly trained volunteer students who specialized in the treatment of schizophrenia were able to participate in the program to receive practicum credits while serving their internships there.

Jim Otterman had just gotten off work early for the afternoon and was driving down the narrow, windy, two-lane road leading from Ocean Bluff to his home at the annex where he lived with his wife Sheree. The late afternoon sun shone through the row of aging cypress trees beside the road. Jim never tired of traveling the scenic route where glimpses of the ocean could be had in-between the trees as he passed. It was March 22, 2023. Tomorrow would mark the anniversary of the recovery of Joyce Troglite's and Veronica Jensen's remains seven years earlier. An annual celebration in their honor had come to be known as the Oceanview Festival and was held each year on March 23rd. Last year alone, the celebration had been attended by over 14,000 people.

For many of the merchants and small shop owners in town, it was their busiest retail day of the entire year, even surpassing Black Friday by several percentage points.

Every hotel, motel, cottage, RV park, campground or bed and breakfast in the entire area had been booked to capacity. The only two rooms left were in the newly refurbished attic of the annex, and construction had not been completed until yesterday. Jim would be anxious to see whether the rooms were rented yet. Most likely they were. Too often, disappointed tourists would have their names on standby for possible cancellations this time of year. Some would drive in from Ocean Bay for the day, just to avoid the hassle and expense of having to stay somewhere overnight.

If only Carolyn could see all this, thought Jim as he pulled into the access road that led to the new Silver Creek Golf Course. One would never guess that it could cost so much – just to put in a golf course – though it had turned out to be a far more lucrative investment than the rundown trailer park that had preceded it. And, to give the place rustic appeal for would-be historians and sentimentalists in the local area, the original Silver Creek Trailer Park Store was now used as a golf pro shop and office from which his son-in-law Ted Jensen ran and maintained the golf course. Killingham ice cream was one of the more popular items on the menu of the small delicatessen sandwich shop built onto one end of it. Ted Jensen ran that, too.

When not working, Ted and his wife Ann lived over on campus in the home that had previously belonged to Ginny Eggersol, and later to Ms. Neilson. Ann Jensen was delighted, of course, to be near her mother Sheree and step-dad Jim Otterman, and was generally kept quite busy helping John and Jeon Murray maintain and operate the Killingham Wildlife Center on campus near the dairy where her colony of feral cats still lived. Many of the felines were descended from the original group prior to Ann successfully being able to capture and get them all neutered.

Jim Otterman had also been instrumental in making sure that the entire campus of Oceanview Academy, as well as the Killingham parcel just north of it where the lighthouse, annex and golf course were located, be given a permanent easement as a wildlife management area. In fact, the beach along both the campus and the Killingham properties had been designated as an official site for bird enthusiasts to come and enjoy watching Snowy Plovers, Lesser Terns, and other endangered species in their chosen nesting grounds.

The Silver Creek Road leading from the golf course up to the lighthouse was finally paved, with an electric security gate that opened by the swipe of a security card. Guests of the Killingham Lighthouse Bed and Breakfast or its annex would be issued key cards – for a small deposit – that enabled them to open the gate without getting out of their cars. After driving through the security gate and up to the

512

lighthouse, Jim slowed to admire some newly planted begonias that were in full bloom by the lighthouse entrance before continuing his drive over to the annex nearby. Jim was glad that Ray and Susan had been able to finally get married and have a good life together. It was a good feeling to know that they were truly happy, too, and would never know the burden of financial worry again. Carolyn would have been glad for them, as well. Strange that she had never chosen to return for a visit.

When Jim arrived at the annex, he pulled into his privately marked parking space. The sign on it simply said "Jim" and its reflective letters were large enough to be easily noticed by anyone searching for a possible parking space. Jim's bright red 2023 AWD Jeep Cherokee was a comfortable vehicle for him, though most of the roads in the area had already been paved, and it was rare that Jim needed off-road capabilities anymore.

While Jim still maintained his aging Cessna as a patrol plane for occasional flights over the beach, and to take up guests wishing to participate in occasional skydiving adventures, Jim's plane of choice was now a Learjet aircraft. Not only did this make Jim's periodic trips to the home office of his mortgage brokerage firm more enjoyable, but featured the best-in-class ease of mobility available with ample leg and headroom, and seating for up to eight passengers.

"Turn off engine," commanded Jim after pressing a button on his smartwatch. As he waited for his new Jeep to shut itself off, Jim noticed a young couple carrying a kite. They were headed from the guest half of the annex toward the access steps Jim had commissioned contractors to install the previous year. The steps gradually descended to the beach after switching back and forth several times down the side of the bluff. Enclosed handrails on the steps ensured the safety of guests while negotiating them. Built to last, the steps and their handrails were made of synthetic wood. Though more expensive than regular wood, synthetic wood was constructed of recycled plastic and wood fibers, pressure treated to withstand water damage and other rigors of time.

"There you are!" flirted Sheree as she came out to greet him.

Jim reached his head through the open window of his vehicle to kiss his wife Sheree on the mouth. "So, what's up?"

"Whatever do you mean?" questioned Sheree rather coyly.

"It isn't every day that my lovely wife races out to greet me when I drive up, and before I've even had a chance to get out of my vehicle," smiled Jim suspiciously.

"Susan was helping Ann get that trunk out of the attic area where the new guest rooms are," informed Sheree rather mysteriously.

"What trunk?" frowned Jim. "Didn't the contractors get the rest of that old junk out of there yet? I'm just not paying 'em enough."

"Actually, the interior decorator thought the trunk gave the area an authentic old world look," explained Sheree, "but it clashed horribly with the new furniture."

"An old trunk?" grinned Jim. "That's what this is all about?"

"Wait until you see what was in it," tempted Sheree as she opened the door to Jim's Jeep, pulled him up, and slipped her arm through his.

"Okay, I give up," responded Jim as he gingerly closed the door to his Jeep with his free arm, pressed the button on his smartwatch, and commanded, "Windows up. Lock car." Jim then turned to Sheree and asked, "What did they find?"

"Oh, I can't tell you that just yet," smiled Sheree as they walked together toward their private south entrance to the annex.

"We're not overbooked for the festival, are we?" Jim suddenly asked as they reached the front door.

"Why would you say that?" responded Sheree.

"I just thought maybe you were moving the trunk out to make room for another rollaway bed," assumed Jim. "I'd actually rather turn guests away than have the ones there feel crowded."

"It's nothing like that," assured Sheree.

Surrounding the annex was a hearty mat of creeping succulent ice plants with hot pink blossoms accented along its outer edge by golden yellow coreopsis, lavender and sedum plants, giving the structure a quaint last-century type of charm.

"Your daughter has a surprise for us," added Sheree as they entered their home.

Since the marriage of Jim Otterman to her mother Sheree, Ann had referred to him as Dad. No further mention of Jon Roth had been made by anyone.

"Dad!" exclaimed Ann as she ran over to give Jim Otterman a hug of greeting.

It made Jim feel good inside to hear Ann call him that, especially after the doctors had finally concluded that Sheree would never be able to have another child of her own, for health reasons. Jim loved Sheree with all his heart, so the fact that she would never be able to bear his child seemed unimportant. In many ways, Jim was grateful to Carolyn for steering him in the right direction. And, though Jim did still have feelings for Carolyn – even after all these years – the point was now moot. Jim knew he would never see Carolyn again, anyway.

"So, what's this all about?" questioned Jim.

"You'll see," promised Ann as she led him to the living room and over to his favorite recliner.

"Hello!" greeted Susan as she came into the room, still wearing an apron. "Ray should be here soon, too."

"Susan and Ray are joining us for an early dinner tonight," explained Sheree as she took Jim's jacket from him and hung it on a rack over by the door. "Hopefully before the guests start checking in."

"And so are we," added Ann. "Ted should be here any minute."

"The festival's not until tomorrow," pointed out Jim suspiciously as he sat down in his recliner.

"Ted has already taken care of everything outside, too," volunteered Ann. "Even the electronic gate log."

Jim nodded with approval. "So, what's for dinner?"

"Shish kabob with rice pilaf," revealed Sheree.

"And cucumber, tomato and onion salad," mentioned Susan.

"With baklava for dessert," grinned Ann.

"This must be a special occasion," smiled Jim. "Is someone going to tell me what's going on, or are you just going to keep me in suspense?"

"There they are!" noticed Ann as she ran over to open the front door.

"Something sure smells good," commented Ray as he and Ted came inside.

"Everyone sit down," invited Ann. "We need to have a quick family meeting before dinner."

"They may want to eat first," cautioned Susan with a crooked smile as she came over to give Ray a welcoming kiss.

"Just get on with it," urged Ted. "I'm starving! It took me almost four hours to mow that golf course today."

"And we do appreciate it," acknowledged Jim.

Susan and Ann quickly handed out cold bottles of water to everyone while Sheree brought out a plate of hors d'oeuvres and placed them on the coffee table to tide everyone over until dinner. The items included crackers, slices of cheese, and freshly washed grapes already removed from their stems.

"You probably should share your news now," recommended Sheree. "Check-in time is around 5:00 for tonight, and some people always show up early."

"Very well," agreed Ann. "Shall I share with them what I found in the trunk first? Or tell them our other good news?"

"Definitely the trunk," suggested Susan excitedly.

"The trunk actually belonged to Helen," revealed Ann mysteriously.

"Edith's sister Helen?" asked Ray with surprise.

"The same," assured Susan.

"She must have been almost a hundred years old when she finally passed," guessed Ray.

"Ninety-seven," clarified Ann.

"That is old," grinned Susan.

"Anyway," resumed Ann, "remember how Ray never knew who his real birth father was?"

The room became quite still.

"We found this old journal kept by Ray's birth mother in that trunk," smiled Ann as she held it up. "Not to be confused with Ginny Eggersol's old journal that Dad keeps hidden in a faux book in his study labeled 'Laws of Probability.'"

Jim was flabbergasted. "How did you know about that?"

Ann innocently shrugged her shoulders in response and struggled not to grin too much.

"Carolyn finally told me in an email that she gave it to you, so it was only a matter of time until we finally found Ginny's journal again," confessed Ann. "It was the title that gave it away."

"The Laws of Probability?" nodded Jim.

From Sheree's smirk, Jim could tell that she already knew about it, too. Jim just shook his head.

"Anyway, Carolyn's been helping me with my genealogy, and we've been emailing and skyping each other for seven years now," revealed Ann.

516

Jim suddenly looked most uncomfortable, and it did not go unnoticed by Sheree.

"What's your genealogy got to do with my real birth father?" interjected Ray, impatient to find out what Ann had been about to say.

"Oh, well, to make a long story short," continued Ann. "According to Linda Dixon – that was Cathy Dixon's sister and also your birth mother – she once had a torrid love affair with a man named Jon Roth. Obviously Jon Roth, Sr."

It was Ray's turn to look as if someone had hit him in the gut with a bowling ball and he was literally speechless.

"So, that would make you my Uncle Ray," beamed Ann, delighted to finally know that she and Ray were related. She had always liked Ray and thought he would be as thrilled as she was with the news.

"Ray?" questioned Susan as she waved her hand in front of his face and snapped her fingers a couple of times. "Ray?"

"I don't believe it!" spat Ray as he stood up to leave. "I've got to get out of here."

"Wait!" commanded Jim Otterman. "Sit down! Let's hear what else she has to say first before we overreact."

"Overreact?" demanded Ray. "Just how would you feel about finding out that Birdboy was your half-brother?"

"I'm sorry, man," Jim shook his head with empathy.

Ray was so angry he feared he might say something he would regret, so held his peace. Susan had never seen him so upset.

"Hey," said Susan as she tenderly put her hand on Ray's arm. "Ann is our niece! And she's almost like a daughter to us anyway."

"I'm sorry," apologized Ray. "It was kind of a shock."

"Tell them your other news," encouraged Sheree.

"Ted and I are going to have a baby!" Ann proudly announced.

Jim leaned forward in his chair and gave Ann a stern glance. "What do you mean you're having a baby?"

"We're having a baby!" corroborated Ted as he got up and gave Ann a proud hug.

"I thought we talked about this," objected Jim.

"He's right," interjected Ray. "Since apparently I am your uncle, let me give you some friendly family advice...."

"Hold it!" interrupted Sheree. "Let her finish."

"Ann has some very interesting theories about the Borden case," informed Ted, "that we think you all should hear."

Jim and Ray each took a deep breath, folded their arms, and sat back in their respective chairs to listen.

"As I mentioned earlier, I've been doing some research on my family lines," reminded Ann seriously. "I'm convinced after what I've learned that Lizzie Borden was as sane as you or I, and that the murders she committed were crimes of passion she was driven to with extremely compelling motives."

"Go on," prompted Sheree. She was as anxious to have Ann share what they had learned about the Borden family line as Ann was to share it. Only Ray and Jim had yet to be educated.

"We all probably know that Lizzie Borden was never actually married," began Ann.

"Then who was the father of her son?" questioned Ray.

"There are theories that she was molested by her father, while others believe they were involved in an illicit romantic affair," answered Ann. "Either way, the common consensus is that they had sexual relations that ended in Lizzie Borden becoming pregnant."

"No wonder her father sent her away on an extended vacation like he did," interjected Susan.

"Exactly!" agreed Ann. "For you see, Mr. Borden was a man of high social and financial status in the community and could not afford for his reputation to be tarnished in the eyes of his business associates once his daughter Lizzie began showing from her pregnancy."

"An extended vacation?" asked Ray rather dubiously.

"She's right! I do remember that part of the story," admitted Jim. "Something about Lizzie Borden being sent away after a huge family argument or something."

"Lizzie giving birth to her own father's illegitimate child would have been pretty huge," pointed out Susan. "No wonder she was forced to remain on vacation until after the baby was born!"

"Nothing I've read says anything about her coming back with a baby when she returned home," recalled Jim.

"Ah, but you have read about what happened to the child," reminded Ann as she held up Ginny's journal for everyone to see. "Sorry, but I needed to borrow this again. I will put it back, Dad."

"No problem," assured Jim.

"I remember when we read that," stated Susan. "Lizzie's father insisted that she give her baby up for adoption by one of his colleagues, some man whose wife was unable to have any children of her own. It really does say that in Ginny's journal."

"Precisely!" Ann took a deep breath and then let it out.

"Wasn't it while Lizzie was away having her baby that her father remarried and brought home some hussy that turned out to be nothing but a gold digger?" questioned Susan.

"That sounds like quite a bit of motive to me," opined Sheree.

"That was only the tip of the iceberg," continued Ann. "Like me, Lizzie loved animals, especially her pigeons."

"Ann does have a really nice pigeon coop down there by the dairy," pointed out Susan with a wry grin.

"Lizzie had even built a special roost for her pigeons in her father's barn," described Ann. "So after losing her child, and then losing her father's affections to the new step-mother, the pigeons were about all poor Lizzie had left. Sadly, her father apparently felt the pigeons were a nuisance and wanted them gone."

"Mr. Borden then went out to the barn and killed them all with a hatchet," added Susan for effect as she grinned at Ray.

"Believe me," assured Ray, "I'll never ever lay a hand on any of Ann's pigeons or their coops, or any other creature she has over there by the dairy! I promise!"

"That's good to know," teased Ann.

"That's a very interesting theory," noted Jim. He had also studied the Borden case, for reasons of his own. So far, Jim had noticed nothing unusual about Ann's behavior to cause him any concern but he did find her sudden interest in the Borden case troubling.

"Everything we know about Lizzie indicates to me that she was quite sane and knew exactly what she was doing when she whacked her step-mother 19 times on the back of her head with that hatchet," described Ann.

"Or the 11 times she whacked her old man," said Sheree.

"Probably one whack for each pigeon," surmised Susan as she gave Ray a knowing look.

"You may have something there," admitted Jim. "Losing her child, her father, and then her pigeons on top of it. That's a lot of motive. I've seen people do much worse over a lot less."

"The jury that acquitted her was comprised entirely of men," commented Sheree.

"Probably her father's business associates," guessed Susan. "Any jury of women would have convicted Lizzie Borden in a heartbeat with all that evidence! Clearly, one of the jurors was the culprit who adopted Lizzie's baby, and probably convinced the other jurors to acquit her as quickly as possible so they could sweep the whole thing under the carpet before their good names got dragged into the mud along with it."

"That actually sounds rather feasible," agreed Jim after listening to the arguments being presented.

"Then when Lizzie was acquitted, she lived alone for the rest of her life," continued Ann. "Some of the jurors and their friends had spread rumors of Lizzie having an inappropriate relationship with the family maid, a woman named Sullivan. But, if that were the case, then why didn't they take up with each other following Lizzie's acquittal? I'll tell you why! Because those men were just trying to cast the public eye toward another direction so they could get it off of them!"

"That is pretty sad that she had to lose her child like that," commented Sheree. "But, I agree, a jury of women would have convicted her. There's still no excuse for what she did."

"True," nodded Susan, "though she apparently never did anything else like that again."

"She also inherited her father's fortune," mentioned Jim.

"Maybe so, but when she finally died," concluded Ann, "Lizzie Borden left $30,000 to the Fall River Animal Rescue League. That would be the equivalent of over half a million dollars today!"

"And the point of all this?" asked Ray.

"To reassure all of you that there is no mental illness to worry about from the Borden line," replied Ann.

"What about Birdboy?" pressed Ray.

"I'm glad you asked," answered Ann. "In doing my genealogy, the only evidence I've found of mental illness actually came from the Roth side of the family, though that was several generations ago. You're welcome to come over and look at my book any time you wish. I'm still working on getting it on-line."

"Hey, we're all related," reminded Susan.

"How do you figure?" frowned Ray.

"Adam and Eve?" teased Susan. "Remember them?"

"There's also a theory called the 'six degrees of separation' where everyone and everything in this world is only six or fewer steps away from anyone else in the world, by way of introduction or personal contact of some kind, so that a chain of friend-to-friend statements can be traced back to connect them with each other by no more than six degrees of separation," elaborated Ann.

"Well, I'm a Killingham now!" informed Ray with finality. He had no interest in learning anything more about the Roth family. It was a big enough step for Ray to abandon the Dixon name he had been raised with for Susan's sake when he married her six years ago. Susan had insisted that Ray's step-dad – old man Killingham – would have wanted it that way, especially after raising him on his own like he had for all those years. So, Ray was not about to change his name again, and definitely not to Roth!

"Anyway, we're going to have a baby!" beamed Ann.

"And we plan to name her Elizabeth Ann Jensen," added Ted with a twinkle in his eyes.

"And you know for certain it's a girl?" pressed Jim.

"Ultrasound," grinned Ted proudly.

"Well, congratulations," acknowledged Jim.

"Then, after Lizzie is born, we plan to name our next children Emma and Alice," revealed Ann with a mischievous twinkle in her eyes.

Jim's eyes opened wide for a moment. "Did you know that Elizabeth Andrew Borden's sisters were named Emma and Alice?"

"You know, I think they were," teased Ann.

"How 'bout that," Ray shook his head and laughed sardonically.

"Guess we'll need to keep our doors locked, our weapons handy, and never turn our backs on 'em," laughed Susan with a wicked grin.

"I hate to ask this, but what was the third thing you were going to tell us?" urged Jim.

"Oh, yes," Ann smiled mischievously. "Have you looked at your guest register lately?"

"Our guest register?" frowned Jim. With everything being on-line now like it was, Jim never bothered much with it anymore and usually just let Sheree or Susan handle all the reservations.

"When Susan and I were up there putting new sheets on the beds in those two new rooms up in the attic today," described Ann, "we just happened to pull up the guest register on our smartwatches to see who would be staying in them. Imagine our surprise when it was someone we knew!"

Jim suddenly pulled up his sleeve, activated his smartwatch to revive it from sleep mode, and commanded, "Guest register for today."

Almost immediately, the current day's guest register was displayed on Jim's smartwatch. Since the screen on his smartwatch was so tiny, Jim normally preferred using his laptop for such things.

"Doctor and Mrs. Lenny Owens?" read Jim after putting on his glasses. "Is this for real? Is this some kind of a sick joke or something?" Jim then looked over in time to see Susan give him a crooked smile.

"Too bad there's only one bathroom up there," chuckled Sheree. "That means the two couples will have to share it."

"Well, we eventually will have to have a second one put in," assured Jim with a troubled look on his face.

"Look at the other name," suggested Sheree rather smugly.

Jim then became quiet when he glanced again at the guest register displayed and saw who it was. Jim deliberately put his smartwatch back into sleep mode and rolled down his sleeve. It was suddenly as if a cloud of despair had descended upon him.

"Who did it say?" demanded Ray. "I don't have my smartwatch with me."

"Carolyn Bennett-Hunter and her husband will be staying in the other room," said Sheree matter-of-factly. Sheree had been with Susan and Ann when they had pulled up the register previously and had been waiting ever since to see how Jim would react.

"Oh, this oughta be good," chuckled Ray. "Did you want us to see if we can switch one of them with someone in the lighthouse?"

"Not a chance!" responded Sheree as she gave Jim a pointed grin. "Just how would you feel if you had a nice room at the lighthouse and suddenly found out you were being moved over to the old servants' quarters instead?"

"Hold it!" commanded Jim. "I know I should have shared this with all of you at the time, but we had already been through so much."

"What are you talking about?" Sheree became serious.

"Just two short months after the day we recovered Joyce's and Veronica's remains," began Jim, "I learned of some other tragic news." Jim was always careful not to mention the tragedy involving Jon Roth when talking about that day, especially in front of Sheree or Ann.

After an awkward silence, Jim continued. "Lenny Owens had some sort of medical situation on March 23, 2016. It was most likely a stroke, but the man at the hospital absolutely would not share any further details with me."

"How awful!" exclaimed Ann.

"Not on that exact same day?" Susan could not believe it.

Everyone else was dumbfounded.

"Lenny died just a few short weeks later," added Jim.

"And you didn't think any of us would have wanted the chance to say goodbye to him?" demanded Susan.

"Well, I can't go back and change it now, can I?" retorted Jim. "I feel bad enough as it is."

"Let him finish," insisted Sheree.

"Well, Lenny's funeral service was almost two months to the day after that," added Jim. "That's really all I know."

"And what about Carolyn? You didn't think she would want to know?" demanded Susan.

"Frankly," replied Jim, "I didn't expect to ever see her again."

"Well, as you now know, I've been emailing and skyping with Carolyn regularly for seven years," pointed out Ann. "I could certainly have told her! In fact, I'm the one who let her know about the new rooms we have available upstairs."

"And that's another thing!" snapped Jim. "Why was I never told that you were keeping in contact with Carolyn?" Jim did not like being kept in the dark about such things.

"You're one to talk!" accused Sheree.

Then, unexpectedly, the sound of someone's vehicle pulling up outside could be heard. "Someone must be early," pointed out Susan.

Jim suddenly felt his heartrate increase exponentially and experienced a high level of anxiety when he heard the car doors shut and the sound of steps on the pavement outside.

Jim was well aware that the fight-or-flight response is a physiological reaction that occurs in response to a perceived harmful event, attack, or threat to survival, and was irritated at himself for reacting so irrationally.

A brisk knock on the front door could be heard.

"Carolyn will have to be told about Lenny," reminded Sheree rather evenly as she approached and opened the door.

A tall, dark, handsome young man in his early forties smiled and nodded at Sheree. Beside him was a tall, attractive blonde woman who bore a striking resemblance to what Carolyn had looked like in her forties. The two made a remarkable pair.

"Dr. Owens, I presume?" questioned Sheree.

"Yes, ma'am," confirmed the stranger. "And this is my lovely wife, Lila."

Lila's shapely physique and timeless presence seemed to command the attention of others, yet she also had a shy and demure quality about her, too. Jim was astounded at how much she reminded him of Carolyn, and could not help but be drawn toward her.

"Hello," greeted Lila with a warm, inviting smile.

"Please, come in," invited Sheree, after covertly jabbing her husband Jim in the side with a warning elbow.

"You wouldn't be related to a Lenny Owens who once went to school over there at Oceanview, would you?" asked Susan.

"He was my father," revealed the man. "I'm Lenny, Jr."

"This should be interesting," Susan suddenly smiled a crooked smile. "My name is Susan Rives, and I knew your father and his cousin Pete quite well. In fact, my friend Carolyn – who also knew them – should be arriving any minute."

Jim Otterman approached and warmly shook Lenny Jr.'s hand before taking Lila's hand and briefly holding it as he finished the introductions. "I'm Jim Otterman. This is my wife, Sheree, our daughter Ann, and her husband Ted."

"And that is my husband Ray," added Susan.

"I'm afraid you all have me at a disadvantage," admitted Lenny, Jr. "But, it is very nice to meet all of you."

Just then a second vehicle could be heard approaching.

"You'll be all right," assured Sheree as she gave her husband Jim a challenging look. "Trust me!"